Military Identities

Military Identities

The Regimental System, the British Army,
and the British People, c.1870–2000

DAVID FRENCH

OXFORD
UNIVERSITY PRESS

OXFORD
UNIVERSITY PRESS

Great Clarendon Street, Oxford OX2 6DP

Oxford University Press is a department of the University of Oxford.
It furthers the University's objective of excellence in research, scholarship,
and education by publishing worldwide in

Oxford New York

Auckland Cape Town Dar es Salaam Hong Kong Karachi Kuala Lumpur
Madrid Melbourne Mexico City Nairobi New Delhi Shanghai Taipei Toronto

With offices in

Argentina Austria Brazil Chile Czech Republic France Greece
Guatemala Hungary Italy Japan Poland Portugal Singapore
South Korea Switzerland Thailand Turkey Ukraine Vietnam

Oxford is a registered trade mark of Oxford University Press
in the UK and in certain other countries

Published in the United States
by Oxford University Press Inc., New York

British Library Cataloguing in Publication Data

Data available

Library of Congress Cataloging in Publication Data

Data available

Typeset by Kolam Information Services Pvt. Ltd, Pondicherry, India
Printed in Great Britain
on acid-free paper by
Biddles Ltd. King's Lynn, Norfolk

ISBN 0-19-925803-1

1 3 5 7 9 10 8 6 4 2

Acknowledgements

I have amassed a considerable number of intellectual debts in the course of writing this book. I would especially like to thank Christine Bielecki, Nicholas Black, Dr Tim Bowman, Simon Fowler, and Peter Hart for making material available to me, and Major-General David Tyacke and Lieutenant-Colonel R. J. Binks for corresponding with me about some of the issues discussed in this book.

The staffs of the Bedfordshire Record Office, the Essex Record Office, the Imperial War Museum (both the Department of Documents and the Sound Archive), the Public Record Office, the Liddell Hart Centre for Military Archives at King's College London, the National Army Museum, the Suffolk Record Office (Bury St Edmunds Branch) gave me every possible assistance. Ian Hook and the staff of the Essex Regiment Museum, and Kate Thaxton and her colleagues at the Royal Norfolk Regiment Museum, not only allowed me to consult their archives, but also supplied me with numerous cups of tea and biscuits while I did so. Working in all of these institutions was a pleasure. For the fifth time, Professor Keith Neilson has placed me in his debt by taking the time and trouble to read a draft of my manuscript, and to give me the benefit of his suggestions. Professor Richard Holmes also read the manuscript and thus saved me from committing many solecisms. None of the above is responsible for what appears here, but I am grateful to them all. I alone am responsible for any errors of fact or interpretation. I am also most grateful to my editors at Oxford University Press, Anne Gelling and Ruth Parr, and to their colleagues for their patience and assistance.

The following institutions and individuals have kindly given me permission to quote from material to which they own the copyright: the Bedfordshire and Luton Archives and Record Services; the Essex Record Office; the Trustees of the Essex Regiment Museum; the Trustees of the Liddell Hart Centre for Military Archives, King's College London; the Trustees of the National Army Museum; the Trustees of the Royal Norfolk Regiment Collection and Norfolk Museums and Archaeology Service; the Department of Documents and the Department of Sound Archives of the Imperial War Museum; the Suffolk Record Office, Bury St Edmunds Branch; Mrs Lionel Baker; Mrs Elizabeth Fletcher;

Mr Douglas Gill; Mr H. Glasby; Mr Andrew Phillips, Secretary, Colchester Recalled; Mrs Rosemary Philips; Mr Len Waller; Mr Dunkin Wedd; Major Neil Wimberley. Lt.-Col. Miles Templer gave permission for me to quote from his father's letter to Colonel Hamilton. Despite my best efforts I was unable to contact the holders of the copyrights to the papers of the Earl of Cavan, Col. K. C. Weldon, E. Lye, and A. R. Gaskin. I apologize to them and to anyone else whose copyright I have unwittingly infringed.

Finally, this book is dedicated to my goddaughter, Elizabeth Anne Russell, because she asked for it.

D.F.

29 August 2004

Contents

Abbreviations

ACI	Army Council Instruction
Adj.-Gen.	Adjutant-General
ASC	Army Service Corps
AWOL	absent without leave
BAOR	British Army of the Rhine
BSM	Battery Sergeant-Major
Capt.	Captain
CB	Confinement to Barracks
CCC	Churchill College Cambridge
CDS	Chief of Defence Staff
CIGS	Chief of the Imperial General Staff
C-in-C	Commander-in-Chief
CO	Commanding Officer
Col.	Colonel
CPGB	Communist Party of Great Britain
Cpl.	Corporal
CQMS	Company Quarter-Master Sergeant
CSM	Company Sergeant-Major
DCGS	Deputy Chief of the General Staff
DCIGS	Deputy Chief of the Imperial General Staff
DCLI	Duke of Cornwall's Light Infantry
DGAMS	Director General of the Army Medical Services
DGMT	Director General of Military Training
DGTA	Director General of the Territorial Army
DMT	Director of Military Training
DPS	Director of Personnel Services
DSD	Director of Staff Duties
DTA	Director Territorial Army
ECAB	Executive Committee of the Army Board
ECAC	Executive Committee of the Army Council
ERM	Essex Regiment Museum
ERO	Essex Record Office
Gen.	General
GOC	General Officer Commanding
GSO	General Staff Officer
HQ	Headquarters

IWM	Imperial War Museum
IWMSA	Imperial War Museum Sound Archives
KR	*King's Regulations and Orders for the Army*
KRRC	King's Royal Rifle Corps
l/cpl.	lance-corporal
LHCMA	Liddell Hart Centre for Military Archives
Lt.	Lieutenant
Lt.-Col.	Lieutenant-Colonel
Lt.-Gen.	Lieutenant-General
Maj.	Major
Maj.-Gen.	Major-General
MML	*Manual of Military Law*
MOD	Ministry of Defence
NAM	National Army Museum
NCO	non-commissioned officer
PBI	Poor Bloody Infantry
PRO	Public Record Office
PSC	passed staff college
PSI	Permanent Staff Instructor
Pte.	Private
PUS	Permanent Under-Secretary
QMG	Quarter-Master General
QR	*Queen's Regulations and Orders for the Army*
RA	Royal Artillery
RAC	Royal Armoured Corps
RAEC	Royal Army Education Corps
RAMC	Royal Army Medical Corps
RAOC	Royal Army Ordnance Corps
RAPC	Royal Army Pay Corps
RASC	Royal Army Service Corps
RCS	Royal Corps of Signals
RE	Royal Engineers
REME	Royal Electrical and Mechanical Engineers
RFA	Royal Field Artillery
RGA	Royal Garrison Artillery
RHA	Royal Horse Artillery
RMAS	Royal Military Academy Sandhurst
RNRM	Royal Norfolk Regiment Museum
RQMS	Regimental Quartermaster Sergeant
RSM	Regimental Sergeant-Major
RTC	Royal Tank Corps
RTR	Royal Tank Regiment
RUR	Royal Ulster Rifles

(S)	(Service)
Sgt.	Sergeant
SAS	Special Air Service
SRO	Suffolk Record Office (Bury St Edmunds Branch)
S/Sgt.	Staff Sergeant
(TF)	(Territorial Force)
(VB)	(Volunteer Battalion)
VCIGS	Vice Chief of the Imperial General Staff
WO	War Office
WO1	Warrant Officer Class 1
WO2	Warrant Officer Class 2
2i/c	second-in-command
2/Lt.	Second Lieutenant

Introduction

In 1917 a cockney sergeant in the Norfolk Regiment who was based at the Infantry Base Depot at Étaples in France marched his squad across the sand dunes and ordered them to sit down. His job was to give them a short lecture on the meaning and significance of *esprit de corps*, or the feeling that a soldier should entertain towards his regiment. The subject was a vital one in the view of the military authorities as it formed the foundations of military discipline and morale. '"Sprit de corpse"', he explained, 'is like this 'ere. If you was in the canteen and I come in and you said, 'what you going t' 'ave, sergeant, that's "sprit de corpse". Now you can smoke.'[1]

Not every soldier or writer has treated the subject of the place of the regiment in British military history so pithily or so flippantly. But those who have written about it have been in no doubt about its importance. Few would disagree with John Keegan's contention that the regimental system is 'the most significant of British military institutions, the principle vehicle of the nation's military culture'.[2] What this book will try to do is to determine the nature, significance, and influence of that culture, and the means by which the regiment transmitted it from one generation of soldiers to the next in the century after 1870.

This is an area of some contention, something that is reflected by the fact that the literature and commentaries on the regimental system fall into three broad categories. Some soldiers and writers have celebrated its virtues. In the eyes of generations of senior soldiers, *esprit de corps* was a product of the regimental system. When a soldier, be he officer or other rank, enlisted he joined a particular regiment or corps, expecting to remain in it for the whole of his military career, and to identify with it as closely as he identified with his own family. Indeed, in the view of many senior regimental officers and NCOs, the regiment should become his family. Speaking in February 1881 when he received the Freedom of the City of London, Sir Frederick (later Lord) Roberts, who had established a formidable reputation fighting in Afghanistan, insisted that 'Soldiers have hearts and imaginations like other men. Therefore it is that regiments are proud of their traditions. Therefore it is that the men are proud

---

[1] IWMSA, Accession No. 000737/16, Private F. Dixon, Reel 8.

[2] J. Keegan, 'Regimental Ideology', in G. Best and A. Wheatcroft (eds.), *War, Economy and the Military Mind* (London: Croom Helm, 1976), 16.

of a regiment that has made a conspicuous name, and look forward to adding to its reputation. This is *esprit de corps*.'[3]

A century later Sir John Hackett, a cavalryman and paratrooper turned academic, echoed Roberts's assessment of the importance of the regimental system in sustaining morale and explained something that often puzzled or irritated laymen, the small differences in military customs and modes of behaviour between one regiment and another. Like the system of localized recruiting that was supposed to ensure that the officers and men of a regiment came from the same city or county, they created a sense of common identity and were

directed to the development of coherence in the group. It is used first of all to demonstrate a unity of context to the members of the group. It also indicates a difference between this group and other groups—that this regiment, which wears its hat back to front, is not the same as that, which does not. Once you have established an awareness of difference, of otherness, you are some way towards creating a feeling of betterness, and if you can develop that in your group, your unit, you can jack up your standards. 'This may be good enough,' you can say, 'for those Queens Park Rangers or the Loamshire Fusiliers but it simply will not do in the Fortieth Foot and Mouth', or the Royal Death Watch, or whatever it happens to be.[4]

Some commentators have, therefore, celebrated the virtues of the regimental system, seeing a strength in the sense of 'otherness' and 'betterness' that it created because they constituted powerful props to battlefield morale.[5] This view has been endorsed at the highest level of British society. Replying to a toast in her honour at a gathering of regimental colonels assembled in November 1956, Queen Elizabeth II told them that the British army

more perhaps than any other in the world, has always lived through the regiment and the regimental tradition. In the hour of battle it has repeatedly relied on it, on the pride and comradeship of men who would sooner die than betray the traditions of their corps or be unworthy of the men of old who fought before them under its colours.

There is no first among the regiments and corps of my Army and there is no last; all are bound in the same spirit of brotherhood and proud service to sovereign and country and each regards itself—with every reason—as second to none.[6]

But where some commentators have seen the sense that each regiment possessed its own unique and separate identity as a source of strength, others have argued that it was a major weakness. The critical literature on

---

[3] NAM 7510–94. Scrapbook of Maj.-Gen. W. O. Barnard, *The Times*, 15 Feb. 1881.

[4] Gen. Sir J. Hackett, *The Profession of Arms* (London: Sidgwick & Jackson, 1983), 223–4.

[5] J. Baynes, *Morale: A Study of Men and Courage. The Second Scottish Rifles at the Battle of Neuve Chapelle 1915* (London: Leo Cooper, 1967); Maj. R. M. Barnes, *A History of the Regiments and Uniforms of the British Army* (London: Seeley Service, 1950, repr. 1962), 314.

[6] *The Times*, 28 Nov. 1956.

the regimental system has been a product of a wider critique of British society that has sought to explain Britain's 'decline' by reference to a culture of gentlemanly amateurism that grew increasingly out of place in the twentieth century.[7] The regiments, led as they were by scions of the public schools, were easily regarded as the quintessentially 'gentlemanly' institution. While agreeing that the regimental system helped to sustain morale, its critics have argued that in at least four other respects it was a major handicap. First, because their mental horizons were confined to their own regiment, the British army was not led by a professional officer corps. Officers continued to exhibit an easy-going amateurism that set them apart from their civilian contemporaries, who were more likely to take their profession seriously.[8] Officership was a pleasant pastime which offered plenty of sport and leave in return for minimal duties.[9] Secondly, the overwhelmingly powerful sense of loyalty to their regiment the system created produced a parochial mindset that was positively dangerous. It meant that soldiers of different regiments and arms of service too often failed to realize that they had to cooperate on the battlefield if they were to gain maximum advantage from their different weapons.[10] Thirdly, their commitment to tradition made regiments conservative and backward-looking institutions, suspicious of change and reluctant to adopt new ways of doing things and new technologies with which to do them.[11] The cavalry have been the subject of particular criticism for their supposed inclination to cling to their regimental identities rather than embrace technology in the shape of the tank.[12] Finally, by confining promotion up to and including the rank of major to a series of separate regimental lists, the regimental system ensured that some officers were likely to be promoted more rapidly than others, depending entirely on their regiment. This meant that the system of promotion did not allow officers of equal ability equal opportunity to rise to high command and so failed to ensure that the best officers got to the top of the army.[13]

---

[7] M. Collins, 'The Fall of the English Gentleman: The National Character in Decline, c.1918–1970', *Historical Research*, 75 (2002), 90–111.

[8] C. Barnett, *The Desert Generals* (London: Allen & Unwin, 1983), 103–4; G. Harries-Jenkins, *The Army in Victorian Society* (London: Routledge & Kegan Paul, 1977), 1–3.

[9] Capt. J. R. Kennedy, *This, Our Army* (London: Hutchinson, 1935), 116–17.

[10] D. Graham, 'Sans Doctrine: British Army Tactics in the First World War', in T. Travers and C. Archon (eds.), *Men at War: Politics, Technology and Innovation in the Twentieth Century* (Chicago: Precedent Publishing 1982), 75; P. Griffith, 'The Extent of Tactical Reform in the British Army', in P. Griffith (ed.), *British Fighting Methods in the Great War* (London: Frank Cass, 1996), 6.

[11] P. Dietz, *The Last of the Regiments: Their Rise and Fall* (London: Brassey's, 1990), 1–3.

[12] S. Bidwell and D. Graham, *Fire-power: British Army Weapons and Theories of War 1904–1945* (London: Allen & Unwin, 1982), 191–2; W. Murray, 'Armoured Warfare: The British, French and German Experiences', in id. and A. R. Millett, *Military Innovation in the Interwar Period* (Cambridge: Cambridge University Press, 1996), 22.

[13] Kennedy, *This, Our Army*, 80–6.

There is nothing particularly original about any of these criticisms. Radical writers looking for sticks with which to beat the aristocratic state during the Crimean War voiced the same criticisms.[14] Furthermore, neither the celebrants nor the critics of the regimental system have emerged unscathed. Peter Simkins has analysed the composition and performance of the British divisions of the BEF in the final hundred days of the First World War and concluded that some of those that fought most successfully had very largely lost their locally recruited character, and had been almost entirely rebuilt after suffering heavy losses in the spring of 1918.[15] While endorsing the generally positive impact of the regimental system in sustaining morale, John Lee has suggested that during the First World War such loyalties were not endogenous, and that they were sometimes complemented by a parallel loyalty to the division.[16] In his study of the development of armoured doctrine in the British army between the world wars, R. H. Larson pointed out that the series of offensives that the BEF mounted during the 'Hundred Days' of August to November 1918 were a brilliantly successful series of combined arms operations.[17]

These comments were made in passing, and as part of examinations of a variety of wider issues. A smaller group of commentators have looked at the regimental system and tried systematically to analyse its functions.[18] Scholars in general have perhaps shunned the subject because of its overtly antiquarian overtones. The history of individual regiments has given rise to a plethora of works, but, as a subsequent chapter in this book will demonstrate, they were intended to create and perpetuate a particular vision of 'the regiment', not to place it in its social or historical context.[19] Most consist of one part parochialism and one part hagiography. There are only a handful of scholarly accounts of the place of the

[14] See e.g. *The Times*, 15 Feb. 1855, 21 Apr. 1855.

[15] P. Simkins, 'Co-stars or Supporting Cast? British Divisions in the "Hundred Days", 1918', in Griffith (ed.), *British Fighting Methods*, 50.

[16] J. Lee, 'The British Divisions at Third Ypres', in P. Liddle (ed.), *Passchendaele in Perspective: The Third Battle of Ypres* (London: Leo Cooper, 1997), 224–5.

[17] R. H. Larson, *The British Army and the Theory of Armoured Warfare, 1918–40* (Newark, NJ: University of Delaware, 1984), 32.

[18] D. Weston, 'The Army: Mother, Sister and Mistress: The British Regiment', in M. Edmonds (ed.), *The Defence Equation: British Military Systems—Policy, Planning and Performance since 1945* (London: Brassey's, 1986), 139–55; Keegan, 'Regimental Ideology'; E. Lummis, 'The English County Regiments', *Journal of the Society for Army Historical Research*, 74 (1995), 221–9; P. Mileham, 'Moral Component—the "Regimental System" ', in A. Alexandrou, R. Bartle, and R. Holmes (eds.), *New People Strategies for the British Armed Forces* (London: Frank Cass, 2002), 70–90. There are some indications that this group may soon grow larger. Timothy Bowman's study of the Irish regiments during the First World War stands as a model that future scholars would do well to follow. See T. Bowman, *Irish Regiments in the Great War* (Manchester: Manchester University Press, 2003).

[19] A bibliography of regimental and unit histories published in 1965 listed some 2,500 titles. See J. M. Brereton, 'Records of the Regiment: A Survey of Regimental Histories', *Journal of the Society for Army Historical Research*, 74 (1995), 107–20.

regimental system within the structure of the British Army. They have traced its history from the establishment of the first permanent regiments as they emerged in Britain after the Restoration in 1662, when Parliament permitted the establishment of a standing army. By the mid-nineteenth century, even before the Cardwell–Childers reforms, some of the essential components of the regimental system were already in existence. For most soldiers 'the army' was a vague legal abstraction. They enlisted in a particular regiment, often for twenty-one years, and could not be transferred outside it against their will. They learnt that they now belonged to a distinct corporation, with its own traditions, and that they had a duty to fight to uphold its reputation.

The Cardwell–Childers reforms did not create the regimental system. They built on these foundations and extended their scope. By 1881 every regular infantry battalion bar one was linked to another and they were firmly rooted in the local community. Every regiment had a permanent depot and a geographically defined recruiting area from which it was supposed to draw all of its recruits. By a complex system of linking regular county and city regiments with the auxiliary forces, that is the semi-professional Militia and the amateur soldiers of the Volunteers, a bridge was supposed to be created between civilian society and the regular army. This process of localization was significant because it created a local pride in the regiments that was new. After 1881 the civilian population came to perceive 'their' local regiment as part of the wider community. This bore fruit in both world wars when men were willing to enlist because they knew that they were not joining some faceless bureaucracy, but a local institution that was as familiar to them as their local football team. Whether or not loyalty to the regiment became so all-encompassing that it also diverted soldiers from following the example of many of their Continental neighbours and intervening in politics is a question that remains unresolved.[20]

A marked social hierarchy also developed amongst the regiments. Because of their long lineage and close connections to the Royal Household, the Brigade of Guards and the Household Cavalry were at the top, followed by some of the line cavalry, and the rifle regiments that had distinguished themselves during the Peninsular War. Next came the remaining cavalry regiments, the Scottish Highland Regiments, the Light Infantry, the Fusiliers, the southern English county regiments, the Lowland Scots, the Irish, and Welsh regiments and then the remaining county regiments. But this hierarchy quickly became of more than merely social significance, for, it was claimed, officers in the socially more prestigious

[20] H. Strachan, *The Politics of the British Army* (Oxford: Clarendon Press, 1997), 195–233; J. Keegan, 'Always a World Apart', *Times Literary Supplement*, 24 July 1998.

regiments were far more likely than their less fortunate comrades to reach high rank.

Culture is an elusive concept, and military culture perhaps doubly so.[21] In broad terms this investigation will adopt an anthropologist's definition of culture as 'A set of rules or standards shared by members of a society, which when acted upon by the members produce behaviour that falls within a range of variation the members consider proper and acceptable'.[22] These rules and patterns of behaviour do not spring into existence fully formed.

Like all cultures, the culture of the regimental system did not just exist. It had to be manufactured, and then transmitted from generation to generation. This book will therefore begin by examining in Chapter 1 the origins of the reforms that transformed the structure of the British regimental system between 1870 and 1881, labelled here for the sake of convenience the Cardwell–Childers reforms after the Secretaries of State for War who instituted them. It will also analyse the factors that shaped them, and the goals their architects hoped to achieve. One of their objectives was to create regimental communities rooted in existing civilian communities. The second chapter will therefore consider who enlisted in the regular army and the extent to which the Cardwell–Childers reforms succeeded in creating regiments able to fill their ranks with recruits from the same locality. The third chapter will examine how, through the process of basic training, the military authorities began to impose the identity of a soldier onto men who had hitherto been civilians.

One vitally important aspect of that process was to imbue each recruit and young officer with the idea that he belonged to a uniquely significant community, the 'regiment'. Chapter 4 will consider how the notion of 'the regiment' was constructed. Both regimental officers and the military authorities were agreed about the utility of regimental identities in helping to sustain discipline and morale. But, as Chapter 5 will show, that did not mean that they imbued the regimental system with the same degree of emotional commitment. Most regular soldiers spent most of their working lives not on the battlefield, but in barracks or cantonments. The sixth chapter will examine how their everyday lives were regulated within the structures created by the regimental system. Chapter 7 will scrutinize the quality of the management of the regiments by looking at the selection, training, and professional progression of its leaders, both officers and non-commissioned officers, in an attempt to discover whether the army did lack a professional leadership cadre. Chapter 8

---

[21] W. Murray, 'Does Military Culture Matter?', *Orbis*, 43 (1999), 27–42.

[22] W. Haviland, *Cultural Anthropology* (Fort Worth: Harcourt Brace College Publishers, 1996), 32.

will measure one way in which the army did, or did not, succeeded in imposing an all-embracing military identity on regimental soldiers by looking at the operation of the formal disciplinary code and by examining the propensity of officers and other ranks to step outside it.

In Chapter 9 the focus will shift to the auxiliary army, the Militia, Volunteers, and Territorials. It will assess the extent to which they did indeed form a bridge between civilian society and the regular army by forming a single, seamless regimental community. Chapter 10 will explore still further the relationship between the army and the civilian world by assessing the extent to which civilian society took their 'local' regiments to their hearts. One of the great paradoxes that requires explanation was why so many civilians were willing, both metaphorically and literally, to cheer the army on, but so reluctant to join it themselves. Chapter 11 will consider the role of the regimental system in inhibiting the adoption of new technologies, in sustaining morale on the battlefield, and in determining the extent to which it was, or was not, responsible for inhibiting all-arms cooperation.

The heyday of the Cardwell–Childers system extended from 1881 to the Second World War and therefore the focus of the analysis in the preceding chapters will be on that period. But the final chapter will examine how and why the system withered and was transformed in the twenty-five years after 1945.

A Note on Terminology

Before embarking on this analysis, it is necessary to explain some of the nomenclature used in this book. 'Officers' were men who held the King's or Queen's commission as officers in the land forces of Great Britain. 'Other ranks' consisted of all those members of the army who were not officers, ranging from the most-recently recruited private soldier, up through the several ranks of non-commissioned officer, to the most senior of the non-commissioned ranks, that of Warrant Officer Class 1.

British military terminology is cursed by words that have multiple or imprecise meanings, and none more so than the word 'regiment'. The *Concise Oxford Dictionary* defines it as 'a permanent unit of an army, typically divided into several smaller units and often into two battalions'. In the context of the British army this is both misleading and incomplete, and indeed the language of 'the regiment' is so shot through with anomalies that to talk of a 'regimental system' is itself almost a misnomer, for there was much about it that was anything but systematic. After 1881 most infantry regiments had three elements. They contained two line (i.e. regular) battalions (although a handful of regiments had four), which consisted of full-time professional officers and other ranks. They also usually had two Militia battalions (renamed Special Reserve battalions in 1908), consisting of semi-professional soldiers who were called up for several weeks of full-time training each year, but were then released to go about their normal civilian occupations for the remainder of the year. And finally, they contained a varying number of Volunteer, or after 1908 Territorial, battalions. These were composed of civilians who undertook military training in the evening or at weekends. An infantry regiment was an administrative organization. The battalion, a force with an establishment of between 800–1,000 officers and other ranks and commanded by a Lieutenant-Colonel, was the army's basic tactical infantry unit.[23] Even in peacetime, as we will see, regular battalions in the same regiment rarely served together, and, except in the opening stages of the First World War, it was rare for Regular, Militia, or Territorial units of the same regiment actually to fight side by side.The regular cavalry, and its part-time associates, the Yeomanry, used some of the same terminology, but it had different meanings. The Yeomanry, like the infantry, was raised on a local basis. The regular cavalry was not. Both were organized into regiments and each regiment was commanded by a Lieutenant-Colonel. In the late nineteenth century a regular cavalry regiment had an establishment of about 600 all ranks. Neither the cavalry nor the Yeomanry was subject to linking by the Cardwell–Childers reforms.

A further range of anomalies arises from the fact that the late Victorian Army also had two 'Corps' regiments, the Royal Artillery and the Royal Engineers. The principal way in which they differed from the infantry and cavalry was in how they recruited their rank and file. After 1881 recruits joined a particular cavalry or infantry regiment and could not be transferred to a different one without their consent. However, recruits for sappers (engineers) joined the corps of Royal Engineers and could be freely transferred between its constituent tactical units, although not into another corps, as the military authorities saw fit. Before the Boer War the Royal Regiment of Artillery was, for purposes of enlistment, divided into two corps. The Royal Field Artillery and Royal Horse Artillery, both of which accompanied the army into the field, constituted one Corps, and the Royal Garrison Artillery, which manned fortress artillery, constituted the second. Other ranks who enlisted in either corps could be posted at will between any unit within that corps.[24]

---

[23] This remains the case today, although the number of men in a battalion has shrunk to about 650 all ranks.

[24] Lt.-Gen. W. H. Goodenough and Lt.-Col. J. C. Dalton, *The Army Book of the British Empire: A Record of the Development and Present Composition of the Military Forces and their Duties in Peace and War* (London: HMSO, 1893), 100, 224.

In 1920 the Army Council agreed to amalgamate the RFA and RGA, although it retained the RHA as a corps d'elite.[25] Henceforth not only other ranks but also officers could be posted at will between all parts of the Corps. The basic tactical unit of the Royal Artillery was the battery, and of the Royal Engineers the field company. Both were normally commanded by a major, and at the end of the nineteenth century consisted of between 150 and 200 officers and other ranks.

The Household troops, the cavalry, infantry, Royal Artillery, and Royal Engineers constituted the 'teeth arms', that is those soldiers who could expect actually to engage the enemy in battle. In the main, this book will examine the significance and development of the regimental system from their perspective. However, they did not constitute the entire army. In 1898 approximately 4 per cent of the army was organized into a number of Services, principally the Army Service Corps, responsible for supplies and transport, and the Army Medical Corps, responsible for providing troops with medical attention. There were also a number of smaller departmental corps such as the Army Ordnance Corps, the Army Pay Corps, the Corps of Army School Masters, and the Corps of Military Police, whose duties were indicated by their name. In the course of the twentieth century the ratio of 'teeth' to 'tail' shifted in favour of the latter and the number of 'Services' and 'Departmental Corps' multiplied. By 1941 slightly more than one in four soldiers was serving in one of the Services or Departmental Corps.

The word 'unit' also has an ambiguous meaning. In the case of the cavalry, infantry, and after 1923 the Royal Tank Corps, it denoted a Lieutenant-Colonel's command, be it a battalion of infantry or tanks, or a regiment of cavalry. In the case of the Royal Engineers, the 'unit' was the company. In the case of the Royal Artillery it was the battery until 1938, when the gunners conformed to the infantry and cavalry, and batteries were grouped into permanent regiments, each commanded by a Lieutenant-Colonel. And finally, the phrase 'the military authorities' has been used as a collective noun to denote all of those senior officers and layers of command who, in rank at least, stood above the regimental soldier, and attempted to direct his and his regiment's destiny. They ranged from District Commanders, usually Major-Generals, at the bottom, to the C-in-C or CIGS, usually a Field-Marshal, at the top. Their powers and responsibilities were delineated in great detail in the opening chapter of successive editions of *King's* or *Queen's Regulations*.[26] To anyone serving with a regiment, they were definitely 'they' and not 'us'.

[25] PRO WO 163/25, Précis No. 1023, Organisation of the Royal Regiment of Artillery (Reports of Lord Byng's and Brigadier-General De Brett's committee), 16 July 1920.
[26] War Office, *KR, 1912* (London: HMSO, 1912), pp. xvi, 1–37; War Office, *KR, 1928* (London: HMSO, 1928), 1–27; War Office, *KR, 1940* (London: HMSO, 1940), pp. xiv, 1–33; War Office, *QR, 1955* (London: HMSO, 1955), 1–39.

CHAPTER ONE

The Cardwell–Childers Reforms and the Re-creation of the Regimental System

In 1854 an anonymous cavalry officer told *The Times*:

The peculiarity of the English army has always been what I may term the regimental system, and its excellence is intimately connected with it. Our expeditions at various times may have been badly planned, our commanders bad, our commissariat bad, but the regiments themselves—that is, the men and officers—have invariably been good. The honour, the fair name of the individual regiment, the desire of all in it to maintain that name, has ever been the keystone of our military arch.[1]

Cardwell and Childers did not, therefore, create the regimental system. What they did was to recreate it in a different form.

In the 1860s the land forces of the Crown were divided into four parts. The largest single component consisted of the Regular Army. In 1861, when it numbered about 220,000 NCOs and other ranks, it was composed of three regiments of Horse Guards, twenty-eight regiments of line cavalry, three regiments of Foot Guards, 110 line infantry regiments, and two Corps Regiments, the Royal Artillery and the Royal Engineers. The first twenty-five line infantry regiments consisted of two battalions; two others (the King's Royal Rifle Corps and the Rifle Brigade) had four battalions each, while the remainder had only a single battalion. From 1847 volunteers could enlist in the ranks of one of the line infantry regiments of the Regular Army for an initial period of ten years, followed by a second period of eleven years. Soldiers who served for the whole twenty-one years became eligible for a pension. *Esprit de corps* was the product of long service in a single regiment. Regiments could be posted to anywhere in the world, but soldiers could not be cross-posted to another regiment without their consent. In 1782 most line regiments had been given county titles in an effort to overcome the recruiting crisis that accompanied the War for American Independence. But in most cases the link was more nominal than real. Regiments had no permanent base in their county, and they continued to find recruits from wherever they could.[2]

---

[1] *The Times*, 1 Dec. 1854.

[2] PP (1881), XXI C. 2792. *General Order 32 of 1873*, 1 Apr. 1873; Lummis, 'The English County Regiments', 221–9.

Aspiring soldiers who did not wish to sever all connections with their civilian associations could volunteer to join the Militia. In 1868 it numbered about 130,000 men, and was organized into 138 infantry battalions and thirty-one artillery units that manned coastal defence batteries. It had been created as a home defence force and its members could not, unlike regular soldiers, be compelled to serve overseas. Militiamen normally enlisted in the ranks of a regiment for a period of five years, and, like the regulars, could not be posted away from their regiment unless they consented. After a few months' full-time initial training, they were released into civilian life but recalled for a period of a few weeks' annual refresher training. Recruiting for the Militia was organized on a county basis and numbers were set according to population density. Although the state retained the power to conscript men for the Militia through the use of the ballot, it was never applied and recruits were attracted by the offer of cash bounties.[3] It had no cavalry arm, but a part-time reserve mounted force did exist, in the shape of forty-six Yeomanry regiments.

Finally, men with martial aspirations who could not afford to leave their civilian responsibilities behind them even for more than a few days could join the Volunteers and carry out their training in the evening, at weekends, and during a short annual camp lasting no more than two weeks. The Volunteers had been formed in 1859–60 as a patriotic response to the imagined threat of a French invasion. In 1862 the Volunteers consisted of 134,000 riflemen, 24,000 gunners, 2,900 engineers, and a handful of mounted troops. The riflemen were organized into eighty-six consolidated battalions and 134 administrative battalions. Like the Militia and Yeomanry, the Volunteers were recruited on a local basis. Most consolidated battalions were raised in densely populated urban areas, where it was possible for the men of the whole battalion to come together for training. Some administrative battalions existed in more sparsely populated parts of the country, where it was difficult for more than a company to meet regularly for training, while others were a device to persuade self-contained companies that had a strong local identity to merge it into a larger organization for the sake of military efficiency. Like the Militia and Yeomanry, the Volunteers could not be compelled to serve overseas.[4]

In view of the praise that the anonymous cavalry officer quoted above heaped on the regimental system as it existed in the mid-1850s, it might seem strange that Cardwell and Childers thought it necessary to make

---

[3] PP (1890), XIX. C. 5922. *Report of the committee appointed to enquire into certain questions that have arisen with respect to the Militia*, xi; Col. G. Jackson Hay, *An Epitomized History of the Militia (The 'Constitutional' Force)* (London: United Services Gazette, 1908), 155–7.

[4] PP (1862), XXVII. C. 5067. *Report of the Commissioners appointed to inquire into the condition of the Volunteer Force in Great Britain*, i–ii.

any changes. But by the 1860s the agglomeration of regiments that was the British army was the target of growing criticism, both from Radicals, who saw in aspects of army organization some of the worst features of the aristocratic state that they so detested, and from some army officers who had considerable doubts about its military efficiency. Between 1864 and 1869 funding for the Army and Ordnance was, after debt charges, easily the largest single item of public expenditure, exceeding spending on the Navy by an average of about £4m per annum.[5] But a considerable proportion of these costs did not go to buy effective military power but to pay the pensions of retired soldiers. Second, the Crimean War and the Indian Mutiny had demonstrated that the army lacked the power of rapid expansion in wartime. When an expedition of any size left Britain, the army did not have a reserve that could be quickly mobilized to make good the losses.[6] Efforts made in 1867 to create an Army Reserve of 20,000 men failed lamentably.[7] Third, respectable working-class men were willing to fight for their country, as witnessed by their readiness to join the Volunteers in the 1860s, but they were not willing to join the Regulars. Two royal commissions that examined recruiting in the 1860s showed that most regular recruits were drawn from the dregs of society, attracted by a mixture of financial bounties, drink, and unrealistically rosy descriptions of army life.[8] Serving officers were particularly worried that too many of the recruits they were getting came from the slums of the great cities and lacked the physical strength and amenability to discipline of their rural cousins.[9]

Finally, for all the money spent on it, there were growing doubts about the army's military effectiveness. While Bismarck united Germany with blood and iron, Britain did nothing, abdicating its position as a Great Power because of the ineffectiveness and inefficiency of its army.[10] Radical critics of the system in which officers in the Regular Army could purchase their initial commission and then each step in rank up to Lieutenant-Colonel had long maintained that it diminished the army's effectiveness by degrading the quality of the officer corps. Purchase, in

---

[5] B. R. Mitchell and P. Deane, *An Abstract of British Historical Statistics* (Cambridge: Cambridge University Press, 1976), 397.

[6] PRO WO 33/19. Reserve Forces. Report, 1868–9, 1 Apr. 1869.

[7] T. F. Gallagher, 'British Military Thinking and the Coming of the Franco-Prussian War', *Military Affairs*, 39 (1975), 19.

[8] R. L. Blanco, 'Army Recruiting Reforms, 1861–67', *Journal of the Society for Army Historical Research*, 46 (1968), 217–24.

[9] PP (1861), XV. C. 2762. *Report of the Commissioners appointed to inquire into the present system of recruiting in the Army*, QQ. 173–6, 649, 993.

[10] PRO 33/22. Brig.-Gen. J. Adye, Army Organisation, Dec. 1870; Anon. [Douglas Galton], 'Article VIII. The Military Forces of the Crown', *Edinburgh Review*, 133 (1871), 207–42.

their estimation, attracted the lazy and gave little incentive to the able.[11] Some regular and auxiliary officers were also concerned about the absence of any formal institutional links between the different parts of the Crown's land services, and wanted to create closer connections between them.[12] The poor showing of volunteer units in the opening stages of the American Civil War, and the success of Prussian conscripts in the wars of 1864, 1866, and 1870, emphasized how important discipline and thorough professional training for both officers and other ranks were on the battlefield.[13]

Critics of existing arrangements were also struck by the advantage the Prussians reaped from their system of territorial recruiting and mass conscription, which linked together the Line, Reserve, and *Landwehr* (militia) into a single consolidated force. 'Each regiment of the [Prussian] army', Maj.-Gen. James Lindsay, the Inspector General of Reserve Forces, wrote in April 1869, 'belongs to a district from which it recruits and where it is quartered. Its own Landwehr battalion is attached to it, bearing the same number and designation; and the Reserve who have served in its ranks belong to it.'[14] In wartime the Reserves were used to bring Line regiments up to their full establishment, the Landwehr garrisoned fortresses, and within weeks the Prussians could double the size of their field army.

The regimental system that was put in place by Cardwell was intended to address these problems. The major institutional reforms that they enacted are easily summarized. In introducing the Army Estimates in March 1870 Cardwell explained that his objectives were 'in time of peace to maintain a force which shall be moderate in amount and susceptible of easy expansion, and the reserve of which shall be so within reach as to be immediately available on the occurrence of any public emergency'.[15] Short service and the reduction in the number of soldiers serving overseas would, Cardwell hoped, popularize service in the Regular Army, attract a better class of recruit, and reduce losses from desertion by doing away with the prospect that soldiers could expect to spend

[11] T. F. Gallagher, ' "Cardwellian mysteries": The Fate of the British Army Regulation Bill, 1871', *Historical Journal*, 18 (1975), 335–47; A. Bruce, *The Purchase System in the British Army 1660–1871* (London: Royal Historical Society, 1980), 75–85, 115–24; Sir C. E. Trevelyan, *The British Army in 1868* (London: Longman, Green & Co., 1868).

[12] Maj. A. Leahy, 'Our Infantry Forces and Infantry Reserves', *Journal of the Royal United Services Institute*, 12 (1868), 310–58; PP (1862), XXVII. C. 5067. *Report of the Commissioners ... vii. On the Militia* see the discussion at the Royal United Services Institute that followed Leahy's lecture.

[13] H. Cunningham, *The Volunteer Force* (London: Croom Helm, 1975), 84–8; Anon. [Douglas Galton], 'Article VIII', 215–16.

[14] PRO WO 33/19. Reserve Forces. Report, 1868–9, 1 Apr. 1869.

[15] Parl. Debs. (series 3) vol. 199, col. 1159.

most of their adult lives in colonial exile. Between 1869 and 1871 the size of overseas garrisons was therefore reduced by more than 25,000 men. Henceforth the white settlement colonies would have to raise their own militia for local defence. And in 1870 the Army Enlistment Act reduced the normal period of service from twenty-one years to twelve years. But most men would pass into the Army Reserve after only six years' colour service, being liable to recall for a further six years only in the event of a serious national emergency. This would give the army the power of expansion it had lacked in the past, but would also reduce the estimates by cutting the size of the pension bill, for most men could expect to leave the army in their mid or late twenties, still young enough to take up another occupation.[16]

The Localisation Act of July 1872 and General Order 32 issued on 1 April 1873 were intended to solve the problem of finding drafts for units overseas without completely destroying regimental *esprit de corps* by having recourse to cross-posting men from one regiment into another. They did so by imposing linking and localization on the line infantry regiments of the army. The first twenty-five regiments on the Army List already had two battalions. The remaining line infantry regiments, from the 26th to 109th Foot (the 79th excepted) were linked in pairs, although they retained their own cap-badges, numbers, and titles. To facilitate drafting, other ranks, but not officers, were liable to be drafted between the linked battalions. This gave soldiers the psychological comfort of knowing that they could expect to soldier amongst friends while enabling the military authorities to solve the problem of how to maintain units serving overseas. One battalion of the linked battalions would normally serve at home and would supply recruits for its linked battalion serving overseas. After 1881 the normal length of a foreign tour for a battalion was no more than sixteen years. However, no matter how long their unit was overseas, officers and other ranks would normally spend no more than eight years abroad.[17]

General Order 32 also divided the country into sixty-six sub-districts. Each pair of linked line battalions was allocated its own sub-district, where it established a permanent depot. Together with two affiliated Militia battalions and the Volunteer battalions that already existed within its sub-district, they were to form a Brigade under the command of a regular Colonel. Henceforth the regulars were expected to draw their recruits from their own sub-district and their depot was to become the headquarters of their associated Militia and Volunteer units. Cardwell also hoped that if militiamen were trained side by side with the

---

[16] Parl. Debs. (series 3) vol. 201, col. 788.
[17] Goodenough and Dalton, *The Army Book of the British Empire*, 130.

regulars, they would recognize the advantages of full-time service, and freely transfer into the line.[18]

Localization was also designed to sustain morale and discipline. As early as 1842 one British officer, Sir J. E. Alexander, had noted that discipline in those units that recruited from the same part of the country tended to be better than in units that took their men from wherever they could find them.[19] British officers who observed the Prussian army in 1870 were impressed by the same practice. They were particularly struck by the almost suicidal bravery that the Prussian infantry showed during the Battle of Spicheren. They believed that it was due

to the system of localizing the regiments and corps of the North German Army in time of peace. It also follows from this arrangement that the Generals and their Staff know the character of the officers they have to work with in time of war; and the men in the same regiment are fellow townsmen or villagers, and know that their conduct in battle will form the subject of many a home conversation on their return.[20]

Cardwell hoped 'that recruiting & training in Scotland for Scotch Regiments, Wales for Welch etc. will improve and popularize the Army'.[21] While a soldier was serving in his local regiment, and knew that in a few short years he would be returning to his local community, he would be careful of his conduct lest bad reports got back to his friends and family and damaged his prospects when he returned to civilian life.[22]

Cardwell attempted to improve the military efficiency of the auxiliary forces by drawing them closer to the Regular Army. The regulars were to supply adjutants and NCOs as permanent staff instructors to their associated auxiliary units. Henceforth when the Volunteers were brigaded with Regulars they would come under the terms of the Mutiny Act, and so could be disciplined just like regulars. He also tried to weed out inefficient Volunteer Corps by ensuring that the government grant they received depended on their efficiency. Each Volunteer unit would be required to attend brigade training once a year and be liable to forfeit their capitation grant if fewer than 50 per cent did so.[23] When he transformed Cardwell's linked battalions into territorial regiments a decade later, Childers was intent on giving effect to the same principle.

[18] PRO 30/48/1/3/250. Cardwell to the Queen, Dec. 1871; Biddulph, *Lord Cardwell at the War Office*, 173.

[19] Alexander, 'On Desertion in Canada', 473.

[20] PRO WO 32/22. Capt. C. W. Wilson, Notes on a visit to Metz and Strasbourg in November 1870.

[21] PRO 30/48/1/3/f 257. Cardwell to Ponsonby, 23 Dec. 1871.

[22] Parl. Debs. (series 3) vol. 213, col. 443 (5 Aug. 1872).

[23] E. M. Spiers, *The Army and Society 1815–1914* (London: Longman, 1980), 194; Cunningham, *Volunteers*, 90–1.

As he explained to his constituents at Pontefract, he hoped 'To see the line and the auxiliary forces closely bound together, the men in the one feeling themselves to be comrades of the men in the other, drawn from the same classes, wearing the same uniform, proud of the same colours and badges.'[24]

Finally, officers were no longer permitted to purchase commissions, or to transfer willy-nilly from regiment to regiment in search of faster promotion. In July 1871, after the House of Lords had rejected a government bill, Cardwell persuaded Queen Victoria to enact an Order-in-Council abolishing the practice whereby officers in the line could purchase their first commission and each subsequent step up to Lieutenant-Colonel. Lords Lieutenant retained the right to nominate officers in the auxiliary forces to their first commission, but after that, Militia, Yeomanry, and Volunteer commissions and promotions would, like commissions in the line, actually be granted by the Crown.[25] Like the rank and file, unless they were promoted above the rank of Lieutenant-Colonel, they could expect to spend their entire career in a single regiment.

Several aspects of Cardwell's reforms aroused intense criticism in the late 1870s. First, they caused a crisis in recruiting, retaining, and disciplining trained soldiers. Whereas between 1861 and 1865 the Regular Army had needed about 12,500 recruits per annum, short service meant that between 1876 and 1879 it needed 28,800 each year.[26] Although the numbers enlisting did grow, the increase was not sufficient to make good wastage caused by death, discharge, and desertion. The introduction of short service was also accompanied by a steep increase in the number of deserters. The figure rose from 3,332 in 1870 to 7,493 in 1878.[27] There was also an increase in disciplinary offences committed by young soldiers in the first two years of their service. They were driven to desperation by excessively harsh living conditions and a disciplinary code that one regimental officer candidly described in 1874 as a system of 'petty tyranny'. A soldier who, for example, was only a few minutes late returning to barracks was liable to be placed in the cells rather than allowed to go to bed. Knowing that he faced the cells, he might be tempted to remain out of barracks all night, or even longer, and so

---

[24] *The Times*, 20 Jan. 1882.

[25] E. M. Spiers, *The Late Victorian Army, 1866–1902* (Manchester: Manchester University Press, 1992), 14–19; War Office, *Regulations for the Volunteer Force. War Office 1881* (London: HMSO, 1881), 198.

[26] PP (1881), XXI. C. 2791. *Report of the Committee of General and other officers of the army on army reorganisation*, 23.

[27] A. R. Skelley, *The Victorian Army at Home: The Recruitment and Terms and Conditions of the British Regular, 1859–1899* (London: Croom Helm, 1977), 321.

became a deserter.[28] Young soldiers found the constraints of military discipline impossible to bear and were more likely to break the rules than more experienced men because they did not know what the rules were.[29] According to a former NCO in the 79th (Cameron) Highlanders, the system taught the rank and file that

A soldier's motto while he is in the service is, 'Know nothing'. On his silence depends not only his promotion, but his happiness. If it is ever found out that he chatters about the inner life of the regiment, his life is made a hell by his superior officers, and he is liable to be punished on the most paltry excuse. In a regiment crimes are even committed and punished of which the public never hears. It is best for the army's sake that it does not.[30]

Soldiers were also three times more likely than civilians of the comparable age group to commit suicide.[31]

One reason frequently mentioned as an explanation of these problems was that the post-Cardwell army lacked sufficient NCOs who, through dint of experience born of long service, knew how to manage men. In 1877 nearly 12 per cent of the rank and file of the German army were NCOs. The comparable figure in the British army was only 7 per cent. Under the long service system, this imbalance had mattered little because there were enough experienced soldiers in the ranks of most British regiments to act as a steadying influence. But under short service they had been lost. Before 1871, promising soldiers were appointed as lance-corporals only after three or four years' service, and sergeants were mature and experienced men. With the introduction of the short-service system, many privates saw little advantage in accepting the extra responsibilities of a step-up in rank to lance-corporal. The army seemed to offer them little prospect of a long-term career to compensate them for the added responsibilities and the enforced break from their friends in the ranks that promotion entailed.[32] Consequently, in order to fill the gaps this left in their NCO cadres, COs had little option but to appoint men who were willing to accept promotion, even if this meant appointing junior NCOs with only six or eight months' service.[33]

---

[28] Anon., 'Desertion and Recruiting', *United Services Magazine* (July 1874), 296–307.

[29] PRO WO 32/8731. Wolseley to GOC-in-Cs Home and Abroad, 23 Feb. 1884.

[30] Sgt. A. V. Palmer, 'What I saw at Tel-el-Kebir: A Rejoinder', *Nineteenth Century*, 28 (1890), 149.

[31] W. M. Millar, 'Statistics of Deaths by Suicide among Her Majesty's British Troops Serving at Home and Abroad during the Ten Years 1862–1871', *Journal of the Statistical Society of London*, 37 (1874), 187–92; W. Ogle, 'Suicides in England and Wales in Relation to Age, Sex, Season and Occupation', *Journal of the Statistical Society of London*, 49 (1886), 101–35.

[32] PP (1881), XX. C. 2817. *Report of the Committee appointed to consider the conditions of a soldier's service as affected by the introduction of the short service system and other matters in connection therewith*, 15–17.

[33] PP (1881), XXI. C. 2791. *Report of the Committee ...*, QQ. 766, 1631.

Cardwell's critics insisted that inexperienced NCOs were a positive danger. The rank and file had too little respect for men who were barely older than themselves, and young NCOs often lacked the experience and tact to handle recalcitrant characters.[34] They might so throw their weight around and abuse their authority that their men rebelled, and found themselves in front of their commanding officer on a charge of insubordination.[35] Alternatively, according to Maj. Francis Clery, who served as a staff officer in Zululand in 1879,

the men were, in the first place, careless about obeying orders given them by those young non-commissioned officers, and in the next place, which was more serious still a non-commissioned officer was often wary of giving an order, because possibly it would not be obeyed. For with young soldiers an order derives most of its weight from the personal character of the man giving it.[36]

The second major criticism directed at Cardwell's work was that it lowered the quality of the rank and file and threatened to produce an over-age officer corps. Such were the insatiable demands of units overseas for drafts that home service battalions became mere training units for their linked battalions abroad. Their rank and file consisted of two kinds of soldiers, youths under 20 years of age who were not yet sufficiently physically mature to bear the burden of active service without breaking down, and men at the end of their engagement awaiting their release into the reserve.[37] There were equally pressing problems amongst the commissioned ranks. Under the purchase system a reasonably rapid rate of promotion had been secured in the purchase corps, the line infantry, cavalry, and Brigade of Guards, because officers were often willing to sell their commissions to fund their retirement. But soon after the abolition of purchase it became apparent that, in lieu of some other system for regulating promotions and retirements, officers would grow old and grey before they were promoted. By the middle of the 1870s it was estimated that in the line infantry officers would on average serve seven years longer than before the abolition of purchase before reaching the rank of captain, and ten years longer before becoming a major. This meant that they would probably be 35 when they became

---

[34] Field Marshal Lord Roberts, *Roberts in India: The Military Papers of Field Marshal Lord Roberts 1876–1893*, ed. B. Robson (London: Alan Sutton for the Army Records Society, 1993), 271.

[35] Anon., 'Desertion and Recruiting', 304; Anon., 'Remarks on the Present Condition of the Army', *United Services Magazine* (June 1876), 210.

[36] PP (1881), XXI. C. 2791. *Report of the Committee* ..., Q. 4886.

[37] Anon., 'On Recruiting and Forming Reserves for the British Army', *United Services Magazine* (1875), 285–314; Anon., 'The Cost of the British Army and Recruiting', *United Services Magazine* (1875), 497–507.

captains, 49 when they became majors, and 53 when they took command of their battalion as a Lieutenant-Colonel.[38]

Finally, as a consequence of the Regular Army's failure to fill the ranks of home service battalions with enough trained soldiers, the Cardwell reforms did not obviate the evil of cross-posting. In the decade after 1872, the army fought a series of small campaigns, against the Ashanti (1872–3), the Zulus (1879), the Afghans (1879–80), the Boers (1880–81), and the Egyptians (1882), which together were enough to dislocate the system of linking. In 1872 there had been a balance between the number of battalions at home (70) and abroad (71). The Ashanti War tipped the scale to 69 to 72, and by 1879 there were only fifty-nine battalions at home trying to feed drafts to eighty-two abroad.[39] The committee under Sir Patrick MacDougall that devised the details of the localization scheme had foreseen this possibility. They recommended that when both regular battalions of a brigade were overseas, their depot should be raised to the strength of a full battalion so that it could provide both of them with the necessary drafts. But no government ever did this, presumably on the grounds of cost.

Another alternative would have involved calling out the Army Reserve. But to attract men to enlist in the Regular Army, and to minimize the difficulty reservists had in finding civilian employment, Cardwell had decreed that they were to be recalled to the colours only in the event of a grave national emergency. This was done in 1878, during the crisis with Russia, and again in 1882 for the invasion of Egypt. But it could not be done to make up numbers during the many smaller colonial campaigns that did not constitute a grave national emergency. These had to be fought by men already serving with the colours. The consequences of this were made all too plain in South Africa in 1879. The battalions that were dispatched from Britain to confront the Zulus all required large numbers of men to bring them up to war strength, and they could only be found by recourse to 'volunteering', that is by drafting large numbers of men from one regiment to another, a practice widely condemned as destructive of discipline and *esprit de corps*.[40]

By 1881 critics of Cardwell's work had become so vocal that the majority report of a committee of general officers that examined the working of

[38] PP (1876), XV. C. 1569. *Report of the Royal Commission on Army promotion and retirement.*

[39] PP (1881), XXI. C. 2791. *Report of the Committee …*, 9–10.

[40] Ibid. 11; PP (1890), XIX. C. 5922. *Report of the Committee …*, QQ. 8593–8; PRO WO 33/35. C. H. Ellice, Minute by the Adjutant General, 23 June 1880; Lt-Col. W. W. Knollys, 'Boy Soldiers', *Nineteenth Century*, 6 (1879), 6–7; B. Bond, 'The Effect of the Cardwell Reforms in Army Organization, 1874–1904', *Journal of the Royal United Services Institute*, 105 (1960), 516–17; Anon., 'Army Reform', *Edinburgh Review*, 153 (1881), 191–9.

the system wanted to abandon linking entirely and to enlist all soldiers for general service.[41] Cardwell's Liberal successor, Hugh Childers, rejected their advice, just as he did the recommendation of the Adjutant-General, Sir Charles Ellice, who suggested that regimental *esprit de corps* might be preserved and cross-posting avoided if all units followed the example of the Rifle Regiments and were linked into regiments of four, rather than two, battalions.[42] Cardwell had earmarked three and a half million pounds to build the brigade depots and most of it had already been spent. No government could afford to write off such a large programme of public investment.[43] Hence Childers's decision to proceed in the only possible direction and hope that by establishing territorial regiments he could create a new and stronger *esprit de corps* that would withstand the stresses of drafting. Rather than destroy the linking system, he took it a step further, amalgamating the linked battalions into territorial regiments. Each regiment was given a territorial designation corresponding to the locality to which it was connected. The Militia battalions of the sub-district became the third and fourth battalions of the new territorial regiment, and the Volunteer battalions took their numbers and titles after them.[44] After 1881 there were sixty-seven territorial regiments in the army, forty-five with their depots in England, three in Wales, eleven in Scotland, and eight in Ireland. Depending on the density of population in their district, some had only one Volunteer battalion, but most had three and one (the Royal Scots) had eight. To cement the links between the Regulars, Militia, and Volunteers, and to improve the military efficiency of the auxiliaries, the Regulars were to be required to supply Adjutants and NCO permanent staff instructors to train their Militia and Volunteer battalions.[45]

Childers announced three other innovations to humanize service in the Regular Army and overcome the recruiting and retention problem. By lengthening the period of colour service from six to seven years and by reducing the period of reserve service to five years, he tried to meet the criticism that short service deprived the Regular Army of soldiers just as they reached their prime. Soldiers under the age of 20 were not allowed to serve overseas.[46] More specifically, he tried to improve the conditions

---

[41] PP (1881), XXI. C. 2791. *Report of the Committee* ..., 33.

[42] PRO WO 33/35. Memo. by the Adjutant-General. Re-organization of the infantry of the line, 13 Nov. 1880.

[43] PRO WO 163/3. War Office Council meeting, 21 Oct. 1880.

[44] PP (1881), LVIII. C. 2826. *Memorandum showing the principal changes in Army organisation intended to take effect from 1st July 1881* and PP (1881), LVIII. C. 2922. *Revised Memorandum showing the principal changes in Army organisation intended to take effect from 1st July 1881*; PRO WO 32/6091. Composition and title of Territorial Regiments of Infantry, 11 Apr. 1881.

[45] Parl. Debs. (series 3) vol. 204, cols. 350–1 (16 Feb. 1871).

[46] Skelley, *The Victorian Army at Home*, 255; Parl. Debs. (series 3) vol. 259, cols. 195–204.

of service of NCOs so that the Regular Army could retain the services of experienced men to fill these vital roles.[47] It was, the PUS at the War Office concluded in 1881,

more than ever indispensable that what may be called the permanent portion of the Army—i.e. the non-commissioned officers upon whom devolves, in so large a measure, the duty of maintaining discipline among the Reserve men when called up, & of training the men passing to the Reserve—should be in the highest possible state of efficiency. The non-commissioned officers must be picked men, upon whom thorough reliance can be placed, and the terms offered must be such as to attract the best men among the rank & file to come forward for promotion, & to look to the Army for a permanent career.[48]

In 1881 Childers improved their pay, prospects, and pensions.[49] Their rates of pay were raised, an increase that was in part funded by using the money generated by fining drunken soldiers. After one year's probation corporals were given the right to extend their colour service to twelve years and, on completion of that period, could, with their CO's permission, extend it for a further nine years, so as to complete twenty-one years and become eligible for a pension. Sergeants were given an absolute right to serve for twenty-one years and to get a pension, although after fifteen years they were liable to be transferred as an instructor to a unit of the auxiliary forces to ensure that field units did not contain NCOs who were past their physical prime. Sergeants were also induced to remain with the colours by being granted more liberal marriage provisions. Whereas only between 4 and 7 per cent of the rank and file could enjoy the advantages of marrying on the strength of their regiment, half of all sergeants and all NCOs above the rank of sergeant could do so. Sergeants were also given their own separate living accommodation so that they no longer shared the same quarters as their men. Henceforth the task of maintaining discipline in barrack rooms fell on the shoulders of corporals and lance-corporals. Finally, the status of the profession of NCO was raised by transforming the most senior of all NCOs, the RSMs and RQMS, into

a class of regimental warrant officer holding an intermediate position between Commissioned and non-commissioned officers. This class will include all regimental and other sergeant-majors & non-commissioned officers holding similar or analogous rank. It will afford a prospect of promotion to all non-commissioned officers of lower rank, & the rates of pay are such as will give adequate remuneration for the very important duties performed.[50]

---

[47] PP (1881), XXI. C. 2791. *Report of the Committee* . . . , 27–31.
[48] PRO WO 32/6673. PUS War Office to Secretary of the Treasury, 24 Feb. 1881.
[49] PP (1881), LVIII. C. 2826. *Memorandum* . . .
[50] PRO WO 32/6673. PUS War Office to Secretary of the Treasury, 24 Feb. 1881.

In parallel with his attempts to create a long-service professional cadre of NCOs, Childers also tried to improve the professional skills and commitment of the officer corps. In doing so he instituted the system of officer promotion and retirement that was to remain largely unchanged until the eve of the Second World War. In 1881 he accepted the conclusions of a Royal Commission chaired by Lord Penzance that had reported in 1876 and recommended the introduction of a combination of compulsory retirement ages coupled with pensions for officers who had served for a set number of years.[51] Henceforth Captains were obliged to retire at the age of 40 if they had not already been promoted to Major, Majors had to retire at the age of 48, and Lieutenant-Colonels at the age of 55. The latter were also not to be allowed to command their unit for more than four years.[52] He also wanted to double the number of field officers in each infantry regiment, thus improving the subalterns' chances of promotion and reducing pension costs by ensuring that fewer officers retired as captains.[53] Before 1881 the proportion of field officers to subalterns had been 1 to $8\frac{2}{3}$. After 1881 it was to become 1 to $3\frac{2}{3}$. However, in 1886, on the grounds of the extra cost, only half of this plan was implemented. Most two-battalion line regiments did have eight majors, compared to four before 1881, but they only had two, rather than four, lieutenant-colonels.[54]

The Penzance Commission would have liked to regulate promotion for regimental officers by merit, but it could not devise a scheme that would work equitably in peacetime. Military qualifications, it asserted, really made themselves known only in action, and no amount of examinations in peacetime could test them. It therefore reverted to a second-best system, which it believed at least had the advantage of being equitable. Childers agreed and after 1881 promotion for regimental officers was governed by seniority within a regimental list, tempered by the rejection of those who failed their qualifying examinations, or who were reported on by their commanding officer as being unfitted for further advancement. The only concession that the Commission or Childers were prepared to make to merit was to accept the continuation of brevet promotion. Especially deserving officers, who had demonstrated their competence and zeal on the battlefield or in a staff appointment, were given a rank in the army higher than the one they enjoyed in their regiment. This meant that a major who was promoted to brevet lieutenant-

---

[51] PP (1876), XV. C. 1569. *Report of the Royal Commission* ...

[52] PP (1881), LVIII. C 2826. *Memorandum* ...; PP (1881), LVIII. C. 2922. *Revised Memorandum*.

[53] Hansard, HC (series 5) vol. 583, cols. 196, 207–9.

[54] Gen. Sir J. Adye, *Recollections of a Military Life* (London: Smith, Elder & Co., 1895), 326; id., 'The Glut of Junior Officers in the Army', *Nineteenth Century*, 27 (1890), 263, 266.

colonel would do the work of a major when serving with his regiment, but would serve as a lieutenant-colonel, with a lieutenant-colonel's pay, when he was employed outside his regiment.[55]

Finally, Childers codified the system of military law that the new and, he hoped, more professionally skilful officer corps and cadre of long-service NCOs would have to administer. In 1881 a committee examining the terms and conditions of the short-service army concluded that the existing system of punishments and rewards was out of date. It had been developed piecemeal over a long period, and was intended to meet the needs of a long-service army. What the short-service army needed was a system that was sufficiently simple so that even the newest recruit could understand the advantages to be gained by good conduct.[56] Childers agreed, partly because of what he and some officers perceived to be changes in the kind of men whom they hoped to attract to the ranks, but also because of changes in the way soldiers would have to behave on the battlefield. The introduction of universal primary education would lead to changes, because as one officer had noted in 1869:

our Armies have hitherto been chiefly composed of the crude uneducated soldier, having no aspiration beyond his immediate duties, and perfectly subjected by drill and discipline. But this staple of the old system of British force is gradually disappearing; it is daily becoming less and less possible even were it expedient, to have again an Army composed of such human material. The staple 'private' of former English Armies will be gradually displaced and supplanted by a man of a very different stamp, more educated, more thinking, more reasoning, who will require an altogether different mode of treatment, which, if foreseen and thoroughly understood, will secure a greater military efficiency, and enable our Armies to achieve even more astonishing results than heretofore. In a country where the classes are rapidly becoming informed, as well as supplied with increased material comforts, the unquestioning implicit obedience of the aboriginal soldier will have to be exacted by other means than by sheer despotic coercion ... [57]

These changes coincided with important developments in military technology. Hitherto infantry had fought in compact masses, each man standing shoulder to shoulder with his comrades, and able to derive the maximum moral support from their close physical proximity. But the introduction of breech-loading rifles made such tactics suicidal. Unless soldiers dispersed they would present an easy target to the enemy. Dispersion, however, brought its own drawbacks. It made it impossible for

---

[55] PP (1876), XV. C. 1569. *Report of the Royal Commission* ...

[56] PP (1881), XX. C. 2817. *Report of the Committee* ..., 3.

[57] Capt. W. Cave Thomas, 'The Establishment of County Military Training Schools; a Suggestion for Improving the Recruiting System', *Journal of the Royal United Services Institute*, 13, (1869), 145.

senior officers to exercise direct personal control over their men. One officer in 1889 even went so far as to predict that under the new conditions of the battlefield, no commander would be able to control the fire of more than eight men. Once fighting began, control of the troops passed from brigade and regimental commanders to company officers and NCOs. This meant that unless the rank and file were imbued with high morale and self-discipline, any advance under fire would quickly grind to a halt.[58] What was required was not the rigid discipline of the barrack square, but discipline based on intelligence and self-reliance, modes of thinking and behaviour that were quite incompatible with a system of 'petty tyranny'.

Childers introduced three innovations in his efforts to create a disciplinary system to meet these new challenges. Before 1879 military law was embodied in the Mutiny Act and the Articles of War. By the second half of the nineteenth century it had become so complex and was so much in need of codification that in 1879 Parliament approved the Army Discipline and Regulation Act, which consolidated the Mutiny Act and the Articles of War. In 1881 Childers took the process of codification a stage further by replacing it with the Army Act. The Act defined the various military offences for which officers and other ranks could be tried by court martial, but most importantly it classified them 'in a manner intended to impress the soldier with their relative military importance'. Meriting the most serious punishments, including the death penalty, were offences 'in respect of military service', such as treachery, cowardice in the face of the enemy, plundering, and sleeping on duty, followed by mutiny and insubordination. These were followed by desertion, fraudulent enlistment, going absent without leave, committing fraud or embezzlement, and being drunk.[59] Potential offenders were now more likely to understand what constituted a military crime and thereby more inclined to avoid committing an offence. But if they did offend, Childers also ensured that punishment would follow swiftly upon commission of the crime. In 1868 a Royal Commission on the constitution and practice of courts martial recommended that COs be allowed to impose fines for drunkenness, a recommendation that was accepted.[60] In the early 1880s their powers to deal summarily with a number of other common offences, rather than delay matters by sending the offender before a court martial, were also increased. Thirdly, Childers dealt with the difficult issue of how to punish offenders on active service. Fines were no real

---

[58] Capt. J. F. Daniell, 'Discipline: Its Importance to an Armed Force and the Best Means of Promoting and Maintaining It', *Journal of the Royal United Services Institute*, 33 (1889), 302–4.

[59] War Office, *MML, 1899*, 18–19.

[60] P. Burrows, 'Crime and Punishment in the British Army, 1815–1870', *English Historical Review*, 100 (1985), 559.

punishment to a soldier facing danger, and he might actually prefer a prison sentence to the perils of active service. Many regimental and more senior officers believed that they had to have a means of punishing wrong-doers in the field that administered swift and exemplary justice, but did not deprive the army of scarce manpower or encourage recalcitrant soldiers to commit offences in the hope that the punishment would provide them with an escape route from the front line. Flogging had once provided the solution. Its advantages were summarized by Lord Chelmsford, who had employed it during his campaign in Zululand in 1879.

Corporal punishment was frequently inflicted by sentence of court-martial. It did not much come under my cognisance; but it was and is the only punishment that I can see that is available on active service. We could not afford to lose the services of the men by sending them to prison, and we could not afford to keep them, and it would have been no punishment to keep them, in the guard room, or the guard tent when we were marching every day.[61]

But since 1829, under a growing weight of public criticism that suggested it degraded good men and deterred others from enlisting, flogging had gradually been restricted until in 1868 it was applied only in cases of mutiny and offering violence to a superior officer on active service. In 1881 Childers finally abolished it.[62] In its place he introduced a series of new field punishments. Soldiers convicted by a court martial and given a summary punishment could be awarded Field Imprisonment (more commonly referred to as Field Punishment) Number 1. They were placed in irons and attached to a fixed post for up to two hours each day for a maximum of twenty-one days, and at other times made to perform hard labour. Lesser offenders might serve a sentence of Field Imprisonment Number 2, which also involved an offender being kept in irons, but not tied to a post.[63]

The Cardwell–Childers reforms did not occur in a political vacuum. Their quest to create a cheaper yet more efficient and militarily effective army was part of a wider political and social programme. The 1867 Reform Act, which had given the Parliamentary franchise to a significant minority of urban working-class males, promised to transform the political landscape of Britain. The Liberal government's quest to elevate the standing of the regular soldier and to make the army a profession for the respectable working class was one small part of their larger

---

[61] PP (1881), XXI. C.2791. *Report of the Committee* ..., Q. 4699.

[62] P. Burroughs, 'An Unreformed Army? 1815–1868', in D. Chandler and I. Beckett (eds.), *The Oxford Illustrated History of the British Army* (Oxford: Oxford University Press, 1994), 174; J. R. Dinwiddy, 'The Early Nineteenth-Century Campaign against Flogging in the Army', *English Historical Review*, 97 (1982), 308–31; Hansard, HC (series 3), vol. 49, col. 212.

[63] *MML*, 1899, 'H. C. E. Childers, "Rules for Summary Punishment made under the Army Discipline and Regulation (Annual) Act 1881", 30 July 1881', 760.

programme of integrating the working classes into the political nation as respected members of the community. In 1868 the Radical MP and committed army reformer Sir Charles Trevelyan hoped that short service might effect a veritable social transformation. In his first few months in the army, the physique of the raw recruit improved markedly, he acquired a sense of duty 'and a just appreciation of the value of character, and he learns both to obey and to command'. If a regular soldier was allowed to return to civilian life before he had served for so long that he had sunk irremediably into vicious habits, he would have little difficulty in adjusting to civilian life. In that case the army could become 'a powerful instrument of national education in a large and high sense. It would be to the body of the people much more than our public schools and universities are to the upper class.'[64] The Brigade depots, he told the Commons in 1872, would be 'schools of discipline, where young men were carefully watched by non-commissioned officers—married men, who had risen from the ranks by their steadiness and good conduct and whose characters were as valuable to them as that of an accountant at Manchester was to him'.[65] Gladstone himself told the Commons in July 1872 that the establishment of Brigade depots was intended 'to diminish to a minimum immorality in the standing army'.[66]

But it was Childers who made the most explicit statement that military service might act as a school for the nation, when he told his constituents in January 1882 that

I wish to see the people of England in the best sense military, but not warlike. It is one of the happiest results of the short service system, and of the general spread of volunteering, that they produce in a large number of the Queen's subjects, a military rather than a warlike spirit (hear, hear). By a military spirit I mean habits of discipline, respect for lawful command, and at the same time independence of character, and that dislike of slovenliness, which, as a general rule, marks the man who has served. I should therefore rejoice if, as I have said elsewhere, our schoolboys were taught more drill, and if it was the exception for a young man who could afford it not to be a Volunteer. And I should not regret were such a state of feeling about military service to prevail, as would justify the Government and Parliament in establishing a system under which a much larger proportion of the youth of the country might, if they wished, voluntarily spend a short time, at or soon after the age of 20, in the ranks (hear, hear). In an army really representing the average intelligence and right feeling of the country, such a short experience of military service would benefit our youth of every class, whether in town or country, whether artisan, mechanic or peasant.[67]

[64] Trevelyan, *The British Army in 1868*, 52.
[65] Hansard, HC (series 3) vol. 213, cols. 93–4.
[66] Hansard, HC (series 3) vol. 212, col. 1646.
[67] *The Times*, 20 Jan. 1882.

This vision of an army and a whole social class transformed by short service and localization was not confined to Radical back-benchers or Liberal Cabinet Ministers. It also appealed to some army officers. Colonel A. Cunningham Robertson, the commanding officer of 2/8th Foot, wanted a military training organization that 'shall render military training a powerful instrument of popular education, so that the same process which renders a young man an efficient soldier shall also improve his character, and develop his bodily and mental capacities, rendering him in every respect a more perfect man and a better citizen'.[68] But perhaps even more significantly, it underpinned the report of the committee that produced the details of the localization scheme.

The details of localization and linking were worked out by a War Office committee of senior officers presided over by Major-General P. L. MacDougall. In its final report the Localisation Committee hoped that

one of the beneficial effects hoped for from the formation of these small recruiting and training establishments [i.e. depots] all over the country, is the removal of a large proportion of the idle male population from the streets of towns and cities to the more healthful moral atmosphere of military discipline. While the advantages that will result to good order and morality, by abolishing the system hitherto prevailing of billeting Militia Battalions during training on the inhabitants of cities and towns, can hardly be exaggerated.[69]

By 1881 the main structural features that defined the late nineteenth-century regimental system were in place. Infantry units in the regular and auxiliary forces were linked and were supposed to recruit on a territorial basis. Regular officers knew that henceforth they could expect to serve their entire careers in a single regiment, unless they were fortunate enough to be promoted above the rank of Lieutenant-Colonel. A cadre of long-service NCOs and Warrant Officers was being created that could similarly expect to spend most of their service career in the same regiment. Steps had been taken to humanize the disciplinary system to fit it to the needs of a short-service army.

However, the description of this organization as constituting the 'Regimental System' should not blind us to the fact that these arrangements contained elements that were anything but systematic. In 1881, 63 per cent of the rank and file of the Regular Army were serving in the line infantry, in regiments where the writ of the Cardwell–Childers system was supposed to run without let or hindrance.[70] But on closer inspection

[68] Col. A. Cunningham Robertson, 'The Constitution of our Military Forces, and the Conditions of Military Service', *Journal of the Royal United Services Institute*, 13 (1870), 478.
[69] PP (1881), XXI. C. 2792. *Final report of committee on the organisation of the various military land forces of the country*, 51.
[70] These statistics are derived from PP (1882), XXXVIII. C. 3405. *General Annual Return of the British Army for the Year Ending 30 Sept. 1881*, 11.

anomalies were apparent even there. The Irish regiments had no Volunteer battalions. In 1881 there were an odd number of regular battalions on the establishment and so one, the Cameron Highlanders, was left without a partner until 1897.[71] But the biggest anomalies amongst the infantry were the Rifle Regiments and the Foot Guards. They remained outside the territorial recruiting system. They had permanent depots, but they continued to take their recruits from across the country. The Rifle Regiments had associated Militia and Volunteer battalions, but the Guards did not. More significantly, localization, territorialization, and linking was only very incompletely applied to the two large Corps regiments, the Royal Artillery and Royal Engineers. Although they were both subdivided into different branches, batteries, and companies, they remained wedded to the principle that both officers and other ranks enlisted for general service within the corps and could be transferred at will between its different branches. The only significant exception to this was that until 1920 the Royal Garrison Artillery operated as a separate corps within the Royal Artillery. Localization was only belatedly applied to the artillery, which constituted nearly 18 per cent of the rank and file of the Regular Army in 1881, and then it proved to be but a temporary expedient. It was not until 1882 that the UK was divided into eleven territorial divisions, each with its own depot. They served as HQs for the regiments of militia artillery, and they also received and trained recruits for all branches for the Royal Field and Royal Garrison Artillery. The Royal Horse Artillery maintained a separate depot at Woolwich.[72] However, as early as 1883 regular battery commanders were complaining that the recruits they were being sent from the depots were not properly trained and in 1884 four new depots, each associated with one of the four artillery brigades in the UK, were established to train recruits and provide drafts for overseas service. In 1922 even this tenuous form of localization was ended when the need to economize meant that all artillery recruits were trained at a single centralized depot at Woolwich.[73]

In the late nineteenth century the smaller Departmental corps, such as the Army Medical Corps, the Military Police, the Army Pay Corps, and the Army Ordnance Corps, departed even further from the model of the line infantry. They recruited most of their men by accepting transfers from other regiments. When the RTC was placed on a permanent footing in 1923 it followed the post-1922 Royal Artillery model. It took recruits

[71] Ibid.; Goodenough and Dalton, *The Army Book of the British Empire*, 124–6.

[72] PP (1882), XVI. C. 3168. *Report of Committee on Artillery Localisation*.

[73] PRO WO 32/11361. Establishment of Royal Artillery Depots, Dec. 1919; Maj.-Gen. B. P. Hughes (ed.), *History of the Royal Regiment of Artillery: Between the Wars 1919–1939* (London: Brassey's, 1992), 45.

from across the nation and trained them at a central depot at Bovington before posting them to one of its battalions.[74]

The cavalry fell somewhere between the infantry and gunners. In 1871 MacDougall's Localization committee divided the country into two recruiting districts for the regular cavalry, but it did not attempt to link regular regiments together for drafting purposes, or to create a close connection between regular regiments and the Yeomanry.[75] In the 1870s cavalry regiments, which constituted 9 per cent of the regular rank and file, had no permanent depots, nor any links that allowed them to call on another regiment for drafts. Each regiment did its own recruiting and trained its own recruits at its regimental HQ. When a cavalry regiment was ordered overseas, it left behind a detachment at the Cavalry Depot at Canterbury to train recruits and remounts.[76]

The weaknesses of this system were illustrated clearly in 1882. The three regiments mobilized for despatch to Egypt with Wolseley's army were so short of men that they could be made up to strength only by wholesale cross-posting from other regiments. But it was another eleven years before the War Office took steps to overcome this problem. The idea of linking cavalry regiments on the infantry model was mooted in the early 1880s, but rejected on grounds of cost—each double regiment would require its own depot—and because a linkage of only two units would probably be too small. The eventual solution was to begin a process that was to transform the cavalry into a corps regiment in all but name. In March 1893 the existing regiments were organized into four corps: Household, Dragoons, Hussars, and Lancers. Within each corps two regiments, one serving overseas and one at home, were linked for drafting purposes, and other ranks, but not officers, could be transferred between regiments in the same corps.[77]

In 1897 the depot at Canterbury was closed, and thereafter regiments in Britain were divided between those that were kept full of men and used to find drafts for units overseas, and those that were maintained on little more than a cadre basis. In 1905 the War Office toyed with the idea of

[74] PRO WO 33/1509. Report by a committee assembled to consider the organization of the mechanized cavalry and the RTC, 29 Apr. 1938.

[75] PRO 30/48/1/3/250. Cardwell to Ponsonby, 23 Dec. 1871; PP (1881), XXI. C. 2792. *Memo by HRH the FM C-in-C on the proposal of the S of S for War for the organization of the various military land forces of the country; and report of a committee on the details involved therein*, 4–8.

[76] Goodenough and Dalton, *The Army Book of the British Empire*, 191; PP (1882), XVI. C. 3167. *1882 Report of the Cavalry Organisation Committee*.

[77] PRO WO 33/42. Cavalry re-organisation. Proposals submitted to the Secretary of State on 7698/494, n.d. but c.1884; PRO WO 33/52. Papers and memos prepared by Sir A. Haliburton in connection with the report of the committee on the terms and conditions of service in the army, n.d. but c. Jan. 1893; PRO WO 32/6724. Annual Report of Inspector-General of Cavalry, 17 Nov. 1897.

establishing two large depots to train recruits and hold men waiting to be drafted overseas.[78] But in 1907 it opted to establish six cavalry depots, each with its own affiliated group of regiments. However, this did not mean that the cavalry had, belatedly, adopted the principles of localization and territorialization. Recruits continued to be enlisted for general service in one of the four cavalry corps. Nor was there any attempt to localize Irish regiments to Ireland or English regiments to England. Three English regiments were allocated to the Irish depot, and three Irish regiments were affiliated to English depots.[79] In 1927, as part of an exercise in cutting costs, the central depot at Canterbury, which had been reopened after the war in place of the six pre-war depots, was closed. Regiments reverted to training their own recruits and, in order to provide the necessary drafts for units overseas, the rank and file of the cavalry were constituted into a single corps, so that men could be freely transferred between every regiment.[80]

Thus by the early 1880s the British army possessed not one but four regimental systems. The first consisted of the line infantry regiments created by Cardwell and Childers. They constituted the largest single component of the army and had been the subject of a thoroughgoing process of linking and territorialization. The second consisted of the two large corps regiments, the Royal Artillery and Royal Engineers, and the much smaller departmental corps. They had hardly been affected by localization or territorialization. The third system consisted of the Horse Guards and line cavalry. They sat awkwardly between the line infantry system and the larger corps system. The fourth consisted of the Rifle Regiments—the King's Royal Rifle Corps and the Rifle Brigade—and the regiments of Foot Guards. Parts of their organization were modelled on that of the line infantry, but other aspects were anomalous.

In the early 1880s there were two major question marks still hanging over the army. It was as yet uncertain whether or not it could make a reality of localized recruiting, for it was unclear in 1881 to what extent regiments would in fact be able to rely on their own districts to supply them with the recruits, both officers and other ranks, which they required. And it was equally uncertain if the new regiments that Cardwell and Childers had established could create a new regimental *esprit de corps* to replace that which their critics claimed their reforms had destroyed. The first of these issues will form the subject matter of the next chapter.

---

[78] PRO WO 32/6783. Minute, AG2 to AG, 28 Jan. 1907.
[79] PRO WO 32/6785. Minute by QMG, 12 Feb. 1909.
[80] PRO WO 32/3059. Army Order 261/1927, 14 Apr. 1927.

CHAPTER TWO

Recruiting for the Regiments

Cardwell did not abolish the purchase of commissions because he hoped it would effect a social transformation of the officer corps. The Gladstone government ended purchase because they saw its abolition as part of a wider programme of remodelling aristocratic institutions to ensure their survival in a new age of mass politics.[1] By contrast Cardwell and Childers did hope that their reforms would so elevate the status of the rank and file that the Regular Army would not only attract the extra numbers it needed to make the short-service reforms work, but would also draw growing numbers of the 'respectable' working class.

Their first expectation was fulfilled. There was no significant change in the social composition of the regimental officer corps. It continued to be dominated by men drawn from the ranks of the gentry and professional upper middle classes. Their second hope was only partially fulfilled. More men did enlist in the late nineteenth century. But as the Regular Army's establishment also increased, it continued to struggle to find sufficient men to fill the ranks, and it had the utmost difficulty in attracting men from the 'respectable' working class. Exactly why this was so will be one of the issues considered in Chapter 9, in which the changing attitudes of the civilian population to the Regular Army will be examined. But one reason is abundantly clear: the attractions of serving in a local regiment were far less of a magnet than the reformers had hoped. In order to explain the comparative failures of the Cardwell–Childers reforms to fill the ranks of the Regular Army with the number and quality of men that they sought, three related questions will be considered: who joined the Regular Army in what might be called 'peacetime'—which is to say in periods other than the Boer War and the two world wars—why did they do so, and why they opted to join a particular regiment.

In the mid-nineteenth century the regular officer corps was overwhelmingly drawn from the sons of gentlemen, and the professional and propertied classes. The only significant shift in the class profile of the officer corps after the Cardwell reforms was the growing proportion of officers who were 'hereditary' soldiers, in that their fathers too had

---

[1] Gallagher, '"Cardwellian mysteries"', 348.

been officers. This generalization remained true down to 1939 and beyond.[2] Second, no matter whether a subaltern's father was a peer, a barrister, a clergyman, or a soldier, the great majority of young officers had undergone a common process of socialization at a public school. In this the army was no different from the civil service, most of whose senior cadres had also been educated at public schools. The major public schools exercised, if not a stranglehold, certainly a very great deal of influence over the pre-cadet education of the regular officer corps until 1939 and beyond. Nearly four of every five cadets at Sandhurst and Woolwich had attended a public school before the Second World War, and the dominance of the public schools abated only slightly in the two decades after 1945.[3] Only a handful of ex-rankers received Regular Army commissions, and most of them were commissioned into the socially marginal roles as Quarter-Masters or Riding Masters, not as combatant officers.[4]

The families who sent their sons to public schools continued to be regarded by the military authorities as constituting the 'officer class'.[5] But too much weight has sometimes been placed on this fact in trying to explain the army's shortcomings. Public school educated officers have been criticized because the schools they attended were apparently more interested in developing their pupils' 'character' than their intellects.[6] As a consequence, their subsequent professional attainments have been unfavourably contrasted with the supposedly more 'professional' officer corps of the German army. Such criticisms, however, overlook the fact that before 1914 the German army also placed 'character' and social status before brains in selecting its officers. Many German regular officers had not studied at a Gymnasium, nor did they possess the *Abitur*, a certificate of eligibility to study at a university. They had attended one of several cadet colleges, where they received a fairly low standard of academic education, but were prepared for the examination they had to pass in order to enter the army, and where, just as at British public schools, the emphasis was on forming character rather than on academic learning.[7] If British officers seemed backward in their professional

[2] C. B. Ottley, 'The Social Origins of British Army Officers', *Sociological Review*, 18 (1970), 225; Harries-Jenkins, *The Army in Victorian Society*, 12–58.

[3] C. B. Ottley, 'The Educational Background of British Army Officers', *Sociology*, 7 (1973), 197.

[4] PP (1907), XLIX. *Army Commissions. Return as to the number of commissions granted during each of the years 1885 to 1906*; PRO WO 32/3773. Minute n.d. but *c.*2 Feb. 1930; Military Sec to PUS and Secretary of State, 13 Aug. 1930; Milne to Secretary of State, 1 Nov. 1930.

[5] PRO WO 163/456. Committee on the supply of officers, Mar. 1937.

[6] C. Barnett, 'The Education of Military Elites', *Journal of Contemporary History*, 2 (1967), 15–35.

[7] D. J. Hughes, *The King's Finest: A Social and Bureaucratic Profile of Prussia's General Officers, 1871–1914* (New York: Praeger, 1987), 62–5; D. E. Showalter, ' "No officer rather than a bad officer": Officer Selection and Education in the Prussian/German Army, 1715–1945',

attainments compared to their German counterparts, the reason had little to do with their pre-school education, and much to do with how they were trained after they entered the army.

Regimental communities were anything but socially homogenous, for the contrast between the social origins of the commissioned ranks of the Regular Army and the rank and file could hardly have been greater. Short service, coupled with localization and territorialization, was intended to overcome the chronic shortage of recruits that the army suffered from in the nineteenth century, and to attract a more 'respectable' class of men into the Regular Army. Before 1914, on two out of three counts, it failed. Enlistment for short service was popular. By 1899 fewer than one soldier in ten elected to serve a full term of twelve years with colours. But in both other respects it failed. In 1876 an anonymous author writing in the *United Services Magazine* lamented that

It is beyond dispute that the better portion of the working classes, and the lower middle class of this country fail in taking that interest in the manning and welfare of the Army and Navy which it is so desirable that they should do. It is to these classes of the community that we should principally look for our recruits, and it is to be regretted, besides it is probably a source of danger to the future, that our forces should depend, for their very existence, mainly on the lowest stratum of the population, the denizens of the slum and out-of-the-way corners of our great towns.[8]

Three years later the Inspector-General of Recruiting ruefully admitted: 'The recruits who join the army belong, to a considerable extent, to the lower classes. No inquiry is made as to their antecedents, and it is undoubtedly the fact that many of them are men whose character would not bear investigation.'[9] Between 1874 and 1880, 61 per cent of recruits described themselves as being unskilled labourers.[10] That figure actually rose to 65 per cent between 1896 and 1898, and had fallen to only 63 per cent by 1911.[11]

Recruiting for the rank and file frequently failed to maintain the Regular Army up to establishment despite the willingness of the military

---

in G. C. Kennedy and K. Neilson (eds.), *Officer Education: Past, Present and Future* (Westport, Conn.: Praeger, 2002), 43–4.

[8] Anon., 'Remarks on the Present Condition of the Army', 209.

[9] PP (1881), XXI. C. 2791. *Report of the Committee* ..., QQ. 76, 388–9, 1526.

[10] Between 1874 and 1880 about 61 per cent of all the regular recruits described themselves on enlistment as being unskilled labourers, servants, or farm labourers, 11 per cent as artisans, 18 per cent as mechanics, 7 per cent as shop assistants or clerks, and 1 per cent had been employed in professional occupations, often as students. The remainder were boys under the age of 18. See PP (1881), XX. C. 2832. *Annual Report of the Inspector-General of Recruiting, 1 Feb. 1881*.

[11] Skelley, *The Victorian Army at Home*, 297; D. French, 'Some Aspects of Social and Economic Planning for War in Great Britain, c. 1905–1915' (Ph.D. thesis, University of London, 1979), 21.

authorities to lower height and medical standards to induct more men. Between 1859 and 1901 the male population of the UK aged between 15 and 24, the normal age range for recruits, grew by 57 per cent. But army recruitment grew by only 45 per cent. Although the actual numbers of recruits increased, it was usually not enough to make good the losses from discharge, desertion, and death.[12]

The typical Regular Army recruit before 1914 was a young, unskilled, and poorly educated urban labourer. In 1878, 13,467 recruits out of a total of 28,035 were under 20 years of age.[13] It was because so many of them could not withstand the physical burdens of active service that Childers raised the minimum age of enlistment in 1881 from 18 to 19.[14] It made little difference. The age profile of recruits remained largely unchanged. In 1929 nearly half of all recruits claimed to be aged 18 or 19.[15] They were probably even younger. Recruits lied about their age, and recruiting officers turned a blind eye to the fact so they could find enough men to fill the ranks. When Kenneth Black tried to enlist in Huddersfield in 1949 he was only 17. The recruiting sergeant told him to go outside, walk around the building, 'and if you're seventeen and a half when you come back, we'll get things going'.[16] Recruits were also increasingly likely to be Englishmen, rather than from Wales, Scotland, or Ireland. Whereas in the mid-nineteenth century the rank and file had contained a disproportionate number of Irishmen, after 1870 it came to include a disproportionate number of Englishmen.[17] By 1937 Englishmen accounted for 77 per cent of the rank and file, Irishmen and Welshmen 5 per cent each, and Scotsmen 10 per cent. (The remainder of the rank and file had been born overseas.)[18]

These facts did not particularly worry most regimental officers. What did concern them, particularly before 1914, was that most of their recruits came from the urban slums. Their ideal recruit was a sturdy rural labourer, for not only was he reckoned to be physically fitter than his urban cousin, he was also thought to be more docile and amenable to discipline.[19] However, their wishes flew in the face of demographic realities. As Britain

[12] Skelley, *The Victorian Army at Home*, 237–8, 260.

[13] PP (1881), XXI. C. 2791. *Report of the Committee* ..., 14–18.

[14] PP (1881), LVIII. C. 2826. *Memorandum showing the principal changes in army organisation* ...

[15] PP (1929–30), XIX. Cmd. 3498. *General Annual Report for the British Army for the Year Ending 30 September 1929*, 16.

[16] IWMSA. Accession No. 18022/6. K. W. Black, reel 1.

[17] T. Denman, ' "Ethnic soldiers pure and simple"? The Irish in the Late Victorian British Army', *War in History*, 3 (1996), 57–9; H. J. Hanham, 'Religion and Nationality in the Mid-Victorian Army' in M. R. D. Foot (ed.), *War and Society: Historical Essays in Honour and Memory of J. R. Western, 1928–1971* (London: Paul Elek, 1973), 159–82.

[18] PP (1929–30), XIX. Cmd. 3498. *General Annual Report* ...; PP (1937–8), XVII. Cmd. 5486. *General Annual Report for the British Army for the Year Ending 30 September 1937*.

[19] PP (1881), XXI. C. 2791. *Report of the Committee* ..., QQ. 1064–6; PRO WO 33/47. Report of the Committee on army schools and schoolmasters, QQ. 426, 427, 777.

became an increasingly urban society, the supply of agricultural labourers dried up.[20] By 1892, the Inspector-General of Recruiting had accepted that

> in almost every rural district in the British Isles the population has decreased in the last decade; whilst in the towns in which any manufacture on a large scale has been established the numbers of the inhabitants have increased to an astonishing extent. To such a degree has this depopulation of rural districts taken place, in some regimental recruiting areas, that it has become impossible for them to furnish from their own resources the requisite number of recruits.[21]

Regimental officers were quick to complain that they were receiving too many recruits who were too physically immature to be trained or sent overseas. Their concerns were justified when it is remembered that by 1892 such men made up nearly one-third of all recruits and large numbers of them had to be discharged within three months of enlistment for medical reasons.[22]

They were also concerned about the low educational standards of many recruits. In 1881 the CO of the 2/18th (The Royal Irish) Foot estimated that over a third of his recruits were illiterate and that 10 per cent of them were of the 'criminal class'.[23] The small number of recruits who had enjoyed a comparatively good education tended to be concentrated in particular regiments and arms of the service. The Guards attracted some men from the 'respectable' sections of the working class, probably because Guardsmen could serve for as short a period as three years with the colours, and many did so in the hope that when they were discharged they would be able to find employment in the Metropolitan Police.[24] In the late nineteenth century better-educated recruits also opted for the cavalry and other arms of the service in preference to the infantry.[25] Even so, a cavalry officer who had served with his regiment in the 1890s looked back from the perspective of the middle of the twentieth century, and concluded that

> The N.C.O.s and men of those days do not compare favourably with the modern, well-educated and alert cavalrymen. They were 'tough nuts' all right, mostly of the artisan class with a sprinkling of well-educated men among them. Perhaps just as useful in a scrap as the moderns, but they were more difficult to teach map reading, signalling, reporting, scouting and other things that cavalry soldiers have to learn.[26]

[20] K. Hoppen, *The Mid-Victorian Generation 1846–1886* (Oxford: Clarendon Press, 1998), 11–12.

[21] PP (1892), XX. C. 6597. *Annual Report of the Inspector General of Recruiting for 1891*, 3.

[22] Anon., 'On Recruiting and Forming Reserves', 287–8; Knollys, 'Boy Soldiers', 1–9; Spiers, *The Army and Society*, 35–7, 40.

[23] PP (1881), XXI. C. 2791. *Report of the Committee ...*, QQ. 1338, 1347.

[24] PP (1904), XLI. Cd. 1791. *Minutes of Evidence taken before the Royal Commission on the War in South Africa*, Q. 16941.

[25] PP (1881), XXI. C. 2791. *Report of the Committee ...*, Q. 166.

[26] Maj.-Gen. J. Vaughan, *Cavalry and Sporting Memoirs* (London: The Bala Press, 1954), 11–12.

It took about a generation after 1870 for there to be a significant improvement in the quality of men enlisting in the ranks. By 1900 recruits were probably better educated, more amenable to discipline, and less inclined to be drunken than their predecessors had been in 1870. By 1910, for example, only fourteen out of 178 recruits who enlisted in the Oxford and Buckinghamshire Light Infantry were officially classified as illiterate, although a further fifty-four were classified as having an 'inferior' education.[27] By 1920 only half of all recruits described themselves as unskilled labourers.[28] They were also probably more physically robust than they had been before 1914. But even in 1928, 12.4 per cent of recruits in depots were discharged for medical reasons.[29]

Such improvements as did occur were probably due more to wider social trends, such as the spread of compulsory elementary education, than to the Cardwell–Childers reforms. By the Edwardian period officers believed that the educational standards of recruits 'keeps pace with the intelligence and education of the people of England'.[30] Even so, following the onset of mechanization, the army's demand for men with a reasonable education continued to exceed the supply. In the early 1920s the army had such difficulty in attracting skilled mechanics that it had to establish its own training school for apprentices, and in 1924 establish a Supplementary Reserve of men with technical skills in order to fill gaps in its establishment on mobilization.[31] In the 1930s better-educated recruits were habitually posted to the more technical arms such as the Royal Engineers or the RTC.

The infantry continued to have to make do with what was left. By 1937 the Adjutant-General estimated that the infantry was losing about 600 recruits annually because they could not read, spell, or do simple arithmetic.[32] But the army was so short of recruits that the CIGS decided that 'I have no objection to any man who is not an imbecile being enlisted, i.e. I do not consider rejection on educational grounds alone should be a sine qua non, but I should not proclaim it loudly.'[33] Instructions were therefore issued to recruiting officers 'which in effect means that any recruit who is not actually mentally deficient can be enlisted'.[34] This policy continued

[27] The Oxford and Buckinghamshire Light Infantry Chronicle 1910: An Annual Record of the First and Second Battalions, formerly the 43rd and 52nd Light Infantry, 19 (1910), 53.

[28] K. Jeffery, 'The Post-War Army', in I. F. W. Beckett and K. Simpson (eds.), A Nation in Arms: A Social Study of the British Army in the First World War (Manchester: Manchester University Press, 1985), 224.

[29] PRO WO 32/4643. Maj. W. A. S. Turner to Maj. C. W. Baker, 6 Apr. 1936.

[30] PP (1904), XL. Cd. 1790. Minutes of evidence taken before the Royal Commission on the War in South Africa, QQ. 9113–14, 9118; PRO WO 32/8699. GOC-in-C Aldershot, to War Office, 30 Jan. 1906.

[31] The Times, 7 Mar. and 14 Aug., 15 Oct. 1924.

[32] PRO WO 32/4354. Sir H. Karslake to CIGS, 24 Sept. 1937.

[33] PRO WO 32/4354. Minute by CIGS, 11 Oct. 1937.

[34] PRO WO 32/4354. Director of Recruiting and Organization, WO to GOC Southern Command, 21 Dec. 1938.

after 1939, at a time when the infantry was being issued with increasing numbers of more complex weapons and transport. Many battalions struggled to find the men capable of operating them to their fullest extent. They had, as the Adjutant-General admitted in 1942, 'received in effect the rejects from other arms of the Service'.[35]

The fact that the officer corps took its recruits from the top of the social pyramid, and that the rank and file were predominantly recruited from those at the very bottom, might suggest that the former opted for a career in the army to confirm their social status, and that the latter were driven to it from desperation. There is more than a modicum of truth in both assertions. But they do not provide a complete explanation of why either officers or men decided to enlist, and nor do they even begin to explain why they opted to join a particular regiment.

Unemployment did drive many men into the ranks of the Regular Army. In 1874 a Sergeant-Major of 77/Foot asked a recruit if he had ever previously served in the army. He replied 'No' and added 'Aw were niver hard enough up, to list, afoor'.[36] Robert Edmondson, who enlisted in the late 1880s, thought that 'Empty pockets and hungry stomachs are the most eloquent of recruiting sergeants'.[37] Officers in search of recruits often behaved as if they agreed with him.[38] When, in 1892, Colonel G. C. Swiney, the commanding officer of the DCLI depot at Bodmin, sent a package of recruiting literature to the Reverend J. J. Hunt, the Vicar of St Pauls, Penzance, he asked him to distribute it amongst 'Young Men in your neighbourhood who are at times thrown out of work, or, being unable to obtain regular employment, fall amongst bad companions and get into trouble; and that there are others who, in search of work, go to large towns with the same result'.[39] Despite the existence of the dole, unemployment continued to drive men into the army after 1918. In 1925 60 per cent of recruits from the London area were unemployed when they enlisted.[40] Herbert Burnett enlisted in 1930 because he was unemployed and he wanted to cease being a burden on his mother.[41] A. R. Gaskin left school at 14 and worked as a pot-boy in a restaurant, an errand boy, in an ice-cream factory, and in a shoe factory before he became unemployed and enlisted.[42] And when J. E. Bowman joined the

[35] PRO WO 163/88. Minutes of the proceedings of 58 meeting of the Executive Committee of the Army Council, 8 May 1942.

[36] NAM 94-5-181. Sgt.-Maj. J. White, Ts Memoirs, 'Reminiscences of my Army Life'.

[37] R. Edmondson, *John Bull's Army from Within: Facts, Figures, and a Human Document from One who Has Been 'Through the Mill'* (London: Francis Griffiths, 1907), 3.

[38] Captain R. D. Gibney, 'Recruiting', *United Services Magazine* (1874), 344.

[39] NAM 8202-55. Colonel G. C. Swiney to Reverend J. J. Hunt, 1 Mar. 1892.

[40] *The Times*, 12 Mar. 1926.

[41] IWMSA. Accession No. 000925/05. H. W. Burnett, 1.

[42] IWM 87/44/1. Pte. A. R. Gaskin MSS Ts memoirs. 'The little bit of green or the light infantryman'.

Royal Artillery in early 1939 many of his fellow recruits 'looked as if they had been transferred from a Dr Barnado's soup kitchen in the late nineteenth century'.[43]

Similarly, there is evidence that public school boys were attracted to the army because a commission would confirm their social status. In the late nineteenth century there were few careers open to a young man from a gentlemanly family. Business was not regarded as a fit occupation, for it required too much time from its initiates, and did not leave them sufficient leisure to pursue the true vocations of a gentleman.[44] They could, therefore, only seek an opening in one of the few professions that allowed them to retain the status of a gentleman, such as the Church, the law, the higher civil service, or the army. As the Conservative MP Lt.-Col. Sir Richard Lloyd-Lindsay, who had won a VC fighting with the Scots Fusilier Guards in the Crimea, told the House of Commons in March 1871, regular officers did not belong to a special caste that set them apart but, 'That they behaved like gentlemen might be inferred from the fact that the Queen's commission, even to an ensign, was a passport to the best society—intellectual or social'.[45] In 1888 Francis Warre-Cornish, a 17-year-old schoolboy at Winchester, wrote to his father: 'I do not think you would approve of my going "into business" or banking or any sort of those fortune making professions, and they are not professions to be proud of or on which you can become as keen as you can become and as I am becoming on the army.'[46] The Church did not appeal to him for the same reason that he abandoned the idea of becoming a professional painter, namely that the financial prospects of both occupations were too insecure.

But a moment's consideration suggests that such a one-dimensional characterization of men's motives oversimplifies a much more complex reality. The number of unemployed males frequently exceeded the number of men willing to present themselves at the recruiting office. The search for a job, therefore, was only one reason why men enlisted in the ranks, and there were a plethora of others. Some men joined the army because it offered them an opportunity to travel.[47] Others left steady civilian jobs because they were bored and hoped that soldiering would offer them more excitement.[48] The glamour of a soldier's uniform was a

---

[43] J. E. Bowman, *Three Stripes and a Gun* (Braunton, Devon: Merlin Books, 1987), 22.

[44] J. Harris, *Private Lives, Public Spirit: Britain, 1870–1914* (London: Penguin, 1993), 124.

[45] Parl. Deb. (series 3) vol. 204, cols. 1403–4 (6 Mar. 1871).

[46] NAM 6412-143. Captain F. Warre-Cornish MSS. Warre-Cornish to his father, 24 Oct. 1888.

[47] G. Horton, *A Brief Outline of my Travels and Doings whilst Serving in the Army from 1884 to 1918*, ed. A. E. Horton (Ts memoirs. Produced by RHQ, Royal Irish Rangers, Belfast, 1982), 2; NAM 8210–13. Warrant Officer I. W. H. Davies, Ts memoirs; IWMSA. Accession No. 006524/02. Pte. R. Jago, reel 1.

[48] IWMSA. Accession No. 000188/07. E. G. White, 3; A. Dixon, *Tinned Soldier: A Personal Record, 1919–26* (London: The Right Book Club, 1941), 28–9.

powerful attraction to men engaged in tedious and repetitive occupations.[49] Peter Gorman, who was working as a farm labourer in Ireland, enlisted in the Leinster Regiment in 1898 because when he was working on the land, 'You see, the way it was, yer finished up so late at night that you nearly met yourself going in the morning again'. One day some troops marched through his village and he 'heard the band playing and I was near, working near, and I left me work And I RUN to see the soldiers . . . and I took a wonderful fancy there and then for the soldiers'.[50]

For some men employed in hard manual labour, the army seemed to promise an easier life. In 1928 a coalminer, Richard Clemens, enlisted because 'I was just fed up with the mines, that's all'.[51] When a trooper in the 10/Hussars was asked in 1932 why he had enlisted, he replied candidly: 'Because I was fed up with working.'[52] Others saw the army as a means of escaping from their domestic surroundings. J. T. Hammond, who was underage when he enlisted in the Essex Regiment in 1899, did so because he was unhappy at home and 'I'd run away from home. That's all there was to it.'[53] Peter Saunders, who was 17 when he volunteered in 1950, did so because 'In my day the only way you left home was either you got married or you went in the army, that was it in those days'.[54]

Potential officers like Warre-Cornish were no more activated by a single motive than were the rank and file. Indeed, their reasons for choosing a military career were sometimes remarkably similar to those of some of the men they were to command. Like many ranker recruits, Warre-Cornish hoped that the army would offer travel, glamour, and excitement, claiming: 'I should like the change of scene and the interest & out door life & roughing it & the soldiering & pipeclaying immensely.' Nor did the prospect of signing what was in effect an unlimited liability contract deter him: 'As to getting oneself killed I should look upon it as a sort of superior hunting, if such a chance came for promotion I think really I could make the army a profession & pride.'[55] Potential officers could also be seduced by the glamour of the army. Vacey Carlyle Magill-Cuerden decided he wanted to be a soldier when he was six years old. He saw a battalion marching past his parents' front gate 'and I stood there with my small drum and bugle and decided then I was going to be a soldier'.[56]

---

[49] 'C. V. B.', 'Days long Ago', *The Sherwood Foresters Regimental Annual*, 1929, 192.
[50] IWMSA. Accession No. 006512/2. Pte. P. Gorman, 1–2.
[51] IWMSA. Accession No. 000923/04. R. Clemens, reel 1.
[52] *The Xth Royal Hussars Gazette*, 13 (1933), 9.
[53] IWMSA. Accession No. 006521/02. J. T. Hammond, reel 2.
[54] IWMSA. Accession No. 18748/4. P. Saunders, reel 1.
[55] NAM 6412-143. Captain F. Warre-Cornish MSS. Warre-Cornish to his father, 24 Oct. 1888.
[56] IWMSA. Accession No. 004485/05. Lt.-Col. V. C. Magill-Cuerden, 1.

Two common factors that encouraged both officers and rankers to enlist were parental encouragement and the influence of their schooling. Not all parents were happy to see their sons in uniform. But it would be wrong to ignore the fact that many positively encouraged them to enlist. It was commonplace in the late nineteenth century for sons to follow their fathers into the same occupation or profession, and for fathers to exert considerable influence upon their son's choice of career.[57] They continued to do so well into the twentieth century. Consequently, both the officer corps and the other ranks contained men who were 'hereditary soldiers', a fact that gave some reality to the familial rhetoric that surrounded the regimental system. Their forefathers had been soldiers and they were consciously following in their footsteps. David McCulloch, who served in the Royal Scots Fusiliers between 1867 and 1888, was the third generation of his family to serve in the regiment.[58] Joe Packer enlisted in the ranks of the Middlesex Regiment in 1898 because his brothers and uncles were serving soldiers 'and I suppose it was in my blood, as you might say...'.[59] Frank Mason's father and grandfather had both been soldiers and when Frank reached the age of 14 in 1907 his father put him into the army as a boy soldier.[60] C. H. Ditcham's father had served in the Argyll and Sutherland Highlanders; Ditcham himself was born in the regiment, and in 1911, 'being a son of the regiment, I joined the regiment'.[61] George Hogan joined the Hampshire Regiment in 1918 aged 15. Hogan had six brothers and sisters and his father had only a soldier's pay to support them.[62] CQMS R. E. Faithorn, who received a Long Service and Good Conduct medal in 1921, was the fourth generation of his family to serve in the Norfolk Regiment.[63]

'Hereditary' soldiers encouraged to enlist by their parents were equally common amongst the commissioned ranks. Hubert Gough, who was commissioned in 1889, came from a highly distinguished family of soldiers. One of his ancestors had been C-in-C in India, and his father had won a VC serving with an Indian Army cavalry regiment during the Indian Mutiny. He decided that his son should leave Eton and attend an

[57] F. M. L. Thompson, *Gentrification and the Enterprise Culture: Britain 1780–1908* (Oxford: Oxford University Press, 2001), 135–6; J. Tosh, *A Man's Place: Masculinity and the Middle-Class Home in Victorian England* (New Haven, Conn.: Yale University Press, 1999), 114–15.

[58] D. J. Oddy, 'Gone for a Soldier: The Anatomy of a Nineteenth-Century Army Family', *Journal of Family History*, 25 (2000), 39–62.

[59] IWMSA. Accession No. 006537/1. Pte. J. Packer, 1.

[60] IWMSA. Accession No. 000049/08. Col. F. O. Mason, reel 1.

[61] IWMSA. Accession No. 000374/06. Maj. C. H. Ditcham, 1.

[62] G. Hogan, *Oh, to be a Soldier: Recollections and Reflections of Seventy Years* (Braunton, Devon: Merlin Book, 1992), 42–3.

[63] RNRM. R. 99. Some Interesting Events connected with the Norfolk Regiment. Scrapbook compiled by Lt. R. D. Ambrose, 1/Norfolk Regiment, 1921. Special Battalion Orders—1st Battalion, 19 Apr. 1921.

army crammer to prepare for the Sandhurst entrance examination because 'my parents were most anxious that we should get into the army with the least possible delay'. In Gough's case family tradition and paternal insistence paralleled his own inclinations. 'I became a soldier', he concluded, 'like several thousand others, because soldiering was a tradition in my family and because I felt a certain aptitude for it.'[64] His was only an exceptional example of a commonplace phenomenon that could easily be multiplied. When Harry Thwaytes went to Sandhurst in 1908, his father had served for twenty years in the West India Regiment before transferring to the Army Pay Corps.

[Harry] had never really seen anything of the outside world except from a military point of view. It never occurred to me to be anything else . . . We were brought up in this sort of military atmosphere, with a lot of ceremonial to look at and bands and all that kind of thing. The Army had a kind of glamour about it and my two brothers also went into the Army.[65]

Frederick Morgan believed that by making his son become a soldier he was achieving vicariously one of his own ambitions. He had become a timber merchant because a downturn in the family's fortunes had prevented him from following a military career himself.[66]

The losses sustained by the 'officer class' during the First World War may have dissuaded some parents from putting their sons into the army, but there is evidence that some continued to do so. S. J. L. Hill was commissioned in 1931 because 'in my generation your family always decided what you were going to do. My father was a soldier and his father, and it was automatically assumed that I would join the Army so I never really thought of doing anything else. And I had no other ideas really.'[67] James Scott-Elliot sought a commission in the army after failing the eyesight test for the navy and 'in the end I joined the Army because my father was a soldier and one really drifted that way'.[68] J. R. V. Thompson came from a line of officers stretching back to 1740. His father was a Royal Engineer, and he 'went to school at Wellington which was a great forcing-house for soldiers', with the result that 'when the time came at school, what was one going to do, there didn't seem to be very much choice in the matter. One had always assumed that one would go on—rather unenterprising perhaps—in the same line but I always felt that I was going to be a soldier and I'm very glad I was.'[69]

[64] Sir H. Gough, *Soldiering On* (London: Arthur Baker, 1954), 16, 24, 27, 36.
[65] IWMSA. Accession No. 000917/07. Lt.-Col. H. D. Thwaytes, reel 1.
[66] Gen. Sir F. Morgan, *Peace and War: A Soldier's Life* (London: Hodder & Stoughton, 1961), 15.
[67] IWMSA. Accession No. 006348/05. Brig. S. J. L. Hill, reel 1.
[68] IWMSA. Accession No. 004449/06. Maj.-Gen. J. Scott Elliot, 1.
[69] IWMSA. Accession No. 004403/06. Lt.-Col. J. R. V. Thompson, 1.

But not everyone had the good fortune to have parents who recognized their son's real aptitudes, and family pressure could sometimes push a potential recruit in the wrong direction. The January 1947 intake at Sandhurst contained many cadets from families with a long tradition of military service. At least one cadet, who was there because of family pressure rather than personal inclination, went to the extreme length of disabling himself by shooting off a finger so that he could escape.[70]

Schoolmasters could be almost as influential as parents in determining that a young man entered the army. Many Victorians prided themselves that theirs was not a militaristic society. In reality, the public schools, which most middle- and upper-class boys attended between 1870 and 1914, inculcated a range of militaristic and imperialistic ideas in their pupils, most notably what one historian has called the sense of a 'self-sacrificial warriorhood'.[71] They were taught that the British empire was a force for moral good in the world, and it was the destiny and the duty of all British men, if necessary, to sacrifice themselves in its service. By the Edwardian period most of them had their own cadet corps where boys received elementary military training.[72] James Marshall-Cornwall was 12 years old when the Boer War broke out in 1899. 'My early schooldays were thus passed in an atmosphere of patriotic fervour and martial enthusiasm. We all wore in our buttonholes little souvenir portraits of our favourite Generals—Roberts, Kitchener, Methuen, Baden-Powell, etc.' His father encouraged him to seek an army career. 'This accorded well enough with my own inclinations, and my early enthusiasm for a military career was stimulated by the books which I used to devour. They included Rudyard Kipling's earlier works which were then appearing, G. A. Henty's historical romances and W. H. Fitchett's *Deeds that won the Empire.*'[73]

After 1870 the spread of compulsory primary education ensured that working-class children were also exposed to a similar range of ideas. Their education not only instilled in them a basic grasp of the '3 Rs', but also habits of obedience, order, sobriety, and respect for the established social structure. One study of recruitment during the Boer War suggests that soldiers' own accounts indicated that they believed that the war would offer them excitement and adventure, ideas that drew heavily upon the tradition of militaristic patriotism that had been instilled in

[70] C. Millman, *Stand Easy or the Rear Rank Remembers* (Edinburgh: The Pentland Press, 1993), 18.

[71] J. A. Mangan, 'Duty unto Death: English Masculinity and Militarism in the Age of the New Imperialism', *International Journal of the History of Sport*, 12 (1995), 10–28.

[72] C. B. Ottley, 'Militarism and Militarization in the Public Schools, 1900–1972', *British Journal of Sociology*, 29 (1978), 321–339.

[73] Gen. Sir J. Marshall-Cornwall, *Wars and Rumours of Wars* (London: Leo Cooper/Secker and Warburg, 1984), 1–2. See also Lt.-Gen. Sir P. Neame, *Playing with Strife: The Autobiography of a Sapper* (London: George Harrap, 1947), 15–16.

them at school and in the popular media in the 1880s and 1890s.[74] Thomas Painting, who was the son of a railway labourer, left school aged 12 and was employed during the Boer War running a railway bookstall at Litchfield, where he admitted that he was

fired with what the army did, you see. And not only that, I could read the 'Wide World' Magazine, the 'Royal' and all the magazines, you see, and also the 'Sheffield Weekly Telegraph' which had an article about a British soldier's adventure in India. And I wanted to go to India and see that.[75]

Furthermore, by 1914 four out of ten male children belonged to at least one of several youth movements, such as the Boys Brigade, the Boy Scouts, and the Church Lad's Brigade, that had developed in Edwardian England, each of which had adopted the military trappings of drill, uniforms, and annual camps.[76] However, it would be a mistake to exaggerate the proportion of the young male population who were sufficiently enthused by what they learned at school or in the Boy Scouts that they were driven to enlist.[77] Between 1908 and 1912 only 4 per cent of former members of school cadet corps took commissions in the Territorial Force and 2 per cent in the Special Reserve, the successor to the Militia.[78] There was also a persistent tradition of resistance to any form of organized militarism in working-class communities.[79]

The youth movements' greatest influence was on the sons of artisans and clerks, people who were unlikely to join the Regular Army or the Militia, but who did enlist in the Volunteers or Territorials. One such was J. W. Milne, who served in South Africa with a Volunteer company of the Gordon Highlanders. Milne claimed that he volunteered because he had read books such as

Darkest Africa, and Lord Clive in India. The stirring tales of his heroic defence of Arcot, and other thrilling incidents imbued a spirit in me to see such things as they were told in those books for myself. Ever since the Jameson Raid I had watched the trend of events in South Africa.

On the call of Her Majesty's Government for volunteers to serve in South Africa, I felt that now was the opportunity for me to see a bit of the World.[80]

[74] M. D. Blanch, 'British Society and the War', in P. Warwick and S. B. Spies (eds.), *The South African War: The Anglo-Boer War 1899–1902* (London: Longman, 1980), 210–38.

[75] IWMSA. Accession No. 000212/14. T. H. Painting, 1.

[76] P. Simkins, *Kitchener's Army: The Raising of the New Armies, 1914–16* (Manchester: Manchester University Press, 1988), 19–20; Blanch, 'British Society', 211–15.

[77] The literature as it concerns the early 20th c. is ably summarized in W. Nasson, *The South African War 1899–1902* (London: Edward Arnold, 1999), 237–41.

[78] G. D. Sheffield, *Leadership in the Trenches: Officer-Man Relations, Morale and Discipline in the British Army in the Era of the First World War* (London: Macmillan, 2000), 15.

[79] J. O. Springhall, 'The Boy Scouts, Class and Militarism in Relation to British Youth Movements 1908–1930', *International Review of Social History*, 16 (1971), 39–41.

[80] http://www.jwmilne.freeservers.com/speech.htm. Accessed on 8 July 2001. 'No 8080 Private JW Milne, 1st Service Company Volunteers, Gordon Highlanders (1900), 'Looking back on the Boer War'.

The First World War undermined any notion of the glamour of war and the nobility of unquestioning patriotism. But a considerable number of young men joined the army after 1918 despite the fact that close relations had died fighting between 1914 and 1918. T. W. Nickalls's father was killed leading a brigade of 21st Division at Loos, but that did not dissuade his son from going to Sandhurst in 1922.[81] David Belchem opted for a military career in 1929, despite the fact that his father had been badly wounded on the Somme, and that four of his uncles had been killed.[82] R. King-Clark's romantic notions of soldiering—plus his headmaster's insistence—survived the death of his father, who was killed during the First World War, and induced him to go to Sandhurst in 1932.[83] H. M. Liardet's father was a senior Terrritorial Army officer and successful City businessman, and initially opposed his son's wish to take a regular commission, 'because he thought I would do better for myself in those days of peace in civil life in his firm. But I hated that and in the end he agreed that I should go in the regular army.'[84] For some regulars their reasons for enlisting after 1918 did not differ significantly from those of their pre-war predecessors. John Hackett, who was commissioned into the 8/Royal Irish Hussars in 1931, believed that young men wanted commissions, 'thinking that it was worthwhile doing something for the empire and hoping to have an interesting and exciting life, while they did it, into the bargain'.[85]

Once a recruit, be he destined for a barrack room or the officer's mess, had made his decision to join the army, or had it made for him, the next question he had to decide was which regiment to join. Unless he opted for general service, in which case he could be posted to any regiment, the intending ranker signed a contract that led to his enlistment into a particular corps or regiment. Young officers, once they had completed their cadet training, were commissioned into the monarch's land forces, but were gazetted into one particular corps or regiment. Cardwell and Childers hoped to attract both officers and men to regiments because of local and family loyalties. There are no army-wide statistics to measure their success in doing so among the officer corps. But there is considerable statistical evidence for the late nineteenth century that indicates that their success in exploiting local loyalties to attract men to fill the ranks was both limited and variable.

Sir Patrick MacDougall's committee, which devised the details of the localization scheme, hoped to exploit local loyalties by producing a recruiting system in which county boundaries and brigade sub-district

[81] IWMSA. Accession No. 00962/4. Lt.-Col. T. W. Nickalls, 1.
[82] Maj.-Gen. D. Belchem, *All in the Day's March* (London: William Collins, 1978), 15.
[83] IWMSA. Accession No. 004486/7. Lt.-Col. R. King-Clark, 1.
[84] IWMSA. Accession No. 000862/05. Maj.-Gen. H. M. Liardet, 2.
[85] Hackett, *The Profession of Arms*, 142.

boundaries coincided. But this ran counter to demographic realities and the actual needs of each regiment. The committee calculated that a community would require an adult male population of about 200,000 to feed the two regular and two militia battalions of the sub-district with recruits. Some counties had more than enough people to meet this criterion, but many others did not. Lancashire, for example, had over 1.3 million males in 1873, but Dorset had only 95,500.[86] Although in some parts of England the committee achieved a rough fit between a county and a regiment, in others it did not. In England the counties of Lancashire, Yorkshire, Staffordshire, Kent, and Surrey, and in Scotland Lanarkshire, had such large populations that they were assigned two or more brigade sub-districts. By contrast, all the counties in Ireland and Wales, and all the counties in Scotland except Lanarkshire, contained so few inhabitants that two or more counties had to be amalgamated to form a sub-district.[87] Thus, of the sixty-six territorial regiments created in 1881, only twenty-nine had a regimental district that was confined to a single county. The remainder drew their men from two or more counties.

Cardwell and Childers recognized that the distribution of the population was unlikely to remain static, and that ways had to be found to provide recruits for the non-localized corps, and so they built into the recruiting organization the means to equalize the distribution of recruits. Cardwell established the cities of Dublin, London, and Liverpool as special recruiting districts outside the territorial system. They acted as magnets for large numbers of men from other parts of the country who came to them in search of work and who, if they could not find it, might enlist.[88] By 1879 it had become commonplace for the Inspector-General of Recruiting to direct that recruits should be sent from 'the great recruiting centres such as London or Liverpool' to regiments in need of men and whose own sub-districts could not supply them.[89] The result was that by the mid-1880s the Dorset Regiment, which could not find enough recruits from its own district, was being completed with men from London, and the KOSB, which was supposed to draw its recruits from the region between Newcastle and southern Scotland, was receiving considerable numbers of Irish immigrants who had enlisted in Glasgow.[90]

Childers added a further refinement that marked another step away from localized recruiting. Britain was already divided into ten military

<hr />

[86] PP (1881), XXI. C. 2792. *Final Report of the Committee* ... In 1881, as a result of the Childers reforms, sub-districts were renumbered and renamed regimental districts.

[87] PP (1881), XXI. C. 2792. *Supplementary report of Committee on the organisation of the various military land forces of the country*, 36–7.

[88] PP (1881), XXI. C. 2791. *Report of the Committee* ..., Q 159.

[89] Ibid., QQ. 15–21.

[90] PRO WO 33/47. Report of the Committee on army schools and schoolmasters, QQ. 424, 1868–9.

districts. Three of them (Chatham, Aldershot, and Woolwich), consisted of military bases. But the remaining seven districts (Northern, South Eastern, Eastern, Western, Southern, Home, and North British) consisted of several counties, or in the case of North Briton, the whole of Scotland. After 1882, if a regiment could not find enough recruits from its own regimental district, it could draw upon recruits from the other regimental districts within the same military district. 'It is hoped', the Inspector-General of Recruiting declared in 1882, 'that in time each general's district will be able to keep its own territorial regiments supplied, even if each regimental district is not able to meet the demands made upon it.' Only if that did not suffice, would recruits be sent from one of the great cities that were administered as independent recruiting districts.[91]

It was a measure of the failure of localized recruiting to become a reality that between 1883 and 1900 territorial regiments could find an average of only 38.5 per cent of their recruits from amongst men born in their own regimental district. This figure, however, concealed considerable variations, for some regiments did much better than others. At the two extremes, the Royal Warwickshire Regiment, the Suffolk Regiment, and the Hampshire Regiment could claim that over 70 per cent of their recruits were born in their regimental district. At the other extreme, sixteen regiments could find less than a quarter of their recruits from men born in their own districts.[92] Overall, forty-six regiments, or nearly two-thirds of the total line infantry regiments, found less than half of their recruits from their own district.

There were also significant national and regional variations. English and Irish regiments were more successfully localized than their Welsh or Scottish counterparts. Whereas on average 43 per cent of soldiers serving with regiments whose depots were in England were born in their regimental district, and the corresponding figure for Irish regiments was 40 per cent; it was only 28 per cent for regiments with their depots in Wales, and 23 per cent for regiments with depots in Scotland. Within England there were also marked regional variations. Regiments with depots in East Anglia topped the table with 54 per cent of men serving with their regiments having been born in their regimental district; regiments from the South and West of England came second, with an average of 47 per cent; they were followed by regiments with depots in Lancashire and North West England and London and the Home Counties, both of which raised 44 per cent of their recruits from their own districts. At the bottom came regiments from North East England (from Leicestershire through

---

[91]   PP (1883), XV. C. 3503. *Annual Report of the Inspector-General of Recruiting*, 2.

[92]   The conclusions are based on statistics calculated from evidence presented annually to Parliament by the Inspector-General of Recruiting. The detailed figures are given in the App. to this chapter.

Yorkshire to Durham and Northumberland), which could raise only 32 per cent of their recruits from amongst men born in their regimental district.

The fact that localized recruiting had in effect become regional recruiting was tacitly acknowledged by the military authorities. Between 1905 and 1907 they amalgamated individual regimental districts into a dozen grouped regimental districts. Recruiting for each regiment was placed in the hands of the major in command of its depot, but the colonel in command of each district had the power to transfer recruits from regiment to regiment to where they were most needed.[93] In 1906, 26 per cent of recruits joined the regiment of their district, 32 per cent enlisted in another infantry regiment, and 42 per cent enlisted in a corps other than the line infantry.[94] The Royal Welch Fusiliers, whose depot was at Wrexham, were known as the 'Birmingham Fusiliers' because they took so many recruits from the Midlands.[95]

In 1921, recruiting became even more divorced from the regiments. The War Office decided that depot commanders and their staff were too inclined to place the interests of their own regiments before the needs of the army as a whole and so responsibility for recruiting was removed from their hands and became the job of specialist recruiting staffs.[96] What had before 1914 been regional recruiting now became national recruiting. Recruits from several parts of the country might be assembled at a depot and then posted en bloc to a regiment most in need of them.[97] Between 1920 and 1937 the proportion of recruits posted to the regiment of their own district remained more or less steady at 28 per cent.[98] Some regiments, such as the Loyal North Lancashire Regiment, sometimes received whole platoons of recruits enlisted in London.[99]

Regiments that before 1914 had made a reality of localized recruiting were resentful that their local identity was being diluted. In 1928 a former battalion commander in the Hampshire Regiment complained that whereas in the Edwardian period nearly 90 per cent of his men had come from Hampshire, the changes meant that the figure had now

[93] PP (1906), XIV. Cd. 2693. *Annual Report of Recruiting for the year ended 30th September 1905*, 2, 5; J. B. M. Frederick, *Lineage Book of the British Army: Mounted Corps and Infantry, 1660–1968* (New York: Hope Farm Press, 1969), 68–9.

[94] PP (1907), IX. Cd. 3365. *General Annual Report on the British Army for the Year ending 30 September 1906*, Table 1.

[95] F. Richards, *Old-Soldier Sahib* (London: Faber & Faber, 1936), 79.

[96] PP (1923), XIV. Cmd. 1941. *General Annual Report for the British Army for the Year Ending 30 September 1921*, 8.

[97] *The Times*, 24 Dec. 1930.

[98] PP (1923), XIV. Cmd. 1941. *General Annual Report ...*, 29–36; PP (1937–8), XVII. Cmd. 5486. *General Annual Report for the British Army for the Year Ending 30 September 1937*, 10–12.

[99] Brig. G. R. R. Williams, 'The Regimental System', *The Lancashire Lad: The Journal of the Loyal Regiment (North Lancashire)*, 12 (1968), 74.

dropped to only 40 per cent.[100] Faced with a shortage of nearly 10,000 infantrymen in 1930, the War Office experimented with a return to localized recruiting under the slogan 'County Men for County Regiments'.[101] The campaign did produce an increase in recruits presenting themselves, but county connections played little part in inducing men to enlist. The Oxford and Buckinghamshire Light Infantry received a considerable number of extra men, but few had any previous connection with Oxfordshire or Buckinghamshire. The CO of the regimental depot thought the increase was because of the attendant publicity campaign, not the appeal of territorial sentiments.[102]

The administrative structure of the recruiting system was never the only impediment to localized recruiting. A further one was the fact that Parliament each year set strict limits on the overall size of the army, and in order to regulate the flow of manpower the War Office periodically closed or opened particular regiments to recruiting. Consequently, men who wanted to join a particular regiment were sometimes denied the choice. They had either to opt for another regiment or another job. When Albert Bradshaw tried to enlist in the ranks in 1926 only two regiments were open for recruits, the Royal Artillery and the Loyal North Lancashire Regiment. As he did not want to be a gunner, he opted for the Loyals.[103] Charles Whitewick wanted to follow his father into the Royal Artillery in 1933, but as they had no vacancies the recruiting sergeant suggested that he join his county regiment, the East Surrey's. But 'I said no to that because I wanted to get away from home, away from the influence of my parents and felt that it would be better all round'. He eventually joined the Royal Berkshire Regiment, which was short of recruits and was being filled up with men from across the country.[104]

Nor did recruits always share Cardwell and Childers's enthusiasm for joining their local regiment. In 1931 the Director of Organisation at the War Office estimated that only half of them expressed a strong wish to join a particular regiment.[105] There were examples of recruits whose reasons for choosing a regiment fulfilled the Cardwell–Childers ideal. They were powerfully influenced by family ties or local loyalties. In 1923, 108 men in 1/Cameron Highlanders had relations who had served with the battalion in the past.[106] Henry Horsfield joined the Royal Artillery as a boy of 15 in

[100] G. H. Nicholson, 'The County System', *The Times*, 29 Sept. 1928.
[101] *The Times*, 3 Jan. 1931.
[102] *The Times*, 18 May 1931.
[103] IWMSA. Accession No. 000811/11. A. H. Bradshaw, 21.
[104] IWMSA. Accession No. 004474/03. E. O. L. Whitewick, 1–3.
[105] *The Times*, 3 Jan. 1931.
[106] IMM PP/MCR/182. Maj.-Gen. D. N. Wimberley MSS, Scottish soldier. 'The Memoirs of Maj.-Gen. Douglas Wimberley', vol. 1.

1920 because he had an uncle who was in the regiment and 'I fell in love with his uniforms, of course, his spurs, riding whip, bandolier, all the rest of them, all the rest of the things'.[107] In 1930 Herbert Burnett confessed to knowing nothing about the regimental system, but he joined the East Yorkshire Regiment because it was his local regiment.[108]

For many men joining the local regiment was the last thing they wanted to do. Dugald McIver's local regiment was the Argyll and Sutherland Highlanders. But in 1919 he joined the Highland Light Infantry. His mother had died, and he could not get along with his step-mother; the Highland Light Infantry, with their headquarters in Glasgow, offered him an escape from his family.[109] A few years later Frederick Mitchell, who came from Folkestone in Kent, opted to join the Northamptonshire Regiment because he hoped that the regiment 'will take me out the rut of Folkestone'.[110] Sometimes family members worked actively to dissuade relations from joining their regiment. On Christmas Eve 1899 Lieutenant L. D. Wedd of the 2/Queen's Royal West Surrey's wrote to his mother that 'I don't think I want Reggie [his brother] in the Queen's, brothers being a bore according to everybody, but will let him know what to put down for and would suggest the Devons'.[111] Reggie was in fact commissioned into the Buffs in May 1901.

Recruits enlisted in regiments with which they had no local connection for a variety of reasons. John Fraser joined the Northumberland Fusiliers in July 1877 because the drill sergeant of his Volunteer Battalion, who was a member of the regiment, persuaded him to opt for it rather than his initial preference, a Highland Regiment. The Northumberland Fusiliers were, the sergeant insisted, the 'Finest Regiment in the British Army. See their roll of Battle honours. No regiment has a longer one, nor a better reputation extending over years and years.'[112] Some men joined a regiment for casual or apparently frivolous reasons. George Horton was born in Kent and had no connection with Ireland. He enlisted into the 1/Royal Irish Rifles in 1883 simply because they happened to be stationed on his doorstep at Deal.[113] In 1901 Frank Richards joined the Royal Welch Fusiliers rather than his local regiment, the South Wales Borders, because he thought he would have more chance of serving overseas with the former.[114] Thomas Painter enlisted at the depot of the Royal Warwickshire Regiment in 1906, where the recruiting sergeant

[107] IWMSA. Accession No. 000780/05. H. L. Horsfield, 1.
[108] IWMSA. Accession No. 000925/05. H. W. Burnett, 1.
[109] IWMSA. Accession No. 00897/09. Maj. D. C. McIver, 1–2.
[110] IWMSA. Accession No. 004513/06. Sgt. F. E. Mitchell, reel 1.
[111] NAM 1999-06-94. Lt. L. Wedd MSS. Wedd to mother, 24 Dec. 1899.
[112] J. Fraser, *Sixty Years in Uniform* (London: Stanley Paul, 1939), 41.
[113] Horton, *A Brief Outline of my Travels*, 2.
[114] Richards, *Old-Soldier Sahib*, 21.

tried to persuade him to join the regiment. He refused on the grounds that its soldiers wore a red marching-out uniform and, 'Well, I didn't want to be a pillar-box, you see, red coat. All due respect to the red coat regiments. But I didn't want a red coat. I said "What's that regiment has a green jacket?" "Oh," he said, "the King's Royal Rifle Corps, four battalions, plenty of foreign service." I said, "That's the regiment for me".'[115]

The route by which aspiring officers and regiments came together was a two-stage process. On the one hand, young men seeking a commission could express a preference for a particular regiment or corps. But their acceptance into it was not automatic. Some officer cadets were drawn towards a particular regiment by family or territorial connections. In 1873 Ian Hamilton sought a commission in his father's old regiment, the Gordon Highlanders.[116] In 1888 Fred Ponsonby was commissioned into the 2/Duke of Cornwall's Light Infantry. However his father, General Sir Henry Ponsonby, a Grenadier Guardsman and Private Secretary to Queen Victoria, insisted that this was only a temporary arrangement until a vacancy appeared in his old regiment, which it did in 1889, and Fred duly transferred.[117] G. F. H. Stayner joined the Leicestershire regiment in 1919, 'chiefly because my uncle had been in it and so I had some family connection with it'.[118] S. J. L. Hill joined the Royal Fusiliers in 1931 because several uncles had fought and died with the regiment in the First World War, 'and so it seemed absolutely normal that I should go into my father's regiment. Of which of course he was also Colonel of the Regiment.'[119] In 1937 J. Sykes-Wright confessed that 'I have been brought up from childhood to think of "The Queens" as the one and only regiment for me. I had an uncle serving in the regiment.'[120]

Family friends could be almost as important as blood relations in easing the passage of a young officer into a regiment. H. E. N. Bredin was able to join the Royal Ulster Rifles in 1936 thanks to the good offices of a friend of his father who commanded one of its battalions.[121]

Local pride could be an equally powerful incentive. For W. O. Walton joining the Green Howards in 1922 seemed the natural thing to do. He had been born and brought up in Richmond, Yorkshire, within sight of their depot.[122] Similarly, E. G. Hollist was commissioned into the Royal Sussex Regiment in 1929 because his family came from Sussex, 'and it was natural that I should want to go into the county regiment where

[115] IWMSA. Accession No. 0007212/04. T. H. Painting, 3.
[116] Gen. Sir I. Hamilton, *Listening for the Drums* (London: Faber & Faber, 1944), 13, 15.
[117] Sir F. Ponsonby, *Recollections of Three Reigns* (London: Eyre and Spottiswoode, 1951), 4–5.
[118] IWMSA. Accession No. 003999/05. Brig. G. F. H. Stayner, 1.
[119] IWMSA. Accession No. 006348/05. Brig. S. J. L. Hill, 1.
[120] PRO WO 32/4477. Southern Command report, App. 2, 17 Mar. 1937.
[121] IWMSA. Accession No. 004550/05. Maj.-Gen. H. E. N. Bredin, 2.
[122] IWMSA. Accession No. 004948/04. Lt.-Col. W. O. Walton, 1.

I would have county friends'.[123] Peter Barclay had no family connections in the Norfolk Regiment, but joined them because 'Norfolk's my county. My roots go jolly deep in the county and I have several very special friends in Norfolk and in fact when I joined the county regiment three others joined together. And we had a wonderful time through the years.'[124]

But local and family connections did not always override other factors in persuading young men to seek a commission in a particular regiment. Aspiring officers sometimes picked their regiments in the same almost casual manner as did some of the men they were to command. Montague Cooke had a nomination from the Duke of Connaught, the Colonel-in-Chief of the Rifle Brigade, to join his regiment, but opted instead for the Royal Artillery after he had seen a section of the Royal Horse Artillery and was mightily impressed by their 'gold jackets, polished harness and black-blue shining twelve-pounder'.[125] J. F. McNab's father was an Indian army doctor and wanted his son to be commissioned into an Indian cavalry regiment. But when he was aged 6 McNab acquired 'Cameron Highlander lead soldiers' and decided he wanted to wear a kilt and join the regiment.[126] Nigel Poett's father had once commanded a battalion of the Dorset Regiment, but when his son came to choose a regiment he chose the Durham Light Infantry. They had the reputation for being an accomplished polo-playing regiment, and love of that sport outweighed family tradition.[127] Young officers like R. H. Harding-Newman, whose uncle was Colonel of the Essex Regiment, also sometimes ignored family tradition when they decided to join newly established corps like the RTC in the 1920s.[128]

In making their initial choice of regiment, young officers had always to take account of one consideration that did not affect the rank and file: that was the question of mess and living expenses. Junior officers in the Royal Artillery and the Royal Engineers could expect to be able to live on their pay, although some extra cash from outside sources such as their parents never came amiss.[129] In 1899 W. A. Tilney, with an allowance of £1,000 per annum, had no difficulty in gaining a commission in the 17/Lancers.[130] But John Vaughan, who joined the 7/Hussars a year later, found that he could just about afford to pay his way on an allowance of

---

[123] IWMSA. Accession No. 000938/05. Lt.-Col. E. G. Hollist, 1.
[124] IWMSA. Accession No. 8192. Brig. P. Barclay, reel 1.
[125] Col. M. Cooke, *Clouds that Flee* (London: Hutchinson, 1935), 35.
[126] IWMSA. Accession No. 004427/04. Brig. J. F. McNab, 1.
[127] Gen. Sir N. Poett, *Pure Poett: The Autobiography of General Sir Nigel Poett* (London: Leo Cooper, 1991), 10.
[128] IWMSA. Accession No. 000834/08. Brig. R. N. Harding-Newman, 4.
[129] IWMSA. Accession No. 004465/07. Maj.-Gen. H. P. W. Hutson, 1.
[130] W. A. Tilney, *Colonel Standfast: The Memoirs of W. A. Tilney 1868–1947. A Soldier's Life in England, India, the Boer War and Ireland*, ed. N. Murray-Philipson (Norwich: Michael Russell, 2001), 16–17.

£400 per annum, but that 'It was not a lot of money for a young soldier to live on'.[131] It was, in fact, the approximate equivalent of the average annual earnings of a General Practitioner.[132]

In 1903 a Parliamentary Committee discovered that infantry subalterns, who were paid just over £95 per annum, needed a private income of between £60 and £150 per annum to meet their mess bills and other necessary expenses. A cavalry subaltern was paid slightly more (£121 per annum), but as he was expected to maintain at least two chargers at his own expense, he needed a private income of between £350 and £700 per annum.[133] The precise size of the supplement depended upon the regiment in question. As one battalion commander admitted in 1937, 'It is notorious that some Regiments are much more expensive than others'.[134]

Anecdotal evidence for the inter-war period suggests that few regiments were very expensive and that it was easier for a frugal subaltern to live on his pay. Even so, marked discrepancies between regiments remained. A subaltern in the Cameron Highlanders, for example, was paid £16 per month, but his mess bills alone came to £25 per month, and if he wished to hunt even a private allowance of £100 was not sufficient.[135] By contrast in 1921 only one of three newly commissioned officers in the Royal Scots Fusiliers had even modest private means, and in the mid-1930s subalterns in the DCLI could lead a reasonably comfortable existence with a private income of £50 per annum.[136]

This meant that aspiring officers of modest means found their choice of regiment more constrained than those with deeper purses.[137] In 1882 Arthur Richardson, who had a private income of only £100 per annum, opted to serve in an inexpensive English line infantry regiment, the East Yorkshire Regiment, and specifically asked to be posted to India, where he knew the cost of living was much less than it was in Britain.[138] In the 1930s K. C. Cooper and Gregory Blaxland both toyed with the idea of joining the cavalry, but opted instead for the RTC and the Buffs

---

[131] Vaughan, *Cavalry and Sporting Memoirs*, 3.

[132] A. Digby, *The Evolution of British General Practice 1850–1948* (Oxford: Oxford University Press, 1999), 41.

[133] PP (1903), X. Cd. 1421. *Report of the committee appointed by the Secretary of State for War to inquire into the nature of the expenses incurred by officers of the Army and to suggest measures for bringing commissions within reach of men of moderate means*, 7–10.

[134] PRO WO 32/4477. Report of Southern Command committee, 17 Mar. 1937. Evidence of Lt.-Col. V. E. C. Dashwood, 2/Royal Sussex Regiment.

[135] IWMSA. Accession No. 004427/04. Brig. J. F. McNab, 1.

[136] K. Strong, *Intelligence at the Top* (London: Cassell, 1968), 3; IWM 83/46/1. Maj. W. G. Blaxland, Ts Memoirs, 'Unready for war. A Memoir of a journey through Sandhurst and Dunkirk'; IWMSA. Accession No. 006367/05. Brig. E. G. B. Davies-Scourfield, 2; Maj-Gen. David Tyacke to the author, 22 July 2002.

[137] IWMSA. Accession No. 000893/03. Col. G. W. Draffen, 4.

[138] NAM 7712-3. Lt.-Col. A. J. Richardson, Ts memoirs, 'A Person of No Importance'.

respectively, partly because they were cheaper.[139] Officers who joined a regiment and then found that they could not meet their expenses had several options. They could seek to transfer to their linked battalion in India or to a colonial corps, such as the Royal West African Frontier Force, where the cost of living was much cheaper. Or they could transfer to another, less expensive, regiment. In 1890 2/Lieutenant St. J. W. T. Parker, who had been commissioned into the Essex Regiment in 1887, wrote imploringly to his brother:

Will you drop me a line to say how that damm concern is getting on & when we may expect some return in the form of a dividend or is it going into bankruptcy. Can you possibly lend me about £20 as I do not know how to meet my next month's mess bill & I must try to hang on till I get my lieutenancy which ought to be soon now & then I will forward an application to join the Army Service Corps which is slightly better paid & none of the expenses of being with a regiment. I may of course have to wait some time for a vacancy but it is not a popular service except for the slight increase of pay.[140]

He could not 'hang on' and transferred to the Army Service Corps in 1892.

But however much an aspiring officer might wish to join a particular regiment or corps, his acceptance into it was not automatic. Until 1947, when it was amalgamated with the Royal Military College at Sandhurst, young men seeking regular commissions in the Royal Engineers or Royal Artillery had first to pass through the Royal Military Academy at Woolwich. Commissions in the Royal Engineers were amongst the best-paid posts in the army. There were, consequently, always more applicants for commissions in the engineers than vacancies, and they were usually filled by those passing out at the top of the order of merit from Woolwich.[141] Those who did not pass out sufficiently high became gunners.

Officer cadets seeking regular commissions in the Household Brigade, line cavalry, or line infantry were trained at Sandhurst, and they were required to express a preference for particular regiments. Shortly before the end of their course, cadets 'having a special family or territorial connection with a regiment' were invited to apply for a commission in it. The Military Secretary, the War Office official responsible for guiding officers' careers, retained the right to post newly commissioned officers according to the needs of the service. However, he did his utmost to accommodate them, even allowing them to wait for up to six months for a vacancy. Cadets without such connections were allowed to apply to two regiments, raised to three in 1924, but were not allowed to wait for a vacancy. Only if the

[139] IWMSA. Accession No. 00000788/04. Maj.-Gen. K. C. Cooper, 3; IWM 83/46/1. Blaxland, 'Unready for war'.

[140] NAM 8303-32. Major St. J. W. T. Parker MSS. Parker to his brother, 17 Jan. 1890.

[141] Morgan, *Peace and War*, 23; IWMSA. Accession No. 00000954/07. Brig. W. R. Smijth-Windham, 3.

claims of cadets for a particular regiment were evenly balanced was any consideration given to a cadet's performance in his final examinations.[142]

However, of even more importance in ensuring a match between aspiring officers and regiments was the semi-official machinery of selection. Regiments identified potential officers in one of several ways, through personal contacts between serving officers and the sons of friends or acquaintances, by maintaining semi-official contacts with particular schools, or through members of the regiment who were serving on the staff at Sandhurst. Asked to describe how this was done in the 1920s, an officer remembered: 'Nobody actually came round to recruit, it was all done on what you sometimes know as the old boy net. Someone said "What about your son, would he like to join the regiment?" or "Would he like to be considered?", that's how it went as a rule.'[143] In most years between 1907 and 1943 the KRRC had so many Old Etonian officers that it was able to produce 'a team of Old Etonian Officers to play the School in the Field'.[144] An ability to play games well was attractive to many regiments. In 1949 D. J. Holdsworth was invited to join the Gloucestershire Regiment because of his prowess at rugby.[145] In 1960 the Royal Highland Fusiliers decided to carry the hereditary principle to its perhaps logical extreme. They decided that one of their main sources of future officers would be the sons of officers, and so began to maintain a 'baby-book' in which their names were entered.[146]

Once a regiment had identified a potential officer, he was then vetted by its representatives. The abolition of purchase led some officers to fear that the social status of the officer corps would deteriorate. Capt. C. B. Brackenbury, a gunner who had witnessed the performance of the Prussian army in 1866 and 1870, commended the Prussian system by which the social suitability of new officers was ensured by allowing the whole of the regiment's existing officers to vote on their nomination. 'No inconvenience is found to result from it,' he asserted, 'and I would venture to ask whether some such principle might not be adopted with advantage in England.'[147]

The British system was less formal and rigid, but equally effective in maintaining social harmony in the officers' mess. Each regiment had its own Colonel, usually a senior serving or retired officer. One of his duties

---

[142] PP (1902), X. Cd. 982. *Report of the Committee appointed to consider the education and training of officers of the Army*, Regulations respecting admissions to the RMC Sandhurst, 1899; PRO WO 32/3771. Army Council, 351 meeting, 31 May 1926.

[143] IWMSA. Accession No. 000933/04. Col. K. E. Savill, 2.

[144] *The King's Royal Rifle Corps Chronicle 1943*, 30.

[145] IWMSA. Accession No. 15428/4. D. J. Holdsworth, reel 1.

[146] Anon., *The Royal Highland Fusiliers: Regimental Standing Orders* (Glasgow: Robert MacLehouse & Co. Ltd, c.1960), 46.

[147] Capt. C. B. Brackenbury, 'The Military Systems of France and Prussia', *Journal of the Royal United Services Institute*, 15 (1871), 239–40.

was to appraise potential officers to ensure that they would be acceptable to the other members of the officers' mess. Before they left Sandhurst, and in some cases even before they had entered it, promising candidates were interviewed by the Colonel or Colonel-Commandant of the regiment or corps and perhaps invited to visit one of its units in order to determine their suitability.[148] Only if a cadet passed this test was it worth his while placing the regiment on his list of choices. Thus Reginald Stephens's passage to a commission in the Rifle Brigade in 1890 was eased by the fact that in 1883 his father had persuaded the Colonel of the Regiment, the Duke of Connaught, to place his name 'on his list of candidates'.[149]

For much of the period under consideration some Regimental Colonels had an effective veto over who was or was not commissioned into their regiment. From the War Office's point of view this had advantages and disadvantages. In the late 1920s the Military Secretary defended the system, minuting that

If commissions were given entirely by order of seniority in passing out, the best regiments would get all the top cadets, and the worst regiments all the bottom cadets, which would be very undesirable.

Cadets at Sandhurst all know that, if they want a particular regiment, they must get nominated by the Colonel. This in itself creates a feeling of esprit de corps in a boy before he ever joins. Moreover it is clearly in the interests of a boy to join a regiment where he is wanted than one where no one has any interest in him.[150]

But it also had its disadvantages. The army often had too few candidates to fill the available commissions and so cadets who had a Colonel's nomination in their pocket knew that they only had to scrape a bare pass at Sandhurst to be sure of receiving a commission in the regiment of their choice.[151] And secondly cadets who missed out on their preferred choices often found themselves posted by the Military Secretary willy-nilly. This sometimes worked out well. J. R. V. Thomson was born in Kent but when he was about to be commissioned in the mid-1920s 'both the county regiments were over strength with young officers and took nobody at all in my term. So I went into the North Staffs in which I'd had an uncle and there I found myself very happy.'[152] Samuel Phillips was born in Ireland and in 1948 hoped to join the Royal Irish Fusiliers. But there was only one vacancy and that was given to a cadet who passed out higher in the order of merit than he did. Philips was eventually commissioned

---

[148] Maj.-Gen. D. Tyacke to the author, 22 July 2002; Anon., *The Royal Highland Fusiliers*, 48.

[149] NAM 8902-201-40. Sir R. B. Stephens MSS. Sir H. Elphinsone [?] to Capt. Stephens, 17 Oct. 1883.

[150] PRO WO 32/3771. General Sir D. Campbell to Milne, n.d.

[151] Gen. Sir Cecil Blacker, *Monkey Business: The Memoirs of General Sir Cecil Blacker* (London, 1993), 16; PRO WO 32/3771. Minute by Milne, 23 Feb. 1926.

[152] IWMSA. Accession No. 004403/06. Lt.-Col. J. R. V. Thompson, 1.

into the Northumberland Fusiliers, a regiment with which he had no territorial or family connections, because they happened to have a vacancy.[153] But sometimes the result was not so happy. This was often the case with cadets who had sought commissions in the infantry or cavalry but found themselves posted instead to one of the services such as the RASC or the RAOC, and felt disappointed and even aggrieved.[154]

National Service saw a brief shift in the power of selection away from Regimental Colonels towards the Military Secretary. Regimental representatives on the instructing staff at Sandhurst continued to play an important role in identifying likely candidates and advising Regimental Colonels about their suitability or otherwise.[155] But for the first time other than during the World Wars National Service gave the military authorities ample numbers of officers and thereby diminished the power of Colonels to pick and choose who they wanted. By 1951 the Army Council had ruled that the allocation of officers to regiments would be made firstly according to the needs of the service, and secondly according to the order of merit in which candidates passed out from Sandhurst. Only after these criteria had been met would they take account of any family or territorial claim that a cadet put forward that was supported by the Colonel of the Regiment.[156] A committee of Cavalry Colonels was so alarmed at this that they actively recommended cadets who aspired to join their regiments to work harder at Sandhurst to ensure that they passed out sufficiently high in the order of merit to secure their first choice.[157]

But the abolition of National Service, and the consequent fall in the number of candidates for commissions, saw power swing back towards the Regimental Colonels.[158] By 1967 the Director of Manning had to admit that 'the wishes of colonels have tended more and more to override the order of merit'. The reason for this was simple. It was the case that 'a considerable number of the officers in certain arms, particularly RAC and Infantry, are recruited by the regiment in the first place and offered a place by the colonel (subject to satisfactory completion of the RMAS course). Under another system this material might well be lost to the Army altogether'.[159] When officer manpower was scarce, the military

[153] IWMSA. Accession No. 17688/3. S. A. S. Phillips, reel 1.

[154] Millman, *Stand Easy*, 22.

[155] See e.g. the correspondence between Maj. Peter Forrest, who was the regimental representative on the RMAS Staff, and Brig. C. J. Wilkinson, Colonel of the Royal Suffolk Regiment, in RNRM. R. 133. Amalgamation file.

[156] PRO WO 163/531. Report of the Committee on the standard of officer cadets, Oct. 1951. See also RNRM. R. 133. Amalgamation file. Adjutant-General to Brig. C. J. Wilkinson, 19 Oct. 1956.

[157] PRO WO 32/14215, AG 17, War Office to Colonel E. H. Tinker, 21 Feb. 1951.

[158] ERM. ER 8579–8610. Brig. C. M. Paton MSS. 3. Royal Anglian Regiment. Standing Instructions, n.d., but c. Sept. 1964.

[159] PRO WO 32/20995. Director of Manning (Army), Draft paper on officers for Committee on Future Structure of the Army, 15 Feb. 1967.

authorities could not afford to be too dictatorial lest they deter potential applicants from seeking commissions.

In the 1870s one-third of the army had been placed outside the territorial system. But by the end of the century, even for the majority of regiments that stood inside it, localized recruiting was failing to provide them with more than a fraction of their men. The result was that, with the minimum of public fanfare, the military authorities transformed localized recruiting into regional recruiting and, after the First World War, into national recruiting. 'Why cannot the authorities be honest about it and drop this eyewash?' one of their critics wrote in 1928. 'If the county system is wrong, do away with it, and designate these general service regiments by numbers, as formerly. The fact is that they are afraid to do away with the county titles openly, in view of the outcry which it would occasion, and the non-military public is deceived into thinking that an organisation still exists which is really a hollow sham.'[160]

As early as 1877 the Duke of Cambridge had recognized the root cause of their failure. '[N]o Brigade Depot can ever keep up its own recruiting without such [outside] assistance. It may for a time do so, but you can never depend on it doing so. It is voluntary; it depends on trade and various things; but you can never have anything of a system of this sort without conscription, if you are to carry it out in its integrity.'[161] Without the ability to compel men to serve and the power to post them to their local regiments, it was always likely that many regiments would struggle to fill their ranks with local men.

Defenders of the regimental system who have claimed that it was the envy of foreign armies have overlooked the fact that as long as the latter relied upon conscription, they were more, not less, likely than the British army to have made a reality of localization.[162] The regimental system was not a uniquely British institution. Elements of it could be found in many other armies before 1914, and some of them institutionalized it far more thoroughly than did the British. During the American Civil War both the North and South raised volunteer regiments drawn from specific localities or ethnic groups.[163] The Prussian, and after 1871 the German, army was recruited on a local basis. Even in wartime it made great efforts to preserve localized recruiting until the catastrophic casualties that the

[160] *The Times*, 29 Sept. 1928.
[161] PP (1877), XVIII. C. 1654. *Report of the committee appointed to inquire into certain questions that have arisen with respect to the militia and the present Brigade Depot system*, Q. 8598.
[162] Lt.-Col. G. Kennard, *Loopy: The Autobiography of George Kennard* (London: Leo Cooper, 1990), 88.
[163] J. M. McPherson, *Battle Cry of Freedom: The Civil War Era* (Oxford: Oxford University Press, 1988), 326.

Wehrmacht suffered in Russia after 1941 made it impossible.[164] The Austrian army opted for localized recruiting after 1886, and by the late 1880s the French army had adopted a broadly similar system.[165] The Tsarist army raised regiments on a localized basis, although each regiment only took three-quarters of its recruits from its own district. The remainder came from outside the district, a policy designed to ensure that potentially disaffected recruits drawn from the non-Russian population were never in a majority in any regiment.[166] But even if only three-quarters of the men in a Russian regiment came from its own district, it still meant that Tsarist regiments were more successfully localized than almost any regiment in the British army.

The British army's failure to make a reality of localized recruiting had significant implications for the evolution of the regimental system. Sustaining discipline and morale were fundamental to the successful functioning of the army. The abolition of long service and its replacement by short service meant that the military authorities could no longer rely on long years in the ranks to instil in soldiers an instinctive obedience. The need to attract more men to the ranks also meant that the system of discipline had to be reformed. Regimental authorities could no longer rely upon the sometimes draconian sanctions they had employed in the past to extract obedience when it was no longer freely given. Cardwell and Childers had hoped that localization and short service would enable them to maintain morale and discipline, and to transcend the deep social divisions that divided the officers' mess from the rank and file. It would transplant into the army the communal roots that bound soldiers to the civilian society from which they sprang, and to which they would return at the end of their colour service. Regiments would become reflections of their parent communities. But only a minority of regiments struck such deep roots in their local communities that they could recruit the majority of their men from their own districts. Most did not and the incomplete success of localization placed a heavy burden on the regimental authorities. If they were to rely upon communal ties to sustain discipline and morale, it meant that where no primordial communities existed, they had to construct them. The next two chapters will begin to explain how they went about instilling a military identity, enforcing obedience, and manufacturing a sense of *esprit de corps* in their recruits.

[164] O. Bartov, *Hitler's Army: Soldiers, Nazis and War in the Third Reich* (Oxford: Oxford University Press, 1991), 30–7.

[165] PRO WO 33/19. Lt.-Col. Cooke and Col. Sir H. James, System of recruitment and of the organisation of the Reserves of France, Prussia, Austria, Russia and the German States, Nov. 1868; D. Porch, *The March to the Marne: The French Army 1871–1914* (Cambridge: Cambridge University Press, 1981), 29–32; PRO WO 106/6200. *Handbook of the French Army, 1906.*

[166] PRO WO 106/6222. *Handbook of the Russian Army 1908.*

Appendix

The average percentage of soldiers serving with territorial regiments who were born in the regimental district between 1883 and 1900

70 per cent or more

Royal Warwickshire Regiment	72.3
Suffolk Regiment	71.3
Hampshire Regiment	71.0

50 to 69 per cent

Norfolk Regiment	66.2
Gloucestershire Regiment	66.1
Royal Munster Fusiliers	62.1
Lancashire Fusiliers	58.5
Royal Sussex Regiment	56.9
Royal Fusiliers	54.9
South Staffordshire Regiment	54.4
Middlesex Regiment	54.2
Wiltshire Regiment	53.3
Royal Dublin Fusiliers	52.7
Buffs	52.2
King's Own Yorkshire Light Infantry	52.0
Somerset Light Infantry	51.0
King's Liverpool Regiment	50.5
North Staffordshire Regiment	50.4
Essex Regiment	50.3

25 to 49 per cent

Bedfordshire Regiment	48.8
Loyal North Lancashire Regiment	48.7
Royal Irish Regiment	48.0
Royal Berkshire Regiment	47.8
Devon Regiment	46.7

South Staffordshire Regiment	46.5
Sherwood Foresters	44.4
York & Lancaster Regiment	43.4
Royal Irish Rifles	42.3
King's Own Royal Lancaster Regiment	40.0
Royal West Kent Regiment	38.5
Cameronians	38.1
Leicestershire Regiment	37.7
East Lancashire Regiment	37.3
King's Shropshire Light Infantry	37.2
Welsh Regiment	37.0
Duke of Wellington's Regiment	36.6
East Surrey Regiment	36.5
Black Watch	36.4
Queen's Royal West Surrey Regiment	36.2
Northamptonshire Regiment	35.8
Connaught Rangers	33.9
Royal Inniskilling Fusiliers	33.2
Lincolnshire Regiment	32.0
Manchester Regiment	31.8
Oxfordshire Light Infantry	31.8
West Yorkshire Regiment	29.5
South Wales Borderers	26.8
Dorset Regiment	25.7
Highland Light Infantry	25.4

Less than 25 per cent

Cheshire Regiment	24.8
Leinster Regiment	24.4
Green Howards	24.0
Royal Scots	23.8
Durham Light Infantry	23.0
King's Own Scottish Borderers	21.8
Royal Irish Fusiliers	21.3
Gordon Highlanders	21.1
Seaforth Highlanders	19.7
Argyll & Sutherland Highlanders	19.1
Royal Welch Fusiliers	18.9
Border Regiment	16.5
East Yorkshire Regiment	12.5
Duke of Cornwall's Light Infantry	12.1
Royal Scots Fusiliers	10.6
Cameron Highlander	9.6

CHAPTER THREE

Basic Training

In 1950 a draft of soldiers who had just completed their basic training were about to leave Park Hill Camp near Oswestry for the last time. As they did so one of them leant out of the truck taking them away and yelled at his training sergeants 'I hope that as you slide down the banister of life you get plenty of big splinters in your arse.'[1] This story epitomizes a widely accepted view of the nature of basic training. Foul-mouthed NCOs bullied young recruits, forcing them to endure long periods of mindless drill, so that by its conclusion they had discovered that army life was irksome and unpleasant. That was the experience of basic training that many recruits remembered. John Lucy, who joined the Royal Irish Rifles in 1912, found basic training 'the worst six months of my life. We became insensitive, bored and revolted, and talked seriously of deserting after three months of the life.'[2] But their reaction was not universal. In 1877 John Fraser found that 'Drilling under "Sloper" Burns was exhilarating for he was full of cheerful repartee which was always to the point, and his language had, by years of practice, become rich and colourful.'[3]

Throughout the whole of their working lives all soldiers, be they officers, NCOs, or privates, were pre-eminently men under discipline. It was that which set them apart from the civilian community. A bank clerk, a railway engine driver, or a farm labourer might have to obey his superiors during his working hours. But once he had left his workplace for the day, he was his own master. A soldier was not. Throughout the twenty-four hours of every day his whole being was regulated by those the army had set over him. The military legal code gave superiors immense power over their subordinates, and the military authorities were never inclined to allow soldiers to forget that fact. It was common for COs to read on parade sections of the Army Act. One recruit who enlisted in 1914 was given

a recital of Army Law—there was great emphasis upon those paragraphs which read 'and the penalty is death or some such punishment'. In those days I was a sensitive boy and began to wonder how one could possibly survive enemies both

[1] E. G. Barraclough, *National Service: An Insider's Story* (Durham: Pentland Books, 2001), 18.
[2] J. F. Lucy, *There's a Devil in the Drum* (Sussex: Naval and Military Press, 1993), 37.
[3] Fraser, *Sixty Years in Uniform*, 48–9.

at home and abroad. This was of course to instil the idea of unquestioning obedience ... [4]

But any army that could rely only on overt power to regulate relations between superiors and subordinates was unlikely to be able to withstand the stresses of the battlefield. One of the main functions of basic training was to instil into young soldiers, both officer cadets and other rank recruits, the belief that the military authorities possessed the legitimate authority to govern their every action. The army wanted not only disciplined bodies, but also disciplined minds. Men enlisting in the army, according to two senior officers writing in 1893, 'have probably not been accustomed in civil life to do exactly and immediately what they are told to do'.[5]

The most important function of basic training was to transform a civilian into a soldier by inculcating in him certain habits of behaviour and mental qualities that the military authorities deemed essential. 'The first thing the recruit has to learn on joining his regiment', according to the *Standing Orders* of 2/Cheshire Regiment, 'is discipline. Discipline means the knowledge how to obey, how to conform to orders and regulations, how to carry these out with cheerfulness, alacrity, and punctuality.'[6] Or, as Lord Wolseley explained in 1878, 'A man may be perfect in all that the drill instructor can impart, but unless his mind is as disciplined as his body, unless he has learned self-control, unquestioning obedience and respect for his superiors, and habits of order and of method, he never can be a really successful soldier in the field.'[7] In this chapter I will analyse how the military authorities began to establish control over the lives of regimental soldiers, both officers and other ranks, through the process of basic training. The machinery employed was different in the case of officers and other ranks, but the purpose was the same. It was designed to ensure that all soldiers accepted that they were part of a disciplined hierarchy stretching from the monarch at the top to the newest-joined private soldier at the bottom.[8]

The organization and experience of basic training remained remarkably constant in the century after 1870. The recruit left his civilian family and home and together with a group of other recruits submitted himself, day and night, to a programme of instruction. This was designed to

[4] IWM Misc. 220/3152/2/24. The Jesse Short Collection. Lt.-Col. T. L. Loveday to D. Gill, 11 Oct. 1965.

[5] Goodenough and Dalton, *The Army Book of the British Empire*, 136.

[6] Anon., *The Standing Orders of the 2nd Battalion 22nd (Cheshire) Regiment* (2nd edn., Madras, Dec. 1906), 1.

[7] Sir G. Wolseley, 'England as a Military Power in 1854 and 1878', *Nineteenth Century*, 3 (1878), 444.

[8] Much of what follows is informed by M. Foucault, *Discipline and Punish: The Birth of the Prison* (London: Penguin, 1977), *passim*.

demonstrate to him his inadequacies as a soldier, to teach him the customs and practices of the army, to test his physical and mental ability to adjust to this new role, and finally, in most cases, to signify that he was accepted into his new military family. The birth of his new identity was usually marked by a ceremonial parade at which the newly emerged soldier could show off his new identity.[9]

Most cadets seeking regular commissions were trained at either Sandhurst or Woolwich. Other ranks usually did their recruit training at their regimental depot. The time they spent on basic training differed. The length of courses at the cadet colleges varied from between twelve and twenty-four months over the course of the century after 1870. The period was shorter for other ranks, ranging from twenty-six weeks on the eve of the First World War to eighteen weeks in the early 1930s, to ten weeks in the mid-1950s. In both cases the process began in similar fashion. Their initiation into the army started when they symbolically shed their civilian identities by surrendering their civilian clothes, accepted the kit that was issued to them by the quartermaster, and donned a uniform for the first time. If they had not already done so, they were also made to have their hair cut very short.[10] The military authorities thus began the process of making a man at least look like a soldier.

Most officer cadets had been boarders at a public school, and so they were already accustomed to communal living. Indeed, it was likely that they had been at school with some of their fellow cadets.[11] At Sandhurst or Woolwich they usually slept in single rooms, messed together, and had servants to perform menial tasks. For other ranks, basic training was perhaps their first experience of communal living, and some found it a rude shock, for in the late nineteenth century some older barrack rooms were overcrowded and squalid.[12] But the more modern ones were a visible expression of the determination of the military authorities to instil order and discipline into the rank and file. 'Its looks, its smell, its general air', one recruit remarked of his barrack room in the early 1880s, 'all meant cleanliness.'[13] More prosaically a recruit who joined the Royal Artillery Depot at Woolwich in 1939 likened his barrack room to a well-ordered and hygienic cowshed.[14] Daily routine in barracks also quickly taught recruits that henceforth the army would determine how they performed even the most basic human functions. The army dictated

[9] R. Jolly, *Changing Step: From Military to Civilian Life. People in Transition* (London: Brassey's , 1996), 35–6.

[10] http://www.britains-smallwars.com/korea/Queens.htm. J. Copsey, 'Two Years for the Queen'. Accessed on 28 Apr. 2002.

[11] NAM 7402-28-13. Lt.-Col. W. Lockhart MSS. Lockhart to mother, 3 Sept. 1882.

[12] NAM 7008-13. Anon., MSS. Experiences of a soldier, n.d.

[13] Edmondson, *John Bull's Army*, 25, 28.

[14] Bowman, *Three Stripes and a Gun*, 23, 25.

when they slept, when they woke up, and when they ate. It also dictated how they dressed and how they kept their rooms clean and tidy.[15]

A training manual issued in 1911 explained that basic training had three functions: '(i) The development of a soldierly spirit. (ii) The training of the body. (iii) The training in the use of rifle, bayonet, and spade.'[16] It was not accidental that the army placed the purely technical aspects of learning how to use rifle, bayonet, and spade last in this list. Mechanical skills could be imparted comparatively easily. Far more important, in the eyes of the military authorities, was the need to impose the elements of a new identity, 'a soldierly spirit', on each recruit. This process began on the parade ground, where both officer cadets and other rank recruits spent hours learning close-order drill. It taught discipline in the most fundamental sense by forcing recruits to hold their bodies as the army required them to do. Soldiers had to learn that 'The exact squareness of the shoulders and body to the front is the first and great principle of the position of a soldier', according to the army's drill manual in 1870.[17]

It also taught the cadet and recruit that he was a member of a team, and that he had to subordinate his own selfish egotism to the larger goals of that team. According to *Infantry Training 1932*,

The first and quickest method of teaching discipline is close order drill. The soldier begins his drill by being taught the 'position of attention', which in itself is the key to the purpose for which drill was invented. It secures the whole attention of the man to his commander by requiring:
  i. Absolute silence.
 ii. The body controlled and motionless.
iii. Eager expectation of the word of command and instant readiness to obey it.

While in the position of attention the unit places itself at the unlimited disposal of its commander. In drill movements it adds to this the instant, unhesitating, and exact obedience of orders.

Thus close order drill compels the habit of obedience, and stimulates, by combined and orderly movement, the man's pride in himself and in his unit.[18]

In the case of officer cadets, parade-ground drill also meant that they experienced at least briefly some of the indignities that were routinely heaped upon the private soldiers they would command.[19] A cadet who went to Sandhurst in 1909 commented that 'we learnt to accept the sort of harsh treatment that we saw put across to the ordinary recruit because

---

[15] Lucy, *There's a Devil in the Drum*, 22; Richards, *Old-Soldier Sahib*, 30, 36.

[16] General Staff, *Infantry Training 1911* (London: War Office, 1911), 1.

[17] Adjutant-General, *Field Exercises and Evolutions of Infantry (1870)* (London: HMSO, 1870), 4.

[18] General Staff, *Infantry Training. Vol. I. Training, 1932* (London: HMSO, 1932), 11.

[19] PP (1902), X. Cd. 982. *Report of the Committee appointed to consider the education and training of officers of the Army*, QQ. 2107–9, 2116.

we ourselves had had it, even in a more sarcastic way than even you had heard the shouting sergeant-major on the parade ground'.[20]

Drill sergeants had a legendary reputation for summoning invective when all else failed them. The recruit who was described as resembling 'a drowned duck in the family way', or 'a bag of manure tied up with pink string!' needed to retain a sense of humour.[21]

Some training NCOs lived down to the stereotype of foul-mouthed and sarcastic bullies. John Hillier described the corporal in charge of his recruit hut in 1940 as 'Hitler'.[22] But if an NCO treated his men firmly and fairly, addressed them without malice or sarcasm, used humour to teach lessons, and knew his job, he could win their respect and even affection. There were men like Sgt. Thompson who served with the Royal Scots Fusiliers in the early 1890s. 'He was', according to one soldier he trained, 'a strict disciplinarian—at first, indeed, I thought him inclined to be far too martinet-like in disposition, until I was subsequently convinced of my mistake. He had a name in the Company for being perfectly "straight"—that is, a man of his word, and consequently no one ever presumed to take liberties with him.'[23] Another such was Sgt. Grace, who trained recruits at the Depot of the York and Lancaster Regiment at Pontefract in the mid-1890s. He was 'a splendid specimen of a soldier, and although a severe disciplinarian he was well liked by us all. At times when dealing with dull and awkward recruits he would sink down on his knees and exclaim "Oh Lord send some sense into these poor fellows' empty skulls".'[24]

Soldiers had to be physically fit and so cadets and recruits spent a great deal of time doing physical training, playing team games, and, in the case of officer cadets, learning equitation or, in the case of recruits, going on route marches.[25] This was not always done with imagination. In 16/ Lancers in the late 1870s, 'Every recruit was expected to do the same thing in an equally proficient way, no allowance being made for differences in age, build, or general physical capacity.'[26] The excessive physical demands placed on recruits in the late nineteenth century, many of whom were undernourished when they entered the army, was one reason why so many deserted.[27] By the early twentieth century the military authorities

[20] IWMSA. Accession No. 000917/07. Lt.-Col. H. D. Thwaytes, reel 1.

[21] Lucy, *There's a Devil in the Drum*, 32; Gen. Sir M. Gow, *General Reflections: A Military Man at Large* (London: Souvenir Press, 1991), 51.

[22] J. Hillier, *The Long Road to Victory: War Diary of an Infantry Despatch Rider 1940–46* (Trowbridge, Wilts.: privately published, 1995), 6.

[23] H. Wyndham, *The Queen's Service: Being the Experiences of a Private Soldier in the British Infantry at Home and Abroad* (London: Heinemann, 1899), 21.

[24] NAM 8210-13. Warrant Officer I. W. H. Davies, Ts memoirs, n.d.

[25] War Office, *QR*, 1892, 216.

[26] Field Marshal Sir W. Robertson, *From Private to Field Marshal* (London: Constable, 1921), 6.

[27] PP (1881), XXI. C. 2791. *Report of the Committee …*, 24–5.

had recognized that physical training had to be progressive and that physical-training instructors must not bully recruits into undertaking exercises that they were not physically capable of performing.[28] Even so, when Richard Clemens passed through the Depot of the East Yorkshire Regiment in 1928 he found that gymnastic training was physically demanding 'because you really got slapped around a bit by the PT instructor, you know, if you slacked a bit. Otherwise it was OK. It kept you fit. It really did.'[29] 'The purpose of this excessive physical exertion', one Sandhurst cadet concluded, 'was either to build or break us. One or two would fail to make it and were removed, but the great majority of us survived and were the better for it.'[30]

When they were not on the parade ground, the gym, or the playing fields, recruits spent a great deal of their spare time polishing their equipment and cleaning their uniforms. 'Bull', the regular and repetitive cleaning of equipment and uniforms, had several functions. It served to emphasize that the soldier had a duty to keep himself and his equipment clean. Even in 1949 Kenneth Walsh found that some men in his recruit squad would not wash, shave, or keep their clothes clean unless ordered to do so.[31] It taught recruits domestic skills they had not learned at home, where their mothers had taken care of sewing, darning, washing, and ironing clothes.[32] It took up time that recruits might otherwise have spent moping about their lot. But above all it reinforced the message that the other aspects of their training were intended to inculcate, that now they were soldiers and therefore they had at all times to subordinate their individual will to that of their superiors. The slightest infringement of regulations, such as a dirty button, was liable to lead to swift punishment with the object of instilling the need to obey each and every order.[33] One Guards recruit concluded that 'Nothing in the army is ever done without a good reason. This "small-circling" [i.e. polishing boots] must have been devised as part of the grand strategy for reducing thinking persons to the level of mindless morons.'[34]

It was that last aspect of basic training that was problematic. Regiments had always needed officers and other ranks who were disciplined and who were trained to perform the technical aspects of their job. Some officers waxed lyrical about the discipline that close-order drill could impart. In 1934 one of them wrote that if it was well done, close-order drill

[28] War Office, *Manual of Physical Training (1908)* (London: War Office, 1908), 19.
[29] IWMSA. Accession No. 000923/04. R. Clemens, reel 1.
[30] Maj.-Gen. G. Kitchen, *Mud and Green Fields* (St. Catherines, Ontario: Vanwell Publishing Ltd., 1992), 25.
[31] IWMSA. Accession No. 18022/6. K. W. Black, reel 1.
[32] IWMSA. Accession No. 18489/4. N. Potter, reel 1.
[33] IWMSA. Accession No. 000569/18. Col. U. B. Burke, reel 7.
[34] IWM 87/42/1. Guardsman Len Waller MSS. Ts memoirs, 'How ever did we win?'

becomes a thing of beauty, a source of mutual satisfaction, an expression of military pride, and, in short, a form of disciplined self-expression: a military work of art. It has, indeed, the spirit of the morris dance, and it has survived the morris dance just because it has continued to be a natural expression of real feelings.[35]

However, there was also a growing school of thought that believed that if basic training inculcated only instant and unhesitating obedience to orders and nothing else, it could produce soldiers who lacked skills that were essential if they were to survive and fight successfully on the modern battlefield. Too much emphasis on close-order drill and obedience training could be counter-productive because it crushed the individual intelligence and initiative that the dispersed tactics of the modern battlefield required.[36] In November 1900 Lord Roberts, reflecting on his experience in South Africa, concluded that

under the existing conditions of war individual intelligence is of infinitely greater importance than the machine-like soldier who did so well when it was only necessary for him to obey orders and not to think for himself.

To secure this individual intelligence we must try and induce a better class of recruit to enter our ranks, and to improve the education of those whom it will, I fear, be still necessary to take from the dregs of the population.[37]

A year later a committee of senior cavalry officers in South Africa recommended that 'The training generally should be such as to develop more initiative than it does at present, without injuring discipline, and should tend more towards making the man an intelligent unit than a mere automaton.'[38]

In an effort to balance discipline with initiative, educational training became part of the basic training syllabus. In the late nineteenth century policy had alternated between obliging recruits to attend educational classes until they had acquired at least a Third Class education certificate, which was fixed at a very minimal level of literacy and numeracy, and merely encouraging them to do so.[39] In the twentieth century attendance became compulsory and a soldier was not deemed to be fully trained unless he had a Third Class certificate. In 1928 the CIGS emphasized the importance of devoting more effort during basic training to educating, rather than merely training, recruits, writing that educational training

[35] Maj. M. K. Wardle, 'A Defence of Close Order Drill: A Reply to "Modern Infantry Discipline" ', *Journal of the Royal United Services Institute*, 79 (1934), 717.

[36] 'A Field Officer', 'Modern Infantry Discipline', *Journal of the Royal United Services Institute*, 79 (1934), 469.

[37] PRO WO 108/411. Roberts to St. John Broderick, 9 Nov. 1900.

[38] PRO WO 32/6781. Report on the organisation and equipment of Cavalry by GOC Cavalry Division, 8 Nov. 1901.

[39] Fraser, *Sixty Years*, 49; Skelley, *The Victorian Army*, 94–6. A fourth-class certificate had been in existence between 1871 and 1888 but was then abandoned.

was intended 'to give the soldier at the beginning of his service the ability to learn, and subsequently encouraging him to work by himself. This principle of the individual learning and acting for himself is the basis of modern education, and is particularly applicable to the Army, which aims at the creation of initiative as well as mental development.'[40]

By 1937 it was officially accepted that the twin functions of basic training for other ranks was to produce a soldier with the individual cunning of 'an expert hunter', and a man who was 'determined, inquisitive and self-dependent', but who was also '*highly disciplined*, for by discipline alone can morale be maintained'.[41] Consequently, some of the more rigid aspects of depot discipline were relaxed. At the Sherwood Foresters Depot at Nottingham in 1938, 'More attention is being paid to the development of initiative and self-reliance and, with those objects in view, our youngsters are not wet nursed so much and proceed to all places of instruction, meals, &c., entirely under their own steam instead of being paraded and marched on every conceivable occasion.'[42]

A training manual issued in 1940 echoed the same idea. It was still essential to teach recruits discipline through parade-ground drill, for without such discipline his morale would collapse under the stress of battle, but it was equally important to teach him to use his intelligence and initiative. 'The modern battlefield calls for controlled dispersion, which requires both obedience and initiative.'[43] But the extent to which these injunctions informed actual training received by the rank and file, at least in the 1920s and 1930s, is questionable. In 1924 a recruit who had failed to perform a parade-ground manoeuvre to the satisfaction of his drill sergeant and was asked why replied

Sorry, sarge, I thought you said ...'
Oh, you thought, did you! Now who the hell gave you permission to think? You ain't got time to think in the army, mate. You just ACT. You act on the executive word of command.[44]

Similarly, many of the better-educated recruits who joined the Territorial Army in 1938–9 were dismayed not just at the paucity of Regular Army instructors, but also at their poor quality and the fact that the training system seemed to have been designed 'to suit the stupidest class of recruits, e.g. the rural ploughman'.[45] As late as 1966 an Army Board examination

[40] PRO WO 32/2382. Milne to Sir William Birdwood, 26 Nov. 1928.
[41] General Staff, *Infantry Training (Training and War)* (London: War Office, 1937), 10.
[42] Anon., *Regimental Annual. The Sherwood Foresters 1938*, 102.
[43] General Staff, *Training in Fieldcraft and Elementary Tactics. Military Training Pamphlet No. 33* (London: HMSO, 1940), 5.
[44] S. Mays, *Fall Out the Officers* (London: Eyre & Spottiswoode, 1969), 62.
[45] PRO WO 32/4610. Memorandum on the Territorial Army, 24 June 1938.

of basic training criticized the fact that educational training still took second place to drill and physical training in the recruit syllabus.[46]

The content and structure of the educational syllabus for officer cadets was even more problematic than the education delivered to the other ranks. The education that aspiring gunners and engineers received at Woolwich received little criticism, even immediately after the Boer War when officer cadet education was the subject of intense inquiry.[47] The educational syllabus, particularly at Sandhurst, oscillated between an emphasis on training officer cadets to perform the practical skills that subalterns needed to know, and providing them with a level of post-school education that would fire their intellectual curiosity and give them the intellectual skills that they would need to continue their own education once they had joined their regiment. At one pole there were those who thought that it should be a military training college, and at the other those who believed it should become a military university.

In the late nineteenth century the syllabus at Sandhurst, in addition to drill, equitation, and gymnastics, consisted of a mixture of military engineering and topography, tactics, military administration, military law, French or German, military history, and geography. Most cadets enjoyed their time there, finding the regime pleasantly free of restrictions after the irksome regulations of public school life.[48] A cadet who passed through the College in the mid-1880s believed that 'the education was sound and good and it was one's own fault if one did not join a Regiment with enough grounding in military affairs to make a respectable start'.[49] But Thomas Montgomery-Cunninghame, who graduated from the College in the mid-1890s, thought that he was taught 'Little to indicate how to cope with an astute enemy under modern conditions in a fire-fight, still less to prepare us for the far-reaching changes just ahead of us, which have revolutionized soldiering both in barracks and in the field'.[50]

The debacles of the Boer War seemed to prove the critics right. In 1902, an official enquiry concluded that Sandhurst was failing both as a place of learning and as a place of training. It failed to instil intellectual curiosity in the cadets, to develop their powers of reasoning, and killed any inclination they might have to continue to study their profession once they left the college. It also failed to prepare cadets for their duties as subalterns.

---

[46] PRO WO 32/17361ECAC/P(58)47. DCIGS. 'The length of recruit training', 24 June 1958; PRO WO 163/683/ECAB/P(66)1. ECAB, Committee on recruit handling, 6 Jan. 1966.

[47] PP (1902), X. Cd. 983. *Report of the Committee ...*, 15.

[48] N. R. Wilkinson, *To All and Singular* (London: Nisbet & Co., 1933), 2.

[49] CCC. Field Marshal Lord Cavan MSS. CAVN 1/3/I. Ts Memoirs, Recollections Hazy but Happy.

[50] Sir T. Montgomery-Cuninghame, *Dusty Measure: A Record of Troubled Times* (London: John Murray, 1939), 12.

Too much instruction in subjects such as tactics, military engineering, and riding took place indoors and there was a lack of sufficient practical training in subjects such as musketry and signalling. Cadets left the college knowing a great deal of drill, but little about the interior economy of the unit they were about to join. Finally, cadets had little real need to work, knowing full well that provided they could scrape a pass mark at the end of the course, they were bound to be commissioned.[51]

But if Sandhurst's critics could agree on what was wrong with the college, they could not agree on the proper direction it ought to take. Sir Coleridge Grove, a former Military Secretary, recommended that it should leave their training as subalterns in the hands of their regimental commanders after they joined their first unit. Sandhurst could then become a military university designed to open cadets' minds to the higher aspects of their profession.[52] But other senior officers, including Sir Evelyn Wood, the Adjutant-General, thought that the lessons of South Africa pointed in the opposite direction. Subalterns needed to know about the practical aspects of their calling before they joined their regiment, because most regiments lacked the facilities to train them. Wood insisted: 'If then, it comes to a choice between two systems, the theoretical and the practical, I should unhesitatingly decide in favour of the latter.'[53] It was Wood's vision that, temporarily, won the day.[54] After 1903 the courses at both Sandhurst and Woolwich became more practical, with greater emphasis on outdoor work, tactics, engineering, and topography. To encourage cadets to apply themselves to their work the War Office decreed that commissions in the Indian Army would be granted to those cadets who passed out highest in the final order of merit, rather than, as in the past, according to how high they had passed into the College. That at least ensured that those cadets whose parents were too poor to subsidize them to the extent necessary to enable them to join a British regiment had to exert themselves.[55]

However, Grove's vision of the cadet colleges found a new champion after 1918 in the shape of Lord Haldane. The First World War seemed to show that the post-Boer War reforms had gone too far in their emphasis on purely professional training. James Marshall-Cornwall, who graduated from Woolwich in 1905, felt in later years at a disadvantage compared to men who had received a wider education at university.[56] The

[51] PP (1902), X. Cd. 982. *Report of the Committee* ..., 10, 19–24; *Minutes of evidence of the Committee appointed to consider the education and training of officers of the Army*, QQ. 1263, 2300.

[52] PP (1904), XL. Cd. 1790. *Minutes of evidence* ..., Q. 9401.

[53] PP (1902), X. Cd. 982. *Report of the Committee* ..., *Appendix XXXVII*. Sir E. Wood to Akers Douglas, 23 Apr. 1901.

[54] PP (1902), X, Cd. 982. *Report of the Committee* ..., 24–5.

[55] Sir J. Smyth, *Sandhurst: The History of the RMA, Woolwich, the RMC, Sandhurst, and the RMA, Sandhurst, 1741–1961* (London, 1961), 135, 142; Parl. Debs. (series 4) vol. 119, col. 137.

[56] Marshall Cornwall, *Wars and Rumours of Wars*, 4.

cadet colleges were blamed for having limited the mental horizons of young officers, leaving them with little knowledge of the civilians turned soldiers they would have to lead, and ignorant of recent scientific developments as they might be applied to war.[57] The 1934 *Training Regulations* explained that officers needed a far broader base of knowledge if they were to cope with the complexities of modern war:

[A] knowledge of purely military subjects is no longer sufficient for an officer. He should also possess a wide range of general knowledge; the study of such subjects as psychology applied to war, political economy, scientific, industrial, and mechanical developments and finance, is of great value both in its practical application to military problems and in serving to widen the mental outlook.[58]

In 1923 Haldane presided over a committee to make recommendations to broaden the education provided by the colleges.[59] He recommended broadening the mental horizons of the majority of officers who went from school to the cadet colleges by raising the age of entry from 17 and a half to 18, the age at which most public schoolboys left school. That would ensure that cadets had completed a full sixth-form education before they joined the army. Once they arrived at the colleges, he wanted the syllabus to place greater emphasis on general education and less on purely military training. Cadets should study modern British history, the geography of Europe and the Empire, and a range of optional subjects including modern languages, the political and economic history of Britain and the Great Powers, or a science. The object, according to Colonel E. D. H. Tollemache, the Assistant Commandant of Sandhurst in 1929, would be that the colleges would become 'the university which gives the best general education and which best develops a boy's character and personality'.[60]

These ambitions were never achieved. Most of the staff were not qualified to teach to degree level, and the course was too brief, lasting only eighteen months, compared to the three years of an undergraduate degree course.[61] Woolwich had always attracted more academically able candidates than Sandhurst because of the need for gunner and engineer officers to have a good grounding in mathematics, and it continued to do so. But when Board of Education Inspectors visited Sandhurst in 1937, they reported that the standard of teaching was comparable only to that of an

[57] PRO WO 279/65. Report on the Staff Conference held at the Staff College, Camberley, 14–17 Jan. 1929.

[58] General Staff, *Training Regulations, 1934* (London: HMSO, 1934), 24.

[59] PRO WO 32/4353. Report of the Committee on Education and Training of Officers, 28 June 1923.

[60] PRO WO 279/65. Staff Conference held at the Staff College, Camberley, 14 to 17 Jan. 1929.

[61] D. French, 'Officer Education and Training in the British Army, 1919–39', in G. C. Kennedy and K. Neilson (eds.), *Officer Education: Past, Present and Future* (Westport, Conn.: Praeger, 2002), 105–28.

average public school.[62] The educational syllabus was so broad that it tended towards superficiality. It ranged from 'an explanation of the principles and terminology of modern political and economic life to world questions such as the League of Nations, &c.'[63] Between the wars the cadet colleges did try to broaden the mental horizons of young officers, but the reluctance of the War Office to spend the money that would have been required to transform them into a real university stymied their efforts. A cadet who graduated from Sandhurst in 1935 believed that 'To anyone possessed of a reasonable level of intelligence, Sandhurst then was, intellectually, an almost complete waste of an important 18 months of his life. There were plenty of physical, but no mental challenges.'[64] The corollary of placing more weight on the general education of the cadets was a reduction in their professional military instruction. Cadets received only a broad training in strategy and tactics in their first two terms, but were not introduced to the elements of platoon and section work until their final term.[65] As one Sandhurst graduate later commented on the syllabus, 'I thought it was splendid, excellent. Thinking back the only thing they didn't teach us much about was soldiering.'[66]

The appropriate balance between educational and purely military training remained a bone of contention even after Sandhurst and Woolwich were merged in 1947. The College retained its ability to instil physical fitness, obedience, and *esprit de corps* in cadet officers.[67] But by the late 1950s there were widespread complaints that even after eighteen months at Sandhurst, young officers sometimes did not have the professional skills and knowledge that they required. They were criticized for lacking initiative, self-confidence, powers of leadership and man-management, and for having too little a grasp of scientific subjects to understand the full potential and limitations of the weapons they would be required to use. In 1958 a committee planning the structure of the all-Regular Army that was to replace the National Service army suggested that all officers who were not university graduates, but who were capable of studying for a degree, should take a London University External degree at the Royal Military College of Science at Shrivenham. The idea was rejected for the same reason that Haldane's attempt to transform the cadet colleges into universities failed, the reluctance of the War Office to provide the necessary funding.[68]

[62] LHCMA. Liddell Hart MSS 11/1937/28. Maj.-Gen. A. C. Temperley, 'Sandhurst's Aim as Army's University', *Daily Telegraph and Morning Post*, 19 Nov. 1937.
[63] PRO WO 279/65. Staff Conference held at the Staff College, Camberley, 14 to 17 Jan. 1929.
[64] Blacker, *Monkey Business*, 16.
[65] PRO WO 32/2371. CIGS periodical letter to Dominions and India, no. 1, Jan. 1926.
[66] IWMSA. Accession No. 004510/03. Lt.-Col. M. R. L. Grove, 1.
[67] Millman, *Stand Easy*, 23.
[68] PRO WO 32/17698. Report of the Committee on the New All-Regular Army (Whistler Report), May 1958; PRO WO 32/17361. Sub-committee on the Scientific and Technical Education of Officers, 26 Aug. 1958.

Although the success of the cadet colleges in inculcating their members with the necessary intellectual skills and professional knowledge they required may be open to question, their ability to impose a new identity on them is not. By the end of their basic training officer cadets had learned important lessons that would help them to perform their duties as regimental officers, lessons that went beyond the purely technical knowledge they had acquired about tactics, military law, and administration. They had learned to subordinate their own wishes and inclinations to the needs of the group, and to channel their energy and aggression to meeting the goals of the group. Most cadets had no difficulty in accepting these lessons, because the cadet colleges were only repeating what they had been taught through the games-oriented syllabus of their public schools. R. H. Bright, who went to Woolwich in 1931, remembered that cadet NCOs generally exercised their authority fairly, 'provided you didn't get yourself disliked then you would get very fair treatment I would say'.[69]

At the end of their course newly commissioned officers were fit and disciplined, and had been socialized to think of themselves as an elite whose first loyalty was to a group. The constant hustling to which they were subject ensured that most could cope well under at least a moderate degree of stress.[70] A cadet who graduated from Sandhurst in the late 1920s remembered: 'I think they were really looking for what you might call stickability. You were kept at it the whole time. You were really fully stretched for everything.'[71] Equally important, the common experience of the hardships of the cadet college meant that

we grew up in the Service with true friends with whom we never lost touch and with whom we frequently came into close contact again on operations, in the same garrison or station, at some establishment like the Staff College, in the Ministry of Defence and so on. We could, therefore, always seek friendly advice or a helping hand when the need arose.[72]

Basic training for other ranks could be an uncomfortable and difficult experience. In the late nineteenth century the incidence of desertion was highest amongst soldiers in their first two years of service as they struggled to come to terms with the demands of their new way of life.[73] A minority found the experience intolerable. In 1956 a National Serviceman who had begun training only a week previously wrote a letter to his parents explaining that 'I am sick of being called names I wouldn't call my worst enemy,

[69] IWMSA. Accession No. 000787/05. Brig. R. H. Bright, 6.
[70] Smyth, Sandhurst, 143; Kitchen, Mud and Green Fields, 28; IWMSA Accession No. 004550/05. Maj.-Gen. H. E. N. Bredin, 1–2; IWMSA. Accession No. 000787/05. Brig. R. H. Bright, 5; Field Marshal Lord Carver, Out of Step: The Memoirs of Field Marshal Lord Carver (London: Hutchinson, 1989), 20, 22.
[71] IWMSA. Accession No. 000822/07. Lt.-Col. A. C. Jackson, 2.
[72] Millman, Stand Easy, 23.   [73] Skelley, The Victorian Army, 132.

and I'm sick of food I can't bear to look at. I just can't stand it any longer. I would rather be dead.' He then committed suicide on a railway line.[74]

But most recruits did not desert or kill themselves. For them basic training was a positive experience that saw them accept a new military identity. They responded positively to the challenges and opportunities that the training regime placed before them. A. M. Man, who passed through the Buffs Depot in 1926, remembered:

After interminable 'square-bashing', P.T. and the many fatigues which seemed never ending and to embrace every form of drudgery, so little time to oneself, and even less 'passes' (since each had to be earned by good work with the result that some of us hardly got away at all), and after taking and eventually passing many rifle and other tests (when failure could result in relegation to a later Squad and a [material missing,] really begun to be members of a team, and a good team too, for were not all who wore the Dragon badge in their caps the best soldiers in the best Regiment in the best of all Armies?[75]

An officer who served at the RTC's depot at about the same time as Man was doing his recruit training thought that

The transformation was absolutely staggering. Chaps used to come in down at heel, badly fed, out of work, dispirited and broken: 16 weeks after you would see the same man walking, going out to join a unit, clean, smart and tidy with quite an amount of knowledge behind him, and what's more the beginnings of an enquiring mind into soldiering which is really the whole secret of the thing from start to finish.[76]

A committee that investigated the attitude of soldiers to their work in 1949 found that for the average National Service man

His first ten or twelve weeks in the Army are highly organized and functional and even if not enthusiastic, he is at least prepared to make an energetic endeavour. Almost without exception these men said they enjoyed their initial training. Although the discipline is strict, it is not severe, and it is reasonable in its application. A personal interest is taken in the individuals by instructors, both Officers and NCOs. The training is hard but it is progressive and there is a purpose apparent to all. There is a comparative absence of irritating fatigues and chores, and there is a competitive spirit.[77]

Soldiers who had passed through basic training looked back on their experiences as one of the most important formative experiences of their lives. Most recruits were youths in their late teens. For them basic training marked the moment not only when they passed from being civilians to soldiers, but also when they ceased to be boys and became men. F. H.

[74] *The Times*, 1 Feb. 1956.
[75] NAM 9404-436. Colonel A. M. Man, Ts Memoirs, 1966.
[76] IWMSA. Accession No. 000829/12. Maj.-Gen. N. W. Duncan, 48.
[77] PRO WO 163/497. First Report of the Army Working Day investigation team, 23 July 1949.

Maitland, a gentleman-ranker who enlisted shortly before the First World War, was severely taxed by the physical exertion required of him as a recruit. But he also gained a sense of achievement from surmounting the physical and mental obstacles confronting him: 'Between them the drill instructors, musketry instructors, rough riders, blasphemous lot that they are, make us into soldiers, instil into us a new sense of manhood.'[78] Similarly Spike Mays believed that learning parade-ground drill left recruits dripping with sweat but that it taught them 'the value of timing and about loyalty and manhood'.[79] And after the Second World War Russell Edwards believed that what the army succeeded in doing during basic training was, in six to eight weeks, transforming 18-year-old boys into men.[80] Put very simply, 'It made me grow up, I suppose.'[81] Basic training was a rite of passage into manhood for many young men. Being admitted into their regiment as a fully-trained soldier marked them out as adults.

Just as in the case of officer cadets, so with other ranks; the experience of living and working in a small group that was geared towards reaching a common goal bred a fierce sense of loyalty that united each recruit squad. One Second World War recruit concluded that

common hardship, shared by a group of people tends to bind them together and develop a sense of comradeship, then it certainly worked so far as we were concerned. It taught us to work as a group, with the strong helping the weak, and in a strange way it became a matter of personal pride to each one of us that we were able to cope with the extreme demands which were made upon us.[82]

However, this intensely focused conception of loyalty to the members of the same barrack room was too narrowly focused for the military authorities' purposes. As one recruit remembered, outside the little 'self-protective union of friends was the jungle, the anarchy, the "sauve qui peut" of selfish individualism where the instinct for survival was epitomised in the immortal army principle, "Fuck you Jack, I'm all right".'[83] The barrack room was a transient community that had been hastily brought together and might, just as hastily, be dissolved by disease or death on the battlefield. The military authorities had to find another larger and more permanent focus for their soldiers' loyalties, and one for which they would, if necessary, fight and die. What that focus was, how it was created, and how the military authorities tried to instil it in soldiers, will be examined in the following chapters.

[78] F. H. Maitland, *Hussar of the Line* (London: Hurst & Blackett Ltd., 1951), 43.
[79] Mays, *Fall Out the Officers*, 60.
[80] IWMSA. Accession No. 18613/3. R. F. Edwards, reel 1.
[81] IWMSA. Accession No. 18489/4. N. Potter, reel 1.
[82] P. Hennessy, *Young Man in a Tank* (privately published, 1995), 12.
[83] N. Craig, *The Broken Plume: A Platoon Commander's Story, 1940–45* (London: Imperial War Museum, 1982), 17–18.

CHAPTER FOUR

The Construction of the Idea
of 'the Regiment'

The problems confronting the military authorities in the early 1880s in the wake of the Cardwell–Childers reforms were manifold. In the 1840s the army had required about 12,000 recruits annually to maintain its establishment. The introduction of short service meant that by 1883 it needed about 32,000 men. Some of the more draconian disciplinary sanctions of the past were relaxed to assist it in doing so. But some officers doubted whether short-service soldiers would ever be able to match the steadiness of their long-service predecessors. It was 'loosening the old ties of camaraderie that existed in the old days between Officers and men' and because soldiers served in the ranks for such a short time that they 'have not the service to have had ingrained into their nature the value of discipline'.[1] This was especially dangerous because the establishment of the territorial regiments had in many cases apparently destroyed existing notions of regimental *esprit de corps* that had been created over many years.

Both the military authorities and regimental officers were agreed on one thing, that if the new generation of recruits was ever to match the discipline and morale of its predecessors, it behoved them to imbue them with a new sense of regimental *esprit de corps* as quickly as possible. In 1887 the Adjutant-General reminded officers that in the case of recruits

it is desirable to appeal rather to their higher and better feelings, than to their dread of punishment.

Love of his regiment, and a regard for its reputation, soon come to the young soldier, and he should be impressed with the conviction that it is his interest, and should therefore be his object, to maintain its high name and character by his own individual good conduct. He should learn to feel, through the manner in which he is dealt with by his Capt. and his Lt. Colonel, that they are solely actuated by this regimental feeling; by their love of the army and the deep interest they take in the reputation of all their comrades of every rank. Nothing tends more to impress soldiers with this conviction than the maintenance of a healthy, manly discipline with the minimum of punishment.[2]

---

[1] M. Laing Meason, 'The Reorganization of our Army', *Dublin Review*, 6 (1881), 104–5; Col. M. Gossett, 'Battalion Command', *Journal of the Royal United Services Institute*, 35 (1891), 470.
[2] PRO WO 32/8731. Circular, A. Alison to GOC's Districts and Corps, 1 Jan. 1887.

The practical utility of instilling into every recruit 'Love of his regiment' was that it facilitated the task of disciplining its members by encouraging them to accept that it represented a legitimate source of authority. This task was easier for some regiments than for others. Technical corps such as the Royal Artillery or Royal Engineers could instil in each recruit the notion that he was a man with special skills and a member of a 'scientific corps'. Other regiments, such as the Parachute Regiment, could impose a rigorous selection system on their recruits, and passing that alone encouraged them to believe that they belonged to a 'special' regiment. But the line infantry and cavalry had no such advantages. They had to rely upon the notion that every regiment was special, and that its 'specialness' was marked by its own peculiar habits, customs, codes of behaviour, and dress, 'in a word traditions, in which the individual can share and take pride'.[3]

In 1884 Childers told Sir Frederick Roberts that his aim should be 'to impress on your men that they belong to a Regiment not a Battalion; that they are supplied on this system with Regts., and this is their family'.[4] But the willingness of officers and other ranks to invest the same emotional commitment in their regiment as they did in their family did not spring ready-made from the ground in 1881. Although regiments had been given territorial titles in 1782–3, most were known by their numbers. The linking of line regiments into sub-brigades in 1873 caused one general to warn that they would 'obliterate the name and number of the regiment, its past records, its future history, and . . . annihilate or absorb that individuality which constitutes a power in itself'.[5] In 1881 Childers preserved the existing titular connections of fifty-six regiments. He gave nine regiments titles that shifted their local connection to an adjacent county or riding; fourteen had their connection shifted to a more distant county, eleven (including nine regiments taken over from the establishment of the East India Company) were in effect transferred to other portions of the empire, two regiments lost their local designations entirely, and eighteen regiments had no existing local titles and were given entirely new ones.

This was the reinvention of 'tradition' with a vengeance, and it caused a good deal of soul-searching.[6] The Queen gave her formal sanction to

[3] Maj. C. E. Jarvis, 'Regimental Tradition in the Infantry of the Line', *Journal of the Royal United Services Institute*, 96 (1951), 102.

[4] Roberts, *Roberts in India*, 289–90.

[5] *The Times*, 20 Apr. 1873.

[6] PRO WO 33/37. Memo by D.R., 12 Dec. 1881; Field Marshal Lord Birdwood, *Khaki and Gown: An Autobiography* (London: Ward Lock, 1941), 143; PRO WO 32/6092. CO 2/25th Foot to War Office, 31 Dec. 1880; *The Sherwood Foresters Regimental Annual*, (1929), 202, 208–9.

the new titles but also informed Childers that 'although Her Majesty sanctioned the adoption of Territorial designations for the New Regiments, she has always thought numbers more suitable for common use and now fails to understand why long names are preferred to convenient numerals'.[7]

The notion that each and every one of the territorial regiments that Childers had created constituted a 'community' or 'family' was largely bogus. The first twenty-five regiments on the army list already had two battalions, so the process of amalgamation was, for them, almost painless.[8] But, the remaining regiments sometimes found themselves amalgamated with uncongenial bedfellows. When 27/Inniskilling Fusiliers was brigaded with 108/Madras Infantry in 1873, it caused one critic to remark that the latter 'has no more to do with Ireland than the Russian Guards'.[9] Similarly the 35/Royal Sussex Regiment did not welcome amalgamation with 107/Bengal Infantry Regiment to form the Royal Sussex Regiment in 1881. The resulting resentment at these shot-gun marriages lingered into the 1930s.[10]

One reason why some regiments took so long to make a reality of territorialization was that they rarely constituted face-to-face communities in which officers and men of the two line battalions served together. On the contrary, the fact that one battalion was supposed to be at home, feeding its linked battalion with an annual draft of recruits, almost always ensured that they were separated by several thousand miles. In 1908, when 1/ and 2/Royal Scots met in Bombay, it was the first time they had done so for nearly twenty years.[11] The two regular battalions of the Sherwood Foresters had an even longer record of physical estrangement. They did not meet at all between 1899 and 1938, while the two battalions of the Wiltshire Regiment met only twice between 1881 and 1947.[12]

To counter these dangerous tendencies that threatened to undermine discipline and *esprit de corps*, the regimental and military authorities manipulated symbols, rituals, ceremonies, and 'histories', to create a new regimental *esprit de corps*. In doing so they constructed what Benedict

[7] PRO WO 32/6089. Ponsonby to Childers, 26 May 1881.

[8] Lt.-Col. G. Le M. Gretton, *The Campaigns and History of the Royal Irish Regiment from 1684 to 1902* (Edinburgh and London: William Blackwood, 1911), 227; C. T. Atkinson, *The South Wales Borderers, 24th Foot* (Cambridge: University Press, for the Regimental History Committee, 1937), 362–3.

[9] Capt. R. Trimen, *The Regiments of the British Army, Chronologically Arranged* (London: William Allen & Co., 1878), p. v.

[10] PRO WO 32/4622. Lt.-Gen. Sir Travers Clarke to Adj.-Gen., 7 Apr. 1937; PRO WO 32/4477. Southern Command report, 17 Mar. 1937 Appendix 2.

[11] IWMSA. Accession No. 4935/05. Maj. E. S. Humphries, 4.

[12] *Regimental Annual. The Sherwood Foresters 1938*, 234; Col. N. C. E. Kenrick, *The Story of the Wiltshire Regiment (Duke of Edinburgh's) The 62nd and 99th Foot (1759–1959)* (Aldershot: Gale and Polden, 1963), 110.

Anderson has called 'imagined communities'. The ideal regimental community, like the ideal nation, was meant to be 'the domain of disinterested love and solidarity'.[13] The 'regiment' was conceived as being based upon a shared comradeship that transcended the inequalities of power and rewards that existed within it. It was something so fundamentally pure that it could call upon its members to lay down their lives for it. At a dinner to mark the end of his command of 2/Essex in 1939, Lt.-Col. C. C. Spooner said that

To me, the Regiment is a living soul, something more than what the casual person calls a Regiment. For its welfare there is nothing I would not do, and I believe those are the sentiments of us all here to-night. It is really the Essex Regiment that counts. We must subordinate ourselves to the interests of the Regiment if it is to be successful. In other words, the Regiment lives on where we pass on.[14]

Leading the effort to propagate and disseminate these notions was usually the Colonel of the Regiment.[15] Colonels of Regiments held a post that was one of 'honour and influence'. Between 1881 and 1920 the Colonel, who was appointed for life from amongst serving or retired senior officers, acted as the unpaid titular head of the regiment. He had no specific duties or authority, but exercised his personal influence to a degree that varied according to his capacity, energy, and interest in his regiment.[16] He usually had the assistance of a full-time regimental secretary, generally a retired officer, who was based at the regimental depot. The Colonels' role in selecting officers for their regiment has already been considered. In 1920 the Army Council regularized their position, deciding that henceforth they should play a more active role in 'knitting together all the battalions and fostering the spirit of comradeship and regimental pride'. To ensure that they were sufficiently active to do so, they were to retire on reaching the age of 70.[17] They were expected to liaise between the various battalions, both regular and auxiliary, of their regiment and to oversee the workings of regimental charities and associations. Battalion commanders were ordered to keep their Colonels informed 'of any questions which may arise from time to time in respect

---

[13] B. Anderson, *Imagined Communities: Reflections on the Origins and Spread of Nationalism* (London: Verson, 1983; rev. edn. 1991), 7, 141–6.

[14] *The Essex Regiment Gazette. New Series*, 7 (Sept. 1939), 65.

[15] The precise title of this officer varied between different regiments and corps. In most infantry and cavalry regiments he was known as the Colonel of the Regiment. In the King's Royal Rifle Corps, the Rifle Brigade, and in Corps regiments such as the Royal Artillery, he was more commonly referred to as the Colonel Commandant. Some of the larger Corps regiments had several Colonels Commandant.

[16] PRO WO 163/273. Committee on functions & conditions of service of Colonels of Regiments (RAC & Infantry), 5 Nov. 1945.

[17] Ibid.

of Regimental customs, memorials, changes in dress, or any other subject on which, for the sake of maintaining uniformity, he should be consulted'.[18] In 1945 the Army Council added to their duties that of 'ensuring local interest in the Regiment by liaison with the civil population'.[19]

Regimental colonels presided over the institutions that created the image of the regiment as a community. The most important of these were Regimental Associations. In the nineteenth century the officers of many regiments raised subscriptions and established charitable funds for the support of the rank and file of their regiments and their families who had fallen on hard times. In 1849, for example, the officers of both the Scots and Coldstream Guards created charitable trusts for serving and former soldiers of their regiments and their wives, widows, and children.[20] In 1884 the officers of the King's Royal Rifle Corps and the Rifle Brigade established the Rifleman's Aid Society 'to look after the welfare and interests of Riflemen, past and present, and their families'.[21] The Highland Light Infantry formed an association with similar functions in 1889.[22] The services followed their example. In 1919 senior officers of the RASC formed a Memorial Fund committee to raise £50,000. They spent the money not just on erecting a memorial to their dead, but also to provide educational and charitable assistance to past and present members of the corps and their families.[23] By 1931 the RASC Regimental Association had over 5,400 members, had found work for 330 former members of the regiment, and provided relief for over 1,250 members or their families.[24]

Typical of these associations was the Royal Fusiliers Old Comrades Association. Apart from assisting former members of the regiment or their families who had fallen on hard times or were seeking work, it also sought 'To promote esprit de corps among all ranks of the Royal Fusiliers, past and present'. It charged a modest subscription, established a network of branches, held an annual dinner in London attended by serving and past members of the regiment, and organized an Old Comrades Day at the regimental depot. The work of the Association was carried on by a committee presided over by the Colonel of the Regiment. He was assisted by past Colonels, the honorary Colonels of its Territorial

[18] PRO WO 32/3771. Appendix A. Functions of colonels, 1920; PRO WO 163/273. Annex to CCR/M(45)1. H. J. Creedy, Responsibility of Colonels of Cavalry and Infantry Regiments and Colonels Commandant (or representative Colonels Commandant) of other corps. 9 Apr. 1936.

[19] PRO WO 32/12142. Lt.-Gen. Sir H. Colville Wemyss, Military Secretary, to Maj. E. C. Ashton, 21 Aug. 1946.

[20] PRO WO 32/6241. The Bowles Charitable Trust, 6 May 1881.

[21] *The King's Royal Rifle Corps Chronicle 1943*, 9.

[22] *Highland Light Infantry Chronicle*, 1 (1892).

[23] *The Times*, 11 Mar. 1919, 19 Aug. 1922.

[24] *The Times*, 17 Oct. 1932.

battalions, representatives of the COs of its regular and Territorial battalions, and a handful of other serving and retired officers.[25]

Most Regimental Associations held annual meetings that gave past and serving members of the regimental community the opportunity to meet and renew their ties of comradeship. In 1904 the Cameron Highlanders Association held their annual dinner in the Trades Hall, Glasgow, and 'During the evening many excellent songs were sung, and with toasts and sentiment a very enjoyable night was spent.'[26] The military authorities welcomed their efforts, particularly the extent to which they could assist Reservists in finding jobs after they left the Colours.[27] Most regiments also formed separate officers' dining associations that met annually to foster *esprit de corps* amongst serving and retired members of the officers' mess.[28] The officers of the Connaught Rangers, whose regiment was disbanded in 1922, held their last dinner in 1967.[29]

Associations also undertook two other activities intended to bind regimental communities together: the erection of memorials to members of the regiment who had died serving with it, and the publication of regimental journals and regimental histories. In 1882 the officers and men of the South Wales Borderers paid for the installation of a memorial window in the Priory Church at Brecon to commemorate their comrades who had died in Zululand in 1879.[30] A year later the officers and men of the Black Watch erected a memorial brass plaque to their comrades who had died in Egypt in 1882.[31] Memorializing their dead comrades was not an activity confined to the infantry and cavalry. The corps regiments and services also fostered it. Thus in 1880 the Royal Artillery Institution agreed to erect a memorial to those members of the regiment who had died in the recent operations in South Africa and Afghanistan.[32]

One of the earliest journals appeared in 1863, published by the Suffolk Regiment, although regular publication did not begin until 1890.[33] The Northumberland Fusiliers' journal, the *St George's Gazette*, made its first

[25] Anon., *Rules of the Royal Fusiliers Old Comrades Association and Royal Fusiliers Aid Society* (n.d. or publisher). See also Anon., *Rules of the Royal Artillery Association, 1946* (n.d. or publisher given).

[26] *The 79th News*, Jan. 1905.

[27] PP (1892), XIX. C. 6582. *Report of the Committee on the terms and conditions of service in the army*, 5.

[28] ERM. ERCB 7. Cutting book, Capt. Leslie, 56/Essex Regiment. Maj. Robert T. Thompson, 56/Regiment, Warley Barracks, Essex, to officers of regiment, 17 Apr. 1878; Maj. D. A. Blest to officers 1 & 2 Essex, 21 Mar. 1888.

[29] NAM 7609-35-2. A. Y. McPeake MSS. The Connaught Rangers Regimental dinner. Army and Navy Club, 2 June 1967.

[30] *The Times*, 15 Apr. 1882.

[31] *The Times*, 5 Nov. 1883.

[32] *The Times*, 28 Dec. 1880.

[33] SRO, Bury St Edmunds. MS copy of the 1st number of *Suffolk Regiment Gazette*, 1863.

appearance in 1883. It had two avowed purposes, 'to be a fast bond and lasting link between Fusiliers—Regular and Auxiliary—home and Abroad—Past and Present'[34] and

As there are many young soldiers now serving with the Battalion who are probably not acquainted with the traditions and achievements of the Regiment with which they are now serving, it is intended to publish, with every issue of St. George's Gazette, extracts from the Historical Records of the Regiment, and, it is hoped, that by holding forth the bright example of their predecessors, the young soldier will strive to emulate the meritorious and gallant conduct in camp and quarters of their predecessors in the 'Old and Bold'.[35]

Regimental journals were usually edited by a serving officer of the regular regiment, assisted, at least after 1918, by helpers in each of its Territorial units. They contained accounts of the doings of the various units of the regiment, both military and, in particular, sporting, together with articles relating to its history and traditions, and obituaries of former members. Sales were usually confined to past and former members of the regiment. In the 1890s, for example, *The Black Horse Gazette*, the journal of the 7/Dragoon Guards, sold about 300 copies per edition.[36]

Regimental histories fell into two categories. Some were lengthy tomes of several hundred pages, giving detailed accounts of the regiment's doings. Many of those produced before 1914 were little more than regurgitations of the regiment's official Digests of Service.[37] They were produced under various auspices. The writing of some was overseen by a committee led by the Colonel of the Regiment. They were funded by subscriptions raised from serving and retired officers, who were also invited to submit any papers, diaries, or reminiscences to the authors.[38] Others, particularly those produced after 1918, were written under the oversight of County Territorial Associations, which established a historical committee to produce histories of both the regular and territorial battalions of the regiment.[39] They were intended to sustain and perpetuate *esprit de corps*. According to the historical committee of the Bedfordshire and Hertfordshire Regiment, one of the most important functions of these works was 'to treat the history as a family history of the Regiment.

[34] *St George's Gazette*, no. 3, 31 Mar. 1883.
[35] *St George's Gazette*, no. 1, 31 Jan. 1883.
[36] *The Black Horse Gazette. The Journal of the 7th Dragoon Guards*, 4 (Apr. 1906).
[37] Brereton, 'Records of the Regiment', 113.
[38] *The Times*, 7 Aug. 1909.
[39] SRO, Bury St Edmunds Branch. GB 554/A2/6. Revision and writing up to date of the History of H.M. 12th Regiment (now Suffolk Regiment), 1 Mar. 1911; ERO. D/DU 346/9/6. Records compiled by J. W. Burrows for 'The War 1914–1919'. Essex Territorial Army Association, June 1927.

Mention should be made in it of all the great families of *other ranks* who had served in it, as well as other outstanding individuals.'[40]

The second kind of regimental history was much briefer. It was commonplace for a recruit to be issued with a brief history of his regiment, prepared by the Association.[41] Regiments were expected to keep their histories up to date and earned a gentle rebuke from the War Office if they failed to do so.[42] Although these small pamphlets were far removed from the weighty tomes produced by professional historians in the late Victorian period, their authors shared a common attitude towards the writing of history. They took pride in past national achievements and in the innate superiority of the British people. In their hands history became a tool for justifying existing institutions and for imbuing the reader with a sense of moral righteousness.[43]

Most volumes presented a chronological account of the significant achievements of the regiment, concentrating on wars and battles, rather than on the dreary years of garrison service that was the lot of most soldiers. All of them stressed the antiquity of the regiment—the history of the Northumberland Fusiliers emphasizing, for example, that the regiment had been raised in 1674.[44] They also laid claims to connections with as many heroes as possible. The history of the Cheshire Regiment, published in 1906, made great play of its connection with Sir Charles Napier, the victory of Scinde, and then, stretching a point, tried to lay equal claim to both Sir John Moore and the Duke of Wellington on the grounds that Napier had served under both.[45] Most histories also gave brief accounts of members of the regiment who had so distinguished themselves in action that they had been awarded the VC.

The histories that regiments created for themselves may have smacked of antiquarianism, but the way in which they used them was anything but backward looking. Regimental Associations produced these pamphlets with the explicit purpose of influencing the behaviour of men in the present and the future. They were intended to bolster pride in the regiment amongst its members, to encourage the present generation to enlist, and then to emulate the heroic deeds of their predecessors.[46] In 1926

[40] Bedfordshire Record Office. X550/15/31. Regimental Association. The Bedfordshire and Hertfordshire [Regimental] Association. The Regimental History Committee, 3 May 1957.

[41] Anon., *The Standing Orders of the King's Royal Rifle Corps* (Aldershot: Gale & Polden, 1930), 57.

[42] PRO WO 32/2382. Memorandum on Army Training. Collective Training period, 1928.

[43] P. Levine, *The Amateur and the Professional: Antiquarians, Historians and Archaeologists in Victorian England, 1838–1886* (Cambridge: Cambridge University Press, 1986), 4–5, 71–6.

[44] Anon., *A Short History of the Fifth Fusiliers from 1674 to 1911* (n.d. or publisher given, but c.1912), 1.

[45] Anon., *The Standing Orders of 2/Battalion 22nd (Cheshire) Regiment*, 2–17.

[46] NAM 7609-35-6. A. Y. McPeake MSS. *The Connaught Rangers* (London: HMSO, n.d., but c. late 1881).

recipients of the Royal Fusiliers' history were told by the Colonel of their Regiment that 'To you is entrusted the History of the Future, into your keeping is placed the fame won by your predecessors. If you manfully carry out the Fusilier traditions, you will be playing your part in the Service of your Regiment, your King, and the Empire.'[47] Regimental authorities thus mobilized the past in the service of the present and the future. Each regiment tried to create for itself a martial reputation and tradition in the hope that it would enhance the combat motivation of men currently serving with it. According to the author of the history of the Somerset Light Infantry, for 250 years 'the Regiment has served its King and Country. That it has done so with a loyalty, courage and devotion to duty unsurpassed by any other regiment of the British Army, will be shown in its history here set forth.'[48] Recruits and serving soldiers in 13/Hussars were given the stern warning that 'The past is the heritage which nothing can take from you, but the present and the future are in your hands, see that you are worthy of these great traditions.'[49]

Much of what passed for regimental history consisted of the legends the regimental authorities developed to make members of the regiment feel content about who they were, the functions they had to perform, and the hardships they had to endure. When history might tell them what they did not want to hear, it was rewritten in a more acceptable form. Defeats, when they were mentioned, were always redeemed because they were accompanied by acts of individual and collective heroism.[50] Few regimental histories made mention of events that showed their regiment in a poor light for, as one regimental historian candidly confessed:

writing about what is virtually his own family, he is bound to present its best face to the world. Obviously, many subjects cannot be frankly set down: personal failures under stress; difficulties with higher commanders; unhappy relations with other units; moments of confusion. Fortunately such things are not too common, but they are an inevitable part of military life. They can be recorded only by later generations, if the diaries and letters in which they occur are given into safe keeping.[51]

Thus the author of the short regimental history of the Black Watch published in 1912 explained away the awkward fact that the regiment had mutinied in 1743 by reference to the pernicious activities of 'paid

---

[47] Anon., *The Royal Fusiliers in an Outline of Military History 1685–1926* (Aldershot: Gale & Polden, 1926), 1.

[48] Anon., *A Short History of the Somerset Light Infantry (Prince Albert's)* (Taunton: n.p., 1934), 6; see also Anon., *Royal Welch Fusiliers* (Aldershot: Gale and Polden, c.1919), 1.

[49] Anon., *A Short History of 13th Hussars* (Aldershot: Gale & Polden, 1923), 63.

[50] See e.g. the account ibid. 7 for the battle of Prestonpans.

[51] Lt.-Col. R. L. V. ffrench Blake, *A History of the 17th/21st Lancers 1922–1959* (London: Longman, 1962), p. ix.

agitators'.[52] And the historian of the Royal Sussex Regiment published in 1927 forgot to mention that in June 1917 men of its 4, 5, and 6 battalions helped to form a Soldier's Soviet in Tunbridge Wells.[53]

These historical pamphlets thus embodied myths in the sense that anthropologists have used the concept of myth, meaning a story about the past that served as a 'charter' for the present.[54] But they also pointed towards the future. Accepting that changes in the structure and organization of the regimental system were inevitable, regimental authorities employed tradition to make them more palatable. In 1935 the Colonel of the King's Own Hussars wrote in the preface to the new regimental short history that, faced by the imminence of mechanization

Today we have entered a new period of our history.

To the ordinary individual it is not easy to cope with the onrush of new ideas and values. None of us can foresee the limits of mechanization either on our lives or on the strategy or tactics of war.

There have been great changes in military armament and tactics during the period embraced by this History, namely, 1688 to 1935. All who read it will realize how courage and training have surmounted every difficulty, every change.

It is not for us to question the wisdom or necessity for changes, but faithfully to carry them out to the best of our ability.[55]

But if traditions were to be made manifest and handed on from generation to generation within the regiment, it was not enough to rely on the written word. They had to be given more concrete and visible embodiments. This was achieved through a combination of physical symbolism and public ceremonial. Regiments relied heavily on totems, badges, and buttons, to provide their members with a ready means of identification and solidarity. No two regiments in the British army wore exactly the same uniform. Variations might in some cases be quite minor—a different pattern of button or cap-badge—but the functions of the differences were quite deliberate. They were a visible symbol of the common identity that each member of the regiment shared, and they enhanced each regiment's sense of separateness. According to one battalion commander, 'anything that separates a regiment from the mass has always the effect of increasing *esprit de corps*. Call it what you will, they take a pride in it.'[56] Evidence of how important such symbols could be in uniting regimental communities, and of how slow some regiments were

---

[52] J. Stewart, *A Brief History of the Royal Highland Regiment: The Black Watch* (Edinburgh: T. & A. Constable, 1912), 8.

[53] PRO WO 32/5455. H. B. Butler to Brade and enc., 19 July 1917.

[54] P. Burke, *History and Social Theory* (Oxford: Polity Press, 1999), 101–3.

[55] Lt.-Col. F. R. Burnside, *A Short History of the King's Own Hussars* (Aldershot: Gale and Polden, 1935), 1.

[56] PP (1877), XVIII. C. 1654. *Report of the Committee*, Q. 1395.

to make a reality of the 1881 amalgamations, is shown by a Battalion order published by 2/Essex in 1933, fifty-two years after it had been formally amalgamated with 1/Essex to form the Essex Regiment:

In order to bind the two Regular Battalions and the Depot more closely together, it has been decided, with the approval of the Colonel of the Regiment, that in future, both Batt[alio]ns and the Depot will play games under the same Colours, and fly the same flag over Barracks.

The Colours of the Regimental teams will be as follows:

(a) Purple shorts (or vests) with a yellow eagle on the left breast.
(b) White drill shorts.
(c) Plain purple stockings.

The Regimental Flag to be flown over Barracks etc will be a plain purple flag with a yellow eagle in the centre.[57]

The chivalric motifs and heraldic symbols of regimental cap-badges and buttons asserted a social vision of a hierarchical, feudal society in which there was an organic link between past and present, and between every different rank in the regiment. Plain uniforms were associated with low status and little honour, whereas smart uniforms were likely to attract recruits.[58] The introduction of battle dress in the late 1930s understandably horrified some senior officers. Lord Gort, the commander of the BEF in 1939–40, feared 'that esprit de corps, particularly in the infantry, will suffer if soldiers in battle dress are not permitted to carry on them an emblem showing the regiment to which they belong'.[59] Gradually units were allowed to embellish their battle dress with their own badges and symbols.[60]

All line infantry regiments, with the exception of the light infantry and rifles, and all Dragoon and Dragoon Guard, but not Lancer and Hussar regiments—had their own heavily embroidered Standards (in the case of the infantry) or Guidons (in the case of the cavalry).[61] These Colours had once formed a visible rallying point in the midst of the smoke and confusion of battle, marking the position of the commander of the regiment, and all soldiers were taught that it was the ultimate disgrace if they fell into enemy hands.[62] However, after 1882, 'in consequence of

[57] ERM. ER 4656. Historical Record. 2/Essex, 19 Jan 1920 to 8 Mar. 1939, 4 Nov. 1933.
[58] PP (1892), XIX. C. 6582. *Report of the Committee on the terms and conditions of service in the army*, 66.
[59] PRO WO 163/65. The Army Council War Committee, 41 meeting, 23 Nov. 1939.
[60] PRO WO 163/48/ACM(AE)15. Minutes of the Proceedings of and précis prepared for the Army Council, 6 Aug. 1940.
[61] Anon., *First Battalion of the York and Lancaster Regiment. Disbandment Ceremonies* (n.p., 1968), 4; Anon., *A Short History of the Royal Sussex Regiment (35th Foot–107th Foot), 1701–1926* (Aldershot: Gale & Polden, 1927), 2.
[62] ERM. ERB 117. Lt.-Col. Hon. A. A. Spencer, *Standing Orders of the 44th or East Essex Regiment by Lt Col. Hon. A. A. Spencer* (Bombay: Education Society Press, Byculla, 1862), 8.

the altered formation of attack and extended range of firing', they were no longer taken into action.[63] But recruits were instructed about the symbolic value of their regiment's Colours, and all ranks were enjoined to pay the Colours the utmost respect.[64] Their design was regulated by an Inspector of Regimental Colours, a post usually filled by a Herald of the College of Arms, the Army Council, and ultimately the monarch.[65] They were presented in a public ceremony that passed into the collective memory of the unit. Grandeur and solemnity were lent to the occasion by the presence of higher-ranking political and/or military figures and by a drum-head service at which the Colours were consecrated by a senior cleric.[66] To symbolize the relationship of subordination and deference to the monarchy, Colours were usually presented by the monarch or his nominee.[67]

Colours were normally replaced at about thirty-year intervals when they had become worn out.[68] Old Colours were never discarded, but were usually laid up in a church associated with the regiment in a ceremony intended to cement the association of the regiment with its recruiting district.[69] The meaning that such ceremonies were meant to convey was made apparent by the addresses that accompanied them. When the Prince of Wales presented new Colours to 1/Norfolk Regiment in 1887 he reminded them that their regiment had always had a reputation for being well disciplined.[70] Twenty years later, after receiving new Colours from the new Prince of Wales, the CO of 2/Royal Inniskilling Fusiliers told the assembled parade that

I can assure your Royal Highness that every officer and man who is fortunate enough in the future to serve under these new colours, just consecrated to the service of our Sovereign and our country, will use his utmost endeavour to maintain the good name which the Inniskilling Regiment has always borne—in peace and in war, and thus carry on our glorious traditions of the past.[71]

---

[63] PRO WO 32/6701. Ellice to GOCs at Home, 17 Jan. 1882.

[64] General Staff, *Cavalry Training 1912* (London: HMSO, 1912), 323; Anon., *The Standing Orders of the 2nd Battalion The Royal Warwickshire Regiment* (Aldershot: Gale & Polden, 1934), 1.

[65] PRO WO 32/13901. Unsigned and undated minute, but *c.*30 Aug. 1950.

[66] Adjutant General, *Field Exercises and Evolutions of Infantry (1874)* (London: HMSO, 1874), 341–2 ;War Office, *KR . . . 1940*, 332–3.

[67] PRO WO 32/19018. Sir Michael Adeane to Lord Herbert, 5 Nov. 1959.

[68] NAM 6005–60. Records of the 88th Regiment (Connaught Rangers).

[69] PRO WO 32/12840. ACI No. 368 of 1948, 1 May 1948; PRO WO 68/257. 4th (West Essex) Militia. Digest of Service, 26 June 1908.

[70] RNRM. R.103. Records of Service. 1 Battalion Norfolk Regiment, 24 Sept. 1887.

[71] NAM 7003/1. Scrapbook, Officer's Mess, 27th Foot, 2nd Battalion Royal Inniskilling Fusiliers, *The Egyptian Morning News*, 31 Mar. 1906. For similar occasions and speeches see: NAM 68-7-310. Historical Records, 97th Regiment of Foot, 1808–1896, 16 Nov. 1880 and NAM 7510–94. Scrapbook of Maj. Gen. W. O. Barnard. Presentation of Regimental Colours. 2nd Battalion Manchester Regiment, 21 Jan. 1886.

Regimental Colours were revered as 'affording a record of the services of the Regiment and furnishing to the young soldier a history of gallant deeds'.[72] Embroidered on them was the regiment's battle honours, that is the list of battles at which the regiment had been present. Deciding which regiments had been present at which battles might appear to be an uncontentious task, but that was anything but the case. By the late 1870s, when the process of rebuilding regimental identities following the Cardwell Reforms was under way, some regiments that could trace their existence back to the eighteenth century were resentful that they did not carry any battle honours on their Colours, or that some to which they thought they were entitled had been omitted.[73] In 1882, less than six months after the promulgation of the Childers reforms, Cambridge established the first of the four committees that were to regulate the granting of battle honours. The first committee was chaired by Maj.-Gen. Sir A. Alison and was charged with determining which regiments had a right to commemorate their participation in Marlborough's victories, Dettington and the fall of Louisbourg and Quebec.[74] In 1909 another War Office Committee examined the award of honours for battles and campaigns ranging from Tangier (1662–80) to the Peninsular War.[75] The reason for granting honours retrospectively was explained by the Adjutant-General, Sir Ian Hamilton: 'Bit by bit the position of giving no honours for ancient wars has been surrendered and it is not logical to stop half way.'[76] By 1913 most regiments carried about twenty battle honours on their Colours.[77]

The principles employed to decide which battles each regiment should be allowed to commemorate widened significantly between the 1880s and the 1950s. Before 1914 awards were commonly governed by three rules: no battle honour was awarded for a defeat or an unsuccessful war, and the HQ of the regiment claiming the honour had to have been present at the battle. Moreover the Alison committee decreed that 'the names of such victories only should be retained, as, either in themselves or by their result, have left a mark in history which renders their name familiar, not only to the British Army, but also to every educated gentleman'. But Alison also discovered that the documentary evidence con-

---

[72] PRO WO 32/6701. Ellice to GOCs at Home, 17 Jan. 1882.

[73] See e.g. NAM 6005–60. Records of the 88th Regiment (Connaught Rangers). Lt.-Col. R. Hughes to Maj.-Gen. Sir E. Grethed, GOC Eastern division, Colchester, 30 Mar. 1874.

[74] PRO WO 33/38. Report of the committee on the claims of regiments to commemorate certain unrecorded victories, 13 Mar. 1882.

[75] WO 32/9249. Honours and Distinctions Committee. Report of a meeting held at the War Office on 15th Dec. 1909.

[76] PRO WO 32/9249. Minute by Sir I. Hamilton, 15 Dec. 1909.

[77] Col. H. C. B. Cook, 'British Battle Honours', *Journal of the Society for Army Historical Research*, 59 (1979), 158–9.

cerning the early eighteenth-century wars was so slender that some regimental claims had to be rejected.[78] After both World Wars the War Office produced a list of all the battles that it considered might constitute battle honours, and then ordered regiments to convene a committee, presided over by the Colonel of the Regiment, and including representatives of its regular, Territorial, and war-raised units, to prepare a list of those honours it wished to claim. In every case, it had to be able to establish that the headquarters and at least half of one of its units had taken part in the battle in question. No limit was placed on the number of battle honours a regiment could claim, but reasons of space meant that they were allowed to emblazon no more than ten of them on their Colours. The remainder were preserved for posterity by being printed in the *Army List*. In an important decision intended to emphasize the unity of regimental communities, the Murray committee, which examined claims for honours after the First World War, agreed that battle honours earned by one battalion would be borne on the Colours of all of its battalions, whether regular or auxiliary.[79]

Regimental claims were vetted by War Office committees before being allowed. They hoped that regiments would make claims only for engagements in which one or more of their units had played a meritorious role. 'A Battle honour is a public commemoration of a Battle, Action, or Engagement, of which not only past and present but also future generations of the regiment can be proud', Sir John Crocker explained in 1955. 'There is no question of an Honour being awarded merely because a unit was present at a battle. It must have taken an active and creditable part in it.'[80]

However, Regimental Colonels viewed matters differently. Their priority was to enhance the status of their own regiment by claiming the maximum possible number of honours. By 1958 the Crocker Committee had awarded 3,549 battle honours to regiments that took part in the Second World War. It might have awarded even more but for the fact that the CIGS, Sir Gerald Templer, objected that many regiments had put in claims for actions in which they had not done any serious fighting. 'The conclusion', he crossly insisted, 'cannot help being drawn that the object is to claim the maximum number of awards irrespective of merit.' 'I am sure you will', he wrote in a circular to all Regimental Colonels, 'agree with me that this is to be deplored.'[81]

---

[78] PRO WO 33/38. Report of the committee, 13 Mar. 1882.
[79] PRO WO 32/11360. Recommendations, 1921–2; PRO WO 163/570. Battle Honours Committee, 18 May 1955.
[80] PRO WO 163/570. First Report of the Battle Honours Committee, 18 May 1955.
[81] PRO WO 163/578. Sir G. Templer to Colonels of Regiments, June 1956.

Ceremonial parades such as those when regiments were given new Colours also made visible to every soldier the fact that the regiment embodied notions of authority, duty, and subordination. Parades presented an ordered regimental world extending from the commanding officer down to the newest-joined recruit. They were a celebration of a hierarchical and harmonious vision of the regiment. Private soldiers stood rigidly to attention in straight ranks and files. NCOs were positioned a little apart from them. Officers stood in front to symbolize their role as leaders, or to one side or behind to symbolize their control over the unit.[82] When a unit was on parade

the Corporal would report to the Orderly Sergeant, the Orderly Sergeant would then report to the Sergeant Major and the Sergeant Major would report to the Company Commander. And when the Company arrived on the parade ground of the Battalion he would then start reporting all over again.[83]

Parades also gave regiments a public opportunity to affirm their status. In 1911 the officers of the Royal Munster Fusiliers were upset because it appeared that their regiment was not to be represented at the Delhi Durbar. They had been present at the taking of Delhi '& we made a tremendous name there, & so it will be an awful slight if we don't go, but we probably wont'.[84] The precise position and order that different regiments should assume on the parade ground could cause a good deal of soul-searching. In the eighteenth century it had been established that when different regiments paraded together, the order in which they stood or marched past during a review was determined by their precedence. The regiment with the oldest pedigree, measured by the date it was raised, was always on the right of the line, the second most senior on the left, the third most senior on the right centre and fourth most senior on the left centre. Even so, squabbles between regiments still continued as they vied with each other to establish their status.[85] In 1920 a dispute arose at Aldershot when the four COs of units in the same brigade could not agree on their relative precedence. The Adjutant-General consulted the King, who was the ultimate arbiter of such matters, but he decided that the question was too difficult for him, and it was finally settled by a War Office committee.[86] The creation of several new regiments and corps shortly after the First World War only added further confusion, and it was not until 1930 that the War Office's Honours and Distinctions committee stated categorically that 'that fighting corps, i.e. those corps which give expression to the

---

[82] Adjutant-General, *Field Exercises . . . (1874)*, 302–3.
[83] IWMSA. Accession No. 4935/05. Maj. E. S. Humphries, 43.
[84] PRO 30/71/1. G. W. Nightingale to mother, 8 Jan 1911.
[85] IWMSA. Accession No. 20494/12. Col. P. Featherby, reel 7.
[86] PRO WO 32/4789. Stamfordham to Macdonogh, 21 Dec. 1920.

raison d'etre of an army, have the precedence of all other corps'. They were followed by administrative departments and then administrative corps. Within each category, corps took precedence according to the date they were established, or, if they were the outgrowth of an existing corps, according to the precedence of their parent corps. Thus the Royal Corps of Signals, which was established shortly after the First World War, took its precedence immediately after its parent corps, the Royal Engineers.[87]

Nor were senior officers above trying to manipulate the system to enhance the standing of their own arm of service. In 1946, for example, the Director of Infantry at the War Office, Maj.-Gen. D. N. Wimberley, tried to have the status of the whole of the infantry raised by suggesting that they should take precedence immediately after the Royal Armoured Corps, thereby downgrading the Royal Engineers, Royal Artillery, and Royal Corps of Signals. The Honours and Distinctions committee dismissed his claim on two grounds. The infantry would hardly have won Alamein without the support of the gunners and if the precedence of the latter were downgraded 'it might breed "bad blood" between the gunners and the PBI, which might not be too good for co-operation'. Secondly, it tacitly admitted that all notions of precedence were far removed from modern military realities and ought to remain so. 'Precedence of the old regiments and corps', it concluded, 'has passed into the historical stage: to treat the matter "realistically" now might not be worthwhile.'[88]

If the parade ground was one forum where regiments struggled to assert their separate identities and superior status, their officers' and sergeants' messes were two others. They were far more than the place where officers and senior NCOs spent their off-duty time and ate their meals. The officers' mess, according to a War Office report in 1947, was 'the focus of regimental life, the repository of tradition; without it esprit de corps cannot thrive'.[89] Each mess proclaimed the regiment's distinct and separate identity by collecting and displaying regimental relics, such as its silver plate, trophies, and Colours, and by maintaining its own distinct mess customs. In 1910, for example, the officers' mess of 2/ Oxford and Buckinghamshire Light Infantry acquired a sword presented to Sir John Moore, a bound volume of historical records of the regiment, and a series of medals awarded to former members of the regiment.[90]

The requirement that regiments construct, maintain, and enhance their traditions was not confined to the cavalry and infantry. The older Corps

[87] PRO WO 32/2861. Creedy to Maj.-Gen. Sir E. Carter, Colonel Commandant RASC, 22 Oct. 1930.

[88] PRO WO 32/11979. Minutes Joint Secretary of the Honours and Distinctions Committee, 7 Nov. 1946.

[89] PRO WO 32/12554. Committee on the future of officers' messes, 14 Aug. 1947.

[90] The Oxford and Buckinghamshire Light Infantry Chronicle 1910, 145.

that existed in the nineteenth century and the new regiments and corps established in the twentieth century followed suit. The Royal Artillery had its own superstructure of Colonels Commandant who oversaw, amongst other things, the work of the Royal Artillery Institution and its Historical Committee.[91] By the early 1860s gunner officers were holding a regular annual dinner organized by the Royal Artillery Club, under the patronage of the Duke of Cambridge, to celebrate their regiment.[92] In 1873 the regiment published its own history, intended to inspire future gunners to emulate the deeds of their forefathers.[93] Batteries did not carry regimental Colours, but in 1925 individual batteries were granted honour titles, usually the name of a famous battery commander or battle. But gunner recruits were taught that 'though "G" Battery RHA, 3rd Battery RFA or 45 Company RGA may have some particularly glorious deed in its history, this deed is not the property of that particular unit alone; the whole of the Royal Regiment shares in it and takes pride in it'.[94]

After the First World War the Army Service Corps, the Army Chaplains Department, the Army Ordnance Corps, the Army Pay Corps, the Army Veterinary Corps, and the Tank Corps, when it was placed on a permanent footing in 1923, all received the 'Royal' prefix before their titles in recognition of their recent service and in expectation that it would help sustain morale and recruiting in the future.[95] Like the other teeth arms, the RTC quickly drew on its past achievements as a way of creating *esprit de corps*. As early as November 1919 officers of the corps were dining together to commemorate the battle of Cambrai.[96] The RTC's Colonel Commandant, Sir Hugh Elles, also decided that it needed its own march, and he assembled a group of senior officers and the band outside the depot mess to choose a tune. 'They had', according to an officer who was present, '"Land of Hope and Glory" and all that sort of business to pick this tank battle song which turned out to be "My boy Willie" which was written by a German, I believe! That's the march-past now of the regiment.'[97] By the late 1920s newly commissioned officers in the RTC

were told all about the Battle of Cambrai and how the tanks were used in the First World War, and all about Sir Hugh Elles, and all the various senior officers and what they'd done and who they were. And all the commanding officers of the regiments as they were, where they'd come from, who they were. It was a very comprehensive affair...[98]

[91] Hughes (ed.), *History of the Royal Regiment of Artillery*, 11–12.
[92] *The Times*, 29 May 1863.
[93] *The Times*, 4 Feb. 1873.
[94] IWM 86/33/3. Papers of Lt.-Col. G. E. A. Granet. Notes for Lectures. Regimental history and Tradition, n.d. but post-1918.
[95] Maj. T. J. Edwards, *Military Customs* (Aldershot: Gale & Polden, 1950), 70.
[96] *The Times*, 21 Nov. 1919.
[97] IWMSA. Accession No. 000870/09. Maj.-Gen. H. L. Birks, 53.
[98] IWMSA. Accession No. 000833/04. Colonel W. B. Blain, 15.

The Corps quickly established its own emblem in the shape of its distinctive black beret headgear. The result, according to the Inspector of the RTC, was that by 1927 the Corps had its own *esprit de corps*, based not upon a long history, but what it regarded as the crucial role it had played 'in the winning of the greatest war the world has ever known. They think it is impossible to have a greater tradition than this. They also look upon themselves as more modern, more scientific and more efficient force for war than anyone else.'[99]

The process of territorialization and linking imposed by Cardwell and Childers may have caused a good deal of upset amongst those personally affected by it. But within thirty years most regiments had settled down, and officers and men had in many cases developed a fierce loyalty to what had become their military family. By the eve of the First World War a generation of officers had grown up who had never known anything different, and for whom the 'rightness' of a system that divided the line infantry, cavalry, and Household Brigade into a large number of small organizations was something that they took for granted. In 1912 Brig.-Gen. J. A. L. Haldane could claim that the system worked because it reflected 'the individuality of the British race, which is a marked feature of our Army, and is a characteristic which, though it may possibly possess some disadvantages, has raised the British nation to the place which it now holds in the world'.[100] In 1936–7 an extensive survey conducted amongst subalterns to discover if they supported organizing regiments into a dozen larger groups in order to hasten their promotion found that the idea met with little support. There was near unanimity that officers had joined a particular regiment because it had certain clearly defined attractions for them, that each regiment was different, and that those differences should be cherished even at the cost of stultifying their career prospects.[101]

The process of instilling the official notion of what constituted 'the regiment' began during recruit training. Shortly after he took command of 1/Dorsets in 1887, Lt.-Col. M. Gossett began to lecture his men on the history of their regiment. Gossett's purpose was not to fill his men's heads with antiquarian knowledge. It was

---

[99] LHCMA. Liddell Hart MSS. 15/12/3. Brigadier G. M. Lindsay, Inspector, RTC, to DMT, 12 Dec. 1927.
[100] PRO WO 279/25. Report of a conference of General Staff Officers at the Staff College, 15–18 Jan. 1912.
[101] PRO WO 32/4477. Grouping of regiments of infantry of the line for promotion purposes, 1936–7.

by enforcing that the honour gained in so many years could not be attained without good discipline, self-denial, ready obedience, and pluck, I do not think I am wrong in saying that the knowledge gained by the men of their regimental history raised their tone, and I could afterwards observe a steady advance in good conduct.[102]

Two years later, this became official War Office policy. Regimental officers were required to teach recruits the history of their regiment.[103] This course of instruction was later extended to include simple lessons in the 'privileges which he inherits as a citizen of a great Empire' and 'he should be taught to appreciate the honour which is his, as a soldier, of serving his King and country'.[104] In the evening recruits sat on their beds polishing their equipment while NCOs catechized them in the great deeds of their regiment. Regimental history also came to form a substantial part of the work that recruits were expected to do for their Third Class education certificate. At Maryhill barracks in Glasgow in 1911 the recruits of the Argyll and Sutherland Highlanders were taught about the past exploits of the regiment, including 'when the regiment was formed and all the various things about it actually, including the Battle of Balaclava'.[105] By the eve of the First World War all recruits were supposed to attend a series of lectures given by their officers during basic training on 'regimental distinctions, the meaning and importance of a military spirit; Good name of the regiment and army'; 'Regimental colours'.[106] And company commanders were expected to 'take every opportunity of teaching the men the glorious traditions of the regiment, and thereby animate them with that true pride of regiment which is the inseparable link between themselves and discipline'.[107]

But, merely because the military authorities recognized the utility of the regimental system with its customs and traditions, that did not mean that they regarded it with the same almost sacerdotal attitude as the members of the regiments themselves. That fact became a fruitful source of conflict between the regiments and the military authorities. The latter had a strictly utilitarian view towards the regimental system and the distinctions of dress and customs that were so much a part of it. Writing in 1886, the Adjutant-General, Sir Garnet Wolseley, insisted that

No man who knew soldiers or their peculiar way of thinking, or who was acquainted with the many little trifles that go to make up pride of Regiment,

[102] Gossett, 'Battalion Command', 472.
[103] Goodenough and Dalton, *The Army Book of the British Empire*, 137.
[104] General Staff, *Infantry Training (4-Company Organisation) 1914* (London: HMSO, 1914), 2, 12; General Staff, *Cavalry Training 1912*, 323.
[105] IWMSA. Accession No. 000374/06. Maj. C. H. Ditcham, 17.
[106] General Staff, *Cavalry Training 1912*, 323.
[107] Anon., *The Standing Orders of the 2nd Battalion 22nd (Cheshire) Regiment*, 25.

and form as it were the link between it and discipline, would ever deprive a soldier of any peculiarity that he prided himself on, without some overpowering reasons for doing so.

The soldier is a peculiar animal that can alone be brought to the highest efficiency by inducing him to believe that he belongs to a regiment which is infinitely superior to the others around him.[108]

Their attitude had changed little when one of Wolseley's successors wrote in 1922 that to abolish all regimental distinctions would be to destroy 'the "soul of the regiment" '.[109] The military authorities were willing to pander to regimental proclivities partly because, as Wolseley hinted, they believed that they helped to maintain morale and discipline. But they also did so because the British army relied on voluntary recruiting. And that meant, as the Duke of Cambridge explained in 1876, that 'what you do in conscription [*sic*] you do by authority and by order; [but] what you do with a volunteer army you must do by good feeling and by judicious arrangements'.[110]

However, their willingness to tolerate diverse habits between regiments had its limits. The War Office issued voluminous rules, encompassed in such books as *Kings* or *Queen's Regulations* and the *Manual of Military Law*, which laid down in great detail how regiments were supposed to organize their domestic affairs.[111] Units were inspected annually by senior officers and if they detected that officers or other ranks had departed significantly from the regulations they were liable to be rebuked.[112] But even the most voluminous regulations left room for discussion and divergence in practice, and it was here that politics and the regimental system sometimes intersected.

Childers's organizational reforms were accompanied by the imposition on many regiments of new badges and 'facings' (the coloured collars and cuffs of their dress uniforms) and his diktat caused considerable anger in some regiments. The final arbiter in such matters was the Crown, and some regiments were quite prepared to lobby the monarch vigorously on their own behalf. The Colonel of the Highland Light Infantry complained to one of Queen Victoria's private secretaries about 'the Badge proposed for his regiment the Highland Light Infantry—a small shepherd on a bugle which among his officers and men is already called the Pig and Whistle'.[113] The Norfolk Regiment was so incensed at the new white

---

[108] Sir G. Wolseley, *The Soldier's Pocket Book* (London: Macmillan, 5th edn., 1886), 3–4.

[109] PRO WO 32/11368. Précis for the Army Council No. 1110. June 1922.

[110] PP (1877), XVIII. C. 1654. *Report of the committee . . .* , Q 8740.

[111] See e.g. NAM 6005–60. Records of the 88th Regiment (Connaught Rangers). Horse Guards issued Gen. Order No. 79 Officers Dress, 1 Sept. 1868.

[112] War Office, *KR . . . 1912*, 287; S. H. Myerly, *British Military Spectacle from the Napoleonic Wars through the Crimea* (Cambridge, Mass.: Harvard University Press, 1996), 34–42.

[113] PRO WO 32/6090. Ponsonby to Ellice, 1 Sept. 1881.

facing that it was forced to wear that it went on lobbying for twenty-five years until finally, in 1905, the King agreed it should be allowed to revert to its original yellow facing.[114]

In 1923 an officer in the Cameron Highlanders complained that 'The Sporran question is getting acute'. The staff at Aldershot Command had insisted that the regiment was flouting dress regulations by wearing sporrans.

Who is responsible for this piece of galling interference? Is it jealousy or what. If ever I rise to any exalted rank I shall do my damnedest to unite the Highland Brigade. It is only because we are not united that they (the Aldershot Staff) are able to mess us about. They dare not 'monkey' with the Guards' Dress because they are too strong, why the hell should they interfere with us.[115]

The regiment took matters into its own hands and wore sporrans on parade before the King. They were reprimanded by a senior officer but were unrepentant. 'When will these Englishmen learn that they cannot ride rough shod over the traditions and customs of a Highland Corps?'[116]

To the outside observer there is something almost comic about grown men concerning themselves with 'the Sporran question'. But what was at stake was something far more important than whether or not a particular regiment could or could not wear a special item of clothing. The underlying issues were much more fundamental: what exactly constituted 'the regiment', and to what extent were they self-regulating corporations or merely subdivisions in a larger bureaucracy governed from the War Office? The resolution of these issues was sometimes played out in public, but more often in private. But in either case the struggles were intensely political. The fact that in 1920 forty-five regiments persuaded the War Office and the King to agree to changes in their names, and that by 1931 only sixteen line infantry regiments were still wearing the white facings that had been imposed on them in 1881, and that the rest had obtained permission to revert to their pre-1881 facings, might suggest that in this struggle the regiments exercised more power than the War Office.[117] That was true, but their victory over a matter so fundamentally unimportant as the design of buttons, badges, and dress uniforms suggests that the military authorities were, if pressed, prepared to humour regimental susceptibilities by compromising over trivia. It did not necessarily demonstrate that, in larger questions that had a direct bearing on the army's combat capability, the balance of power was firmly tilted towards the regiments and away from the military authorities.

---

[114] RNRM. R. 96. Digest of Service, 1857–1904, 2nd Battalion, 9th Regiment, 29 Mar. 1905.
[115] IWM PP/MCR/182. Maj.-Gen. D. N. Wimberley MSS. 'Scottish soldier. The Memoirs of Maj. Gen. Douglas Wimberley', vol. 1, diary entry 3 May 1923.
[116] Ibid., 19 May 1923.
[117] *The Times*, 9 Dec. 1920, 25 Apr. 1931.

In 1880 the Duke of Cambridge wrote bitterly that 'the individuality of regiments—derived from fixity of tenure, strengthened by community of service, and founded on the memory of great deeds in olden times—is slowly being sapped, and surely passing away'.[118] The Duke's pessimism was unjustified. The Cardwell–Childers reforms were accompanied by the wholesale recreation of regimental traditions. In 1933 the Old Comrades Association of 10/Hussars held their annual dinner in London. The toast to the regiment was proposed by Captain R. C. Gordon-Canning, who had joined the regiment in 1910 and served with it through the First World War:

The 10th Hussars are not merely a Cavalry Regiment or a Hussar Regiment, they are THE TENTH, and that signifies an individuality, and in these days of mass movement and mass psychology, an individuality, is a precious heirloom which all Tenth, past and present, must strive to retain.

Amid the fluidity of present day conditions, it is most valuable for everyone to possess some Loyalty, and to be guided by some sound traditions. It is because these two factors have been characteristic of Englishmen during the last centuries that England is to-day, in the words of Winston Churchill, still the best country to live in for either Duke or Dustman. The glory of England does not reside in our politicians, in our financiers or in our journalists with the vulgarity of the popular press, but in the Royal Family, in the landed aristocracy, in the constable and in the rank and file of such Regiments as the 10th Hussars. People who, in a position of responsibility, in the words of Shakespeare 'Hold their honour higher than their life'.[119]

Gordon-Canning's peroration summed up the widely accepted view of the role of tradition in the British regimental system. It was essentially backward-looking, insular, and conservative. When regimental spokesmen found that the military authorities at times of change such as the Sandys Reforms of 1957 rejected past associations as the basis for future policy and thereby threatened the future of their regiments, they were understandably bitter.[120] But such attitudes represented the past of the regiment in a quite literal sense. Gordon-Canning had retired from the army in 1919. While his attitude was tinged with the kind of nostalgia that made him an effective after-dinner speaker, it was not typical of the attitude of serving officers. They constructed and construed regimental traditions as a prop for morale and discipline. For them, traditions had a distinctly utilitarian and therefore forward-looking function.

In 1945, an officer of 1/Essex candidly admitted that regimental loyalty was not, and given the shortcomings of localized recruiting could

---

[118] PRO WO 33/35. Memorandum by HRH the Field Marshal Commanding-in-Chief, 15 Nov. 1880.

[119] *The Xth Royal Hussars Gazette*, 13 (Sept. 1933), 7.

[120] Anon, 'Editorial', *The Regimental Chronicle. The South Lancashire Regiment (Prince of Wales Volunteers)*, 25 (Mar. 1957).

not, be primordial. It had to be manufactured: 'We are now reduced to comparatively few genuine Essex men... We have some younger Essex blood recently out from home who were most welcome. Fortunately, we know now that you need not be Essex bred to make a good "Essex soldier".'[121]

Regiments were culturally defined organizations that were bound together by shared historical memories, customs, and a myth of descent, not by the common ethnic or local origins of their members. They were the product of a particular set of historical circumstances, the Cardwell–Childers reforms, and of the need identified by the military authorities to find a way of instilling morale and discipline into the large number of short-service recruits that the Regular Army needed. The idea of 'the regiment' was something that was artificially constructed by the Colonels of Regiments and their senior officers. In many cases their efforts were rewarded with success. Plenty of Regular Army recruits came to accept part or all of the official interpretation of the meaning of the regimental communities to which they belonged, and in doing so they took on new identities as members of their regiment. Before 1914 there were, for example, large numbers of Birmingham-born Englishmen in the Royal Welch Fusiliers but 'on Taffy Day, as we called St. David's Day, they proved themselves as good Welshmen as could be desired'.[122] Many recruits came from impoverished backgrounds, and life in their regiment offered them the first stable environment they had known. Playing in the band at an official function in the officers' mess of the 1/Royal Dragoons, when the regimental standards and mess silver were on display, Spike Mays realized that 'There is no doubt about the way I felt. For the first time in my life I belonged to something of consequence and I could not tear my eyes away from the symbols of that importance.'[123] So close became their identification with their regiment that they used familial language to describe it. Having joined 8/Hussars in 1950, Kenneth Black found the dignity and stability that had been lacking in his impoverished civilian life and decided that 'It was a real good regiment, it was. And you thought more of the regiment then than you did of your relations. You know, that was your... in my opinion that was my home, and everything and I really loved it.'[124] When one long-serving regular Warrant Officer came to retire, he simply said 'I had left the family'.[125] The next chapter will consider how the regimental family lived its life together.

[121] *The Eagle. The Journal of the Essex Regiment*, 8 (Sept. 1945), 30.
[122] Richards, *Old-Soldier Sahib*, 79.
[123] Mays, *Fall Out the Officers*, 24.
[124] IWMSA. Accession No. 18022/03. K. Black, reel 1.
[125] IWMSA. Accession No. 16593/29. T. Chadwick, reel 29.

CHAPTER FIVE

Barrack Life

Regiments were not only military organizations. They were self-contained societies. When John Lucy joined 2/Royal Irish Rifles at Dover in 1912 he likened his battalion to

a little town, and viewed in this way [it] has many attractions. The seven or eight hundred men and the thirty or so officers are not solely and at all times engaged in training for war. Working hours are not long, and holidays are numerous. A duty soldier, that is, one fully trained, may ease his boredom by finding employment in various stores and workshops, by looking after horses, by making himself expert in specialized jobs like machine-gunnery or signaling, or by educating himself in the regimental school. While still in the army he may become, among other things, a cook, a waiter, a valet, a clerk, a butcher, an armourer, or a storekeeper, if he so wishes. He may also compete for promotion.[1]

The daily life of every member of the regiment was organized in such a way that he was never allowed to forget for a moment that he was part of a hierarchical society and that he owed instant obedience to his superiors.

At the top of every unit was its CO. He was responsible for every aspect of its efficiency, discipline, and training, and for all of the public property that was allocated to it. His authority was paramount 'and all orders emanating from him must receive an unhesitating and cheerful obedience'.[2] He was assisted by a senior major who acted as his 2i/c, and an Adjutant, usually a Captain, who performed the functions of his staff officer.[3] Each unit was divided into a number of sub-units. They were called companies in the infantry, squadrons in the cavalry, and batteries in the Royal Artillery, and each was commanded by a Captain or Major. The number of sub-units in a unit varied. Until the eve of the First World War infantry battalions were organized on an eight-company basis. But in 1914 they were reorganized into four double-companies. Sub-units in turn were divided into platoons in the infantry, troops in the cavalry, and sections in the artillery. Each was commanded by a subaltern, assisted by a sergeant. In the infantry the smallest organization was a section,

---

[1] Lucy, *There's a Devil in the Drum*, 56.
[2] Anon., *The Standing Orders of the 2nd Battalion The Royal Warwickshire Regiment*, 4.
[3] SRO. GB 554/B3/1. Anon., *The Standing Orders of the 1st Battalion, the Suffolk Regiment* (Chatham: Gale and Polden, 1888), 14–16.

usually consisting of about a dozen men, and under the command of a corporal, or a gun detachment in the artillery.

These organizational structures were important for they determined how and where soldiers lived. Living arrangements mirrored the military structure of the unit. 'In order effectually to carry out discipline, and to facilitate continual superintendence', the Standing Orders of the 2/Royal Warwickshire Regiment explained in 1934, 'which is never to be dispensed with, men of each Section, Platoon or Company are at all times, as far as practicable, to occupy the same room, tent or billet.'4 Men who lived together fought together.

Daily routine in every unit was governed by its standing orders. They regulated in minute detail every soldier's deportment, appearance, and daily routine. Soldiers were expected to discipline their bodies, and 'must never loaf or slouch about. Whatever they are doing they must go about smartly and well set up.'5 They had to wear their hair short and to sport a moustache.6 Other ranks were issued with cleaning kit free and could be placed on a charge if their uniforms and accoutrements were not spotlessly clean.7 The lower a soldier's rank, the more minutely was his behaviour controlled. Boy soldiers were not permitted to enter the barrack rooms of private soldiers or to purchase alcohol, and had to be in their barrack room by 8.30 p.m. each evening. Privates and NCOs were not permitted to enter each others' rooms or messes unless they were on duty.8 Discipline was not relaxed at mealtimes. In 1882, 1/Norfolks were reminded that 'Men are to sit down to breakfast and dinner with their faces neatly brushed, and in serge frocks buttoned up.'9 Sergeants were allowed out of barracks until midnight without a pass, but COs granted the same privilege only to well-conducted trained private soldiers.10 Men who broke out of barracks after tattoo were liable to be punished if they were caught.11 Even a soldier who wanted to report sick had to do so according to strict regulations.12

Immediately reveille was sounded, soldiers were to leave their beds, brush their clothes, black their boots, shave, wash, and clean their arms and equipment.13 Floors were to be washed at least once a week, and the

---

4 Anon., *Standing Orders ... 2nd Battalion The Royal Warwickshire*, 94.

5 Anon., *Standing Orders of the 5th (Royal Irish) Lancers* (Aldershot: Gale and Polden, 1904), 1.

6 Anon., *QR ... 1892*, 169, 351–4.

7 IWMSA. Accession No. 000569/18. Col. U. B. Burke, reel 7; Anon., *The Standing Orders of the 2nd Battalion The Royal Warwickshire Regiment*, 93.

8 Anon., *Standing Orders ... King's Royal Rifle Corps*, 29.

9 RNRM. R 65. Permanent Order book, 1st Battalion, 1831 to 1907, 3 Jan. 1882.

10 Anon., *QR ... 1892*, 169, 357.

11 Robertson, *From Private to Field Marshal*, 7–8.

12 IWMSA. Accession No. 004473/04. Lt.-Col. E. G. Brice, 40.

13 Anon., *The Standing Orders of the 47th (The Lancashire Regiment) of Foot* (Aldershot: William Clowes, 1876), *passim*.

latrines and ablutions were to be kept clean at all times. Bedding was to be aired for an hour and then folded up, and beds were not to be made up again until 7 p.m.[14] Some men undoubtedly found this irksome, but plenty took a real pride in their appearance. In the Royal Dragoons in the 1920s, one trooper recalled that 'there was something almost sacramental about daily turnout and the wearing of uniform, and to us professional soldiers this became an end in itself; a strange combination of regimental and personal pride, an art, ritual, ceremony, almost a religion'.[15]

These regulations were enforced by a system of careful surveillance. A Captain of the Week, assisted by a Subaltern of the Day, a Regimental Orderly-Sergeant, and a Regimental Orderly-Corporal inspected every part of the unit to ensure that standing orders were being enforced. They looked at the men's rations, the cookhouse, the dairy, the Regimental Institute, the recreation room, the hospital, the guards and the guard room, the sergeants' mess, and the latrines. They visited every barrack room in the morning to ensure they were cleaned, and a Medical Officer inspected them once a week to make certain that the sanitation was adequate.[16] Finally on a Saturday morning, the CO inspected the accommodation of the entire unit. This gave rise to an extraordinary amount of preparation. In 1911, when 2/Argyll and Sutherland Highlanders were stationed at Maryhill Barracks in Glasgow, the men 'used to have on the Friday afternoon what we used to call the barrack sports— get down on your knees and scrub the place out. And the floor had to be snow white. And to keep it snow white you used to put a blanket from your bed down on the floor so that the floors wouldn't get dirtied.'[17]

Junior officers were not exempt from this system of regulation and surveillance. They did have a batman, a military servant, to tidy their room and clean their uniforms. But they were expected to purchase a long list of uniform clothing and accoutrements from approved regimental tailors.[18] Any deviation from accepted uniform patterns, or any dirt on buttons, belts, or boots, was likely to earn them a stern rebuke from the Adjutant. Even when they were off duty their appearance was regulated and they were expected to buy their clothes from a 'good tailor' and 'avoid buying flashy or highly coloured clothes'.[19]

The daily routine of every unit was regulated by a strict timetable. In the 1890s soldiers in an infantry battalion in the UK were roused from

[14] Anon., *Standing Orders … The Royal Warwickshire Regiment*, 92.
[15] Mays, *Fall Out the Officers*, 78.
[16] Spencer, *Standing Orders of the 44th or East Essex Regiment*, *passim*.
[17] IWMSA. Accession No. 000374/06. Maj. C. H. Ditcham, 8.
[18] ERM. ER 2459. *The Essex Regiment. Officers' Dress Regulations* (Brentwood: H. George Allis, 1938); PRO WO 33/40. Committee on furnishing officers' quarters and messes, 8 Feb. 1883.
[19] War Office, *Customs of the Army (1956)* (London: War Office, 1956), 8.

their beds at 6 a.m. After cleaning their rooms they did physical training on the barrack square until 7.45 a.m. Breakfast was at 8 a.m. Defaulters were summoned to the orderly room for disposal by the CO between 10 and 11 a.m. each morning. In the morning the battalion held parades, and took part in route marches and other forms of training until dinner time, usually at 1 p.m. Other ranks then had their main meal of the day, while officers had lunch.[20] Recruits would do another drill parade in the afternoon, but it was common for soldiers who had completed their recruit training and who were not on guard duty or other fatigues to be free of duty thereafter. They whiled away time playing football, in the canteen, or sleeping on their beds until tea at 4 p.m., although men who wanted promotion might attend the regimental school to gain the necessary army educational certificate. In the evening most soldiers went to the canteen or left barracks, either to meet girls, to drink in local pubs or beer shops, or to attend a theatre or a music hall. Tattoo and roll-call, the time when all soldiers without a pass had to be back in barracks, was normally at 9.30 p.m., and lights were put out at 10.15 p.m.[21]

The daily routine of units stationed overseas in places such as India or Egypt varied according to the time of year. In the summer months on the plains of India it was reckoned to be so hot in the middle of the day that parades were held early in the morning and in the cool of the evening. Troops were confined indoors for the rest of the day. In cavalry regiments, for example, reveille might be at 5.30 a.m., riding school from 6.15 to 8.30 a.m., feeding and grooming horses from 9.30 a.m. to 11 a.m., and drill from 5 p.m. to 6.30 p.m.[22] When the 2/Seaforth Highlanders were stationed at Lahore in the summer of 1928 the men were roused at 5 or 6 a.m. They washed, shaved, and had breakfast and then did PT, cross-country running, or highland dancing. At 8.30 or 9 a.m. there was a drill parade. But from 10 a.m. to 4 p.m. their time was their own because it was too hot to go outdoors. Men lay on their beds, read books or newspapers, played cards, or slept until about 4 p.m., when it was cool enough for them to go outside to play games and sports or go for a walk.[23]

Soldiers were housed in barracks or cantonments, each surrounded by walls or fences. Entrance and egress was through a carefully guarded gate.[24] Soldiers and civilians had to report to the Guard Room for permission to enter or leave the barracks. The regimental community was thus physically cut off from its civilian neighbours. The quality of

[20] 'A British Officer' [Captain W. E. Cairnes], *Social Life in the British Army* (London & New York: Harper Brothers, 1899), 68; Richards, *Old-Soldier Sahib*, 30–6.

[21] Wyndham, *The Queen's Service*, 42–3.

[22] NAM 7104-31. Pte. P. Y. Grainger, Diary entry, 15 Apr. 1903.

[23] IWMSA. Accession No. 00906/06. Set. M. Finlayson, 30.

[24] ERM. M16/79/57/C. Maj. C. A. Webb, A few memories of soldiering in the nineteen twenties and thirties.

accommodation varied. In the middle of the nineteenth century barracks in the United Kingdom were often unsanitary and overcrowded and posed serious health risks to the soldiers who lived in them. Lack of money meant that the War Office only slowly modernized them.[25] They consisted of a mixture of barrack rooms, sergeants' and officers' messes, recreation rooms and canteens, workshops, and an orderly room and guard room. In India a regimental bazaar, where native shopkeepers supplied the troops with local services and products, was usually attached to them. The whole comprised a self-contained community.[26]

A typical barrack room in Britain in the late nineteenth or early twentieth century was about 150 feet long and 60 feet wide. It contained sixty soldiers' beds. Each bed could be folded up when not in use. The men slept on three coir-filled mattresses, known as 'biscuits', with coarse linen sheets and thick blankets. Behind each bed was an iron shelf or metal locker where each soldier was required to fold his kit neatly. The furniture consisted of 'six foot plain wooden tables with polished steel rims round the corners, six foot wooden forms, also with black enameled iron legs and struts; a large iron coal box; a long handled dry scrubber; a hand scrubbing brush and a poker and fire tongs and a shovel'.[27] Rooms were kept spotlessly clean: 'Its looks, its smell, its general air, all meant cleanliness. You felt you might be happy in it.'[28] However, they were inadequately heated, and the stench in the morning was appalling, generated by a mixture of stale sweat and the stink of the urine tubs that were placed in each room.[29]

In India officers and other ranks usually enjoyed more spacious accommodation. After inhabiting cramped quarters at Chatham, the men of 2/Northumberland Fusiliers, who moved to Agra in 1880, were impressed by their new barrack rooms, recognizing that

There was a certain nobility about them; a certain affinity in size and shape to a cathedral. One for each company. Long and wide and spacious, they were cut-off in the middle by a transept like messroom fitted with tables and forms where the whole company could sit down at table at one time. The two halves for sleeping accommodation consisted each of a long, high space, fifty feet to the roof and twenty feet wide, the walls interspersed with arches. The bare stone slabs of the floor added to the effect of cloistered coolness. The customary shelves, cots and kit-boxes were fitted between each arch of the room, while through the arches on either side was a corridor about fifteen feet wide with open doors opposite the

[25] Skelley, *The Victorian Army*, 36–41.
[26] NAM 7104–31. Pte. P. Y. Grainger, diary entry, 8 Apr. 1903; A. C. Kennett, *Life is What you Make it* (Edinburgh: The Pentland Press Ltd, 1992), 65.
[27] ERM. M16/79/57/C. Maj. C. A. Webb, A few memories of soldiering in the nineteen twenties and thirties.
[28] Edmondson, *John Bull's Army*, 25.
[29] IWMSA. Accession No. 000374/06. Maj. C. H. Ditcham, 21.

arches. Outside this was a veranda of the same width, supported by a row of pillars on the outer edge, and beyond this was a plinth of five steps running right round the building. Add to this, extreme cleanliness, for it was made of stone that was almost white in colour and was lime washed inside once a year, and you will have some idea of the simple austerity of the place.[30]

Over each bed there was a 'punka', a large fan operated through a system of ropes and pulleys by an Indian servant, a punkah-wallah. It was kept constantly in motion during hot weather in an effort to cool the temperature in the barracks.[31] Every bed also had a mosquito net, and soldiers were under strict instructions to ensure that the net was pulled over the bed before they turned in for the night.

Soldiers were not kept in physical isolation from the civilian community just to facilitate discipline. In the empire, cantonments were sited outside large towns because the military authorities sought to preserve their health by ensuring that they inhabited islands of order and cleanliness, supplied with clean water and piped sanitation, in what was otherwise a sea of dirt.[32] A British soldier who was stationed at Dum Dum, outside Calcutta, in 1901 informed his family that 'There is enough fever here to stock a few of the stars if they want a sample in fact they can have any disease they want. Everywhere is out of bounds for troops ...'.[33] In the 1930s men drafted to Egypt were warned about a whole variety of tropical diseases they might catch if they did not take proper precautions. But they were also assured that 'If you keep your head covered, your tummy warm and your bowels open you'll be perfectly all right always.'[34]

For practical reasons, and reasons of morale, the complete and permanent segregation of soldiers and civilians was impossible. The military authorities therefore tried to impose strict control over their contacts. Troops in tropical cantonments were often forbidden to visit the indigenous quarters of local towns.[35] Most other ranks came into contact only with barrack servants or shopkeepers in the regimental bazaar. Officers might learn a smattering of Arabic or one of the Indian languages,

[30] Fraser, *Sixty Years*, 80.   [31] Richards, *Old-Soldier Sahib*, 190–1.

[32] S. Guha, 'Nutrition, Sanitation, Hygiene, and the Likelihood of Death: The British Army in India, c. 1870–1920', *Population Studies*, 47 (1993), 390; M. Harrison, 'Medicine and the Management of Modern Warfare', *History of Science*, 34 (1996), 395; id., *Public Health in British India: Anglo-Indian Preventive Medicine 1859–1914* (Cambridge: Cambridge University Press, 1994), *passim*; Maj. A. T. Moore, *Notes for Officers Proceeding to India. Revised and Corrected to March 1912* (Chatham: Royal Engineers Institute, 1912), 61.

[33] ERO. D/DU 730/1. Records of Samuel Watson of Shenfield. Pte. George Watson, B. Company, 1/Norfolk Regiment, 23 May 1901.

[34] IWMSA. Accession No. 004449/06. Maj.-Gen. J. Scott Elliot, 3; IWMSA. Accession No. 004473/04. Lt.-Col. E. G. Brice, 2–3.

[35] IWMSA. Accession No. 000923/04. R. Clemens, reel 2; IWMSA. Accession No. 004534/02. Lt.-Col. W. H. Hyde, 4.

but other ranks rarely bothered to learn more than they needed to give orders to a servant or to purchase goods in a bazaar.[36] Otherwise, they resorted to the time-honoured methods that monoglot Englishmen had always employed to make themselves understood abroad, for 'he knew that if he shouted loudly enough the other fellow would understand what he was saying'.[37]

Relations between British officers and soldiers and the indigenous population of the empire they garrisoned did little to break down the mental isolation of regimental life. Officers were expected to be tactful but reserved towards natives of high social status with whom they came into contact on official business.[38] If relations between the races became too close, it would threaten the foundation of British rule. In 1927 one gunner officer believed that the main reason a handful of Europeans could rule India was because 'we have kept apart from the natives [and] we have not mixed with them nor intermarried with them, but we have always remained as a race apart'.[39] They were not required to be so considerate towards servants and shopkeepers. Royal Engineer officers proceeding to India before 1914 were told that they should not be

too considerate for a servant's feelings; they have no sense of gratitude as a rule, and will think you are afraid if you request them to do a thing instead of ordering them; on the other hand some of them are the best-tempered and most faithful servants in the world. Also do not praise. Natives should never be struck, as a very large number suffer from enlarged spleens and other complaints, and a blow, or even sometimes only a shove, may be fatal.[40]

British officers rarely met Indians of even high social status on a footing of social equality, or invited them into their clubs, messes, or hill stations as guests. In Karachi in the 1930s the British had their clubs and the Indians had their own, something that the British persuaded themselves was both natural and preferred by both races.[41] In Cairo officers might meet wealthy Pashas at the Muhamed Ali Club, but 'any officer in a British regiment was regarded with some reserve if he was known to have many Egyptian friends'.[42] Similarly, in India, 'except for polo playing', a former cavalry

[36] IWMSA. Accession No. 000314/12. Capt. P. Snelling, 60; IWMSA. Accession No. 00962/4. Lt.-Col. T. W. Nickalls, 26; Richards, *Old-Soldier Sahib*, 143–4. This was not true of British officers serving with Indian Army regiments. They were expected to master the vernacular of their men.

[37] IWMSA. Accession No. 004486/7. Lt.-Col. R. King-Clark, 17.

[38] RNRM. Anon., *Memorandum on the subject of social and official intercourse between British Officers and Indians* (Calcutta: Superintendent Government Printing, India, 1919).

[39] IWM 86/33/1. Papers of Lt.-Col. G. E. A. Granet. Granet to his wife, 27 Apr. 1927.

[40] Moore, *Notes for Officers Proceeding to India*, 26.

[41] IWMSA. Accession No. 000938/05. Lt.-Col. E. G. Hollist, 22–3; IWMSA. Accession No. 004465/07. Maj.-Gen. H. P. W. Hutson, 55.

[42] IWMSA. Accession No. 004527/06. Gen. Sir J. Hackett, 9.

officer who served in India recalled, 'maharajas and people one met like that, we had very little contact with Indian civilians other than what you might call employees, shikaris, you know, grooms, servants, etc.'.[43]

British NCOs and other ranks were expected to treat native servants temperately, but cases of bullying, abuse, and refusing to pay debts to tradesmen were not uncommon.[44] As Viceroy between 1898 and 1905, Lord Curzon made himself unpopular with the garrison by insisting that troops who mistreated Indians should be punished.[45] This flew in the face of the fact that many soldiers stationed in the sub-continent believed that the only way to ensure the continued respect of the indigenous population was to treat them harshly.[46]

The subservience often displayed by servants, and the suspicion that shopkeepers were out to cheat them, only encouraged British soldiers to regard most of the indigenous population of their empire disdainfully. 'You never got close linked with them', one soldier who served in India remarked. 'Putting it bluntly, you weren't supposed to do, anyhow. They were the natives and you were the rajahs, the sahibs, you see.'[47] A private in the 21/Rifle Brigade put the same idea more succinctly. Writing of his experiences in Egypt and India, he concluded that 'The natives [in India] are more respectful than those in Egypt. Perhaps this is due to Egyptians being more interconnected with English, proves the old proverb: *Familiarity breeds Contempt*'.[48]

There were, however, some peoples they did not disparage. In Palestine, they had considerable respect for the Jewish farmers who, thanks to their industry and intelligence, seemed to have created prosperity from a wilderness.[49] And on the North West Frontier of India, they admired the masculine virtues of the Pathan tribesmen they fought. The Pathans showed none of the servility of the servants and shopkeepers they otherwise encountered. They were, according to one soldier who fought them, 'Real men. I liked them. Fellows who would look you straight in the eye, you know, and smile at you, say "Salem, sahib." They wouldn't bow.'[50]

---

[43] IWMSA. Accession No. 000946/05. Lt.-Col. R. L. V. ffrench Blake, 17; IWMSA. Accession No. 00962/4. Lt.-Col. T. W. Nickalls, 26.

[44] IWMSA. Accession No. 000780/05. H. L. Horsfield, 22–3; IWMSA. Accession No. 004523/07. Capt. F. J. Powell, 31; NAM 7104–31. Pte. P. Y. Grainger, diary entry, 7 Mar. 1903.

[45] K. Ballhatchet, *Race, Sex and Class under the Raj: Imperial Attitudes and Policies and their Critics, 1793–1905* (London: Weidenfeld & Nicolson, 1980), 141–3.

[46] Richards, *Old-Soldier Sahib*, 74.

[47] IWMSA. Accession No. 000780/05. H. L. Horsfield, 43.

[48] ERM. ER 2178:1. Diary of Pte. R. A. Newbury, 31 Jan. 1919.

[49] IWMSA. Accession No. 004550/05. Maj-Gen. H. E. N. Bredin, 12.

[50] IWMSA. Accession No. 00897/09. Maj. D. C. McIver, 24. In India the British developed an important distinction between the 'martial' and 'non-martial races' that had an important influence on the recruiting strategies of the Indian Army. See D. Omissi, *The Sepoys and the Raj: The Indian Army, 1860–1940* (London: Macmillan, 1994), 1–46.

Service in some overseas garrisons did have its compensations. Impecunious officers who could not afford the cost of living in a mess in Britain sought a posting to India or Egypt because the cost of living was much cheaper. In 1890 Frederick Ponsonby wanted a posting to India because he had lost money gambling and racing.[51] Once he arrived he found that 'Living on my pay, I could afford to keep two polo ponies, a pony cart, and two Indian servants, which in England would have been out of the question.'[52] In Britain a junior officer usually had a soldier servant, a batman, and, if he was a mounted officer, a groom. In India, his retinue of servants was likely to consist of a bearer, who was his personal servant and who looked after his clothes and bungalow, a *chokra*, who was a boy who was being trained to be a bearer, a water-carrier, and a cook. A married officer might have an even more lavish establishment. Lt.-Col. Harry Thwaytes, who served with the Dorset regiment in India between the wars, and his wife had ten servants 'and of course we lived in a higher standard than you would have done in England. One never thought of walking across the room to pour out one's own whiskey and soda, you clapped your hands or shouted out and somebody was there ...'.[53]

In India and Egypt the cost of living was so low that even private soldiers could afford servants to do the menial tasks that they had to do themselves in Britain. Native sweepers cleaned their rooms and latrines, and native cooks, under the supervision of British soldier-cooks, prepared their food. Early in the morning the *nappy* (barber) shaved men in bed before reveille. *Dhobis* (washermen) did their washing and every section had a boy who cleaned boots, buttons, and buckles.[54] Food was so cheap that the rank and file could supplement their official rations with locally bought produce, although locally produced meat was often tough.[55] Provided they did not mind the heat and distance from home, 'Life in [a] Barrack Room', in India before 1914, 'was a pleasant business. Our Parades were not too arduous, except when we went on manoeuvres or on battalion exercises, and in the main, life passed like a dream of roses compared with soldiering at home.'[56]

To an outsider much of the daily activity of a unit in barracks must have seemed purposeless because it was apparently far removed from the main function of an army, preparing to fight. That was not so. What set an army apart from an armed mob was its sense of discipline, and unit routines were organized so that soldiers never forgot that they were men

[51] Ponsonby, *Recollections of Three Reigns*, 8–9.   [52] Ibid. 8–10.

[53] IWMSA. Accession No. 000917/07. Lt.-Col. H. D. Thwaytes, reels 1–2; IWMSA. Accession No. 000938/05. Lt.-Col. E. G. Hollist, 9.

[54] Richards, *Old-Soldier Sahib*, 192–3; IWMSA. Accession No. 4935/05. Maj. E. S. Humphries, 14–15; IWMSA. Accession No. 004611/03. Sgt. F. T. Suter, reel 2.

[55] RNRM. NMS RM 5053. Memoirs of L/Cpl. C. Mates, 5 Mar. 1889.

[56] IWMSA. Accession No. 4935/05. Maj. E. S. Humphries, 16.

under discipline. Units consisted of hundreds of mostly young, unmarried men living in close proximity to each other. Some regulations were essential to ensure harmony. A cursory reading of regimental standing orders might suggest that officers regarded their men as akin to children who had to be disciplined if they misbehaved, who would misbehave if they were left unsupervised, and who lacked any basic commitment to thrift, honesty, and cleanliness, so that these qualities had to be impressed upon them by constant inspections.[57] Colonel M. Gossett, who commanded 1/Dorset Regiment from 1887 to 1891, believed that 'With all his good qualities, tommy in peace time is a very helpless and careless man as regards his own good, and has in many cases to be treated like a child. He comes of a thriftless class, and, while he accepts everything that is done for him, he does but very little for himself.'[58]

COs like Gossett enforced whole books of regulations with exacting accuracy because they were concerned to ensure that their unit functioned effectively in action. They believed that if men learned to keep themselves and their weapons and equipment clean in barracks, they would do the same in the field, and if that happened, casualties from sickness and jammed weapons would be minimized.[59] They also shared the obsession of the late Victorian middle classes with cleanliness. They knew at first hand the often devastating effects that disease could have on a unit. Typical was the experience of 1/Connaught Rangers, stationed at Moltan in India. In 1882 they were struck by 'a severe epidemic of fever and ague' and out of a ration strength of about 800, they recorded a daily sickness rate for some time of 300 men.[60] 'It is a fact', noted the author of the *Manual of Elementary Military Hygiene 1912*, 'not always recognized that the risks which are run on service are almost invariably far greater from disease than from the enemy's bullets.'[61] Late nineteenth-century medical science, with its discovery of germs and microbes, helped to create a real undercurrent of unease about the dangers of communal living. Practical experience taught regimental officers that cleanliness and efficiency went hand in hand in barracks and in the field and it was their duty to promote both.[62]

---

[57] Sheffield, *Leadership in the Trenches*, 8.   [58] Gossett, 'Battalion Command', 472–3.
[59] Lt.-Gen. Sir B. Horrocks, *A Full Life* (London: Collins, 1960), 77.
[60] NAM 6005–60. Records of the 88th Regiment (Connaght Rangers), July 1882.
[61] War Office, *Manual of Elementary Military Hygiene 1912* (London: War Office, 1912), 3.
[62] P. D. Curtain, *Death by Migration: Europe's Encounter with the Tropical World in the Nineteenth Century* (Cambridge: Cambridge University Press, 1989), *passim*; D. Anderson, *Colonizing the Body: State Medicine and Epidemic Disease in Nineteenth-Century India* (Berkeley: University of California Press, 1993), 61–98; War Office, *Manual of Elementary Military Hygiene 1912*, 4; War Office, *Handbook of Military Hygiene 1943* (London: War Office, 1943), 4–5; L. A. Sawchuk, S. D. A. Burke, and J. Padiak, 'A Matter of Privilege: Infant Mortality in the Garrison Town of Gibraltar, 1870–1899', *Journal of Family History*, 27 (2002), 399–429; Guha, 'Nutrition, Sanitation, Hygiene', 397–8.

The main problem confronting the regimental authorities was that the rhythms of garrison soldiering meant that for many hours of the day soldiers had too few military duties to keep them fully occupied. To a civilian, accustomed to the long working hours that characterized the experience of labour for the working classes, one of the most striking features of the daily life of a trained soldier was how little work he was required to do.[63] Boredom was an endemic problem, particularly for soldiers stationed in remote colonial garrisons with few amenities to amuse them. Posted to the Connaught Rangers then serving in India in 1884, one officer discovered that 'The life of the British soldier in the 'eighties was monotonous.'[64] The military authorities were understandably concerned that officers and men might do themselves harm, and so reduce their value to the army, if they relieved their boredom and filled their leisure hours with harmful recreations. As one former NCO remembered, 'there are three things that human beings, at any rate men, WILL indulge in, and no amount of restrictive laws will ever stop them—or can ever stop them. These three things are gambling, drinking, and fornicating.'[65]

There was ample evidence to justify their concerns. In 1860 the incidence of venereal disease in the army reached 369 cases per 1,000 men.[66] In 1868 there were no fewer than 10,966 courts martial for drunkenness, and many other offences were committed by men who, if they had been sober, would probably have not offended in the first place.[67] According to one battalion commander,

The vice of drunkeness may justly be looked on as the chief source of every crime, and consequent punishment, which occurs in a Regiment: it debases the mind, enervates the body, and by creating a want which a Soldiers' pay is not able to supply induces the commissioning of dishonest acts, and renders a man as contemptible in his character as he is from debility of body unfit for the profession of a Soldier.[68]

Significant events in the life of the unit, be it Christmas, or the occasion when it was posted to a new station, were invariably accompanied by heavy drinking and drunkenness.[69] Nor were officers immune from boredom and its related dangers. Stationed at Mhow in Central India during the hot season in 1879, one officer remembered that 'Barrack life in India at that time was apt to cause boredom. A good part of the afternoon was spent in sleep. Card games and gambling instincts also

[63] PP (1867), XV. C. 3752. *Report of commissioners appointed to inquire into the recruiting for the army*, QQ. 887–902.
[64] General Sir G. de S. Barrow, *The Fire of Life* (London: Hutchinson, 1941), 7.
[65] Fraser, *Sixty Years in Uniform*, 149; Daniell, 'Discipline', 320.
[66] Skelley, *The Victorian Army*, 53–5.
[67] PP (1881), LVIII. C. 3083. *General Annual Return for the British Army for the Year 1880*, 44.
[68] Spencer, *Standing Orders of the 44th or East Essex Regiment*, 29.
[69] RNRM. NMS RM 5053. Memoirs of L/Cpl. C. Mates, 1883–96.

had a fine opportunity for being developed', so much so in his case that he could not meet his debts and had to leave the regiment.[70]

In 1863 a Royal Commission on the Sanitary Condition of the Army in India concluded that the best way to improve the health and discipline of the troops was to wean soldiers away from drink, prostitution, and dissipation by providing them with a better diet and with opportunities for rational recreation such as reading rooms, educational classes, and organized games.[71] Some regiments had been trying to do this even before the Crimean War, although they received only sporadic assistance from the military authorities. In 1842, Parliament passed a Savings Bank Act. Regiments could now establish their own savings banks to encourage soldiers to save their surplus pay rather than drink it away.[72] If they wanted to drink, by the 1840s they were being encouraged to do it in the regiment's own wet canteen, where they could buy beer which they drank under the eyes of their own NCOs. A few units also acquired playing fields in the hope that organized games would absorb the men's surplus energies. The army appointed a handful of chaplains to look after the spiritual welfare of the troops and by the 1850s there were also about 150 garrison libraries, where soldiers could borrow books that in the main encouraged them to adopt sober and moral habits.[73]

All of these innovations were designed to give the regimental authorities a greater degree of control over the behaviour of the rank and file in their off-duty hours, and the pace and extent that they were introduced accelerated in the post-Crimean Army. At one extreme the military authorities and some regimental officers tried to encourage their men to forswear drink entirely. Some regiments had established their own temperance societies before the Crimean War. In 1881 the War Office gave official encouragement to their efforts when a committee recommended issuing medals to soldiers who avoided an entry for drunkenness in the regimental defaulters book for six and twelve years' service. They would be testimonies of the soldier's good character and would help him to secure a job in civilian life after his discharge.[74] In 1884 Lord Roberts, who believed that drink was one reason why many soldiers committed crimes, wrote to the Reverend J. G. Gregson, the secretary of the Soldiers' Total Abstinence Association, that 'I am quite convinced that all who

[70] J. Robson Scott, *My Life as Soldier and Sportsman* (London: Grant Richards, 1921), 67.

[71] R. Hess, '"A Healing Hegemony": Florence Nightingale, the British Army in India and a "Want of exercise"', *International Journal of the History of Sport*, 15 (1998), 1–17.

[72] H. Strachan, *Wellington's Legacy: The Reform of the British Army 1830–54* (Manchester: Manchester University Press, 1984), 65–8, 85–93; ERM. ER 15250. Sgt. W. H. Green MSS. Lt.-Col. H. R. Bowen to Company Commanders, Dec. 1928.

[73] M. D. Calabria, 'Florence Nightingale and the Libraries of the British Army', *Libraries and Culture*, 29 (1994), 367–88.

[74] PP (1881), XX. C. 2817. *Report of the Committee ...*, 17.

have the welfare of the soldier at heart, cannot do better than to sub-scribe to your association, and thus assist to promote discipline, content-ment and health in the ranks.'[75] In 1887 Roberts was instrumental in uniting the various denominational societies involved in temperance reform into a single body, the Army Temperance Association.[76]

But most senior officers knew they could never create a whole army of total abstainers. They therefore determined to try to regulate the con-sumption of alcohol by the rank and file and to provide alternative ways for them to spend their leisure. That might at least minimize the discip-linary problems caused by excessive alcohol consumption. 'What is wanted', Roberts affirmed in 1886, 'is a building sufficiently large to include the canteen, recreation-room, and coffee-shop, and to admit of the greater number of the men being able to spend their evenings in a respectable and rational manner.' They did this by establishing in every unit and garrison a regimental or garrison institute. Their object was to supply the soldier with almost everything he required, at moderate prices, to provide for his recreation and amusement, and to do it under the supervision of his military superiors in the hope that the number of men falling foul of the army's disciplinary code would be reduced.[77]

Regimental and garrison institutes were divided into four parts. They consisted of a wet canteen that sold beer, but not spirits, and where NCOs kept a careful watch on the men's conduct; a refreshment room or coffee shop that sold non-alcoholic beverages and food, a shop that sold groceries and other articles, and a recreation room where a soldier 'writes letters, reads papers, and where amusements can be provided calculated to keep soldiers in barracks and away from the temptations of the public-houses outside'.[78] When the suggestion was mooted in 1885 that soldiers be forbidden to play cards in the recreation room on Sundays, the CO of 1/Suffolks riposted: 'The soldiers being for the most part uneducated, I do not see that his playing cards or other games on a Sunday in the recreation room interferes with any one or with discipline, and he certainly might be more harmfully employed.'[79]

Each institute was regulated by the CO. Profits were redistributed to support games and sports in its parent unit.[80] However, the standard of

[75] Roberts, *Roberts in India*, 300.

[76] Ibid. 376–7; S. Wood, 'Temperance and its Rewards in the British Army', in M. Harding (ed.), *The Victorian Soldier: Studies in the History of the British Army 1816–1914* (London: National Army Museum, 1993), 86–96.

[77] Roberts, *Roberts in India*, 366–7, 399–400.

[78] PP (1903), X. Cd. 1424. *Report of the committee appointed to consider the existing conditions under which canteens and regimental institutes are conducted*, 1.

[79] SRO. GB 554/B13/4. Lt.-Col. H. P. Pearson, to Adjutant General, India, 14 Jan. 1885.

[80] War Office, *QR ... 1892*, 365–6; Goodenough and Dalton, *The Army Book of the British Empire*, 164.

service and the goods on offer frequently left something to be desired. In the late nineteenth century accommodation was often cramped.[81] In most wet canteens patrons could drink but they could not play games or buy food.[82] Some men suspected, unjustly, that officers siphoned off profits from the canteen for their own purposes, or, with more justice, that canteen managers swindled them by watering the beer. The goods on sale in the grocery shop were often shoddy and more expensive than in nearby civilian shops, and the refreshment room often lacked such basic facilities as cups with handles.[83] Whilst some institutes, such as the Colchester Garrison Institute that was reformed by Sir Evelyn Wood in the late 1880s, were so successful that they spoilt the trade of neighbouring pubs, a good many soldiers still preferred to seek their pleasures in nearby civilian pubs.[84] The reform of regimental and garrison institutes probably did help to reduce the incidence of drunkenness and drink-related crime. But it happened only slowly, and was part of a wider social trend that saw alcohol consumption in society at large decline markedly after reaching its peak in 1875–6.[85]

Institutes themselves could create quite different problems. They were managed by one of two systems. They were either under the direct supervision of a committee of officers and NCOs, or they were let out under contract to a commercial tenant, who remitted a proportion of his profits to the regiment.[86] Both systems were open to abuse. Under the regimental system inexperienced or careless officers sometimes allowed the caterer, a long service NCO, scope for peculation.[87] In order to avoid this, by 1913 most units had opted for the tenant system. But it was then discovered that one of the largest military canteen contractors, Liptons, who by 1910 had contracts with eighty-seven canteens in the UK, Malta, and Egypt, had created a business worth £5–600,000 annually by employing systematic bribery. Between 1904 and 1912 their illegal activities touched at least sixty-nine units, and involved nearly 150 military personnel. Bribes were given to Quarter-Masters, Warrant Officers, and NCOs to influence their COs against existing contractors and in favour of Liptons. In at least three instances there were suspicions that unit commanders themselves had

[81] PP (1903), X. Cd. 1494. *Minutes of Evidence* ..., Q. 1475, 3328.

[82] Ibid., Q. 3217, 3234.

[83] Wyndham, *The Queen's Service*, 101; PP (1903), X. Cd. 1494. *Minutes of Evidence*, QQ. 789, 1260.

[84] Richards, *Old-Soldier Sahib*, 25–6; PP (1903), X. Cd. 1494. *Minutes of Evidence*, Q. 3002.

[85] D. J. Oddy, 'Food, Drink and Nutrition', in F. M. L. Thompson (ed.), *The Cambridge Social History of Britain* (Cambridge: Cambridge University Press, 1990), ii. 265–6.

[86] PRO WO 32/8702. Change in system of canteen management. War Office, Rules for the management of the Refreshment Branches of Regimental Institutes, 22 June 1903.

[87] Wyndham, *The Queen's Service*, 102; SRO. GB 554/B13/4. 1/Suffolks. CO's letter and memoranda book, 1883–1903. E. Wood to GOC Malta, 14 Oct. 1897; PP (1903), X. Cd. 1424. *Report of the committee*, p. viii.

received bribes ranging from £100 to £300. In April 1914, seventeen defendants (nine soldiers and eight civilians) were committed for trial, a former CO of 2/KOYLI was found guilty of accepting bribes and imprisoned, and several civilians were fined.[88] To avoid further such scandals, in 1921 the Army Council handed the management of canteen facilities to the Navy, Army, and Air Force Institutes. [89]

In 1861 nearly a third of all hospital admissions at Aldershot were related to venereal disease. It was evidence like this that persuaded Parliament in 1864, 1866, and 1869 to pass the Contagious Diseases Acts, which gave police the powers to inspect women suspected of being prostitutes in garrison towns and to detain them for compulsory medical treatment, or deport them. In 1868 similar legislation was applied in India.[90] However, the Acts encountered powerful opposition from civilian purity campaigners and feminists in Britain, who objected to the double standard enshrined in the Acts. Some of the rank and file in India referred to them derisively as 'the Exeter Hall "Shrieking Sisterhood"', but their opposition forced governments in Britain to abandon the legislation and in India temporarily to suspend it, although it was reintroduced at the end of the century.[91]

Given the fact that regulations forbad most soldiers to marry, the problem was unlikely to disappear. For many young soldiers their first sexual experience was an inevitable rite of passage to manhood.[92] Some senior officers, steeped in Christianity and the spartan ethos of public schools, deplored regulated prostitution. Others regretted it, but believed that it was the most effective way of reducing manpower losses from sexually transmitted diseases.[93] Medical officers frightened some soldiers into avoiding brothels by their lurid lectures on the dangers of venereal disease.[94] But many regiments overseas organized, or at least tolerated, licensed prostitution. At Agra in the late 1890s prostitutes who produced a 'clear certificate from their last place of residence' were given a list of bungalows where they could carry on their trade.[95] Other regiments that acted similarly included 2/Royal Welch Fusiliers at Schwebo in Burma in 1907, 2/Essex in Turkey in 1922 and at Khartoum in 1936, the 2/South

---

[88] PRO WO 32/5497. Report by Mr Archibald Read on bribery and other irregularities in connection with canteen contracts, 13 Nov. 1913; *The Times*, 28 May 1914.

[89] Jeffrey, 'The Post-war Army', 225.

[90] Harrison, *Public Health in British India*, 72–6.

[91] J. R. Walkowitz, *Prostitution and Victorian Society: Women, Class and the State* (Cambridge: Cambridge University Press, 1980); Fraser, *Sixty Years in Uniform*, 147.

[92] Maitland, *Hussar of the Line*, 94.

[93] Harrison, 'Medicine and the Management of Modern Warfare', 391.

[94] ERO. T/G 266/1. W. G. Green, The well travelled life of a Great Baddow Man, 32.

[95] NAM 8210–13. Warrant Officer I. W. H. Davies, Ts. Memoirs.

Lancashire Regiment at Quetta in 1937, and 1/Bedfordshire and Hertfordshire Regiment in Syria in 1941.[96] Where regulated brothels did not exist, the troops made their own arrangements, and rates of venereal disease rose sharply.[97]

Regulating access to drink and prostitutes were only two means adopted by regimental authorities to wean the rank and file away from potentially harmful pursuits. The regimental authorities also tried to provide them with alternative ways of spending their leisure time, and the most important of these was organized sports. Team games, and in the case of more wealthy officers, field sports such as fox hunting, polo, and shooting wild game, were deliberately employed as a way of luring officers and other ranks away from more harmful leisure activities. Team games were also deemed to foster regimental *esprit de corps* and leadership.[98] In 1907 Captain C. E. Kinahan of 1/Royal Irish Fusiliers contrasted two different types of soldier. On the one hand there were those men who, having finished their day's work at 3 p.m., spent the rest of the afternoon asleep on their beds, had tea, and then went into town, where they frequented pubs, got into trouble, and brought discredit on themselves and on their regiment. But

Now see the other side of the picture, where games are arranged for all. Instead of going to bed in the afternoon the man goes out and plays a game in the open air, comes back to tea and feels healthily tired, goes over to the reading room and reads or plays draughts with a chum, perhaps before going to bed spends some money on supper, which, with the 'tunic brigade', would have been spent on drink and disease traps. Compare the health and subsequent efficiency of this man with the tunic brigade.[99]

Junior officers were just as likely to get into trouble if they had too much time on their hands, so two years later, the Inspector-General of Cavalry, Douglas Haig, thought that everything possible should be done to encourage cavalry subalterns with private means to hunt and play polo. These sports absorbed their surplus energies and trained them for war and were infinitely to be preferred to 'buying expensive motor cars and similar luxuries which have precisely the opposite tendency'.[100]

[96] ERM. 15248.1/2. Sgt. W. H. Green MSS. Proforma to accompany every man sent to the D.A.P.M. for identification of the infected woman, 13 Apr. 1922; Bedfordshire Record Office. X550/15/31. Regimental Association. B. R. Thomas to Lt.-Col. John Barrow, 12 June 1987.

[97] IWMSA. Accession No. 000780/05. H. L. Horsfield, 17; Sir Neville Macready, *Annals of an Active Life* (London: Hutchinson, 1924), i. 65–6.

[98] Anon., *The Standing Orders of the 2nd Battalion 22nd (Cheshire) Regiment*, 22; IWMSA. Accession No. 4405/9. Lt.-Col. R. C. Glanville, 50.

[99] Capt. C. E. Kinahan, 'The Need of Games in the Army: How they should be Organised', '*Faugh-a-Ballagh*'. *The Regimental Gazette of the 87th Royal Irish Fusiliers*, 6 (Jan. 1907).

[100] PRO WO 279/30. Cavalry Divisional Training, 1909, 6 Oct. 1909. For other senior officers expressing similar sentiments, see PRO WO 163/26. 281 meeting of the Army Council,

Regimental officers hoped that by getting men out of the wet canteens, beer halls, and brothels and into the gym and playing fields they would improve their minds, morale, morals, and fighting capabilities.[101] 'Manly games', the *Cavalry Training* manual insisted in 1912, 'have a great effect on the military spirit, especially if they are arranged so that all ranks generally, and not only selected teams, take part.'[102] Participating in team games and country sports also gave officers the opportunity to create networks of contacts that helped them to integrate into the local community where they were stationed. By hunting with the West Meath fox hunt in 1882, the officers of 1/Northumberland Fusiliers were able to mix with 'all the *elite* of the country'.[103] An aptitude for games and sports could also help an officer to gain approval from his comrades. When H. C. H. Hudson joined the 11th Hussars as a 2/Lieutenant in 1911 he was already 25 years old and, as a university graduate, his commission was backdated, so he immediately found himself senior to several other subalterns. This might have caused much jealousy, but he quickly gained acceptance because of his enthusiasm for hunting, polo, and steeplechasing.[104]

Games and field sports not only occupied time and energies that might otherwise have been spent in more harmful pursuits. They also prepared soldiers for war. After 1880 the army's tactical doctrine placed a much greater emphasis than hitherto on mobility, scouting, and open order tactics. This transformation required fitter and more nimble soldiers, the very qualities that sports and games developed. The 1932 edition of *Infantry Training* explained that

Fighting spirit, discipline, esprit de corps, and mobility are bound up with physical fitness. [Emphasis in original]

The efficient fighting man requires a sound mind in a fit body. For this the physical exercise of drill and physical training are most valuable for developing quickness of mind and eye, but are not by themselves sufficient. Fitness of body and contentment of mind come more readily in the free atmosphere of games. The platoon commander should organise in the afternoon football, cricket, boxing, and cross-country running, especially in competition with other platoons, and take part in them himself. The men will respond wholeheartedly, and will carry the spirit of their games into their work. A platoon which plays

---

2 June 1921; Maj.-Gen. C. H. Miller, *History of the 13th/18th Royal Hussars (Queen Mary's Own) 1922–1947* (London: Chisman, Bradshaw Ltd., 1949), 19.

[101] J. D. Campbell, '"Training for sport is training for war": Sport and the Transformation of the British Army, 1860–1914', *International Journal of the History of Sport*, 17 (2000), 27–58.

[102] General Staff, *Cavalry Training 1912*, 16.

[103] *St George's Gazette*, 4 (30 Apr. 1883).

[104] Anon., 'Obituary notice of Lieutenant Colonel H. C. H. Hudson', *Eleventh Hussars Journal*, 13 (1929).

football, runs, and boxes, will be qualified to meet and overcome the stress and strain of battle and of long marches.[105]

In 1958 a Ministry of Defence committee justified spending public money on providing sporting facilities on the grounds that they encouraged recruiting and that sports called for 'fortitude, rapid decisions and the ability to take calculated risks. These are very valuable Service qualities.'[106]

Which games and sports officers played depended in part on the length of their purse. Although they might indulge in some rough shooting, officers without considerable private means were largely confined to playing team games alongside their men. The officers of 2/King's Regiment were not rich and when they were stationed at Colchester in the mid-1890s they played cricket, rugby, association football, tennis, racquets, and hockey.[107] Wealthier officers could afford to indulge in more expensive pastimes, such as hunting, polo, or in India, pig-sticking. Some regiments and corps pursued particular sports to raise their status in the eyes of their comrades. In 1920, for example, the RASC began to hold its own annual race meeting, although *The Times*'s racing correspondent was inclined to be dismissive of it, deciding that 'it really does not amount to very much'.[108]

Field sports enthusiasts claimed that they were character forming because they required their participants to put themselves at some physical risk and demonstrate their stamina, fitness, courage, and skill with horse or firearms.[109] Officers who could afford to indulge in them insisted that hunting, on horseback, or steeplechasing were the ultimate manly pastimes. In 5/Inniskilling Dragoon Guards in the 1930s

It was, also, understood that every officer must risk his neck in some sport or other, and these sports were hard and competitive. Anyone who hunted seriously—as we all did—or competed on a horse, found himself having to make quick decisions which only he could make, to assess rapidly the best way across a piece of country, and to get used to hard knocks and unpleasant accidents.[110]

And deaths did occur. The 14/20th Hussars lost one officer killed in a steeplechase in 1929 and two more killed playing polo in 1935 and 1937.[111]

[105] General Staff, *Infantry Training, 1932*, 13–14.
[106] PRO DEFE 7/1217/MISC/P(58)4. Ministry of Defence, Amenities in the forces. Report of a working party, 29 Apr. 1958.
[107] Sir C. Harington, *Tim Harington Looks Back* (London: John Murray, 1940), 12.
[108] *The Times*, 29 Jan. 1920 and 12 Apr. 1922.
[109] Capt. E. D. Miller, *Modern Polo* (London: Hurst and Blackett, 1911), 79–81, 86–7, 294–5; Anon., 'The Army, the Officer and the Horse', *Cavalry Journal*, 27 (1937), 244–5.
[110] Blacker, *Monkey Business*, 27.
[111] Lt.-Col. L. B. Oatts, *Emperor's Chambermaids: The Story of the 14th/20th King's Hussars* (London: Lock, 1973), 423, 425.

Taking part in such activities on a frequent and regular basis also helped to teach soldiers that violence was a natural part of life.[112] According to one enthusiastic hunter, soldiers needed to cultivate a certain amount of ferocity and what he called 'preventable cruelty' and hunting allowed them to do so.[113] This in turn undoubtedly coloured their attitudes towards fighting and war. Even a cursory glance through the army's doctrinal publications illustrates the propensity for officers to use the same language to describe games, field sports, and war. In 1916 the GOC of 17th Division, Maj.-Gen. Philip Robertson, likened the war to a 'test cricket match in which the final result was inevitable; but the proceedings had lost all interest'.[114] When one gunner officer stumbled across a German soldier in a trench in August 1917 and shot him at very close range with his pistol he believed that it was 'The most exciting day I have had since I came out. It brackets with the first time I shot a rhino in East Africa.'[115] Before D-Day Montgomery spoke to large numbers of units about to go to France, and ended his perorations with an injunction right out of the field sports handbook: 'Good luck to each one of you. And good hunting on the mainland of Europe.'[116]

It is difficult to determine whether this propensity to mix sport and war made men better or worse soldiers. A junior officer serving in a British cavalry regiment in India in the 1930s believed that if a regiment had a reputation for being good at polo playing any small faults in its training were apt to be overlooked by inspecting officers. 'But the worst thing of all was to be a bad polo regiment and not efficient in the field—or not considered efficient in the field. We tried to be both and we have always been terribly professional about our soldiering.'[117] Skill at fox hunting did not automatically breed skill in tactics. This was inadvertently admitted in 1869 by the Earl of Cork and Orry. Addressing a banquet given by the officers of the Household Brigade he said, without any apparent trace of irony: 'He thought the hunting-field a good training-ground for soldiers, and any who had ever witnessed the straight way the late Lord Cardigan was in the habit of going over Leicestershire country could not have been surprised at his performance in the famous Balaklava charge.'[118]

[112] J. M. MacKenzie, *The Empire of Nature: Hunting Conservation and British Imperialism* (Manchester: Manchester University Press, 1988), 10–13, 133–4; P. Horn, *Pleasures and Pastimes in Victorian Britain* (Stroud, Glos: Sutton, 1999), 96–9.

[113] Montgomery-Cuninghame, *Dusty Measure*, 68.

[114] Col. W. N. Nicholson, *Behind the Lines: An Account of Administrative Staffwork in the British Army, 1914–1918* (London: The Strong Oak Press & Tom Donovan, 1939), 127.

[115] The Master of Belhaven, *The War Diary of the Master of Belhaven 1914–18* (Barnsley: Wharncliffe Publishing Ltd, 1990), 374.

[116] Montgomery, *Memoirs*, 244.

[117] IWMSA. Accession No. 00962/04. Lt.-Col. T. W. Nickalls, 31.

[118] Anon., 'Her Majesty's Staghounds: The Royal Hunt—the Farmers Banquet', *The Journal of the Household Brigade for the Year 1869* (London, 1869), 87.

In some men familiarity with the apprehension that field sports could breed did not make them less apprehensive about the dangers of the battlefield. In August 1914, as his battalion mobilized, Captain James Jack wrote in his diary: 'All ranks are in high fettle at the prospect of active service. But hating bloodshed as I do, and having had a hard if not dangerous fifteen months in the South African War (1901–02), together with many racing, hunting and polo accidents, I personally loathe the outlook.'[119]

Nor was it necessarily the case that a commitment to sports and games meant that officers shunned more cerebral pursuits. The 8/Royal Irish Hussars were a wealthy regiment. In 1934, when they were earmarked for service in Egypt and India, the officers of the regiment were able to raise enough money to purchase no fewer than 120 high-class polo ponies. However, their love of field sports was not all-consuming. Amongst the officers of the regiment one was a keen follower of the ballet. Another spent parts of his leave in Syria and in the Bodleian library at Oxford and the British Museum Reading Room writing an Oxford University B.Litt. on the campaigns of Saladin. These were the first steps on a career that was to take him to promotion to General and to the Principalship of King's College London. 'From birds to music, wine, pictures; you were allowed your interest.'[120]

The regimental authorities also used team games to breed *esprit de corps* and to cement good inter-rank relations.[121] By the 1880s about fifteen organized sports were played in the army. They included soccer, rugby, cricket, hockey, athletics, billiards, rackets, water polo, and boxing. By the early 1890s most regiments had a regimental sports day, usually the anniversary of one of its more famous battles. Regiments could create a distinct sporting identity for themselves by concentrating on being good at one particular sport. The Leicesters, Welch, and Duke of Wellington's Regiment were pre-eminent at rugby, the Royal Fusiliers and the Queens at cricket, the Duke of Cornwall's Light Infantry at cross-country running, and the Durham Light Infantry was one of the few infantry regiments that could take on the cavalry at polo and expect to win.[122] In the 1930s 2/RTC was noted for its prowess in swimming and boxing, the 3/RTC was known as the 'Athletics Regiment', the 4/RTC specialized in soccer, and 'the 5th Battalion was always known as the "Rugby Union Regiment"'.[123] Winning games against other regiments

[119] Brigadier-General J. L. Jack, *General Jack's Diary 1914–1918: The Trench Diary of Brigadier-General J. L. Jack, DSO*, ed. J. Terraine (London: Cassell, 2000), 22.

[120] IWMSA. Accession No. 004527/06. Gen. Sir J. Hackett, 4.

[121] ERM. ERB 397. Anon., *Standing Orders of the 56th (West Essex) Regiment* (Bombay: Education Society Press, Byculla, 1874), 25; Daniell, 'Discipline', 320–1.

[122] Maj.-Gen. D. Tyacke, letter to the author, 8 Sept. 2002; Poett, *Pure Poett*, 12–13, 15.

[123] IWMSA. Accession No. 000833/04. Col. W. B. Blain, 13; IWMSA. Accession No. 000822/07. Lt.-Col. A. C. Jackson, 10.

became a matter of collective pride. In the early 1930s in the 1/King's Royal Rifle Corps 'If the battalion team lost at all there was a great gloom about it, and if they won everybody was happy and cheering like mad.'[124] Sport thus became yet another way in which regiments established and maintained their separate identities.

Some officers glorified in the belief that sport brought officers and other ranks together on a basis of common interest.[125] In the 1920s junior officers of 2/King's Own Scottish Borderers were told that after parades their first duty was to play sports and games with their men, and only when they had done so were they free to indulge in their own pastimes.[126] But it was an ideal that was not universally pursued. When 2/Lt. G. W. Nightingale joined his regiment in 1911, he found that he was one of only two officers who regularly played team games with his men.[127]

Furthermore, particular sports were divided, sometimes quite sharply, between officers and other ranks. Soccer was the favorite game of the rank and file. Its rules were first codified at the public schools, and the game was then brought into the army by public school educated officers.[128] But very soon, when players were chosen on merit, few officers managed to gain a place in their unit team. In 1883 the soccer team of 1/Royal Irish Fusiliers contained only two officers.[129] A decade later the soccer team of 1/HLI did not have a single officer.[130] If an officer was good enough to play on his merits, he gained great kudos in the eyes of his men. When 2/Lt. S. J. Martin proved himself to be an expert soccer player who was good enough to gain a place in the 1/Hampshire Regiment's team in the mid-1920s, he 'was made from then on as far as the troops were concerned, to see an officer turn out and play football because whilst they would compulsorily take part in most sport with the men, to see one in the regimental team was really something'.[131] Most regimental cricket teams, on the other hand, contained a disproportionate number of officers. Of the fourteen cricketers who represented the Northumberland Fusiliers in Ireland in 1882, seven were officers, three were sergeants, one was a corporal, and only four were privates.[132] Similarly, in 1905 the cricket team of 2/Cameron Highlanders contained two privates, but five officers.[133]

[124] IWMSA. Accession No. 004299/04. J. E. Heyes, reel 1.
[125] Gough, *Soldiering On*, 15.
[126] IWMSA. Accession No. 004464/04. F. M. V. Tregar, reel 3.
[127] PRO 30/71/1. Nightingale to his mother, 25 Jan. 1911.
[128] SRO GB 554/W/1. MS copy of the 1st number of *Suffolk Regiment Gazette*, 10 Dec. 1863.
[129] 'Faugh-a-Ballagh'. *The Regimental Gazette of the 87th & 89th Royal Irish Fusiliers*, 1 (31 Mar. 1883).
[130] *Highland Light Infantry Chronicle*, 1 (Jan 1893).
[131] IWMSA. Accession No. 004514/04. Maj. W. Parrott, 14.
[132] *St George's Gazette*, 1 (31 Jan. 1883)
[133] *The 79th News*, Jan. 1905.

As spectators, regimental sporting events gave other ranks the temporary licence to criticize their seniors, as 2/Lt. J. H. Finch found when he joined his platoon football team in 1940. The spectators 'gave me a raspberry whenever I touched the ball'.[134] But too much should not be made of the fact that the sports field provided one of the few places where officers, NCOs, and other ranks could stand in positions of equality. Rank and status were never entirely abandoned. The senior officer in any team was invariably the captain, and spectators did not always intermingle freely. When 11/Hussars held their regimental sports day in August 1912, officers, sergeants, and private soldiers each watched them from their own separate enclosures.[135]

By the inter-war period sports had become highly organized at regimental level. Units had a sports officer who was responsible for overseeing the organization of all team games, and particular officers were responsible for organizing teams for different games. During the individual training season in the winter all NCOs and other ranks were expected to take part in some form of organized games or athletics competitions several times a week. Most regiments held tournaments at company level.[136] In 1918 the Army Council established the Army Sport Control Board to organize sports and games throughout the army and to provide capital for sports facilities. The Board provided permanent fixtures like playing fields and goal posts, but units continued to have to raise subscriptions for sports kit and equipment.[137] The military authorities hoped that their sponsorship of army sports and games would inculcate into the rank and file modes of behaviour that were akin to the ethics of amateurism that regular officers had imbibed at their public schools. According to the Board,

Our definition of a Sportsman is one who—

(1) Plays the game for the game's sake.
(2) Plays for his side and not for himself.
(3) Is a good winner and a good loser, i.e., modest in victory and generous in defeat.
(4) Accepts all decisions in a proper spirit.
(5) Is chivalrous towards a defeated opponent.
(6) Is unselfish and always ready to help others to become proficient.

---

[134] IMM 90/6/1. Maj. J. H. Finch MSS, *The wanderings of a transport officer before Dunkirk, 1939–1940*; J. G. Fuller, *Troop Morale and Popular Culture in the British and Dominion Armies 1914–1918* (Oxford: Oxford University Press, 1990), 90–4; Maitland, *Hussar of the Line*, 34.

[135] NAM 7003/1. Scrapbook, Officer's Mess, 27th Foot, 2nd Battalion Royal Inniskilling Fusiliers, Aug. 1912.

[136] Anon., *The Standing Orders ... The Royal Warwickshire Regiment*, 68–70; IWMSA. Accession No. 000938/05. Lt.-Col. E. G. Hollist, 16.

[137] PRO WO 33/976. Report of the proceedings at a conference in connection with the Territorial Force recreation scheme, 22 Nov. 1920.

Service games are modelled on the above. If we keep these six points always before us, we shall not go far wrong.[138]

But their attempts to colonize sport and to inculcate the rank and file with the ideology of 'sportsmanship' largely failed.[139] The rank and file imparted quite different meanings to their games. For them sport usually embodied older ideals of masculine toughness and rudeness that pre-dated the muscular Christianity of their officers. Fairness and good manners were far less important to them than winning.[140]

In the late nineteenth century boredom was not the only reason why soldiers drank too much alcohol. The other reason was that they were often hungry.[141] The government ration provided for private soldiers consisted of 12 ounces of beef or mutton (including bone), and a pound of bread. After 1874 this was issued free of charge.[142] British soldiers ate more meat than any of their continental counterparts, and probably more than most of their civilian contemporaries, but its quality was often poor.[143] The sergeants' mess and married families usually received the best cuts, and the rank and file had to make do with the remainder. After deducting the bone content of the ration, and after shrinkage during cooking, each man only received about half of the official ration. Ration bread was also widely disliked. It was badly baked, quickly went stale, and a great deal was thrown away. Until 1898, when groceries were issued free of charge, 3d. a day was deducted from the pay of each soldier, pooled on a company basis, and used to pay for tea, coffee, salt, sugar, potatoes, flour, jam, cheese, and, if the funds were used carefully, small quantities of 'luxuries such as bacon, eggs, and fish'. These deductions were a cause of resentment to the troops, because recruiting literature implied, although it did not specify, that all rations would be issued free of charge.[144] The quality of cooking varied between units.[145]

---

[138] Army Sports Control Board, *Games and Sports in the Army 1943–44* (London: War Office, 1944), 24.

[139] J. A. Mangan, '"Muscular, militaristic and manly": The British Middle Class Hero as Moral Messenger', *International Journal of the History of Sport*, 13 (1996), 30–44.

[140] R. Holt, *Sport and the British: A Modern History* (Oxford: Oxford University Press, 1989), 74–202.

[141] Capt. C. E. D. Telfer, 'Discipline: Its Importance to an Armed Force and the Best Means of Promoting and Maintaining It', *Journal of the Royal United Services Institute*, 33 (1889), 362–3.

[142] NAM 94-5-181. Sgt.-Major J. White, Ts Memoirs, Reminiscences of my Army life.

[143] D. J. Oddy, 'Working Class Diets in Late Nineteenth Century Britain', *Economic History Review*, 23 (1970), 318.

[144] Wyndham, *The Queen's Service*, 31; War Office, *QR ... 1892*, 190; Goodenough and Dalton, *The Army Book*, 150.

[145] D. Smurthwaite, 'A Recipe for Discontent: The Victorian Soldier's Cuisine', in M. Harding (ed.), *The Victorian Soldier: Studies in the History of the British Army 1816–1914* (London: National Army Museum, 1993), 74–85.

In a typical unit in the early 1890s the rank and file were served three meals a day. At 8 a.m. breakfast consisted of tea or coffee and bread, plus any extras the men purchased for themselves. Dinner was served at 1 p.m. and consisted of combinations such as pea soup and meat, meat pies and potatoes or cabbage, stewed meat and potatoes, or curry, rice, and potatoes. Finally, tea, consisting of tea and bread, and any extras the men purchased for themselves, was served at 4 p.m.[146] Some soldiers were content with what they ate, but many were not.[147] Food could be monotonous because cookhouses were equipped only to bake or steam meat and vegetables. In 1899 one private likened his meat ration to 'leather, nobody can eat it scarcely'.[148] In 1908 an official report estimated that the official ration provided only enough calories for a man doing a moderate amount of physical work.[149] That meant, according to Percy Snelling, who enlisted in 1906, that 'From the time I was a trooper till I was a sergeant in the sergeants' mess, I never got up from a meal that I couldn't have eaten as much again, except when I was on furlough, at home.'[150]

Improvements happened, but they happened only slowly, and as they did occur, so they reduced the need soldiers felt to fill their bellies with beer. Sometimes the initiative for improvements came from the War Office, but on other occasions it was the work of individual COs. In 1889 a War Office committee recommended that regimental officers should receive training in meat inspection so they could ensure that the meat supplied to their men was of a proper standard and that ration bread should be baked with improved yeast and in 2lb loaves to make it more palatable.[151] Cooking was done under the direction of a sergeant cook, and after 1890 he was required to have a certificate from the School of Cookery at Aldershot. The 2i/c of each unit was usually given special responsibility for overseeing the preparation of the soldiers' food. In 1917 one such wrote: 'I dabble in dripping, and should know the capabilities of a cook-soldier for varying the diet of his company.'[152]

In the 1880s individual COs began to take steps to bridge the long gap between tea and breakfast by providing their men with supper which could be supplied by reducing the often considerable wastage of

[146] PRO WO 33/49. Report of the committee appointed to enquire into the questions of the soldiers dietary, Q. 544; *Highland Light Infantry Chronicle*, 1 (Jan. 1892).

[147] ERM. Transcript of oral history interview, Harry John Staff.

[148] PRO WO 33/49. Report of the committee appointed to enquire into the questions of the soldiers dietary, Q. 1741.

[149] PRO WO 32/3207. Minute by QMG, 11 Jan. 1921.

[150] IWMSA. Accession No. 000314/12. Capt. P. Snelling, 12.

[151] PRO WO 33/49. Report of the committee appointed to enquire into the questions of the soldiers dietary, 15 May 1889.

[152] IWM Con Shelf and 95/21/1. Letters of Brigadier E. E. F. Baker. Baker to parents, 9 Aug. 1917.

government-issued rations.[153] By 1910 a War Office inquiry was struck by how much standards of messing differed between regiments: 'Where the system is satisfactory, it is, as a rule, due to the individual efforts of an officer who has made the study of soldiers' messing a hobby and has devoted much of his time to it.'[154] It recommended that the level in all units could be raised to the standards in the best if cookhouses were issued with the means to fry large quantities of food, and if pies and puddings were prepared in individual portions. This would reduce wastage and the savings used to provide a more varied diet within the existing budget.[155]

These recommendations were slowly put into practice, despite attempts by the Treasury in the early 1920s to save money by reducing the quantity and variety of rations issued.[156] Menus did become more varied. By 1927, for example, breakfast for privates in 2/Buffs consisted of tea, bacon and beans, bread, margarine and marmalade, with eggs on Sunday. There were still plenty of complaints about the quality of army cooking.[157] But the fact that canteen profits fell in the late 1920s, because troops had less need to supplement their rations with private purchases, suggests that regimental food had improved.[158] By 1944 US personnel who were attached to British units in the UK noted: 'Although their [i.e. British units'] ration lacks variety and quality such as we have, their preparation is superior and the food is served in an appetizing manner.'[159] By the mid-1950s recruits at Winston Barracks in Lanark, the depot of the Cameronians, each put on four and a half pounds in weight during their basic training.[160]

In the same way that units serving in the Empire were physically isolated from their host communities, so they also endured, or enjoyed, culinary isolation. Meals in India or Egypt differed little from the food served in the UK.[161] Soldiers demanded and received much the same food as they were accustomed to eat in Britain, although it was supplemented with the occasional dish of rice and curry.[162] In Egypt and India

---

[153] PRO WO 33/49. Report of the committee appointed to enquire into the questions of the soldiers dietary, 20 Dec. 1888; RNRM. R 65. Permanent Order book, 1st Battalion, 1831 to 1907, 22 and 29 Sept. 1888.

[154] PRO WO 32/4921. Report of the committee on system of messing, 4 Feb. 1910.

[155] Ibid.

[156] PRO WO 32/3207. Minute by QMG, 11 Jan. 1921; ERM. ER2285. Cpl. A. E. Cooper. AB 136. Information re Rations, etc. AO 300/1921. Daily entitlement, 1921.

[157] NAM 9404–436. Colonel A. M. Man, Ts. memoirs (1966).

[158] PRO WO 32/3932. Canteen Service. History and development of, 3 Dec. 1928.

[159] PRO WO 163/53/AC/G(44)19. Adjutant-General, Inter-attachment of British and American Army Personnel in the United Kingdom: 1944, 6 May 1944.

[160] Anon., *Handbook of the Cameronians (Scottish Rifles)* (Winston Barracks, Lanark: 1957), 41.

[161] PRO WO 33/49. Report of the committee appointed to enquire into the questions of the soldiers dietary, QQ. 15–19.

[162] IWMSA. Accession No. 00897/09. Maj. D. C. McIver, 42.

they were rarely served salad or fresh fruit because it was thought that they would spread disease. In Egypt beef was imported from Britain and kept in frozen store. Similarly, canteens imported beer from the UK rather than serve locally brewed ales, which were usually unpopular with their patrons.[163] A signaller who served in Egypt in the early 1930s remembered: 'The whole point about the food, the rations were universal throughout the Army. It didn't matter whether you were in India, Egypt, or in England. You had very, very little change in your actual menu.'[164]

The rank and file were not the only part of the regimental community whose lives were subject to regulation and surveillance to prevent them from getting into mischief or harming themselves. The same was true of both officers and NCOs. They were no more immune from the temptations of alcohol and women than were the men they led. In 1874, for example, the officers of 92/Foot and their guests became uproariously drunk when several officers filled a large silver salt cellar with spirits and drank the contents.[165] Some officers became addicted to alcohol. In 1895 the batman of a major in the York and Lancaster regiment was required to rouse his master at 6 a.m. with a glass of whisky and then to serve him breakfast, accompanied by a second glass.[166] Officers who were known to be heavy drinkers could have their promotion delayed or blocked.[167]

Separate messes for both officers and sergeants existed to restrain and regulate such behaviour and to sustain the formal hierarchy of the regiment. When an officer was on parade he addressed all of his seniors as 'Sir'. But when he entered the officers' mess he removed his sword and belt to signify that he was off-duty. In most regiments in order to emphasize the common identity of the officer corps, an officer addressed all other officers 'of whatever seniority in the regiment by his Christian name, except the colonel. You called him "Colonel". This was by way of emphasising the family nature of it.'[168] In 1947 a War Office committee concluded: 'We are convinced that the status of the officer has so important an influence on the discipline and efficiency of the Army that the restoration and maintenance of high mess standards must be accorded the highest priority.'[169]

[163] IWMSA. Accession No. 004524/05. L. H. Porter Harper, 16–17; IWMSA. Accession No. 000923/04. R. Clemens, reel 1.

[164] IWMSA. Accession No. 004473/04. Lt.-Col. E. G. Brice, 7.

[165] Hamilton, *Listening for the Drums*, 35–6.

[166] NAM 8210–13. Warrant Officer I. W. H. Davies, Ts. Memoirs.

[167] Bedfordshire Record Office. X550/6/76. Out letter book of Lt.-Col. Victor Russell, 2/5th Beds. Russell to Orlebar, 27 Mar. 1916.

[168] IWMSA. Accession No. 004527/06. Gen. Sir J. Hackett; Anon., *Durham Light Infantry Standing Orders* (Newcastle-upon-Tyne: J. & P. Beals Ltd, 1941), 13.

[169] PRO WO 32/12554. Committee on the future of officers' messes, 14 Aug. 1947.

Similarly, in the opinion of one Regimental Colonel, 'the Sergeants Mess is just as important as the Officers Mess—in fact more important in some ways since if the junior NCOs consider that belonging to the Sergeants Mess is a real privilege, they will all try the harder to reach the rank of sergeant.'[170] The sergeants agreed. To emphasize their superior status, they too held formal mess nights once each week. Members dressed for dinner in their own mess kit 'and', according to one RSM, 'that just kept us that little bit above the others and gave a boost to discipline again. These little things helped discipline.'[171]

Officers' and sergeants' messes resembled the gentlemen's clubs that burgeoned between 1870 and 1914. They largely excluded women and created a bachelors' ambiance by having smoking rooms, billiard rooms, card tables, and male servants. They were organized around a veneer of democracy in that mess meetings, chaired by the RSM in the case of the sergeants' mess and the Mess President, a senior officer below the CO, in the case of officers' messes, were held regularly to discuss catering and entertainments.[172] However, in practice their autonomy was limited by the power of the CO to veto behaviour that he deemed unacceptable. The RSM was responsible to the CO for the orderly conduct of the sergeants' mess and the mess accounts were regularly audited by a senior officer.[173] All food and drink had to be purchased from contractors approved by the CO. To inhibit excessive drinking the sergeant in charge of catering was required to keep an account of every drink consumed by each member of the mess, and the mess could not hold any collective entertainments without the CO's permission.[174]

Officers' and sergeants' messes also helped regiments to establish their own identity and place in the army's social pecking order by the lavishness or otherwise of their furniture and fittings and the quality of the food and wine they offered. In 1892 a subaltern serving with 1/Somerset Light Infantry at Gibraltar noted that in terms of the hospitality its mess offered 'we go in for being rather crack and are on much better terms with the 60th & 42nd than we are with the more "scug" 82nd.'[175] This

---

[170] NAM 8201–25. Field Marshal Sir G. Templer MSS. Templer to Lt.-Col. G. J. Hamilton, 7 Dec. 1954.

[171] IWMSA. Accession No. 00897/09. Maj. D. C. McIver, 48.

[172] SRO. GB 554/D2/1. Proceedings of [Officers] Mess meetings, 12th Regiment Depot, Bury St Edmunds, 6 Oct. 1888 to 5 Sept. 1930.

[173] Essex Regiment Museum. ERB 2.5. 1/Battalion Essex Regiment (44th Foot). Warrant Officers' and Sergeants' Mess Rules (Aldershot: Gale & Polden, 1926).

[174] War Office, QR ... 1892, 130, 185; War Office, QR ... 1955, 311–15.

[175] NAM 6412-143-4. Capt. F. Warre-Cornish MSS. Warre-Cornish to mother, 20 May 1892. Warre-Cornish's father was Vice-Provost of Eton. The Oxford English Dictionary defined 'scug' as Eton schoolboy slang for 'a boy who is not distinguished in person, in games, or social qualities. Positively, a boy of untidy, dirty, or ill-mannered habits; one whose sense of propriety

did not always meet with the approval of the military authorities, who believed that the high cost of messing in some regiments was a reason why the Regular Army was short of junior officers. Consequently they periodically attempted to restrain mess expenses.[176] But they also recognized that if gentlemen were compelled to live below their income, they might not serve at all, and so their injunctions were more honoured in the breach than in the observance.[177] The War Office provided furniture and billiard tables for the sergeants' messes, but plates, china, glass, and cutlery was provided by the members themselves. A sergeant who entered the mess of 2/Northumberland Fusiliers in 1879 described it as a 'very-well appointed club, and [where he] sit[s] down to dinner served at a well-appointed table.'[178]

Social life in both the officers' and sergeants' mess was organized according to an elaborate protocol. Behaviour likely to cause dissention, such as practical joking or gambling, was forbidden. Officers were 'required to preserve the same decorum in the Mess as they would in any gentleman's house', and the senior officer present 'will, without hesitation, put a stop to any conduct which is likely to interrupt for a moment the general harmony'.[179] Officers were not allowed to talk 'shop', and anyone who did so was likely to be rebuked.[180] Discussion of contentious subjects such as politics or religion was also forbidden, and 'ladies' names are not to be lightly used at the Mess table'.[181] Military and civilian guests could only be introduced into the mess according to strict rules.[182] Before 1914 most regiments held a formal dinner five nights each week and a regimental guest night on one night a week.[183] Even in the inter-war period officers wore mess kit on all but

is not fully developed.' The 42nd were the 1/Black Watch, the 60th were 2/King's Royal Rifle Corps, and the 82nd were 2/South Lancashire Regiment.

[176] SRO. GB 554/B13/4.CO's letter and memoranda book, 1883–1903. CO, 1/Suffolks to AAG, Meerut division, 8 Sept. 1884; PRO WO 32/8670. Report of committee on the deficiency of officers in the cavalry, 17 May 1905; War Office, KR ... 1912, 208.

[177] PRO WO 32/4927. Roberts to Secretary of State for War, 16 Apr. 1901.

[178] Fraser, Sixty Years in Uniform, 58.

[179] Anon., The Standing Orders of the King's Royal Rifle Corps, 14; Anon., The Standing Orders of the 2nd Battalion The Royal Warwickshire Regiment, 22; Anon., 5th Royal Inniskilling Dragoon Guards. Officers Mess Rules (Sennelager, Germany, no publisher, 1957), 3.

[180] Anon., Standing Orders of the 47th (The Lancashire Regiment) of Foot, 22; Anon., Standing Orders of the 1st Batt. "The Queen's Own", late 50th Regiment (Chatham, Gale & Polden, 1891), 1, 24.

[181] Anon., Rules of the Officers' Mess 1st Battalion South Staffordshire Regiment (Aldershot: Gale & Polden, 1924), 18; Anon., The Subaltern's Handbook of Useful Information (London: Gale & Polden: first published Apr. 1916; 3rd edn. Jan. 1918), 61–2; ERM. ERB 41. Anon., Officers' Mess Rules. 1st Battalion The Essex Regiment (44th/56th) (Depot. Archive Copy, 1955), 2, 5.

[182] Anon., Rules of the Officers' Mess 1st Battalion South Staffordshire Regiment, 8–11, 16, 18.

[183] IWMSA. Accession No. 000569/18. Col. U. Burke, reel 5.

two or three evenings each week; dinner was a parade and no officer could leave until all had finished.[184]

Both officers and NCOs had a collective obligation to uphold the decorum and dignity of their messes.[185] In 1876 the Standing Orders of 47/Foot insisted that 'The Sergeants' Mess is an institution highly conducive to the respectability and comfort of the Sergeants, who must feel that any irregularity or improper conduct therein would be an injury to it, and reflect discredit on all its members.'[186] Heavy drinking was no longer thought to be compatible with the status of a gentleman, although occasional collective lapses were permitted. The officers of one regiment in India in the 1930s decided that their guest nights were so boring that they required enlivening. Therefore, when they entertained a dozen officers from a newly arrived infantry regiment, after dinner they suggested that the officers of the two regiments should play a game of draughts using drinks (port and brandy) as pieces. 'And all I can remember is that the commanding officer of the visiting regiment went home with nothing on but his black bow tie. He was driven away.'[187] But if the mess secretary noticed that a particular officer's drinks bill was regularly excessive, he was obliged to report the fact to the CO.[188]

The purpose of these regulations was to socialize officers and NCOs in the modes of behaviour that the regimental authorities thought were appropriate to their rank. As the CO of 10/Hussars explained in 1902, young officers 'have to give way to the regiment, and do what the regiment really wishes, and a man very soon gets out of the disinclination to do what his regiment teaches him is the proper thing to do, and how to behave'.[189] Much the same happened in the sergeants' mess:

If you could follow the man's career from the time he enlists, and watch him, you could not make much of him if you are in contact with him constantly until he is a sergeant. He is a rough and ready man, because he has to be. When he comes to mess he gets a little bit better refinement, he has a tablecloth to have his meals on, and a glass to drink out of, and it makes a different man of him altogether.[190]

To outsiders a mess could resemble 'a sort of secret society, full of many mysterious rites and ceremonies, and full of pains and penalties for the

---

[184] ERM. Lt.-Col. H. C. N. Trollope, Take it or Leave it, 217; PRO WO 32/12554. Committee on the future of officers' messes, 14 Aug. 1947.

[185] ERM. ERB 41. *Officers' Mess Rules. 1st Battalion The Essex Regiment (44th/56th)*, 1.

[186] Anon., *The Standing Orders of the 47th (The Lancashire Regiment) of Foot*, 29; ERM. ERB 23. *2/Battalion Essex Regiment (The Pompadours). Sergeants Mess Rules* (Aldershot: Gale & Polden, 1931), 1–2.

[187] IWMSA. Accession No. 000946/05. Lt.-Col. R. L. V. ffrench Blake, 26.

[188] IWMSA. Accession No. 000569/18. Colonel U. B. Burke, reel 5.

[189] PP (1902), X. Cd. 983. *Minutes of evidence ...* Q. 1701.

[190] PP (1903), X. Cd. 1494. *Minutes of Evidence ...* QQ. 307, 312.

uninitiated'.[191] Newly commissioned officers were indeed nervous of committing a social solecism. 'We didn't know anything about how to behave and were terrified of dropping bricks through ignorance', one officer wrote about when he joined the 2/Rifle Brigade in 1916.[192] It was the job of the senior subaltern to instruct newcomers in the customs of the mess. Such behaviour did not represent some mindless obeisance to antiquity or an excuse to embarrass the uninitiated. They served the important function of giving every officer a sense that he belonged to a special and separate institution whose very existence was hallowed by tradition.[193]

Another way in which regiments established their separate identity, at least from civilian society, was by the way in which they virtually excluded women. The late Victorian army was a patriarchal society, and the military authorities preferred officers and other ranks to remain unmarried during their colour service. The regiment was their family, and they wanted officers and men who were free of other intimate ties so that they could devote themselves to its corporate good.[194] In return the regiment promised to provide them with the support network they would otherwise have received from their extended family. But the military authorities knew that it was impossible to enforce this ideal completely. Forbidding all contact with women was impossible and so women had to be incorporated into regimental life without hampering military efficiency and discipline.

All ranks had to seek their CO's permission before marrying. Before 1914 young officers were actively discouraged from marrying before they reached the age of 30. Given their slender means many could not afford to do so in any case before they were promoted to Captain. After 1918 the War Office granted officers over the age of 30 a marriage allowance, and although they could marry below that age, they would not receive the allowance.[195] Individual regiments also made their own rules. In 1931 a subaltern in 2/RTC who was aged only 23 asked his CO, Lt.-Col. Percy Hobart, for permission to marry. Hobart thought that he ought to learn to box instead. Undeterred, the subaltern learnt to box and still got married.[196]

---

[191] Anon., *The Subaltern's Handbook*, 61.

[192] J. Nettleton, *The Anger of the Guns: An Infantry Officer on the Western Front* (London: William Kimber, 1979), 57.

[193] Nicholson, *Behind the Lines*, 101–2.

[194] IWMSA. Accession No. 000569/18. Col. U. Burke, reel 6; M. Trustram, *Women of the Regiment: Marriage and the Victorian Army* (Cambridge: Cambridge University Press, 1984), *passim*.

[195] IWMSA. Accession No. 000917/07. Lt.-Col. H. D. Thwaytes, reel 4.

[196] Gen. Sir H. Pyman, *Call to Arms* (London: Leo Cooper, 1971), 19.

Cardwell had hoped that the short-service system would reduce the cost of the married roll because young men would enlist for a short time and leave the army in their mid-twenties before they married. What he had not bargained for was that so few men would remain in the army after their initial period of service that regiments would find it increasingly difficult to promote suitable men to serve as senior NCOs. In 1881 the War Office tried to persuade NCOs to extend their service by granting them extra marriage privileges. Henceforth all staff sergeants and colour sergeants, half of all sergeants provided they were over the age of 24, and 12 per cent of the rank and file, provided they were over the age of 26, were allowed to marry on the strength, if they were men of proven good conduct and 'they being the persons to whom it is considered desirable to offer special inducements to remain in the Service'.[197]

The advantage to a soldier of marrying with his CO's permission and 'on the strength' was that his family was transported as part of the regiment and at the government's expense every time it changed station.[198] There were 12,000 men on the married rolls occupying married quarters and their rent and transport expenses cost the taxpayer £128,000 per annum. This was not a privilege that was given easily. COs often enquired carefully into the character of prospective wives.[199] When Mary Clearly of Fermanagh applied to marry Sgt. John Lynch of 2/ 27th Foot in 1875, her employer could 'testify my belief that she will be an acquisition to the regiment. She possesses a fair education in reading, writing & arithmetic—can sew well, wash well—cook well, and is a queenly girl.'[200] The military authorities also operated an effective colour bar. COs usually demanded to see a fiancée's birth certificate before granting permission to marry, and officers or soldiers stationed overseas who asked for permission to marry an Indian or Eurasian woman often found themselves hastily posted to another station hundreds of miles away.[201]

Soldiers who married without their CO's consent could not be punished for doing so, but they forfeited all right to be placed on the married establishment.[202] This often exposed their wives and families to poverty, even when they lived with them in Britain, and to separation and

---

[197] PRO WO 33/38. Committee on the future of the Married Establishments, 19 Dec. 1881; PRO WO 33/37. J. Adye, Married establishments of the army, Aug. 1881.

[198] Adye, *Recollections of a Military Life*, 263.

[199] Anon., *The Standing Orders of the 2nd Battalion 22nd (Cheshire) Regiment*, 66.

[200] NAM 7003/1. Scrapbook, Officers' Mess, 27th Foot, 2nd Battalion Royal Inniskilling Fusiliers. Mr Trimble to Capt. Urquhart, 2 Sept. 1875.

[201] IWMSA. Accession No. 00836/06. Maj. H. J. Smith, 68–9; IWMSA. Accession No. 000911/03. Mrs P. M. Hopkins, reel 1; IWMSA. Accession No. 17936. Reverend Maj. D. Davies, reel 1.

[202] War Office, *QR ... 1892*, 197.

destitution when they were posted overseas.[203] An enquiry carried out in 1913 could not find an exact figure but believed that the numbers concerned were, in some regiments, considerable. This was detrimental to both the health of married soldiers, because they had to feed their families by sharing their own rations with them, and their morale, for their families could afford only the meanest of lodgings near their barracks.[204]

For most of the nineteenth century even married families on the strength of a regiment led a spartan existence. Initially the only married quarters they were allotted was a curtained-off corner of a barrack room, which afforded minimal privacy and comfort.[205] By 1912 a family with two children was allotted two rooms plus a scullery.[206] But married quarters were sometimes far from luxurious. When Albert Bradshaw's wife and two children joined him at Calcutta in 1931, their quarters consisted of a single-room flat, which was about the size of an army hut. It was divided into rooms by hessian screens. The family slept on basic army beds and it was infested with insects.[207] Others were more fortunate. In 1935, Phyllis Hopkins married a sergeant in 1/Buffs, then stationed in Burma, and she and her husband were allocated a large detached house with three bedrooms, a drawing room, a dining room, a bathroom, and a kitchen.[208]

Wives who married on the strength were usually quickly accepted into the regimental community. Elizabeth Harrington, who married a lance-sergeant in the Royal Artillery in the mid-1920s, believed that 'The Army always helps its own. It always shields its own, it always helps its own and it always looks after its own. You were sort of protected when you joined it.'[209] But the incorporation was such that they were never allowed to forget that their needs had to be subordinated to those of the regiment and their husband. They took their status within the regiment according to their husband's rank. Relationships between wives were dominated by the same hierarchy that determined the lives of their husbands. As one private who served before 1914 remembered,

I often did a grin at some Battalion outdoor function, such as Regimental Sports, to watch the ladies according to their different social classes collect in groups apart from one another: one group of officers' wives with the Colonel's wife in

  [203] NAM 7008–13. MSS. Anon., *Experiences of a soldier*, n.d.
  [204] PP (1914), LI. Cd. 7441. *Report of an inquiry by Mrs Tennant regarding the conditions of marriage off the strength*, passim.
  [205] Anon., 'Remarks on the Present Condition of the Army', 211.
  [206] War Office, *KR ... 1912*, 200–1.
  [207] IWMSA. Accession No. 000811/11. A. H. Bradshaw, 40–2.
  [208] IWMSA. Accession No. 000911/03. Mrs P. M. Hopkins, reel 1.
  [209] IWMSA. Accession No. 000898/06. Elizabeth Harrington, 4.

command, another of senior N.C.O.s' wives with the Regimental Sergeant-Major's wife in command, and then the wives of the sergeants, corporals and privates, each group parading separately. It was class distinction with a vengeance.[210]

The conduct of family life was closely supervised by regimental officers. Married soldiers were responsible for the behaviour of their wives and children, and wives who misbehaved could be evicted from their quarters. Wives of private soldiers were expected to supplement the family income by doing washing and sewing for the regiment.[211] Officers regularly inspected their quarters and officers' wives were expected to establish the same paternal relationship with the wives and children of other ranks that their husbands did with the men under their command. It was commonplace for officers' wives to organize Christmas parties for the wives and children of their regiment. In 1899, Mrs Stephenson, the wife of the CO of 1/Essex, organized classes in dairying. The battalion was due to be posted to India, and she hoped to reduce the incidence of enteric fever and diphtheria by teaching the men how to produce uncontaminated milk products for the regiment. She also played a leading role in organizing charitable relief for the wives and families of Essex Regiment reservists recalled to the Colours during the Boer War, and in establishing a 'Soldiers Home' near the regimental depot at Warley in Essex.[212]

Marriages that collapsed were also of concern to the military authorities, not least because they could disrupt that harmony of regimental life that it was their goal to maintain. Fearful that marital discord, especially if it involved men in the same regiment, could harm morale and discipline, the military authorities forbade unmarried soldiers to enter married quarters unless they were on duty or had been specifically invited to do so by the head of the household.[213] Single soldiers therefore had little contact with married families in the regiment except on formal social occasions.[214]

In some regiments the wives of senior officers ran an unofficial marriage guidance service. Soldiers who were accounted bad husbands were

---

[210] Richards, *Old-Soldier Sahib*, 159.
[211] ERM. ERB 397. Anon., *Standing Orders of the 56th (West Essex) Regiment*, 41–3; SRO. GB 554/B3/1. Anon., *The Standing Orders of the 1st Battalion, the Suffolk Regiment*, 44–5; RNRM. R 65. Permanent Order book, 1st Battalion, 1831 to 1907. Entries for 21 Mar. 1870, 20 Nov. 1878, 1 Oct. 1881.
[212] ERM. ERPA 30. A military dairy class, 1899; ERM. CB1. Mrs Stephenson to ?, n.d. but *c*. late 1899; Essex Regimental Museum. CB1. Warley soldiers' home opened by Maj.-Gen. W. F. Gatacre, 31 July 1900.
[213] RNRM. R 65. Permanent Order book, 1st Battalion, 1831 to 1907. Entry for 12 July 1892; Anon., *The Standing Orders of the King's Royal Rifle Corps*, 56–7.
[214] IWMSA. Accession No. 000923/04. R. Clemens, reel 4.

liable to be given a dressing down by their CO and told to mend their ways. If the wife of a soldier began an affair with another member of the regiment, 'the fellow was on the mat within twenty-four hours' and an officer warned the wife concerned about her future behaviour.[215] If they persisted in misbehaving, all the parties involved were liable to find themselves separated by being posted to other units.[216]

Officers who got into marital difficulties were treated even more severely. For much of the period examined by this book divorce, in the eyes of middle-class observers, carried a serious social stigma. But in the eyes of the military authorities divorce, if it involved an officer and another officer's wife, was little short of a military offence, for it was the kind of behaviour that could disrupt the harmony and comradeship of the mess. In the 1920s if such cases were brought to the attention of the Army Council, the 'guilty' officer could be required to resign or retire. '[W]hile an officer's private code of morals may normally be no business of ours,' the CIGS insisted in 1931, 'we consider that once it affects his relations with a brother officer the whole fabric of Army and Regimental life is undermined.'[217] In cases that did not involve an officer's wife, the Army Council merely issued the officer concerned with a note of its displeasure, or banished him to the colonies. He was allowed 'to serve temporarily under the Colonial Office in order to live down any scandal caused'.[218] In 1936 the Army Council warned all officers that if they became involved in divorce proceedings that fact would be noted on their records, a decision that was reiterated in 1950 and again in 1961.[219]

Although the military authorities might have been misogynistic, they did not promote same-sex desire and overt homosexuality. Same-sex relations were discouraged and could be severely punished.[220] In 1950 one BSM told a squad of gunners: 'If any of you are ever caught in bed with another man your feet will never touch the ground again.'[221] Giving evidence to a Parliamentary Committee considering a new Army and Air Force Disciplinary Bill in 1952, the Adjutant-General insisted that punishing homosexual activities was essential because 'Once you get it started in a barrack room you get the whole lot corrupted, and we want to protect the individual. It is an offence that we have to stop

[215] IWMSA. Accession No. 00897/09. Maj. D. C. McIver, 58.

[216] IWMSA. Accession No. 004524/05. L. H. Porter Harper, 28–30.

[217] PRO WO 32/15274. Montgomery-Massingberd to all GOC-in-C, 4 May 1931.

[218] Ibid.

[219] PRO WO 32/15274. Extract from the minutes of the ECAC, 9 June 1950; War Office to all C-in-C and GOC-in-C, 14 Apr. 1961.

[220] A. D. Harvey, 'Homosexuality and the British Army during the First World War', *Journal of the Society for Army Historical Research*, 79 (2001), 313–19.

[221] Barraclough, *National Service*, 21.

because otherwise you get corrupt barrack rooms, just like the vicious type of public school dormitory where vice spreads widely.'[222]

However, prosecutions for indecency were comparatively rare. Between 1909, when separate figures for indecency were first published, and 1913, they averaged only twenty-six a year. Between 1920 and 1937 they rose, but there were still an average of only forty each year.[223] There is also anecdotal evidence suggesting that in some regiments, provided that their behaviour was not blatant, homosexual acts, or at least the existence of homosexuals, was tolerated.[224] 'Well, we knew it went on but we didn't go out to look for it', one RSM admitted. 'Let me put it that way. Obviously it went on. You can't have eight hundred troops living together and something of that not being practised. But so long as we didn't stumble on it then we didn't go looking for it.'[225] But there were limits to toleration. Each infantry or cavalry regiment contained a small number of band boys, who enlisted at about 14 years of age. To prevent them from being corrupted by their elders they were forbidden to enter barrack rooms occupied by older soldiers, or to associate with them in or out of barracks.[226] Officers or NCOs who were suspected of making sexual advances to them were almost invariably prosecuted.[227]

The physical and mental isolation of regimental communities also served another purpose. To an extent it helped to ensure the political quiescence of the army. As the Director of Personnel Services at the War Office wrote in 1943: 'So long as we retain the Regimental system, there will be no "Invergordon" in the Army.'[228] Even before the Russian revolution of 1917 made the army an obvious target for communist subversion, the military authorities had taken steps to insulate soldiers from politics. *King's Regulations* specifically forbade officers, NCOs or other ranks to participate in political meetings, demonstrations, or processions.[229]

---

[222] PP (1952–3), III. *Reports of Committees. Army and Air Force Act. Report with Proceedings, Evidence and Appendices, Annex 36 (M.45(1952–53),* Q. 615.

[223] PP (1911), XLVI. *General Annual Return for the British Army for the year ending 1910,* 70–1; PP (1914), XVI. *General Annual Return for the British Army for the year ending 30 Sept. 1913,* 68; PP (1921), XX. *General Annual Reports on the British Army (including the Territorial Force from the date of embodiment) for the period from 1 October 1913 to 30 Sept. 1919,* 82–6; PP (1930–1), XIX. *General Annual Report for the British Army for the year ending 30 Sept. 1930,* 67–8; PP (1937–8), XVII. *General Annual report for the British Army for the Year ending 30 Sept. 1937,* 61.

[224] IWMSA. Accession No. 20494/12. Col. P. Featherby, reel 3; M. Houlbrook, 'Soldier Heroes and Rent Boys: Homosex, Masculinities, and Britishness in the Brigade of Guards, c. 1900–1960', *Journal of British Studies,* 42 (2003), 351–88.

[225] IWMSA. Accession No. 00897/09. Maj. D. C. McIver, 61.

[226] Anon., *The Standing Orders of the 2nd Battalion The Royal Warwickshire Regiment,* 7.

[227] IWMSA. Accession No. 000780/05. H. L. Horsfield, 18.

[228] PRO WO 32/11061. Minute, DPS, to DMS(B), 25 Nov. 1943.

[229] War Office, *KR ... 1912,* 94–5.

Prosecutions for such offences were rare but not unknown. In 1952, for example, an 18-year-old trooper in the Royal Armoured Corps was sentenced by court martial to a year's imprisonment for attempting to pass information to a potential enemy.[230] Nor was it only lowly privates who were prosecuted. In October 1919, Lieutenant-Colonel John Sherwood-Kelly, who had won a VC at Cambrai, and who was commanding 2/Hampshire Regiment in North Russia, was court-martialled for publishing letters in the *Daily Express* criticizing the political purposes of the campaign.[231]

Canvassing and the holding of political meetings inside barracks were always forbidden, although officers and other ranks were permitted to attend political meetings away from barracks in mufti.[232] Before 1914 few other ranks could vote because they found it almost impossible to meet the complex residence qualifications necessary to secure the franchise. The 1918 Representation of the People Act greatly simplified the voting registration system, with the result that far more soldiers could qualify to vote than ever before. In 1918 the presence of so many civilians in uniform persuaded the military authorities to relax some of their regulations. Officers and other ranks were allowed to take an active part in the general election as candidates or on a candidate's behalf provided they were in mufti. But with the return to a fully professional army these concessions lapsed. In May 1921 an inter-service committee decided that although every facility had to be given to officers and other ranks to cast their votes, henceforth they were forbidden to organize or address political meetings unless they were adopted as candidates. But they were permitted to attend such meetings if they were in mufti, and they were allowed to vote.[233]

Before the Second World War both regular officers and other ranks who were properly qualified were permitted to stand as candidates in local and general elections. There were no known cases of other ranks being elected to Parliament, at least before the First World War. In the case of officers the War Office's practice before 1914 was that officers below the rank of Lieutenant-Colonel were either seconded or placed on half pay if they were elected as an MP. It was only in July 1925, following the report of the Blanesburgh committee, which considered the regulations governing the candidature for Parliament and municipal bodies of persons in the service of the Crown, that candidates were required to resign their commission or, if another rank, take their discharge, when

[230] *The Times*, 3 Dec. 1952.
[231] *The Times*, 29 Oct. and 5 Nov. 1919; 19 Aug. 1931.
[232] War Office, *QR* ... *1892*, 87; War Office, *KR* ... *1912*, 94.
[233] PRO WO 32/3946. PUS, WO to all GOC-in-C at home, 17 Nov. 1923 and WO to all GOC-in-C Home Commands, 2 Apr. 1928; Minute, AG3, 13 Dec. 1927.

they became a candidate.[234] Once elected, the military authorities had to concede that soldier-MPs had a perfect right to express views on any 'political or national subject with absolute freedom', but they hoped that they would not use Parliamentary privilege to cast slurs on their military superiors.[235]

However, after the Second World War, the onset of the Cold War meant that the civil liberties of regular soldiers were significantly reduced. By 1955 serving regulars were no longer permitted to stand for election to either local or national office, nor were they allowed to take any active part in party politics by joining a political party, speaking for it, or writing for it. National Servicemen, however, enjoyed greater freedoms. They could stand as a candidate for election, although not as serving soldiers. A month before the election, any soldier who had been adopted as a candidate was discharged from the army for the duration of the election.[236]

Evidence indicating the party political opinions of the regular rank and file is sparse. The Regular Army was recruited from amongst very young men from deprived backgrounds and so they were unlikely before they enlisted to have been politicized by being a member of either a trades union or a political party. There does seem to have been scant support for extra-Parliamentary parties of the left. In 1912 a Syndicalist agitator who tried to suborn troops at a barracks in Northern Command was seized by soldiers of the garrison, stripped of his clothing, ducked in a pond, and forced to leave the barracks naked.[237]

Soldiers who took part in strike duty during the General Strike in 1926, like Corporal Lewis Porter of 12/Lancers, did not enjoy the experience, but regarded it as part of their duty, 'because when you look at your own kin and you're saying "Right, we've got to break you up" [but] this is a part of soldiering which you musn't shirk and you musn't have any sentiment at all otherwise the whole system would collapse'.[238] During the strike it was difficult for the CPGB to transmit propaganda to troops because of the extra guards on duty in barracks and because emergency regulations made it an offence for anyone to try to cause mutiny or spread sedition or disaffection amongst serving members of the forces. But their 'difficulties were also added to by the hostile attitude displayed by the troops generally to any appeals made to them not to do their duty'.[239] Some troops recruited from mining districts were known

[234] PRO WO 32/3946. Memorandum by the War Office on Parliamentary Candidature and political activities by officers and soldiers of the Regular army, n.d.; *The Times*, 18 May 1925.

[235] PRO WO 32/18555. Minute by DPS, 13 June 1915; Extracts from *Hansard*, 29 June 1915.

[236] War Office, *QR* ... 1955, 158.

[237] PRO DPP 1/18. *Pall Mall Gazette*, 27 Feb. 1912.

[238] IWMSA. Accession No. 004524/05. L. H. P. Harper, 6.

[239] PRO WO 30/143. CB 1751. Aspects of the General Strike, May 1926. Produced by New Scotland Yard, SW1, June 1926.

to have expressed some sympathy with the strikers, but not to an extent that the military authorities felt they had to take action against them. A careful watch was kept on a handful of other ranks suspected of harbouring communist sympathies, but no action was taken against them, except in the case of one private 'who had openly expressed his approval of acts of violence, committed at Newcastle [who] was dealt with by his C.O. Men of the unit gave evidence, voluntarily against him.'[240] The same unwillingness to consider the political implications of their calling was apparent even amongst men who did come from a background that might have politicized them. Albert Bradshaw, who enlisted in 1920, was the son of a trade union official in Liverpool. When his father pointed out to him that once in uniform he might be called upon to shoot strikers, he simply denied the very possibility.[241]

A secret War Office Intelligence summary compiled in the middle of the General Strike suggested that the attitude of the troops called out on strike duty could be divided into two camps:

The older soldiers, looking ahead, hope that the present struggle will render it possible for ex-soldiers, and non-unionists to find work without difficulty along-side trade unionists.

The younger soldiers are anxious to defeat the strike, and get back to their amusements.[242]

Most regular soldiers had not been encouraged to question the status quo before they joined the army, and they certainly were not after they had done so. Brig. George Lindsay, who commanded 7 Infantry Brigade between 1932 and 1934, addressed each overseas draft before it left for India. What he told them must have reinforced their easy acceptance of what they were being called upon to do. According to Lindsay, the British were in India not only for their own benefit, for India was of great commercial importance to Britain, but also for the benefit of the Indian people. India was 'A great conglomeration of peoples which we are welding into a Country'. More generally, in India and elsewhere, the British were God's chosen instrument 'to help evolution of [the] World to better things'. Trade, freedom, and prosperity would each grow under the protection afforded the people of the empire by the British army. 'What [was] good for [the] British Empire [was] good for [the] World. Therefore Britain first.'[243]

With these and similar ideas echoing in their minds, few soldiers in imperial cantonments felt much need to take an informed interest in the

---

[240] PRO WO 30/143. WO Intelligence summary no. 12, WO, MI1, 11 May 1926.

[241] IWMSA. Accession No. 000811/11. A. H. Bradshaw, 3.

[242] PRO WO 30/143. War Office Intelligence summary no. 16. 1400 hrs 13th May to 1400 hrs 14th May [1926].

[243] LHCMA. Liddell Hart MSS 15/12/2. 'Address to Indian Draft', n.d., but c.1932–4.

domestic politics of the countries in which they were stationed. Drummer Richard Clemens, who served in India in the late 1920s, thought that 'We weren't interested in politics one little bit.'[244] Nor did they question the existence of the British Empire or the fact that it was so organized that a small number of privileged Europeans governed a much larger number of inhabitants. In India few British soldiers seem to have been more than dimly aware of the significance of Ghandi's Congress movement.[245] Henry Horsfield, who was posted to an artillery battery in India in 1923, was, like most of his comrades, not interested in Indian politics. 'All we knew we were the Indian Army, the English Army in India. And we were there to protect people, as far as that goes; in case of any uprising we were there on the spot, weren't we? That's all there was to it. We were there to soldier.'[246] Cpl. E. G. Brice, who served with the Royal Signals in Egypt between 1930 and 1933, thought that 'we take it as part of our jobs. What we joined the Army for and as far as we were concerned we were sent out there and didn't even consider ourselves an army of occupation. We thought well it wanted doing and that was that.'[247]

Until shortly before 1914 the authorities took a generally relaxed attitude towards left-wing politicians and trades union leaders who urged soldiers to refuse to obey orders if they were deployed on strike duty. In August 1911, for example, the Labour politicians George Lansbury and Ben Tillet addressed a meeting of 1,500 people in Trafalgar Square that passed a resolution condemning the use of troops by the government during the railway strike. Another speaker encouraged people who had friends in the army to write to them telling them to refuse to shoot their own countrymen 'and that if they were charged with mutiny, and were bound to shoot, then to shoot in the right direction'.[248] But as the War Office did not complain about it, the PUS at the Home Office, and Winston Churchill, the Home Secretary, agreed that the right course was 'No action'.[249]

However, shortly thereafter, the military authorities ceased to be so complacent. They gradually recognized that they could no longer rely on the way in which the regimental system impeded the growth of political consciousness amongst the rank and file to prevent the spread of subversion. With a minimum of publicity they therefore began to take more active counter-measures. Between 1911 and 1914 industrial unrest was

[244] IWMSA. Accession No. 000923/04. R. Clemens, reel 4.
[245] IWMSA. Accession No. 000811/11. A. H. Bradshaw, 87.
[246] IWMSA. Accession No. 000780/05. H. L. Horsfield, 44–5.
[247] IWMSA. Accession No. 004473/04. Lt.-Col. E. G. Brice, 43; IWMSA. Accession No. 004611/03. Sgt. F. T. Suter, reel 3.
[248] PRO HO 144/1163/2135. *The Times*, Monday, 28 Aug. 1911.
[249] PRO HO 144/1163/2135. Minute by Churchill, 2 Sept. 1911.

becoming more commonplace and troops were called out on strike duty with increasing frequency. No longer were the military authorities content to take for granted the political passivity of the rank and file, or to believe that loyalty to regiment would override the competing calls of class loyalty. The emergence of quasi-revolutionary left-wing groups seemed to pose a potential threat to military discipline.

In February 1912 Syndicalist agitators tried to persuade troops to disobey orders when they were called out on strike duty by issuing handbills claiming that

We work long hours for small wages at hard work because of our POVERTY. And both YOUR poverty and OURS arises from the fact that Britain, with its resources, belongs to only a few people. These few, owning Britain, own OUR jobs. Owning OUR jobs, they own OUR very LIVES. Comrades, have we called in vain? Think things out, and refuse any longer to MURDER YOUR KINDRED. Help US to win back BRITAIN for the BRITISH and the WORLD for the WORKERS![250]

In March 1912 the handbills' publishers and printers were found guilty of trying to incite mutiny and sentenced to prison, and in April the Syndicalist leader Tom Mann was sent for trial in Manchester on a charge of inciting troops to mutiny by refusing to obey their officers if they were called out on strike duty.[251] A distributor of Syndicalist literature was apprehended at Aldershot, found guilty at Winchester Assize under the 1797 Incitement to Mutiny Act, and given four months' hard labour.[252]

During the later stages of the First World War the authorities began to maintain a close and regular oversight of subversive activities that might threaten military discipline. By the summer of 1917, in the wake of the first Russian Revolution and the wave of strikes that affected the engineering industry in Britain in May, some senior members of the War Office were becoming concerned about the political reliability of their troops. On 24 June 1917 a meeting was held at Tunbridge Wells of representatives of 4/, 5/, and 6/Royal Sussex, 10/Middlesex, and certain battalions of the Royal West Kent Regiment and the Buffs, 'and constituted a branch of the Soldiers' and Workmen's Council which they named the Home Counties and Training Reserve Branch'.[253] In late 1918 the Soldiers, Sailors and Airmen's Union was formed and, together with the *Daily Herald* newspaper, gave support to veteran soldiers who were striking and demonstrating in favour of faster demobilization. By May 1919 they were also encouraging troops to refuse to serve in the forces

---

[250] PRO DPP 1/18. Open Letter to British Soldiers, n.d. but c.Feb. 1912.
[251] *The Times*, 23 Mar. and 1 Apr. 1912.
[252] PRO DPP 1/18. F. Crowsley. Offence: Incitement to mutiny, 18 June 1912.
[253] PRO WO 32/5455. H. B. Butler to R. H. Brade, 19 July 1917.

sent to intervene in the Russian Civil War, to seize ports, and to join the police in a general strike.[254]

On receiving a report of the Tunbridge Wells Soviet, the Adjutant-General minuted that

In view of the fact that the army of today is by no means as highly disciplined as that in existence before the war, and also that the classes of men serving at the present moment include individuals of every shade of education and opinion, it is probable that the movement to encourage soldiers to take part in political questions will be fanned by certain political factions for their own ends.[255]

Conscription meant that discontented and disaffected men could be inducted into the army where they could threaten morale and discipline. The War Cabinet decided they had no option but to enforce the strictures in King's Regulations forbidding soldiers to join political parties and banned Soldiers and Sailors' Councils in the army and navy. The Metropolitan Police's Special Branch, MI5, and Military Intelligence were also ordered to watch 'militant' trade unionists, pacifist and anti-conscriptionist organizations, and socialist activists and isolate them from the rest of the organized labour movement and the armed forces. By 1919 the War Office Intelligence Department had established a special department, A2, run by Lt.-Col. Vere Isham, to counter Bolshevik agitation in the army.[256] Isham's branch did so under the cover of a

'Welfare Scheme'. Briefly, a number of Officers were selected and trained in Security Intelligence, and attached to each command to work under the general direction of the Security Service. These 'Welfare Officers' as they were called, had no other duties than to visit every unit in their respective command at frequent intervals; to explain to Commanding Officers the nature of the dangers to be guarded against; the necessity of watching for and reporting the slightest indications of subversive activities or discontent among the men; to collect all possible information about such activities and to carry out any local investigations required.[257]

Isham also cooperated with a variety of private sector organizations such as the National Stability League and the Anti-Bolshevik Society to gather information on ex-servicemen's organizations, trades unions, and other left-wing groups in the immediate post-war period.[258]

Threats to the political loyalty of the rank and file did not disappear with the demobilization of the wartime army. Throughout the 1920s and

[254] S. R. Ward, 'Intelligence Surveillance of British Ex-servicemen, 1918–20', *Historical Journal*, 16 (1973), 179–88.
[255] PRO WO 32/5455. Minute by Macready to Secretary of State, 19 July 1917; Ward, 'Intelligence Surveillance', 181.
[256] J. Hope, 'Surveillance or Collusion? Maxwell Knight, MI5 and the British Fascisti', *Intelligence and National Security*, 9 (1994), 663–4.
[257] PRO ADM 1/27314. The Naval Security Service. Memorandum for the Board, 7 July 1932.
[258] Hope, 'Surveillance or Collusion?', 663–4.

into the 1930s the Comintern and the CPGB tried to subvert the loyalty of troops to pave the way for a Bolshevik revolution in Britain.[259] Their efforts reached a crescendo in the ten months before the General Strike of May 1926. They wrote slogans on walls near barracks, posted propaganda to soldiers, and accosted them as they went to and from leave and in pubs in garrison towns. Immediately before the strike bundles of a propaganda pamphlet addressed 'To the Men of H.M. Forces' were thrown into Chelsea barracks and a couple of days later others were posted to soldiers in barracks in Manchester, Warrington, Ashton-under-Lyne, and Aldershot. After urging men to tell their officers that they would not take part in strike-breaking activities, it asserted

You are WORKERS IN UNIFORM. Your officers are BOSSES IN UNIFORM, and you know the vast difference between you: the food, the leave, the right to wear 'civvies'; the wide differences in pay and countless other privileges. They lead a far better life than you. Why? Because they are of the BOSS CLASS. They can join clubs, may join Conservative or Liberal parties and play their part in politics. Can you? Not bloody likely!! Why shouldn't you be allowed to join a political party or form a definite organisation inside the Army and Navy to fight in your interests? The answer is simple, comrades. The officer is well cared for and his wants are all provided for, so he has no grouse. But with you it is different.

You could do with better food, longer leave, the right to wear 'civvies' on your leave, and higher wages. You must do C.B. 'pay stop' or detention if you happen to incur the dislike of any snotty little officer. REMEMBER McCAFFERTY!!!

You could also put a stop to the whole damned show if you'd only set up your SOLDIERS' AND SAILORS' COUNCILS.[260]

In 1923 the 'Welfare Scheme' had been curtailed as an economy measure but it was revived shortly before the start of the General Strike.[261] By August 1925 the Secret Intelligence Service had discovered that the Comintern had instructed the CPGB to continue working to organize a general strike of miners, railway workers, and textile workers, and at the same time agitate amongst the armed forces in the hope that an alliance of workers and soldiers could overthrow the government.[262] In June 1925 the War Office ordered officers whose troops were called out on strike duty to appoint their own counter-intelligence officer, independent

---

[259] C. Andrew, *Secret Service: The Making of the British Intelligence Community* (London: Heineman, 1985), 318. See also PRO WO 32/3948. Minute, W. H. Bartholomew, 5 Oct. 1921.

[260] PRO WO 30/143. CB 1751. Aspects of the General Strike, May 1926. Produced by New Scotland Yard, SW1, June 1926.

[261] Andrew, *Secret Service*, 320. The best assessment of the army's internal security activities in the 1920s and early 1930s is K. Jeffrey, 'The British Army and Internal Security 1919–1939', *Historical Journal*, 24 (1981), 377–97.

[262] PRO WO 32/3948. Special Branch, New Scotland Yard, Report on Revolutionary Organisations in the UK, 13 Aug. 1925.

of the 'Welfare Officer' scheme. One of their tasks was to report on the morale of government forces and 'Undesirables present in Government forces'.[263] A security officer was posted to the staff of each Army Command to act as the link between the Command and the Security Service. By the middle of the 1920s each CO was his own Security Officer. If he learnt of any subversive activities, he was expected to report it to the Command Security Officer, who forwarded the report to the Security Service.[264] He was also warned: 'Don't think that, because a soldier laughs at Communism with you, he may not think twice about it alone. To-day's joke may be to-morrow's grievance.'[265]

The authorities were also increasingly willing to prosecute those suspected of trying to undermine the loyalty of the rank and file. In 1925 twelve defendants, all members of the CPGB and associated with its newspaper *Workers' Weekly*, were charged with sedition and incitement to mutiny.[266] During the General Strike a speaker in Liverpool was prosecuted for sedition for misleading an open-air meeting by telling his audience that the Welsh Guards were confined to Chelsea Barracks for refusing to entrain for a mining area, and that troops at Aldershot had also refused to obey orders.[267] In 1930 an ex-soldier who had served for twelve years in the army and joined the Communist party when serving in Shanghai was successfully prosecuted for distributing pamphlets to troops telling them to refuse to fire on Indian workers and peasants and calling on them to turn their weapons on representatives of the British capitalist classes.[268]

But prosecutions had to take place under a piece of antiquated legislation, the Incitement to Mutiny Act, passed as long ago as 1797. The Directorate of Military Intelligence had been anxious since 1921 to modernize the law and in the early 1930s, MI5 prepared a bill to do so, which finally became law in late 1934.[269]

The cases of soldiers whom the Security Service suspected of harbouring communist tendencies were usually referred to the Secretary of State for War. If he agreed they were then discharged, 'services no longer required', rather than prosecuted. This course of action was deliberately chosen because had the military authorities given the real reason for their dismissal, they would have opened themselves not only to complaints

---

[263] PRO WO 32/5314. AG3, WO. Memo. No. 1. Duties in aid of the civil power. Revised memorandum. June 1925 to GOC-in-C Home Commands.

[264] PRO ADM 1/27314. The Naval Security Service. Memorandum for the Board, 7 July 1932.

[265] PRO WO 33/1310. Internal Security Instructions (1933) (Army).

[266] *The Times*, 24 Nov. 1925.

[267] PRO HO 144/9237. *British Gazette*, 12 May 1926.

[268] PRO DPP 2/44. Clerk of Assize Courts, Winchester, to Attorney General, 5 July 1930.

[269] Andrew, *Secret Service*, 359–66; *The Times*, 7 Nov. 1934.

from the soldier concerned, but also to embarrassing Parliamentary questions, because 'there are very few cases indeed where the evidence could be produced or even quoted without exposing the secret system under which it was obtained'.[270] Communists who were members of the Territorial Army and members of the British Union of Fascists were dealt with in a similar way.[271]

After 1945 and the onset of the Cold War it became common practice for soldiers about to be posted to potentially sensitive appointments to be vetted by the Security Service. By 1948 those subject to vetting included all candidates for commissions, all officers or other ranks who were aliens or who had close alien connections through birth, parentage, or marriage, and all soldiers who were posted to intelligence staffs, interpreters, cipher and signals staffs, welfare and educational staffs, as well as officially sponsored civilian lecturers. Personnel who showed up in its records were dealt with in one of several ways. They were posted to a non-sensitive job, discharged 'services no longer required', refused an application for a commission, or had their call-up for National Service deferred.[272] But vetting was not an infallible means of detecting potentially subversive personnel. The Security Service sometimes paid little attention to membership of youth organizations such as the Young Communist League. It was perhaps for that reason that it was not until a private soldier tried in 1963 to establish a Campaign for Nuclear Disarmament cell in an army camp at Shoeburyness, abutting the atomic weapons research establishment at Foulness, that the military authorities discovered that he had been an active member of CND before he enlisted.[273]

The military authorities did not, therefore, believe that they could automatically depend on loyalty to Crown and regiment to maintain discipline in the face of active efforts to subvert the loyalty of their troops. But neither did they think it necessary to pursue a large-scale witch-hunt against subversives. The number of serving soldiers whose cases were investigated by the Security Service was usually very small. In 1929, for example, MI5 investigated eighty-two cases of soldiers suspected of Communist activity. Forty-six men were cleared, five cases were dropped, sixteen remained under investigation, and fifteen men were discharged, which was one fewer than in 1928. In the five years between

[270] PRO WO 32/4514. Major C. T. Tomes (AG3) to Maj.-Gen. J. K. Dick-Cunyngham, 19 June 1933.

[271] PRO WO 32/4608. Conditions under which members of the British Union of Fascists are permitted to join the Territorial Army, 1936.

[272] PRO ADM 1/27314/MISC/P(48)14. MOD. Security Vetting of Service Personnel, 1 Sept. 1948.

[273] PRO WO 32/21706. Press cutting, Daily Telegraph, 11 Jan. 1963.

1951 and 1956 only twenty-seven regular soldiers were discharged on security grounds.[274]

By organizing life in barracks, by promoting games and sports, canteens and recreation rooms, and even by the food it served, the regimental system replicated, under military control, what one historian has defined as the conservative 'boisterous working-class culture'. It was a culture that was more concerned with pubs, football, horse-racing, boxing, and music-hall entertainments, which was enthusiastic for the monarchy and the empire, and suspicious of all foreigners, than it was with supporting trades unions or the Labour party or threatening the political status quo.[275] Except during the two world wars, when a much wider cross-section of society was drawn into the army, the Regular Army recruited its rank and file from amongst very young men from deprived backgrounds who were unlikely to have been exposed before they enlisted to forces that might have encouraged them to question the status quo. The regimental system, by providing a focus for the loyalty of the rank and file of the Regular Army, helped to ensure that the hardships and inequalities of army life did not politicize them. However, it would be a mistake to conclude that the military authorities believed that it alone would suffice to keep troops loyal to the Crown, and the army free from the taint of politics. When the loyalty of the rank and file was subject to direct threats from extremist extra-Parliamentary groups, they responded in an equally direct manner by establishing a security system independent of the regimental system to detect and combat the threat.

The outstanding feature of regimental life in barracks was the extent to which regiments were isolated, both physically and, at least when overseas, mentally, from the civilian communities that surrounded them. Ensconced in its barracks or cantonments, regiments were largely self-contained communities. They lived in the military equivalent of splendid isolation. This served two functions. It facilitated the imposition of discipline, and it helped build *esprit de corps*. Discipline is one of the factors that distinguished an army from an armed mob, and in the British army the existence of the regimental system ensured that subordinates, both officers and other ranks, were never allowed to forget that they were men under discipline. Officers were no more exempt from the system of surveillance that enforced these codes of behaviour than were NCOs or other ranks. Not only were the working lives of all members of the regiment minutely regulated, but their leisure was organized in such a

---

[274] *The Times*, 18 July 1956.
[275] M. D. Pugh, 'The Rise of Labour and the Political Culture of Conservatism, 1890–1945', *History*, 87 (2002), 517.

way as to minimize the possibility that they might do themselves, or the reputation of their regiment, any harm. The management of daily life also served a second purpose, that of helping to cement a pervasive sense of community that ran from the top to the bottom of each unit, thus making an everyday reality of *esprit de corps*.

CHAPTER SIX

The Leadership of the Regimental System: Officers and NCOs

In 1937 three senior regimental officers, two of whom commanded their units, wondered 'whether the Army was a purely professional affair, or whether it might not be regarded by many officers as a series of clubs. Such officers did not want to be compulsorily uprooted from their club and forced into a new one. We had achieved very good results by what might be termed this club spirit.'[1] That 'club spirit' was under threat in 1937 because the Army Council was toying with the idea of equalizing the rate of promotion between different line regiments by grouping them for promotion purposes. The senior subaltern in each group would be promoted when the first vacancy occurred in another regiment in the group.[2] The response of a committee of subalterns in Aldershot Command was typical. They insisted that 'The proposed Grouping system struck at something that vitally affects the happiness of subaltern officers as a body—the regimental or "club spirit"—and the dissatisfaction caused by the introduction of the system would not be compensated by the prospect of earlier promotion to Captain.'[3] The criticism, therefore, that at least before 1939 the British army was not led by a homogenous officer corps is justified. The regimental system fragmented the officer corps into a large number of small groups. For many officers their regiment provided a more powerful focus for their loyalty than did the more remote and abstract concept of 'the army'.

But the regimental system has also been criticized for producing officers with the wrong mental attributes. The army needed officers who were not only trained to perform the technical functions of their profession, but also sufficiently intelligent and educated that they could solve the many unexpected problems that confronted them on the battlefield. But, it has been claimed, regiments recruited most of their officers from public schools that placed 'character' above intellectual attainments.

---

[1] PRO WO 32/4477. Report of Aldershot committee, n.d. but c.31 Mar. 1937.

[2] PRO WO 32/3747. Minute by CIGS, 15 Apr. 1936; WO to GOCs all home commands, Palestine, Egypt, China, etc., 2 Oct. 1936.

[3] PRO WO 32/4477. Grouping of regiments of infantry of the line for promotion purposes. Report of Aldershot committee, n.d. but c.31 Mar. 1937.

Their cadet colleges failed to instil in budding subalterns any ambition to study their profession. The regimental system, with its glacially slow rate of promotion, did nothing to promote professional zeal. It produced officers with, at worst, no commitment to taking their profession seriously or, at best, an inward-looking professionalism that encouraged them to believe that the regiment was the centre of their profession. The only institution that could break down the mental insularity that the regimental system fostered was the Staff College at Camberley. But few officers tried to go there, and some who might have were discouraged from doing so by their commanding officers.[4]

The upshot was that the regular officer corps became an anomaly. Whereas by the final quarter of the nineteenth century what one historian has identified as the 'professional ideal' was becoming pervasive in the rest of British society, regimental officers remained sunk in an easy-going aristocratic amateurism.[5] Historians, however, should perhaps be suspicious of laying too many of the army's shortcomings at the door of its junior officers. Many of the most astringent criticisms of the lack of professional commitment of officer cadets and regimental officers were made in the wake of the setbacks of the Boer War. They were made by senior officers who were facing hostile interrogators in the series of official enquiries that had been established to discover why the army had experienced so much difficulty in defeating the Boer Republics. Some generals found irresistible the opportunity to direct attention towards the system of educating and training regimental officers, for in doing so they could deflect criticism away from their own conduct.[6] The result was that their testimony has produced a distorted vision of the professionalism of the regimental officer corps. In this chapter I will suggest that some of the criticisms directed against them were justified. However, it will also be demonstrated that some were exaggerated and others were not universally applicable. Moreover the military authorities acted on these criticisms, and, even before 1899, they had tried to impose structures on the

[4] See e.g. Harries-Jenkins, *The Army in Victorian Society*, 1–3; M. Ramsay, *Command and Cohesion: The Citizen Soldier and Minor Tactics in the British Army, 1870–1918* (Westport, Conn.: Praeger, 2002), 57–60; Bidwell and Graham, *Fire-Power*, 159–63; G. de Groot, *Blighty: British Society in the Era of the Great War* (London: Longman, 1996), 17–18; B. Bond, *British Military Policy between the Wars* (Oxford: Clarendon Press, 1980), 60–4; D. Fraser, *And We Shall Shock Them: The British Army and the Second World War* (London: Hodder and Stoughton, 1983), 22–3; Barnett, *Desert Generals*, 103–9; M. Howard, 'The Liddell Hart Memoirs', *Journal of the Royal United Services Institute*, 111 (1966), 58; Barnett, 'The Education of Military Elites', 16–31; Hamilton, *Listening for the Drums*, 119–20.

[5] H. Perkins, *The Rise of Professional Society: England since 1880* (London: Routledge, 1989), 2–8.

[6] PP (1902), X. Cd. 982. *Report of the Committee...*, Q. 15 (Sir E. Wood), Q. 691–2, 825 (Sir I. Hamilton), Q. 8431 (Lord Roberts); PP (1904), XLI. Cd. 1791. *Minutes of evidence*, Q. 14268. (Lord Methuen), Q. 16772 (Sir W. Gatacre).

officer corps that would encourage regimental officers to take a more professional attitude towards their job.

Secondly, I will examine a layer of the regimental system that constitutes a real 'unknown army'. These were the men who comprised the army's cadre of Warrant Officers and NCOs, the men whom one officer described as being the 'engine room' of every unit.[7] Without some understanding of how they were selected, trained, and promoted, and how they related both to the commissioned officers who served above them, and the other ranks who served below them, it is impossible to understand how units actually functioned.

The function of commissioned officers was to offer leadership; the role of Warrant Officers and NCOs was to provide supervision. In other words, commissioned officers decided what had to be done and provided the necessary inspiration for their subordinates, and Warrant Officers and NCOs ensured that it was done. Whether on the battlefield or in barracks, the most important person in any unit was its CO. His knowledge and leadership qualities could make or break his unit. In the opinion of one former battalion commander, 'a battalion is as good as its CO'.[8] In 1952, for example, the men of 1/Black Watch successfully withstood a major Chinese communist attack, and afterwards 'There was a great love of our Colonel. We used to call him Colonel Davey and he was everywhere and his one concern was the Jocks. Look after the Jocks.'[9] In this case the regimental system had served its purpose. It had bred such a high degree of respect between leaders and led, that the latter would willingly follow their officers.

Before it is possible to understand the relationship between officers and NCOs, it is necessary to examine the command structure of a unit. Each unit, be it an infantry battalion, a cavalry regiment, or a brigade in the Royal Artillery, was divided into a number of sub-units. Before 1914 cavalry regiments were usually organized into three active and one reserve squadron, each commanded by a major, assisted by a captain and four subalterns. Until the eve of the First World War infantry battalions were divided into eight companies, each normally commanded by a captain, although sometimes by a major, and assisted by two subalterns. Every captain, if his company was at full strength, was responsible for the work of about 100 NCOs and men.[10] In 1913 the organization of the infantry

---

[7] Millman, *Stand Easy*, 149.

[8] IWMSA. Accession No. 18047/4. Brig. W. C. Deller, reel 3; Nicholson, *Behind the Lines*, 152.

[9] IWMSA. Accession No. 18267/3. R. J. Carriage, reel 2.

[10] Lt.-Col. J. M. Grierson, *Scarlet into Khaki: The British Army on the Eve of the Boer War* (London: Greenhill Books, 1899), 31–58.

was transformed when the British belatedly followed the example of most Continental armies, and organized their battalions into four 'double-companies', each usually commanded by a major or senior captain.

Units had a large cadre of leaders and supervisors, although the precise ratio of officers to NCOs and other ranks varied according to whether or not a unit was overseas, and therefore at or near its full establishment, or at home. This was essential if the system of regulation analysed in the preceding chapters was to work effectively.[11] Units at home and low on the roster for foreign service usually had something like their full complement of officers and NCOs, but only a proportion of their other ranks. On paper, between the Cardwell Reforms and the Boer War, the ratio of officers to other ranks in an infantry battalion varied between one officer to twenty-seven other ranks, to one officer to forty-nine other ranks. The introduction of the double-company system did little to alter this. In artillery batteries the variation was smaller, ranging from 1:32 to 1:34. Cavalry regiments had a more favourable ratio, ranging from 1:20 to 1:22, and it had fallen to 1:16 on the eve of the First World War.

However, owing to the frequency with which officers were given leave, the number actually serving with their unit at any moment was often less than these figures suggest. But this was more than compensated for by the presence of large numbers of Warrant and Non-commissioned officers. After finding drafts for their sister battalion overseas, units at home might have as many as one NCO to every five rank and file. Infantry battalions overseas typically had between one NCO for every eight to one NCO for every ten men. Artillery batteries made up for their comparative lack of officers by having a ratio of NCOs that varied between 1:7 and 1:8. But again, cavalry regiments enjoyed on average a more favourable ratio, of something between one NCO to every six or seven men, depending upon whether it was serving at home or in India. Little changed between the world wars. Infantry battalions in the late 1930s maintained a ratio of one officer to between twenty-seven to thirty other ranks, and one NCO to every seven or eight other ranks, depending on whether the battalion was at home or overseas.[12] By the Second World War, supervision of the rank and file became even more close and continuous. By 1944 infantry battalions had one officer to every twenty-two other ranks and one NCO to every 6.6 other ranks.[13]

---

[11] The statistics in this and the next paragraph are derived from RNRM. R. 103. Records of Service I/Battalion Norfolk Regiment, 14 May 1870 and 1 Oct. 1888; ERM. ER6005. Historical Record, I/Battalion, Essex Regiment, 44/Foot, 27 Sept. 1871; ERM. ER3251.Digest of Service 56/Foot, 1844 to 1881, and 2/Essex 1881 to 1900, 31 Dec. 1875; Grierson, *Scarlet into Khaki*, 44–5, 52; War Office, *Field Service Pocket Book, 1914* (London, 1914), 20–2.

[12] PP (1937–8), XVII. Cmd. 5681. *Army Estimates, 1937–38*, 14, 16, 24.

[13] These figures are derived from PRO WO 171/1262. War Diary, 2 Argyll & Sutherland Highlanders, Field Return, 27 May 1944.

It is easy to find evidence to support many of the criticisms levelled against the lack of professional commitment of the regimental officers who worked within this structure. The military authorities did indeed place great emphasis on 'character', and rather less on technical skills. In October 1940 the Secretary of State for War, Anthony Eden, insisted that 'the Army officer must be a leader first and a technician second'.[14] Senior officers were sometimes scathing about the education of junior officers. Shortly after the Boer War, Sir Archibald Hunter, who had served as a staff officer and field commander in South Africa, asserted: 'The only officers in the Army who receive a fair military education are Engineers and Artillerymen—even they are no better trained than they ought to be, if as well.'[15] In 1903 a committee examining the education of officer cadets at Sandhurst concluded that few of them showed much keenness to study their profession because they knew that they would be commissioned even if they received low marks in the passing-out examinations.[16] Once a young officer had joined his regiment and undergone a period of recruit training, unlike young men in other professions, his daily duties were so light that he had little to do except to amuse himself.[17]

There is also a good case for suggesting that the system of officer promotion did too little to encourage professional zeal. After the abolition of the purchase of commissions, promotion for regimental officers was governed by two separate systems. Purchase had never determined the promotion of officers in the artillery or engineers, and their promotion continued to be governed by seniority tempered by the overriding principle of time promotion. By 1906 a 2/Lieutenant in the Royal Artillery or Royal Engineers was automatically promoted to Lieutenant after three years' service irrespective of the existence of a vacancy, to Captain after eleven years' service, and to Major after twenty years' service.[18] By the early 1930s these periods had been slightly extended.[19] Promotion in the other arms of service was governed by seniority within a regimental list, tempered by the rejection of officers who were reported on by their commanding officer as being unfitted for further advancement.[20] But, before the Boer War, an officer's faults had to be so egregious that, as Sir Evelyn

---

[14] PRO WO 163/48/ACM(AE)23. Minutes of the Army Council, 10 Oct. 1940.

[15] PP (1904), XLI. Cd. 1791. *Minutes of evidence...*Précis of evidence by Lt.-Gen. Sir A. Hunter, 29 Jan. 1903.

[16] PP (1902), X. Cd. 983. *Report of the Committee....*

[17] PP (1904), XL. Cd. 1790. *Minutes of evidence...*, QQ. 4306–7.

[18] War Office, *Royal Warrant for the Pay, Appointment, Promotion, and Non-effective Pay of the Army, 1906* (London: HMSO, 1906), sections 29–32.

[19] War Office, *Royal Warrant for the Pay, Appointment, Promotion, and Non-effective Pay of the Army, 1931* (London, 1931), section 119.

[20] PP (1876), XV. C. 1569. *Report of the Royal Commission on army promotion and retirement.*

Wood, the Adjutant-General between 1897 and 1901, explained, the system was 'seniority tempered by rejection in very bad cases'.[21]

The system of regimental promotion was also unfair to some deserving officers, for promotion in some regiments was considerably faster than it was in others. The Household Brigade and the cavalry usually enjoyed more rapid promotion than the infantry.[22] They attracted the sons of wealthy men who were apt to resign their commissions voluntarily when their fathers died and they inherited his property, thus creating vacancies for those below them in their regiment.[23] Other regiments attracted poorer men who had to endure sometimes frustratingly slow rates of promotion. By 1932 the average age at which a subaltern in a line infantry regiment became a Captain was 32; captains did not become majors until they were 39, and majors did not become lieutenant-colonels until they were 47.[24] These were only averages and even within the line infantry there were wide variations. In 1936 the senior subaltern in the Royal Irish Fusiliers had only seven years' service, whereas his counterpart in the Royal Sussex Regiment had sixteen years'.[25]

After the Boer War Kitchener criticized the system for producing too many unit commanders who were too old for their jobs. Experience in both world wars showed that the best age for unit commanders in the teeth arms was between 28 and 36.[26] Both time promotion and regimental promotion were, therefore, open to the same criticisms. They did too little to reward merit, they promoted good officers far too slowly, and they deadened the enthusiasm of many otherwise competent officers.[27] As one officer who had been a subaltern for fifteen years remarked, 'When you've done orderly officer for that length of time it does rather take the energy out of you. You're rather apt to become rather lethargic and not to have any vision, and just to carry on your duties as best you can and hope that one day you'll be a captain.'[28]

The alternative would have been to employ a thorough-going system of promotion according to merit that would have advanced able and energetic officers over the heads of their less deserving colleagues. The Penzance

---

[21] PP (1904), XL. Cd. 1790. *Minutes of evidence*, Q. 4166.

[22] Kennedy, *This, Our Army*, 83.

[23] IWMSA. Accession No. 000822/07. Lt.-Col. A. C. Jackson, 13.

[24] PRO WO 32/3742. First Report of the committee on promotion of regimental officers (Line Infantry), 2 May 1934.

[25] PRO WO 32/4477. War Office to GOC-in-C Home and Overseas, 2 Oct. 1936.

[26] PP (1904), XL. Cd. 1790. *Minutes of evidence*, Q. 174; PRO WO 32/13253. Memo by Military Secretary, 25 Nov. 1946.

[27] NAM 8202-55. Colonel G. C. Swiney MSS. Scrapbook, Sept. 1872 to June 1913. 'The officer of the day', *The World*, 25 July 1894; PRO WO 163/456. Committee on the supply of officers (Willingdon Committee), Mar. 1937.

[28] IWMSA. Accession No. 000822/07. Lt.-Col. A. C. Jackson, 13.

commission had shunned this, convinced that military qualifications only really showed themselves in wartime and that peacetime examinations could not test them. The Duke of Cambridge agreed. He shared the fear that was widespread amongst regimental officers themselves that promotion by merit would become promotion by political jobbery and favouritism.[29] In 1908 a former Military Secretary, the officer responsible for guiding officers' careers, suggested a cautious application of the principle of selection by merit.[30] The CGS, Sir William Nicholson, was quick to reject the idea. Selection might advance the career of deserving junior officers, but the cost of doing so would be the destruction of one of the foundations of the regimental system, for it would 'cause serious unrest in the Army, disturb the cordial relations which ought to exist between officers belonging to the same regiment, and weaken that esprit de corps which is so conducive to fighting efficiency'.[31] The Director of Personnel Services at the War Office echoed the same sentiments in 1943. He opposed the idea of creating a general list of suitably qualified majors from which unit commanders could be selected because 'General List promotion has always been objected to on the grounds that it would break up the Regimental system. I am convinced that this system contains much of inestimable value which would be lost by plain General List promotion.'[32] The most that the Army Council was prepared to do was to apply more rigorously the principle of rejecting officers who were manifestly unfitted for promotion.[33]

There were two ways, however, in which a junior officer could break free of the stranglehold over the speed of promotion exercised by the regimental system. Officers who demonstrated their competence and zeal on the battlefield or in a staff appointment on active service might be given a brevet promotion.[34] Or officers who had demonstrated 'outstanding proof of brains and industry together with capacity for command combined with initiative, tact, reliability and loyalty' might be offered accelerated promotion to fill a vacancy in another regiment.[35] But the application of such narrow categories ensured that the principle was applied sparingly. In 1927, for example, no cavalrymen and only

[29] Col. G. Poulett Cameron, 'The Royal Army Warrant and Explanatory Minute', *United Services Journal* (Dec. 1871), 475–88; Maj. W. W. Knollys, 'The Army Promotion and Retirement Warrant', *United Services Magazine* (Oct. 1877), 217.

[30] PRO WO 32/5056. Report of Sir C. Grove's Committee on the promotion of regimental officers, May 1908.

[31] PRO WO 32/5056. Minute, W. G. Nicholson, CGS, 10 June 1908.

[32] PRO WO 32/11061. Minute, DPS, to DMS(B), 25 Nov. 1943.

[33] PRO WO 32/5056. Brade to Secretary of the Selection Board, 5 Apr. 1909.

[34] PP (1876), XV. C. 1569. *Report of the Royal Commission on army promotion and retirement.*

[35] PRO WO 32/3740. Promotion of officers. Accelerated promotion Major to Lt.-Col., 8 June 1926.

thirteen infantry officers were granted accelerated promotion.[36] Regiments regarded it as a mark of shame if they could not themselves produce at least one major who was capable of rising to command, resulting in the job having to be given to an officer granted accelerated promotion from another regiment.[37]

Many officers shunned promotion by merit not only because it threatened one of the foundations of the regimental system; they also recognized that it raised the intractable practical issue of how to identify 'merit'. After April 1873, commanding officers were required to compile an annual confidential report on every officer, giving 'a full and exhaustive report upon the personal efficiency, conduct, character, acquirements [sic] and service of every officer in the unit...'.[38] However, the reports had numerous defects. Some Commanding Officers found the whole system irksome.[39] Many reports were either unduly favourable or so vague as to be practically useless. Reporting officers were frequently unwilling to submit an adverse report on a comrade with whom they had served for many years.[40] Some commanders used the system to promote an officer nearing retirement age in order to keep him in the service, and so enhance his pension.[41] Others employed bizarre criteria in assessing the fitness of their subordinates for promotion.[42] In 1926 the CIGS, Sir George Milne, complained:

It is really comic some of the reasons given in confidential reports as to why an officer is really considered fit for promotion. I recognize the importance of every officer playing games, but I cannot see why, because a young officer plays polo or is a good cricketer, he is going to be of great advantage to the staff.[43]

There is also evidence that the regimental system could narrow an officer's mental outlook. In the 1870s the ethos of the Gordon Highlanders was, according to one of its officers, that 'We went where we were told; we fought where we were told; we sought no personal reward; a very proud stand to take up in face of a pushing, self-seeking world; there was a great deal to be said for it and it was said, freely—to me.'[44] Nearly

[36] PRO WO 32/3734. Maj.-Gen. Boyd to Adjutant-General, 7 May 1928.
[37] Bedfordshire Record Office. X550/15/29 Regimental Association. Lt.-Col. P. Young to Lt.-Col. A. C. Young, 19 Feb. 1955.
[38] War Office, QR... 1892, 66.
[39] PP (1902), X. Cd. 982. Minutes of evidence, Q. 892.
[40] PRO WO 32/5056. Report of Sir C. Grove's Committee, May 1908; PRO WO 32/17698. Report of the Committee on the New All-Regular Army (Whistler Report), May 1958.
[41] PRO WO 32/3737. Report of Lord Plumer's committee on the promotion of officers in the army, 7 Jan. 1925.
[42] PP (1904), XL. Cd. 1790. Minutes of evidence, Q. 4246.
[43] PRO WO 279/57. Report on the Staff Conference held at the Staff College, Camberley, 17–20 Jan. 1927.
[44] Hamilton, Listening for the Drum, 61.

seventy years later, some regiments retained much the same outlook. R. King Clark, who served as a subaltern with 1/Manchester Regiment in Egypt in 1937, remembered that, after overseeing his platoon doing weapons training in the morning and playing sport with them in the afternoon, he

wasn't a professional soldier. I mean my mind wasn't wrapped up in my job at all really and I don't think it was with very few officers, junior officers. It was a sort of police job with a sort of social angle thrown in. You got paid half a day's pay for half a day's work. And I think we all had a very high sense of duty in that we would do what we were told. But very few of us had any real initiative about trying to develop our own small units, you know, to improve them beyond the scope of the general attitude of the day.[45]

Some commanding officers regarded subordinates who wanted to widen their knowledge by attending the Staff College as being disloyal to their regiment and anxious to spend two years in idleness rather than take their proper turn at regimental duties.[46] When W. N. Nicholson of the Suffolk Regiment decided to apply to go to Camberley in 1910, his company commander asked him 'Why do you want to leave the battalion?', adding that 'The Regiment should be good enough; only wasters go away.'[47] Even in the early 1930s some infantry regiments were said to boast that none of their officers had ever been encouraged to leave the regimental family in order to attend the Staff College.[48]

However, the idea that regimental officers had little commitment to their profession betrays an incomplete and partial understanding of how they were educated and trained, and how their career paths developed. It overlooks the attempts that began in the late nineteenth century to overcome some of the more obvious defects in the system and to break down the mental parochialism of regimental officers and broaden their intellectual horizons. The military authorities did try to inculcate a degree of professional zeal in regimental officers, they did try to widen their mental horizons, and they did try to provide outlets for able and ambitious officers. They did this by a combination of pre- and post-commissioning compulsory education, and by offering young officers the opportunity to serve away from their regiments for short periods so that they could widen their experience of practical soldiering. Although experience in South Africa suggested that their efforts were not uniformly successful, the fact that they were being made should not be overlooked.

[45] IWMSA. Accession No. 004486/7. Lt.-Col. R. King-Clark, 11.
[46] Spiers, *The Late Victorian Army*, 109.
[47] Nicolson, *Behind the Lines*, 168.
[48] Belchem, *All in the Day's March*, 17.

In 1874 the CO of 56/Foot told his officers that 'Diligence and zeal in the performance of all duty will be productive of their own rewards.'[49] However, the military authorities were never so optimistic about human nature that they acted as if they believed that to be the case. An officer's formal training and education did not stop when he left Sandhurst or Woolwich and joined his regiment. All regimental officers underwent post-commissioning compulsory training. It fell into two parts. In the first phase, subalterns in the Royal Artillery, Royal Engineers, and after the First World War, the Royal Corps of Signals and Royal Tank Corps, were sent for periods varying from several weeks to several months to their arm of service school. There they were taught the technical aspects of their profession. In the 1880s, for example, newly commissioned gunners did a six- to eight-week course at the School of Artillery at Shoeburyness.[50] The engineers received the longest post-commissioning training. Before 1900 they spent two years at their Depot at Chatham. This was reduced to ten months after 1918, but was then followed by two years at the University of Cambridge, where they completed an honours degree in engineering.[51]

This phase of their training meant that officers in the more technical arms of the service joined their unit with an understanding of the professional demands of their job, and some sense of a common tactical doctrine. The infantry and the cavalry were not so well served. Before 1939 neither arm had its own junior officers' tactical school. Instead, subalterns were posted either to their regimental depot or straight to their unit, where they spent several months doing drill and learning about the interior economy of their unit. Infantry subalterns also spent three months at the School of Musketry at Hythe, where they learned to become musketry instructors.[52] It was left to their COs to instil some knowledge of tactics in them after they had joined their unit.[53] Suggestions were made from time to time that the infantry and cavalry ought to copy the other arms of service and send newly commissioned subalterns either to special classes organized in some of the larger garrisons, or to an

[49] ERM. ERB 397. Anon., *Standing Orders of the 56th (West Essex) Regiment*, 22.

[50] Goodenough and Dalton, *The Army Book of the British Empire*, 224.

[51] Spiers, *Late Victorian Army*, 101; Col. M. A. Wingfield, 'The Supply and Training of Officers for the Army', *Journal of the Royal United Services Institute*, 69 (1924), 437; IWMSA. Accession No. 000954. Brig. W. R. Smijth-Windham, 4–6; IWMSA. Accession No. 000944/03. Maj. A. H. Austin, 5.

[52] LHCMA. Liddell Hart MSS 15/8/284. *Small Arms School, Hythe, June 1922. Memorandum 2. Training Junior Leaders as Instructors* (London: War Office, 1922); PRO WO 279/70. Report on the Staff Conference held at the Staff College, Camberley, 13–16 Jan. 1930; IWMSA. Accession No. 000968/02. Col. Sir Douglas Scott, 6.

[53] PRO WO 279/65. Staff Conference held at the Staff College, Camberley, 14 to 17 Jan. 1929.

arm-of-service school before they joined their unit.[54] But they usually met with a frosty reception, not just on grounds of the cost involved, but also because they ran counter to one of the most fundamental principles that guided training at all levels of the army. Schools existed to train instructors, but COs wanted to retain their autonomous power to train the subordinates they would lead in battle.[55]

All subalterns were on probation for the first three years of their service. At the end of that period their commission might be terminated if the three senior officers in their unit did not agree that they were likely to become efficient officers. Each officer then had to pass two sets of examinations to demonstrate that he was qualified for promotion, the first for the step up from Lieutenant to Captain, and the second from Captain to Major. When the examinations were first introduced after the abolition of purchase, they attracted a good deal of opprobrium from senior officers who fulminated that they would favour the bookworm over the practical soldier, but they were there to stay.[56] Before 1899 the subjects in which candidates were examined included regimental duties, which involved the study of *Queen's Regulations*, military law, the interior economy of their unit, the regulations governing the pay of their men, drill, and tactics.[57] Lieutenants seeking promotion to Captain were expected to answer questions concerned with the deployment of a reinforced company, and Captains seeking promotion to Major faced questions concerned with the leadership of a reinforced battalion. In 1936 this test was made stiffer. Henceforth Lieutenants were required to write orders for a mixed force of battalion strength, and Captains were expected to show how they would command a mixed force of brigade size.[58]

Finally, majors who aspired to reach the rank of lieutenant-colonel had to pass an examination designed to test their tactical fitness for command of a unit. Candidates were required to answer written questions concerning the deployment of a mixed force of brigade strength, and then to conduct a practical tactical exercise under the eye of a board of senior officers in which they took command of an imaginary mixed force no smaller than a battalion of infantry, a battery of artillery, and a squadron

[54] NAM 8202-55. Col. G. C. Swiney MSS. Scrapbook, Sept. 1872 to June 1913. Suggestions for a military college for officers on long leave or half-pay, 27 Feb. 1872.

[55] Gossett, 'Battalion Command', 476; LHCMA. Lord Alanbrooke MSS 14/67/MCL/3. WO file 43/Infy/389, 31 July 1937.

[56] Hansard, HC (series 3) vol. 204, col. 1401; S. M. Miller, *Lord Methuen and the British Army: Failure and Redemption* (London: Frank Cass, 1999), 50–1; PP (1902), X. Cd. 983. *Minutes of evidence*, QQ. 2295–6.

[57] War Office, *QR... 1892*, 249.

[58] LHCMA. Liddell Hart MSS 15/8/97. War Office, Examination of Army Officers for Promotion. Paper set in Oct. 1936.

of cavalry.[59] These examinations were not solely meant to discover academic excellence. Their purpose, as the author of a textbook published to assist candidates wrote, 'is not so much to ensure a simple passing of the tests, which are in reality fixed at a fairly low standard, as to encourage officers to improve themselves, by reading and practice, in professional knowledge and attainments'.[60]

Experience in South Africa showed that the system had some significant defects, and after the Boer War some major changes were introduced. First, the format of the examinations became more practical. Hitherto, the examinations had been largely paper exercises. After 1903 the examinations in tactics, topography, and military engineering were conducted partly on paper, but partly orally and on the ground and by a Board of Officers especially nominated for the job. Second, efforts began to force regimental officers to widen their mental horizons. Two further examinations, in strategy and military history, were added. They were set for lieutenants seeking promotion to captain and were taught with a strongly didactic bent.[61] 'The object of this paper', *King's Regulations* explained in 1912, 'is to elicit from the candidates their knowledge of tactical principles and to test their power of applying those principles, while discriminating between the methods by which those principles were applied during the campaign in question and the methods by which they would be applied at the present time.'[62]

This was the first measure the military authorities took to require officers to look beyond the narrow boundaries of a body of knowledge that was entirely confined to their duties as regimental officers. This process was carried a step further after 1918, when, in a further effort to broaden the mental horizons of all officers, they were also required to pass examinations in 'Imperial Military Geography', a subject that today would be analogous to strategic studies.[63]

It is difficult to judge the extent to which this system represented a serious test of professional competence. Some junior officers welcomed the greater emphasis on formal training that developed in the late nineteenth century, believing that 'the complications which science has intro-

[59] War Office, *KR... 1912*, Appendix XII.
[60] Maj. R. F. Legge, *Guide to Promotion for Officers in Subjects (a)(i) Regimental Duties* (London, 1915), p. xv; War Office, *King's Regulations and Orders for the Army* (London, 1912), 168–70, 384–406.
[61] PRO WO 32/8704. Memorandum, Director General Military Training and Education to C-in-C, 28 July 1903.
[62] War Office, *KR... 1912*, Appendix XI.
[63] War Office, *King's Regulations... 1928*, 482; Maj. D. H. Cole, *Imperial Military Geography: General Characteristics of the Empire in Relation to Defence* (London: Sifton Praed, 1937) was a popular textbook that went through numerous revisions before 1939; General Staff, *Training Regulations 1934*, 111–12.

duced into the art of war render it necessary that Officers should have a professional education as thorough and as profound as that which is usually possessed by members of one of the learned professions'.[64] However, there was also a suspicion that the hurdle faced by subalterns at the end of their three years of probation was a farce because many senior officers were reluctant to blight a young man's career at its outset and so gave candidates the benefit of any doubt.[65] But that was not always the case. Some senior regimental officers were not so tender-hearted and did present adverse reports on young officers under their tutelage, who then received a formal letter from the C-in-C telling them to mend their ways and were dismissed if they did not.[66]

The system of confidential reporting probably did encourage some officers to take their profession seriously who might not otherwise have done so, if only because a series of poor reports could lead to the premature end of a career. In 1892 Major J. L. Fraser of 1/Suffolk Regiment decided to retire after being told that his confidential reports were so unsatisfactory that he would receive no further promotion. Two years later, another officer in the same battalion was refused promotion because of poor confidential reports.[67] Promotion examinations had a similar effect because the penalties for failure were similar. Lieutenant Bathurst of the Royal Sussex Regiment discovered this when he failed his promotion examinations in 1883, and subsequently had to resign his commission.[68] In October 1926, over 150 candidates, including several with gallantry awards, could not pass one or more of their promotion examinations.[69] That the demands placed on officers by these examinations were real was shown by the degree of resentment that some officers expressed at the pressure they placed upon them.[70]

Even so, the system of promotion examinations had its shortcomings. Most important, it was doubtful whether they encouraged more than a minority of regimental officers to study their profession in a sustained

[64] Telfer, 'Discipline: Its Importance to an Armed Force', 361.
[65] PP (1902), X. Cd. 983. *Minutes of evidence*, QQ. 8247, 8250; PRO WO 32/5056. Report of Sir C. Grove's Committee on the promotion of regimental officers, QQ. 864, 866.
[66] PP (1902), X. Cd. 983. *Minutes of evidence*, QQ. 2310–11, 2315; War Office, *QR... 1892*, 68.
[67] SRO. GB 554/B13/4.CO's letter and memoranda book, 1883–1903. AAG, Eastern District to OC 1/Suffolks, 21 Nov. 1892; AAG, Eastern District to OC 1/Suffolks, 2 June 1894.
[68] Col. Benjamin D. A. Donne, *The Life and Times of a Victorian Officer, being the Journals of Colonel Benjamin D. A. Donne*, ed. A. Harfield (Wincanton: The Wincanton Press, 1986), 138; PRO WO 32/3786. Minute, Military Secretary to Director of Staff Duties, 17 May 1926.
[69] PRO WO 33/1138. Examination for promotion, Oct. 1926.
[70] Maj. Lord Douglas Compton, 'The Shortage of Officers in the Army', *Journal of the Royal United Services Institute*, 50 (1906), 788; Col. the Earl of Erroll, 'The Defence of Empire. IV. The Dearth of Officers', *Nineteenth Century*, 339 (1905), 745–50; PRO WO 32/8669. Précis for Army Council No. 191, Mar. 1905.

fashion. Officers might work hard to pass the examinations, but many took to their books only in the few months before they sat them, and closed them with a sigh of relief once they had passed.[71] Secondly, by the 1920s the examinations were successful in encouraging officers in the artillery, engineers, and RTC to think in terms of combined arms tactics. But they were less successful in the case of the infantry. This was because, according to one General Staff officer who acted as an examiner, 'officers of other arms are compelled, in the ordinary course of their work, to study the infantry problems, and in many cases I think that the training of the infantry officer is rather narrow-minded and rather liable to be confined only to his own arm'.[72]

There was no doubt, however, that the examination to determine an officer's fitness to command his unit was a real test of competence, for in 1912 no fewer than 38 per cent of candidates failed.[73] However, this also highlighted a major structural defect in the way in which the continuation training of regimental officers was conducted. Unit commanders were responsible for training their own officers, but few had themselves been trained how to do so. Whether or not a regimental officer studied his profession seriously and continuously depended largely on his CO. Some units were fortunate in that they had a CO who was anxious to educate his subordinates. In the winter of 1901 Lt.-Col. C. F. Annesley of 4/Royal Fusiliers made his subalterns write weekly examination answers on military law, administration, fortifications, and interior economy. Every officer who produced the wrong answer had to retake the paper.[74] But many officers were not so fortunate. By 1913 only a quarter of all teeth arm units had a CO or a second-in-command who was a Staff College graduate and, therefore, reasonably well qualified to instruct his subordinates. Officers in many units had to get through their examinations either by their own unaided efforts, or by paying one of the 'crammers' who specialized in preparing candidates for the examinations.[75] Some of the senior officers who were so critical of the performance of their juniors before the post-Boer war enquiries might have done well to reflect upon their own shortcomings as leaders able to inspire their subordinates to study their profession seriously.

[71] PP (1902), X. Cd. 983. *Minutes of evidence*, Q. 2153; PRO WO 279/48. Report of a conf. of General Staff Officers at the Staff College, 15 Jan. 1913.

[72] PRO WO 279/57. Report on the Staff Conference held at the Staff College, Camberley, 17–20 Jan. 1927.

[73] PRO WO 279/48. Report of a conference of General Staff Officers at the Staff College, 15 Jan. 1913.

[74] PP (1902), X. Cd. 983. *Minutes of evidence*, QQ. 1358, 1367–9.

[75] SRO. GB 554/B13/4. CO's letter and memoranda book, 1883–1903. Lt.-Col. R. H. Grady O'Haley to AAG Rawlpindi division, 27 Oct. 1886.

The establishment of the General Staff as the 'brain' of the army in 1906 did lead to some, albeit hesitant, steps towards centralizing the continuation training of regimental officers. In December 1906 the General Staff agreed that the responsibility for training regimental officers would remain with unit commanders, but that General Staff officers in each Command would henceforth assist them by organizing lectures, classes, and staff rides to help promotion candidates. In 1908, for example, the GOC 3 division, Maj.-Gen. W. E. Franklyn, organized an ad hoc 'War School' for forty officers. It was run by his General Staff officers, lasted for two weeks, and consisted of a mixture of lectures and practical problems.[76] However, such innovations made little headway before 1914 in the face of the determination of most COs to retain the power of training their own officers, in their own methods, themselves.[77] This principle was not abandoned until the rapid expansion of the army during the First World War showed up the shortcomings of many officers promoted rapidly from Captain to Lieutenant-Colonel and given command of New Army units. From 1916 onwards the military authorities therefore organized a series of short courses to train unit commanders. These were placed on a permanent footing in 1920–1 with the establishment of the Senior Officers School.[78]

Promotion examinations thus played some part in compelling regimental officers to acquire wider professional knowledge. But they were not the only factor that helped to break down the mental parochialism of regimental soldiering. An equally important force in achieving that goal was the opportunity to serve overseas. As one subaltern explained, 'If an officer finds life irksome, and is hard up or becoming stagnant, he already has an outlet by going away for a few years, such as Africa, Iraq, etc.'[79] By the turn of the century, nearly 150 British officers were serving with the Egyptian Army, and another 700–800 were seconded to the various colonial forces, such as the King's African Rifles or the West African Frontier Force, that the British had raised in tropical Africa.[80] The financial incentives to seek these posts were obvious. In 1906 a subaltern or captain serving with the West African Frontier Force received an allowance of £110 per annum in addition to his ordinary regimental

---

[76] PRO WO 279/18. Report of a conference of General Staff Officers at the Staff College, 7–10 Jan. 1908.

[77] PRO WO 279/48. Report of a conference of General Staff Officers at the Staff College, 15 Jan. 1913.

[78] Brig. B. D. Fisher, 'The Training of the Regimental Officer', *Journal of the Royal United Services Institute*, 74 (1929), 252.

[79] PRO WO 32/4477. Grouping of regiments of infantry of the line for promotion purposes, 17 Mar. 1937.

[80] PP (1904), XL. Cd. 1790. *Minutes of evidence*, QQ. 9457, 9461, 9464.

pay, thus almost doubling his emoluments.[81] Secondments also carried with them increased responsibility and greater opportunity for practical soldiering. In the Egyptian Army in the 1890s, for example, British army captains commanded battalions.[82] J. F. McNab sought a secondment to the King's African Rifles in Uganda in 1929 because he had been told that he, another officer, and the District Commissioner would be the only Europeans in a place twice the size of Wales. 'So I thought, "Oh yes, what a feeling of adventure."'[83] In 1936 R. C. Glanville secured a similar posting because 'you had bags of scope and the chance of using your initiative which at Aldershot you didn't really have'.[84] Some senior regimental officers positively encouraged their juniors to serve in one of the colonial forces for a short period. This prevented them from becoming stale, and gave them the opportunity to exercise more responsibility than they could hope to do if they remained with their own regiment.[85]

After an officer had passed his Captain to Major promotion examinations his compulsory education stopped. However, there was one more rung on the army's educational ladder that could be ascended by able and ambitious officers, the Staff College entrance examination. Entrance to the college was carefully controlled. In the 1890s all candidates had to have completed at least five years' service and their CO had to certify that they were a thoroughly efficient regimental officer.[86] Ambitious officers realized that attendance at the College was one way of breaking free of the shackles of promotion by seniority. In 1890 Capt. Edwin Montagu of 1/Suffolks thought it worthwhile to spend the whole of his life savings so that he could study for the entrance examination.[87] It was evidence that regiments contained a growing proportion of officers committed to rising in their profession that the ratio of applicants to places increased considerably in the early decades of the twentieth century. Whereas in 1904 there were four candidates for each vacancy, by 1928 the ratio was nine to one.[88] The prejudice against the College that had once existed was

[81] War Office, *Royal Warrant... 1906*, sections 218, 223B.

[82] G. Stevens, *With Kitchener to Khartoum* (London: William Blackwood & Sons, 1898), 19.

[83] IWMSA. Accession No. 004427/04. Brig. J. F. McNab, 1–2.

[84] IWMSA. Accession No. 4405/9. Lt.-Col. R. C. Glanville, 1–2.

[85] IWMSA. Accession No. 003835/06. Col. P. R. M. Mundy, 5–6; IWMSA. Accession No. 6188/5. Maj.-Gen. G. F. Upjohn, 3, 4, 8.

[86] War Office, *QR... 1892*, 245–6.

[87] SRO. GB 554/B13/4. CO's letter and memoranda book, 1883–1903. Lt.-Col. R. T. E. Down to Military Secretary, Malta, 26 Feb. 1898.

[88] B. Bond, *The Victorian Army and the Staff College* (London: Eyre Methuen, 1972), 134, 138, 195; PRO WO 279/60. Report on the Staff Conference held at the Staff College, Camberley, 16–19 Jan. 1928; Maj.-Gen. Sir E. Ironside, 'The Modern Staff Officer', *Journal of the Royal United Services Institute*, 73 (1928), 441; PRO WO 32/3093. Bonham-Carter to All GOC-in-Cs, 26 July 1929.

already fading by the Edwardian period. Some regimental officers who appeared as witnesses before a War Office committee investigating the system of promotion for regimental officers in 1908 believed that no officer should be given command of his unit unless he had already passed the Staff College entrance examination.[89] After 1918 increasing numbers of officers recognized that the initials 'p.s.c.' were becoming an indispensable passport to the higher ranks.[90] In 1931 John Vaizey, a subaltern in the RHA, was so determined to get into the College that he paid a 'crammer' 20 guineas, or only a little less than one month's pay, to coach him for the examination, even though he knew that he was competing against about 800 other candidates for one of only eighty places.[91]

Like the cadet colleges and promotion examinations, the syllabus at Camberley reflected the perceived lessons of previous wars. After the Boer War, the emphasis of the course became more practical as work on the ground increasingly supplemented study in the classroom. The course began to include tours of the battlefields of the Franco-Prussian War, the study of the South African and Russo-Japanese Wars, and students were also required to pay more attention than in the past to logistics. After 1918, both in the entrance examination and in the work they did at the College, students were required to demonstrate not only that they understood the technical aspects of their profession, but also that they had a wider understanding of the historical, economic, and contemporary political and strategic issues connected with imperial defence. The courses in the second year included such subjects as inter-service cooperation, industrial mobilization, imperial defence, and the grand strategy of the empire.[92] The Staff College Drag Hounds were not some throwback to a more leisurely age when prowess at field sports was considered to be more important than professional knowledge. On the contrary, they enabled the directing staff to discover which of their students were able to combine physical fatigue with the mental effort required of a successful staff officer.[93]

Both before and after 1918, Staff College students found that the two-year course stretched them mentally and physically.[94] The College brought together the most able and ambitious officers from all arms and fostered personal connections between junior officers who were later to rise to high command. They learnt from their teachers, and

---

[89] PRO WO 32/5056. Report of Sir C. Grove's Committee, May 1908.

[90] PRO WO 279/57. Report on the Staff Conference held at the Staff College, Camberley, 17–20 Jan. 1927.

[91] ERO. D/DVz/376. Vaizey to his mother, 20 Sept. 1930.

[92] PRO WO 32/3098. War Office, *Staff College Regulations* (Camberley, 1921).

[93] IWM PP/MCR/182. Maj.-Gen. D. N. Wimberley MSS. Scottish Soldier. The Memoirs of Maj.-Gen. Douglas Wimberley, vol. 1.

[94] Morgan, *Peace and War*, 90–1.

they learnt from each other.[95] By the inter-war period a post as an instructor at the college had become, for an ambitious major or brevet Lieutenant-Colonel, one of the most highly sought after jobs in the army as their holders were marked out for rapid promotion.

The Staff College, for the minority of officers who attended it before 1939, therefore helped to a limited extent to overcome the mental parochialism of the regimental system. But it had two major shortcomings. By 1899 it was producing only thirty-two PSCs annually and after 1918 its output rose to only sixty.[96] These figures were only just sufficient to meet the needs of the peacetime army. They were far too few to meet the demands of the army as it expanded in both world wars.[97] The paucity of trained staff officers in peacetime also meant that a divide opened between staff and regimental officers. PSCs were required to return to their regiment for only a year before becoming eligible for staff posts, and by the early 1900s ambitious and energetic young officers had better prospects of promotion if they could secure staff appointments at the earliest possible age.[98] The best-qualified staff officers gravitated to staff posts and did not remain with their regiments and rise to command them. Many staff officers, therefore, had comparatively little experience of regimental soldiering. In 1908, for example, of seven infantry generals at the War Office, only one had commanded a battalion.[99] It was not until after 1945, when there was a larger supply of PSCs, that the Military Secretary was able to ensure that Staff College graduates regularly returned to their units for a reasonably long period of duty before being taken for other staff jobs.[100]

The second shortcoming of the Staff College was that it existed 'for the purpose of affording selected officers instruction in the higher branches of the art of war and in staff duties'.[101] This meant that it took officers in their early thirties, when most were too young to have commanded more than a company, and devoted too much time to preparing them to command armies and to considering the wider issues of imperial defence.

---

[95] PP (1904), XL. Cd. 1790. *Minutes of evidence*, Q. 9450; IWM PP/MCR/182. Maj.-Gen. D. N. Wimberley MSS. *Scottish Soldier. The Memoirs of Maj.-Gen. Douglas Wimberley*; Harington, *Tim Harington Looks Back*, 32; Vaughan, *Cavalry and Sporting Memoirs*, 94; Horrocks, *A Full Life*, 161.

[96] Bond, *The Victorian Army and the Staff College*, 182.

[97] J. Hussey, 'The Deaths of Qualified Staff Officers in the Great War', *Journal of the Society for Army Historical Research*, 75 (1997), 246–59; N. Evans, 'The Deaths of Qualified Staff Officers, 1914–1918', *Journal of the Society for Army Historical Research*, 78 (2000), 29–37.

[98] War Office, *QRs... 1892*, 76; PRO WO 32/4840. Maj.-Gen. Ironside, Higher Education for War, 15 Dec. 1925; PRO WO 32/3093. Maj.-Gen. C. Bonham-Carter, to all GOC-in-C home and abroad, 26 July 1929.

[99] PRO WO 32/5056. Report of Sir C. Grove's Committee, May 1908.

[100] PRO WO 32/14215. Meeting of Colonels of Cavalry Regiments held in the Cavalry Club 1415 hrs 3 May, 1952.

[101] War Office, *KR...*, 1912, 144.

When Sir William Robertson became Commandant in 1910 he thought that the title Staff College was a misnomer and that it ought to have been called a 'War School'.[102] In the inter-war period the first six months of the course were spent learning routine staff duties and the second half of the year in studying tactics at the level of the division. But, perhaps in an effort to avoid in the future the problems that soldiers and politicians had during the First World War in working together, in the second year Captains and Majors were expected not only to study how to command corps and armies, but also to consider the political and strategic issues that faced imperial defence planners.[103] One result was that the British army often produced excellent grand strategists, but was sometimes seriously short of able divisional and corps commanders.

Determining the influence of the regimental system on who did, or did not, rise to senior rank is beset by difficulties. In theory it should have played no part, for if the military authorities had qualms about applying the principle of selection below the rank of major, they had no such qualms in applying it when it came to choosing men for regimental or higher commands. In December 1886 they explained to the Treasury that

It is daily becoming more essential that Officers for high command should be selected with reference to their qualifications; and the more frequently that such selection can be exercised before the grade of Major-General is reached, the greater will be the security that the interests of any considerable force will not be entrusted to incompetent hands.[104]

A Selection Board, sitting at the War Office and composed of the Commander-in-Chief, the Adjutant-General, the Quarter-Master General, the Inspector-General of Fortifications, the Director General of Ordnance, and the Military Secretary, considered the case of every senior major to determine his fitness for promotion to lieutenant-colonel and command of a unit.[105] It carefully perused the confidential report of each officer whose case came before it. Sir Evelyn Wood, who served on the board for several years, did not think that favouritism ever entered into its decisions. 'I do not think that I ever saw in eight years any disposition to slur over or to try to do anything but to get at the back of every officer's character. The mistakes I saw made were because we were not drastic enough.'[106]

---

[102] Robertson, *From Private to Field Marshal*, 170.

[103] PRO WO 32/3098. *Staff College Regulations* (Camberley, 1921).

[104] PRO WO 33/47. Correspondence relative to the Royal Warrant for promotion and retirement of combatant officers, dated 31 Dec. 1886.

[105] PRO WO 32/6187. Memorandum defining the constitution and duties of the Army Board, Selection Board and Promotion board, 28 May 1900.

[106] PP (1904), XL. Cd. 1790. *Minutes of evidence*, Q. 4332.

Not everyone agreed with him. H. O. Arnold Forster, the Secretary of State for War between 1903 and 1905, believed that the Board's deliberations resembled an exercise in log-rolling: '"A" can always agree to accept "B's" man if "B" accepts "A's", and so on.'[107] In the late nineteenth century officers who had the good fortune to demonstrate their prowess in some of the innumerable small colonial campaigns that the British army fought could gain command of their unit, and, if they also attracted the patronage of a senior officer, could rise still further.[108] But the war in South Africa demonstrated that unit commanders needed more than 'mere physical bravery, a strong will, nerves of iron and a body impervious to fatigue'.[109] Too many of them could not solve the larger administrative and tactical problems that confronted them on the veldt. The result, according to Sir John French, was 'that he has notorious duffers commanding regiments under his orders who neither he, nor apparently anyone else, can get rid of, except by private and back stairs means, which are subversive of everything that stands for efficiency!'[110]

However, the notion that some regiments enjoyed a higher status than others, and that officers in 'smart regiments' were more likely to get to the top of the army than their counterparts in less smart ones, was a commonplace. To military insiders the social hierarchy of the regimental system seemed so obvious that they took it for granted. Writing in 1946, an officer in the Royal Ulster Rifles who had been commissioned in 1927, remarked that

There was a time, and that not so very distant, when a regiment's 'social' reputation marched hand in hand with its professional reputation, when certain regiments, classified as 'smart' or 'expensive', were viewed by hostesses and mothers as a pool of dancing, bridge, and tennis partners, and even as a pool of potential husbands. Such regiments could be relied upon to 'support the Hunt' and were to be found at full officer strength at the covert-side, slaughtering pheasants, and at every point-to-point and steeplechase meeting.[111]

The fact that the existence of the hierarchy has been taken for granted has meant that few soldiers bothered to comment upon it. It has, therefore, been left to outside observers to try to delimit it. John Keegan has

[107] NAM 8704/35-68. Lt.-Gen. Sir Gerald F. Ellison MSS. H. O. Arnold Forster, Secretary of State for War, For the personal information of Sir John Fisher and his colleagues only, 7 Dec. 1903.
[108] I. F. W. Beckett, 'Command in the Late Victorian Army', in G. D. Sheffield (ed.), *Leadership and Command: The Anglo-American Military Experience since 1861* (London: Brassey's, 1997), 37–56.
[109] NAM 8704/35-85. Lt.-Gen. Sir Gerald F. Ellison MSS. Ellison, Considerations influencing the selection of officers for command, July 1900.
[110] Ibid. Memorandum by Fisher to Esher and Clarke, 15 Jan. 1904.
[111] Maj. M. J. P. M. Corbally, 'The Officer-Producing Class', *Journal of the Royal United Services Institute*, 91 (1946), 204.

suggested that a regiment's place in the social pecking order of the army was determined only in part by its military reputation. Other factors that had nothing to do with military efficiency were equally, if not more, important. They included its lineage, its proximity to the royal family expressed through patronage in the form of Royal Colonels-in-Chief, and its regional affiliations. At the top of the hierarchy were the Household Brigade, four or five of the more exclusive cavalry regiments, the King's Royal Rifle Corps, and the Rifle Brigade. Then came the rest of the cavalry, the Highland Regiments, the Light Infantry, and the Fusilier regiments. They were followed by English county regiments with regional affiliations in the south of England, Lowland Scottish regiments, and then regiments whose regional affiliations were in Ireland, Wales, the north of England, and the Midlands. The technical corps, which counted as teeth arms, the Royal Artillery and the Royal Engineers, came somewhere in the middle. The artillery, until all three branches were amalgamated in the early 1920s, was further subdivided into the most socially desirable branch, because of its connections with the cavalry, the Royal Horse Artillery, the rather less desirable Royal Field Artillery, and the distinctly unglamorous Royal Garrison Artillery.[112] The service corps, such as the Army Service Corps, the Army Ordnance Corps, and the Army Pay Corps, came at the very bottom of the ladder.[113]

The superior prestige of the teeth arms over the 'tail' was never in doubt: 'it is a principle established from the very inception of the army, that fighting corps, i.e. those corps which give expression to the raison d'etre of an army, have the precedence of all other corps', wrote the Permanent Under Secretary of the War Office in 1930.[114] This was reflected in the army's official order of precedence that fixed the position of regiments and corps relative to each other on ceremonial parades.

However, other generalizations rest on uncertain foundations. Before proceeding to examine the military implications of the social hierarchy of the regimental system, it is essential to try to provide a more objective measure for establishing the social pecking order of that hierarchy. This has been done by analysing the system at four selected dates, each set apart by about twenty years. The analysis begins in 1890, a generation

---

[112] Morgan, *Peace and War*, 23.

[113] Keegan, 'Regimental Ideology', 6; K. Simpson, 'The Officers', in I. F. W. Beckett and K. Simpson (eds.), *A Nation in Arms* (Manchester: Manchester University Press, 1985), 66; K. M. Macdonald, 'The Persistence of an Elite: The Case of British Army Officer Cadets', *Sociological Review*, 28, (1980), 637; M. Garnier, 'Power and Ideological Conformity: A Case Study', *American Journal of Sociology*, 79 (1973), 349–50; Weston, 'The Army: Mother, Sister and Mistress', 149–50.

[114] WO 32/2861. Creedy to Maj.-Gen. Sir Evan Carter, Colonel Commandant RASC, 22 Oct. 1930.

after the inauguration of the Cardwell reforms, and is followed by three further 'snapshots' of the regiments, taken in 1910, 1930, and 1951. At each date the number of titled officers serving with each regiment was counted; also noted is whether or not the regiment had attracted a royal patron, in the shape of a royal Colonel-in-Chief. These criteria were chosen on the assumption that the more titled officers, and the greater the willingness of royalty to patronize a particular regiment, the higher was its status.[115] Each regiment was then placed in one of eight categories, depending on how highly it 'scored' according to the number of times it attracted at least one titled officer or a royal patron. Thus the Grenadier Guards, which had at least one titled officer and a royal Colonel-in-Chief on each of the four occasions noted, scored 8. By contrast, the Suffolk Regiment, which failed to attract a royal patron or a titled officer on any of the four occasions, scored 0.

When the results are analysed, they present a picture of the regimental hierarchy that is broadly in accordance with the accepted picture, but which also displays some significant deviations from it. Measured by their ability to attract titled officers and royal patrons, the Household Brigade, the King's Royal Rifle Corps, and the Rifle Brigade outstripped all other regiments. The line cavalry must be treated as a distinct part of the system rather than be conflated with the line infantry. Service in even a relatively unfashionable cavalry regiment was an occupation that was restricted to the comparatively wealthy, whether or not the officer possessed a hereditary title. The line cavalry can be divided into two groups, ten regiments with greater prestige,[116] and another eleven that possessed a lesser status.[117] There were also some clear differentiations in the line infantry. At the top of the hierarchy stood eight regiments. No fewer than five were Highland regiments,[118] one was the Royal Welch Fusiliers, and the other two were the King's Own Yorkshire Light Infantry and the Buffs. The next ten regiments also confirmed the prestige of the Scottish regiments, for one was a Highland Regiment[119] and three others were Scottish Lowland Regiments.[120] This group also contained the

---

[115] Titled officers were defined as those shown in the *Army List* as possessing a peerage, baronetcy, or with a courtesy title denoting that they were the eldest son of a peer.

[116] They were (giving their post-1922 titles): 1/Dragoon Guards, 1/Royal Dragoons, 2/ Dragoons (Scots Greys), 5/Dragoon Guards, 7/, 10/, and 11/Hussars, 13/18 Hussars, 9 Lancers, 16/5th Lancers, 17/21 Lancers.

[117] They were (again using their post-1922 titles): 1/, 2/, 3/ and 6/Dragoon Guards, 4/, 7/ Dragoon Guards, 12/Lancers 3/, 4/, and 8/Hussars, 14/20 Hussars and 15/19 Hussars.

[118] Black Watch, Cameron Highlanders, Highland Light Infantry, Gordon Highlanders, Seaforth Highlanders, Royal Welch Fusiliers, King's Own Yorkshire Light Infantry, and the Buffs.

[119] The Argyll and Sutherland Highlanders.

[120] The Cameronians (Scottish Rifles), King's Own Scottish Borderers, and the Royal Scots Fusiliers.

highest-ranking Irish Regiment, the Royal Irish Fusiliers, together with five English county regiments.[121] The third group of thirteen regiments consisted of eight English county regiments,[122] the Royal Scots, which was the only Scottish Regiment outside the top two groups, the two remaining Welsh Regiments, the Connaught Rangers and the Royal Inniskilling Fusiliers.[123] The final two groups consisted of fifteen[124] and twenty[125] regiments respectively: a mass of English regiments and all of the remaining Irish regiments.

There was no automatic correspondence between regimental prestige and regimental titles. Light Infantry regiments were not positioned immediately behind the more prestigious Highland Regiments but were found in all five groups. The King's Shropshire Light Infantry was in the least prestigious group, whereas the King's Yorkshire Light Infantry was in the most prestigious. By contrast, fusilier regiments did enjoy a modicum of prestige, four out of seven appearing in the first two cohorts. But their high standing was not shared by the other two fusilier regiments, both of which were positioned in the last cohort. The high prestige accorded to Scottish Regiments, and in particular to Highland Regiments, is readily apparent, and Welsh Regiments came before the great mass of English county regiments. In England there was some correspondence between territorial affinity and regimental prestige. Although the bulk of English county regiments was found in the last two cohorts, they can be further divided according to their territorial affiliations, with South of England county regiments outstripping those whose depots were in the north of England, and they in turn outstripping those with depots in the Midlands.

The regimental system thus constituted a variegated social hierarchy. But that fact was of military significance only if the social hierarchy of the

---

[121] Oxford and Buckinghamshire Light Infantry, Gloucestershire Regiment, Somerset Light Infantry, Norfolk Regiment, and the Royal Fusiliers.

[122] Duke of Wellington's Regiment, King's Liverpool Regiment, Royal West Surrey Regiment, Duke of Cornwall's Light Infantry, East Yorkshire Regiment, Northamptonshire Regiment, Manchester Regiment, Royal Berkshire Regiment.

[123] The Royal Scots, South Wales Borderers, Welsh Regiment, Royal Inniskilling Fusiliers, and the Connaught Rangers.

[124] Wiltshire Regiment, West Yorkshire Regiment, Middlesex Regiment, Bedfordshire Regiment, Hampshire Regiment, Royal West Kent, South Lancashire Regiment, Royal Sussex Regiment, Green Howards, Sherwood Foresters, Essex Regiment, King's Own (Royal Lancaster Regiment), Durham Light Infantry, Royal Dublin Fusiliers, Royal Ulster Rifles.

[125] Royal Warwickshire Regiment, North Staffordshire Regiment, Northumberland Fusiliers, Lincolnshire Regiment, Devonshire Regiment, York and Lancaster Regiment, Suffolk Regiment, Border Regiment, Lancashire Fusiliers, South Staffordshire Regiment, King's Shropshire Light Infantry, Cheshire Regiment, Loyal North Lancashire Regiment, Worcestershire Regiment, East Lancashire Regiment, East Surrey Regiment, Dorsetshire Regiment, Leicester Regiment, Leinster Regiment, Royal Dublin Fusiliers, Royal Munster Fusiliers.

regimental system corresponded to the army's professional hierarchy. In other words, social prestige only mattered if it meant that high-status regiments such as the Household Brigade, the line cavalry, and the rifle regiments produced a disproportionate number of senior officers. An attempt to determine whether this was the case has been made by looking at four cohorts of senior officers at four selected dates, 1890, 1910, 1930, and 1951. Senior officers have been defined as all officers holding the rank of Field Marshal, General, Lieutenant-General, and Major-General, but excluding medical officers and members of the Royal family whose ranks were honorary. In 1881 the establishment of Field Marshals and General officers was fixed and remained so until shortly after the First World War, when the number of Major-Generals was slightly reduced, although it was raised to something close to its previous limit in 1938. There was to be a total of no more than six Field Marshals, chosen without reference to their arm of service, ten generals (one sapper, two gunners, and the remainder drawn from the Household Brigade, cavalry, or line infantry), thirty-five Lieutenant-Generals (22 from the Household Brigade, cavalry, or line infantry, 8 gunners, and 5 sappers), and ninety-five Major-Generals (11 sappers, 19 gunners, and 65 drawn from the Household Brigade, the cavalry, and the line infantry).[126] Therefore, 67 per cent of the establishment of general officers was supposed to be drawn from the Household Brigade, the cavalry, and the line infantry, 21 per cent from the Royal Artillery, and 12 per cent from the Royal Engineers.

In 1890 there was a strong correspondence between the social hierarchy of the regimental system and the senior officer corps. In both 1890 and 1910 the Royal Artillery and Royal Engineers were represented in the proportion laid down by the establishments fixed in 1881. However, in 1890 no fewer than thirty out of 142 senior officers (21 per cent) were drawn from the Household Brigade, the King's Royal Rifle Corps, and the Rifle Brigade. If general officers from the line cavalry are included, their share of the senior ranks accounted for no less than 29 per cent. By contrast, the thirty-five least fashionable line infantry regiments provided only 19 per cent of the senior officer cohort. The dominance of the Household Brigade, the King's Royal Rifle Corps, and the Rifle Brigade had hardly been dented a generation later. In 1910, 17.8 per cent of the senior officer cohort was drawn from their ranks. Again, if the cavalry are included in the social elite of the army, it shows that the professional dominance of the social elite was still very apparent, accounting as they did for 28.6 per cent of all senior officers. The thirty-five least fashionable regiments continued

[126] PP (1881), LVIII. C. 2826. *Memorandum showing the principal changes in army organisation...*; PRO WO 32/3785. Minute by R. Patterson, 7 Apr. 1926; PRO WO 32/4466. Minute Military Secretary, 3 Feb. 1938.

to be underrepresented in the ranks of the senior officer cohort, providing just 17 per cent of their number.

However, after 1918 the overrepresentation of the social elite of the army in the ranks of the senior officer corps was significantly reduced. By 1930 the proportion of senior officers drawn from the Household Brigade, the King's Royal Rifle Corps, and the Rifle Brigade had fallen to 11 per cent, and the proportion of this group combined with the cavalry had dropped to 19 per cent. The proportion of senior officers drawn from the thirty-five least fashionable line regiments had risen marginally, but it was still only 22 per cent. The real gainers were the gunners. They had benefited from the expansion of their arm during the First World War, and their share of the senior officers' ranks now stood at 24 per cent. If their share was added to that of the Royal Engineers, these two technical arms together provided 36 per cent of the senior officer cohort. These trends were greatly magnified in the next two decades. By 1951 the share of the Household Brigade, the King's Royal Rifle Corps, the Rifle Brigade, and line cavalry had slumped to only 8.7 per cent. The share of senior officers drawn from the thirty-five least fashionable line infantry regiments had also fallen, to only 15.7 per cent. The numerically dominant force in the senior ranks was now the generals from the 'teeth' corps regiments (the Royal Artillery, Royal Engineers, RTR, and RCS), who now accounted for 56 per cent of the senior officer corps, the gunners alone accounting for 28.9 per cent of the senior officer cohort.

The strong grip that the socially most prestigious regiments within the regimental system had on the senior ranks of the army in the late nineteenth century thus grew weaker after 1918, and had all but disappeared by the middle of the twentieth century.[127] In its place, however, another institution was asserting an increasingly powerful dominance over the higher echelons of the army. It was the Staff College. In 1890 only 7 per cent of the senior officer cohort were staff college graduates. By 1910 the figure had risen, but was still only 39 per cent. However, after the First World War the dominance of PSCs in the ranks of general officers increasingly became apparent. Sixty-four per cent of general officers in 1930 were Staff College graduates, a figure that had risen to 80 per cent by 1950. Under the stimulus of the enormous expansion of the army in both world wars, there was a clear shift in the composition of the army's most senior leadership cohort. It moved from being an elite

[127] I am grateful to Keith Neilson for pointing out to me that the army was not unique in this respect, and that after 1918 a broadly similar trend was discernable in the senior ranks of the Foreign Office, marked by a gradual infusion of men from outside the magic circle of Eton and Harrow. See Z. Steiner and M. L. Dockrill, 'The Foreign Office Reforms, 1919–21', *Historical Journal*, 17 (1974), 144–5.

based upon social prestige to an elite based on the kinds of management skills required by a large and multifarious organization.

Any analysis of the leadership of the regimental system that was confined to commissioned officers would be hopelessly incomplete. For most private soldiers staff officers were infinitely remote beings, and, at least in barracks, even their company and battalion commanders were people they saw infrequently. For most private soldiers authority and leadership on a daily basis was personified by junior NCOs (corporals and lance-corporals), senior NCOs (sergeants), and warrant officers. They were an everyday presence in their lives in a way that officers rarely were.

At the apex of this system stood the usually formidable figure of the RSM. His superior status was marked out by the fact that whereas other NCOs were addressed by their inferiors according to their rank, the RSM, like commissioned officers, was addressed as 'Sir'.[128] (This privilege was later extended to all Warrant Officers). He received the orders of the commanding officer through the Adjutant and issued them to the various company orderlies, he detailed non-commissioned officers and men for duty, he organized all the minor parades, he instructed young non-commissioned officers in their duties, and he superintended the conduct of the sergeants' mess. He could even place NCOs or private soldiers under arrest.[129] He was meant to be a symbol to be emulated by every NCO and other rank in the regiment.[130]

The supervisory duties of other Warrant Officers and NCOs were more limited. The Bandmaster was responsible for the conduct of the regimental band, the Regimental Quartermaster Sergeant was the right-hand man of the Quarter-Master, and had daily oversight over the unit's stores.[131] Each unit had a sergeant cook, who oversaw the preparation of all meals, a master-tailor, who had charge of the tailor's shop, and a provost sergeant, who was responsible to the Adjutant for the conduct of the regimental police and had charge of all defaulters while they were serving their sentences.[132] The orderly room sergeant acted as the confidential clerk of the CO and Adjutant. The remaining sergeants and corporals acted in turn, usually for a week at a time, as battalion orderly sergeant and orderly corporal. Their main function was to assist the

---

[128] Anon., *The Standing Orders of the 47th ... Foot*, 23.

[129] Goodenough and Dalton, *The Army Book of the British Empire*, 144; Anon., *Standing Orders ... late 50th Regiment*, 14–15.

[130] Anon., *Standing Orders ... 5th (Royal Irish) Lancers*, 21.

[131] Anon., *The Standing Orders ... Warwickshire Regiment* , 25.

[132] Anon., *The Standing Orders of the Durham Light Infantry* (Newcastle: J. & P. Bealls Ltd, 1933), 14–17; ERM. ERB 397. Anon., *Standing Orders of the 56th (West Essex) Regiment*, 26–32.

subaltern of the day and the Captain of the week in ensuring that the rank and file complied with battalion standing orders.[133]

By 1892 there were no fewer than twenty different grades of Warrant Officer, ninety-eight different grades of sergeant, and sixteen different grades of corporal and lance-corporal. Their precise title varied between the different arms of service.[134] Whereas officers had some, albeit slight, opportunity to gain accelerated promotion by moving outside their own regiment, before 1946 the promotion of NCOs and Warrant Officers took place entirely within their regiment. This was undoubtedly a significant weakness of the regimental system, because it did nothing to equalize the quality of NCOs between different regiments. During the Boer War one divisional commander concluded that units that recruited in urban areas had far less difficulty in finding intelligent and appropriately educated men to fill NCOs' appointments than did units that recruited in rural areas.[135]

On the other hand, promotion through the non-commissioned ranks was more dependent upon merit than it was for officers. The latter knew that, provided they passed the necessary qualifying examinations, time promotion or promotion by regimental vacancy would ensure that they would usually reach the rank of major. Before 1914 most NCOs enjoyed no such privilege. COs had sole charge over the promotion of NCOs in their unit.[136] Seniority conferred no automatic right to promotion, although some COs took account of it when choosing between equally meritorious candidates.[137] The only exception was a small number of NCOs in particular trade groups, such as other ranks in the RAPC, skilled tradesmen in the Royal Engineers, and, after 1919, Orderly Room Clerks. They were given time promotion because they had such a limited rank structure that promotion by vacancy would have meant that most would have languished as private soldiers long after men of comparable experience but with less scarce skills had risen through the ranks of the non-commissioned officers.[138]

This began to change in the 1930s. As the army became more mechanized, and the need to recruit and retain a wider range of skilled tradesmen grew, so the number of NCOs eligible for time promotion also had to be increased. By the late 1930s men in seventy-nine

[133] Anon., *The Standing Orders... King's Royal Rifle Corps*, 47–8.

[134] War Office, QR... *1892*, 23–7.

[135] PP (1904), XLI. Cd. *1791*. *Minutes of evidence...*, QQ. 16018, 16024.

[136] War Office, KR... *1912*, 55–7, 178.

[137] ERM. ERB 397. *Standing Orders of the 56th (West Essex) Regiment*, 36–8; Anon., *Standing Orders... King's Royal Rifle Corps*, 25–6; Anon., *The Standing Orders... The Royal Warwickshire Regiment*, 35.

[138] PRO WO 32/17657. Colonel AAG, AG17 to PA3, 13 Oct. 1958.

specialized trades received time promotion. Provided they had gained the requisite trade qualifications and their CO's recommendation, such skilled men as blacksmiths, armourers, carpenters and joiners, various types of clerks, dental technicians, gun fitters, electrical fitters, millwrights, moulders, riveters, saddlers, and tailors could expect to be promoted to lance-corporal after three years' service, corporal after six years' service, and lance-sergeant after nine years' service.[139] Such men had always been required in corps like the Royal Engineers, but mechanization meant that they were increasingly needed even in the infantry and cavalry. They not only had to know how to command others, but also had to possess a growing degree of technical knowledge. This could have a profound impact on a unit's NCO cadre, as exemplified by the experience of 12/Lancers. In 1928 it became one of the first cavalry regiments to exchange its horses for armoured cars. Some Warrant Officers and senior NCOs opted to transfer to other regiments rather than lose all connection with horses. The remainder 'adapted themselves', although in the opinion of one of the regiments' officers, few of them ever became really skilled drivers or mechanics. It was left to more junior and younger NCOs to lead the way in acquiring the necessary driving and mechanical skills, and in doing so to gain comparatively swift promotion by proving their technical competence by instructing others.[140]

Like officers, prospective NCOs also had to pass formal qualifying examinations, but they gave no guarantee of future promotion. NCOs had to be literate, and therefore the military authorities insisted that all aspiring corporals had to possess a Third Class Army Education certificate, all sergeants a Second Class Certificate, and all NCOs and Warrant Officers senior to them a First Class certificate.[141] After 1918 the standard for corporals was raised to a Second Class certificate. Soldiers anxious for promotion had to work hard to garner the essential qualifications and demonstrate the necessary zeal.[142] This produced a particular relationship between NCOs that was largely absent from the officers' mess. Comradeship existed, but it was often tempered by a sense of competition.[143] The ideal NCO needed 'to be highly trained in all technical matters, to be possessed of intelligence, superior attainments,

---

[139] PRO WO 32/13706. Director of Personnel Administration to WO Directors, 17 Sept. 1948; War Office, *Royal Warrant for the Pay, Appointment, Promotion, and Non-effective Pay of the Army, 1940* (London: War Office, 1940), 232–40.

[140] IWMSA. Accession No. 000892/06. Col. G. J. Kidston-Montgomerie, 11–12.

[141] War Office, *QR . . . 1892*, 182–3; War Office, *KR . . . 1912*, 58.

[142] Anon., *Standing Orders of the 47th . . . Foot*, 27; SRO. GB 554/B3/1. Anon., *The Standing Orders of the 1st Battalion, the Suffolk Regiment*, 58–9.

[143] Lucy, *There's a Devil in the Drum*, 63.

force of character, firmness, tact, and judgment'.[144] Senior NCOs such as colour sergeants were

selected by commanding Officers from the serjeants; they should be men whose devotion to duty, integrity, and general soldier like qualities are conspicuous. They should have a good knowledge of accounts, and will invariably be the pay serjeants of their troops or companies, from which they are not to be detached... [145]

Before being promoted, prospective NCOs were usually obliged to attend a cadre course, run by the Adjutant. Its rigour varied from unit to unit, depending on the supply of potential NCOs and the energy of the officers running it.[146] In the Cheshire Regiment aspiring corporals had to pass practical tests conducted by a board of regimental officers—leading a section in the field, musketry exercises, barrack and guard duties— before being eligible for promotion. Corporals who aspired to become sergeants had to pass further examinations in regimental history, elementary sanitation, and leading a half company in the field.[147] This system produced a cadre of Warrant Officers and senior NCOs who were relatively young men but who had considerable experience of regimental soldiering. In the late 1930s, for example, the average age at which Warrant Officer IIs were appointed in the Sherwood Foresters was between 30 and 32.[148]

The basic function of all Warrant Officers and NCOs was to ensure that the other ranks carried out the orders that were passed down through them from their officers, and they did so without hesitation or question.[149] In barracks they oversaw most of the daily routine in their unit. Each company had a senior NCO, a colour sergeant, or, after 1914, a company sergeant-major, who as well as being responsible for the discipline of the rank and file of his company also kept the pay accounts. He was assisted by three or four sergeants and several corporals, all of whom were answerable to him for ensuring that their company commander's orders were performed to the letter.[150] The NCOs had a far more intimate knowledge of their men than the company officers, and formed the vital link that mediated relations between officers and other ranks. It was their duty to report any improper behaviour to their

[144] Anon., *The Standing Orders... (Cheshire) Regiment*, 38.
[145] War Office, *QR... 1892*, 180.
[146] Goodenough and Dalton, *The Army Book of the British Empire*, 384; Col. H. E. Franklyn, 'Training Troops on Foreign Service', *Journal of the Royal United Services Institute*, 79 (1934), 561.
[147] Anon., *The Standing Orders... (Cheshire) Regiment*, 78–9.
[148] *Regimental Annual. The Sherwood Foresters 1938*, 28, 101.
[149] Anon., *Standing Orders... 50th Regiment*, 23.
[150] Ibid. 20.

sergeant-major or company commander.[151] As a sergeant in the Seaforth Highlanders explained, 'if you took promotion you had to keep control over them. Another old saying in the Army: "as an NCO you can only be two things—either a bastard or a stupid bastard", because of the fact that if you allowed laxity it was taken advantage of. But you could always strike a happy medium.'[152]

The first step up the promotion ladder, from private to lance-corporal, represented a major change in the life experiences of a soldier. It meant the breaking of friendships, for lance-corporals could no longer associate with their former comrades as their social equals, and any lance-corporal who was caught mixing freely with private soldiers was liable to be demoted. On the other hand, rather than being the recipient of all orders, lance-corporals, for the first time in their military career, were given a small modicum of authority. Promotion to lance-corporal relieved the soldier of having physically to carry out many of the more onerous chores around barracks.[153] Henceforth, as Horace Wyndham discovered when he became a lance-corporal in 1892, 'instead of performing what were really menial tasks, I superintended their execution by others'.[154] Promotion thus became a test of the lance-corporal's character and ambition. Large numbers of young lance-corporals found the burdens of being a junior NCO were not commensurate with the meagre rewards on offer and resigned their stripe.[155] But if a lance-corporal were sufficiently strong-minded he could usually exert the necessary authority, particularly because his superiors would invariably support him in any clash with his inferiors.[156] NCOs who could not enforce discipline, or who could not ensure that their officers' orders were obeyed, were liable to be demoted or even court-martialled.[157]

An effective NCO had to earn the respect of the other ranks below him and the confidence of the officers above him.[158] In most units the relationship between NCOs and other ranks was characterized by mutual respect, tinged, on the part of private soldiers, with a sense of wariness. Some NCOs gained their respect and obedience because of their longer service and man-management skills. At the Royal Artillery Depot in

[151] Anon., *Standing Orders... (Cheshire) Regiment*, 47.
[152] IWMSA. Accession No. 00906/06. Sgt. M. Finlayson, 3.
[153] RNRM. NMS RM 5053. Memoirs of L/Cpl. C. Mates, 1883–1896.
[154] Wyndham, *The Queen's Service*, 156.
[155] PP (1892), XIX. C. 6582. *Report of the Committee...*, 19–20.
[156] Wyndham, *The Queen's Service*, 159.
[157] IWM 77/118/1. Papers of Colonel K. C. Weldon, Army Book 152. Weldon to OC 49th Infantry Brigade, 9 Jan. 1917; ERM. ERCB3. Warley WO's and Sergeant's Mess Scrap Book, 1898–1939. Cutting from *Mid Essex Recorder*, 'Warley Barracks Tragedy. Essex Sergeant Major Shot', 24 May 1924.
[158] Anon., *Standing Orders... (Cheshire) Regiment*, 38.

1939 Sergeant Hardy 'was a very humane man, devoid of malice or sarcasm. He expressed no favouritism. Very quickly he gained our respect and we obeyed his slightest wish. We had no option, I know, but his firm but fair manner, coupled with his efficiency, encouraged us to work together as a unit, as well as individually.'[159] The very best NCOs 'had the priceless gift of being able to get the best out of men, by means of a shrewd admixture of discipline, humour and plain common sense'.[160] But even if they lacked some of these skills, most NCOs were obeyed if only because their subordinates knew that they could mete out punishments if they were not.[161]

Private soldiers did not usually resent NCOs who were strict disciplinarians, provided that they dealt with their men fairly. In July 1941 the RSM of 3/London Scottish 'was a ruthless disciplinarian, but what RSM isn't? Nevertheless, he was highly respected by all. He would play football in the recreation hours, enter wholeheartedly into the game, and expect no quarter from anybody.'[162] However, NCOs who were capricious, foul-mouthed, or bullying were detested by their men.[163] Harry Smith, who served on the Western Front during the First World War, knew some 'real pleasant and helpful sergeant-majors; [but] I've known one or two that were pigs'.[164] NCOs who swaggered on the parade ground but proved incapable of overcoming the stresses of the battlefield earned the silent contempt of their men.[165] Sometimes bad blood did develop between NCOs and other ranks, and it could occasionally spill over into outright violence and, in exceptional cases, even murder.[166] In 1932 enmity between a trooper in 12/Lancers and one of his sergeants culminated in the trooper shooting the sergeant with his pistol.[167]

Many newly commissioned subalterns relied heavily on their NCOs in running their sub-unit, and remained grateful for what they had taught them.[168] Senior NCOs had the advantage that they not only knew their men more intimately than any newly joined officer, but they also had a better grasp of the daily practicalities of running the sub-unit. Newly commissioned officers were reminded that

[159] Bowman, *Three Stripes*, 26–7.

[160] Maj.-Gen. D. Tyacke, *A Cornish Hotchpotch* (King's Lynn: privately printed, 2002), 114.

[161] G. Coppard, *With a Machine Gun to Cambrai: The Tale of a Young Tommy in Kitchener's Army 1914–1918* (London: HMSO, 1969), 6.

[162] J. M. Lee Harvey, *D-Day Dodger* (London: William Kimber, 1979), 14.

[163] W. Gore-Browne, 'Life in a Cavalry Regiment', *Nineteenth Century*, 28 (1890), 847–8.

[164] IWMSA. Accession No. 0000/46/6. H. Smith, 39.

[165] IWM 81/9/1. E. Lye Ts. memoirs, A Worm's eye view of Suvla Bay, 29.

[166] NAM 6005-60. Records of the 88th Regiment (Connaught Rangers). Entries for 5 June 1887 and Aug. 1889.

[167] PRO WO 141/79. JAG to Secretary of State, 2 Jan. 1933; IWMSA. Accession No. 004473/04. Lt.-Col. E. G. Brice, 53–4.

[168] IWMSA. Accession No. 000944/03. Maj. A. H. Austin, 16.

It must be realised that the Company, Squadron or Battery Sergeant-Major is a man of considerable service and experience. In view of this the officer should not hesitate to ask for advice on matters to do with the routine of the unit or sub-unit. Furthermore, when offered advice by the Company, Squadron or Battery Sergeant-Major the officer should accept it in the spirit in which it is given. Although the officer holds the Queen's Commission, whereas the Warrant Officer does not, the latter has both service and experience behind him.[169]

Ideally, officers and NCOs were expected to maintain a tone of polite reasonableness in their professional relations. In 8/Royal Irish Lancers in the 1930s officers

never for example called a man 'Sergeant'. You never said, 'Sergeant So-and-So do this'. You had to call him by his name. That was the form. You said, 'Sergeant Jenkins, will you please do so-and-so', and of course that was an order but it was conveyed in this way because this was the civilised way of doing it.[170]

Officers were also expected never to reprove NCOs in the presence of their inferiors for fear of undermining their authority.[171] If a junior officer behaved badly in public towards an NCO, his CO was likely to take the part of the NCO. Experienced NCOs were hard to replace; new subalterns were not.

The British aristocracy, and their supposedly pernicious influence, have frequently been singled out as convenient whipping boys for the wider failings of British society and the British economy in the century after 1870.[172] In the same way that the aristocracy were supposed to have undermined the enterprising spirit of British capitalists, so it has been supposed that when they donned khaki, they and their clients infused the regular officer corps with an anti-modern and anti-professional spirit that served the army ill in the late nineteenth and twentieth centuries. In 1903 Sir Archibald Hunter told the Royal Commission on the War in South Africa: 'Neither "Duke's son, cook's son, nor son of a millionaire" should go beyond the rank of captain unless he be recognised as fit to be trusted with the fate of other men. I hope to live to see this—hitherto I have not.'[173] But Hunter's critique ignored several factors. Just as social historians have begun to detect members of the aristocracy and gentry who were every bit as commercially enterprising as any city merchant or Manchester manufacturer, so it is equally possible for military historians

---

[169] Anon., *Customs of the Army (1956)*, 18.
[170] IWMSA. Accession No. 004527/06. Gen. Sir John Hackett, 14.
[171] Anon., *Standing Orders... (Cheshire) Regiment*, 21.
[172] See e.g. M. J. Weiner, *English Culture and the Decline of the Industrial Spirit, 1850–1980* (Cambridge: Cambridge University Press, 1981).
[173] PP (1904), XLI. Cd. 1791. *Minutes of evidence*, Précis of evidence by Lt.-Gen. Sir A. Hunter, 29 Jan. 1903.

to find army officers who adopted a professional attitude towards their duties.[174] Before the First World War the Regular Army did place a high emphasis on regimental officers who possessed all of the attributes of a gentleman. Membership of a socially elite regiment was of considerable assistance to those officers anxious to climb the promotion ladder. But these factors were not something that was unique to the British army. German officers, who have never been accused of being unprofessional, required similar attributes. In both armies the pay of junior regimental officers rarely covered their expenses; both required private incomes, although German officers required less than their British counterparts and suffered a lower standard of living. And in both armies the zeal of regimental officers had the edge taken off it by chronically slow promotion.[175] But even before 1914, in the British army just as in the German army, there was a growing emphasis on requiring gentlemen to acquire professional attainments. In Britain, the military authorities demanded that officers achieve at least a minimum standard of competence in the essential technical skills of their profession. Looking back on his career from the tranquillity of old age, Percival Marling, who was gazetted into that most aristocratic of regiments, the King's Royal Rifle Corps, in 1880, remembered his feelings on discovering that he had passed the entrance examination for Sandhurst, and also the surprise that was in store for him:

When I read my name in the *Times* as one of the successful candidates, I said, 'No more lessons or work for me', little dreaming that I had two examinations to get out of Sandhurst, and examinations for Lieutenant, Captain, Major, and Lieutenant-Colonel, to say nothing of musketry, veterinary, gunnery, transport and other courses in the Army to pass.[176]

Where the British and German armies differed was that German officers received a more thorough and perhaps more uniform training than their British counterparts. The German army relied more than the British did on a school, rather than a unit-based, education system to prepare regimental officers and NCOs for their jobs. And unlike in the British army, studying for and taking the entrance examination for the General

---

[174] Thompson, *Gentrification and the Enterprise Culture*, 23–43; S. Pollard, 'Reflections on Entrepreneurship and Culture in European Societies', *Transactions of the Royal Historical Society*, 5th ser. 40 (1990), 153–75.

[175] S. E. Clemente, *For King and Kaiser! The Making of the Prussian Army Officer, 1860–1914* (New York: Greenwood Press, 1992), 160–3; PRO WO 32/4927. Col. Walters, British Military Attaché, Berlin, to Sir F. Lascelles, British Ambassador, Expenses of Prussian Officers. Emperor's orders respecting, 15 Jan. 1901 and Memo by J. E. Edmonds. 'Amplification of the two papers enclosed', n.d. but *c*.15 Jan. 1901.

[176] Col. Sir Percival Marling, *Rifleman and Hussar* (London: John Murray 1935), 22.

Staff was compulsory for all German officers, not an option for the ambitious few.[177]

Radical critics of the regular officer corps in the late nineteenth century were wrong to dismiss them as aristocratic amateurs. They did constitute a profession, albeit one whose intellectual horizons were, for the most part, confined to the regiment. But within those confines, officers were required to possess appropriate knowledge that would enable them to manage their men effectively in barracks and to lead them in small-scale actions on the battlefield. What the scale and scope of the Boer War did was to demonstrate that brave officers who were well versed in the intricacies of the routines of regimental soldiering were not enough. The army always needed such men. But it also needed officers who could manage large and intricate organizations, recognize the problems that confronted them, and find practical solutions to them. After 1902, and even more so after 1918, the military authorities tried to find such people by making a serious attempt, although not always a successful one, to produce officers who had been educated to think beyond the confines of their regiments. The syllabus of compulsory promotion examinations was modified accordingly. They were not only intended to inculcate in regimental officers the professional knowledge they needed to fulfil their regimental duties. They were also intended to ensure that regimental officers did not mentally stagnate by thinking that the regiment was the be-all and end-all of their profession.

Regimental soldiering could impede the promotion of able officers. Many preferred the comfort of their own regiment to accepting accelerated promotion into another regiment. But this willingness to stagnate was never universal. Regimental officers anxious to extend their professional experience—and to stretch their exiguous incomes—volunteered in considerable numbers to serve in one or other of the colonial forces. And for the most ambitious there was the Staff College, which took the most zealous of the regular officer corps and, in their early 30s, prepared them to become staff officers and senior commanders. And increasingly, it was possession of the initials 'PSC', rather than membership of a socially elite regiment, that determined who arrived at the top of the army.

Finally, critics of the way in which the regimental system impeded the growth of effective leaders have overlooked what was probably its most significant shortcoming. The British army possessed an excellent cadre of long-service professional Warrant and Non-Commissioned officers. But to a considerable extent it wasted their talents. Despite their experience, they were usually relegated merely to supervising the activities of the

[177] A. Bucholz, *Moltke, Schlieffen and Prussian War Planning* (Oxford: Berg, 1993), 73.

rank and file. They were not trained to lead them. In the Regular Army, except for relatively brief periods in the two world wars, leadership qualities were supposedly confined to the 'officer class'. The reason the distinction between officers who were leaders and Warrant Officers and NCOs who were supervisors persisted for so long was that it conferred a corresponding advantage. Officers did not always invoke unhesitating and unquestioned obedience. But Warrant Officers and NCOs who knew their job, and could handle their men with the right blend of firmness and tact, could often absorb or defuse the resentment felt by the rank and file at what they regarded as unfair or unreasonable orders, so that dissatis-faction did not become rebellion. How the regimental authorities dealt with soldiers who did express their resentment too loudly, or who broke into outright rebellion, is the subject of the next chapter.

CHAPTER SEVEN

Deviancy and Discipline in the Regimental System

On 11 August 1865 Major Francis De Vere, the commanding officer of a sapper company, was on parade at Brompton Barracks, Chatham. Nineteen-year-old Private John Currie, who had enlisted nine months earlier, took aim at him with his rifle and fired a single shot. The major fell wounded into the arms of a brother officer, lingered for eleven days, and died. At his trial, it became apparent that Currie acted because of a festering grievance against his company commander. Three months earlier De Vere had been the cause of his losing a day's pay, being confined to the guard room for six days, and being forced to undergo a second period of recruit training. The major was, according to Currie, 'a rogue, a tyrant and a thief in his heart'. Currie made no secret of his guilt. He was tried before a civilian court, found guilty of murder, and executed.[1]

The regimental system has been likened to a Victorian family, presided over by a powerful paterfamilias. De Vere's murder indicates that the military and regimental authorities were not always successful in their efforts to transform the power that they could legally exercise over the members of every regiment into legitimate authority. The communal life of the regiment was intense, claustrophobic, and minutely regulated, and some soldiers rebelled against some of the restrictions that were placed on them. Currie's behaviour was an extreme form of rebellion. In the first part of this chapter I will analyse how the military authorities defined deviant behaviour and examine the main forms that it took. In the second part I will explore the ways in which the army's formal disciplinary structures evolved to deal with the problem of soldiers who broke the rules. In the third section I will determine the extent to which soldiers believed that the disciplinary regime was legitimate and treated them fairly, and in the final section I will analyse how the military authorities dealt with instances of mass disobedience.

Soldiers were subject both to the ordinary law of the land and to a special code of military law. The administration of that code was, until the

---

[1] *The Times*, 21 Sept. 1865.

mid-1960s, almost exempt from civilian scrutiny.[2] For most of the nineteenth century deviant behaviour in the army was defined by the Mutiny Act and the Articles of War. By the second half of the nineteenth century, military law had become so complex and was so much in need of codification that in 1879 Parliament approved the Army Discipline and Regulation Act, which consolidated the Mutiny Act and the Articles of War.[3] But in 1881 a committee of senior officers concluded that the existing system of punishments and rewards was still too complicated. It had developed piecemeal over a long period and was intended to meet the needs of a long-service army. It was unnecessarily complicated to administer and what the new short-service army needed was a system that was so simple that even the newest-joined recruit could understand the advantages to be gained by good conduct.[4] Consequently, the 1879 Act was repealed and replaced in 1881 by the Army Act.

The new Act defined military offences for which officers and other ranks could be tried by court martial and classified them 'in a manner intended to impress the soldier with their relative military importance'. First came offences 'in respect of military service', such as treachery, cowardice in the face of the enemy, plundering, sleeping on duty, followed by mutiny and insubordination. They were followed by desertion, fraudulent enlistment, going absent without leave, committing fraud or embezzlement, and being drunk. Lest this long string of offences was thought to be insufficient, under the heading of miscellaneous military offences Section 40 of the act gave the military authorities powers to punish offenders found guilty of 'any act, conduct, disorder, or neglect, to the prejudice of good order and military discipline'.[5] This could cover a multitude of military sins. In September 1919, for example, a corporal of 2/Bedfordshire and Hertfordshire Regiment was found guilty of this crime because he had shouted and used obscene language in the streets of Colchester.[6] A year later a private in 2/Royal Dublin Fusiliers was charged with the same crime, 'Fighting civilians, [being] improperly dressed, [and] using obscene language to [a] M[ilitary] P[oliceman]'.[7] Lest any offender might try to plead ignorance of the law, the relevant sections of the Army Act were explained to the troops and read out to

[2] G. Rubin, 'United Kingdom Military Law: Autonomy, Civilianisation and Juridification', *Modern Law Review*, 65 (2002), 36–57.

[3] *The Times*, 29 July 1878 and 28 Feb. 1879.

[4] PP (1881), XX. C. 2817. *Report...*, 3.

[5] War Office, *MML, 1899*, 18–19, 359.

[6] Bedfordshire Record Office. 2/Bedfordshire & Hertfordshire Regiment. X550/3/18. Battalion Orders—Part II Orders, 1919–1920, 4 Sept. 1919.

[7] ERM. ER 15247. Sgt W. H. Green MSS. Herewith receipt for four soldiers confined in the Detention Barracks, Haidar Pasha, 11 July 1920.

them on parade every three months.[8] Finally, the legislation also established a fundamental principle that should underpin punishments: offences committed on active service were to be punished more severely than those committed in barracks.[9]

Deviant behaviour could take different forms, but measured by court-martial statistics, there was a steady improvement in the army's behaviour. Between 1868 and 1893 an average of 77 men per 1,000 were court-martialled each year. That statistic fell to 30 per 1,000 men on average between 1902 and 1913, and to only 19 per 1,000 men per year between 1919 and 1935.[10] Unfortunately, the way in which court-martial statistics were gathered and tabulated was not consistent, and therefore generalizations across the whole period are difficult to make. Between 1865 and 1898, for example, the court-martial statistics indicated that the most common form of protest against the army's disciplinary regime took the form of 'miscellaneous military offences'. They included not only conduct to the prejudice of good order and military discipline, which was the largest single offence listed under this heading, but also offences that ranged from uttering traitorous or disloyal words to disclosing the position of troops or future operational plans, or attempting to commit suicide. However, having noted this caveat, some generalizations are apparent. The first is that, if the Boer War and the two world wars are excluded, the most common offences for which soldiers were court-martialled were desertion and being absent without leave. Second, the incidence of soldiers being court-martialled for drunkenness declined. Between 1865 and 1898 it was the third most common offence, after miscellaneous military crimes and desertion/AWOL. It then slipped down the league table of offences until it was the fifth most common in the inter-war period.

It is also apparent that the paternalism of the regimental officer corps did not always evoke an automatically deferential response. In the late nineteenth century confrontations between soldiers and their superiors in which the former refused to obey a lawful order, and sometimes accompanied their refusal with threats, obscene language, or even violence, rose up the scale of court-martial offences. By the Edwardian period they

---

[8] Anon., *QR . . . 1892*, 89.   [9] *The Times*, 29 Sept. 1881.
[10] The statistics in this paragraph are derived from PP (1882) XXXVIII. C. 3405. *General Annual Return for the British Army for 1881*, 49; PP (1894), LIII. C. 7483. *General Annual Return for the British army for the year 1893*, 59; PP (1907), IX. Cd. 3365. *General Annual Return for the British Army . . . 1906*, 82–5, 87; PP (1914), XVI. *General Annual Return . . . 1913*, 75–8; PP (1899), LIII. C. 9426. *General Annual return . . . 1898*, 40; PP (1897), LIV. C. 8558. *General Annual Return . . . 1896*, 35–40; PP (1924–5), XVII. Cmd. 2342. *General Annual Report, . . . 1924*, 52; PP (1930–1), XIX. Cmd. 3800, *General Annual Report for the British Army for Year ending 30 Sept. 1930*, 67–8; PP (1935–6), XVI. Cmd. 5104. *General Annual Report . . . 1935*, 63; PP (1937–8), XVII. Cmd. 5681. *General Annual Report . . . 1937*, 61.

were the second most likely cause of a soldier being court-martialled, coming behind desertion and being AWOL. But after 1918 they slipped back to third place, to be replaced in second place by crimes against army property. Finally, the least common crimes throughout the whole period were offences committed in the face of the enemy, such as shamefully abandoning a post or casting away weapons, treachery, or cowardice and mutiny. Between 1865 and 1898, for example, only five soldiers were tried for offences committed in the face of the enemy (all in 1898) and only ninety-four for mutiny.

But these statistics conceal almost as much as they reveal about the nature and extent of deviant behaviour. They understate the real extent of desertion, for many deserters were never apprehended and therefore did not figure in the court-martial statistics. Others who were apprehended were dealt with by their CO, rather than sent for court martial. In 2/ Bedfordshire and Hertfordshire Regiment, for example, in 1919 and between 1926 and 1938 when the unit was in the UK, 190 men deserted. The majority of deserters who were apprehended or who surrendered themselves never appeared before a court martial. They were tried summarily by their CO, who sentenced them to CB or detention for up to twenty-eight days. Only a handful were court-martialled. The typical deserter in the regiment was a private soldier, aged under 21, and with less than two years service. A frequent cause of desertion seems to have been reluctance on the part of the soldier who had just completed his basic training to join a draft going overseas.[11]

Court-martial statistics also understate the actual extent of the problem of alcohol-related offences. In 1868, following the recommendation of a Royal Commission on the constitution and practice of courts martial, COs were given powers to deal summarily with most cases of drunkenness. Henceforth, most offenders were fined by their CO rather than sent for court martial.[12] Between 1870 and 1893 an average of 232 soldiers per 1,000 per year were fined by their CO for being drunk.[13] However, this average concealed a significant downward trend, which continued after the Boer War, so that between 1902 and 1913 only 50 per 1,000 soldiers per annum were being fined for this offence. This points to the problem that confronts the historian trying to establish the extent of deviant behaviour in the regiments: court-martial statistics give only a limited and partial picture. After 1868 there was a growing tendency to devolve the power to try and punish offenders onto unit commanders, and statistical evidence

---

[11] Bedfordshire Record Office. X550/3/33. Register of deserters, 1919–38.
[12] Burrows, 'Crime and Punishment', 559.
[13] PP (1881), LVIII. C. 3083. *General Annual Return...*, 44; *PP (1899) LIII.* C. 9426. *General Annual Return... 1898*, 56.

for the less serious misdemeanours that they dealt with was either not collected on an army-wide scale or is incomplete. But where they do exist on an army-wide scale, as they do for the period from 1869 to 1893, statistics for the number of summary punishments imposed by COs do show a similar trend to court-martial statistics. There was a significant drop in the number of punishments inflicted by COs. They fell from an average of 1,405 per 1,000 men in 1869 to 1,050 per 1,000 men in 1893.[14]

The operation of the court-martial system at the regimental level can be illustrated by the case of 1/Norfolk Regiment. Following army regulations, details of every court martial in the regiment were entered into *Army Book 160*. The surviving register records brief details of every court martial of a soldier serving with the battalion between 2 February 1905 to 29 July 1914, from 26 May 1919 to 26 March 1940, and finally from 21 January 1948 to 16 December 1957.[15] It shows that officers and men in the battalion were arraigned at 406 courts martial, and that on average 10.5 men serving with the battalion were tried annually. But this average conceals some significant shifts over time. While the period from 1905 to 1914 conforms almost exactly to the average, the period from May 1919 to August 1922, when the battalion was on active service in Belfast, witnessed no fewer than seventy-three courts martial, or an average of 4.25 per month. The experience of the 1/Norfolks in this respect was similar to that of the rest of the army. Whereas in each year between 1915 and 1919 there were only seventeen courts martial per 1,000 men in the army as a whole, the figure rose to forty-five per 1,000 in 1920 and forty-two per 1,000 in 1921. Clearly, in the immediate aftermath of the First World War the military authorities struggled to reassert discipline and were ready to use all of the formal means at their disposal to do so.

Thereafter, as conscripts passed out of the battalion's ranks to be replaced by volunteers, the annual average of courts martial in 1/Norfolks declined steeply, falling to only 6.66 courts martial annually from October 1922 to March 1940. However, the fall was not permanent. Between January 1948 and December 1957, the battalion saw 119 courts martial, an average of 13.2 per annum. This was perhaps some indication of the problems that the regimental authorities encountered in trying to discipline their sometimes reluctant National Servicemen.

Finally, statistical averages also conceal another important truth about the extent of misbehaviour in the battalion. Much of it could be laid at the door of a comparatively small number of recidivists. Fifty soldiers

---

[14] PP (1875), XLIII. C. 1323. *General Annual Return . . . 1875*, 37; PP (1890), XLIII. C. 6196. *General Annual Return . . . 1889*, 53; PP (1899), LIII. C. 9426. *General Annual Return . . . 1899*, 59.

[15] RNRM. R. 140. Extracts of Court Martial. *Army Book 160*.

between them accounted for no fewer than 114 courts martial. There were, therefore, at any one time, a small number of malcontents in the unit who could not adjust to the demands of army life. The great majority of soldiers were well behaved, or at least they did not commit misdemeanours for which they might be court-martialled, or if they did they escaped detection.

The accused were not drawn evenly from across the whole of the battalion. Only two officers, a Captain (Quarter-Master) and a Lieutenant, two Warrant Officers, a CSM, and one CQMS were tried. The remainder consisted of twenty-five sergeants or acting or lance sergeants, thirty-four corporals, fourteen lance-corporals or acting lance-corporals, and all of the remainder were private soldiers. The men of the Norfolks were charged with 641 separate offences. The most common offences were AWOL and desertion (77 and 46 cases respectively), offering violence, threatening, or striking a superior officer (49), disobeying a lawful order (26), and being insolent or using insubordinate language to a superior officer (24). The widespread utility of Section 40 of the Army Act was demonstrated by the fact that the Norfolks faced no fewer than sixty-eight charges of conduct to the prejudice of good order and military discipline.

The evidence of courts martial in the Norfolks also supports the contention that drunkenness was becoming less of a problem in the army after the First World War. Whereas there were fifteen courts martial for drunkenness between 1905 and 1914, there were only eleven between 1919 and 1940 and three between 1948 and 1957. Finally, the Norfolks' courts martial conformed closely to the army's norm. They brought in guilty verdicts to 93 per cent of all charges.

The comparatively low incidence of courts martial and the declining incidence of both courts martial and summary punishments suggest that the regimental authorities enjoyed a growing measure of success in transforming their formal powers into legitimate authority. Their efforts to evoke obedience through a combination of instilling *esprit de corps* and by maintaining a close surveillance over the rank and file usually succeeded. But their success was not universal, and when they failed to achieve this aim by these methods, they were thrown back upon the more formal sanctions enshrined in the military legal code. Military law was designed to deter soldiers from breaking the rules and to punish and rehabilitate those who did so. To achieve these objectives, trial and punishment had to follow quickly upon the offence. Courts martial, especially if they were held too frequently, were seen as an inefficient instrument to do this. According to the Adjutant-General, their very frequency detracted from their effectiveness: 'The awe which they ought to inspire is wanting and without it, their effect as a deterrent loses much of its value.' Consequently, from the late nineteenth century, they were increasingly reserved as a means of punishing hardened criminals, not men guilty of youthful delinquencies.[16]

At the same time the locus of discipline shifted towards the CO's orderly room. In 1893 the maximum sentence of detention that a CO could impose was increased from seven to fourteen days, or twenty-one days in cases of AWOL, and was further increased to twenty-eight days in 1910.[17] Any qualms that jurists might have entertained about the notion of COs acting as judge and jury in their own court were brushed aside by a committee of general officers who announced in 1881:

But it must be recollected that military offences are very different from civil crimes, and that in the orderly room a Commanding Officer knows all about the men he is dealing with, and the men know one another, while, on the other hand, in civil life, a magistrate is dealing with strangers. Besides this, the existence of military law is due entirely to the necessity of permitting military authorities to administer substantial justice under less rigid and formal rules than obtain in ordinary courts of law, and in a manner more suitable to the conditions and exigencies of the Army.[18]

If a soldier was accused of an offence, he, together with any witnesses, was brought before their CO in his orderly room. The charge was heard before not only the CO, but also the Adjutant, RSM, Provost Sergeant, Company Orderly Sergeant, and the Company Commander of the accused. The latter brought with him his Company Defaulters Book, which contained a list of the prisoner's previous offences.[19] As a safeguard against tyrannous COs, prisoners charged with an offence that made them liable to detention or imprisonment could opt for trial by a court martial, although few did so, on the justifiable grounds that courts martial upheld a very high conviction rate and had the powers to impose heavier sentences than their CO.[20]

In any case, in opting to increase the summary powers of unit commanders to deal with minor offences, the military authorities were only following in the footsteps of civilian society, where the powers of magistrates were also increased in the late nineteenth century.[21] Sentencing

[16] PRO WO 32/8701. Minute, Director of Personnel Services, 13 Nov. 1909; Minute Hamilton, 3 Feb. 1910; Minute by Haldane, 24 Nov. 1909 and 7 Feb. 1910; Anon, *KR...1912*, 101.

[17] PRO WO 32/8701. Report of the Committee appointed to consider the New edition of the Manual of Military Law, 21 Jan. 1893; Procedure on offences committed by soldiers, n.d. but *c.* 1910.

[18] PP (1881), XX. C. 2817. *Report...*, 3.

[19] Anon., *The Standing Orders... Warwickshire Regiment*, 105–6.

[20] Wyndham, *The Queen's Service*, 238; PRO WO 32/8701. Minute by Hamilton, 3 Feb. 1910.

[21] F. M. L. Thompson, *The Rise of Respectable Society: A Social History of Victorian Britain, 1830–1900* (London: Fontana, 1988), 328–30.

policy also followed the same trend as in civil society. In the mid-nineteenth century, the majority of criminologists and lawyers believed that if punishments were to be effective in reforming a delinquent, they had to be swift, certain, and uniform in their application. If the offender knew that he was bound to be caught, and could predict accurately the punishment he would face, he would, they reasoned, be deterred from offending.[22]

In September 1885 the Adjutant-General published a circular laying down a tariff of sentences that courts martial should inflict for different offences.[23] Two years later he published a second circular, seeking to achieve a similar uniformity in the conduct of summary proceedings in orderly rooms. Offenders with less than a year's service should not be remitted to a court martial for offences that did not involve desertion, fraudulent enlistment, gross insubordination, or 'disgraceful conduct'. Soldiers accused of using insubordinate language, neglect of duty, going AWOL, and minor disobedience should be disposed of by their CO. They should also remember that indulgence in liquor, ignorance, thoughtlessness, and inexperience of the restraints of discipline might cause a young soldier to commit an offence that looked serious on paper but was in fact trivial. In such cases a CO's powers of summary punishment would suffice to 'prevent a recurrence of crime injurious to discipline'.[24]

However, at the end of the nineteenth century civilian jurists were increasingly convinced that men were pushed into crime not by their natural propensity, but by their environment. Henceforth criminals were less likely to be regarded as wicked individuals, and more likely to be seen as the products of their environment. This in turn opened the way for a greater differentiation in their treatment and a slow and hesitant acceptance that different kinds of offenders should be treated differently.[25] In the army this meant that by the Edwardian period COs were expected to know the character and the previous service of their men sufficiently well so that they could determine where leniency might achieve better results than a severe punishment.[26] Thus when Private Richard Jago of the Royal Dublin Fusiliers was arrested for being drunk in the field in South Africa in 1900, he was not tried on a capital charge. He was instead merely admonished by his CO. His company commander

---

[22] M. J. Wiener, *Reconstructing the Criminal: Culture, Law and Policy in England, 1830–1914* (Cambridge: Cambridge University Press, 1990), *passim*.

[23] PRO WO 32/8731. Adjutant-General to GOCs-in-C, 18 Sept. 1885.

[24] PRO WO 32/8731. A. Alison to GOC's Districts and Corps, 1 Jan. 1887.

[25] Wiener, *Reconstructing the Criminal*, 185–215; V. Bailey, 'English Prisons, Penal Culture, and the Abatement of Imprisonment, 1895 to 1922', *Journal of British Studies*, 36 (1997), 285–324.

[26] Anon., *The Standing Orders ... (Cheshire) Regiment*, 25; Anon, War Office, *KR ... 1912*, 92.

had interceded with his CO and pleaded for clemency on the grounds that he was a young soldier and that this was his first offence.[27]

The Adjutant-Generals' efforts to devolve disciplinary powers onto COs and ensure uniformity in the conduct of trials and sentencing failed. In practice, it meant that COs had considerable discretion in how they administered discipline, and that the severity with which the code was imposed varied considerably between different units. In 1880 Lt.-Col. G. H. Adams, the CO of the 86/Foot, admitted: 'I think there is a great difference in regiments; some regiments are very much stricter than others, and naturally the men prefer an easy regiment, or at least one in which they are not quite so tightly kept.'[28] There could also be considerable variation within the same unit depending who commanded it. In 1884 Lt.-Col. Hugh Pearson of 1/Suffolks was critical of his predecessor for the supposedly lenient way in which he had disciplined the regiment and was determined not to follow his example, especially as he believed that most crime in his unit was committed by a handful of bad characters.[29]

COs usually awarded sentences of detention only for comparatively serious offences. For more minor offences they had powers to inflict a series of lesser punishments. These ranged from fines for drunkenness, extra duties, stoppages of pay, and confinement to barracks.[30] Company commanders also had the power to impose lesser punishments, including a maximum of seven days CB. What this meant was described by a private in 2/Royal Welch Fusiliers who was sentenced to seven days CB by his CO in 1902 for the crimes of having a dirty rifle and being insolent:

I was now a defaulter, or 'on jankers' as the troops called it. Every time the bugle sounded the Defaulters' call, unless I was already on parade, I would have to answer my name at the Guardroom and be marched off with the other defaulters to do some fatigue or other, in or about the barracks. Defaulters also had to parade every afternoon in full marching order under the Provost-Sergeant, who for one whole hour marched them backwards and forwards over a space of ground no more than ten yards in length. The old 'shoulder arms!' was not yet abolished, and carrying our rifles at the shoulder with bayonets fixed numbed the middle finger and made the right arm ache unbearably: the bayonet seemed to make the rifle twice as heavy. At the end of this hour, which was no joke, we had to show our kit, which we carried in our valises. If any man was short of any article he was tried for the crime on the following morning and generally given an additional three days confined to barracks. Between six o'clock in the evening

[27] IWMSA. Accession No. 006524/02. Pte. Richard Jago, reel 1.

[28] PP (1881), XXI. C. 2791. *Report of the Committee...*, Q. 1808.

[29] SRO. GB 554/B13/4.CO's letter and memoranda book, 1883–1903. Lt.-Col. H. P. Pearson, CO to Adjutant-General, India, 17 Nov. 1884.

[30] Anon., *The QR... 1892*, 97–9.

and Last Post the bugle sounded the Defaulters' call every half an hour and at every call the Defaulters had to answer their names to the Sergeant of the Guard. They were not allowed in the Canteen at noon, though they could visit it between eight and nine at night, with an interruption at half-past eight of going to the Guardroom to answer their names. The Defaulters concluded their day by falling in on staff-parade outside the Guardroom at Last Post: this was when the Regimental Sergeant-Major took the reports of the Orderly Sergeants and the N.C.O.s who had been on duty in the barracks during the evening.[31]

Some commanding officers put their defaulters to doing more constructive work. Men sentenced to CB in 2/York and Lancaster Regiment in 1902 built tennis courts, ornamental gardens, and a miniature rifle range.[32]

Offences that were of such a serious nature that they could not be dealt with summarily were tried before one of four different kinds of courts martial: a Regimental Court Martial, a District Court Martial, a General Court Martial, or a Field General Court Martial. In every case the judge and jury consisted of a body of officers, varying in number from a minimum of three in the case of a Regimental Court Martial to a maximum of five or more in the case of a General Court Martial. A Regimental Court Martial could not impose a sentence of more than forty-two days' imprisonment, a District Court Martial could not impose a sentence of more than two years' imprisonment, and only a General Court Martial or a Field General Court Martial (which was convened only on active service) could try a Warrant Officer or a commissioned officer, or impose a death sentence.[33] Offenders found guilty had no right of appeal to an independent civilian tribunal. All guilty verdicts were instead reviewed by the senior officer who had convened the court martial, who had the power to confirm or set aside the sentence and verdict of the court.

Like COs acting summarily, courts martial were expected to vary their sentences according to the nature of the offence and the particulars of the accused. Sentences were expected to rehabilitate first offenders, to deter others by making an example of particular wrongdoers, and to avoid depriving the army of scarce manpower by consigning men to prison for unnecessarily long periods. In the 1890s courts were recommended to show leniency to first offenders on the grounds that a short sentence was likely to be as effective as a long one. Sentences of imprisonment for between twenty-eight and fifty-six days were held to be effective for

[31] Richards, *Old-Soldier Sahib*, 54–5.
[32] NAM 8210–13. Warrant Officer I. W. H. Davies, Ts. memoirs.
[33] Spiers, *Late Victorian Army*, 32; Anon., *MML, 1899*, 377–81.

soldiers found guilty for the first time of offences such as leaving a guard, using insubordinate or threatening language to a superior officer, breaking out of barracks, neglecting duty, losing kit, or conduct prejudicial to good order and military discipline. Soldiers found guilty of such offences for a second or subsequent time could expect an extra seven to twenty-eight days for each previous conviction. Offences that were held to be more serious, such as striking a superior officer, disobeying a lawful command, desertion, fraudulent enlistment, theft, or fraud, could expect a sentence of between three to six months.[34] In the late 1890s the regimes in military prisons and detention barracks were also modified to rehabilitate offenders rather than merely punish them and deter others.[35]

Courts martial were not independent legal tribunals. The officers who sat upon them were themselves part of the army's chain of command. This became apparent when they came to determine the sentences to be meted out to offenders. In reaching their verdict and determining the sentence members were often expected to take account of the extent to which particular offences were prevalent in particular units or formations, and to pass sentences designed to deter such behaviour. If they did not, as Major E. E. F. Baker discovered in 1917, they were liable to be castigated by their superiors, sometimes the very officers who had convened the tribunal in the first place.[36]

During the First World War it was also noticeable that death sentences tended to increase in the weeks preceding a major offensive as the military authorities worked to stamp their authority on the troops.[37] A similar trend may also have been apparent in the case of lesser penalties summarily inflicted by COs. The Essex Yeomanry landed in France in December 1914. It lost heavily at the Second Battle of Ypres in May 1915 and was thereafter rebuilt. Between landing in France and 30 May 1916 the yeomen received sixteen sentences of field punishments, or less than one a month. Offences ranged from insolence, disobedience, ill-treating a horse, to being drunk. The severity or frequency of punishments did not appear to vary as new COs or Adjutants assumed office. But in June 1916, in the month preceding the Somme offensive, the men of the regiment received no fewer than eleven field punishments.[38] Although there is no direct evidence that the COs were ordered to tighten discipline

[34] Anon., QR... 1892, 114–15.

[35] PRO WO 32/8733. Report of the Committee to consider certain questions relating to the treatment of military prisoners, 28 June 1895; PRO WO 32/8734. Report of the Committee on the proposed alterations in the military penal system, 4 Oct. 1899.

[36] IWM Con Shelf. Letters of Brigadier E. E. F. Baker. Baker to his parents, 13/14 Dec. 1917.

[37] G. C. Oram, Military Executions during World War One (Basingstoke: Palgrave, 2003), 53–56.

[38] ERM. Loan from private collection. Essex Yeomanry Order Books, 1914–1918.

just prior to the battle, the experience of the Essex Yeomanry suggests that they had been, and that they acted accordingly.

Not every offender was dealt with according to the letter of the law. Alongside the army's formal disciplinary structure there existed a more shadowy system of unofficial punishments and sanctions. They rarely surfaced in the official record, and then only as incidents when officers or NCOs were court-martialled for striking or ill-treating a soldier. Between 1940 and 1945 an average of 153 officers or NCOs were tried annually on this charge.[39] But unofficial sanctions probably did play a significant part in enforcing conformity. Regimental officers and NCOs were not always above taking the law into their own hands. In South Africa in 1900 an officer of the London Irish Rifles discovered two sentries who were asleep. Rather than bring them before their CO on a charge that might have carried the death penalty, he woke them and promptly knocked them down. The men did not bear him any grudge, 'And they worshiped him after that. They called him the "big oar"'[40]

Such behaviour was probably more common in the field than it was in barracks, but unofficial punishments were used when soldiers were not on active service. In 1906 Tom Painting and a fellow recruit at the King's Royal Rifle Corps depot at Winchester were caught fighting by a corporal. Rather than report them to their company commander, the corporal insisted that they finish their fight the next day behind the latrines and that he would referee the bout. At the end of the proceedings Painting and his opponent shook hands and no more was said of the matter.[41]

However, some COs took a dim view of such behaviour and readily punished NCOs who, for example, assaulted men under their command. A lance-corporal attached to a battalion of the Norfolk Regiment in South Africa in 1901 was reduced to the ranks when it was discovered that he had pushed a private who had sworn at him.[42] The operations of unofficial sanctions could sometimes degenerate into outright brutality. In one infantry battalion in Germany in 1948, it was not unknown for men confined to the guard room to be beaten up by the regimental police. When the matter was investigated some other ranks alleged that their officers connived in this, and one officer when questioned admitted that 'he encouraged it as "the only way to keep down the toughs"'.[43]

[39] PRO WO 277/7. Discipline, Appendix 1a.
[40] IWMSA. Accession No. 6532/2. T. Pain, reel 1.
[41] IWMSA. Accession No. 0007212/04. T. H. Painting, p. 4.
[42] RNRM. R. 5058 Cpl. P. C. Richards to his parents, 1 May 1901.
[43] PRO WO 163/497. Second Report of the Army Working Day investigation team, 17 Oct. 1948.

Clever NCOs could impose discipline on recalcitrant individuals by turning their own comrades against them. During basic training in 1950, one National Service recruit refused to obey an order during an exercise. His sergeant did not put him on a charge because a court-martial sentence would have added to his time in the army. Instead he imposed an extra drill-parade on the entire troop, explaining that

Gunner H...needs to be taught that in the Army, and especially in action, one man can fuck it up for all his comrades by disobeying a direct order. I don't put men on a charge because if they get 156 days in Shepton Mallet or Colchester it will add the time to their military service. So I give the whole troop a lesson...in turn the troop will give the offender a lesson.[44]

That night Gunner H. found his bed deposited in the washroom and his boots full of urine.

On paper the army's judicial system was fair, impartial, and uniform. The majority of offenders were arraigned before their CO in his orderly room and at least some soldiers believed that their CO dispensed justice tempered by common sense. Francis Maitland, a gentleman-ranker serving with the 19/Hussars on the eve of the First World War, thought that 'There is rarely, if ever, a case of injustice. The officers appear to have an instinct to judge exactly how far a man has been provoked, how far a man has travelled along the road to being "fed-up" and thus driven to do or say something that ordinarily he would not.'[45]

Many regular soldiers expected to be punished for their misdemeanours and accepted what was coming to them. When Ernest Whitewick sailed with the Royal Berkshire Regiment to Palestine in 1934 he was so seasick that he was unable to perform any fatigues on board ship, and on arrival he was reprimanded by his company commander. But he did not resent his treatment, accepting that

despite being seasick things have still got to go on. It is that sort of thing that makes the discipline in the Army so necessary and so essential, especially under stress. The discipline that you've been brought up in obviously comes to the fore and helps you to do things. You don't even question it because by this time you've realised that it's all being done for a very good reason.[46]

Some men could calculate to a nicety how much each misdemeanour would cost them. When 2/Royal Sussex Regiment was stationed in India in the 1930s, the men knew that if they got drunk they would be fined 5 rupees. If they were fined 10 rupees they would make their ill-feelings known, and, one of their officers concluded, if they were fined less than

---

[44] Barraclough, *National Service*, 41, 44.
[45] Maitland, *Hussar of the Line*, 20.
[46] IWMSA. Accession No. 004474/03. Ernest O. L. Whitewick, 4.

5 rupees 'they'd imply that you were a lunatic and didn't know your stuff'.[47]

Other soldiers were less philosophical and accepting of the system. When William Green fell off his horse during his recruit training in 1921, and his riding instructor had him charged with dismounting without permission, for which he received five days' CB, he vowed that 'if I met that Sergeant Tross again, I would do him some injury'.[48]

Many of the rank and file held the operation of the courts-martial system in considerable suspicion. A soldier who faced one in 1943 concluded: 'The military authorities are treacherous and unpredictable.'[49] Their proceedings were likely to overawe the average ranker. Few of them could afford a counsel and so might only be represented by an officer with no legal qualifications. The court also usually gave precedence to the evidence of officers or NCOs before that of rankers.[50] Even soldiers who had enjoyed a successful career in the army had serious doubts about their impartiality. One Sergeant Major candidly admitted in 1904:

They [the courts martial] take the evidence of the sergeant major or colour sergeant of a company, but do not hear the truth about the case. Many men have got long terms of imprisonment for crimes which the court considered were very serious, while if the truth had really been known, the men have been driven to commit the offence.[51]

Another NCO concluded that 'from the standpoint of impartial justice, they [courts martial] are as a rule no better than a farce'.[52]

But in the eyes of senior officers, these matters were of comparatively little consideration. The main function of courts martial was to ensure that discipline was enforced. Doing justice to the individual sometimes took second place to that. Soldiers who were arraigned before a court martial had little chance of being found not guilty, as they maintained a conviction rate that hovered around 90 per cent.[53] It was not until 1951 that convicted soldiers had the right of appeal to an independent civilian tribunal against their conviction.[54]

---

[47] IWMSA. Accession No. 000938/05. Lt.-Col. E. G. Hollist, 16.

[48] ERO. T/G 266/1. W. G. Green, The well travelled life of a Great Baddow Man.

[49] B. Mills, One For Grandad: The Really, Really, Real Dad's Army (Salford, privately published, 1998), 5.

[50] Skelley, The Victorian Army, 139.

[51] PRO WO 32/4512. Report of the committee on punishment on active service, Q. 1532.

[52] Edmondson, John Bull's Army, 74.

[53] This statistic is calculated from PRO WO 32/4512. Report of the committee on punishment on active service, 5 Jan. 1904; PP (1952–3) Reports of Committees, III. Army and Air Force Act. Report with proceedings, evidence and appendices, Annex 28. (M31(1952–3).

[54] War Office, MML, Part 1, 1956, 587–622.

The introduction of the short-service system probably was accompanied by an increase in indiscipline. In 1/Essex, for example, between 1873 and 1875 there was an annual average of twenty-two courts martial. But between 1877 and 1881, as long-service NCOs and other ranks retired and were replaced by young, short-service volunteers under the immediate charge of inexperienced junior NCOs, the number nearly trebled to an annual average of sixty-three. Thereafter, as the disciplinary system evolved to take account of the new conditions created by short service, the average fell. Between 1887 and 1895 it was down to forty-two courts martial per annum in the regiment.[55] By the end of the Boer War Lord Roberts believed that the soldier 'is more intelligent. He is more temperate. He knows his duties better. He has more self-respect, and he is more readily amenable to discipline.'[56]

There is statistical and anecdotal evidence to support his contention, and it does appear that the disciplinary regime was doing what it was designed to do by 1914, to produce an obedient and deferential rank and file. Thus whereas in 1894 7,543 men were tried by a General or District Court Martial, in 1908 the corresponding figure was only 1,352. In 1904 there was a daily average of 1,540 soldiers in detention barracks. By 1909 that figure had fallen to only 650.[57] The drop in the numbers of men court-martialled or sent to prison cannot be accounted for by any corresponding fall in the number of men serving in the army. Sir Evelyn Wood asserted that the improvement was due to the fact that 'our people are very amenable and education has made them yearly more amenable; there is not one-tenth of the crime and the men are much easier to handle than ever they were before, and with each decade I think it becomes easier. I see it every decade; the men are easier to handle.'[58]

What they had been educated to believe was that it was wisest to obey regulations, for if they did not, retribution was likely to be swift and certain. Horace Wyndham, who served as a private in 1/Royal Scots in the 1890s, recalled that although private soldiers knew that they had the right to raise any grievances with the inspecting officer when he conducted his annual inspection of their unit, they rarely did so. Their complaints would have been fairly dealt with, but thereafter they would have become marked men in the eyes of their superiors.[59] Giving

[55] These figures are calculated from ERM. ER6005. Historical Record, 1 Battalion Essex Regiment.
[56] PP (1904), XL. Cd. 1790. Minutes of evidence... Q. 10442.
[57] PRO WO 32/8701. Procedure on offences committed by soldiers, n.d. but c.1910; Minute, Director of Personnel Services, 13 Nov. 1909.
[58] PP (1904), XXI. Cd. 2063. Minutes of Evidence..., Q. 21682.
[59] H. Wyndham, 'General's Inspection: Old Days and Old Ways', Army Quarterly, 74 (1957), 62.

evidence to a War Office committee examining messing arrangements, Sergeant Sibbald, 2/Royal Scots Fusiliers explained in 1889: 'A soldier very seldom asks for anything; he always lets things go on in the regular way, and he does not bother himself much, he has only a short time to do, and the quieter he lets it pass the better.'[60]

Ernest White, who served in the ranks of the Edwardian army, believed that the orderly officer's appearance at meal times to ask if the men had any complaints about their food was an empty formality for 'you daren't make a complaint'.[61] Several privates who gave evidence before a committee examining how regimental institutes and canteens were run echoed the sentiments of Private Sidney Minchin. When asked what he thought would happen if he and other soldiers went to the president of their battalion canteen committee, an officer who was usually the 2i/c of the battalion, and suggested how the profits should be spent, he replied

Ever since I have been in the army I have made it a rule never to make myself a spokesman.

Major-General Eaton: That is what it amounts to. The fact is you are rather afraid?—Yes, I am afraid.[62]

Private Joseph Hancocks was even more succinct: 'The best is to keep my tongue between my teeth and say nothing at all to him.'[63]

Many thoughtful rankers believed that, despite the modifications in the army's disciplinary code that had followed the Cardwell–Childers reforms, it continued to manufacture crime. It made the lives of many soldiers one of constant worry that they would fall foul of its regulations. The regiment did not always provide the nurturing atmosphere that the familial rhetoric that surrounded it suggested it should have done. For some suicide became an escape route from the stress that was imposed on them by the regulations of army life. In India by 1887 so many soldiers were either committing suicide or trying to murder comrades that an Army Order was issued that soldiers were no longer to have ball ammunition in their possession when in barracks. In 1886–7, the last year in which soldiers had free access to ammunition, there were no fewer than fifty cases of suicide in India. There was a significant reduction in the number thereafter, but even so by 1904 the rate of suicides amongst soldiers was more than three times what it was amongst the civilian population.[64] When questioned in the Commons about the rate of

[60] PRO WO 33/49. Report of the committee appointed to enquire into the questions of the soldiers' dietary, Q. 1704.

[61] IWMSA. Accession No. 000188/07. E. G. White, p. 18.

[62] PP (1903), X. Cd. 1494. *Minutes of Evidence...*, QQ. 1388–9.

[63] Ibid., Q 1252.

[64] *The Times*, 19 Nov. 1890; Edmondson, *John Bull's Army from Within*, 93–7; NAM 9010-31-600. N. Hallam, diary entry, 10 Mar. 1907.

suicides amongst serving soldiers in 1909, the War Office's spokesman replied that in the last few years between fifty and sixty soldiers per annum stationed throughout the world had killed themselves. In the preceding sixty years, if losses for the Indian Mutiny and Boer War were excluded, the army had lost 26,100 other ranks in action.[65] If the rate of suicides was constant over the same period, between 3,000 to 3,600 men may have taken their own lives, a figure that represented a significant proportion of the army's manpower losses.

NCOs seem to have been particularly susceptible to such pressures, probably because of the extra responsibilities that were heaped on their shoulders. In 1871, shortly after their regiment arrived at Cork, two sergeants in 9/East Norfolk regiment shot themselves with their own rifles.[66] Six years later a sergeant of 77/Foot, then stationed at Dundalk, who had 'given way to drink', cut his throat.[67] In 1885 a troop sergeant major in 16/Lancers shot himself because he had got his troop accounts into a muddle and could not stand the disgrace of a court martial and demotion.[68] In November 1917 a sergeant in the Essex Yeomanry became so depressed when he was left in charge of his troop that he shot himself.[69] And in 1924 an RSM at the depot of the Essex Regiment committed suicide because he was about to be demoted and could not stand the disgrace and humiliation.[70] Another cause of stress that could be fatal was the restrictions that the military authorities placed on soldiers wishing to marry. In April 1887 a corporal at Woolwich barracks shot himself because he had been denied promotion to sergeant, and therefore could not marry his fiancée.[71]

But if some rankers thought that the army's disciplinary code was a vehicle that officers used to oppress them, they might have spared a thought for those officers who transgressed the army's rules. Officers found guilty of an offence were just as likely as other ranks to be punished, and in some cases to be punished with much greater severity. A private soldier found guilty of drunkenness, for example, was likely to be fined by his commanding officer. But in 1886 Lord Roberts discovered that

---

[65] *The Times*, 25 June 1909.

[66] RNRM. R111. Journal of Colour Sgt. J. Wall, 1/9 East Norfolk Regiment, 1857–1878, 140–1.

[67] NAM 94-5-181. Sgt.-Maj. J. White. Ts. Memoirs, Reminiscences of my Army life.

[68] Robertson, *From Private to Field Marshal*, 28.

[69] ERM. Loan from private collection. EY Files KBM 37. Court of Inquiry held at Naours on 18th Nov. 1917.

[70] ERM. ERCB3. Warley Warrant Officers' and Sergeants' Mess Scrap Book, 1898–1939. Cutting from the *Mid-Essex Recorder*, 'Warley Barracks Tragedy. Essex Sergeant Major Shot', 24 May 1924.

[71] *The Times*, 8 Apr. 1887.

An unpleasant affair has occurred at a ball given in Delhi the evening before last. I was there for a short time and observed nothing wrong, but after I left there was some disturbance and more than one officer was the worse for liquor. I have only been able to bring it home to one, Lieut. [R. W. H.] Macdonald of the Border Regiment (34th). He does not bear a very good character, and as he committed himself before the Foreign officers, I have put him under arrest, and have given him the option of retiring or being tried by a Court Martial. I hope he will send in his papers, if not, he must be tried, as it is necessary to make an example.[72]

Macdonald refused to send in his papers. He was therefore court-martialled, and sentenced to be dismissed from the service. This was not an isolated case. Other officers who committed offences for which, had they been other ranks, they would have received relatively minor punishments were dealt with far more severely. In December 1881 a lieutenant in the 1/Essex Regiment was found guilty of issuing a dud cheque to his Mess President. He was cashiered. In 1913 an officer in the same unit was found guilty of embezzlement and of going AWOL and received the same sentence.[73] In 1920 2/Lt. Alfred Joseph Guy of the RASC was found guilty of using insubordinate language to a superior officer and of an act prejudicial to good order and military discipline and was dismissed from the army. He had told his CO that 'I wont be buggered about and I will take the first boat back to England' and then wrote to him that he was unwilling to 'tolerate such incompetent senior officers, and the continual reshovelling [sic] of duties'.[74] Similarly, in 1921 Lt. D. P. Harman of 2/Wiltshire Regiment was found guilty of being AWOL for a week, issuing a dud cheque, and disobeying his CO's order not to frequent any nightclubs until he had cleared his debts, and was sentenced to be cashiered.[75]

The rank and file were not always content to remain passive victims of the workings of the army's disciplinary code. Protests could take either individual or collective forms. Malingering, that is feigning illness or incapacity or exacerbating an existing condition, was a favourite gambit to avoid unpleasant duties or punishments.[76] In 1922 a private in 2/Essex reported to the medical officer with an abrasion on his toe. The doctor placed a dressing on it. He then asked the doctor to excuse him from wearing boots, probably because he could then avoid having to complete some defaulters' drill that he had been awarded. But the medical officer

[72] Roberts, *Roberts in India*, 338.

[73] ERM. ER2725. Officer's Court Martials. Charges: against Lt. C. D. Rosser, 1/Essex, 3 Dec. 1881; Extract from the proceedings of a GCM held at Quetta on 4th March 1913 by order of Lt.-Gen. Sir M. H. S. Firer Commanding 4th (Quetta) Division, 26 Feb. 1913.

[74] PRO WO 209/23. Proceedings of a General Court Martial, 7 Nov. 1920.

[75] PRO WO 209/36. Proceedings of a General Court Martial, 4 Aug. 1921.

[76] J. Bourke, *Dismembering the Male: Men's Bodies, Britain and the Great War* (London: Reaktion Books, 1996), 76–89.

198 DEVIANCY AND DISCIPLINE

refused to agree and consequently, as soon as he left the medical hut, he removed the dressing in the hope that the toe would turn septic. The ploy failed. The doctor dressed the toe again and reported him to the battalion provost sergeant.[77]

Soldiers who were more seriously disgruntled with army life sometimes resorted to committing minor crimes, such as theft of a bicycle or breaking a shop window, knowing that if they were found guilty by a civilian court and sentenced to a period of imprisonment, the army would have to discharge them. In 1876 Private James Little of the Royal Artillery broke a jeweller's window in Greenwich and stole two watches because he 'would sooner be hanged than remain any longer in the Army'.[78] In 1932 the War Office asked the Home Office to request magistrates to remand such offenders to military custody so that they could be tried by a court martial, thus ensuring that they were punished but not discharged.[79]

Collective protests against discipline were less common but represented a far more serious threat to military authority. The boundaries between what soldiers regarded as strict but fair discipline and outright bullying were constantly shifting. But they were essentially consensual, a fact that was revealed when that consensus temporarily broke down. Officers who bullied their men were detested, and their behaviour might actually precipitate the breakdown in discipline that they wished to avoid. Thus in May 1899 there was mass insubordination in 2/Royal Guernsey Militia when nearly 150 men refused to parade for their annual training. When the Lieutenant Governor of the island investigated the causes of the problem he discovered that whereas in each of three other battalions doing their training on the island, the CO had inflicted an average of nine punishments, the Adjutant of 2/Battalion had imposed thirty on his men.[80] On a smaller scale, in 1928 one battery commander based near Secunderabad in India was such a martinet that his Adjutant resigned his commission, several senior NCOs who had completed six years' service in India asked to be posted to the UK, and one of his captains committed suicide.[81]

But probably the biggest breakdown of the consensus occurred in the aftermath of the First World War. By 1919 most soldiers had either volunteered or thought that they had been conscripted to defeat the Germans. Having fulfilled their part of the bargain, they believed that

[77] ERM. ER 15249. Sgt. W. H. Green MSS. Capt. T. Starton [?] RAMC to Provost Sgt., the Essex Regiment, n.d., but c.1 June 1922.

[78] *The Times*, 25 Aug. 1876; Lucy, *There's a Devil*, 32.

[79] PRO HO 45/24648. Col. C. T. Tomes, AAG, to A. Locke, Home Office, 28 June 1932.

[80] PRO WO 32/8621. Lieutenant Governor of Guernsey to Under Secretary of State for War, 16 May 1899.

[81] IWMSA. Accession No. 000780/05. H. L. Horsfield, 26–7.

the military authorities now had to fulfil their part by demobilizing them as quickly as possible. When they seemed reluctant to do so, authority in many units began to disintegrate. As one regular battalion commander in France noted on 11 November 1918, 'the men, or many of them, will be difficult to hold now,—the purpose which has held them together is gone, discipline as a power in itself is not a very strong one in our army.'[82] Attempts by the military authorities to impose regular-style peacetime discipline were particularly resented.[83] Within a few days of the Armistice GHQ in Egypt issued an order 'telling officers and N.C.O.S to use *tact* in dealing with men. "Give them sports and make duties as light as possible."'[84]

The wisdom of that order was shown a few weeks later when it was ignored and the infantry of 75th Division were ordered to work at labouring duties building roads. Many men refused, complaining that Egypt 'is not a country for white men to work hard and they are quite right. Having fought out here they ought to be given plenty of time off now.'[85] Similar protests took place in Britain. When a senior officer was sent to Shoreham demobilization camp in January 1919 to talk to a large group of soldiers who had mutinied, released prisoners from the guard-room, and pelted the orderly officer with potatoes, he was heckled and shouted down.[86] Sometimes the protestors evoked the sympathy of their officers. When the 2/Rifle Brigade refused to go on a route march in January 1919 in protest against their slow demobilization and poor rations, one of their officers described the incident as 'just a little explosion of discontent about quite legitimate grievances'.[87] Even the most highly disciplined troops were not immune. During the war Haig had regarded the Guards division 'As our *only* really reliable reserve' but even they could be driven too far. In June 1919 a battalion of the Grenadier Guards mutinied at Pirbright Camp because of the tactless handling by their officers, who required them to work in the afternoons.[88]

[82] W. Fraser, *In Good Company: The First World War Letters and Diaries of the Hon. William Fraser, Gordon Highlanders*, ed. D. Fraser (Salisbury, Wilts: Michael Joseph, 1990), 332; IWM Misc 220/3152/2/23. The Jesse Short Collection. Lt.-Col. T. L. Loveday to Gill, 30 Sept. 1965; IWM 84/46/1. Captain M. Hardie MSS. GHQ, Italy, Report on Postal Censorship. Italian Expeditionary Force, n.d. but *c.* early 1919.
[83] IWM Misc. 220/3152/323. The Jesse Short Collection. Edward Pointon to Gill, 7 July 1965.
[84] A. Pryor and J. K. Woods (eds.), *Great Uncle Fred's War: An Illustrated Diary 1917–20* (Whitstable, Kent: Pryor Publications, 1985), 47.
[85] Ibid. 51.
[86] IWM Misc. 220/3152/2/20 & /21. The Jesse Short Collection. L. Laurence to Gill, 30 Sept. 1965.
[87] Nettleton, *The Anger of the Guns*, 184.
[88] LHCMA. Kiggell MSS II/15. Haig to Kiggell, 4 Jan. 1918; PRO WO 32/9543. OC Grenadier Guards to GOC London District, 12 June 1919.

The course of these mutinies demonstrated, for good or bad, the key part that COs played in maintaining discipline in their unit. In February 1919, for example, by showing that he was willing to listen to his men's grievances and to put right those that it was in his power to alter, the CO of 14/Stationary Hospital near Boulogne was able to defuse a potentially mutinous situation.[89] By contrast, in India in 1920 some men of 1/ Connaught Rangers mutinied ostensibly because of the treatment being meted out to some of their relatives in Ireland by British troops and police. But in the opinion of a former Adjutant who had served with the battalion only a few months before the mutiny, the real cause was that 'the senior officers [of the battalion] were quite out of touch with their men and the junior officers were kept in their place and not asked for their opinion'.[90] The whole sorry episode, which led to the execution of one mutineer, left much the same impression on a junior soldier in the regiment, who noted: 'That mutiny did not spread to the other Southern Irish Regiments was I think due to the fact that their officers had got the situation in hand. It came like a bolt from the blue to us, and our officers knew nothing at all, so maybe the other regiments learned a lesson from us.'[91]

The military authorities drew some important conclusions from this explosion of unrest. Coercion could only be employed if a small minority of soldiers refused to obey orders. In February 1919, when most of the troops at the Base Depot at Kantara went on strike, the local commander had little option other than to listen to their grievances and pass them on to the War Office.[92] By April 1919 the situation had become even worse. Demobilization had been stopped as troops were required in Egypt to put down a rising against British rule. The men resented this and went on a strike again.[93] The GOC in Egypt, Sir Edmund Allenby, ruefully accepted that 'I can't shoot them all for mutiny; so I must carry on as best I can, & must resume demobilisation.'[94] The CIGS, Sir Henry Wilson, was afraid that discipline throughout the army might be about to collapse completely.[95] Wilson realized that

[89] IWM Misc. 220/3152/3/30. The Jesse Short Collection. P. Rumens to Gill, 18 Oct. 1965.
[90] IWM P15. Colonel F. W. S. Jourdain MSS. Jourdain to Field Marshal Sir Gerald Templer, 20 May 1971.
[91] IWM Misc. 220/3152/1/6. The Jesse Short Collection. G. Byrne to Gill, 4 Oct. 1965; A. Babington, *The Devil to Pay: The Mutiny of the Connaught Rangers, India, July 1920* (London: Leo Cooper, 1991).
[92] IWM Misc. 220/3152/4/18. The Jesse Short Collection. H. Williams to Gill, 18 Oct. 1965.
[93] IWM Misc. 220/3152/3/3. The Jesse Short Collection. W. S. Mead to Gill, and enc. The Mutiny at Kantara 1919 by one who took part, 19 Oct. 1965. IWM Misc. 220/3152/2/26. The Jesse Short Collection. P. McCormack to Gill, ? June 1965.
[94] Sir H. Wilson, *The Military Correspondence of Field Marshal Sir Henry Wilson 1918–1922*, ed. K. Jeffery (London: Bodley Head for the Army Record Society, 1985), 99.
[95] Ibid. 73–4.

We live in very difficult times in 1919, after the bloodiest war that the world has ever seen, to what we did in 1914, and we must be careful what we do. Methods & practices which were desirable & possible in 1914 are often wholly unadvisable & impracticable in 1919. True discipline *must* be maintained, but we must adjust ourselves to the times & maintain it, often, by means other than those we employed before the war.[96]

When faced by groups of soldiers expressing collective grievances, the military authorities had to calculate whether they could afford to deal summarily with them, or whether more tactful methods were required. In some cases they were able to exploit the sectionalized loyalties of the regimental system to their advantage. When several thousand RAOC soldiers at 5 Base Ordnance Depot at Tel-el-Kebir in Egypt mutinied in November 1946 in protest at the slowing down of their demobilization, the local military authorities felt able to deal robustly with them because they had to hand a battalion of loyal troops, 2/King's Royal Rifle Corps. The attitude of the riflemen, dragged out of bed in the middle of the night, was summed up by one of their number, who was heard to mutter 'Rotten b-s getting us aht at this...hour...I'll give 'em Mutiny...'. The Riflemen deployed throughout the camp with fixed bayonets, 'and firmly pushed about those who tried to be tiresome'. But after this show of effective force, the military authorities dealt leniently with the offenders. Most of the identified ringleaders were dealt with summarily by their CO and only two men were sent for court martial.[97]

The military authorities adopted a similar approach in 1956. The Suez crisis led to several mutinies on Cyprus amongst reservists recalled to the Colours and National Servicemen retained after their demobilization date. In October, 21 RAOC men were arrested for refusing to leave an unofficial meeting called to voice their grievances. The military authorities made an example of the more egregious cases, but were concerned that 'Considerable publicity has been given by the Press during recent weeks of the present emergency to incidents arising from corporate representation of alleged grievances. Many Ministerial questions have also been submitted.' The War Office therefore reminded commanding officers and their men that the Army Act laid down specific means by which soldiers could make their complaints, and warned them that it would not countenance their employing methods that stepped outside the confines of military law.[98]

---

[96] PRO WO 32/9543. Wilson to Churchill, 22 June 1919.
[97] PRO WO 261/469. RAOC. 5 Base Depot. July–Dec. 1946, 8–11 Nov. 1946; IWM 74/147/1. J. C. Slater, Account of the mutiny at Tel-El-Kebir Base, Nov. 1946.
[98] PRO WO 32/16639. War Office to all GOCs-in-C, 12 Oct. 1956; *The Times*, 5 Oct. 1956.

The regimental system established a series of norms and patterns of behaviour against which the conduct of every soldier in the regiment could be measured. Soldiers who fell short of these standards were disgraced because they could be held to be letting down their regiment. This was typified in the late 1890s when troopers guilty of minor disobedience in 16/Lancers were admonished by being told by their officers that '"he had disgraced the regiment"—"Lancers do not do that."'[99] Similarly, the men of 1/Suffolks were reminded in 1925 that

Each individual soldier must remember that he has his duty to perform by the Regiment. A good soldier is obedient, regular in his quarters, and attentive to the care and cleanliness of his arms. He must be smart in his appearance and orderly in his behaviour. He must endeavour at all times by his personal example and influence with others to uphold the good name of the Regiment, which he must place above everything else.[100]

At the same time soldiers who did behave in ways that the military authorities deemed to be deviant were also subject to a series of punishments of escalating severity. Evidence from the incidence of courts martial suggests that there was a marked increase in the willingness of soldiers to accept the constraints of military discipline, or at least that the military authorities came to believe that it was becoming less necessary for them to utilize the full majesty of military law to extract obedience. Over the century after 1870 the efforts made by the military authorities and regimental officers to improve the tone of the soldiers' life, by humanizing disciplinary structures and providing constructive outlets for energies that might otherwise have been directed towards dangerous pastimes that were disruptive of discipline, had a positive effect.

However, the very fact that the Regular Army had its own disciplinary code set it apart from civilian society, and that ran contrary to one of Cardwell's and Childers's most cherished aims, to narrow the gap between soldiers and society. They hoped that by linking regular battalions with units of the auxiliary forces they would be able to build bridges between civil society and the army. The extent to which they were able to create regimental communities that extended beyond the Regular Army and to encompass Militia, Volunteer, and Territorial Force units will be examined in the next chapter.

---

[99] Gough, *Soldiering On*, 33.
[100] SRO. GB 554/Y1/128a. Anon., *Standing Orders of the Suffolk Regiment (The Twelfth Foot)* (n.p., 1925), 48.

CHAPTER EIGHT

The Auxiliary Regiments

A few days after the start of the Second World War two officers of a London Territorial regiment were waiting for a bus. A Rolls Royce drew up and the driver enquired if he could give them a lift. The driver was their company sanitary orderly. Both officers were Old Etonians. The sanitary man was Old Harrovian.[1] It is difficult to imagine a similar occurrence happening in a regular unit. That it could happen in a unit of the auxiliary army suggests that for all the attempts made by Cardwell, Childers, and their successors to create homogeneous regimental communities that transcended the distinctions between regulars, Militiamen, Volunteers, and Territorial soldiers, wide differences in many aspects of their behaviour persisted.

One of the objectives of the Cardwell–Childers reforms was to establish the auxiliary armies—the Militia, Yeomanry, and Volunteers—as a reserve for the Regular Army, and as a bridge between the regulars and civilian society. In January 1882 Childers spoke of his goal as being

> to see the line and the auxiliary forces closely bound together (cheers), the men in the one feeling themselves to be the comrades of the men in the other, drawn from the same classes, wearing the same uniform, proud of the same colours and badges (cheers). I want to see the permanent staff of all having the same origin, with the district colonel at their head, selected from those who have spent their lives in the regiment.[2]

The extent of their success depended on the ability and willingness of regulars and auxiliaries to forge close and meaningful links. Some were obviously willing to do so. In July 1882 Colonel Moore, the CO of the Royal South Lincolnshire Militia, and five of his officers attended a regimental dinner with the officers of the two regular battalions of the Lincolnshire Regiment. The dinner was also attended by Prince Edward of Saxe Weimar, the Colonel of Regiment. 'This being the first occasion in which the officers of all four Battalions have met together since they were

---

[1] B. Sheridan, 'What Did You Do in the War, Dad?' (Lewes, Sussex: The Book Guild, 1993), 23–4.

[2] NAM 8202-55. Colonel G. C. Swiney, Scrapbook, Sept. 1872 to June 1913. *Standard*, 20 Jan. 1882.

united in the Territorial Lincolnshire Regiment, Colonel Moore trusts that the amalgamation so pleasantly and happily begun may be long perpetuated to the honour and satisfaction of all four Battalions.'[3] But in many instances relations between the different components of the land forces were characterized by mutual suspicion if not downright hostility, and for a long time their relations were far from being harmonious.

Cardwell and Childers had to overcome a legacy of mutual suspicion that had grown up between the regulars and the auxiliaries long before they began their work of remodelling Britain's land forces. In the mid-nineteenth century, Militia regiments drew their recruits from a clearly defined geographical area. Their officer corps were dominated by county families and they were usually fiercely determined to maintain their separate existence independent of the Regular Army. They distrusted the regulars for the way in which, during the Crimean War, their regiments had been milked by the regulars for recruits. They resented the Volunteers because they were attracting just the kind of respectable working-class men that they wanted to fill their own ranks.[4]

Linking and territorialization did not automatically overcome this legacy of division and suspicion, and in some respects even made it worse. When Militia COs were asked in 1876 about the possibility that their units might become part of newly created Territorial regiments consisting of linked line and militia units, their reactions were mixed. Some were indifferent. The CO of the 1/South Durham Militia stated:

I do not think the Militia would care about it one way or the other. The Line battalions of the Sub-District are in most cases a myth to the men of the Militia. For instance, in our case, we have never seen the Foreign battalion, and we shall probably never see the home battalion, as there is no station for a regiment in the county.[5]

Others gave it a cautious welcome. The COs of the Wexford Militia and the Royal South Lincolnshire Militia embraced it, believing that 'the nearer the Militia is made to assimilate to the Line the more popular it will become'.[6] But others were downright hostile. Their regiments had their own distinct *esprit de corps*, which linking and territorialization threatened to destroy. The COs of units like the Carnarvon Rifles, the North Lincolnshire Militia, and the 2/Cheshire Militia and 2/Northamptonshire and Rutlandshire Militia complained that the creation of

[3] PRO WO 68/131. Royal South Lincs. Militia. Digest of Service, 15 July 1882.

[4] I. F. W. Beckett, *The Amateur Military Tradition, 1558–1945* (Manchester: Manchester University Press, 1991), 151–4, 170–1.

[5] PP (1887), XVIII. C. 1654. *Report of the Committee . . .*, Appendix II. Questions sent to Commanding Officers of Militia Regiments (Great Britain and Ireland), 1 Aug. 1876.

[6] Ibid.

Territorial regiments would mean that their regiments would lose their separate identities, the county gentry who officered them would lose all interest in them, and recruits would be discouraged from joining the Militia for fear that they would be transferred against their will into the line.[7] The CO of the Scottish Borders Militia summarized their objections succinctly. Asked if his men would be proud if their regiment became a numbered battalion of 21/Foot, he expostulated that 'Upon my word, if you ask me, they are just as proud of their regiment as they can be. You cannot make them any prouder.'[8]

For some Militia units, the Cardwell–Childers reforms actually involved the breaking of existing territorial loyalties. Cardwell and Childers hoped to create real bonds of sympathy between regular and Militia units of the same regiment by ensuring that regular and Militia recruits trained side by side at the same depot. However, this was slow to occur, not least because it required some Militia regiments to leave their existing headquarters and move to a different town, or in some cases to a different county. This meant, as Lt.-Gen. Sir George Willis, the GOC Northern District, explained in 1880,

that the keeping up [of] the feeling between the line and the militia regiments is one thing, and keeping up the recruiting connexion is another. In the one case, that is to keep up the feeling between the line and the militia, you have to let them see as much as possible of each other. In the other case the great thing is to let the locality from which you raise the recruits see as much of the battalion as they can. And the only way of carrying that out is to keep the head-quarters at the place where they raise the bulk of the recruits; and at the training period to bring them in contact with the regulars.[9]

Militia officers also disliked a system that deprived them of the right to train their own recruits and meant that they took charge of them only after they had undergone their recruit training at the depot.[10] In 1880 Lt.-Col. Henry Sanford, the CO of the Royal Buckinghamshire Militia, favoured creating closer links between the militia and the line, but objected that recruiting for his battalion would suffer if he was forced to move its headquarters from High Wycombe to the brigade depot HQ of its regular regiment, the Oxfordshire Light Infantry, at Oxford. 'Recruits as a rule only enlist when they are out of work or hard up', he explained, 'and walk into head-quarters from the neighbouring villages'. If his regiment moved to Oxford it would be too far from its recruiting

[7] Ibid.

[8] Ibid., Q. 3010.

[9] PRO WO 33/37. Report of the militia localisation committee appointed by the Secretary of State for War to inquire into the movement of certain militia regiments, 4 Apr. 1881, Q. 41.

[10] Jackson Hay, *An Epitomized History of the Militia*, 160–1.

grounds for the men to walk.[11] Faced by his and similar complaints, a War Office committee investigating the localization of the militia recommended in 1880 that those regiments that had not already moved their HQ to their brigade depot should be required to do so only if the move did not take them out of their own county.[12]

That localization and territorialization happened despite the opposition of many senior Militia officers was symptomatic of the fact that, when the interests of the regulars and auxiliary forces clashed, the military authorities usually sided with the former. This was demonstrated by what happened to the 25/Foot. In 1881 the regiment was localized in the Scottish borders, but the region was underpopulated and the regiment was without an associated Militia battalion. The War Office, therefore, decided, despite the objections of their CO, to transfer the 3/(Militia) Battalion of the Royal Scots Fusiliers to the 25/Foot. This was welcomed by the CO of the 25/Foot, who insisted that the claims of his regiment ('one of the oldest Scottish Regiments of the Line, consisting of two strong Battalions') should have precedence over those of a Militia battalion 'of recent origin'.[13] The Adjutant-General, Sir Garnet Wolseley, agreed, recognizing that 'the question is whether, if the proposal is desirable from the broad point of view of Army organisation, it is to be abandoned in deference to the sentimental objections of a single Militia battalion'.[14] Such 'sentimental objections' counted for nothing and the linking went ahead. The only concession that the Militia could wring from the military authorities was that the title of the regiment would be changed from the King's Own Borderers to the King's Own Scottish Borderers, on the grounds that it would 'materially help to ally the natural feeling of deep regret with which we regard the contemplated change'.[15]

One reason why relations between the regulars and the different branches of the auxiliary forces remained strained for a long time after the Cardwell–Childers reforms was that some of the different branches of the land forces were divided by subtle but significant social distinctions. The Militia and Yeomanry recruited their officers from amongst much the same social classes as did the Regular Army. In the Middlesex Yeomanry, for example, in the early 1890s each of the fourteen officers was sufficiently wealthy to be able to contribute between £20–40 per annum from their own pocket to the regimental band and prize funds. Captains in the Wiltshire Yeomanry were probably £100 out of pocket

---

[11] PRO WO 33/37. Report of the militia localisation committee, 4 Apr. 1881. QQ. 697, 702.
[12] PRO WO 33/37. Report of the militia localisation committee ..., 1–4 Apr. 1881.
[13] PRO WO 32/6092. Lt.-Col. Hope to Wolseley, n.d.
[14] Ibid. Adj.-Gen., 23 Aug. 1885.
[15] Ibid. Walker to Dormer, 2 Oct. 1886.

per annum.[16] Like the Yeomanry, the ideal Militia officers, in the eyes of many commanding officers, were 'county men', and 'men of property accustomed to looking after things, and who have got good heads on their shoulders'.[17] In 1898 about half of all Yeomanry officers were retired cavalry officers, landowners, and fox-hunters.[18]

Some country gentlemen, secure in their place in the county community, regarded a few years' service in their local Militia regiment as a necessary rite of passage. But in the second half of the nineteenth century they became fewer in number. In 1868 Maj.-Gen. James Lindsay, the Inspector-General of Reserve Forces, complained that

We have heard a good deal of 'the county connection'. The 'county connection' has been hitherto a most important element in the militia, but I am afraid that those who study the Army List and look at the requirements of the Militia, will find that the service at the present moment is not quite so popular a service as it should be, with those who live in the different counties. The militia is very short of officers, very short of subalterns, and in some instances, I am afraid, very short of captains.[19]

In an effort to attract more men to take commissions in the Militia, and to make a reality of the link that he wished to forge between the regulars and Militia, Cardwell modified the terms of service of Militia officers. In 1869 he abolished the property qualification for Militia officers, thus widening the field from which they could be recruited. And in 1872, as an inducement to young men to seek Militia commissions, each regiment was allowed annually to nominate one of its subalterns for a regular commission. Applicants had to be aged between 19 to 22, to have attended at least two annual trainings, and to have passed a professional examination. These reforms made a Militia commission a popular back-door into the Regular Army, but they did nothing to enable Militia colonels to officer their units.[20] Militia colonels hoped to recruit their officers from amongst men of good families who were closely attached to their county. In 1880, the Earl of Sandwich, the CO of the Huntington Militia, wanted such men 'because they know most of their men and they are anxious to keep up the corps; they take an interest in it'.[21] But, thanks

---

[16] PP (1892), XX. C. 6675. *Report of the Committee appointed by the Secretary of State for War to consider the conditions of the Yeomanry*, QQ. 10, 16, 205, 363-4.

[17] PP (1904), XXXI. Cd. 2063. *Minutes of Evidence ...*, Q. 15043.

[18] P. Talbot, 'The English Yeomanry in the Nineteenth Century and the Great Boer War', *Journal of the Society for Army Historical Research*, 79 (2001), 55-6.

[19] Lindsay made these comments at the Royal United Services Institute on the occasion of a lecture by Maj. A. Leahy, 'Our Infantry Forces and Infantry Reserves', 338.

[20] Beckett, *The Amateur Military Tradition*, 186-7; PP (1890), XIX. C. 5922. *Report of the Committee, ...*; PP (1907), XLIX. Cd. 3294. *Interim report of the War Office Committee on the provision of officers (a) for service with the regular army in war, and (b) for the auxiliary forces.*

[21] PRO WO 33/37. Report of the militia localisation committee ..., 4 Apr. 1881.

to the impact of the Great Depression on agricultural rents, the supply was drying up. Like many other Militia commanders, he had to accept men from outside the county. They had joined because they wanted a stepping stone to a regular commission, and when they took it they did not invariably transfer into the linked line battalion of their Militia regiment. One Militia CO derided them as suffering from 'scarlet fever', but the very fact that they left so soon after joining caused resentment to be directed towards the regulars.[22]

Nor did the flow of Militia officers into the Regular Army necessarily cement better relations between the regulars and auxiliaries. Between 1874 and 1908 the 3/(Militia Battalion) Somerset Light Infantry supplied forty-five officers to the line. Only eleven of them joined one of the regular battalions of their regiment.[23] The conversion of the Militia into the Special Reserve in 1908 worsened the already serious shortage of officers. The initial training period could be as long as six to twelve months, and few young men could find the time to undertake it, 'for the leisured class, from which the old Militia officers were drawn, is fast disappearing', and the incentive of a regular commission was now closed off to them.[24]

The officers of the Volunteers were divided from their regular and Militia comrades by far more than their part-time status. When they were first raised, many Volunteer units had found their officers from amongst the ranks of established gentlemen of leisure. However, by the end of the nineteenth century there had been a distinct decline in their social status. By the eve of the First World War the overwhelming majority of Territorial officers came from the ranks of the professional middle classes, with a sprinkling of tradesmen.[25] A commission in the Volunteers and Territorials gave them a certain social status in their community that they might not otherwise have enjoyed. In 1878 one Volunteer CO said of his officers:

A good many of them are not in the actual rank of gentlemen. I think that the service very much improves them in that respect. We have had a good number of officers, very young men, commanding company [sic]; my experience has been that they have proved the best officers. Young clerks in the Civil Service and the

[22] PP (1902), X. Cd. 983. *Minutes of evidence* ..., QQ. 6065, 6069, 6073–7, 6091; PP (1904), XXXI. Cd. 2063. *Minutes of evidence*, QQ. 15021–5.

[23] Capt. W. J. W. Kerr, *Records of the 1st Somerset Militia (3rd Battalion. Somerset Light Infantry* (Aldershot: Gale & Polden, 1930), 79–84.

[24] PRO WO 33/505. Committee on the Organisation of the Special Reserve. Second Report, 14 Dec. 1910; War Office, *Regulations for the Officers of the Special Reserve of Officers and the Special Reserve, 1911* (London: War Office, 1911), 43–5; PRO WO 33/498. Organisation of the Special Reserve. Interim Report, 14 Apr. 1910; PRO WO 32/3676. Director of Organisation to Adj.-Gen., 25 Nov. 1919.

[25] Cunningham, *The Volunteer Force*, 55–9; Sheffield, *Leadership in the Trenches*, 15.

like have proved our best officers; it was the only ladder which they had to a little distinction in the town, and they took a great deal of interest in their companies; they worked hard at it and proved very efficient indeed.[26]

Although a commission could put them to considerable expense, a fact that probably deterred some men from seeking one, Volunteer and Territorial officers regarded part-time soldiering as an enjoyable form of recreation.[27] They liked the opportunity to wear martial uniforms and to go to camp and so occasionally to be able to escape from their everyday lives. One former Territorial officer who eventually rose to be CIGS admitted in 1948: 'I started my military career as a T.A. officer in May 1914 and I am sure it was mainly the "club" side of the business that attracted the best chaps in all ranks and held them together. It would be foolish now to disregard the British addiction to clubs!!'[28]

A commission in the Volunteers or Territorials could also be a badge of social respectability and social acceptance. Given the fact that many Volunteer or Territorial units recruited from a restricted geographical area or occupation, it also gave officers the opportunity to replicate in their leisure activities the same relationship of authority and deference that they enjoyed with their subordinates in the factory or office.[29]

There were similar divisions between the social profiles of the rank and file of the auxiliary forces. The Militia drew most of its rank and file from the same sectors of society as the regulars. In the mid-1870s, depending on the economy of its recruiting district, Militia regiments attracted agricultural labourers, carters, colliers, dock labourers, mill operatives, miners, 'a lower class of mechanics, and the migratory portion of the labouring class'.[30] In some agricultural regions, it was easier to recruit artisans and miners than it was agricultural labourers. 'Farmers have great objection to the Militia, even though the times of training have been so arranged as to interfere as little as possible with the requirements of agriculture', wrote a War Office official in 1870. 'The hold which they have over their labourers is strong enough to counterbalance the pecuniary inducements—presumably considerable in comparison with the usual run of wages—held out by government, and to bring it about that the bulk of recruits in most of the agricultural counties consists of the artizan class of townsmen.'[31]

[26] PP (1878–9), XV. C. 2235. *Report of the committee appointed by the Secretary of State for War to enquire into the Internal Organisation of the Volunteer Forces in Great Britain*, Q. 693.
[27] PP (1894), XV. *Report from the Select Committee on Volunteer Acts*, QQ. 365, 1085.
[28] PRO WO 216/250. Harding to Templer, 8 Mar. 1948.
[29] Cunningham, *The Volunteer Force*, 108–13.
[30] PP (1887), XVIII. C. 1654. *Report of the committee …*, 77.
[31] PRO WO 32/21A. O. H. Moreshead, Memo on Militia Recruiting, 10 Mar. 1870.

By the early twentieth century little had changed, except that, as their numbers dwindled, it became even more difficult to recruit agricultural labourers. About three out of ten militiamen were agricultural labourers, two out of ten were 'mechanical labourers', slightly more than one in ten were miners, and slightly fewer than one in ten were artisans. In 1907 of the 288 men of the 5/Royal Irish Fusiliers who assembled for their annual training at Monaghan, 'The majority of the men', according to one member of the regiment, 'are fine specimens of the Irish peasant'. But, he went on to lament, 'It is a matter of regret that recruiting in Co. Monaghan had been falling off for a number of years, due principally to the dearth of young men, and the consequent increase in demand for agricultural labour.'[32]

Two things distinguished the average Militia recruit from his regular comrade. He was more likely to be underemployed rather than un-employed when he enlisted, and he was probably less fit. One depot commander said of one of the Militia recruits he received during the Boer War: 'He is a boy of seventeen years of age; five feet two, hardly able to carry a rifle, and he is no use.'[33] Indeed, some men joined the ranks of the Militia, or after 1908 its successor the Special Reserve, because they could not meet the physical standards of the Regular Army, but hoped that a few months' training with the Militia, accompanied by plenty of food, would enable them to do so.[34] Others did so because Militia pay offered them a form of temporary outdoor unemployment relief. Re-cruits from agricultural regions where employment on the land was seasonal, such as Bedfordshire, Cambridgeshire, and Essex, joined the Militia to tide them over 'during the slack season of the year', and for 'Ready money, and want of employment in frost and cold'.[35] In 1876 the CO of the East Essex Militia was adamant that his men enlisted for the 'Bounty. No man enrols unless he is out of work, and wants money down.'[36]

In urban areas, and also in some rural areas, others were attracted to the Militia because it offered them a temporary escape from the tedium of their daily lives. In the 1870s the men of 2/Middlesex Militia were recruited from cab drivers and costermongers and 'we get a certain number of mechanics, who look upon the training as an outing, that what they lose in money they gain in health'.[37] The men of 1/Durham

---

[32] 'Faugh-a-Ballagh'. The Regimental Gazette of the 87th Royal Irish Fusiliers, 6 (July 1907).
[33] PP (1904), XXXI. Cd. 2063. Minutes of Evidence ..., Q. 19795.
[34] Sgt. C. Arnold, From Mons to Messines and Beyond: The Great War Experience of Sergeant Charles Arnold, ed. S. Royal (Studley, Warwickshire: K. A. F. Brewin Books, 1985), 5.
[35] PP (1877), XVIII. C. 1654. Report of the committee ... Appendix II. Questions sent to Commanding Officers of Militia Regiments (Great Britain and Ireland) 1 Aug. 1876.
[36] Ibid.
[37] Ibid., Q. 1962.

Militia, which recruited heavily amongst the mining and ironworking communities of County Durham, joined 'Chiefly [for] the desire for an "outing" during the hot weather, and a month or two in the country after the hard work of the factories or mines. The men, as a rule earn high wages, and do not mind being out of work for a time.'[38] And the men of the Scottish Borders Militia enlisted because 'They take kindly to the annual training as a pleasant variety from the work-a-day toil of daily life ...'.[39]

If the Regular Army and the Militia failed to find many men from the respectable working classes, the Volunteers had no such difficulty. Before 1914 the rank and file of the Volunteers, and their successors the Territorials, remained socially a cut above the Militia and the regulars.[40] In rural areas with scattered settlement patterns Volunteer units sometimes resembled bands of feudal retainers. But most rural units were centred on small towns and recruited their rank and file from tradesmen, artisans, and craftsmen who were in full-time employment.[41]

However, the heartland of the Volunteer movement lay in the urban centres, where initially they recruited amongst predominantly middle and lower middle-class groups. When the Queen's Edinburgh Rifle Volunteer Brigade was first formed, many of its companies had their own distinctive professional flavour, consisting of lawyers, accountants, civil servants, and bankers.[42] But from 1862, after the initial invasion panic that had caused men to enlist began to abate, Volunteers tended to become both younger and more working class. By 1879, for example, 1/Administrative Battalion, the Derbyshire Rifle Volunteers consisted of a company of agricultural labourers, two strong companies from the Butterley Iron Works, a company and a half from a nearby cotton factory, a company of bank clerks and shop assistants from the town of Derby, and six companies of artisans from the same town.[43] In 1887 nearly half of the rank and file of 2/(VB) of the Royal Fusiliers, with its HQ at Westminster, consisted of urban labourers and porters. But the rest of the battalion was composed of men drawn from skilled manual

---

[38] Ibid., Appendix II.

[39] Col. W. W. Walker, 'Our Militia and How to Improve It', *Journal of the Royal United Services Institute*, 24 (1880), 454·

[40] PP (1904), 30. Cd. 2062. *Report of the Royal Commission ...*, QQ 1210–12; Sheffield, *Leadership in the Trenches*, 14, 19; Col. G. R. Codrington, *The Territorial Army* (London: Sifton Praed, 1938), 113–14; P. Dennis, *The Territorial Army 1906–40* (Woodbridge: The Boydell Press and the Royal Historical Society, 1987), 148; IWMSA. Accession No. 00048/8. Lt.-Gen. Sir P. Neame, 22.

[41] PP (1878–9), XV. C. 2235. *Report of the Committee ...*, Q. 529.

[42] Ibid., QQ. 665, 704.

[43] Ibid., Q. 866.

and white-collar occupations, such as clerks, bookbinders, compositors, engineers, joiners, plumbers, and printers.[44] Finally, there were a handful of Volunteer and Territorial units that were so socially exclusive that they could demand references from would-be recruits. Young men anxious to join the socially prestigious Honourable Artillery Company, which recruited almost exclusively from amongst public school-educated members of the professional classes of the City of London, had either to supply references or be sponsored by an existing member of the regiment.[45]

The social profile of Territorial units did shift downwards between the world wars. One Territorial CO complained in 1935 that in the south of England Territorial Army units were attracting very few skilled artisans and 'the better class of black-coated man'.[46] But, as the Director-General of the Territorial Army had candidly admitted in 1924, beggars could not be choosers, for

In peace-time we have to rely on voluntary enlistment, and cannot afford to be too critical of the type of men who offer themselves. It is necessary to maintain cadres at such a strength as shall allow of the requisite modicum of peace training and of keeping alive at least a spark of military spirit which will serve to kindle and spread a serviceable and enduring glow on an emergency arising sufficiently serious to necessitate the embodiment of the Territorial Army.[47]

In contrast to the regulars and Militia, the Volunteers and Territorials recruited well in periods of prosperity and lost men in times of depression. Some contemporaries liked to believe that men joined the Volunteers/Territorials as an expression of their patriotism. In 1904, Lt.-Col. D. Shaw, the CO of the 1/(VB)Cameron Highlanders, told his soldiers: 'Their forbears had handed down to them the finest Empire ever known, and it was every subject's duty to guard that Empire.'[48] But the fact that he was addressing a meeting called to mark the opening of new reading and recreation rooms attached to their drill hall suggests that his men's reasons for enlisting were more complex than a simple desire to fight for King, Country, and Empire.

Many Volunteers enlisted because volunteering was an enjoyable form of recreation. John Fraser claimed that when he joined the 1/Newcastle Rifle Volunteers in 1876 'I cannot pretend that I did so with any particular patriotic motive, actually I joined rather with the idea of finding some

[44] Lt.-Col. R. W. Routledge, 'A Volunteer Battalion', *Nineteenth Century*, 22 (1887), 742–7.
[45] *Journal of the Honourable Artillery Company*, 14 (1936).
[46] PRO WO 33/1376. Report on the Staff Conference held at the Staff College, Camberley, 7–10 Jan. 1935.
[47] PRO WO 32/2856. Lt.-Gen. H. S. Jeudwine, Précis for the Army Council No. 1186. The peace organisation of the Territorial Army, 14 Mar. 1924.
[48] Anon, 'The Cameron Volunteers', *The 79th News* (1904).

outlet for my physical energies, and also with the idea of being able to meet and mix with other lads of my own age and tastes.'[49] Fraser and his friends were attracted by the colourful uniforms and by the opportunity to attend the annual camp, which for many of them represented the only annual holiday away from their home and place of work they were likely to enjoy.[50] Men joined the Volunteers and Territorials to take advantage of the many different leisure and social activities they organized. Most units held bazaars to raise funds, and entertained their members at theatrical shows, annual dinners, dances, whist drives, sports and athletics meetings, and opened their own club houses.[51] Above all, they offered male companionship to their members.[52] Walter Cousins, who joined 5/ East Surrey Regiment in 1912, 'used it more like a youth club to start with'.[53] James Grant Rodger, who lived in a small village near Perth, joined 6/Black Watch in 1908. There were few entertainment opportunities nearby and he followed many of his friends into the regiment.

You just went there for the fun of the thing, to meet other boys, got to the drill hall at night, winter nights. It was just the same as a club, you might call it. ... You had nothing else to take up your attention. Dark winter nights, you could go up to the Drill Hall and have boxing or anything you wanted, dominos or something of that kind, you had to pass the evening, you see ... What they would term in present day terms a youth club.[54]

However, the pull of patriotism should not be entirely discounted. In the late 1930s, around the time of the Munich crisis, large numbers of men did join the Territorials with more serious motives in mind. L. J. Green, who enlisted in a Territorial Anti-Aircraft unit in south London a few months before the Munich crisis, did so because 'war was on the way whether I liked it or not. So it gradually dawned on me I had a choice: wait to be called up or get myself a bit of pre-war training.'[55]

The rank and file of the Yeomanry was even more socially exclusive than the Volunteers and Territorials. In the early nineteenth century it had recruited from amongst tenant farmers and their sons. But the agricultural depression that began in the 1870s seriously depleted that class.[56] By 1914 it attracted 'respectable' recruits from amongst small tradesmen and

---

[49] Fraser, *Sixty Years in Uniform*, 39.
[50] IWMSA. Accession No. 6714/03. D. F. Cowie, reel 1.
[51] NAM 7305-74. Surrey Yeomanry, B Squadron, Woking Troop, Report Book 1908; L. Jackson, 'Patriotism or Pleasure? The Nineteenth-Century Volunteer Force as a Vehicle for Rural Working-Class Male Sport', *Sports Historian*, 19 (1999), 125–9.
[52] Cunningham, *The Volunteer Force*, 103–22.
[53] IWMSA. Accession No. 000786/06. W. Cousins, 1.
[54] IWMSA. Accession No. 000373/03. Lance-Sergeant J. G. Rodger, reel 1.
[55] L. J. Green, *Gunner Green's War (1938–1946)* (Edinburgh: Pentland Press, 1999), 1.
[56] PP (1892), XX. C. 6675. *Report of the Committee ...*, Q 468.

professionals who lived and worked in rural communities, and also from amongst urban tradesmen. By 1900 a typical Yeoman was a man who owned his own horse. In the countryside he was likely to be a small farmer, the owner of a livery stable, a coach proprietor, a horse dealer, a clerk, or a tradesman.[57] In urban areas such as London, where the Middlesex Yeomanry recruited, Yeomen were found from the 'men who are engaged in business in the City'.[58] In 1911 the rank and file of the Essex Yeomanry were sufficiently well to do that they sometimes took civilian grooms with them to camp to care for their horses.[59] For the rank and file membership gave them the opportunity to parade in a smart uniform and to demonstrate their respectability and standing in the community by allowing them to associate with the social elite who officered their regiment. Each unit had brightly coloured uniforms and no civic public occasion was complete without the pageantry they could provide.[60]

Cardwell and Childers hoped that by creating a close association between the regular and auxiliary units of the same regiments they would encourage Militiamen and Volunteers to transfer into the line. But in view of the different social classes from which they drew their recruits, it was always likely that they would be only partially successful. Unsurprisingly, given their superior employment situations, few Volunteers joined the regulars. However, many Militiamen did so. Between 1882 and 1904, 327,496 Militiamen enlisted in the Regular Army. This represented 35.4 per cent of all regular recruits, and by 1907 nearly a third of all Militiamen were transferring.[61] The Militia also proved to be a fruitful source of officers for the regulars. Between 1885 and 1906 rather more than a third of young officers preferred to enter the army through the Militia because by doing so they could avoid the considerable expense of attending a special 'Army crammer', usually necessary in order to pass the cadet college entrance examination, and the fees that the colleges charged parents.[62]

Linking, therefore, benefited the regulars, but it did not benefit the Militia. Every Militiaman or officer who joined the regulars was a man lost to the Militia, something that Militia officers understandably did not always welcome. Furthermore, the flow of recruits from the Militia to the regulars did not mean that regimental links were real, for not every

---

[57] Goodenough and Dalton, *The Army Book of the British Empire*, 374; ERO. D/DU 783/3. Scrapbook of Brigadier-General Sir Richard Colvin of Waltham Abbey, 'Our Territorial Army', *East Anglian Daily Times*, 1 Oct. 1911.

[58] PP (1892), XX. C. 6675. *Report of the Committee ...*, Q. 17.

[59] ERM. No accession number. MS memoirs of H. R. Wardill, 2.

[60] Talbot, 'The English Yeomanry', 54–6.

[61] Beckett, *The Amateur Military Tradition*, 187; Dennis, *The Territorial Army 1906–40*, 8.

[62] PP (1907), XLIX. *Army Commissions. Return as to the number of commissions granted during each of the years 1885 to 1906.*

Militiaman who enlisted in the line joined his linked battalion. In 1882 only 48 per cent of Militiamen who transferred to the line went to a unit of their linked regular regiment.[63] Many men in the Cornwall Rangers, for example, who opted to become regular soldiers, joined the Royal Marines rather than the DCLI, whilst the men of the Middlesex Militia preferred to enlist at Woolwich for the Royal Artillery.[64]

The multiplicity of social and communal distinctions that distinguished the regulars, Militia, Yeomanry, Volunteers, and Territorials mattered because they had military consequences. Some regular officers respected the patriotism of their Volunteer and Territorial colleagues. Montagu Cooke, posted as an Adjutant to a Territorial artillery ammunition column in 1911, welcomed the opportunity to come into 'direct contact with members of these loyal, patriotic defenders of our beloved country'.[65] But other regular officers held them in disdain. When a Volunteer company joined the 2/Queen's Royal West Surreys in South Africa in 1900, a regular officer wrote that one of his Volunteer colleagues 'is an estimable young man with a fearful cockney accent and we think they might have sent a rather better class man'.[66]

At bottom some regulars feared that because of their background, Volunteer and Territorial officers might lack the necessary hereditary aptitude for command.[67] As one regular wrote in 1889, in order to maintain discipline 'the commissioned ranks of the army should be filled, to a great extent, by gentlemen of education occupying a good social position'.[68] Or, as a regular colonel explained in 1910, 'They should be gentlemen. If a bad class is introduced in a regiment it will be difficult to get the best class to join. Besides, the wrong class will eventually work to the top and then parents will object to their sons joining the unit.'[69] Such disdain went beyond the merely social. It was incorporated into the very fabric of the army and was institutionalized by the military authorities. Thus, when regular officers served alongside Militia or Volunteer officers of the same rank, the former always took command.[70] And in 1909 the Army Council decreed that on parade regular units of the same regiment should always take precedence over the Militia, which in turn should always take precedence before the Territorials.[71]

[63] PP (1883), XV. C. 3503 *Annual Report of the Inspector-General of Recruiting*, 2–3.
[64] PP (1877), XVIII. C. 1654. *Report of the Committee ...*, QQ. 1881, 7555.
[65] Cooke, *Clouds that Flee*, 136.
[66] NAM 1999-06-94. Lt. L. D. Wedd MSS. Wedd to Arthur?, 16 Apr. 1900.
[67] PRO WO 32/3681. Minute by Macdonogh, 7 Aug. 1920.
[68] Telfer, 'Discipline', 360.
[69] PRO WO 32/9192. Report on the relative value of territorial troops as compared with regular troops, by Colonel R. Fanshawe, n.d., but *c.* Oct. 1911; Simpson, 'The Officers', 68.
[70] *QR 1892*, 17.
[71] *KR 1912*, para. 1765.

Nor did the Cardwell–Childers reforms automatically overcome divisions between the rank and file of the different branches of the land forces. In the late nineteenth century some Militia recruits thought that their regular counterparts looked down upon them. Militiamen who were trained at the Suffolk regiment's depot at Bury St Edmunds prior to the Boer War were ridiculed by the regulars, who called them 'half-soldiers'. According to their CO, recruits for the Middlesex Militia who trained at the regimental depot at Hounslow were 'looked down upon I consider by the Regular officer'.[72] If a regular ranker wanted to insult the men of another regiment he might ask 'What Militia is that?'[73] At hogmanay in January 1915 two Territorial battalions of 51 Highland Division fought a pitched battle against each other in the streets of Bedford, 'first with fists, and then with entrenching helves. When the military police arrived, instead of separating the combatants, they joined in. Finally the orderly officer of one battalion appeared; and he, gallant fellow, drew his sword and attacked the other battalion!'[74]

Local feuds were sometimes perpetuated between units of the same regiment long after the Cardwell–Childers reforms. In 1903 the CO of 4/ Suffolks admitted:

Of course you must remember that although it appears to be one regiment the 3rd and 4th battalion have never had anything to do with one another; my regiment is the old Cambridgeshire Militia, and at the time it was a sore subject when that title was taken away because we were turned into 'Suffolk' without any warning at all.[75]

Finally, for their part Volunteer and Territorial units were every bit as sensitive as their regular counterparts to questions of regimental status.[76] In 1921, faced with the choice of converting to either an artillery or an armoured car unit, the CO of the Essex Yeomanry hesitated to agree to his regiment becoming a gunner unit because he knew there was already a Territorial artillery unit at Colchester, and 'they are rather a motley crowd'.[77] And the South Nottinghamshire Hussars humorously derided their neighbouring regiment, the Sherwood Rangers, as 'The Shirk-All-Dangers'.[78]

[72] PP (1904), XXXI. Cd. 2063. *Minutes of Evidence*, QQ. 14857, 15045, 15362.

[73] http://freespace.virgin.net/edward.nicholl/jacksonsdiary.htm. Accessed 18 Mar. 2000. An Experience of Twelve Months Active Service on the Veldt, by 3213 Private John Jackson, 1st Battalion The Yorkshire Regiment (Green Howards).

[74] Nicholson, *Behind the Lines*, 43.

[75] PP (1904), XXXI. Cd. 2063. *Minutes of Evidence* ..., Q. 15140.

[76] PRO WO 32/6556. Lt.-Col. L. Montagu, 1(VB)Devonshire Regiment, to Secretary, Devon County Association, Territorial Force, 16 Mar. 1908; PRO WO 32/15082. Lt.-Col. W. D. Ellis, 7/Middlesex Regiment, to HQ 47 (London) Infantry Brigade Territorial Army, 15 Aug. 1956.

[77] ERM. EY 1900–1920. Lt.-Col. E. Hill to Maj. E. Ruggles-Brice, 29 May 1921.

[78] IWMSA. Accession No. 14230. Sir W. Barber, reel 3.

In view of the social and communal distinctions between the different branches of the Crown's land forces, the creation of regimental communities that transcended the boundaries of its regular, Militia, and Volunteer units was always likely to be a long and difficult process. It was not made any easier because half of the Regular Army was serving overseas at any one time, and most regular units at home were in garrisons rather than stationed in their own recruiting district. Face-to-face meetings between the regulars and their comrades in the Militia and Volunteers were often infrequent.[79] Many regular battalions rarely visited their recruiting district and their presence was only represented by their depot. Ceremonial occasions could provide a brief opportunity for real contacts. Thus in 1886, when the Lord Lieutenant of Berkshire unveiled a monument to the officers and men of the Berkshire Regiment killed at Maiwand in the Second Afghan War, the auxiliaries were allowed to share in the reflected glory. Representatives of the County Militia, Yeomanry, and Volunteers were invited to attend the ceremony alongside officers and men from the regular battalions, the county gentry, and the Mayor and Corporation of Reading.[80] Similarly, in 1906 when the Duke of Connaught, the Colonel-in-Chief of the Highland Light Infantry, unveiled the memorial to those members of the regiment who had died in South Africa, the ceremony was attended not only by the regular 2/ Battalion of the regiment, but also by its Volunteer battalions.[81] Some regular units tried to break down the institutional barriers that separated them from their auxiliary comrades by sending some of their best officers and NCOs to act as adjutants and instructors to their auxiliaries. But others seemed content to allow the barriers to remain.[82] Thus, in 1905 the 3/(Militia) Welch Regiment acquired a new regular adjutant, not from one of their own regular battalions, but from the Essex Regiment.[83]

In some other respects, however, the Cardwell–Childers reforms did achieve the aims of their architects. Cardwell and Childers had hoped that if recruiting became genuinely localized, the social sanctions of civic responsibility would help to sustain discipline and morale. The Volunteers and Territorials very largely, and the Militia to a great extent, fulfilled their ideals. In the early 1880s the CO of the Huntington Militia, the Earl of Sandwich, deliberately exploited local attachments to recruit his regiment. His men

[79] PP (1904), XXXI. Cd. 2063. *Minutes of Evidence* ... Q. 13284.

[80] *The Times*, 20 Dec. 1886.

[81] *The Times*, 29 Sept. 1906.

[82] PRO WO 33/37. Report of the militia localisation committee appointed by the Secretary of State for War to inquire into the movement of certain militia regiments, Q. 251.

[83] ERM. ER 3250. Historical Record MS. 56th Foot, 1844–72. 2 Battalion Essex, 1888–1908, 1914, 1920, 11 Mar. 1905.

like to come to their county town, and show their uniform and see their friends. If you take these men to another place, say to Bedford, they will have no inducement of that kind; you may get the recruits, but they will be a different class of men, tramps and people of that description, whereas we have men who are receiving 30s and 35s a week, who come regularly up to the training for their shilling a day to see their friends and amuse themselves in their own district.[84]

Because their members were in regular daily employment and could not travel long distances to carry out their training obligations in the evenings and at weekends, the Volunteers and Territorials were the most localized of all branches of the army. To a very considerable extent they were able to build on Cardwell's ideal that existing community loyalties could be translated into discipline and military *esprit de corps*. Before 1914, for example, the 6/Black Watch recruited heavily around Perth, where it attracted a cross-section of the population: 'Rich and poor alike it made no difference, only those, of course, you might call upper class, they were more inclined to be recruited as officers for commissions.' Until 1908 a local mill owner, Mr Hally, had been the CO of the battalion. When he retired the family connection was maintained by his son, who became one of its subalterns.[85] Bob Sheridan joined the 2/London Rifle Brigade in late 1938 because a group of his old school friends had done so.[86] A few months later Wilf Saunders joined 48th Division Signals because it was the nearest Territorial unit to his home and because the father of a friend who joined the unit with him knew the adjutant.[87]

The close identification between officers and men of the regiment and their locality meant that discipline and morale were sustained by 'a strong county feeling in the regiment, among the officers and the men'.[88] Or, as another senior officer explained: 'I find that in all the best regiments we have got the best local feeling, and the absentees are much fewer because the sergeants know the men; they are brought constantly in contact with them; they know who are reliable men, and if a man is not reliable they will not enlist him.'[89] Volunteer COs saw no incompatibility between officers and other ranks associating off parade and discipline on parade. The standing orders of 1(VB)/Essex Regiment insisted: 'The strictest discipline is in no way incompatible with the most thorough good feeling and heartiest co-operation throughout

[84] PRO WO 33/37. Report of the militia localisation committee appointed by the Secretary of State for War to inquire into the movement of certain militia regiments, Q. 204.
[85] IWMSA. Accession No. 000373/03. Lance-Sergeant J. G. Rodger, reel 1.
[86] Sheridan, 'What Did You Do in the War, Dad?', 13.
[87] W. Saunders, *Dunkirk Diary* (Birmingham: Birmingham City Council. Public Libraries Department, 1990), 3.
[88] PRO WO 33/37. Report of the militia localisation committee ..., Q. 626.
[89] Ibid., Q. 34.

the Battalion.'[90] The class of men attracted to the Volunteers, Yeomanry, and Territorials also meant that certain crimes common in the regulars were rare in their units. In 1892, for example, the CO of the Middlesex Yeomanry, which recruited a good many of its men from workers in the City of London, believed that crimes like drunkenness or being dirty on parade were unknown in his regiment.[91]

This was probably as well, because Volunteer and Territorial COs had few of the overt and formal disciplinary sanctions that their regular counterparts could employ. Volunteers and Territorials were under military law only when on active service or when called out for training with the Militia or regulars. At other times they could resign with only a few days' or weeks' notice if they disliked any orders they were given.[92] Officers and NCOs usually knew their men in civilian life, and relations between all ranks tended to be less formal than in regular units. Discipline rested on a combination of the tact and social position of the units' officers, peer group pressure, and a shared enthusiasm to become efficient soldiers. Most Volunteer COs were quite content with this and did not seek increased formal powers, and believed that their discipline was every bit as good as that of the regulars.[93] Much, therefore, depended on the respect with which those in authority were held by the men they commanded. There was little that a Territorial drill instructor could do if his platoon decided 'to take the mickey'. Parades could degenerate into a state of humorous chaos if, when the NCO said 'left turn', everyone turned to the right.[94]

But such behaviour only convinced many regulars that the brevity of basic training in the auxiliary forces meant that it was impossible to instil into their rank and file a proper respect for discipline. Men who enlisted in the auxiliaries underwent a much shorter term of basic training than did the regulars. For Militia recruits this lasted seven weeks, and even their own COs thought that this was too short to produce properly disciplined soldiers.[95] Basic training for the Volunteers and Territorials was even briefer. Depending on their arm of service, they were required to undertake a number of hour-long 'drills'. In the late 1870s Volunteer infantrymen had to do thirty drills before they were classed as 'efficient'. By the 1930s this had risen to forty for infantrymen and forty-five for gunners.[96]

[90] ERM. ER 21921. Anon., *Standing Orders and rules of the 1st Volunteer Battalion Essex Regiment* (Brentwood: n.p., 1896), 6.
[91] PP (1892), XX. C. 6675. *Report of the Committee ...*, Q. 41.
[92] War Office, *Regulations for the Volunteer Force*, 178; War Office, MML, 1914, 756.
[93] PP (1878–9), XV. C. 2235. *Reports of the committee ...*, Appendix XIX; Col. R. Loyd-Lindsay, 'The Coming of Age of the Volunteers', *Nineteenth Century*, 10 (1881), 206–16.
[94] Sheridan, *'What Did You Do in the War, Dad?'*, 15.
[95] PP (1890), XIX. C. 5922. *Report of the committee ...*, pp. x, xviii; Col. T. Innes, 'Notes on Training the Militia', *Journal of the Royal United Services Institute*, 25 (1881), 127.
[96] PP (1878–9), XV. C. 2235. *Reports of the committee ...* X; Codrington, *The Territorial Army*, 82.

From the outset the military authorities had recognized that the disciplinary regime in the Volunteers was bound to be different from that of the regulars. In 1859 the Duke of Cambridge wrote that

A Volunteer Organisation, to be effectual, must be subject, as far as practicable, to military discipline, as otherwise no dependence could be placed on it at the hour of need, and the military authorities, under whose direction the force would have to be placed, could not rely with certainty on its assistance and co-operation when required for Garrison or field duty. At the same time, there cannot be a doubt that the service should be made as little irksome to the men as possible, and the object to be attained is therefore clearly to give the force to be enrolled, such an organisation as to combine, as far as practicable, efficiency, with the least amount of trouble or vexation to the parties forming it.[97]

But given the brevity of their training, many regular officers concluded that their discipline was bound to be inadequate. Even Sir Garnet Wolseley, otherwise a strong supporter of the Volunteers, conceded in 1878: 'I think it is generally admitted that the one great defect from which it suffers, and must always suffer, is a want of discipline, which it has a difficulty in acquiring except when collected together by regiments in barracks or camps.'[98]

The apparent weakness of the auxiliary forces' NCO cadre was a particular source of worry, not only for the regulars, but also for some Militia and Volunteer officers themselves. Auxiliary NCOs were selected and promoted in the same ways as their regular counterparts and were expected to maintain the same discipline amongst their men as the regulars did.[99] But in 1877 the CO of the South Lincolnshire Militia opined that 'the Militia or Volunteer non-commissioned officers are, as a rule, worse than useless, and know little, if anything, more than the men, and frequently are afraid to exercise authority'.[100] Ten years later an officer in 3/(Militia) Hampshire Regiment explained:

A regiment is trained for twenty-seven days annually, and at the end of that time the men are dispersed all over the country to their own homes. If a militia sergeant or corporal has reported a private for breach of discipline, he runs a good chance of getting his head punched by the said private the day after the training is over. The remedy for the sergeant is simple; he is only human—he does not report the private.[101]

---

[97] RNRM. R.97A. 'A History of the 4th Battalion of the Norfolk Regiment (Territorial).' Compiled by Col. J. R. Harvey, Dec. 1920, 12.

[98] Wolseley, 'England as a Military Power', 444.

[99] ERM. ER 2991. *Standing Orders of the First Essex Artillery Volunteers (EDRA)* (Stratford: Wilson & Whitworth, 1890), 9, 11–15.

[100] PP (1877), XVIII. C. 1654. *Report of the Committee. . . . Minutes of Evidence*, Appendix II.

[101] Lord Wolmer, 'A Militia Regiment', *Nineteenth Century*, 122 (1887), 567.

A regular officer who had temporarily commanded a Territorial brigade remarked that

the officers and non-commissioned officers do not give their orders in such a way as to ensure instant obedience and action, but rather as if they were asking a favour which they hardly expected to be granted in full, and the men appear to be doing things 'to oblige' often after some delay, as if they had been thinking over before acting whether the action is necessary or not. This all leads to slowness and indecision.[102]

The apparent differences between the discipline of regular and auxiliary units led some senior regular officers to disparage the military worth of the Territorials and Volunteers. In 1910 Sir Charles Douglas, the GOC Southern Command, concluded 'that the valuable quality, born of discipline and training, possessed by regular troops to "stick it out", is not present to any marked degree with Territorials'.[103] What he and others failed to recognize was that Volunteer and Territorial units did not require the same strict and formal disciplinary system as their regular counterparts because they could rely to a much greater extent than the regulars on the fact that their men were genuine volunteers and that any misdemeanours would evoke community sanction. The mindset of many regulars was captured by Maj.-Gen. Sir J. P. Brabazon, a regular cavalry officer who commanded the Imperial Yeomanry in South Africa. While admitting that their discipline left nothing to be desired and that insubordination was almost non-existent, he was critical of their NCOs: 'Being friends, often intimate friends "at home", with the men in the ranks, they did not understand the line of demarcation that ought to exist between the non-commissioned ranks and the men.'[104] He ignored the fact that the very existence of such relationships could produce a powerful bond of discipline amongst the Yeomen once they took to the field. A few of his colleagues were more perceptive. Sir Arthur Paget, the GOC Eastern Command, recognized that 'there was an excellent spirit among a large number of the men [of the Territorial Force], which as far as it can, takes the place of discipline'.[105]

Critics of the auxiliary forces were on firmer ground when they noted that their military efficiency was degraded by their high turnover in personnel. A company commander in 3/Hampshires estimated in 1887

[102] PRO WO 279/480. Reports of GOC-in-C on the physical capacity of Territorial Force troops to carry out the work and endure the hardships which were incidental to the manoeuvres, 1910. 31 Aug. 1910.
[103] Ibid.
[104] PRO WO 108/263. Maj.-Gen. Sir J. P. Brabazon, Report on the Imperial Yeomanry in South Africa rendered to the Field Marshal C-in-C South Africa, 16 Oct. 1900.
[105] PRO WO 279/480. Reports of GOC-in-C on the physical capacity of Territorial Force troops ... 31 Aug. 1910.

that each year half the men in his company were recruits.[106] For many young men service in the Territorials or Volunteers was a rite of passage rather than a permanent leisure commitment. In 1912 only about half of the men who had joined the Territorial Force when it was first raised in 1908 and whose engagements had now ended chose to re-enlist. About a third of the force failed to pass an annual musketry test, and only 155,000 out of 252,000 Territorials had attended an annual training camp for the full two-week prescribed period.[107] Recruiting problems persisted after 1919, and by 1935 the Territorial Army was over 31,000 men below its establishment. Yeomanry, artillery, and armoured car units had comparatively little difficulty in finding recruits.[108] The worst shortages were in the infantry. Recruiting was hampered by government parsimony and public indifference to defence. Married men were probably encouraged to resign because it was not until 1936 that Territorials aged over 21 were granted marriage allowances. In Croydon the 4/Queen's Royal Regiment thought that there was 'a strong element of apathy existent in the town which was hard to break down'.[109]

Regular Army critics of the auxiliaries were also right to point to shortcomings in the unit and formation-level training of the auxiliaries. The facilities available to them were often inadequate. Between 1872 and 1874 the 4/(West Essex) Militia could do no musketry training at their camp at Chelmsford because there was no nearby rifle range. In 1877 a War Office committee discovered that nearly a third of brigade depots did not have adequate training grounds nearby for their Militia battalions.[110] The enthusiasm and commitment of the regular adjutants and sergeant instructors posted to units varied and could have a major impact, for good or ill, on a unit's level of training.[111] Militiamen were given less practice ammunition than the regulars and by the late 1890s some Militia battalions still did not have a trained musketry instructor.[112] In the early 1890s the officers of the Leicestershire Yeomanry had to dip into their own pockets to pay for their men to use a nearby rifle

[106] Wolmer, 'A Militia Regiment', 568.

[107] K. W. Mitchinson, 'Auxiliary Forces for the Land Defence of Great Britain, 1909–1919' (Ph.D. thesis, University of Luton, 2002), 94.

[108] PRO WO 33/1376. Report on the Staff conference held at the Staff College, Camberley, 7–10 Jan. 1935; PRO WO 32/4118. CIGS periodical letter No. 3/1937 to Dominions and India, 28 July 1937.

[109] Journal of the Queens' Royal Regiment, 6 (1935), 24; Dennis, The Territorial Army, 153, 158–9, 164, 176.

[110] PRO WO 68/257. 4/(West Essex) Militia. Digest of Service, 1872–74; PRO WO 33/32. Report of the committee appointed by the Secretary of State for War to visit and report upon the Brigade Depots, 22 Dec. 1877.

[111] Macready, Annals of an Active Life, i, 71.

[112] PP (1890), XIX. C. 5922. Report of the Committee, QQ. 292–8, 307–16, 361–7.

range.[113] The military efficiency of the auxiliaries also suffered because they had little time in which to carry out unit training.[114] The Militia might have up to a month in camp, but the Volunteers, Yeomanry, and Territorials rarely had more than a fortnight, and even then many employers objected if their workers were away for so long.[115] In 1881–2, Militia training in Ireland was cancelled due to the disturbed state of much of the country in the midst of the Land War.[116] Annual camps could be supplemented by weekend camps, but they were difficult to organize in parts of Scotland and Wales before 1914 because of strong opposition from the Churches and Chapels, who insisted that Sunday should be a day of rest.[117] Finally, for much of the period from 1919 to 1939, the Territorials were without a clear idea of exactly what they were supposed to train to do.[118]

Even when the Territorials were supposed to be the basis of the national army during the era of National Service after 1945, shortages of equipment continued to hamper realistic training. In the early 1950s 6/ East Surreys were on manoeuvres when the CO approached the crew of a purely imaginary anti-tank gun, told them that a heavy enemy tank was approaching, and asked them what they would do. They replied in unison '"turn round and run like bloody hell." He came up between us, put his arms round our shoulders and said "I know that. You know that. But we dare not let these young soldiers know that because that would be fatal wouldn't it … "'.[119]

Just as in the Regular Army, responsibility for training fell largely on unit COs, and the methods and standards they imposed varied widely.[120] In 1869 the Inspector-General of Reserve Forces concluded that there was little uniformity in either the interior economy or the drill practised in

[113] PP (1892), XX. C. 6675. *Report of the Committee* …, QQ. 425–6.

[114] PRO WO 32/5451. Report of the Monro committee on musketry training for the Territorial Force, 7 Apr. 1914; PRO WO 32/2382. Memorandum on Army Training. Collective Training period 1928, 26 Nov. 1928; PRO WO 33/1396. First Interim report of the Committee on the readiness of the Territorial Army on mobilization, 30 Nov. 1935.

[115] PRO WO 33/19. Maj.-Gen. J. Lindsay, Reserve Forces. Report, 1868–9, 1 Apr. 1869; IWMSA. Accession No. 000373/03. Lance-Sergeant J. G. Rodger, reel 1.

[116] PRO WO 79/43. Historical Records of the Galway Militia; 4th Battalion Connnaught Rangers, 1881–2.

[117] PRO WO 279/25. Report of a conference of General Staff Officers at the Staff College, 18–21 Jan. 1909.

[118] PRO WO 33/1308. Supplementary Report on the Conference held at the Staff College, Camberley, 9–11 Jan. 1933; PRO WO 279/75. Report on the Staff Conference held at the Staff College, Camberley, 8–12 Jan. 1934; PRO WO 32/4610. Organization and training of Territorial Army. Criticisms of, 16 June 1938.

[119] IWMSA. Accession No. 18463/42. D. F. Barrett, reel 39.

[120] PRO WO 32/9192. Reports (with summary) of GOC-in-C as to the relative value of Territorial Troops as compared with corresponding units and formations of the Regular Army, 1911. Lt.-Gen. Sir B. Hamilton, 28 Oct. 1911.

different regiments.[121] When the Territorial Force was established the military authorities, mindful that the facilities available to different units for training was likely to vary considerably, bowed to the inevitable. They abandoned any idea of imposing uniform requirements on every unit, and left the responsibility for their collective training to individual Territorial divisional commanders.[122] In practice, the state of sub-unit training in most auxiliary units was so poor that much time at annual camps that might have been spent in formation training had to be devoted to remedial work. Thus in 1910 the GOC Southern Command concluded that because Territorial gunners and infantry rarely worked together, 'the co-operation of all arms during a tactical exercise is not very good'.[123] A year later the GOC Eastern Command complained: 'It has been observed that Territorial battalions are inclined to regard themselves as independent units, and forget that one battalion must, not only in theory, but also in practice, co-operate with another.'[124] There was little improvement after 1945. One Territorial gunner who served in the 1950s with 49 (North Midlands) Division remembered: 'It was virtually impossible to get tanks, infantry and gunners firing on the same piece of territory, and therefore we did not do much all-arms training. In fact very little all-arms training.'[125]

Even when field training did occur, it was sometimes far from realistic. In 1906 the 3/ and 4/Norfolk Militia battalions were in camp and conducted a two-handed exercise: 'But the 3rd having taken up a very strong position & our only line of attack being across the open drill field in full view of our opponents. The General naturally decided that the 3rd had held their position, Lieutenant Douglas being censured for showing too great boldness.' The next day the battalions repeated the same exercise and 'The General expressed his opinion that sufficient orders were not given, & that the attack was too rapidly developed, which was natural as the men were fighting in the direction of their dinners.'[126]

The Norfolk's experience highlighted a fundamental shortcoming of the auxiliaries. Their unit and sub-unit commanders were themselves not adequately trained. Some Territorial divisional commanders tried to

---

[121] PRO WO 33/19. Maj.-Gen. J. Lindsay, Reserve Forces. Report, 1868–9, 1 Apr. 1869.

[122] PP (1907), XXXIX. Cd. 3515. *Principles to be kept in view in training the Territorial Force and the Special Contingent.*

[123] PRO WO 279/480. Report by GOC-in-C Southern Command, 23 Aug. 1910.

[124] ERM. Loan from private collection. Essex Yeomanry EY Files. KBM Misc.(2). Brig.-Gen. A. Haldane, BGGS, Eastern Command, Instructions Regarding Training, Territorial Force 1911–12, 1 Sept. 1911.

[125] IWMSA. Accession No. 20494/12. Col. P. Featherby.

[126] PRO WO 68/123. 4th (East Norfolk) Militia. Digest of Service, 14 May. 1906. See also ERO. D/DU 783/3. Scrapbook of Brigadier-General Sir Richard Colvin of Waltham Abbey. Cutting, 'The Battle of Epping Forest', 18 Apr. 1903.

rectify this. They held special courses for their Territorial officers to improve their training, and to disseminate a common understanding of doctrine. In 1911 Maj.-Gen. E. T. Dickson, the GOC of the Home Counties Territorial Division, held a number of weekend exercises for senior captains and majors to prepare them to command their units, 'and thus a uniform system of instruction is maintained and a uniform method of applying the principles inculcated in the training manuals is diffused throughout the Division'.[127] But their efforts were sporadic and came too late. At the outset of both world wars, when the auxiliary forces were augmented, it soon became apparent that they lacked a sufficiently well-trained cadre of regimental officers and NCOs to enable expansion to take place without an alarming drop in the quality of training.[128] Even in the early 1950s, when the Territorials contained a considerable number of officers and NCOs with wartime experience and large numbers of former National Servicemen, combined arms training remained difficult. In 1952 the War Office tried to impose a three-year training cycle on them. In the first year they devoted their annual camp to unit training, in the second year to brigade training, and in the third year to divisional training. Experience, however, soon showed that the rapid run-out of veteran officers and NCOs made this unrealistic, and that units and formations were trying to run before they could walk.[129]

By 1900 some regiments had created a real sense of a regimental community that spanned regulars, Militia, and in some cases the Volunteers. Shortly after the Boer War Lord Grenfell, a former Inspector-General of Auxiliary Forces and C-in-C at Malta, decided that

> My experience is, after some years at the War Office as Inspector-General of Auxiliary Forces, and also as commanding the six or seven battalions of Militia at Malta, which I had the opportunity of doing, that certainly the best regiments I had were those in which they were more intimately connected with the territorial battalion—even socially—the regiments that had their regimental dinner together, etc. In those regiments I found officers of the territorial regiments who had retired into the Militia regiment, and in my opinion they were the best regiments I had.[130]

In many other regiments, however, there were still deep fissures. The best solvent of the mutual suspicions and disdain that so often divided

---

[127] PRO WO 279/481. Report on senior officers' autumn course. Home Counties Territorial Army Division 1911.

[128] PRO WO 163/49. Lt. Gen. Sir R. Adam to WO 21 Jan. 1940.

[129] PRO WO 32/15067. DGMT to GOCs-in-C all Home Commands, 30 Apr. 1953; Millman, *Stand Easy*, 55–6.

[130] PP (1904), XXXI. Cd. 2063. *Minutes of Evidence*, Q. 15612.

the regulars from their auxiliary comrades was provided by shared hardships and dangers in the field. But before 1914 the different branches of the land forces had little opportunity to fight together, and even when they did so, the consequences were not always greater harmony and sympathy. The Volunteers hoped that the fact that during the Boer War they had sent whole companies to South Africa to reinforce their regular battalions would raise their prestige. Addressing the annual dinner of the sergeants of his battalion in December 1900, the CO of 1/(VB)Norfolk Regiment, insisted that the Volunteers represented a huge reservoir of soldiers that the army could draw upon in a national emergency and, 'In passing from the Army to the Volunteers, he remarked that there were no longer two armies, but one army.'[131] Many regulars still did not agree. When a company drawn from one of their Volunteer battalions joined 2/ Gordon Highlanders in South Africa in 1900, the regulars were impressed by their courage, but deplored their lack of training.[132] Nor were the different terms and conditions of service enjoyed by the two services calculated to create harmony. The much higher rates of pay that some Volunteer units, such as the Imperial Yeomanry, received hardly endeared them to their regular comrades. One regular private referred to the Imperial Yeomanry as the '"Five-Bob a day Fellows"—the volunteer crowd that came out with the cavalry. Five shillings a day, you see. The boys used to pass our camp in the morning and they'd go shouting: "Another five bob".'[133]

It was symptomatic of the military authorities' desire to create a common identity that united regular, Militia, and Volunteers in a single regimental community that when R. de M. Rudolph's official *Short Histories of the Territorial Regiments* was published by the War Office shortly after the Boer War, it contained references not only to the roles of regular units, but also to the part played by their Volunteer and Militia units during the war. It also emphasized that the willingness of so many auxiliaries to serve overseas was testimony to their military worth and to the patriotism of their officers and men. Lord Haldane, the creator of the Territorial Force, worked hard to raise their public standing. In 1909 he organized a mass parade at Windsor Castle, attended by 2,000 Territorials and 3,000 regulars, at which the King presented Colours and guidons to every Territorial unit.[134]

---

[131] RNRM. R. 135B.Scrapbook of the Norfolk Volunteer Company from 11 Feb. 1900 to 25 May 1901. '1st VB NR. Staff Sergeants and Sergeants Annual dinner', *Eastern Daily Press*, 18 Dec. 1900.

[132] Macready, *Annals*, i. 97, 99.

[133] IWMSA. Accession No. 0065126/2. P. Gorman, 18.

[134] *The Times*, 21 June 1909.

But the regulars remained almost as reluctant to accept Haldane's new creation as their equals as they had the Volunteers. By 1914 regimental journals were chronicling the doings and histories of their regular battalions and usually also their Militia battalions. But the Volunteers and Territorials remained a half-incorporated part of the regimental community. Some regimental journals carried information about them, but many did not.[135] Similarly, the Territorials were also usually excluded from regimental associations. In 1908 the Essex Regimental association was established to offer help to former regulars, Militiamen, and Special Reservists who had fallen on hard times. But the only Volunteers or Territorials able to claim its assistance were those who had seen active service overseas.[136] Similarly, when the Oxford and Buckinghamshire Light Infantry formed an Old Comrades Dining Club in 1910 with the aim of 'bringing together comrades of the past and present to the mutual advantage and pleasure of all', former Volunteers and Territorials were permitted to join on the same terms as other members of the regiment only if they had seen active service in South Africa.[137]

The attitude of many regulars to the auxiliaries on the eve of the First World War was summarized by one staff officer who believed that 'Before the war it [the Regular Army] took no real trouble to make itself acquainted with these bodies of men or to lend them a helping hand; even during the early stages of the fighting it continued in an attitude of aloofness.'[138] Once the war began, a regular ranker, posted in the course of the war to an auxiliary unit, begged to be transferred to a regular unit, for his new officers were, in his opinion, 'nothing but tin soldiers, sir. My lot are nothing but bun-wallahs and balloon juice drinkers'.[139]

Regimental communities existed on paper before 1914, but in many cases they were very imperfect creations. But as the First World War continued, and regular, Territorial, and New Army units fought side by side, their suspicions slowly evaporated, dissolved by the common experience of the front line. Frank Richards's regular comrades in 2/Royal Welch Fusiliers were often suspicious of the reliability of Territorials under fire, 'but as time went on we got to like the 5th Scottish Rifles very much. They were the best Territorial battalion that I ever saw, and after they had been a few months with us we never worried if they were on the left or right of us in the line or in attacks.'[140] In January 1916

---

[135] *Essex Regiment Gazette*, 1 (1910).

[136] *Essex Regiment Gazette*, 1 (July 1909).

[137] *The Oxford and Buckinghamshire Light Infantry Chronicle 1910. An Annual Record of the First and Second Battalions. Formerly the 43rd and 52nd Light Infantry*, 19 (1910), 134.

[138] Nicholson, *Behind the Lines*, 138.

[139] Sgt. T. Secrett, *Twenty-Five Years with Earl Haig* (London: Jarrolds, 1929), 117.

[140] F. Richards, *Old Soldiers Never Die* (London: Faber & Faber, 1933), 61.

another Territorial unit, the Queen Victoria Rifles, was told that they were to be withdrawn from the regular 5th Division. The Territorials were 'most fed up and sick at having to leave the regiments with whom we have been ever since 1914. The regulars too are very sorry that we are going. In 1914 they looked on us as their pet territorial regiment and we were very popular with them.'[141]

For their part, Territorials recognized the real strengths of their regular comrades, although without necessarily believing that they possessed a monopoly of military virtues. A. R. Bain, a Territorial officer in the 1/7th Argyll and Sutherland Highlanders,

was attached to one regular unit, the 2/Seaforths. And their discipline was absolutely perfect. I mean they were born soldiers. I put it down as the finest battalion of infantry I have ever seen in my life, the 2/Seaforth Highlanders. But there it was just a matter of very strict discipline. They had to do what they were told as they were told. There was no nonsense. Territorials, you had to work round them to their better nature. Because the Territorials had been accustomed to looking after themselves all their life at home and home life. And he liked to do things his own way. And very often his own way was a better way that [sic] his officers told him to do it. And there's be a certain amount of give and take to keep up the morale and make them realise... [sic] and of course they would do anything for each other, the Territorials. A regular soldier just did exactly what he was told and nothing more. But a Territorial if he saw another fellow in trouble he would go and give him a hand even although it was another platoon or another company, it didn't matter. He was a Jock.[142]

The collective experiences and sacrifices of the First World War did create a shared sense of identity between regulars and auxiliaries that in many regiments had not existed before 1914. The war provided a common enemy against whom the different parts of the regimental community could unite, it mobilized regimental sentiments, and it provided a shared store of myths and memories for future generations. By the end of the war, relations between auxiliary and regular units of the same regiment were undoubtedly closer and more harmonious than at any time before 1914. Henceforth, each Territorial unit, 'quite apart from its own history it shares also, in the case of infantry, the history and battle honours of the County Regiment of which it is now an integral portion, and not merely a sort of "Territorial appendage", like an affiliated cadet unit or like the old affiliated volunteer units'.[143] And auxiliaries wanted to be regarded as part of a single army. In 1920 Special Reserve officers opposed reverting to the title 'Militia' to denote their force and wanted to retain the title

[141] F. Hawkins, *Frank Hawkins: From Ypres to Cambrai. The Diary of an Infantryman 1914–1919*, ed. A. Taylor (Morley, Yorks: The Elmsfield Press, 1974), 83.
[142] IWMSA. Accession No. 000375/06. Col. A. R. Bain, 17.
[143] Codrington, *The Territorial Army*, 28.

'Special Reserve' because in their experience regular officers had disdained the Militia before the war and because

It was thought that the title 'Reserve' would serve to emphasise the association between the Regulars and the Reserve Forces far better than the term 'Militia', and they would be regarded as being to a much greater extent an essential adjunct to the Regular Forces instead of being something distinctive—a force of Amateur soldiers, in fact.[144]

Regimental journals, which before 1914 had frequently ignored the activities of Territorial units, now invariably carried extensive reports of both branches of the regiment. In 1926, when it commenced publication after the First World War, the *Essex Regiment Gazette* proclaimed that its function was 'to foster the feeling that whether serving soldier, territorial, or old comrade, all have a bond of fellowship,—the Regiment— and that each should strive to promote its good name.'[145]

Regimental Associations now embraced men of all branches of the regiment. When the Colchester Branch of the Royal Artillery Association held its first meeting, also in 1926, the committee consisted of regular warrant officers from the Colchester garrison and sergeants from the Territorial Army artillery of the 54th division.[146] Regimental histories gave space to the achievements of the regulars and auxiliaries in the Great War. The revised edition of the short history of the Royal Fusiliers published in 1926 gave full weight to the achievements of the regiment's Territorial and New Army battalions between 1914 and 1918.[147] By 1928 one regimental colonel believed that the link that Haldane had created between regular and Territorial units of the same regiment 'has been greatly strengthened by the splendid services of the Territorial battalions during the Great War. Regarded with real pride by all ranks of Territorials, that tie has become a real spiritual force.'[148] In 1934, the regular Adjutant of 6/Sherwood Foresters told a battalion dinner of 'how proud the Line battalions were of their relationship with the Territorial battalions who had so greatly added to the good name and honours of the Regiment of which all battalions formed a comprehensive whole'.[149] His regiment even thought it worthwhile to memorialize 'the debt owed by The Regiment to the numerous "service Battalions" who so worthily

---

[144] PRO WO 32/3681. Duke of Northumberland to Macdonogh, 7 Aug. 1920.

[145] *Essex Regiment Gazette*, NS 1 (Sept. 1926), 2.

[146] *The Abbey Field Review. A Monthly Record of Garrison Life in Colchester*, 1/3 (1926), 108.

[147] Anon., *The Royal Fusiliers, passim*.

[148] Lt.-Gen. Sir E. A. Altham, 'The Cardwell System', *Journal of the Royal United Services Institute*, 73 (1928), 111–12.

[149] *Regimental Annual. The Sherwood Foresters 1934*, 135.

upheld the traditions of the Sherwood Foresters, and of whom all that is left with us to-day is a King's Colour in some Church and memories which will pass away with the regular officers who served with them.' They did so by commissioning two paintings of some of the more memorable feats of their defunct service battalions.[150]

The good relations that developed between the regulars and auxiliaries during the First World War rested above all else on parity of esteem borne of achieving common professional standards. Heavy casualties amongst regular officers and other ranks meant that the standards of professionalism in regular units declined, whereas periods of continuous training and fighting meant that the standards of training in auxiliary units rose. By 1916–17 the army had become a homogeneous mass in which distinctions between 'regular', 'Territorial', and 'New Army' units had nearly evaporated. But they re-emerged quickly after the war. After 1918 the General Staff wanted Territorial Army officers and NCOs to attend the same schools as their regular counterparts to learn how to instruct their men in skills such as musketry and signalling. In the late 1920s the Territorial units of the Essex regiment were fortunate in that one of their regular units, 1/Essex, was actually stationed at Colchester. This meant not only that regulars could easily be posted to Territorial units of the regiment as instructors, but it also meant that regulars and Territorials could maintain a close relationship by socializing together and playing sports against each other.[151] But most territorial units did not enjoy such good fortune. And few Territorials could absent themselves from their normal occupations for the time necessary to attend long training courses. Just as before 1914, they had to acquire what technical training they could from the regular Adjutant and PSIs attached to their unit. Training standards in Territorial units therefore inevitably slipped.

Furthermore, by the late 1920s the number of regular officers and NCOs who had served with Territorial units during the First World War was fast diminishing, and some of the mutual incomprehension and disdain that had characterized relations between regulars and auxiliaries before 1914 was reasserting itself. Regular COs were sometimes loath to part with their best officers and NCOs and second them to train their Territorial comrades. By 1932 Sir Charles 'Tim' Harington, the GOC Aldershot, thought it necessary to remind regular units that it

behoves all units to send the best Officers and N.C.O.'s they can to the Territorial Army. These Officers and N.C.O.'s can not only do so much in helping and

[150] *Regimental Annual. The Sherwood Foresters 1934*, 135.
[151] *Essex Regiment Gazette*, NS 1 (1926), 2.

instructing the Territorial Army, but they can do so much in addition to strengthen the vital link between the Regular and Territorial Army.[152]

But, starved of modern equipment, with miserly training grants, and faced by a shortage of both officers and other ranks, most Territorial units were seriously under-trained.[153] The lowly status of the Territorials in the eyes of senior regulars was emphasized by the fact that it was not until 1937 that the Director General of the Territorial Army became a member of the Army Council. By the eve of the Second World War some regular regimental officers looked upon Territorial officers as men

whose ignorance was such, so it was authoritatively stated, that the officer recently raised to command a new T[erritorial] A[rmy] battalion of Buffs could not even make out a charge sheet. (It never occurred to regulars of the old school that the TA soldier had a different outlook and did not need to be put on charges to be kept up to the mark.)[154]

One of Cardwell and Childers's grand designs was to root the army more firmly in civil society by creating regimental communities that transcended the distinctions between regular and auxiliary units. The auxiliary forces were to form a bridge between civilian society and the regulars. But in order to achieve this they first had to build bridges that would unite the regulars and the auxiliaries. However, the regimental communities that Cardwell and Childers had hoped to establish were, for much of the period after 1881, very imperfect creations. Relations between the regulars and their auxiliary comrades often resembled that between distant cousins rather than blood brothers. In many regiments regular and auxiliary units were never entirely melded into a single homogeneous community. They were closest during the two world wars, but they drifted apart thereafter.

The consequences that had for Cardwell and Childers's efforts to locate the army more firmly in civil society will be considered in the next chapter, which will examine the attitudes of the civilian community to the regimental system and military service.

[152] Codrington, *The Territorial Army*, p. ix.
[153] PRO WO 279/75. Report on the Staff Conference held at the Staff College, Camberley, 8–12 Jan. 1934.
[154] IWM 83/46/1. Major W. G. Blaxland, Unready for war. A Memoir of a journey through Sandhurst and Dunkirk. Ts. memoirs.

CHAPTER NINE

Civilians and their Regiments

In 1879 William Hunt, who had enlisted in 1858 and risen to the rank of Quarter Master, noted regretfully that

It is well known too that there exists among the civil population in this country, to a certain extent at least, a repugnance and antipathy to the soldier. It would be difficult satisfactorily to account for this feeling, but that it does exist there can hardly be any question. Instances have occurred where a non-commissioned officer has found it difficult to enter places of amusement, and public resort, in uniform, and even in church he has not infrequently been relegated to the lowest seat in the synagogue. It is, of course, vain to hope for any sudden or radical change of public feeling in this respect. Time may work wonders, and, aided by the popularity of the volunteer movement the soldier's uniform may, by-and-by, come to be regarded, as it ought to be, with respect, and as the badge and symbol of a noble and honourable profession.[1]

Cardwell and Childers hoped to raise the status of the regular soldier by rooting each regiment in its own local community and using the depot and its linked Militia and Volunteer units as bridges between civilian society and the Regular Army. Speaking to an audience in his constituency at Pontefract in January 1882, Childers explained that

What I want to bring about is a state of public opinion as to our military forces which will make each county, or in some cases, as here, each division of a county, feel a special interest in a particular regiment and the men belonging to it; and I mean by a regiment not only its line battalions but its militia battalions, and also I hope soon to say, its volunteer battalions.[2]

But by the end of the nineteenth century, the Regular Army inhabited a paradoxical position. On the one hand flesh-and-blood rank-and-file soldiers were shunned by much of 'respectable' society. In 1891 a Parliamentary Committee noted: 'The refusal to admit non-commissioned officers and soldiers in uniform to certain parts of theatres, or to the coffee-rooms of hotels, may be taken as sufficient evidence of the feeling with which the manager believes his customers would regard the pres-

---

[1] PP (1881), XXI. C. 2791. *Report of the Committee...*, Q. 1222.
[2] NAM 8202–55. Col. G. C. Swiney, Scrapbook, Sept. 1872 to June 1913. *Standard*, 20 Jan. 1882.

ence of soldiers.'[3] On the other hand, the soldier in the abstract had become an icon held in growing public esteem. His character was construed as being loyal, patriotic, brave, and therefore virtuous. In July 1872 the leading citizens of Norwich organized a banquet to celebrate the stay in their city of the 7/Dragoon Guards and presented a solid silver tankard to the sergeants' mess. In the opinion of the *Norwich Mercury*, 'At all times have they been ready to do all that lay in their power to make their stay amongst us agreeable, and they have proved that though soldiers, they can be and are gentlemen in the strictest sense of the word.' In reply, RSM F. C. Butcher told his hosts that

Gentlemen, what a lesson your magnanimity teaches to such communities as those of Richmond and elsewhere, who object, under the new system of army organisation, to the military being located in their neighbourhood. But more especially [I]would allude to such communities as have designated, and only very recently, the British soldier as 'the scum of the earth' ('Shame'). That 'scum of the earth', gentlemen, fought Crécy, Agincourt, Poitiers and a thousand other battles that culminated in Waterloo—(cheers)—that 'scum of the earth' was the brightest gem that sparkles in the British Crown—the empire of India—(cheers)—that 'scum of the earth' avenged the outrage upon English ladies, the murder of innocents, and upheld the name and honour of England in the terrible crisis of the Indian mutiny...[4]

In this chapter I will first analyse the reasons why soldiers occupied this paradoxical position in the late nineteenth century, and then explore the extent to which the experience of mass military recruiting during the two world wars changed the attitudes of the wider public to service in the Regular Army.

Between the Indian Mutiny and the death of General Gordon in 1885 the public persona of the soldier in the abstract was redefined. He was less likely to be dismissed as a drunken and dissolute reprobate, and more likely, for the reasons that RSM Butcher indicated, to be seen as a Christian hero and martyr, ready to die for the sake of spreading the virtues of British civilization across the globe. The image of the soldier benefited from the fact that there was a pervasive belief that Britain had a mission to do so, and that waging war was an acceptable, if sometimes to be regretted, means of accomplishing it. This mood of overweening imperial self-confidence was reflected and nurtured in many ways. Boys bought and played with toy soldiers. There was a growing mass market for pro-imperial juvenile literature. Manufacturers and advertisers

---

[3] PP (1892), XIX. C. 6582. *Report of the Committee...*, 8.

[4] Extract from the *Norwich Mercury*, 9 July 1872, repr. in *The Black Horse Gazette. The Journal of the 7th Dragoon Guards*, 2 (1895).

discovered that naval and military images and associations could sell their goods.[5] And soldiers like Havelock and Gordon became national heroes, which was perhaps a measure of the extent to which the public wanted to believe that the Empire was a force for moral good in the world, and not merely a money- and power-grubbing commercial enterprise.[6]

The same upper and middle classes who would disdain to sit in the same railway carriage or restaurant with a private soldier were equally capable of holding the virtues of the warrior in the highest esteem. In 1898, when 1/Lincolnshire Regiment departed for Khartoum to revenge Gordon, it was speeded on its way by the prayers of the Bishop of Lincoln, and was received with wild cheers by the British tourists staying at Shepherds Hotel in Cairo, which caused one officer to comment 'Personally, [I] never knew how damn popular I was before!!'[7] When 1/Rifle Brigade was mobilized at Parkhurst on the Isle of Wight for service in South Africa in 1899, and were marched to Cowes and waited for a ferry to take them aboard their troop ship, the inhabitants plied them with so much free beer that hardly a single man was sober by time they embarked.[8] Shared acts of commemoration could also bring a regiment and its parent communities together. In Liverpool in 1907 an annual civic ceremony was instituted to commemorate the role of the King's Liverpool Regiment in the siege of Ladysmith. It was attended by officers and men of the regiment, civic dignitaries, and the families of men who died serving with the regiment in South Africa.[9]

There was a pervasive popular militarism in late Victorian Britain that found expression in many different ways. Military spectacles influenced a wide variety of forms of popular culture and entertainments, including reading, music, the theatre, and fashion. Characters in Shakespeare's plays wore regimental uniforms on stage. Martial memoirs were avidly bought by the reading public.[10] Military spectacles such as reviews, parades, and funerals became a form of public entertainment. They were frequently patronized by local dignitaries and occasionally even

---

[5] R. Stern, ' "To rid the country of a scandal": The Uniforms Act of 1894', *Journal of the Society for Army Historical Research*, 71 (1993), 227–31.

[6] K. E. Hendrickson, *Making Saints: Religion and the Public Image of the British Army, 1809–1885* (London: Associated Universities Press, 1998); M. Paris, *Warrior Nation: Images of War in British Popular Culture 1850–2000* (London: Reaktion Books, 2000), 7–109; J. W. M. Hichberger, *Images of the Army: The Military in British Art, 1815–1914* (Manchester: Manchester University Press, 1988), 59–74.

[7] J. Meredith (ed.), *Omdurman Diaries 1898: Eyewitness Accounts of the Legendary Campaign* (London: Leo Cooper, 1998), 11, 114.

[8] Montgomery-Cuninghame, *Dusty Measure*, 25.

[9] A. King, *Memorials of the Great War in Britain: The Symbolism and Politics of Remembrance* (London: Berg, 1998), 44.

[10] Myerly, *British Military Spectacle*, 143–7.

by royalty.[11] Starting in 1879 a Royal Tournament, organized under the patronage of the Queen and the Prince and Princess of Wales, was held annually at the Royal Agricultural Hall in London to raise money for military charities. By 1888 it had 'taken its place as one of the established events of the year', and by 1894 it was attracting audiences of nearly 123,000 people, who paid £18,725 for admission.[12]

Even mundane parades attracted appreciative audiences. In the 1890s troops in the Colchester garrison marched to church every Sunday morning and one civilian remembered that 'they used to look lovely, you know coming along the roads, and hundreds of people used to be up there Sunday morning to see them go to Church. . . . They were really a wonderful sight.'[13] In June 1883 the presentation of new Colours to the 4/ Lincolnshire Regiment by the Lord Lieutenant of the county at Belton Park near Grantham attracted an audience that cut across class lines. The local gentry in their finery thronged the mansion and its steps, while 150 privates of the regiment kept the lower orders at a respectful distance. After the ceremony the officers of the battalion held a Grand Ball in the Town Hall that, in the opinion of the *Grantham Journal*, was one of the grandest held in the town for many years.[14] On a more private scale, civilian guests in an officers' mess could expect to be played into dinner by the regimental band and seated in front of a display of the mess plate, 'the historical associations connected with many of the principal pieces possibly calling forth a flow of reminiscence from the senior officers and any old members of the regiment who may happen to be present, which cannot fail to have a peculiar fascination for the interested civilian guest'.[15]

Military music was a particular attraction for civilians. Having learnt that 2/Royal Inniskilling Fusiliers would soon be visiting the town of Enniskillen, one inhabitant wrote to the CO in 1879 asking that the soldiers should be accompanied by their fifes and drums: 'The men are sure to be well received as the inhabitants of Enniskillen have always esteemed & respected the military but they are also musical and I am sure a great number of recruits may be obtained if this hint is acted upon.'[16] In 1905 the band of the Royal Irish Fusiliers attracted a paying audience of over 13,000 when it gave four performances in Bangor in aid of the local

[11] Ibid. 139–42.

[12] *The Times*, 15 June 1888 and 23 May 1895.

[13] ERO. SA 25/2/6/1. Colchester Recalled Tape 2159–2. Colchester Museum Service. H. Salmon, Tape 2, side A.

[14] PRO WO 68/131. 4th Battalion Lincolnshire Regiment. Digest of Service, 13 June 1883.

[15] 'A British Officer', *Social Life*, 43.

[16] NAM 7003/1. Scrapbook, Officer's Mess, 27th Foot, 2/Royal Inniskilling Fusiliers, Letter to CO, 108th Regiment, from 'An Enniskilliner', 5 Mar. 1879.

cottage hospital.[17] Field days and manoeuvres also attracted crowds of spectators. Sometimes, however, civilians could be a positive nuisance. In 1908 one staff officer complained that the conduct of the cavalry manoeuvres at Aldershot was impeded because 'people took country houses and brought two horses each and rode about all over the place, constantly interfering with the manoeuvres'.[18]

One reason why military spectacles were so popular was that they had conservative political overtones. The industrialization and rapid urbanization that characterized nineteenth-century Britain created numerous social and political problems that disturbed the order of society. To many observers, the notion of the ordered and hierarchical society that was epitomized by the Regular Army must have seemed deeply attractive. Martial pageants seemed to echo the needs of an industrial community for order, regularity, and uniformity, and the military virtues of discipline and self-sacrifice promised to hold together a fissiparous society.[19] This was epitomized in 1910 when the Soldiers' and Sailors' Help Society, a charity established in 1899 to give relief to men disabled in South Africa, organized a large-scale 'Army Pageant' at Fulham Palace. The ostensible purpose of the pageant was to raise funds for the society. Its underlying meaning was explained by Lord Roberts, who wrote in the foreword to the commemorative booklet that it was designed

to instil a sense of Patriotism into the People, and to impress upon them that it is the duty of every member of our great Empire to endeavour to do something, however small, for the good of their country: that everyone has a definite place in the general scheme which they can suitably fill: and that their country's interest should come before everything else.[20]

Such occasions also provided an opportunity for the crowd to display their loyalty to established institutions. When the King left Horse Guards Parade after the Trooping the Colour in 1903, 'the cheering in the Mall shows how a London crowd is influenced by military display'.[21] At such moments people could imagine society as how they wanted it to be, and not how it was.

There were, however, instances when the interests of the army and the wider civilian community were in open conflict. One of the most common causes of friction came about when the army tried to conduct

---

[17] 'Faugh-a-Ballagh'. The Regimental Gazette of the 87th Royal Irish Fusiliers, 4 (1905).

[18] PRO WO 279/25. Report of a conference of General Staff Officers at the Staff College, 18–21 Jan. 1909.

[19] Myerly, British Military Spectacle, 152–3.

[20] F. R. Benson and A. T. Craig (eds.), The Book of the Army Pageant Held at Fulham Palace (London: Sir J. Causton, 1910), 13.

[21] ERO D/DU 901/1. Papers of Maj.-Gen. Sir Harold Ruggles-Brise. 'The King's Birthday Celebration', The Times, 27 June 1903.

manoeuvres outside the immediate confines of barracks. In 1871 Cardwell decided to hold a large camp of exercise, involving 16,000 regulars, Militia, and Volunteers, on the Berkshire Downs. The immediate response of local farmers was to insist that the government pay them compensation for any damage done to their property by the troops, to erect signs warning troops not to trample their crops, to insist that the government grant them liberal payments for any transports they were asked to provide, and to put money into their pockets by purchasing supplies locally for the troops.[22] In 1873 the War Office leased Plumstead Common, which abutted the Royal Artillery depot at Woolwich, as a training ground. Three years later some of the commoners rioted, partly because some private landowners had erected fences that deprived them of their grazing rights, but also because the constant passage of troops and horses across the common was destroying their pasture.[23] A similar dispute, but on a smaller scale, occurred in 1907 when the trustees of Nazeing Common, near North Weald in Essex, refused the Essex Imperial Yeomanry permission to use the common as part of their training ground. The Yeomanry CO, Sir Richard Colvin, retaliated by using his powers as patron of the local flower show to refuse the commoners permission to exhibit at the show.[24]

However, in general territorialization and localization undoubtedly did help to forge a shared sense of identity between civilian communities and particular regiments. Some civilian communities eagerly accepted the opportunity that localization offered them. In 1873 and 1874 both Pontefract and Halifax in Yorkshire, and Antrim in Ireland, petitioned the War Office to establish depots in their towns.[25] A public meeting held in Glasgow in January 1873, presided over by the Lord Provost, resolved unanimously that they 'would express a strong and decided opinion in favour of army reform, believing that greatly increased efficiency can be obtained with greatly reduced expenditure; and that short service, with localisation of the forces, would promote not only a more honourable position for the soldier but greater morality in the army'.[26] In 1886, 2/ Manchester Regiment deposited their old Colours in Manchester Cathedral because, as their commanding officer remarked during the ceremony,

---

[22] PRO WO 33/23. Papers relating to the proposed Camp of Exercise, 1871.

[23] PRO HO 45/9413/56640. J. W. Boordy MP to R. A. Cross, 3 July 1876.

[24] ERO D/DU 783/3. Scrapbook of Brig.-Gen. Sir R. Colvin of Waltham Abbey. 'The Weekly Telegraph', 12 Apr. 1907.

[25] PRO WO 163/1. War Office Council meeting, 8 Mar. 1873; Anon., *Appendix to the reports of the Select Committee of the House of Commons on public petitions. Session 1874* (London: House of Commons, 1874), 183.

[26] *Appendix to the reports of the Select Committee of the House of Commons on Public Petitions. Session 1873* (London: House of Commons, 1873), 30.

It appears to me to be most desirable to foster everything that could tend to strengthen the bonds of Manchester to her territorial regiment, and what is more likely to do so than placing these old colours, which has accompanied them all over Her Majesty's dominions, in this Cathedral? As years roll by many old soldiers will come here to see the old colours, and I hope their comrades of the Manchester Militia and the Lancashire Volunteers and the citizens of Manchester and Lancashire generally will bestow a kindly glance at them.[27]

The regiment's goodwill was reciprocated by the civic authorities and at least some of the inhabitants of the city. When the battalion returned to Manchester in 1898, after serving overseas, they were given a warm civic welcome. Such a large and cheering crowd filled the railway station yard and platforms that police had to be summoned to control them. The battalion was greeted by the Lord Mayor in the name of the city and then marched out of the station led by the band of the 2/Manchester Volunteers.[28] The 2/Royal West Kent Regiment received a similar welcome a year later when it went on a recruiting march through its regimental district and

A most gratifying reception was met with at the towns and villages visited, and at the principal towns etc, Maidstone, Tonbridge, Tonbridge Wells, Sevenoaks, Westerham, Bromley, Dartford, entertainments were provided for the men. The resident gentry showed much hospitality to all ranks of the Battalion . . . [29]

Units could commend themselves to the community where they happened to be stationed in a variety of ways. In June 1873 the Mayor and Town Council of Newport voted their official thanks to the officers and men of 94/Foot for the assistance they had given the townsmen in putting out a large fire in the town.[30] Regiments often mixed freely with their civilian neighbours on the sports field. In the late 1880s teams from the Colchester garrison began to take part in sporting competitions with teams from the surrounding civilian population. 1/SLI had as its centre forward Lieutenant A. B. Whatman, 'a giant in stature, and a wonderful footballer; and his knowledge of the game revolutionised the style as played locally, incidentally bringing his unit into great prominence'. A little later the Sherwood Foresters, who had an excellent soccer team, joined the garrison, and attracted as opponents other leading teams such as the Woolwich Arsenal, Luton, Stockton, the Casuals, the Old Eton-

---

[27] NAM 7510–94. Scrapbook of Maj.-Gen. W. O. Barnard. Manchester Cathedral. Presentation of Regimental Colours. 2/Manchester Regiment, 21 June 1886.

[28] Ibid. *Manchester Evening Chronicle*, n.d., but *c*.1 Dec. 1898.

[29] NAM 6807–390. Historical Records, 97th Regiment of Foot, 1808–99.

[30] NAM 6807–390. Record of Service of 94th Regiment and 2nd Battalion Connaught Rangers, 18 June 1873.

ians, and the Old Harrovians. Their games often attracted audiences of soldiers and civilians numbering over 5,000 spectators.[31]

The welcomes that the Manchester Regiment and Royal West Kent Regiment received when they arrived in their districts were an expression of a local patriotism that was commonplace before 1914. Politicians, local dignitaries, and civic leaders were ever ready to extol the virtues of their own communities, and to claim that local patriotism was the foundation of the liberty and prosperity that all Britons enjoyed. In July 1877 Mr Rylands, the Liberal MP for Warrington, told the Commons that 'local patriotism and the local spirit' were 'one of the chief elements of the progress, the prosperity, and the power of Great Britain ... '.[32] A year later a Conservative peer, Lord Carnarvon, in opening a new municipal building at Newbury, asserted that 'in the adornment of our provincial towns, in the creation of these public buildings, in their embellishment, in the raising of the standard of taste in art, I see distinctly the fostering of local patriotism and a distinct step towards higher political life'.[33] And in 1924 Winston Churchill, addressing the annual dinner of the Society of Dorset Men in London, told his audience that he believed that 'Local patriotism was the foundation of national patriotism, and national patriotism was the foundation of true citizenship'.[34]

However, even before 1900 some perceptive observers had noted that the strength of local patriotism, and the willingness of people to identify with their local community and its institutions, was starting to wane. In September 1882 Lord Derby told an audience in Preston that although he had no doubt that Englishmen were still willing to do their patriotic duty and make sacrifices for the wider community,

there is another feeling which I may venture to call local patriotism, which, perhaps, under the circumstances of our modern life is not always as active as it used to be. I mean that feeling of attachment to a town or district or to the local community in which one resides which induces every inhabitant to be willing to make sacrifices for that community. We shift about so much, we live so fast, we move so easily, we are so much centralized, not by the operation of law, but in consequences of the circumstances of modern life, that we are in some danger of losing that feeling of what I have ventured to call local patriotism, which was so strong in earlier and simpler days.[35]

This process happened most quickly in the large conurbations with their shifting populations. In 1915 the chairman of Middlesex County

---

[31] 'Bantam', 'Reminiscences of Colchester Garrison', *The Abbey Field Review. A Monthly Record of Garrison Life in Colchester*, 1 (1926), 96–7.

[32] *The Times*, 16 Feb. 1877.

[33] *The Times*, 8 May 1878.

[34] *The Times*, 6 May 1924.

[35] *The Times*, 6 Sept. 1882.

Council publicly regretted the fact that 'The [Middlesex] regiment has not in the past been so much of a county regiment as it might have been. Other county regiments were looked after by the people in the county, and he hoped that this would be the case in the future with the Middlesex Regiment.'[36]

It was also symptomatic of the trend that Derby had identified that by the late 1880s the term 'local patriotism' was increasingly employed to describe loyalty to one of the four nations that constituted the United Kingdom, rather than to denote identification with a particular county or city. Gladstone in 1888, for example, spoke of local patriotism in the sense of the existence of a separate and distinct Welsh nationality.[37] And in November 1895 a future Conservative Prime Minister, Arthur Balfour, identified 'local patriotism' as existing in England, Scotland, and Ireland.[38]

'Local patriotism' in this sense could be just as powerful a force as county or civic patriotism in encouraging a sense of common identity between civilians and soldiers. Nowhere was the attachment between an individual nationality within the British Isles and its regiments stronger than in Scotland in the late nineteenth and early twentieth century.[39] When the existence of Scottish regiments was threatened by policies dictated from London, the campaigns waged to save them reflected a growing public concern that the distinctive Scottish culture that had survived the Act of Union of 1707 was under threat from a combination of emigration, the collapse of much of heavy industry, and the intrusion of alien English values.[40] The first such incident occurred in 1891–2 when the War Office was rumoured to be considering transforming the Cameron Highlanders, the only single battalion regiment left after 1881, into the 3/Scots Guards. The proposal aroused furious objections from the officers of the regiment, from the Highland Society of London, and from Scottish MPs sitting for highland constituencies. One of the latter, in language that was revealing of the underlying national sentiments that drew so many Scots to lend vocal support to their regiments, insisted: 'It would be nothing short of a national disgrace were this historic regiment to be wiped out as a distinctive body of men.'[41]

---

[36] *The Times*, 22 Apr. 1915.

[37] *The Times*, 5 Sept. 1888.

[38] *The Times*, 15 Nov. 1895.

[39] J. M. MacKenzie, 'Empire and National Identity: The Case of Scotland', *Transactions of the Royal Historical Society*, 8 (1998), 215–31.

[40] R. Finlay, 'National Identity in Crisis: Politicians, Intellectuals and the "End of Scotland", 1929–1939', *History*, 79 (1994), 242–62.

[41] *The Times*, 19 and 25 Nov. 1891, 12 Dec. 1892, 10 Jan. 1893.

Another possible national disgrace faced a Scottish regiment in 1937, when the Army Council decided that it was necessary to mechanize the army's remaining horsed cavalry regiments. However, faced by a shortage of tanks and armoured cars, it also decided that for the time being three regiments would retain their horses. The Scots Greys were Scotland's only cavalry regiment and their distinctive grey horses had made them one of the symbols of Scottish national identity. In March 1937, without any apparent action by the regiment, the civic leaders of several Scottish cities petitioned the War Office, insisting that there would be great dismay in Scotland if the regiment lost its horses.[42] Their efforts evoked no apparent response, and so in October 1937 the regiment's Commanding Officer, Lt.-Col. C. G. St. Lawrence, wrote to all Scottish MPs asking them to help to ensure that the regiment would keep its horses. He couched his plea in distinctively nationalistic terms. The regiment 'claim to be a part of Scotland and they and their grey horses are mingled with Scottish history and traditions. For this reason it should be recognised that to do away with the grey horses robs the Scottish people of something which they own and cherish.'[43] His lobbying produced a flood of public petitions and letters to the War Office.[44] The regiment's horses did receive a temporary stay of execution—not because of the lobbying that had taken place on their behalf, but because the Army Council still lacked the money to mechanize them.[45] However, St. Lawrence, who was described by the Colonel of the Regiment, Sir P. Chetwode, as 'an idiot', was also officially reprimanded by the Army Council and received no further employment.[46]

The third campaign to maintain a distinctive Scottish military identity against the meddlesome intrusions of the government in London occurred twenty years later. In 1957, as part of the Sandys reforms, the War Office opted to amalgamate the Highland Light Infantry and the Royal Scots Fusiliers. Seen from the perspective of London, it appeared to be an obvious policy. Their regimental districts were adjacent and both drew the bulk of their recruits from Glasgow.[47] Seen from a Scottish perspective, it seemed less obvious. The Highland Light Infantry were part of the Highland Brigade, and wished to remain a Highland Regiment, with all that entailed in terms of wearing the kilt, whereas the

[42] PRO WO 32/4633. Lord Provosts of Edinburgh, Perth, Glasgow, Dundee, and Aberdeen to Walter Elliot MP, Secretary of State Scotland, 11 Mar. 1937.
[43] Ibid. Lt.-Col. C. G. St Lawrence, to all Scottish MPs, 14 Oct. 1937.
[44] Ibid. Association of Lowland Scots to Hore-Belisha, 13 Oct. 1937.
[45] Ibid. Hore-Belisha to Hardinge, 28 Oct. 1937.
[46] Ibid. Field Marshal Sir P. Chetwode (Colonel, the Scots Greys) to Knox, 2 Nov. 1937.
[47] PRO WO 32/17321. Note on reductions in the Lowland and Highland Brigades, n.d. but c. July 1957.

Fusiliers were a Lowland regiment that wore trews. The proposal provoked vehement opposition from supporters of both regiments. One Scottish peer, Lord Belhaven, who had served as a regular officer in the Royal Scots Fusiliers, tried to enlist the support of Winston Churchill, who had briefly commanded a battalion of the regiment on the Western Front in 1916. 'They are Highland and we are Lowland', he wrote. 'They are townsmen, we countrymen. They are Light Infantry. This "merging" means extinction for both the regiments and the creation of a new regiment which our two colonels can do nothing about and should hand to the War Office if War Office want any Lowland Scots.'[48]

The military authorities in London had overlooked the fact that Glasgow was a city divided on sectarian lines. The Highland Light Infantry had habitually recruited from amongst the Catholic population of Irish descent. The Royal Scots Fusiliers, by contrast, had recruited from amongst Protestants. Belhaven believed that 'the racial and traditional differences of the two regiments will make merger dangerous. Already officers and men of both regiments are in mutual opposition and this must inevitably result in disastrous and probably violent aversion one from another.'[49] Lady Katherine Trenchard, whose son and first husband had died serving with the Fusiliers and whose second husband, Lord Trenchard, had been their Colonel, added her weight to the protests. She wrote to the Prime Minister, Harold Macmillan, that the Fusiliers

have always recruited in Ayrshire and Wigtownshire and are fine men. The H.L.I. the 71st Regiment. From the Gorbals of Glasgow. And to put it fairly, these do not mix—there is a dividing line between N & S of Glasgow. It may be silly but it is so. The two Cols. have both told you they couldn't make a reliable Battalion with that amalgamation.[50]

In March 1957, John Maclay, the Secretary of State for Scotland, heard that rumours that the Army Council was considering disbanding some Scottish regiments had reached Scotland and that consequently 'The glens are already rumbling'.[51] The War Office became the focus of an energetic lobbying campaign that involved not only the leaders of Scottish civic society, but also cultural pressure groups such as the Highland Society of London and MPs who sat for Scottish constituencies.[52] Much of this was orchestrated by the Colonels of the regiments, Maj.-Gen. Roy Urquhart of the Highland Light Infantry and Maj.-Gen.

[48] Ibid. Lord Belhaven to Churchill, 25 July 1957.
[49] Ibid. Lord Belhaven to First Lord of the Admiralty, 28 July 1957.
[50] Ibid. Lady Katherine Trenchard to Macmillan, 24 Aug. 1957.
[51] Ibid. Maclay to Hare, 27 Mar. 1957.
[52] Ibid. Sir S. Campbell to Sir R. Boothby, 30 Mar. 1957; Maclay to Hare, 29 Mar. 1957; Sir D. Robertson to Hare, n.d. but c.30 Mar. 1957.

Edmund Hakewill-Smith, the Colonel of the Royal Scots Fusiliers.[53] Their effort culminated in a deputation to the Prime Minister. It was to no avail. On 15 November, in what must have been an exchange of brutal frankness that exposed where power ultimately lay in the relationship between the War Office and the regiments, the latter lost. The sticking point dividing the two sides was the kilt. The Colonels insisted that if their regiments amalgamated they should be allowed to wear it. But the CIGS, Sir Gerald Templer, refused. The new regiment would be part of the Lowland Brigade, all of whose regiments wore trews. Templer then gave the Colonels a choice, either cooperate or resign so that he could appoint new Colonels who would bring about the amalgamation on the War Office's terms. Neither Colonel would budge, and within four days both had been required to resign.[54]

The War Office had taken little account of the fissures in Glasgow society when it decided on the merger, and even after they had been exposed, it was willing to ignore them and bulldoze the merger through. One reason they could do this was because the Colonels of the other Regiments of the Lowland Brigade studiously remained on the sidelines during the agitation, much to Hakewill-Smith's anger. At a thoroughly bad-tempered meeting on 22 November 1957, he was reported to have 'launched upon a tirade of abusive recriminations', and 'called them all Judases'.[55] There was more to the dispute than the inability of Englishmen to empathize with the symbols of another nation. That the kilt should become the make-or-break issue was symbolic of the War Office's attitude towards individual regiments. It was prepared to indulge their fancies in small matters, but to brush them aside in big ones. And in 1957 the government had far more at stake than did the objectors. If two regiments successfully defied the War Office, others would try to emulate them. The whole package of reforms embodied in the Sandys programme might then unravel. Macmillan had invested enormous political capital in the programme in the wake of the Suez debacle, and could not let that happen.

The popular support for Scottish regiments that was strong in 1891–2, 1937, and 1957 was symptomatic of the readiness with which some communities identified with their local regiments, and in doing so transformed them into icons that transcended their purely military roles. Their

---

[53] Ibid. Maj.-Gen. R. Urquhart to all Glasgow MPs, 22 July 1957; Councillor John Wingate to Hare, 24 Sept. 1957, and Lord Provost Glasgow to Hare, 29 Sept. 1957; John Nixon Browne to Hare, 6 Sept. 1957; London Branch, RSF OCA to PM, 20 Sept. 1957; R. Anderson to Hare, 13 Nov. 1957.
[54] Ibid. Hare to Urquhart and Hakewill-Smith, 19 Nov. 1957.
[55] Ibid. GOC Scottish Command to CIGS, 23 Nov. 1957.

support could go far beyond flag-waving and petition-signing. Press reports of the terrible sufferings of troops in Crimea, and the widespread belief amongst the Victorian middle classes that philanthropy was a wholesome remedy for the nation's ills, meant that the soldier now became a suitable object for charitable assistance. In the second half of the nineteenth century there was a burgeoning growth in charities directed towards relieving the suffering of men at the front and their dependants at home.[56]

Some charities, such as the Soldiers' and Sailors' Families Association, founded in 1885, operated on a national basis, but many others focused their efforts on particular county regiments. One of the advantages of localization and territorialization was that it provided a way of organizing and channelling these sentiments. In 1878–9 the inhabitants of the county and city of Aberdeen raised a fund to support the wives, widows, and children of their local regiment, the 92/Gordon Highlanders.[57] When 2/Essex took part in the failed attempt to relieve General Gordon at Khartoum in 1885, the members of the 'Colchester and Essex Ladies Association' collected a fund worth £50 and sent the battalion a consignment of underclothing and pipes to show their appreciation for its efforts.[58]

In 1899, when the War Office received numerous letters asking how civilians could assist the families of soldiers serving in South Africa, the Secretary of State and the Commander-in-Chief replied that

Such assistance should, in our opinion, be organised so far as possible on local lines. Local agencies can alone distribute the funds which may be available with a thorough knowledge of the merits of each case, and now that a territorial connection has been established between each Line Regiment, with its reservists and Militia battalions, and a particular portion of the United Kingdom, we may hope that on an occasion like the present one every county will readily avail itself of the opportunity of recognising that connection and helping that portion of the Army which is peculiarly its own.[59]

In November 1899 the Lord Lieutenant of Essex called a meeting at the county town of Chelmsford that was attended by the Bishop of Colchester and a clutch of local MPs, County Councillors, and other local worthies. The meeting agreed to establish a county fund to collect subscriptions to support the families of Reservists of the Essex regiment

---

[56] S. Fowler, '"Pass the hat for your credit's sake ... and pay-pay-pay"': Philanthropy and Victorian Military Campaigns', *Soldiers of the Queen*, 105 (2001), 2–5.

[57] *The Times*, 12 Nov. 1879.

[58] ERM. Archives ER3251. Digest of Service, 56th Foot, 1844 to 1881 and 2/Essex, 1881–1900, Nov. 1886.

[59] PP (1900), XLII. Cd. 196. *Report of the Committee on War Relief Funds*, 259. I am most grateful to Simon Fowler for drawing my attention to this report.

serving in South Africa. By March 1900 it had raised £5,000. Furthermore, by early 1900, Mrs Stephenson, the wife of the CO of the battalion serving in South Africa, had raised sufficient funds to send 5,520 pairs of socks, 1,020 shirts, jerseys, and drawers, 3,820 handkerchiefs, 10,000 envelopes and paper, 2,000 pencils, 1,000 pipes, 400lb tobacco, and 300 pairs of mittens to the soldiers serving with her husband.[60] The men of the battalion were almost overwhelmed by the gifts, although no one seems to have told them who had sent them.[61] Efforts on a national scale matched this. By May 1900 national charities had raised over £900,000 to assist wounded soldiers and the families of men in South Africa.[62]

The reality of localization and territorialization was that most regular units spent far more time outside their own recruiting district than inside it. When they were not posted overseas, they were usually stationed in one or other of the major garrison towns in the UK. When 1/Sherwood Foresters visited Nottingham in 1935, it was the first time they had done so for 150 years.[63] Cardwell had hoped that Depots would be the mainstay of the link between the regulars and their communities, but the extent to which regimental depots scattered across the country helped to break down civilian prejudices and ignorance was debatable. In 1874 Capt. R. D. Gibney, the Superintendent of Recruiting on Salisbury Plain, wrote that

The people are prejudiced against the Service. It was supposed some time ago, that much of this ignorance would be overcome by the introduction into the country of brigade depots, where regiments would be quartered, and the training of auxiliaries carried out, and doubtless it would have had this effect had these depots been on a larger scale, and recruits trained thereat with the regiments of their choice.

Countless small brigades without a sufficient staff, working unobserved and unheeded, have done nothing towards the promotion of recruiting. They have only complicated the machinery by increasing workers and channels of communication, and in too many instances have sunk into something very much resembling The Recruit Parcels Receiving and Delivery Company.[64]

In many instances it was therefore left to the auxiliaries to make a reality of the connection between the civil community and its regiment.

[60] ERM. ERPA30. *Essex County Chronicle*, 17 Nov. 1899; CB 1. Cutting from *Essex County Chronicle*, 19 Jan. 1900; Archives ER6005. Historical Record, 1 Battalion Essex Regiment, Herbert Gibson, Essex County Council, to CO, Regimental Depot, Warley Barracks, Brentwood, 14 Mar. 1900.

[61] ERM. ER 2178:1. Diary of Cpl. E. J. Wymer, 19 Apr. 1900.

[62] PP (1900), XLII. Cd. 196. *Report . . .*, 5.

[63] *Regimental Annual. The Sherwood Foresters 1935*, 4.

[64] Gibney, 'Recruiting', 343–4.

This did not happen automatically. On the eve of the Cardwell reforms, the Militia was probably held in lower public esteem than the regulars. That was certainly the impression of Maj.-Gen. James Lindsay, the Inspector-General of Auxiliary Forces: 'While other forces are toasted at public meetings, the Militia is seldom mentioned', he reported in 1869.[65] Little happened in the late nineteenth century to raise its status. The mid-Victorians had an ambivalent attitude towards the Militia. When the bill to revive the Militia was passing through Parliament in 1852 it attracted nearly 800 hostile petitions. Manufacturing districts complained that it would disrupt the industrial labour force and Radical and pacifist propagandists insisted that militia service would be morally corrupting.[66] The behaviour of some Militiamen during their annual training seemed to justify their forebodings. In Richmond in 1869, fifty men of the North Yorkshire Militia won money on a horse race and celebrated on a potent mixture of beer and rum. The next morning nineteen were so drunk that they had to be confined to the guard room, and 'On those who were sober going back to dinner the cook was so tipsy that he fell downstairs (almost in the officers' presence), and upset the whole of the soup of the mess.'[67] Some communities nonetheless welcomed them, but only because free-spending soldiers put money into the pocket of local shopkeepers and tradesmen.[68]

It was the Volunteers and their Territorial successors, rather than the regulars or Militia, that played the most significant part in bridging the gap between the Regular Army and civilian society. By the 1860s and 1870s the Volunteers had become a prominent feature of late Victorian society. Their military pretensions, like those of the Yeomanry, sometimes made them an easy target for lampoons.[69] But no major local function was complete without their presence, their parades and field days attracted crowds of spectators, and their doings were regularly reported in the local and national press.[70] By the mid-1860s any sizeable community without a Volunteer Corps felt itself at a disadvantage compared to its neighbours. Each corps was sustained by a strong sense of community pride. Local notables were willing to patronize their own

[65] PRO WO 33/19. Maj.-Gen. J. Lindsay, Reserve Forces. Report, 1868–69, Apr. 1869.

[66] Beckett, *The Amateur Military Tradition*, 148–9.

[67] PRO WO 33/20. Notes on the system of billeting the Militia, as seen in five English and two Scotch Regiments, during the Training of 1869, 17 July 1869.

[68] PRO WO 33/37. Report of the militia localisation committee appointed by the Secretary of State for War to inquire into the movement of certain militia regiments, QQ. 746–7.

[69] See e.g. P. J. R. Mileham (ed.), *Yeoman Service by W. B and G. D. Giles: Contemporary Cartoons of the Suffolk Yeomanry Cavalry 1870 to 1910* (Tunbridge Wells, Kent: Spellmount, 1985) and L. Raven-Hill, *Our Battalion: Being Some Slight Impressions of his Majesty's Auxiliary Forces in Camp and Elsewhere* (London: Punch Office, 1902).

[70] RNRM. R. 137A. Press cuttings, dated 4 Apr. 1893; *The Times*, 16 Apr. 1881.

units or to defend them in the face of criticism.[71] In 1892, when 1(VB) Norfolk Regiment held a concert at Agricultural Hall, Norwich to clear the debt they had incurred in building a new rifle range, it was patronized by the Mayor, the local MP, and several prominent local families.[72] When Haldane established the Territorials in 1908, one of his objectives was to give wider expression to this willingness by reorganizing 'the military forces of this country in such a fashion as to give the nation what is really a National Army, not separated from itself by artificial barriers of caste or class, but regarded by the people as something that is their very own'.[73]

The Volunteers and the Territorials epitomized some of the values held most dear by the late Victorians: self-help, local pride, and patriotism, discipline, a commitment to healthy and rational recreations, and the orderly mixing of different social classes to form an organic community.[74] In 1908 the Vicar of Christchurch in Hampshire told a congregation of Territorials that 'The day when Britain is driven to rely on conscription or compulsion to fill the ranks of her defenders will mark the wane of her national glory.'[75] The Territorials saw themselves, and were seen by the military authorities, as the essential bridge between the soldier and the civilian. When the Commanding Officer of 1(VB)/DCLI addressed a civilian audience at Truro Town Hall in 1890, he was applauded when he

referred to the absence of that broad line of demarcation which used to be observable between the military and the civilian element. Some people used to think that the interest between the civilian and the military was distinct, and that the interest of the military was a danger to the civilian interest. That idea had now almost entirely passed away. He claimed for the auxiliary forces that they had done something to break down these distinctions and bring about a closer bond of sympathy between the civilian and military element; and for this alone they were to be congratulated (Applause).[76]

But the Volunteers were not readily accepted by everyone. In the early 1860s, many employers had been in the forefront of organizing Volunteer Corps, believing that membership of a disciplined corps would make a man a better worker, and some continued their patronage.[77] But by the

---

[71] Cunningham, *The Volunteer Force*, 68–9; Beckett, *The Amateur Military Tradition*, 178.

[72] RNRM. R. 157. Militia and Volunteers. Bill poster advertising 'Grand Military, Muscular and Musical Fete', 14–15 Oct. 1892.

[73] NLS. Haldane MSS 6108A(1). R. B. Haldane, Fourth Memorandum, 25 Apr. 1906; Second Memorandum, 1 Feb. 1906.

[74] Cunningham, *The Volunteer Force*, 98.

[75] *The Hampshire Regiment Journal*, 3 (1908).

[76] NAM 8202–55. Colonel G. C. Swiney, Scrapbook, Sept. 1872 to June 1913. *West Briton*, 13 Mar. 1890.

[77] PP (1878–9), XV. C. 2235. *Report of the Committee . . .*, Q. 1512.

early 1890s increasing numbers of employers began to feel that Volunteering was no more than a form of amusement, and one that threatened to take men away from their work and that did not necessarily hold the key to better industrial relations or make for a more obedient labour force.[78]

That suggests that while the soldier, be he a regular or a part-timer, and his regiment were held in high public esteem in the abstract by 1914 because of what they represented, the actual flesh-and-blood soldier, particularly if he was a regular, was still regarded by most civilians with some disdain. 'We know that the civilian looks down upon us', wrote F. W. Maitland, a private in the 19/Hussars shortly before the First World War; 'we suffer agonies of stricken pride when we enter a railway carriage and fellow passengers pass our carriage and leave us to solitary meditation'.[79] Learning in 1906 that his son wanted to enlist, Percy Snelling's father told him that 'Soldiers they're the scum of the earth'.[80] There were a multitude of reasons for the prevalence of these attitudes.

The strongest objections to service in the Regular Army came from the very section of the community that provided most of its recruits. Setting aside the long-standing suspicion of many British people towards a standing army, and the fact that the army were still occasionally employed to protect strike-breakers, the objections of large sections of the working class to service in the Regular Army had two foundations. The behaviour of some of the rank and file was contrary to their own notions of 'respectability', and the terms and conditions of service offered to ordinary soldiers were some way below what most hoped to enjoy in civilian life.

Regiments consisted for the most part of young men who were, because of the army's bar on matrimony, unmarried. In their pursuit of female company and entertainment and their resort to pubs, beer halls, and brothels, their behaviour sometimes offended their more respectable neighbours. In 1883 John Killigan wrote to the CO of 2/Royal Inniskilling Fusiliers, then stationed near Belfast:

I beg to call your attention to the misconduct of a large section of your men on frequent occasions about this place. They are in the habit of bringing bad females where we are working and about the lanes leading into the town and acting in the most indecent manner so that the moral families about this place are in terror of them.[81]

---

[78] PP (1894), XV. *Report from the Select Committee on Volunteer Acts*, QQ. 1479, 1517.
[79] Maitland, *Hussar of the Line*, 32.
[80] IWMSA. Accession No. 000314/12. P. Snelling, 1.
[81] NAM 7003/1. Scrapbook, Officers' Mess, 27th Foot, 2/Royal Inniskilling Fusiliers. J. Killigan to 2/Royal Inniskilling Fusiliers, 25 Apr. 1883.

Districts in some garrison towns became notorious for rowdy behaviour by soldiers. Plymouth's Union Street was a mile long, contained no fewer than thirty-seven pubs, and was a frequent site of fights between soldiers and sailors.[82] In Colchester in 1885 there was a major riot one Saturday night when a group of military police under a Provost Sergeant clashed with some civilians outside the Woolpack pub. A series of brawls involving several hundred people developed, and men of the Durham Militia, who were training in the garrison, were observed 'using their belts freely'. Order was restored only by the intervention of a company of infantry with fixed bayonets.[83]

Misconduct like that helped to ensure that service in the ranks of the Regular Army continued to carry a deep social stigma. It was not accidental that the army failed to attract many recruits from English and Welsh nonconformist backgrounds, the backbone of the respectable working class in the late nineteenth century.[84] One spokesman for such a community, Henry Richards, Liberal MP for Merthyr Tydfil, objected to the Cardwell localization scheme because 'it covered the country with a web-work of military institutions, the tendency of which was to make us what we have always deprecated—a military nation' and because 'they were too often schools of immorality and vice. The moral condition of our Army and Navy was simply appalling. Wherever, indeed, a body of soldiers was stationed, it became a corrupting and demoralising agency.'[85] Nearly 14,000 people in Sunderland petitioned against the establishment of a depot in their town because the intrusion of large numbers of young soldiers who were forbidden to marry was bound to lead to an increase in prostitution.[86] And in 1872 the inhabitants of Kirkdale, near Liverpool, petitioned Parliament to repeal the 40th Clause of the Mutiny Act. The clause granted exemption from arrest to any serving soldier for any debt worth less than £30. The petitioners objected, because

the action of this clause is practically very detrimental to morality, and creative of much misery.

That the increase of shorter service in the army, and the proposed more extended localisation of troops, by exposing many more men and many more districts than formerly to the evil influence of such an immoral law, renders its existence in the future a cause of the gravest danger.

That your Petitioners reside in a district which it is proposed to make an 'army centre', and that they view with terror the introduction in their neighbourhood

---

82 IWMSA. Accession No. 000569/18. Col. U. B. Burke, reels 5 and 7.
83 'Bantam', 'Reminiscences of Colchester Garrison', 96–7.
84 Spiers, *The Army and Society*, 49, 52.
85 Hansard, HC (series 3) vol. 213, col. 1210.
86 Ibid., col. 1214.

of any large body of men who are thus exempted by positive enactment from the responsibilities which should attach alike to every member of the community.[87]

The military authorities were fully aware of the burden attitudes like this placed upon them. In 1906 Maj.-Gen. F. Howard, the acting GOC of the Welsh and Midland Command, insisted that the main reason why the Regular Army could not attract recruits from the respectable classes was because,

in the opinion of the men and their parents, the associations of the barrack-room are not morally healthy, and it is an undoubted fact that a few low-minded men who are a discredit to their profession may render the atmosphere of a barrack-room very distasteful to the respectable men who are forced to associate with them.[88]

By 1900 most stations had regimental and garrison institutes specifically intended to wean the other ranks away from the kinds of amusements that might lead to indiscipline and friction with their civilian neighbours. Such developments were not, however, universally welcomed by every civilian. In 1906 a publican in Portsmouth wrote to the Hampshire Regiment complaining that of late years there had been a fall in the number of soldiers who patronized his pub. 'I say it was British Beer beat Bonaparte, and how can we hope to beat Kaiser Bill on tea—I ask you?'[89]

The rowdy behaviour of some soldiers was not the only reason why the 'respectable' classes held service in the ranks of the Regular Army in low esteem. An equally potent factor was the terms and conditions of service that the army offered. They saw the Regular Army, quite simply, as a bad employer. Dishonest recruiting methods and repellent conditions of service conferred a stigma on every man who enlisted. The reliance of the Regular Army on the unemployed and the disreputable to fill the ranks in turn discouraged better-class recruits from enlisting. This created a vicious circle and perpetuated the impression that the Regular Army offered work that was fit only for paupers, criminals, and those too lazy to find proper jobs. The latter was a particular stigma, given the importance that generations of Victorians attached to work as a sign of manly respectability.[90]

A private from Derry who enlisted in the 63/Foot in the late 1850s returned home on furlough to discover that his friends and family called him 'a mean man for being a soldier'. This was because 'Plenty of labouring men at home, what you call the labouring class, on account of their hearing what the army was, the small pay, and everything of that

---

[87] Anon., *Appendix to the reports of the Select Committee of the House of Commons on public petitions. Session 1872* (London: House of Commons, 1872), 32.

[88] PRO WO 32/8699. Report of the Committee on military punishments and the method of recording them, n.d. but *c.*6 June 1906.

[89] *The Hampshire Regiment Journal*, 1 (1906).

[90] Harris, *Private Lives*, 123–4.

kind. Men taking their discharge and going home tell these things, and then the country people all have it that way.'[91]

Little changed over the next sixty years. In 1919 NCOs in the Royal Garrison Artillery complained that at the end of twenty-one years' service they expected to find themselves 'without a trade and a pension of just over 7 s[hillings] per week to keep him and his family'.[92] They had good reason to be disgruntled with their pay. Army recruiting literature tried to present a picture of the army as a reasonably well-paid occupation, and one that compared favourably with many civilian jobs. But in reality army pay consistently lagged behind all but the very worst-paid civilian jobs.[93]

The two Royal Commissions that examined recruiting in the 1860s both pointed to the fact that low pay and too many compulsory stoppages from their pay were reasons why men were reluctant to enlist.[94] In the late nineteenth century a private soldier's pay consisted of four elements: the cash he received each week, the rations, accommodation, and clothing he was given as a free issue, any good conduct pay he might have earned, and the deferred pay he received when he ended his colour service.[95] This meant that in 1881 he received £21.29 in cash, £3.04 in deferred pay, £6.80 in bread and meat and, according to one authority, £3.46 in free accommodation. Deferred pay was introduced in 1876 so that men who served over twelve years received a lump sum when they left the army. In 1898 it was replaced by a messing allowance and a gratuity of £1 for every year of service. A soldier's income was regular and he was not subject to unemployment. But against his total income of £34.59 per annum, he was liable to have deducted from the cash element of his pay compulsory stoppages to pay for his laundry, damages to his barrack room or equipment, and until 1893, 3d. per day that was pooled on a company basis, and used to pay for tea, coffee, salt, sugar, potatoes, flour, jam, cheese, and, if the funds were used carefully, small quantities of 'luxuries as bacon, eggs, and fish...'. These deductions were a cause of resentment for many serving soldiers. Recruiting literature implied, although it did not specify, that all rations would be issued free of charge, but the reality of army rations was that most privates went hungry if they did not have money in their pockets to buy extra food.[96]

[91] PP (1867), XV. C. 3752. *Report of commissioners...*, Q. 3815–6.
[92] *The Times*, 22 May 1919.
[93] NAM 7105–28. *The Army and What it Offers* (1914).
[94] Blanco, 'Army Recruiting Reforms, 1861–67', 217–24.
[95] Goodenough and Dalton, *The Army Book of the British Empire*, 148–9; Col. F. J. Graves, 'Other Ranks Compared with Civilian Working Class Life—II. Recruiting Difficulties—III. The Condition of the Army Reserve', *Journal of the Royal United Services Institute*, 35 (1891), 576.
[96] Wyndham, *The Queen's Service*, 31; Anon., *QR 1892*, 190; Goodenough and Dalton, *The Army Book of the British Empire*, 150; IWMSA. Accession No. 4935/05. Maj. E. S. Humphries, 19.

When all of these elements were taken into account, a private soldier received less than almost any other worker with the possible exception of an agricultural labourer in Ireland. This was one reason why most recruits were below the age of 21. The army was paying just enough to attract teenagers who were capable of earning only a boy's wages. It was paying too little to attract more mature men who were capable of earning a man's wage.[97] In 1881 the pay of non-commissioned officers was sharply increased as part of Childers's efforts to retain such men with the Colours, but even their wages were below those of most men with comparable skills and responsibilities in civilian life. The basic pay of a private soldier was increased slightly in 1902, but an infantry soldier's pay after deductions was still only comparable to a poorly paid agricultural labourer.[98]

Service in the ranks of the Regular Army was not only poorly paid, but it also threatened that most sacred of late Victorian institutions, the family. Forbidden to marry on the strength during their first period of colour service, most soldiers could expect to spend several years abroad without any home leave. They faced not only the dangers of the battlefield, but also the equally terrible and unknown dangers of disease. Sons might never see their parents again, and the wives of men who had married off the strength were regularly deserted by their husbands when they were posted overseas.[99] When 7/Dragoon Guards returned to Shorncliffe in 1894 after a decade in India, the editor of the regimental journal noted wistfully that 'Most of our homes have been broken up since we went abroad, and those that survive seem strange and altogether different from what they used to be.'[100]

Short service also left many soldiers destitute at the end of their colour service. Between 1861 and 1898 only one soldier in three who left the army received a pension. The others had to find work and often had the utmost difficult in doing so. Short service was intended to attract more recruits by ensuring that enlistment would no longer be regarded as a life sentence. But it also created its own problems. At the end of their colour service, most soldiers were confronted with the problem of finding civilian employment, without the skills or patronage that enabled their civilian counterparts to find work. The inability of the military authorities to offer assistance to broken-down or unemployed ex-soldiers did little for the army's public image. Regimental Associations offered what

---

[97] PP (1892), XIX. C. 6582. *Report of the Committee*... 10.

[98] C. Pulsifer, 'Beyond the Queen's Shilling: Reflections on the Pay of Other Ranks in the Victorian British Army', *Journal of the Society for Army Historical Research*, 80 (2002), 326–34; Hoppen, *The Mid-Victorian Generation*, 21, 59, 61–3; Spiers, *Army and Society*, 53–5.

[99] Fraser, *Sixty Years*, 75; NAM 7008–13. Anon., MSS. Experiences of a soldier, n.d.

[100] *The Black Horse Gazette. The Journal of the 7th Dragoon Guards*, 2 (1895).

help they could but their means were limited.[101] By the mid-1930s, many soldiers were reluctant to extend their initial period of colour service because they feared that if they did so they would be too old to find a new job when they did leave the army.[102] Unemployed ex-soldiers, according to one critic of short service, 'carry with them and disseminate regrets that they ever entered so thankless an employment. They will spread the feeling, as expressed by Lord Hardinge, that the nation treats its soldiers like oranges, that having sucked them dry, it throws them aside.'[103] Every time the press reported a case like that of John Tyrell, a veteran of the Crimean War and the Indian Mutiny, who tried to poison himself in 1893 because he could not find work and believed he was a burden on his wife, it did nothing to enhance the image of the army as a worthwhile career.[104]

By 1916 most families in Britain had at least one member who was serving in the army. It was therefore, at least temporarily, no longer possible for civilians casually to dismiss the ordinary 'tommy' as a dissolute ne'er-do-well. The war gave added impetus to the notion of the ordinary soldier as the heroic defender of hearth and home. At Christmas 1914 Queen Alexandra sent a message to each soldier serving in France: 'No words of mine can express the great admiration which we all feel for the splendid endurance and bravery of our gallant soldiers and I wish you and them from the depths of my heart success in the just and righteous cause for which our Country is fighting.'[105] The Lord Mayor of London sent a similar message, and the *Daily News*, to show its appreciation, sent every soldier a Christmas pudding.[106] Soldiers returning home, especially if they had been decorated for bravery, were treated as heroes. When Frank Richards was on leave in August 1917, having been awarded a DCM, his neighbours presented him with a gold watch in recognition of his bravery.[107]

However, what the war did not do was to change the perception of the army as a poor employer. When Bert Reynolds enlisted in 2/5th Somerset Light Infantry in September 1914, his father, who had served in the ranks of the Gordon Highlanders in Egypt and the Sudan in the 1880s, 'got hold of [me] by the ears, to look face to face at him. He was calling me one of the biggest blasted fools in the nation. Here I had a job; no reason

---

[101] Skelley, *The Victorian Army*, 216.
[102] *The Times*, 29 Apr. 1935.
[103] Anon., 'Army Reform', *Edinburgh Review*, 153 (1881), 196.
[104] *The Times*, 25 July 1893.
[105] PRO WO 95/25. Army Routine Orders, 24 Dec. 1914.
[106] Ibid. Army Routine Orders, 10 and 19 Dec. 1914.
[107] Richards, *Old Soldiers Never Die*, 243.

to go. He told me all about his hellish days in the Sudan and the Relief of Gordon and that hadn't done me had it?'[108]

Indeed, the experience of wartime soldiering may only have reinforced the impression that the military authorities dealt with men in a careless and callous fashion. Wartime service meant that far more people than before had personal experience of the inadequacies of army pay and separation allowances.[109] And in 1916 there was growing criticism expressed in the press, in private letters to the War Office, and in the Commons of the manner and frequency with which the authorities inflicted Field Punishment Number One on hapless soldiers who had fallen foul of the disciplinary code in the BEF.[110]

But despite the experiences of the First World War, military spectacles and entertainments seem to have lost none of their pre-war popularity. At Hastings in August 1921, the Royal Engineer's Band held a series of concerts which drew paying audiences of about 5,000 each evening.[111] Nearly 20,000 people watched when the Colours of 4/ and 5/King's Own Royal Regiment were trooped in Lancaster in July 1930.[112] On a much larger scale the Royal Tournament was held annually in London and continued to attract royal patronage and to raise large sums of money for military charities.[113] In 1933 it was visited by 250,000 spectators.[114] The plethora of unveilings of war memorials that characterized the 1920s provided numerous occasions for soldiers and civilians to demonstrate their common appreciation of the sacrifices of their comrades and loved ones. The unveiling of the Buffs war memorial in Canterbury Cathedral in 1921 was attended by representatives of the regular and Territorial battalions of the regiment, the Lord Lieutenant and High Sheriff of Kent, the mayors of its major towns, and nearly 1,500 spectators.[115] Between 1925 and 1935, several borough councils in Essex paid for memorials to be placed in the chapel of the Essex Regiment at Warley to commemorate the men of their towns who had died fighting with the regiment.[116] Similarly, by 1936 the links between 5/North Staffordshire Regiment and the towns of the Potteries had been cemented by the installation in

---

[108] C. P. Mills, *A Strange War: Burma, India and Afghanistan 1914–1918* (Gloucester: Alan Sutton, 1988), 7.

[109] See e.g. *The Times*, 11 July, 2 Aug., 1, 2, 10 Oct. 1917.

[110] PRO WO 32/5460. Field Punishment No. 1 contains a great deal of correspondence on this issue.

[111] *The Times*, 4 Aug. 1921.

[112] *The Times*, 14 July 1930.

[113] *The Times*, 29 May 1930.

[114] *The Times*, 12 June 1933.

[115] *The Times*, 1 Aug. 1921.

[116] Anon., *Essex Regiment, The Essex Regiment Chapel* (Warley Barracks, 1954), 3–7.

the town hall at Stoke-on-Trent of windows commemorating the men who died in the battalion.[117]

However, the willingness of serving soldiers, ex-soldiers, and civilians to come together to commemorate the sacrifices of the war did not translate into more practical contacts between the army and civil society. In 1934 an officer of the Sherwood Foresters believed that one of the reasons so many reservists in his regiment could not find work was because the people of Nottinghamshire and Derbyshire knew little of the doings of their regiment.[118] In Croydon in 1935, 4/Queen's Royal Regiment blamed its poor recruiting record on 'a strong element of apathy existent in the town which was hard to break down'.[119]

The perception of the soldier as the heroic defender of hearth and home faded quite quickly after 1918. In its place the image of the regular soldier as a ne'er-do-well reasserted itself. When Lieutenant-Colonel W. N. Nicholson began to organize a recruiting march of a regular battalion of the Suffolk Regiment through Suffolk in the late 1920s

it was necessary to inquire whether we should be welcome. At a general meeting in a mayor's parlour the civil authorities of the different towns made it clear that they had no need of a Pied Piper of Hamelin; they spoke frankly about the expense to their civic purses; they hinted delicately but decidedly at drunkeness.[120]

It was not just civic leaders who entertained such ideas. Elizabeth Harrington, who was the daughter of a railway porter and herself working as a nurse, remembered that her family initially opposed her marriage to a soldier because in the mid-1920s: 'There was a very vast line between soldiers and civilians. You see, it was a hungry time. And people didn't join the Army unless they were really down and out. And although people did join the Army, quite nice people, it was not considered the thing to mix.'[121]

The army retained its justified reputation for being a poor employer. Families were alarmed at the prospect of a long separation from their sons and lovers if they enlisted and were posted overseas. Serving soldiers told stories of the sometimes irksome disciplinary system that they had to endure. Too many soldiers, after completing a period of colour service, still found themselves cast onto the civilian job market without any useful skills. As the Adjutant-General, Sir Harry Knox, explained in 1936:

[117] PRO WO 32/21589. Secretary of the Staffordshire Territorial & Auxiliary Forces Association to HQ Mid-West District, 8 Aug. 1960.
[118] *Regimental Annual. The Sherwood Foresters 1934*, 246.
[119] *The Journal of the Queen's Royal Regiment*, 6 (1935), 24.
[120] Nicholson, *Behind the Lines*, 271.
[121] IWMSA. Accession No. 000898/06. Elizabeth Harrington, 3.

No man comes into the Army now because he cannot live outside it. Education has had a considerable effect on the outlook of the man in the street. The men who come into the Army now do not lead a hand-to-mouth existence and one reason why we are short of recruits is that young men will not come into the Army because they do not see sufficient prospect of a reasonable life career.[122]

Above all, pay remained poor. On active service, all troops had received free rations and clothing, and in 1914 married men, whether they were married on or off the strength, were given a separation allowance for their wives and children.[123] In April 1919 the military authorities did increase military pay, mainly in order to lessen the discontent amongst soldiers awaiting demobilization and who saw how much higher civilian pay was. But although the Secretary of State for War, Winston Churchill, claimed that three out of four men in the army would soon be demobilized and that he was going to 'pay the fourth man double to finish the job', a private soldier's wage was still low.[124] He was paid only £59.32 per annum. This represented no more than a tiny improvement on the pre-war situation. Whereas before 1914 the average earnings of a private soldier were about 63 per cent of the level of earnings of a semi-skilled worker, by 1920 the position had hardly changed, in that they now stood at 65 per cent of that level.[125] The military authorities continued to place a positive gloss on army pay, insisting that deductions were now negligible. But the reality, as a recruit who enlisted in 1920 discovered, was that 'we lads did not get much pay. Friday was pay-day and, after we had brought our bits and pieces such as soap, toothpaste and boot polish from the N.A.A.F.I. Canteen, by Sunday we were broke.'[126] Troops also continued to be subject to compulsory deductions for barrack damages and some items of replacement clothing.[127]

It was, therefore, hardly surprising that other ranks remained sensitive to anything that threatened their pay. So, for example, there was considerable disquiet amongst the men of 1/Welch Regiment, who were stationed in India in August 1920, when a rumour reached them that the purchasing power of their pay might be cut by a government decision to pay them at the prevailing rate of exchange between the pound sterling and the rupee, rather than at the existing fixed and artificially high rate

---

[122] PRO WO 32/2984. Adjutant-General to Army Council, 15 Sept. 1936.
[123] PRO WO 293/1. Army Council Instructions. ACI 166. Emoluments of Officers, WOs, NCOs, and men, 20 Aug. 1914.
[124] *The Times*, 4 Mar. 1919.
[125] Jeffery, 'The Post-war Army', 214, 224; Anon., 'Army Notes', *Journal of the Royal United Services Institute*, 64 (1919), 757–8; War Office, *Royal Warrant...1931*, 230–1.
[126] Kennett, *Life is What you Make It*, 20; *The Times*, 13 Mar. 1925.
[127] IWMSA. Accession No. 004503/06. CQMS P. C. Munn. Reel 1; IWMSA. Accession No. 004523/07. Capt. F. J. Powell, 4.

that had been used in the past.[128] Furthermore, the pay rates that Churchill announced in 1919 were not intended to be permanent. They were to be revised in the light of changes in the cost of living. Consequently, when in 1925 post-war deflation meant that the cost of living had fallen, wage rates for soldiers enlisting after 1925 were cut by a corresponding amount.

This caused understandable disquiet. It meant that men serving in the same unit and doing the same job might be on different rates of pay. But in September 1931 everyone's pay rates were reduced by 10 per cent in response to the financial crisis that brought about the formation of the National Government.[129] As unemployed men on the dole received 17 shillings per week, army pay offered little incentive to enlist.[130] Pay rates were not raised again until 1938, when a fully qualified private soldier could then expect to earn £91 per annum. Even so, this put his earnings only slightly ahead of those of an agricultural labourer, and still a long way behind any other manual worker.[131]

On the eve of the Second World War James Brough, a journalist who was conscripted into the army as a militiaman in July 1939, described popular attitudes towards service in the Regular Army that would not have been out of place in 1914. There was, he decided, a

complete lack of understanding of life in the Army that exists in the civilian world. Up to now, to the average citizen the Army has been either faintly comic, with a background of jokes about the vocal ability of N.C.O.s, or something to admire in parades and listen to when a military band plays in a seaside bandstand. One of the jobs of the Militia, of course, is to bridge that gap between 'Civvy Street' and the parade grounds and barrack rooms.[132]

The army probably reached the nadir of its public esteem in the middle of the Second World War. By early 1942 there were nearly two million troops under arms in Britain. Unlike the RAF and the Royal Navy, they seemed to be doing little to win the war. As defeat followed defeat in North Africa and the Far East, press criticism echoed the Labour Party's pre-war critique of the officer corps as being class-bound and behind the times. Senior officers were likened to David Low's cartoon character, Colonel Blimp, and accused of incompetence and 'Maginot mindedness'. Some civilians resented what they regarded as the easy life that many

[128] IWM Misc 220/3152/2/8. The Jesse Short Collection. W. Gould to Gill, 13 Oct. 1965.
[129] *The Times*, 23 Sept. 1931.
[130] PRO WO 32/2984. Adj.-Gen. to Duff Cooper, 10 July 1936.
[131] PP (1937–8), XVII. Cmd. 5696. *Statement relating to improvements in the pay and allowances etc of the regular army*; J. M. Brereton, *The British Soldier: A Social History from 1661 to the Present Day* (London: Bodley Head, 1986), 188; G. Routh, *Occupation and Pay in Great Britain 1906–79* (London: Macmillan, 1980), 106–8.
[132] *The Essex Regiment Gazette*, NS. 7 (Sept. 1939), 170.

soldiers stationed in Britain seemed to be enjoying. The soldiers themselves, and their families, had many of the same complaints about the inadequacies of army pay and separation allowances as their fathers had during the First World War.[133]

The military authorities could not ignore such criticisms for they rebounded on the army itself, lowering the morale of many soldiers, who felt that their efforts were unappreciated.[134] The War Office responded by mounting its own publicity campaign in an effort to project a more favourable image of the army. In the spring and summer of 1942 the War Office's Director of Public Relations ensured that more newsreel stories appeared about the army than either of the other two services combined. They emphasized that the army was undergoing continuous and tougher training and that every effort was being made to ensure that the right men were selected for the jobs for which they had the most talent. By October 1942 the DPR wanted to give the maximum possible publicity to the infantry as a whole and to selected regiments by encouraging local newspapers to take a greater interest in their local regiment. He also tried 'to build up public knowledge of the personality of commanders and confidence in them' and above all, to publicize stories of the army in action. 'If we can get more theatres active and more news of the Army fighting, the whole problem of good Army publicity will become infinitely easier. The spotlight will then be shifted from some of the petty boring complaints of and about the Army at home.'[135] For the public image of the army Montgomery, and the Second Battle of Alamein, could not have happened at a more apposite moment.

Cardwell and Childers were thus only partly successful in rooting the regiments firmly in the wider community, and thereby improving the status of the regular soldier and the esteem in which he was held by his civilian counterparts. After 1870 most civilians probably accepted that the army was a necessary institution and that it was doing a worthwhile job. They were willing to cheer the soldier as he marched by, and to dip into their pockets to support his dependants when he was on active service. But the presence of Regular Army depots and Volunteer and Territorial drill halls scattered across the country did not necessarily mean that civilians had much real knowledge of the everyday life of the soldier, and what they did know they generally did not like. The soldier as an imperial icon may have been held in high public regard, but the army as an employer most certainly was not.

[133] Hillier, *The Long Road*, 40.

[134] PRO WO 163/86/ECAC/P(41)96 PUS, The Army and the Public, 31 Oct. 1941; PRO WO 163/88/ECAC/P(42)53. AG. 'Weekly Magazine for the Army ("Soldier")', 29 Apr. 1942.

[135] PRO WO 163/89/ECAC/P(42)138. DPR, The Directorate of Public Relations, 19 Oct. 1942.

CHAPTER TEN

The Regimental System and the Battlefield

One of the most damning indictments of the regimental system was written by a sailor. In 1904 Admiral Sir John Fisher asserted that

On the one hand we have the great sentimental feeling of the sacredness for the regimental system, and on the other we have the terrible consequent evil of Officers being practically ignorant of all other branches of the Service, than of the special unit in which they practically spend their whole lives. So we have Cavalry, Artillery and Infantry Officers all shut up in separate water-tight compartments for their whole career with the inevitable result of 'clique' in its most injurious form . . .'[1]

Some soldiers agreed with Fisher that the regimental system was a barrier to modernity and all-arms cooperation on the battlefield and made it impossible for soldiers to give their loyalty to larger, functional organizations. Before 1914, one officer asserted, 'Pride of Brigade, of Division, of Command, was impossible in the Regular Army, owing to the conditions of service, which were such that a battalion might form part of a different brigade every year.'[2] Such attitudes sometimes permeated the other ranks. Before 1914 cavalry troopers would rarely deign to speak to an infantryman in a pub:

Oh, we despised them. We called them the towies. We despised them. We despised the infantry till the war. Oh, yes, you wouldn't be a towie. Good Lord no! 'Oh he's no good, he comes from the towies.' We were damnably conceited, ridiculously conceited compared to other branches. We thought we were something superior to the Royal Engineers. And the Foot Guards too.[3]

This is only half of the story. It is too easy to exaggerate the extent to which regimental particularism stood in the way of modernity or inhibited all-arms cooperation on the battlefield. Similarly, as will be

---

[1] NAM 8704/35–85. Lt.-Gen. Sir G. F. Ellison MSS. Memorandum by Fisher to Esher and Clarke, 15 Jan. 1904.

[2] Maj. L. I. Cowper, 'Gold Medal (Military) Prize Essay', *Journal of the Royal United Services Institute*, 70 (1925), 208. See also Lord Carrington, *Reflect on Things Past: The Memoirs of Lord Carrington* (London: Fontana, 1989), 31.

[3] IWMSA. Accession No. 000314/12. Capt. P. Snelling, 40–1.

suggested in the second half of this chapter, it is also too easy to exaggerate the extent to which the regimental system acted as a prop to morale on the battlefield.

Officers and men held their own regiment in the highest esteem. Asked how gunner officers rated the Royal Artillery during the First World War, one replied, 'Right at the top, of course. It always has been since 1716, it always has been, I hope it always will be.'[4] It was also true that their disdain for other regiments could breed bad feelings between them. In 1887 the men of 2/Royal Irish Rifles and 3/King's Royal Rifle Corps descended into public brawls in the streets of Gibraltar.[5] Officers in some high-status regiments did regard other units with snobbish disdain.[6] A subaltern in 2/Queen's Royal West Surrey Regiment described the West Yorkshire Regiment as 'slummy' when he discovered in November 1899 that on the South African veldt they had allowed their standards of hygiene to drop so low that they were growing beards.[7]

But too much can be made of social fripperies. Thrown together in isolated colonial cantonments, even regiments of different arms of the service discovered that they had much in common. When the officers of the Scots Greys and 4/Armoured Car Company of the RTC were stationed in Palestine in the early 1920s, a Tank Corps officer remembered that 'They [the Scots Greys] were very good to us indeed, good and hospitable and kind.'[8] The officers of 7/Armoured Car Company and a battalion of the Devon Regiment struck up a similar friendship when they were stationed together in an isolated garrison at Razmak in Waziristan in 1932. 'They used to come into our mess and we used to go into theirs and we were very, very friendly. It was a most awful nice arrangements [sic] and station to be in.'[9] Rivalry between units on the sports field could be intense, but the moment the game was over, regimental teams were usually happy to socialize together.[10] Friendships also extended across regimental boundaries amongst the other ranks.[11] Soldiers were just like other people in that they lived their lives in compartments, and

[4] IWMSA. Accession No. 000490/06. Lt.-Col. M. E. S. Laws, 49.
[5] Horton, *A Brief Outline of My Travels*, 10.
[6] IWMSA. Accession No. 00000788/04. Maj.-Gen. K. C. Cooper, 21–2; IWMSA. Accession No. 000858/05. Maj.-Gen. F. W. Gordon Hall, 14.
[7] NAM 1999-06-94. Lt. L. D. Wedd MSS. Wedd to his mother, 20 Nov. 1899.
[8] IWMSA. Accession No. 000829/12. Maj.-Gen. N. W. Duncan, 32.
[9] IWMSA. Accession No. 000833/04. Col. W. B. Blain, 24.
[10] IWMSA. Accession No. 00906/06. Sgt. M. Finlayson, 6; IWMSA. Accession No. 000892/06. Col. G. J. Kidston-Montgomerie, 46.
[11] NAM 8107–18. Diary of Pte. W. J. Putland, 16 Feb. 1900; Richards, *Old-Soldier Sahib*, 92; IWMSA. Accession No. 004524/05. L. H. Porter Harper, 12.

were quite able to put aside petty rivalries and jealousies when the situation demanded it.

They were equally capable of offering loyalty to more than one institution. Loyalty to regiment did not preclude loyalty to larger military organizations. When they were confronted by a common enemy, regiments could sink their differences and develop a collective identity that transcended their regimental peculiarities. Soldiers who fought together regularly did forge a common identity that transcended their cap-badge identities. A gunner officer whose battery was affiliated to the Bays, and formed part of 2nd Armoured Brigade in North Africa in 1942, decided that

Much of the success of 2nd Armoured Brigade was because all the regimental groups had lived and trained together for three months. All the officers knew one another intimately and could appreciate what the other ones were likely to do. Although we all wore different cap badges we were all intensely loyal to the Bays Group.[12]

Even the suspicions that characterized relations between the RTC and the cavalry in the inter-war period were softened by the experience of fighting together. By 1945 the war had, in the opinion of one former senior RTR officer, bred a new feeling of fellowship between his own regiment and the cavalry. 'I was most impressed when I was in France', wrote Gen. Sir Frederick Pile in June 1945, 'with the feeling of friendship which I found everywhere between the personnel of the Royal Tank Regiment and the personnel of the various Cavalry Regiments. That friendship was no mean achievement and was born of the high regard each had for the other's work.'[13]

Divisional *esprit de corps* may have been difficult to conjure up but it did exist. This was exemplified by the fact that after both world wars many divisions produced their own official histories. Of the sixty-six infantry divisions that saw active service overseas during the First World War, at least forty-five had produced divisional histories before 1939. The proportion that produced divisional histories after the Second World War, sixteen out of the thirty-three divisions that saw active service, was smaller, but was still by no means negligible.

It is equally misleading to assume that regimental particularism caused the British army to shun new technologies. On the contrary, the British either led the world, or at least kept pace with the most advanced armies in the world, in their eagerness to employ the most modern high-technology weapons. By 1900 it had already adopted bolt-action magazine rifles, machine guns, smokeless powder, the electric telegraph,

[12] R. Dunn, *Sword and Wig: Memoirs of a Lord Justice* (London: Quiller Press, 1993), 279.
[13] LHCMA. Liddell Hart MSS 9/28/93. Pile to Elles, 7 June 1945.

observation balloons, and military railways. It was shortly to employ steam and motor lorries, telephones, radios, and aircraft. During the First World War the British were the first army in the world to deploy tanks on the battlefield. They were also ahead of the Germans in taking advantage of the skills of the many civilian scientists and engineers who had enlisted to develop new apparatus and techniques to enable their artillery to 'shoot off the map', thereby allowing them by the end of 1917 to reclaim the priceless asset of surprise.[14]

The army's commitment to developing and deploying high technology did not happen by accident. It was an essential part of policy at the highest level and was never seen as being incompatible with the maintenance of regimental traditions. When he became C-in-C in 1895, Lord Wolseley's objectives were 'to maintain the great traditions of the British Army, to further the well-being of the soldier, and to encourage the progress called for by the unceasing advance in warlike appliances and in military knowledge which marks this age'.[15] It was the very malleability of the regimental system that ensured that it was not an insuperable barrier to technological innovation, or even much of a barrier at all. The Corps of Royal Engineers were habitually the first regiment to be given new experimental technologies. They thus formed the first telegraph company and the first balloon company in the army. But infantry regiments did not have any objections to the adoption of new weapons such as bolt-action magazine rifles. And even a complete change of role did not necessarily disturb them. When 6/Sherwood Foresters were converted into an anti-aircraft unit in 1936, all the officers and 90 per cent of the rank and file opted to remain with the regiment rather than resign.[16]

The cavalry were sometimes regarded as placing regimental identities before the need to change with the times. This is unfair. After the Boer War, for example, cavalry regiments understood that they had to train both for mounted action, which was necessary if they were ever to encounter European cavalry on the Continent, but also as mounted infantry. They therefore adopted the same rifle as the infantry and many regiments took considerable pride in their shooting ability.[17] At least one

[14] I. F. W. Beckett, 'Victorians at War—War, Technology and Change', *Journal of the Society for Army Historical Research*, 81 (2003), 330–8; H. Strachan, 'The Battle of the Somme and British Strategy', *Journal of Strategic Studies*, 21 (1998), 79–95; H. Bailes, 'Military Aspects of the War', in P. Warwick and S. B. Spies (eds.), *The South African War* (London: Longman, 1980), 67; G. R. Winton, 'The British Army, Mechanisation and a New Transport System, 1900–1914', *Journal of the Society for Army Historical Research*, 78 (2000), 197–212; R. MacLeod, 'Sight and Sound on the Western Front: Surveyors, Scientists, and the "Battlefield Laboratory", 1915–1918', *War and Society*, 18 (2000), 23–46.

[15] *The Black Horse Gazette. The Journal of the 7th Dragoon Guards*, 2 (1895).

[16] *Regimental Annual. The Sherwood Foresters 1937*.

[17] S. Badsey, 'Cavalry and the Development of Breakthrough Doctrine', in P. Griffith (ed.), *British Fighting Methods in the Great War* (London: Frank Cass, 1996), 145–6.

Yeomanry regiment was experimenting with motor cars as early as 1906, and by 1913 British cavalry regiments in India were carrying out trials with radios to improve their ability to get reconnaissance reports back to divisional headquarters more rapidly.[18]

Nor did the cavalry's attitude towards mechanization in the inter-war period signify that they suffered from a misplaced sentimental attachment to the horse and an inbuilt technophobia.[19] Representatives of the cavalry called to give evidence to a committee investigating how to mechanize their arm in 1926–7 appreciated that the days of horsed cavalry were numbered, and were quite willing to begin cautious mechanization. But they also recognized that contemporary tanks and armoured cars had serious technological limitations. As RTC officers themselves admitted, armoured cars were road-bound, and tanks were still liable to frequent mechanical breakdowns and were by no means immune to hostile fire.[20] For much of the inter-war period there remained a job for horsed cavalry, particularly in the close reconnaissance role. In the late 1930s many cavalry officers did surrender their horses with some pangs of nostalgic regret. Cavalry troopers, however, often welcomed the change. Tanks did not have to be fed, watered, and mucked out three times a day, and the mechanical skills the army taught them were highly marketable when they returned to civilian life. But for both officers and other ranks, regimental loyalty was a positive spur to excel in their new role. Each believed that his regiment had been the best horsed cavalry regiment, and they were now determined to become the best mechanized cavalry regiment.

The real obstacles to mechanization in the inter-war period were twofold. Mechanization was expensive and it was difficult to meet the cost of new weapons without simultaneous cuts in the army's already exiguous manpower budget. Secondly, it was not necessarily an appropriate solution to all of the army's commitments. As the DSD explained in 1927:

We have to provide drafts for units abroad. It is quite true that the modern unit, as visualised, with fewer men and more effective weapons, may be very suitable under most circumstances; but we have to remember that a large part of our army abroad is practically a police force, that a small unit with small manpower, however effective may be its fire power, is not necessarily what is wanted. You have got to find guards and detachments, you may have to find duties in aid of

[18] ERM. ER 2069. *Essex Yeomanry Magazine*, 11 (Apr. 1914); ERO D/DU 783/3. Scrapbook of Brig.-Gen. Sir R. Colvin of Waltham Abbey. Press cutting 'Cars in Military Service'.

[19] B. H. Liddell Hart, *The Tanks: The History of the Royal Tank Regiment and its Predecessors, Heavy Branch MGC, Tank Corps and Royal Tank Corps*, i: 1914–1939 (London: Cassell, 1959), 200.

[20] IWMSA. Accession no. 000866/08. Maj.-Gen. G. W. Richards, 37.

the civil power, and what you want for these duties is man power and not necessarily fire power.[21]

If the British cavalry did not excel in its new role in the first half of the Second World War, it was not because of a lack of professional commitment. It was because government funding meant that the changeover from horses to tanks and armoured cars came too late for them to be fully trained before the war began.[22] Traditions that had been invented were not allowed to stand in the way of regiments excelling when they adopted new technologies. If they threatened to do so they were reinvented. For a short time after 1928, when they became one of the first two horsed cavalry regiments to be mechanized, the officers of 11/Hussars continued to wear their peaked service cap, riding breeches, and spurs in their new armoured cars. But discovering that their attire was anything but practical—their spurs tended to become entangled in the gear box— they discarded their spurs, adopted overalls and a new headdress, a beret, like that already worn by the RTC, but brown with a red band rather than the RTC's plain black.[23] To have failed to adjust traditions in order to adapt to changed circumstances would have been to fly in the face of everything that regimental tradition meant to the British army. As one regimental officer who had been instructed in regimental history in the 1930s explained, 'tradition's no good to you unless it leads to efficiency'.[24]

There are numerous instances of failures in combined arms cooperation on the battlefield. But to place the blame for them squarely on regimental jealousies is to turn a blind eye to the far more pervasive reasons that brought about such failures. It is to give too much prominence to one relatively minor cause, whilst failing to attempt to understand the far more significant structural problems that often hindered battlefield cooperation. Two factors in particular hamstrung the British army in the opening stages of major wars when units tried to cooperate on the battlefield: the absence of a common understanding of doctrine, and lack of prior combined arms training. A third factor, breakdowns in inter-arm communications, was also sometimes significant.

[21] PRO WO 279/57. Report on the Staff Conference held at the Staff College, Camberley, 17th to 20th January 1927.

[22] D. French, 'The Mechanization of the British Cavalry between the Wars', War in History, 10 (2003), 296–320; Maj. H. V. S. Charrington, 'Where Cavalry Stands Today', Cavalry Journal, 17 (1927), 419–30; Maj. E. W. Sheppard, 'Apprenticeship of Mechanised Cavalry', Cavalry Journal, 28 (1938), 165–70.

[23] IWMSA. Accession No. 000918/04. Lt.-Col. P. M. Wiggan, 11.

[24] IWMSA. Accession No. 000867/06. Col. E. F. Offord, 13.

Neither problems in interpreting doctrine, nor the difficulties in mounting realistic combined-arms exercises, resulted from the regimental system. But like the regimental system, they were products of the most fundamental factor that determined the development of the British army, the fact that it did not have a single clearly defined mission that it could plan for and train to perform. In the century after 1870 the army had a series of roles that it was required to fulfil. However, not all of these missions were of equal importance all of the time. Between 1870 and 1970 the British army fought only four wars in which it found itself fighting against an enemy that was equipped to the same modern standard as itself, and was organized into large combined arms formations. They were the opening months of the Second Anglo-Boer War, the First and Second World Wars, and the Korean War. Yet during the same period, hardly a year went by when it was not engaged in some kind of skirmish on the frontiers of the empire. And even during the 'big' wars, the conditions that troops had to be trained to meet varied enormously. In 1942, in earmarking divisions to be sent overseas, the DSD unhelpfully informed their commanders that, as he could not predict whether they would be sent to North Africa or Burma, they should try to prepare for both contingencies.[25]

The multiplicity of different missions confronting the army had important implications for its organization, doctrine, and training. In the realm of doctrine, it meant that drawing lessons from the army's own past experience was difficult because of the multiplicity of different situations that presented themselves.[26] It also meant that an over-specific doctrine might be a positive danger. In preparing carefully for one possible contingency, it might be learning lessons that would be counter-productive in a different setting. In 1879–80 Sir Frederick Roberts's troops gained considerable practical expertise in hill warfare against Afghan irregulars. But many officers who took part in the invasion of Afghanistan were cautious about applying lessons of the campaign to the quite different circumstances they might encounter if they confronted a regular Russian army across the same terrain.[27] The same point was made by the CIGS, Sir George Milne, who wrote in 1931:

Except that the fundamental basis must remain for all cases, that is to say that the Army must aim at discipline, morale, courage, physical fitness, loyalty and mental alertness, together with technical skill at arms, the different degrees of

---

[25] PRO WO 260/16. DSD to C-in-C Home Forces, 9 Mar. 1942.
[26] Spiers, *Late Victorian Army*, 245–9; M. O'Connor, 'The Vision of Soldiers: Britain, France, Germany and the United States Observe the Russo-Turkish War', *War in History*, 4 (1997), 264–95.
[27] T. Moreman, *The Army in India and the Development of Frontier Warfare 1849–1947* (London: Macmillan, 1998), 38–41.

activity demand large variations in training for leadership, in tactics, and in the application of weapons to war.[28]

Before the Boer War the military authorities were reluctant to issue specific instructional manuals suited to a single theatre of war or a single type of operation. Instead they produced arm-of-service training manuals that stated general principles that were supposedly applicable to any contingency, and then left it to senior officers on the spot to decide how they should be interpreted. The scale of the Boer War, and the fact that it compelled the army to bring together larger formations of units from different arms of the service than ever before, persuaded Lord Roberts, when he became C-in-C, to order the preparation of manuals for the guidance of officers leading combined arms formations.[29] The fruits of his labour appeared in the shape of *Combined Training*, published in 1902. In 1909 the recently created General Staff issued a successor volume, *Field Service Regulations. Part 1. Operations (1909)*. It was revised no fewer than four times between 1920 and 1935, but it never departed from the existing laissez-faire approach to doctrine. Each volume stated general principles, leaving it up to individual commanders to interpret them as they saw fit according to the particular circumstances they confronted.[30] In 1913 the rationale for this was explained by Brig.-Gen. L. E. Kiggell. As the DSD he had oversight of the production of all of the army's doctrinal manuals. He insisted that

we know that the problems of war cannot be solved by rules, but by judgement based on a knowledge of general principles. To lay down rules, rather than principles, for peace training would tend to cramp judgement, not to educate and strengthen it. For that reason our manuals aim at giving principles but avoiding [*sic*] laying down methods.[31]

This could be a recipe for confusion. In 1887, for example, the CO of 1/Suffolks, then based at Rawalpindi, was left wondering whether he should train his battalion according to the doctrine laid down in the latest edition of the *Field Exercises* manual published by the War Office, or according to local instructions issued by the GOC at Rawalpindi.[32]

[28] PRO WO 32/3115. Army Training Memorandum No 4A. Guide for commanders of regular troops at home, 1932, 29 Dec. 1931.

[29] PP (1904), XL. Cd. 1790. *Minutes of evidence...*, Q. 15852.

[30] H. Strachan, 'The British Army, its General Staff and the Continental Commitment', in D. French and B. Holden Reid (eds.), *The British General Staff: Reform and Innovation* (London: Frank Cass, 2002), 75–94; War Office, *Field Service Regulations. Part 1. Combined Training* (London: War Office, 1905); *Field Service Regulations. Part 1. Operations (1909)* (London: HMSO, 1909).

[31] PRO WO 279/48. Report of a Conference of General Staff Officers at the Staff College, 13–16 Jan. 1913.

[32] SRO GB 554/B13/4. CO's letter and memoranda book, 1883–1903. CO 1/Suffolks to AAG Rawlpindi, 2 Nov. 1887.

Doctrine existed only on paper unless units and formations practised it in training so that they could implement it on the battlefield. This was something that the British army found it difficult to do. The military authorities decreed that each year was divided into a cycle of training activities. In the winter in the UK, and in the hot season overseas, regimental officers and other ranks engaged in individual training, honing their particular skills and learning new ones. In the spring and early summer in temperate climates, and in the cold weather in places like India or Egypt, they embarked upon a cycle of sub-unit, unit, and, where possible, formation training.[33]

The time devoted to individual, sub-unit, and unit training could be frustrating for those charged with it. Range facilities and the amount of ammunition supplied for training were often inadequate. Soldiers could become skilled individual shots, but without sufficient facilities for field firing practice, where troops were taught how to fire at targets at unknown ranges, section and platoon commanders could not learn how to direct their fire effectively.[34] But even more disruptive was the fact that units were subject to a great deal of personnel turbulence. Officers and NCOs in home-service battalions might be absent on furloughs during this period. Parties of recruits were posted to home-service battalions from their depot at unpredictable and irregular intervals throughout the year.[35] A large proportion of men in a battalion were often newly joined from the depot, and they sometimes attended command manoeuvres in the autumn without first having done company or battalion training.[36] Home-service battalions were regularly stripped of men for overseas drafts and to perform barrack fatigues, so that companies with a notional strength of a hundred rank and file might have only a handful of men present for duty.[37]

This was a perennial problem. One possible solution was to imitate Continental armies and adopt the double-company system, so that even if a considerable proportion of the rank and file were absent, there were still enough remaining for realistic training exercises. The military authorities considered doing this in 1877 but they rejected it because 'All

[33] Spiers, *Late Victorian Army*, 260–3; General Staff, *Training and Manoeuvre Regulations, 1909* (London: HMSO, 1909), 6–8; General Staff, *Training Regulations, 1934*, 8–10; IWMSA. Accession No. 000905/06. Col. Sir A. Horsbrugh-Porter, 5–6.

[34] PRO WO 33/42. Report of the Committee on the musketry instruction of the army, 25 Oct. 1884.; PRO WO 108/411. Roberts to Under Secretary of State War Office, 20 Nov. 1900; WO 279/48. Report of a conference of General Staff Officers at the Staff College, 13–16 Jan. 1913.

[35] Col.-Sgt. L. Raven, 'A Practical System of Ensuring Progressive Instruction throughout the Year's Training', *Essex Regiment Gazette*, 4 (1912), 50–1.

[36] PRO WO 279/25. Report of a conference of General Staff Officers at the Staff College, 18–21 Jan. 1909.

[37] PP (1902), X. Cd. 983. *Report of the Committee*, QQ. 58, 2176–2217.

modern experience of war shows that troops under fire have a tendency to get into confusion, and that the presence of many leaders in the line of battle is then of the highest importance', and they believed it would spread the available officers too thinly.[38] Experience in South Africa did persuade some brigade and battalion commanders of the advantages of the double company, but it was not adopted until 1913.[39] Double companies were divided into four platoons, each commanded by a subaltern, assisted by a platoon sergeant charged with maintaining constant supervision over all aspects of the men in his platoon.[40] Even so, the problem of too few men in the ranks to enable NCOs and junior officers to practise the art of command persisted. In 1934 a platoon commander with 2/Manchester Regiment stationed at York found that he had only eleven men in his platoon, of whom only two or three were available for training. 'And so in fact you had very little chance to do what you'd joined the Army for, which was to I suppose you'd say to lead—rather pompous thing really—to lead men and particularly as a young officer to lead your platoon.'[41]

It was usually only in the brief period of formation training in the autumn that units participated in all-arms exercises, and even then their extent and frequency was circumscribed. With the exception of Aldershot, where divisional-size formations were permanently concentrated, units were scattered in small and widely dispersed garrisons, both at home and in the empire. In India in 1890, British artillery, infantry, and cavalry units were scattered around fifty-seven separate cantonments. Seventeen of them contained only a single British infantry battalion and only three stations, Meerut, Rawalpindi, and Lucknow, contained British units of all three of the main teeth arms.[42] Sufficient land for manoeuvres, both in Britain and in parts of the empire, was difficult, if not impossible to acquire.[43] Landowners did not welcome their crops being

---

[38] PRO WO 33/32. Col. R. Home, Memo., 14 Dec. 1877.

[39] PRO WO 108/253. Lt.-Gen. Reginald Pole-Carew, Report on organisation and equipment of infantry by the GOC 11th division, 17 July 1900.

[40] Anon., *Standing Orders of the Durham Light Infantry*, 20.

[41] IWMSA. Accession No. 004486/7. Lt.-Col. R. King-Clark, 2; E. Spiers, 'Reforming the Infantry of the Line, 1900–14', *Journal of the Society for Army Historical Research*, 59 (1981), 86–8; Ramsay, *Command and Cohesion*, 93–103; PRO WO 32/2382. Milne to Sir W. Birdwood and enc. Memorandum on Army Training. Collective Training period 1928, 26 Nov. 1928; LHCMA. Sir Basil Liddell Hart MSS. 1/322/32. Gort to Liddell Hart, 31 July 1929; Maj. M. K. Wardle, 'The Development of Regimental Routine', *Journal of the Royal United Services Institute*, 81 (1936), 538–47.

[42] *Army List* for 1890.

[43] H. Bailies, 'Technology and Tactics in the British Army, 1866–1900', in R. Haycock and K. Neilson (eds.), *Men, Machines and War* (Waterloo, Ont.: Wilfried Laurier University Press, 1988), 37; PRO WO 279/18. Report of a conference of General Staff Officers at the Staff College, 7–10 Jan. 1908.

trampled by troops, their fences broken, their woods cut down for firewood, and their livestock frightened or eaten.[44] Exercises were made unrealistic because large parts of the manoeuvre areas were usually marked as being out of bounds to the troops.[45] Some imperial stations, such as Egypt and the Sudan, had ample space for manoeuvres, although units tended to take advantage of it only during the cool season, remaining indoors during the warmest part of the day during the summer.[46] Other stations, such as Gibraltar, Bermuda, and Malta, had little or no space for realistic exercises.

These factors made it difficult for large numbers of units of different arms of the service to be brought together to conduct training manoeuvres and to learn how to cooperate.[47] This had a seriously deleterious impact on the ability of the different arms of the service to work together, something that was shown with painful clarity in 1891, when the army did mount major manoeuvres in Hampshire. According to Sir Evelyn Wood, the GOC Aldershot Command,

The failing most apparent is that of officers considering only the branch of the service to which they belong. Many officers have not sufficient confidence to give decided orders to the other arms of the service; thus officers of the same force were observed working in the immediate vicinity but independently of each other. Commanders of units neither asked for nor gave information to other units operating near them. Infantry when joining Artillery in action seldom or never enquired as to range.

When attacking strong positions it was observed that sufficient reconnaissances were not made, that time was not given for the action of Artillery fire, and that the Staff did not direct the general movement.[48]

The one countervailing force that might have been able to impose a single, coherent vision of doctrine on the army was the General Staff. But it was not established until 1906 and for a long time it failed to impose its will on the army at large.[49] Within months of its establishment, it decreed that unit commanders would remain responsible for the training and education of their officers.[50] This left unit commanders with considerable scope, as exemplified in 1920 when the GSO1 of 6 Division in Ireland issued

---

[44] PRO WO 33/23. Papers relating to the proposed camp of exercise, 1871, n.d. but c.31 July 1871; PRO WO 279/1. Report on autumn manoeuvres, 1891, dated Aldershot 20 Nov. 1891.

[45] LHCMA. Capt. L. C. King-Wilkinson MSS. Extracts from Western Command Admin. Standing Orders (1931).

[46] IWMSA. Accession No. 000918/04. Lt.-Col. P. M. Wiggan, 42–4; IWMSA. Accession No. 004485/05. Lt.-Col V. C. Magill-Cuerden, 11–12.

[47] LHCMA. Sir Basil Liddell Hart MSS, 1/238/6. Dill to Liddell Hart, 22 Mar. 1930.

[48] PRO WO 279/1. Autumn manoeuvres in Hampshire, in September 1891, 20 Nov. 1891.

[49] J. Gooch, ' "A particularly Anglo-Saxon institution": The British General Staff in the Era of the Two World Wars', in D. French and B. Holden Reid (eds.), *The British General Staff: Reform and Innovation* (London: Frank Cass, 2002), 196–7.

[50] Strachan, 'The British Army, its General Staff', 75–94.

training instructions, which, he explained, 'are not issued as an order to be rigidly obeyed, nor are they intended to cramp the style of officers who may have worked out a training scheme of their own'.[51]

The confusion that such a policy engendered was exemplified by Sir George Milne during his period as the CIGS. In 1927 he told a conference of senior General Staff officers that it was up to them to interpret the doctrine in the manuals as they thought appropriate and that 'on the question of training manuals . . . these are guides, purely guides and not to be slavishly followed'.[52] But two years later, he added: 'We avoid giving detailed instructions on every point, but those we publish are decisions authorised by the Secretary of State and we can have no variation from them.'[53] The General Staff could issue written injunctions, but it had only limited means of enforcing them. The post of Inspector-General of the Forces had been created in 1904 to oversee training. But the Inspector-General reported to the Army Council, not to the General Staff, a fact that caused the latter a good deal of resentment until the post was abolished in 1920.[54]

The devolution of authority that this allowed meant that unit commanders could on occasion flout higher directives, and sometimes even the orders of their own immediate superiors.[55] More normally, however, they had to work within a doctrinal framework constructed for them by the senior commander on the spot.[56] Within days of arriving in South Africa in January 1900, Lord Roberts issued his 'Notes for Guidance in South African Warfare'. They were intended to disseminate the tactical lessons of the first three months of the campaign.[57] From 1916 onwards, Haig's GHQ issued a growing number of publications designed to spread a common interpretation of doctrine in the light of the conditions facing the army in France. In 1917 it established a Training Directorate to assist in this process.[58] Individual unit commanders were usually required to

---

[51] ERM. Brig. C. M. Paton MSS 1. ER 8420. Hints on Training and recreation for detachments, 6 Division, July 1920.

[52] PRO WO 279/57. Report on the Staff Conference held at the Staff College, Camberley, 17th to 20th January 1927.

[53] PRO WO 279/65. Staff Conference held at the Staff College, Camberley, 14 to 17 January 1929.

[54] Robertson, *From Private to Field Marshal*, 186–7.

[55] PRO WO 279/57. Report on the Staff Conference held at the Staff College, Camberley, 17th to 20th January 1927 under the orders and direction of the CIGS.

[56] IWM 77/118/1. Papers of Colonel K. C. Weldon. Second Army School of Instruction. Object, 19 Mar. 1917; in author's possession. Capt. the Hon. J. St. V. B. Saumrez, Scots Guards MSS. Senior Officers Course. Bushey. June 1918.

[57] PP (1904), XL. Cd. 1790. *Minutes of evidence taken before the Royal Commission on the war in South Africa*. Lord Roberts, Notes for Guidance in South African Warfare. Chief of Staff circular Memo no. 5, 26 Jan. 1900.

[58] S. Robbins, 'British Generalship on the Western Front in the First World War, 1914–1918' (Ph.D. thesis, University of London, 2001), 261–9.

conform to the decisions of the next tier of command. In July 1918, for example, Maj.-Gen. H. C. Jackson, the GOC of 50 Division, held a divisional tactical exercise to teach his unit commanders a series of standard drills for the company, battalion, and brigade in attack.[59] Similarly, in November 1943 the commander of 4 Brigade gave his battalion commanders his own Standing Orders for War, laying down standard procedures to enable the brigade and its battalions to deploy for battle as fast as possible. They were intended to serve as a guide for battalion commanders to frame their own standing orders in such a way as they conformed to a common brigade framework.[60]

It would, therefore, be an exaggeration to suggest that unit commanders retained a completely unfettered hand to do as they thought best. But it would also be equally wrong to suppose that the military authorities succeeded in disseminating a single, common, interpretation of doctrine throughout every unit and formation in either world war. In 1928 Sir W. Hastings Anderson, the Quarter-Master General, noted that

The normal infantry officer gets his training rather from the mouth than from the book. He is probably training on the idea which has been handed down by tradition from commanding officer to commanding officer, from adjutant to adjutant, from sergeant-major to sergeant-major, and so on, and consequently very often training is more conservative in the battalion than officers are conscious of, while with the progressive issue of new training manuals they are naturally some way behind in actual book training.[61]

The cavalry was no different. A subaltern who served with 12/Lancers in the late 1920s believed that 'The Cavalry used to have manuals, there were Cavalry Training Volume One and Two which...I don't think we ever looked at, but they were there as a basis for good training. And of course we used to rely on being taught by our senior officers what to do, and they in turn had been taught.'[62] The doctrine that units actually trained on in peacetime was often highly personalized, but it was usually formulated at one level above that of a unit commander. In 1901 the CO of 4/Royal Fusiliers, then stationed at Shorncliffe, explained that 'We generally take our idea as to that [i.e. tactics] from the men we are serving under, and as we get enough tactical field days at Shorncliffe, we have a very good idea of what is required.'[63]

[59] IWM 77/118/1. Papers of Col. K. C. Weldon. Notes on divisional Tactical Exercise held on Wednesday, July 31st, 1918.
[60] RNRM. 2/Norfolks. 1939–1945 War. Standing Operation Instructions 1942–45. Various. 4 Infantry Brigade Standing Orders for War, 13 Nov. 1943.
[61] PRO WO 279/60. Report on the Staff Conference held at the Staff College, Camberley, 16–19th Jan. 1928.
[62] IWMSA. Accession No. 000933/04. Col. K. E. Savill, 26.
[63] PP (1902), X. Cd. 983. *Minutes of evidence*, Q. 1372.

This did mean that different units could develop different ways of doing things. In October 1899 2/Royal Dublin Fusiliers were brigaded with a battalion of 60th Rifles and 1/Royal Irish Fusiliers and 1/Leicesters when they attacked Boer forces on Talana Hill in Natal. One of the Dublin's officers recalled that

It was then, as afterwards, that the training of our men told and showed that we had not been dinning into the men's ears for 2.5 years in vain that they must advance in open order formation, take advantage of all cover, and fire independently when they could see anything to fire at. You may have seen in some of the home papers very flattering accounts of the behaviour of the regiment and others that rather cry it down, saying, why, if we did it all, were our casualties so much less in both officers and men than the other regiments. I can only put it down to the different training, and several times during the day it was most noticeable. Our men would, one at a time, get up and rush across the open, never two together, get over behind a stone or in a nullah, the officer, of course, going first. It was different in the 87th and the 60th. I, several times, saw them advance a whole section at a time, à la drill book. It does not do against good shots like the Boers. It may answer in Egypt.[64]

Finally, even when units had trained and worked together, 'friction', often in the shape of failures in communications, could wreck even the best-laid plans. When the Germans raided a company of 2/Leinsters in July 1915, the Leinsters accepted that 'There was no support from our covering battery, as the telephone wires had been cut in the bombardment.'[65] Similarly, an infantry-tank attack mounted in Tunisia in 1943 by 48/RTR and 1/6 East Surreys failed because the orders group to coordinate the operation was broken up by enemy shelling and a liaison officer equipped with a wireless set to link the infantry and tanks never arrived because his scout car became bogged down.[66]

British formations therefore frequently began major wars suffering from a serious training deficit. In 1899 only Sir Henry Hildyard's 2nd Infantry Brigade took to the field in South Africa having trained together as a formation before embarkation.[67] But when 'friction' did not intrude, when units did have the opportunity to train and work together in battle, regimental jealousies vanished. British formations could mount successful

---

[64] Letters of Capt. C. A. Hensley to his father, 20 Oct. 1899. *Journal of the South African Military History Society*, accessed on 20 May 2000 at www://rapidttp.com/milhist/vol66ch.html.

[65] Capt. F. C. Hitchcock, *'Stand To': A Diary of the Trenches by Captain F. C. Hitchcock MC*, ed. A. Spagnoly (Norwich: Gliddon Books, 1937/1988), 48.

[66] P. Gudgin, *With Churchills to War: 48th Battalion Royal Tank Regiment at War 1939–45* (Stroud: Sutton Publishing, 1996), 86.

[67] PP (1904), XLI. Cd. 1791. *Minutes of evidence...*, Q. 15973.

combined arms operations.[68] Even in the opening months of the Boer War, units that had recently fought on the North West frontier of India were able to practise sophisticated fire-and-movement tactics, and infantry could combine successfully with artillery to drive the Boers from their position.[69] By July 1900, for example, Sir Francis Howard's brigade had sufficient experience of operating against dug-in Boer positions that tactics had been reduced almost to a drill, and even recently arrived and inexperienced Volunteers could be successfully incorporated into an attack. At the end of July 1900 a company of Volunteers attached to 1/Manchesters were part of a force attacking a Boer position near Zandspruit, in Natal. One of the Volunteers, Sergeant Harry Hopwood,

heard rifles cracking in the front of us and before we knew where we were the bullets were falling all round us. The Colours [Sergeant] immediately shouted for us to extend to 10 paces and we did and then advanced by short rushes, lying down and rushing again. All this time we could see the puffs of dust in the ground where the bullets were letting [*sic*] and hear the whiz, ping and pay all round, but for my life I could not see a single Boer and could not see whether they came from the right or the left front. We had no cover at all until we got about half way up the hill and then we got to rocks and the Captain (B. C. P. Heywood) who was in front shouted to us to get under cover. The Boers fired a pom pom at our left flank and then our 4.7 which were in rear started on them and they soon quietened them down, and before we got to the summit the Boers were on their horses and off. I never saw a single Boer myself and did not get a chance of a shot but about half a dozen of our section who were round the right flank got some firing in and most of the left flank who had not to go as high as us also got in some shooting but we expect to have another go at them any day and I hope to have a better chance next time.[70]

Hopwood thought that the battalion's success was due to luck. In fact, as his own account demonstrated, it was due to a combination of realistic infantry tactics, good leadership by the company commander and his senior NCOs, and cooperation between the infantry and their supporting artillery.

Units of different arms of the service could reach a similarly effective level of cooperation on the Western Front in 1917–18. In July 1917 6/ Gordon Highlanders, taking part in the opening encounters of Third Battle of Ypres, were delighted with the support they received from their gunners. 'The accuracy and density of the barrage was beyond all

[68] See e.g. Griffith, 'The Extent of Tactical Reform'; D. French, *Raising Churchill's Army: The British Army and the War against Germany, 1919–1945* (Oxford: Oxford University Press, 2000).

[69] N. R. H. Evans, 'Boer War Tactics Re-examined', *Journal of the Royal United Services Institute*, 145 (2000), 71–6.

[70] NAM 7403-29-14. Sgt. H. Hopwood MSS. Hopwood to his family, 28 July 1900.

praise, and the pace was excellent.'[71] A year later a company commander, whose battalion was about to assault the Hindenberg line, noted the careful attention that had been paid to inter-arm cooperation before the attack, and which contributed in large measure to its success:

The army organisation in these days has certainly been brought to a fine art, particularly the cooperation between infantry, artillery, airforce and tanks. For the coming battle, each company commander has a barrage schedule, which when referred to in conjunction with a map, will show the exact position of the barrage at any given time. Every battery has, of course, a similar schedule with ranges and times shown. I am also to have a special 'contact' plane for the benefit of my own company. The duty of the observer is to fly over the ground where I am expected to be and to sound his klaxon horn. I shall then light red flares. He will mark my position on a map tracing, fly back to divisional headquarters and drop it by parachute; and then return to observe me once more.[72]

In both world wars a degree of uniformity in the interpretation of doctrine was gradually introduced by the establishment of school-based training courses. During the First World War a variety of army and corps schools were established in France. They not only taught regimental officers and NCOs the tactics of their own arm of service, but also enabled experienced officers to exchange ideas about how to effect cooperation between different arms of the service.[73]

But the institutionalization of this system was slow and halting. The lead was taken by the gunners, who established the School of Artillery on a permanent footing at Larkhill in 1919. In the 1920s it concerned itself with teaching the technical aspects of gunnery to gunner officers. But in 1929 its new commandant, Brig. Alan Brooke, introduced a new element to the syllabus, the handling of artillery as an integral part of the army, and under his regime officers from other arms came to the school to study the role of artillery.[74] The infantry did not get a similar school until the Second World War.

Finally, in wartime the system of regimental promotion did not invariably stifle the emergence of talented battlefield leaders. Some rigidities remained, but there is also evidence that, particularly in the First World War, there was a relaxation of the stranglehold on promotion governed by seniority within separate regimental lists. In wartime, leadership at

---

[71] W. Fraser, In Good Company, 142.

[72] Hawkins, Frank Hawkins, 113–14.

[73] Belhaven, War Diary, 135; Robbins, 'British Generalship on the Western Front', 249–51; A. Simpson, 'The Operational role of British Corps Commanders on the Western Front' (Ph.D. thesis, University of London, 2001), 40–1.

[74] PRO WO 163/25. Précis No. 1023. Organisation of the Royal Regiment of Artillery (Reports of Lord Byng's and Brigadier-General De Brett's committee), June 1919; LHCMA. Lord Alanbrooke MSS. 14/67/MCL/6/1. Notes by Mrs M. C. Long. Confidential Interviews, 1941–6. Interview with General Sir William Lindsell.

the unit level became far more of a career open to talent than it was at other times, if only because most of the arguments against selection by merit disappeared. There was far less compunction about promoting young officers to command. In the closing stages of both World Wars the average age of unit commanders in the teeth arms was between 28 and 36, an age when in peacetime most teeth-arm officers were still only captains or majors.[75] The military authorities were also far more willing to draft talented leaders into different regiments according to need rather than the shape of their cap-badge. Of the 689 acting, temporary, and substantive Lieutenant-Colonels who were killed during the First World War, 142 (21 per cent) were serving with regiments other than their own at the time of their death.[76] However, this practice was less common during the Second World War, when of the 478 Lieutenant-Colonels killed, only 21 (4 per cent) died fighting with a unit from a regiment other than their own.[77]

One distinction that did remain, however, was that between regular and auxiliary officers. In both world wars regulars had far more chance of rising to command a unit than did their Territorial counterparts.[78] Experienced Territorial officers were passed over. This was partly because they were often older than the regulars they were serving with, but it was also because many regulars were prejudiced against men whom they regarded as amateurs.[79] In March 1940 the Army Council decided that nearly 55 per cent of Territorial Lieutenant-Colonels were either totally unfit to hold their appointments or were too inexperienced to do so.[80] By October 1941, 253 Territorial Lieutenant-Colonels had been removed from their command, compared to only seventy-two regulars.[81] In practice few Territorial officers could hope to rise above the rank of major. Of 17,213 pre-war Territorial officers on the active list in October 1944, only 1,554 had risen above the rank of major, and by 1945 three-quarters of officers holding the rank of Lieutenant-Colonel or above were regulars or regular reservists.[82]

[75] PRO WO 32/13253. Memo. by Military Secretary, 25 Nov. 1946.

[76] These statistics are derived from the CD-Rom edition of *Soldiers Died in the Great War* (East Sussex: Naval and Military Press, 1998).

[77] These statistics are derived from the CD-Rom edition of *Army Roll of Honour: World War Two* (Naval and Military Press, 2002).

[78] PRO CAB 23/5/WC330. Minutes of War Cabinet, 24 Jan. 1918.

[79] Beckett, 'The Territorial Army', 141–3.

[80] WO 163/48. Minutes of the Proceedings of and précis prepared for the Army Council, 29 Mar. 1940.

[81] PRO WO 163/86/ECAC/P(41)94 Military Secretary, Age limits for the appointment of officers to command and their retention in command and employment, 30 Oct. 1941.

[82] PRO WO 163/430. Committee on wartime promotion in the Territorial Army. Report. 21 Oct. 1944; J. Crang, *The British Army and the People's War 1939–1945* (Manchester: Manchester University Press, 2000), 52–3.

The supporters of the regimental system can, therefore, take some comfort from the fact that it was not primarily responsible for the difficulty British formations sometimes had in effecting successful combined-arms cooperation. But they must also accept that their claim that it played a major role in sustaining morale on the battlefield requires considerable qualification.

The regimental system did help to sustain discipline and morale amongst Regular Army units committed to the numerous 'small wars' that characterized so much of their experience. The physical hardships involved in such operations were often considerable, but casualties were usually, at least by the standards of the world wars, comparatively light. The experience of active service could weld officers and men together in a closeness that went beyond the formality of life in barracks. In 1937–8 the 2/RUR took part in operations to suppress the Arab rebellion in Palestine. The battalion consisted of long-service regular soldiers, and an officer who served with them explained that

most of them stayed in the Army for twelve years, and many stayed for twenty-one years. This meant that they were very much, perhaps more, part of the Army and part of the regiment than they are now and it was very much a family affair.

Now in a case like this where a battalion went off on its own, without any wives or families, for eighteen months it actually had a most marvellous beneficial effect on the battalion—and I'm not being rude to the wives or families in this case. It enabled us all to get to know each other very, very well and I reckoned that by the end of the eighteen months that most of the officers knew most of the names of pretty well nearly all the seven or eight hundred men which a battalion then consisted of, and the seven or eight hundred men knew the names of all the officers, and there was a tremendous rapport, we all knew each other and there were no problems. We knew what the task was, which was fairly simply to keep law and order, and, when asked by the civil authority, to bash anybody on the head who broke the law, and if he didn't want to be bashed on the head then he had to be shot. It may sound brutal but in fact it was a reasonably nice, simple objective and the soldiers understood it.[83]

But not every unit succeed in inculcating all of its men with such a high *esprit de corps* that they were willing to suffer the hardships of colonial campaigning without complaint. A soldier who served with 1/South Wales Borderers in operations in Waziristan in 1937 remembered several instances of men wounding themselves because 'mountain warfare is the hardest warfare in the world and they were getting browned off sort of thing, and to get back from the front line they were self-inflicting themselves'.[84]

---

[83] IWMSA. Accession No. 004550/05. Maj.-Gen. H. E. N. Bredin, 9–10.
[84] IWMSA. Accession No. 00912/07. J. E. G. Jones, 25.

The role of localized recruiting in helping to sustain morale in 'big' wars has also been exaggerated. There is some evidence that men did find it easier to volunteer in 1914–15 because they knew that they were joining familiar local institutions. Fred Dixon joined 2/1 Surrey Yeomanry in 1914. He did so even though he had never ridden a horse because, when he was 4 years old, the regiment held their annual camp near where he lived and his mother took him to see their camp. The splendour of their uniforms and horses made a deep impression on him, 'and it took hold of my fancy so that when the war came it was quite natural that I should want to join the Surrey Yeomanry'.[85] But all too often the bureaucratic needs of the military authorities got in the way of the pull of local or family loyalties. When Jack Merewood was conscripted in 1939 he wanted to follow his uncles into the Royal Artillery. The army posted him to the RAC.[86] In 1950 E. G. Barraclough wanted to do his National Service in the RASC so that he could earn a Heavy Goods Vehicle driving licence. He was posted instead to the Royal Artillery.[87]

In large colonial wars, and in both world wars, when casualties mounted, localized recruiting broke down and cross-posting became commonplace. During the Boer War the cavalry had comparatively little difficulty in finding drafts, and the artillery was able to do so, although it had to employ ASC personnel as drivers and transfer RGA personnel to the RFA. But by July 1900, thirty infantry regiments had exhausted their regimental reserve, and could only be made up by cross-posting men from other regiments. The only infantry drafts left in Britain were those men who, month by month, were reaching the age of 20 and could be sent overseas.[88] The result was that localized recruiting collapsed in the second half of the war. In 1901 only 7,920 recruits were raised in regimental districts for service in the territorial line regiment attached to each district. But a further 36,179 recruits were raised in regimental districts who were posted to regiments outside their regimental district.[89]

At the start of the First World War, the military authorities did at least try to preserve local affiliations. In 1914–15 the first two New Armies were formed on the territorial basis. In December 1914 the War Office ordered each locally raised battalion to form a depot company to provide it with drafts to replace casualties. In July 1915 these were grouped together to form reserve battalions. In September 1914 Territorial units

[85] IWMSA. Accession No. 000737/16. F. Dixon, reel 2.
[86] J. Merewood, *To War with the Bays: A Tank Gunner Remembers 1939–1945* (Cardiff: 1st Queen's Dragoon Guards, 1996), 11.
[87] Barraclough, *National Service*, 3.
[88] PRO WO 32/9141. Minute by Col. P. Lake, AAG, 8 Oct. 1901.
[89] PP (1902), X. Cd. 962. *Annual Report of the Inspector-General of Recruiting for the Year 1901*, 32–3.

that had volunteered to serve overseas began to create second-, and later third-line units. The third line was used to feed drafts to their linked units serving overseas.[90] Regular battalions were supposed to draw their drafts from their linked Special Reserve battalions. But local affiliations could not long sustain the strain placed upon them by a combination of demographic realities and mounting casualties. Kitchener's third New Army could not be formed on a local basis. The largest concentrations of population were in the Midlands, the north of England, the Central Lowlands of Scotland, South Wales, and London, not in the rural counties of England, Wales, and Scotland, or in Ireland.[91] Even in the first two New Armies, some battalions from rural areas had to be filled with recruits from the large conurbations. For example, 9/Devons contained only eighty men from Devon. The remainder came from London and Birmingham.[92] Some second-line Territorial units were similarly made up with men from outside their own recruiting district. The 2/4th Seaforth Highlanders had 460 men from Manchester in its ranks.[93]

Once casualties at the front mounted, the military authorities had no option but to make this practice more general. In 1915–16 the War Office went to great lengths to secure powers to transfer Territorials between regiments, much to the disgust of many individuals involved.[94] In the autumn of 1916, following the introduction of conscription, the War Office went much further and deliberately broke the connection between particular localities and the drafting system. All conscripts were enlisted for general service and allocated to where they were most needed irrespective of their local connections. They did this partly because the sudden and heavy incidence of casualties that many units suffered on the Somme meant that the drafting system could not replace losses fast enough. But they were also concerned to spread the resulting misery amongst the civilian population who were bereaved by diluting the local connections of many units.[95]

Mindful of the lessons of 1915–18, the military authorities made far less effort to maintain localized recruiting in the Second World War. In 1933 the War Office abrogated the pledge that it had made to the Territorials after the First World War that in the next war they would not be sent overseas except as part of their own units. Henceforth every

---

[90] PRO WO 163/44. 30th meeting of the Military Members of the Army Council, 9 Sept. 1914; Simkins, *Kitchener's Army*, 313.
[91] PRO WO 163/44. 23rd meeting of the Military Members of the Army Council, 1 Sept. 1914.
[92] Simkins, *Kitchener's Army*, 70–1.
[93] Fuller, *Troop Morale and Popular Culture*, 42.
[94] PRO WO 32/5452. Draft of a bill to amend the Army Act, 11 Feb. 1915; Attorney General to Adj.-Gen., 29 Apr. 1915.
[95] Fuller, *Troop Morale and Popular Culture*, 43–4.

Territorial recruit had to agree to accept a general service liability and to serve after embodiment in any unit of the Regular or Territorial Army. In 1937 the War Office also decided that in order to provide the skilled tradesmen necessary to man a mechanized army, men with the requisite skills in Territorial units would be arbitrarily posted on mobilization to units where they could make full use of their skills.[96] A bill embodying these powers was passed as soon as the war began and by November 1939 the Army Council conceded that

it would be impossible to fill up battalions which were due to move overseas, to provide for transfers of skilled personnel or to provide reinforcements unless the whole Army was treated as a national Army and there was freedom to move personnel from one unit to another to the best advantage.[97]

At least until 1941, however, each infantry regiment retained its own Infantry Training Depot. But following the War Cabinet's decision to cap the size of the army in March 1941, the War Office closed all but twenty-five of them, and those remaining now had to serve several different regiments. The Adjutant-General, Sir Ronald Adam, wanted to go even further, to abolish the link between depots and particular regiments entirely, and to create a homogeneous Corps of Infantry. 'This will', he suggested, 'allow administrative flexibility and economy of personnel, and permit the simplest arrangements to be made for the distribution of reinforcements.'[98] His plan was the greatest single threat to the integrity of the regimental system since the Cardwell–Childers reforms. It was defeated, both because senior infantry officers at the War Office opposed it, and because the Secretary of State, the Conservative MP David Margesson, feared the political furore that its implementation would cause.[99]

But even though the British army avoided establishing a Corps of Infantry, regiments did become more homogeneous. In July 1942 Adam established the General Service Corps. Henceforth, all recruits were posted to a Primary Training Centre and received six weeks' basic training. They also underwent a series of selection tests to determine if they were suitable for more specialist training. Only at the end of his period were they posted to a unit or corps.[100] Men were posted to a unit or corps according to four criteria: their suitability as determined by their

[96] PRO WO 32/4645. Note of meeting at the War Office on 22nd February 1937.

[97] PRO WO 163/48. Minutes of the Proceedings of the Army Council, 27 Nov. 1939; PRO WO 32/2982. Adj.-Gen. to Director of Recruiting and Organisation, 21 June 1929.

[98] PRO WO 163/85/ECC 47. Adj.-Gen., The future of regimental infantry and machine gun training centres, with particular reference to FFC 36 and the formation of separate corps for infantry, machine gun, motor and reconnaissance battalions, n.d. but c.1 July 1941; PRO WO 32/9846. Adj.-Gen., Formation of a Corps of Infantry, 19 July 1941.

[99] PRO WO 32/9846. Minute by Margesson, 2 July 1941; PRO WO 216/66. Gen. G. Liddell, Inspector General of Training, to CIGS, 27 Sept. 1941.

[100] PRO WO 32/11519. Adam to Regimental Colonels, 28 May 1942.

scores in the selection tests; the requirements of the various arms; and their nationality; the 'need for fostering the county, T.A., and regimental spirit' was only the fourth and last criterion.[101] The result was that, by the mid-point of the war, as Adam admitted, the 'drafting of infantry by Regiments had completely broken down'.[102]

The consequences of these decisions can be measured by examining the local connections of the fatal casualties suffered by soldiers serving with line-infantry regiments in both world wars. An examination of the fatal casualties sustained by twenty-one Regular, Territorial, and New Army battalions drawn from seven different regiments during the First World War shows that regiments such as the West Yorkshire and the East Lancashire, which drew their recruits from large and densely populated conurbations, were comparatively successful in maintaining some local character.[103] Such regiments may not have been able to draw their recruits from their own regimental district, but they did at least manage to ensure that the great majority of their men were drawn from their own county. The result was that across the whole of the war, 75 per cent of the men of 1/West Yorkshire Regiment had been born or were resident in Yorkshire, 84 per cent of the men of 1/6th (TF)West Yorkshire were drawn from a similar background, and so were 67 per cent of the men of the 11//(S)West Yorkshire battalion. In these cases local connections obviously existed and meant something.

By contrast, regiments that could not draw upon large conurbations for recruits had greater difficulty in maintaining their local character, even if they began the war with a high proportion of local men. Seventy per cent of men serving with the 2/Essex who were killed in 1914 had been born or were resident in the county. But by 1918 the same figure was only 19.5 per cent. The 1/Hampshire saw a similar fall in the proportion of locally born or resident men in its ranks. In 1914 some 78 per cent of its fatalities were local men. By 1918 the proportion had fallen to only 34.5 per cent. Regiments that were localized in predomin-antly rural areas were filled out with strangers. Between 1914 and 1918, only 27 per cent of the men who died fighting with 2/Royal Welch Fusiliers were born or resident in its recruiting district, and only 20 per cent of the men who died serving with the 1/DCLI were Cornishmen.

---

[101] PRO WO 163/86/ECAC/P(41)106. Adj.-Gen., Common reception centres and basic training and selection of army class intake, 26 Nov. 1941.

[102] PRO WO 32/9804. Posting of officers and other ranks to their National Units. DRM to DAG (B), 27/6/41; PRO WO 205/1c. Minutes of the C-in-C's conference held at GHQ, 17 Mar. 1942.

[103] The units surveyed were 2, 4(TF) and 10(S) Essex, 1, 1/5(TF) and 7(S)Duke of Cornwall's Light Infantry, 1, 1/6(TF) and 11(S) West Yorkshire Regiment, 1, 1/6(TF) and 16(S) Lancashire Fusiliers, 2, 1/6(TF) and 11(S) Northumberland Fusiliers, 2 7(TF) and 9(S) Royal Welch Fusiliers, and 1, 1/8(TF) and 10(S) Hampshire Regiment.

In general Territorial battalions were more likely to have maintained their local character than regular or service battalions. The six Territorial battalions surveyed averaged 67 per cent local men across the whole of the war, compared to 49 per cent of local men in Regular battalions, and 46 per cent of local men who fought in service battalions. By 1918 cross-posting had become commonplace. A survey of other ranks who died in 1918 serving with fifty-six battalions drawn from twenty different line regiments showed that 31 per cent of them had been drafted in from another regiment.[104]

Statistics for men killed fighting in the Second World War show a broadly similar picture of a waning of local connections the longer the war continued. A survey of 8,304 men who died fighting with seven different infantry regiments during the Second World War showed that, at the time of their death, only 43 per cent of them were serving with a regiment with which they had a close territorial connection. In October 1943 battalions overseas could expect a draft of no more than twenty men per month from their own regiment; any deficiency had to be made up with men from other regiments.[105] By 1941 the most that the War Office could do was to try to ensure that Englishmen, Welshmen, Scots-men, and Irishmen were posted to units of their own nationality, and even then they were not always successful.[106] The figure for those in the sample who were killed after 1 January 1944 shows even more clearly the breakdown of localized recruiting. Only 34 per cent were serving with their 'local regiment'.[107] The extent to which this was a reflection of a deliberate policy can be seen when the pattern of service of the 1,198 men born in Essex who were killed during the war is examined. Only 236 were serving with their county regiment at the time of their death. The rest were scattered amongst fifty-nine other regiments, including five Scottish Highland Regiments, three Irish regiments, and all three Welsh regiments. Similarly, only 145 of the 417 Cornish-born infantrymen who were killed in the Second World War were serving with the Duke of Cornwall's Light Infantry at the time of their death. The remainder were

---

[104] These statistics are derived from the CD-Rom, *Soldiers Died in the Great War.*

[105] PRO WO 163/92/ECAC/P(43)109. Adj.-Gen. Infantry of the Line. Regimental System of drafting to units overseas, 4 Oct. 1943.

[106] PRO WO 32/9804. Director of Organisation to all GOC-in-C, Home Commands, 3 June 1941.

[107] These statistics are derived from *Army Roll of Honour: World War Two* and *Soldiers Died in the Second World War.* A 'close territorial connection' is defined as having been born in or being resident in the county in which a regiment was localized. The regiments surveyed were the Essex Regiment, the West Yorkshire Regiment, the Lancashire Fusiliers, the Northumberland Fusiliers, the Royal Welch Fusiliers, and the Hampshire Regiment.

scattered amongst fifty-five other regiments, including three Highland regiments, one Irish regiment, and two Welsh regiments.[108]

Heavy casualties and the collapse of localized recruiting did have a deleterious impact on morale and regimental *esprit de corps*. Soldiers could find themselves shunted from unit to unit, never in one place long enough to create friendships or build a sense of loyalty to a particular unit. In March 1944 Maj. D. A. Philips of 7/Oxford and Buckinghamshire Light Infantry lamented:

I wish that we could be reinforced by officers and men from the Regiment; there must be plenty of Regimental Officers who could be sent out to us. I know that Regimental esprit de corps is of tremendous value in keeping up the morale of troops when they are tired and conditions are not too good; but the policy of treating officers and men as so many numbers and posting them hither and thither at random makes the task of keeping alive a regimental spirit well-nigh impossible. Some of the new officers do their best to conform to our habits and customs; others seem to make no effort at all. Perhaps they are not to be blamed; they did not ask to leave their parent Regiments.[109]

Nevertheless that did not mean that regimental *esprit de corps* was entirely absent and thus failed to play any part in maintaining morale on the battlefield. What it meant was that regimental leaders had to work hard to create a sense of community where none had existed before. It also meant that officers and other ranks often came to construct the idea of the regiment in ways that were subtly but significantly different from the official version. J. M. L. Grover, who was commissioned into the King's Shropshire Light Infantry, and served with them for three years on the Western Front, remembered that the cheerfulness and camaraderie of his unit was

built up of [*sic*] the time in which people live together and if you have very heavy casualties the whole time you are building up a unit with new people.

Looking back to almost the last operation I was in 1918, we filled up then—after one battle—with reinforcements from all sorts of regiments; the Pembrokeshire Yeomanry, the Welsh Regiment, the South Wales Borderers—in addition to my own. And the first thing one had got to do was to try and sort of unite them all as members of your unit. And until you'd got a little bit over that atmosphere you didn't have quite the same spirit because that is what regimental esprit de corps is built on—which is enthusiasm for the team you belong to whether it's the Leeds United or whatever it is.[110]

---

[108] The statistics were derived from the CD-Roms *Army Roll of Honour: World War Two* and *Soldiers Died in the Second World War*.

[109] IWM 95/33/1. Major D. A. Philips MSS. Philips to his mother, 1 Mar. 1944.

[110] IWMSA. Accession No. 000046/8. Maj.-Gen J. M. L. Grover, 22–3.

How this could be done was explained by A. P. B. Irwin, who commanded a New Army Battalion of the East Surrey Regiment on the Western Front. He greeted each draft of reinforcements with a brief lecture on the history and traditions of the regiment and their new battalion. The result, he felt, was that *esprit de corps* in the battalion was maintained even after it had suffered heavy casualties. 'The chaps we got [in 1918] were gradually getting nearer and nearer to the dregs of the nation, of course. But they all seemed to become 8th East Surrey's in an extraordinarily short length of time. I suppose there was an optimism about us. There was certainly a feeling of pride because we never failed to do what we set out to do.'[111]

Regular officers and long-service regular NCOs had an almost metaphysical vision of what constituted their regiment.[112] But many men who volunteered or were conscripted during the world wars came to understand the military community of which they were a part in a different sense. For them the regiment was not an intangible entity with traditions stretching back decades or centuries. It was the men they were fighting alongside. What mattered to them was not the need to maintain the reputation of the regiment, but the comradeship of their mates and the need to stand well in their eyes. In 1916 Bernard Livermore was drafted into 2/20 London Regiment. At the start of the war it had recruited from Blackheath and Woolwich. By the time Livermore joined, heavy casualties meant that it had been made up from drafts culled from across the British Isles. But its morale remained high, largely because of the quality of the human relations that developed between its members. After the war Livermore

wondered if it was just a lucky chance that my bivvy mates were such fine friends—or whether a kindly Providence arranged things so expertly. Throughout my Army life I was continually brought into contact with men who became very dear friends and very close companions. Considering the fact that they hailed from many parts of the British Isles and were derived from all manner of classes, labourers, business men, clerks, professional men, they formed a true cross-section of the population. It was a very real privilege to have enjoyed their friendship.[113]

Similarly, John Gray, who served with the Fife and Forfar Yeomanry during the Second World War, remembered that

You lived, you ate and you died with these fellers. Or they died. I lived. Yes, it was like a big family. It's, it's difficult to describe. There was always somebody to

---

[111] IWMSA. Accession No. 000211/04. Col. A. P. B. Irwin, reel 4.

[112] *The Essex Regiment Gazette*, NS 7 (1939), 165.

[113] B. Livermore, *Long 'Un: A Damn Bad Soldier* (Batley, West Yorks: Harry Haynes, 1974), 97.

help you if there was anything wrong at home or anything like that. You know, you could always go and talk to your officer in private, and he had the means of sorting something out for you. And anything like that. You know, there is no doubt about it. The Army Welfare, even within the regiment, was something to be experienced to be believed, if you know what I mean. It was an incredible thing. I think the word they use is camaraderie, or something of that kind. Yes, you were all mates together. It's an odd thing. When I came out there was this feeling of emptiness.[114]

Soldiers on active service, particularly if their unit had suffered heavy casualties, came to regard their unit not as an impersonal and enduring institution, but as a diminishing group of comrades.[115] F. W. Allen had enlisted in the Norfolk Regiment in 1912 and served with them until the end of 1916, when he was invalided home and then posted to the Royal Dublin Fusiliers. But when he found himself on a draft amongst strangers he was not concerned because 'I soon made friends as all the boys were a decent lot, nearly all Irish, a few English here & there.'[116]

What mattered to Allen was the same thing that came to matter to Rayleigh Trevelyan. In March 1944 he was a young subaltern who had been commissioned into the Rifle Brigade but was then posted as a replacement platoon commander to 1/Green Howards at Anzio. When the possibility of returning to his original regiment emerged a month later he mused that

I'm not sure if my ties with the blokes in this platoon don't outweigh any nebulous loyalty I may have felt towards the traditions of the regiment.

When I originally joined up, straight from school and therefore impression-able, I had it dinned into me day and night that I now belonged to a crack regiment; only Guards regiments and one or two others in the Cavalry could be tolerated. As soon as I went abroad, what happened? Without the smallest apology I and a lot of my contemporaries were doled out as cannon-fodder to any mob that happened to be short of platoon commanders. No wonder at first we were very unhappy, and no wonder now we are bitter with the people who taught us that iniquitous rubbish.[117]

For men such as Allen and Trevelyan, it was the personal relations they had established with the men around them, not loyalty to a particular cap-badge or institution, that was critical in maintaining their morale.

The regimental system did not create an automatic bond of loyalty and trust between officers and other ranks on the battlefield. Soldiers in battle did not give their obedience automatically or unconditionally to an

[114] IWMSA. Accession No. 20202/11. J. Gray. Reel 11.

[115] J. F. Tucker, *Johnny Get your Gun: A Personal Narrative of the Somme, Ypres and Arras* (London: William Kimber, 1978), 110.

[116] RNRM. Diary box. War Memoirs of F. W. Allen.

[117] R. Trevelyan, *The Fortress: Anzio 1944* (London: Leo Cooper, 1956), 48.

officer merely because he had the attributes of a gentleman, despite what some senior officers thought.[118] During both world wars large numbers of young and inexperienced junior officers were posted to units. Like pre-war Regular officers, they had been given no specific training in leadership. 'You grew into it', one such officer thought.[119] Many relied on the quiet advice of their platoon or troop sergeant as they were learning.[120] The more perceptive realized that initially they were on probation in the eyes of their men. Their men might obey them because of their rank, but it would take some time before they were really trusted.[121]

In battle, particularly if they were inexperienced, officers exercised their authority through a process of constant negotiation with the men they were leading. In the autumn of 1943, for example, the 16/DLI received a new platoon commander who had recently been transferred from the Royal Artillery and who knew little about infantry tactics. The first time he took his platoon into action he ordered his men to fix bayonets and charge. 'You got private soldiers shouting "Go and get knotted" or words to that effect.' Fortunately he learned quickly, and a few weeks later 'he was into the groove and he was a first class officer'.[122]

The battlefield brought about subtle but important changes in the relationship between officers and other ranks. In the front line regimental officers continued to enjoy certain creature comforts that their men could only dream about.[123] But the social distance between officers and their men diminished in direct proportion to their proximity to the front line. The prospect of encountering a real enemy and shared privations were powerful unifying forces.[124] Whereas in barracks a private soldier could not speak to an officer except in the presence of an NCO, in the front line such formalities were often forgotten. 'You would get up against the sentry and be talking with him while he was watching and it was dark', Capt. B. G. Buxton of 6/Duke of Wellington's Regiment remembered of his service on the Western Front, 'and you were alone and he would open up with his problems at home. It gave a tremendous sense—at any rate to a very young officer like me—of the humanity, shall I say, of the men one commanded and a very real affection, personal affection, for the men you were talking to as you heard about his problems at home.'[125]

[118] LHCMA. Montgomery-Massingberd MSS 160. Dill to Montgomery-Massingberd, 18 Nov. 1939.

[119] IWMSA. Accession No. 16814. Maj. F. Crocker, reel 2.

[120] IWMSA. Accession No. 17229. F. Hazzell, reel 4; IWMSA. Accession No. 17230. Maj. S. Hornor, reels 3–4.

[121] Jary, *Eighteen Platoon* , pp. xvi–xvii.

[122] IWMSA. Accession No. 16593/29. T. Chadwick, reel 8.

[123] Coppard, *With a Machine Gun*, 69.

[124] Tyacke, *A Cornish Hotchpotch*, 102.

[125] IWMSA. Accession No. 000299/05. Capt. B. G. Buxton, 17.

Other ranks habitually retained a respectful reserve towards their officers and avoided undue familiarity. 'There is', Cpl. Frank Hodges believed, 'that gap, that social gap and you always say sir and salute '.[126] Even in tank crews, where officers lived, ate, and slept beside their men, they were still addressed as 'sir'.[127] But in the front line, regimental officers who were not actively unpleasant to their men, were cheerful, seemed to understand their job, and took an interest in their welfare, had little difficulty in earning their respect.[128] And those who really did act as a father to their men could inspire an intense loyalty. When he served in South Africa in 1901 with the Norfolk Regiment, Lt. W. J. Barton was 'really loved[,] he will talk to anyone like an equal & if you complain about anything he will do his very best to put it right. Any man in the company would do anything for him.'[129] Similarly, John Howard, who served with 2/Essex in 1917–18, had little time for senior officers but thought that the regimental officers he had known

were men. We had an officer who used to walk along the parapet with his cane in his hand as if he was walking down Piccadilly Circus. Really brave men they were, some of them officers. But, when, I couldn't say nothing wrong about the officers, they are brave men, them that was in the line, they were in the line.[130]

Another officer who won the respect of his men was 2/Lt A. Borwick, of 1/King's Shropshire Light Infantry, who was decorated for rescuing a wounded soldier under fire in Korea. One of his platoon thought that 'the lads would go to the end of the earth for [him]. He was a real, a real toff, a real gentleman. But, he had that quality, that aura, I don't know, but the lads, as I say, would follow him anywhere, they would. He was a splendid chap . . . His qualities of leadership were second to none.'[131]

But soldiers also deprecated officers who were recklessly brave, one commenting that 'a little more directing, and less examples of studied bravery, would have suited us better' for it would not have denied his company the leadership they needed.[132] A private in the King's Royal Rifle Corps who served in South Africa asserted that his officers 'Well, like damn fools they *led* their men at the start . . .'. It was only after they suffered serious casualties that 'Then they got more sense . . . The troops should be in front.'[133]

[126] IWMSA. Accession No. 13015. F. Hodges, 9.

[127] S. Dyson, *Tank Twins: East End Brothers in Arms* (London: Leo Cooper, 1994), 29.

[128] ERM. Ts. copy of diary of C. D. Bacon, 3 and 7 May, 13 Oct. 1917; Richards, *Old Soldiers Never Die*, 180.

[129] RNRM. Letters of Cpl. P. C. Richards, 4/VB Norfolk Regiment, to parents, 10 May 1901.

[130] ERM. Transcript of oral history interview of Pte. J. R. Howard, 2/Battalion, Essex Regiment, 1917–1918 by Robin Sharp, Dept of Records, NAM, 6 May 1980.

[131] IWMSA. Accession No. 18497/6. A. R. Bale, reel 2.

[132] Lucy, *There's a Devil*, 189.

[133] IWMSA. Accession No. 006545/2. A. S. Whitton, 6.

And not all regimental officers inspired the respect and confidence of their men. Officers who showed their fear too obviously were regarded with suspicion. One soldier thought that 'the men watch their officers closely for any sign of weakness, inefficiency or indecision. Lack of confidence in one's leader can have disastrous effects on morale.'[134] Marching into Afghanistan in 1879 Pte. John Facer of 30/Foot felt his spirits rising 'as I near Umballa, the only damper on my spirits is the thought of having to meet death with that illustrious of all individuals, Captain Gunter'. Gunter was widely disliked by his company, who took a quiet delight when he was publicly reprimanded by a senior officer.[135]

NCOs retained the same supervisory functions on the battlefield as they had when they were in quarters. But rather than supervise the behaviour of their men in a barrack room, they now supervised their behaviour in a fire-bay or slit trench.[136] Good NCOs, like good officers, tried to offer an example of stoical courage to their men. When he went into the line in September 1915 Pte. George Coppard was grateful that the lance-corporal in charge of his Vickers machine-gun crew was 'a brave cool customer from the forests of Hampshire. He was very fair, with hair almost white, and his cold grey eyes did more than anything else to help me control my fears. Nicknamed Snowy, he was a natural leader, and I treasure the memory of his friendship and courage.'[137] In Normandy in 1944 Sgt. Harris of 1/6 Queen's led his men because he was 'firm, competent, [and] kind-hearted'.[138] One of the most important roles performed by NCOs was to provide reassurance for young soldiers going into their first battle. When Albert Avis went into action in Korea with 1/Middlesex in 1950, he was struck by how his platoon sergeant and section corporal went out of their way to assure their young charges that 'You'll be all right son. You'll get used to it.'[139] It fell to the lot of more senior NCOs such as the CSM to try to maintain a semblance of more formal discipline by insisting, for example, that for their own protection they obey unit standing orders to wear helmets and keep their weapons clean.[140]

Once units went into action, the rapid turnover of NCOs meant that COs had to fill vacancies by promoting men on the spot who had proven themselves in action. Many wartime NCOs in the teeth arms, therefore,

[134] Tucker, *Johnny Get your Gun*, 41.
[135] NAM 8301–131. Diary, no. 975, Pte. J. A. Facer, H. Company 30th Regiment, 29 Oct. 1879.
[136] Coppard, *With a Machine Gun to Cambrai*, 20.
[137] Ibid. 36–7.
[138] R. J. Wingfield, *The Only Way Out: An Infantryman's Autobiography of the North-West Europe Campaign August 1944–February 1945* (London: Hutchinson, 1955), 14.
[139] IWMSA. Accession No. 18746/3. A. G. Avis, reel 4.
[140] IWMSA. Accession No. 19094/5. G. Paterson, reel 1.

had little notion of barrack-room routines. Successful front-line leadership at the level of section commanders depended on the human relationships of the men concerned, and the ability of corporals and sergeants to lead by a mixture of tact and personal example. This was exemplified by the habit prevalent in most units in the Second World War of private soldiers addressing all NCOs up to the rank of corporal by their Christian name: '[T]here was no "corporal sir" and spring to attention. It was Bill and Joe. Up to sergeant. Then you called him "sarge".' It was, in the opinion of one soldier who served in Italy in 1944, 'a totally different discipline, totally, from what one gets in barracks'.[141]

The regimental system thus made a clear distinction between commissioned officers on the one hand, and Warrant Officers and NCOs on the other. Commissioned officers were leaders; warrant officers and NCOs were supervisors. This was a source of weakness, for it meant that when heavy casualties had thinned the ranks of a unit's officers, NCOs sometimes lacked the necessary qualities, training, and authority to step into their place. At Spion Kop in January 1900, for example, the Lancashire Fusiliers began to retire because they 'had lost all their officers & had no one in charge of them that caused their retirement'.[142] Recalling a failed attack that his battalion made on the Somme in August 1916, an officer of 4/Suffolks, thought that

It seems to me hardly credible anyhow for Suffolk yokels to get as far an objective with at most two officers—who were probably both wounded. It also seems fairly obvious that with no officers they would not remain in a highly dangerous and uncomfortable place. It may be suggested that the sergeants and other NCOs should have held the men together. But the suggestion would not come from anyone aware of the ineffectiveness of the average NCO under shell fire. There are exceptions—and then they ought to be officers.[143]

On the battlefield, therefore, the regimental system did not play quite the role that its supporters or detractors claimed. It did not constitute an insuperable barrier to technological innovation. Nor did it completely stifle the development of wider loyalties beyond the regiment. It was only one factor, and not the most important, that inhibited combined-arms cooperation on the battlefield. It did help to maintain morale and discipline in regular units committed to low-intensity operations. But when it was placed under significant pressure during high-intensity colonial wars or both world wars, localized recruiting collapsed and unit commanders

---

[141] IWMSA. Accession No. 16593/29. T. Chadwick, reels 5 and 8.

[142] NAM 8107–18. Diary of Pte. W. J. Putland, 2nd Middx Regiment, 24 Jan. 1900.

[143] Capt. S. Gibbs, *From the Somme to the Armistice: The Memoirs of Captain Stormont Gibbs MC*, ed. R. Devonold-Lewis (Norwich: Gliddon Books, 1986–92), 48.

had to do the best they could to create a sense of community where none had previously existed. Some succeeded, and others did not. Furthermore, the sense of community that those who succeeded did create was in some respects significantly different from official notions of the regimental community. Rather than taking on the identity of a particular institution, officers and other ranks took on an identity as comrades. Some senior officers, albeit those of an iconoclastic bent, realized this. In 1946 Montgomery concluded that

most men do not fight well because their ancestors fought well at the Battle of Minden two centuries ago, but because their particular platoon or battalion has good leaders, is well disciplined, and has developed the feelings of comradeship and self-respect among all ranks on all levels. It is not devotion to some ancient regimental story which steels men in the crisis; it is devotion to the comrades who are with them and the leaders who are in front of them.[144]

[144] Field Marshal Viscount Montgomery, 'Morale in Battle', *British Medical Journal*, 2 (1946), 704.

CHAPTER ELEVEN

The Creation of the Post-modern Regimental System, c.1945–1970

In July 1950 King George VI presented Colours to three battalions of the Parachute Regiment, a new regiment that had been created during the Second World War and remained on the Army List thereafter. The presentation ceremony was surrounded by a reassuring air of historical continuity.[1] It seemed to suggest that the regimental system had surmounted the challenges of the war and that it was unchanged and would remain unchanged. The reality was quite different.

If post-modernism was the creation of a world in which the grand narratives of the nineteenth century, 'capitalism', 'socialism', 'liberalism', 'fascism', and 'communism', were no more, then by the 1970s the British had created a post-modern regimental system. The regimental system that had been fashioned by Cardwell and Childers was the product of one of those grand narratives, 'imperialism'. But by 1970s imperialism, or at least its British variant, was all but over. The transformation of the British regimental system after the Second World War reflected that fact. It still possessed many of the outward trappings of the late nineteenth-century system. Soldiers in different regiments still looked different. They wore buttons and badges that distinguished them from each other. They carried flags with different symbols on parade. Guardsmen still marched at a stately pace while light infantrymen scurried along. But it was not only the structures that Cardwell and Childers had created that were transformed by the amalgamations and disbandments that followed hard on each other after 1945. The inward meaning of the regimental system also changed dramatically in the thirty years after 1945. No longer could officers or senior NCOs confidently expect to spend their entire careers cocooned in the same regiment. No longer was their promotion governed by their seniority on a regimental list. No longer were soldiers expected, or in many cases willing, to regard their regiment as their real, as opposed to their metaphorical, family.

---

[1] *The Times*, 20 July 1950.

In 1966 the Army Board remained convinced that the regimental system was still a barrier to innovation:

a. The first loyalty is inevitably to the corps, regiment or unit; but a loyalty to the Army as a whole is lacking;

b. It is difficult to move men between corps either on recruitment or later, movement sometimes being resisted even when it is in the interests of the Army as a whole;

c. Duplication of function and demarcation problems between corps are difficult to resolve.

d. Any change involving the disappearance of a historic name is very difficult to resolve.[2]

In reaching these conclusions they ignored the fact that in the preceding twenty years the regimental system that had been created by Cardwell and Childers had been transformed almost out of recognition. Many of the regimental titles that they had created had disappeared, or were about to, in the wave of amalgamations and disbandments that accompanied the Sandys and Healey reforms of the 1950s and 1960s. Furthermore, the ethos of the regimental system had to a large extent been transformed by two other developments, both products of the changed strategic situation that Britain confronted after the Second World War. The leadership of the regiments was more visibly professional than it had been before 1939. And the rhetoric that the regiment constituted a family community had been forced to confront the reality that in the post-Second World War era most soldiers were in fact married, and room had somehow to be found for their families.

The regimental system that Cardwell and Childers created enjoyed its heyday between 1881 and the Second World War. During this period the dominant model of the system was the line infantry and cavalry regiments. In 1881, 76.7 per cent of the army's manpower was allocated to these units. Although the figure dropped to only 47.9 per cent in 1918, it quickly rose again after the First World War, so that by 1939 59.7 per cent of the Regular Army's manpower was in the infantry or cavalry. The typical soldier throughout this period was, therefore, a member of such a regiment, with all that implied for his *esprit de corps*. But after the Second World War the dominance of this model withered. By 1991 only 34.3 per cent of soldiers were serving in either an infantry or cavalry regiment. By contrast the significance of the corps regiment model had increased enormously. From accounting for only 23.3 per cent of serving soldiers in 1881, it accounted for 65.7 per cent by 1991.

---

[2] PRO WO 163/686/AB/P(66)33. Committee on the future structure of the Army. Interim Report, 9 Dec. 1966.

These crude statistics also conceal another important truth about the line infantry. Changes in its organization meant that, although the British army never established a single Corps of Infantry, the autonomy and distinctiveness of individual regiments was appreciably eroded after 1945. Officers and other ranks were not freely deployable throughout the infantry as they were within corps regiments, but the powers of the military authorities to post them where they chose, and to do so irrespective of regimental wishes, did appreciably increase.

The regimental system that Cardwell and Childers created was designed to meet the needs of an army whose main daily task was to police a world-wide empire. That task seemed to be about to end in 1947. With Britain about to shed its imperial responsibilities in the Indian sub-continent and Palestine, the Labour government took the opportunity to reap a peace dividend. Convinced that the main task that would henceforth confront the army was centred on the Cold War in Western Europe and the Middle East, they reshaped the army so that its primary mission was to deal with this threat. The army that the Attlee government created was different in four major respects from the army that Cardwell and Childers had constructed. First, in 1948 they reverted to the pre-Cardwell regimental system. Each line infantry regiment lost its second battalion. To provide for drafting, the surviving single-battalion regiments were organized into fifteen Brigade Groups.[3] Each brigade was an affiliation of regiments that were either functional, in the case of the Brigade of Guards or the Light Infantry Brigade, or regional, as was the case with the East Anglian or the North Midlands Brigades. Although regiments retained many of the trappings of their individual identities, each brigade had a shared training centre, one of its battalions being charged with the job of training all recruits for the brigade. But, in a policy that marked a second major departure from the dominance of the Cardwell–Childers model, officers and men could now be freely cross-posted between regiments in the same brigade.[4]

Third, the Cardwell–Childers system had sought to attract youths in their late teens, to keep most of them in the army for only seven years, and then to pass them into the Reserve in their mid-twenties. Only a small cadre of long-service NCOs were required to train and discipline them. But once the Labour government decided that they could not find the larger number of men they required by voluntary recruiting alone,

[3] C. Messenger, *For Love of Regiment: A History of the British Infantry* (London: Leo Cooper, 1996), ii. 156; PRO WO 32/11508. Form of drafting organisation in post-war army, 6 Sept. 1945.

[4] PRO WO 32/11508/APWP/P(46)11. Organisation of infantry groups in the post-war army. Method of drafting. By Vice Adj.-Gen., 22 Feb. 1946; PRO WO 32/11508/ECAC/P(46)62. ECAC. Organisation of infantry groups in the post-war army: APWC 25th interim report, 24 May 1946.

they had recourse to manning the army by a combination of volunteer regular soldiers and National Servicemen. In 1947 legislation was introduced continuing National Service, initially for a period of eighteen months. In 1950, under the pressure from the Korean War, it was increased to two years.[5] The presence of many young and inexperienced junior soldiers in the ranks meant that the army now required larger numbers of trained and experienced soldiers to train them. New terms of service were introduced designed to persuade soldiers to make the army their career. From 1952 they could sign on for a full career lasting twenty-two years, although with the option of resigning at three-yearly intervals. This had a transformative effect on the army that was comparable in its impact to the abolition of second battalions. If the military authorities wanted to retain soldiers for half of their working lives, all barriers to marriage had to be abolished. The regimental system had to be made family friendly.

Finally, the Attlee government transformed the role and organization of the Territorial Army. When the Territorials were reconstituted after the Second World War they formed a very different organization from what they had been before 1939. Between 1948 and 1960 the Territorial Army was manned by a cadre of volunteers and filled out by former National Servicemen who had an obligation to undergo periodic training with their local Territorial units. The strategic rationale behind this force was based upon the perceived lessons of the two world wars. On both occasions the British had been fortunate in that the small Regular Army had been able to hold the line while a much larger national army was raised and trained. In 1948, the CIGS, Montgomery, was convinced that Britain would never again enjoy such a breathing space. The Ministry of Defence assumed that by 1957 the USSR would have recovered sufficiently from the Second World War to constitute a real military threat to Western Europe and the Middle East. Montgomery's objective was to create a 'New Model' or Citizen's army that would enable Britain to put 400,000 men into the field at the start of a major war.[6] Until the mid-1950s, therefore, the Territorial Army had three main roles, and all of them implied that relations between the regular and auxiliary armies would be closer than ever. They were to reinforce British forces in Western Europe and the Middle East, to prepare for general contingencies elsewhere overseas, and to provide forces for home defence and to support the civil defence services in the event of a nuclear attack.[7]

[5] L. V. Scott, *Conscription and the Attlee Governments: The Politics and Policy of National Service 1945–51* (Oxford: Oxford University Press, 1993), *passim*.

[6] PRO WO 216/270. Press conference, the National Army, 30 Sept. 1948; PRO WO 216/236. Notes by Adj.-Gen. on the future army organisation, 6 Oct. 1947.

[7] PRO WO 32/15067. Brig. G. F. Hutchinson to Maj.-Gen. V. G. Campbell, 21 Sept. 1956.

The essentials of the Cardwell–Childers regimental system had endured for nearly seventy years. The Labour government's reforms lasted for barely a decade. The 1948 model of the regimental system was a failure because the strategic premiss upon which it was based was quickly proved to be false. The Cold War was not confined to Western Europe. Britain did not shed its extra-European military responsibilities when India was given its independence. Between 1949 and 1970 the British mounted no fewer than thirty-five overseas military operations in more than twenty countries, in nearly every major region of the world. Some were over quickly and met almost no resistance. But others, such as the campaigns in Malaya, Cyprus, Kenya, and Aden, became prolonged military commitments.[8] The Brigade Group system was designed 'to meet drafting problems without recourse to the introduction of a Corps of Infantry. One of the objects, therefore, was to produce drafting flexibility without dealing too serious a blow against regimental traditions.'[9] The system did give the military authorities a large degree of flexibility in posting men, but at the expense of regimental *esprit de corps*. But it could not meet the demands placed on it by the heavy overseas deployments that characterized the army's experience from the Korean War onwards. Regular soldiers were usually posted to the regiment of their choice, but National Servicemen were arbitrarily posted to one of the regiments in the group into which they had been called up. It was quite possible that a National Serviceman might never serve with the regiment that he originally opted to join because after training he could be posted to any of the regiments in his group.[10]

As the experience of both world wars suggested, it was possible for some units to absorb men from several different regiments and weld them into an effective fighting force. When 1/Suffolks were posted to Malaya in 1949 to take part in counter-insurgency operations against communist guerrillas, the battalion commander explained its success by virtue of the fact that it found ways 'to absorb soldiers from other Regiments and especially to imbue the many National Servicemen (conscripts) with his pride in his Regiment[; this was] the foundation from which success flowed'.[11] But many others did not, and the Korean War showed that even the Brigade Group organization was still too small to meet the drafting needs of infantry regiments. In 1950 several regiments had to be reinforced by drafts from outside their group.[12] When 1/Middlesex

[8] J. van Wingen and H. K. Tillema, 'British Military Intervention after World War Two: Militance in a Second-Rank Power', *Journal of Peace Research*, 17 (1980), 291–303.

[9] PRO WO 32/11534. Minutes, the 227 meeting of the ECAC, 13 Sept. 1946.

[10] Capt. W. K. B. Crawford, 'Future of Regimental Pride', *Army Quarterly*, 58 (1949), 241.

[11] SRO GB 554/Y1/304a. Brig. I. L. Wight, Reflections of a Battalion Commander in Malaya, n.d.

[12] PRO WO 32/14637. Brig. D. S. Gordon to Gen. Sir B. Paget, 18 Jan. 1952.

was posted with only one week's notice from Hong Kong to Korea in 1950, it had to leave behind any National Servicemen under the age of 19 and make up its numbers from two other regiments with which it had no links.[13] When 1/Royal Norfolks were posted to Korea its own East Anglian brigade could not supply sufficient drafts 'and we were then increased by soldiers from the Home Counties Brigade'.[14] Local, regional, and sometimes even national recruiting went out of the window at times. According to a soldier who served with them shortly after the Second World War, 'When I was in the Black Watch they had a saying about the Black Watch that it's a good English regiment. There's more Englishmen in the Black Watch than there was Scotsmen.'[15]

In 1956 a War Office committee chaired by the DCIGS, Sir Richard Hull, suggested the only way to overcome the drafting problem and maintain regimental *esprit de corps* was to organize the line infantry into nineteen large regiments, each of three battalions and a depot. While one battalion was in the UK, another would be in Germany, and the third in another overseas garrison.[16] But before any decision had been taken, the army was overtaken by the Sandys reforms. By 1957, in the wake of the Suez debacle, the Macmillan government decided that defence was consuming too large a share of Britain's gross domestic product. The Cold War struggle against the USSR would be prolonged, and a robust economy was essential if Britain was to stay the course.[17] The Sandys White Paper, published in April 1957, promised to abolish National Service and reduce the army to 165,000 men. A subsequent White Paper, issued in July, explained the consequences of this for the army. It would lose fifty-one teeth-arm units.[18] The number of infantry battalions was reduced from seventy-seven to sixty, the number of cavalry regiments from twenty-six to twenty, and artillery units from fifty-three to thirty-two.[19] About 5,000 officers of the rank of Major and above, and 10,000 regular NCOs, were made redundant.[20]

In the midst of the anguish caused by the reductions and amalgamations forced on the army by Sandys, the CIGS, Sir Gerald Templer, was

---

[13] IWMSA Accession No. 9537/4. Lt.-Col. A. M. Man, reel 1.

[14] IWMSA Accession No. 18047/4. Brig. W. C. Deller, reel 3.

[15] IWMSA Accession No. 18347/5. J. L. Fairhurst, reel 5.

[16] PRO WO 32/17321. Report of the committee on the organisation of the army, 1 Oct. 1956.

[17] W. Rees, 'The 1957 Defence White Paper: New Priorities in British Defence Policy', *Journal of Strategic Studies*, 12 (1989), 215–29.

[18] PP (1956–7), XII. Cmnd. 230. The future organisation of the army, July 1957.

[19] PRO WO 163/634/AC/P(57)16. DCGS, The Long Term Order of Battle of the Army, 19 Mar. 1957; PRO WO 163/634/AC/P(57)20. DCGS, Statement on Disbandments, 29 Mar. 1957.

[20] PRO WO 163/634/AC/P(57)19. Adj.-Gen., Officers and other ranks prematurely retired on redundancy—compensation terms, 25 Mar. 1957.

reluctant to force the infantry into a further series of shotgun marriages to implement Hull's recommendations.[21] He took soundings from amongst up-and-coming officers at the Imperial Defence College and the Staff College, and discovered that only a minority wanted to see the existing brigades evolve into 'large regiments'. He therefore concluded that, as the changes that were about to overtake the infantry were so traumatic, it would be too much to expect them to swallow the 'large regiments' simultaneously. Initially, therefore, he opted to reorganize the Brigade Group system so as to facilitate its evolution towards large regiments at some unspecified date in the future. To facilitate the emergence of a brigade *esprit de corps* each brigade was to have a common cap-badge, but its constituent regiments would retain their identities as named regiments and keep their own special forms of dress, subject to some modification in those regiments that were about to be amalgamated. Officers would be gazetted into a regiment, but other ranks would enlist into a brigade. There would be a common seniority roll for officers of the rank of Major and above, but cross-postings of lower-ranking officers and men between regiments in the same brigade would be kept to minimum.[22] Each of the brigades that came into existence in April 1958 had three or four battalions, one or two of which were formed by amalgamating existing regiments. Eleven of the brigades conformed to a geographical logic, but the remaining four (the Light Infantry, Fusiliers, Green Jacket, Parachute and Brigade of Guards) were the product of historical association or functional criteria.[23]

Templer's goal of a gradual evolution from brigades to large regiments was not achieved. By 1966 only three large regiments had been formed, the Royal Green Jackets, the Royal Anglian Regiment, and the Queen's Regiment.[24] The Ministry of Defence welcomed these developments and continued to recognize the logic of transforming the brigades into large regiments, but the political furore that had accompanied the Sandys reforms made them reluctant to act precipitately.[25] The remainder of the infantry was organized into eleven brigades.

By the mid-1960s this compromise could no longer be sustained. Some battalions had three rifle companies, others could only muster two, the quality of officers attracted to different regiments was variable, and the free movement of officers between regiments in brigades was sometimes

---

[21] PRO WO 32/16852/AC/M(57)13: Confidential Annex to Minutes of the Army Council, 20 May 1957.

[22] PRO WO 32/16852/AC/M(57)14. Confidential Annex to Minutes of the Army Council, 27 May 1957.

[23] The Highland, Lowland, Welsh and Lancastrian, Home Counties, Foresters, East Anglian, Wessex, Yorkshire, Mercian, Northern Irish Brigades.

[24] Messenger, *For Love of Regiment*, ii. 176–7.

[25] PRO WO 163/660/AC/G(61)58. Minute, 27 Feb. 1961.

opposed by the Colonels of regiments. Above all, it was expensive and costly, for each brigade or large regiment had its own training depot.[26] In December 1966 the Army Board therefore charged a committee under the DCIGS, Sir Charles Harington, 'to make a radical examination of the overall structure of the Army and to recommend what the shape of the Army should be in the 1970s within certain limits of size'.[27] It produced an interim report in December 1966 and a second one in June 1967.

This seemed to be an ideal moment to effect major reforms. Since the disbandment of second battalions, the army had struggled to fulfil two missions, to sustain a force inside Western Europe to fight a major conventional and nuclear war, and to sustain another force in Africa and Asia to take part in a series of counter-insurgency operations. But with the empire finally on the verge of liquidation, it seemed as if in future it could focus on just the first of these missions. 'The prospect is that', Harington concluded, 'because of economic pressures and revised political assumptions, the army of the future will be substantially based in the UK and elsewhere in Europe. The changes which are likely to result will be as great as any the Army had yet faced in peacetime.'[28]

The committee's aim was to produce a flexible manning system that would enable the army to expand or contract in the future without producing the upheavals and heart-burning that had characterized previous periods of reorganization. They also wanted a system that would allow the transfer of officers and men between regiments to iron out some of the imbalances in the numbers and quality of personnel serving with different regiments. Such a system would also, the committee hoped, have the additional benefit that it would break down 'the parochialism which is a feature of the present army [and which] would become more serious if the size of the Army had to be significantly reduced'.[29] The Corps regiments already had this and were left largely untouched. The division that had existed in the RAC since 1938 between its Cavalry and RTR wings was ended. Regiments retained their titles and cap-badges but henceforth officers were gazetted, not into a regiment but onto a common RAC roll, although they would normally be allowed to serve with one regiment for as long as possible. Other ranks were also placed on a common corps roll and could be posted at will between regiments.[30]

[26] PRO WO 163/686/AB/P(66)33. Committee on the future structure of the Army. Interim Report, 9 Dec. 1966.

[27] Ibid.

[28] PRO WO 163/691/AB/G(67)33. Committee on the Future Structure of the Army. Second Report, 29 June 1967.

[29] Ibid.

[30] Ibid.; PRO WO 163/691/AB/M(67)10.Confidential annex to the Minutes 48th meeting Army Board, 28 July1967.

Most of Harington's work, however, focused on the infantry. The committee rejected allowing the brigades to evolve into large regiments, convinced that they would still be too small to meet future manning needs. Nor did they embrace a single Corps of Infantry.

20. National and territorial affiliations together with traditional ceremonial continue to play some part in the life and character of the nation. As such they cannot and should not be discarded without convincing reasons.

21. There is no doubt that tradition, regimental history and customs are of considerable help to the maintenance of morale. They probably mean more to the officer and senior NCO than the soldier but it is on the officer and senior NCO that unit morale largely depends. To discard regimental traditions therefore may well have an effect on officer recruiting.[31]

Instead they recommended grouping the existing large regiments and brigades into a smaller number of divisions, each of which would have access to at least one of the army's main recruiting areas. This represented a sensible concession to the demographic realities of mid-twentieth-century Britain. By 1951, 80 per cent of the population were living in towns, and half the population was concentrated in just seven great conurbations—Greater London, the West Midlands, South-East Lancashire, Merseyside, the West Riding of Yorkshire, Tyneside, and Clydeside—and that by 1966 the Regular Army was taking 45 per cent of its recruits from these areas.[32] It also reflected the fact that the growth of a consumer culture and greater physical mobility meant that people tended less readily to identify with local or regional institutions than they had once done. This was reflected in an investigation by the Army Board in 1966 that discovered that only a quarter of recruits expressed a strong preference to join a particular regiment or corps.[33]

Initially each division was to have between eight and ten battalions and eventually, after any reductions in the overall size of the army, not fewer than six. It would have a single depot that would train recruits for the whole division, and a HQ which, under the control of the MOD, would manage postings and recruiting. All officers and other ranks would be on a common divisional roll and free movement of officers, NCOs, and other ranks between regiments in the division would be normal. Almost the only major concession to tradition was that regiments were to retain their existing titles.[34] In 1967 the Army Board accepted a

[31] PRO WO 163/686/AB/P(66)33. Committee on the future structure of the Army. Interim Report, 9 Dec. 1966.

[32] A. Marwick, *British Society since 1945* (London: Penguin, 2003), 15; PRO WO 163/686. AB/P(66)33. Committee on the future structure of the Army. Interim Report. Appendix G, 9 Dec. 1966.

[33] PRO WO 163/686/AB/M(66)13. Minutes of 39th meeting of the Army Board, 21 Dec. 1966.

[34] Ibid.

divisional system composed of six divisions, the Guards, the Queen's, the King's, the Prince of Wales's, the Scottish, and the Light divisions. The Parachute Regiment and the Special Air Service alone stood outside the system.[35]

By 1971, there was little left of the structure of the regimental system that Cardwell and Childers had established. Following another series of reductions announced in 1967, the Regular Army was left with six large infantry regiments each comprising three battalions; there were eleven regiments each of a single battalion that had been formed by the amalgamation of two regiments, and there were eleven regiments each of a single battalion continuing from before 1957.[36] Only five regiments could claim an entirely pure lineage dating back to their foundation,[37] and only six of Cardwell's creations had not suffered some form of amalgamation.[38] This reorganization was followed between 1972 and 1975 by equally far-reaching changes in the structure of local government that destroyed many of the historic county and city communities upon which Cardwell and Childers had tried to localize their regiments. Together they meant that by the early 1970s the close and enduring links between a regular regiment and a particular local community such as Cardwell and Childers had envisaged had been sundered.

The Territorial Army did not escape unscathed from this process of restructuring. If it was to fulfil its role as the cornerstone of the Citizen's Army that Montgomery wanted to establish, it needed to create by April 1949 a cadre of between 150,000 and 175,000 volunteers. Before 1939 Territorial Army volunteers were in their late teens, with no family responsibilities. But in 1947 the force wanted older men with war experience to serve as leaders and instructors for the National Servicemen. The government offered various inducements, which included granting civil servants who joined extra holidays to cover their training, and it exempted the bounty paid to trained men from income tax.[39] But, anxious to re-establish themselves in civilian life, few men came forward. They had already faced long separations from families, and were working long hours for good pay in industry. Even those who did volunteer tended

---

[35] PRO WO 163/691. Report of a Committee on the Future Structure of the Army. Recommendations on the infantry, 15 Feb. 1967; PRO WO 163/691/AB/M(67)2. Minutes of 41st meeting of the Army Board, 23 Feb. 1967.

[36] M. Yardley and D. Sewell, *A New Model Army* (London: W. H. Allen, 1989), 44; PP (1966–7), LIII. Cmnd. 3357. *Supplementary Statement on Defence Policy 1967.*

[37] The Royal Scots, the Green Howards, the Cheshire Regiment, the Royal Welch Fusiliers, and the King's Own Scottish Borderers.

[38] Messenger, *For Love of Regiment*, ii. 189.

[39] *The Eagle. The Journal of the Essex Regiment*, 10 (1947), 112–13.

to serve for only a few years and to give up once they were married.[40] Recruiting began in May 1947, but by the end of the year only 7,040 officers and 31,513 other ranks had enlisted and recruiting had fallen to only 1,500 per month, barely a tenth of what was needed.

Throughout the 1950s Territorial officers had to work hard to fill their establishment of volunteers. In the 1950s a battery commander of the South Nottinghamshire Hussars Yeomanry held recruiting drives at local fetes and spent a good deal of his time with a gun standing in the market place in Nottingham trying to persuade men to join the regiment.[41] At the end of 1961 the regiment was the best recruited Territorial unit in Northern Command, but it was still only 75 per cent up to establishment. Some units, like 4/Norfolks, promoted 'the idea of the Territorial Army as a sort of club rather than a fighting force. I suppose that was to attract people in. But it was not very successful at that.'[42] Although dances and social evenings did promote a sense of comradeship, 'The comradeship which comes from good, hard, interesting training is far more important.'[43] And in too many instances it was that which units could not provide.

Hamstrung by chronic under-recruitment, the Territorials were hardly in a position to resist the changes thrust upon them following the Sandys reorganization of the Regular Army and the abolition of National Service. By the late 1950s it was widely anticipated that nuclear war would be over so quickly that there would be no time to mobilize the existing Territorial divisions, and even if they could be mobilized quickly, there was no money to modernize their ageing Second World War vintage equipment. The consequent reconstruction of the auxiliary army took place in two stages. In 1959–60 the Army Council considered how to reduce it from a force of 400,000 volunteers and former National Servicemen to an all-volunteer force of 123,000 men. In July 1960 they announced that forty-six artillery units, twelve Royal Engineer units, two Royal Signals units, and eighteen infantry battalions would be cut from the order of battle, but that most of the reductions would be carried out by amalgamations rather than disbandments. Units were chosen for disbandment, amalgamation, or survival according to operational needs and their recruiting record and future potential to find recruits.[44]

---

[40] PRO WO 216/250. Responsibility for co-ordinating Territorial Army questions in the War Office, 25 Feb. 1948; Maj.-Gen. G. W E. Erskine, 'The Territorial Army', *Journal of the Royal United Services Institute*, 93 (1948), 570–83; *The Rifle Brigade Chronicle for 1947 (Fifty-Eighth Year)*, 37–39.

[41] IWMSA. Accession No. 20494/12. Col. P. Featherby, reel 4.

[42] IWMSA. Accession No. 16812. A. Barr, reel 10.

[43] PRO WO 32/21323. Report on a preliminary study of wastage in the Territorial Army prepared by Analytical European Surveys Limited on behalf of Colman, Prentis & Varley Ltd, Mar. 1965.

[44] PRO WO 163/649/AC/P(60)23. Army Council, Reorganisation of the Territorial Army. Paper by the DCIGS, 6 July 1960.

This reorganization was largely completed by May 1961. Even before then, however, the Army Council was questioning whether they actually needed such a large force, and whether they could afford it. In May 1960 they estimated that it would cost £135m over the next five years, including £22m needed to modernize its equipment. But the Treasury was reluctant to find the money to enable the Territorial Army to prepare for a global war, and the General Staff could foresee no role for them in a limited war because they could only be called out following the recall of Parliament and after the government had issued a proclamation that a national emergency was imminent. The Territorial Army's continued existence seemed to hang on the slender thread of political expediency. Its future looked bleak when the only reason that the Secretary of State for War could find in 1960 not to suggest further drastic reductions was that 'it was not practical politics at the present time to disband the Territorial Army'.[45]

By May 1965 the Territorials were far below their establishment.[46] The most important cause of the recruiting shortfall and the high wastage rate amongst men who had joined was uninteresting training with out-of-date equipment.[47] Echoing sentiments that might have been voiced by generations of Volunteer and Territorial officers, one Territorial unit commander believed that the Territorials had not been given the facilities, equipment, and adequate pay and allowances to convince potential recruits that they were needed: 'Nobody really said the Territorial Army is absolutely essential to the maintenance of the defence of the UK.'[48]

A year later the Wilson government cast political expediency to the wind and did decide that in its existing form the Territorial Army was not essential to the defence of the UK. Where Macmillan's ministers had feared to tread, Wilson's Secretary of State for Defence, Denis Healey, had fewer qualms. By late 1964 the MOD found it impossible to envisage a situation in which large numbers of Territorial units would be required, or in which the Territorial Army would be employed to form the basis of a much larger national army.[49] In July 1965 a Defence Review announced that it would shed no fewer than seventy-three Territorial infantry battalions, forty-one artillery regiments, and nineteen armoured

---

[45] PRO WO 163/649/AC/G(60)20. Extract from the minutes of a meeting between the Minister of Defence and the Secretary of State [for War] on Wednesday, 4th May 1960.

[46] PRO WO 32/20957. Sir E. Caffyn to Lieutenant-General Sir J. Hackett, 26 May 1965 and enc.

[47] PRO WO 32/21323. Report on a preliminary study of wastage in the Territorial Army prepared by Analytical European Surveys Limited on behalf of Colman, Prentis & Varley Ltd, Mar. 1965.

[48] IWMSA. Accession No. 20494/12. Col. P. Featherby, reel 6.

[49] PRO WO 32/21323/ECAB/P(65)1. ECAB. Defence Planning Studies—Reserve Forces. Paper by DCGS for consideration at a future meeting, 1 Jan. 1965.

regiments. There would be a new Territorial and Volunteer Reserve, but it was to be only 50,000 strong, less than half of the size of its predecessor. This would reduce the cost of the Territorial Army from £34m to £20m per annum, but enable it quickly to provide 11,000 men for the logistic support of the Strategic Reserve, and to furnish 37,000 reinforcements for BAOR. The only remaining territorial teeth units would consist of a single armoured unit, two SAS units, a single parachute battalion, four artillery regiments, and thirteen infantry battalions.[50]

The reduction of the Territorials to an all-Volunteer force in 1960–1 had been effected with little fuss or public opposition. In November 1959 the DSD had minuted that his goal was to ensure that at the end of the process 'there must be nobody with hurt feelings or doubts about the rightness of the final decision. There must if possible be no P[arliamentary] Q[uestion]s or disgruntled pressure groups.'[51] His wish was granted. The chief spokesman for the Territorials, the Council of the Territorial and Auxiliary Forces Association, led by the Duke of Norfolk, told the War Office that although they wanted some detailed modifications to the War Office's plans, they had no objection to them in principle.[52] Their acquiescence rested on the fact that the 1960–1 programme left the structure of the Territorial Army largely intact. Even after the reductions, it still had 195 major teeth-arm units and they were promised modern equipment. Furthermore, by making the cuts through the process of amalgamation rather than disbandment, the War Office went some way towards assuaging regimental susceptibilities. Many Territorials also probably welcomed the return to an all-volunteer force shorn of the presence of sometimes unwilling ex-National Servicemen.

But the 1965 reductions were so large that they threatened the very existence of the Territorials and provoked bitter opposition. By April 1965, as stories of possible cuts were leaked to the press, spokesmen for the Territorials began to lobby vigorously in the press and through local MPs, but to no avail.[53] They extracted only two concessions from the MOD. The first was literally nominal. In June 1965 Fred Mulley, the Minister of Defence for the Army, told Healey: 'Consideration is being given to retaining the title "Territorial" for part at least of the new reserve

---

[50] PRO WO 32/21323. Deputy Secretary of State, MOD, to Secretary of State for Defence and enc., The future of the Army Reserves, 3 June 1965; *The Times*, 30 July 1965.

[51] PRO WO 163/649. DSD, Re-organisation of the Territorial Army. Notes on procedure, 29 Nov. 1959.

[52] PRO WO 163/649/ACTA/M(60)1. Advisory Committee on the Territorial Army, 12 July 1960.

[53] PRO WO 32/20957. Sir E. Caffyn to Lt.-Gen. Sir J. Hackett, 26 May 1965; Col. J. Ellis Evans, Chairman of the T&AFA of the counties of Denbigh and Flintshire to Mrs Eirene White MP, 31 May 1965; Maj. Lennox Paterson, Chairman, County of Lanark Territorial and Auxiliary Forces Association to Secretary of State Defence, 9 June 1965; Harry Legge Bourke MP & Francis Pym MP to Fred Mulley, 1 July 1965.

force, perhaps T.A.V.R. I feel this may help to get Territorial Council support. It would not mean that the existing Territorial Association structure would continue as at present.'[54] Healey agreed that

While I am sure that we must dismantle the Territorial Association structure, I very much agree with you that there may be advantage in retaining, in some way, the title 'Territorial', and that we should do everything possible—short of dropping essential parts of the scheme, or of foregoing any part of the estimated saving of £20m.—to shape our plans in a form that will secure the support of the T.A. Council or, at least, some leading members of it.[55]

The second concession was commonsensical. The MOD was willing to consult with the Associations about which units should be retained to fill the TAVR's order of battle. In July 1965 the DCGS told a group of senior officers that

The guiding principle should be to base units and sub-units on centres of population with good recruiting potential, allowing not more than one training centre for each sub-unit. It is obviously important to retain existing well-recruited units where they fill the bill and you will also bear in mind those units with historic claims. There are, of course, good precedents for converting infantry, gunner and yeomanry units into engineer and signal units.[56]

The Territorial lobbyists failed for three reasons. The Territorials were the inevitable victims of the same economic circumstances that were to cause Healey to cut the Regular Army. Secondly, Labour ministers were less likely than their Conservative counterparts to be influenced by sentimental attachments to either the Territorial Army or the regimental system. One senior staff officer who served under both Conservative and Labour governments in the 1960s and 1970s found that the latter 'did their homework and concentrated on the essentials. Conservatives were fussier over detail and had all too often done their National Service in a "smart" regiment; the military experience thus acquired had given them opinions on how the army worked, or should work, which they often considered more relevant than the views of serving generals.'[57] And thirdly, the Territorials' defenders had no persuasive riposte to the strategic rationale that underpinned the 1965 reductions. Instead their supporters emphasized the social, rather than the military, utility of the force. The *Sunday Telegraph*, for example, insisted that the Territorials provided a socially useful outlet for the energies of young men in cities

[54] PRO WO 32/21323. Deputy Secretary of State, MOD, to Secretary of State for Defence and enc., The future of the Army Reserves, 3 June 1965.
[55] PRO WO 32/20957. Healey to Mulley, 10 June 1965.
[56] PRO WO 32/20957. An address by DCGS to Army Commanders/Chiefs of Staff. Reorganization of the Reserve Army, 27 July 1965.
[57] Blacker, *Monkey Business*, 165.

like London and Birmingham who might otherwise spend their time in pubs or worse, and in country towns it provided a social focus and social cohesion for an otherwise scattered community: 'Here is continuity; this is what Britain outside the great conurbations has always prided itself on.'[58] But such arguments appeared irrelevant to the government, and the military authorities. Their priority was to produce the most effective army they could within a tightly constrained budget, not to perpetuate an organization that lacked a real strategic rationale because it might act as a school for the nation.

The end of National Service and the end of the Territorials' role as a reserve force able to place large formations in the field reopened the gap that had existed before both world wars between the regulars and their comrades in the auxiliary forces, and further undermined the reality of regimental communities that united both parts of the Crown's land forces. By the 1960s some regular officers and NCOs regarded serving with a Territorial Army unit as akin to a punishment. One regular adjutant told an enquirer in 1965 that he regarded his service with the Territorials as 'two years chopped out of my career as a professional soldier. God knows what it will do to my promotion prospects.' A PSI, when asked what he knew about the Territorial Army before coming to it, said: 'enough to try and get out of it. I didn't want to be a flunkey and sweep up the drill hall because no other b . . . . . . would do it.'[59] For their part many Territorials resented the fact that they continued to be treated as a second-class army, equipped with obsolete weapons and clothed in battledress.[60] Relations between the two branches of the army became characterized by much the same ignorance and suspicion as had characterized relations between the regulars, Volunteers, and Militia before the Cardwell–Childers reforms, and which those reforms had done something to lessen.

The post-war era also saw major changes in the relationship between civil society and the army, changes that ultimately were also inimical to the close relationship between the two that Cardwell and Childers had hoped to create. After initially closing the gap between the army and civil society, the period after 1945, and in particular the period after the abolition of National Service, saw a veritable chasm open between them. Between 1948 and 1960 National Service meant that for the first time other than during the world wars, Cardwell's and Childers's hopes that the wider nation would identify with the army

---

[58] PRO WO 32/20957. *Sunday Telegraph*, 'Tuppenny-ha'penny T.A. cuts', 1 Aug. 1965.

[59] PRO WO 32/21323. Report on a preliminary study of wastage in the Territorial Army prepared by Analytical European Surveys Limited on behalf of Colman Prentis & Varley Ltd., Mar. 1965.

[60] Ibid.

came close to fruition. This was demonstrated, for example, in the summer of 1949. During a national dock strike, troops were sent to the docks to unload cargo ships. But far from showing resentment towards the soldiers who were breaking their strike, the local population and the dockers themselves accepted that the troops had no choice in the matter but were just obeying orders. They invited some of them into their homes for Sunday dinner, and according to one National Serviceman who was sent to Tilbury, they were 'gems'.[61]

But the gradual dismantling of the Cardwell–Childers system after 1945 made it increasingly difficult for regiments and the army to maintain meaningful relations with their own civilian communities. The military authorities did try to do so, encouraged by the belief that in a period of full employment it had to do all it could to promote recruiting. Thus in 1946, for example, the War Office decided that small parties of officers and men from units that were about to be placed in suspended animation should be returned to the UK as 'unofficial representative parties' so as to

provide an opportunity for civic welcomes which would be appreciated by the local authorities of the county etc. where the unit was originally raised. It was felt too that such ceremonies would be of value to Army recruiting and that the consequent revival and maintenance of local interest would be an important factor when the auxiliary Army is being built up.[62]

Civic authorities continued to show that they wanted to be associated with their local regiments by offering them the freedom of their towns and boroughs.[63] And for their part the military authorities persisted in trying to project a positive image of army life through a commitment to sport. In 1955 the Adjutant-General persuaded the Treasury that officers and other ranks chosen to represent the UK at the 1956 Olympic Games should be granted paid leave for a period of intensive training and for the games themselves. 'There is an obvious morale and publicity value in members of the Services participating in the Olympic games', he insisted, 'but it is essential to see that no one is penalised financially on account of being selected.'[64] The army also tried to project an image of good neighbourliness towards the civilian community. Thus in 1963 the

---

[61] IWMSA Accession No. 18022/6. K. W. Black, reel 1; *The Times*, 8 July 1949.

[62] PRO WO 32/13371. War Office to C-in-C Middle East, East and West Africa, BAOR, Malta, Gibraltar and all Home Commands, 12 Feb. 1946.

[63] *The Eagle. The Journal of the Essex Regiment*, 10 (Sept. 1947), 64; NAM 9012-28-57. Maj.-Gen. Sir E. Hakewill-Smith, Corporation of Glasgow. Reception of the Officers, NCOs and men of the 2nd HLI (City of Glasgow Regiment), 16 Mar. 1948; PRO WO 32/12803. GOC Northern Command to War Office, 14 July 1948.

[64] PRO DEFE 7/1220/PPo/P(55)5. Note by the Adj.-Gen., Services participation in the Olympic Games, 1956, 4 Aug. 1955.

Adjutant-General, Gen. Sir Richard Goodbody, agreed to ask local commanders 'to deal as kindly as they can with requests for the use of Service sports grounds within their Commands by civilian clubs, particularly those of youth organisations, where this would not be to the detriment of Service personnel'.[65] Territorial Army Associations continued to function as an essential link between the military authorities and the civilian community.[66] But they were no more successful than they had been before 1939 in breaking down the opposition of many employers, especially smaller ones, to the idea of giving their employees who were Territorials extra leave to attend their annual camp.[67]

The abolition of National Service marked the start of a more difficult era for the regiments in their attempts to maintain close links with the wider civilian community, for as the editor of the *Army Quarterly* wrote in July 1959,

It is a saying that bears frequent repetition that to be efficient, loyal and contented the armed forces of a country must be closely identified with the civil population as a whole. This close association is almost automatic under conscription, and is made easier still within living memory of two national wars. It will become more difficult for us when we return to a system of voluntary, long-service enlistment in 1961, and as the two national struggles recede from memory.[68]

Civilians remained curious about the army and army life. In 1959 Northern Ireland Command held an 'At home' at Ballykiner, which was held over two days and attracted 16,000 visitors.[69] But their opportunities to see the army diminished considerably following the abolition of National Service. The sixty-four infantry depots that existed in 1948 were reduced in the early 1960s to only fourteen brigade depots.[70] Many towns that once enjoyed or endured the physical presence of regular soldiers saw them no more. The public visibility and image of the army was hardly helped by the fact that many infantry regiments lost their local titles. In 1968, for example, the creation of the Light Infantry by the amalgamation of the Somerset and Cornwall Light Infantry, the King's Own Yorkshire Light Infantry, the King's Shropshire Light Infantry, and the Durham Light Infantry meant that each shed its county title and

[65] PRO DEFE 7/1220/PPO.1016/13/3/63. Porchester to Principal Personnel Officers, n.d. but c. Mar. 1963 and Goodbody to Porchester, 24 Apr. 1963.

[66] Brig. H. King-Lewis, 'The Role of Territorial and Auxiliary Forces Associations in the Future', *Journal of the Royal United Services Institute*, 98 (1953), 585–93.

[67] PRO WO 216/250. Minute, DTA to VCIGS, DCIGS, 25 Feb. 1948.

[68] Brig. C. N. Barclay, 'Editorial', *Army Quarterly*, 77 (1959), 131.

[69] *The King's Royal Rifle Corps Chronicle* (1959), 19–20.

[70] PRO WO 163/649/CRTA/P(60)2. DWD and DSD, Equipment for the Territorial Army from Regular army, 6 Jan. 1960.

became a numbered battalion within a new Light Infantry regiment. The Brigade Colonel hoped that

the people of Cornwall, Durham, Herefordshire, Shropshire, Somerset and Yorkshire will understand that, although our county names are being dropped and individual regular Battalions will no longer be affiliated to any particular county, The Light Infantry will be none the less their Regiment, relying on their help and support as much as existing Regiments have done in the past.[71]

But the abandonment of titles that readily identified a regiment with a particular geographical location made it difficult for his wish to be fulfilled. In many instances all that was left to mark the association between a locality and a regiment was a place name. When the Essex Regiment's depot at Warley was closed in 1962, with the exception of a regimental chapel and the officers' mess, the depot was demolished, and apart from a few street names, little remained to show that Warley was once 'a garrison of considerable national importance'.[72] However, the Highways Committee of Brentwood Urban District Council did persuade the council to rename Barrack Road 'Eagle Way', 'thus commemorating the long association of the Essex Regiment with the Barracks'.[73]

The amalgamations and disbandments of Territorial units reduced still further the physical footprint of the regiments on the ground, and the likelihood of soldiers and civilians rubbing shoulders more than very occasionally.[74] Those Territorial units that survived the 1960s did so in part because they carefully cultivated good relations with their civilian constituency. This was vital because in order to survive they had to find sufficient recruits to demonstrate their continued viability. In the mid-1960s, for example, the 307 (South Notts Hussars) Regiment, Royal Artillery, were careful to invite local civic leaders to their social events and annual camps. This often bore fruit. At one dinner the CO discovered that the Lord Mayor of Nottingham, who had a reputation for being a pacifist, had been born in Aldershot. His father had been an RSM and 'we were his lads'.[75] The regiment created a vibrant regimental association, which 'was most important for recruiting, for our standing in the county, in the city, the strength of the South Nottinghamshire Hussars

---

[71] NAM 6803–60. Formation of the Light Infantry. The Brigade Colonel, the Light Infantry Brigade, to 1/Battalions, Somerset and Cornwall Light Infantry, King's Own Yorkshire Light Infantry, King's Shropshire Light Infantry, Durham Light Infantry, et al., including members of the Light Infantry Clubs, 1 Mar. 1968.
[72] Brentwood Library Local History cuttings collection, D1/F27/f14–15. John Marriage, 'Back to Barracks'.
[73] *The Wasp and the Eagle. Regimental Journal of the 3rd East Anglian Regiment(16th/44th Foot)*, 1 (1962), 419.
[74] Brig. C. N. Barclay, 'Editorial', *Army Quarterly*, 81 (1965), 1–2.
[75] IWMSA. Accession No. 20493/8. Col. J. Gunn, reel 5.

Association is absolutely critical'.[76] The regiment also worked to perpetuate a link first formed with the regular 1/RHA during the siege of
Tobruk because, according to the commanding officer, 'well it's very
important to us in our connections with the regular regiment and you
say you're RHA people sit up and take notice'.[77]

By 1967 an MOD committee examining the future structure of the
army concluded that while relations between the army and civilian
communities were often excellent, the army had 'an inadequate public
image'. This was partly because the public rarely saw it, and partly
because relations between the army and the press were not always
satisfactory.[78] Every time the press carried headlines such as 'Brawling
Case Sentences' recounting the prosecution of soldiers in BAOR for
fighting with German civilians, they did nothing to project a positive
image of the army.[79] Social surveys carried out in the mid-1960s showed
that public attitudes towards the army had remained remarkably consistent over time. Respondents knew little about the reality of army life,
they had generally positive attitudes towards the soldier, but they were
disdainful of soldiering as a possible career because the terms and conditions of service they thought it offered were not attractive.[80]

The military authorities had recognized the importance of that last point
for a long time. In the late 1930s they realized that if they wanted to
recruit and retain sufficient men, the minutely regulated, constantly
supervised, and largely misogynistic communities that composed the
regimental system after 1870 had to be transformed. In 1936 the Adjutant-General, Sir Harry Knox, identified irksome discipline as one of
many causes why the Regular Army was experiencing difficulty in finding
recruits.[81] In 1937, therefore, all soldiers at home who were over 21 and
had completed their recruit training were given a permanent pass to sleep
out of barracks except when military duties required their presence. They
were also allowed to wear plain clothes when off duty, and they were no
longer expected to polish barrack room utensils and mess tins.[82] The
symbolic significance of these measures was overlooked at the time, but it
was immense. They represented the first significant steps away from the

[76] IWMSA. Accession No. 20493/8. Col. J. Gunn, reel 5.
[77] Ibid; IWMSA. Accession No. 20494/12. Col. P. Featherby, reel 6.
[78] PRO WO 163/691/AB/G(67)33. Committee on the Future Structure of the Army. Second
Report, 29 June 1967.
[79] The Times, 11 and 14 June 1962.
[80] Col. J. C. M. Baynes, The Soldier in Modern Society (London: Eyre Methuen, 1972), 61–4,
189–94.
[81] PRO WO 32/2984. Knox to Duff Cooper, 10 July 1936.
[82] PRO WO 32/4521. Gen. Sir J. F. Gathorne-Hardy, to Sir H. Knox, 13 Mar. 1936; AG3 to
all GOC-in-C at home, 1 Sept. 1937; ERM. ER 4655. Historical Record. 1/Essex, 10 Apr. 1937.

notion that soldiers had to identify with their regiments for every one of the twenty-four hours of each day of their service lives, and that regiments were closed communities that had the right to regulate every aspect of their daily lives.

This process was given further impetus when Leslie Hore-Belisha became Secretary of State for War in 1937. 'We had', he told his first meeting of the Army Council in 1937, 'to take into account the fact that the mentality of the present year differed greatly from that of years ago.'[83] His efforts focused on two major issues, soldiers' marriages and their accommodation.

During the First World War all married soldiers, no matter what their age, had received a separation allowance calculated according to the size of their family.[84] In 1920, with a return to a regular, all-volunteer force, and in the hope of encouraging experienced and trained men to make the army their career, this allowance was continued in a modified form. Soldiers aged over 26 who married during their period of enlistment were granted a marriage allowance. Official permission to marry was no longer a prerequisite for being eligible to be placed on the married roll or to receive the allowance. However, married quarters remained in short supply, and it was not until 1938 that married soldiers over the age of 26 were granted either free quarters or a married allowance, together with extra allowances for their children.[85] But such were the army's difficulties in recruiting and retaining men that in May 1939 the military authorities went a step further and announced they would recognize marriages contracted by all soldiers over the age of 20. They did so, as the Adjutant-General explained, for 'If we do not do this we are shutting out of the Army, at a time when we need recruits, a young class of the population between the ages of 21 and 26.'[86] Each married family was to be given a modern, self-contained house equipped with hot and cold running water, gas, and electricity. Each unmarried soldier was to have a partitioned bed space fitted with a wardrobe, barrack rooms were to be centrally heated, and they were to be equipped with modern sanitation and baths with hot and cold running water. Dining rooms were to be refitted as restaurants and all table equipment, knives, forks, spoons,

[83] PRO WO 32/4195. Informal Army Council meetings, 29 June 1937; Bond, *British Military Policy*, 330; PP (1937–8), XVII. Cmd. 5696. *Statement relating to improvements*, 2.

[84] PRO WO 293/1. Army Council Instructions. ACI 166. Emoluments of officers, WOs, NCOs and men, 20 Aug. 1914.

[85] PP (1937–8), XVII. Cmd. 5696. *Statement relating to improvements*, 2; Jeffery, 'The Post-war Army', 225; RNRM. *Standing Orders of the 1/Battalion The Norfolk Regiment* (Birmingham: The Birmingham Printers, 1925), 109.

[86] PRO WO 32/4680. Adj.-Gen., The married soldier problem, 9 Nov. 1938.

glasses, mugs, and plates were to be kept on the premises, 'so the men have simply to walk into a meal as they would into a restaurant'.[87]

The actual implementation of many of these policies was stalled by the outbreak of the war. But the decision to 'civilianize' everyday life in the army had been taken, and in the post-war era the military authorities had no option but to continue with it. After 1945 they had to make the terms and conditions of service, for both officers and other ranks, more attractive, for they were struggling against a background of a society that was undergoing radical social changes. Between 1945 and the early 1970s Britain enjoyed full employment and that, as social surveys conducted in the mid- and late 1950s showed, produced significant changes in people's social expectations and patterns of behaviour. Some, such as the fall in the per capita consumption of alcohol, were wholly beneficial to the army. But others were not because they posited a divided loyalty in the minds of many soldiers between their identification with their regiment and their identification with their family and home. There was a marked shift away from a 'work-based culture' to one more focused on home life and consumption. For the first time since the industrial revolution, the majority of male workers saw their home, not their workplace, as the main site of companionship and sociability. Having a job was increasingly taken for granted. What mattered more to people was having a home and the wherewithal to furnish it with the latest consumer goods such as televisions, refrigerators, and cars. Within marriage there was a growing gender convergence. Wives were increasingly more likely to work outside the home, and husbands took on a bigger share of domestic chores and childcare. Increasing numbers of parents also wanted to see their children climb the social ladder and better themselves, and were anxious that they received a better education than they had themselves.[88] The army could not remain immune from these trends. As long as it needed long-service volunteers it had to find ways of accommodating officers, NCOs, and other ranks whose aspirations were often markedly different from those of their fathers and grandfathers.

After 1945 the army could no longer rely on the unemployed to fill the ranks, but it did still find most of its recruits from amongst the most disadvantaged sections of society. Youths from stable homes, and youths who had an apprenticeship, were less likely to enlist than those from broken homes or who were working at monotonous jobs with few prospects.[89] Most recruits who enlisted on a regular engagement had left school at the minimum school-leaving age of 15. The men who

---

[87] 'Improvements to Barracks', *Regimental Annual. The Sherwood Foresters 1938*, 111–12.

[88] J. Harris, 'Society and Civil Society in Britain, 1945–2001', in K. M. Burk (ed.), *The British Isles since 1945* (Oxford: Oxford University Press, 2003), 101.

[89] Lt.-Col. A. Barker, 'The Recruiting Problem', *Army Quarterly*, 86 (1963), 195.

enlisted in the all-volunteer army of the 1960s may have been better educated and, thanks to the radio, television, and newspapers, better informed about the world around them than their forefathers. Perhaps because of the heightened awareness of nationhood created by the two world wars, patriotism may have been a more important factor encouraging men to enlist after the dissolution of the Empire than it had been in the late nineteenth century, but some of the old motives for enlisting, such as a desire to travel and escape from the monotony of everyday life, still existed. Asked why he had enlisted in August 1959, David Sextone remembered that the army offered opportunities to travel and to escape from the tedium of his father's career as a small-businessman. But that also

I suppose being suckled to the sounds of World War Two must have had something to do with it. Like most small boys growing up in the aftermath of the Second World War I was fascinated by all things military.

At school I avidly read patriotic tales of England's heroes that I found between tattered covers of history books printed in the years when the sun never set on the British Empire. Most of the earnings from my paper round were spent on second-hand books about the land, sea, and air battles that had raged through both hemispheres while I lay cozy in my pram.[90]

Required to maintain an establishment of 165,000 men, the all-volunteer army of the 1960s needed 27,000 recruits each year, preferably men between the ages of 17 and 19, who were as yet too young to want to marry and settle down. One recruiting officer believed that

Such men have a more sophisticated mentality than their pre-war predecessors. Generally, they are better educated, easier to teach, more apt to reason, but their nervous constitutions are more tense. They expect more from their superiors, are less inclined to give without receiving and more disposed to argue. Greater softness of living has caused them to expect more regard to be paid to their creature comforts. Their mental outlook, coloured by the more sensational tabloid Press, the habits of the cinema and the influence of the television have greatly affected the stolid, patient British character of fifty years ago.[91]

They enlisted for adventure, the chance to travel, and because they hoped to learn a trade that would be useful to them when they returned to civilian life.[92]

But once they had enlisted, the army then had to retain them. That proved to be a besetting problem and the solutions that the military authorities devised accelerated still further the disintegration of the

---

[90] D. Sextone, *Reflections of an Idle Guardsman* (Sussex: The Book Guild, 1991), 11.
[91] Barker, 'The Recruiting Problem', 195.
[92] Ibid.

concept of the regiment as an all-embracing community whose requirements and regulations governed every aspect of its members' lives.

This can be seen in both big and little ways after 1945. Hore-Belisha's decision to transform mess halls into restaurants was implemented. The 'family' system of messing, which had meant that soldiers in a unit or sub-unit had sat down at meals together, and the food was brought to their tables by an orderly, gave way to cafeteria-style eating. Meals henceforth took less time to consume, but, rather to the surprise of some senior officers, discipline in dining halls did not suffer. 'The orderly behaviour of the men without special supervision', one senior officer noted, 'is most marked, and there is a noticeable absence of pushing and noise.'[93]

Similarly, in 1946 a War Office committee reiterated the decision that in order to attract and retain the long-service volunteers that the army needed, an off-duty soldier 'should be free to go where he pleases and return when he pleases … We consider that it is a logical step to free the trained soldier, who is a responsible citizen and a civilised being, from restrictions on his off-duty time.'[94]

This edict was not universally welcomed. Some regimental officers saw it as a threat to their control over their men. In 1949 senior officers told the CIGS that the army was increasingly becoming a five-day-a-week job. Drab barracks and a lack of married quarters meant that few soldiers remained in barracks at the weekend, preferring instead to go home to their families. The result, according to the Adjutant-General, Sir J. S. Steele, was 'a general spirit of laxness, arising partly from weekend leave'.[95] In 1949 the Army Council therefore agreed that for one weekend each month whole units should be in barracks. Communal activities such as dances and games would be organized, followed by a Church Parade on Sunday. These 'Regimental Week-ends' were designed to recreate the kind of communal life that had been commonplace throughout the regimental system before the Second World War. They were intended to build unit *esprit de corps* through developing 'corporate activities, out of normal duty hours' and to bring officers and other ranks together on the pre-war model by enabling them to develop common leisure interests.[96]

But far from enhancing morale, the restrictions that these activities placed on their free time irritated soldiers, both regulars and National

[93] PRO WO 32/12154. GOC Southern Command to War Office, 11 July 1947.

[94] PRO WO 163/481. ECAC, Committee on Army Life. Final Report, 25 July 1946; WO 163/497. First Report of the Army Working Day investigation team, 23 July 1949.

[95] PRO WO 32/13254. Minutes of the CIGS's meeting with Home Army commanders, 7 Jan. 1949.

[96] PRO WO 163/634/AC/G(57)3. Adj.-Gen., Week-end Leave, 24 Jan. 1957.

Servicemen.[97] Many of them particularly disliked serving in West Germany in the early 1950s because the military authorities were intent that the British army had to impress the local inhabitants with its discipline and turnout and so 'it was what we called, sort of, excuse my language, bullshit. You had parades, parades and more parades.'[98] Most servicemen did not resent those aspects of discipline that had an obvious bearing on the efficiency of their unit. But they did resent what they regarded as 'unnecessary parades (such as pay parades), over-frequent kit-inspections, guard duties which have no obvious purpose, excessive fatigues—all these', according to a report compiled in 1957, 'are breeders of discontent'.[99]

Following the creation of an all-volunteer army in the early 1960s, the military authorities had to respond to this. They tried once again 'to remove unnecessary restrictions and irritations from routine service life. Formation and unit commanders have been given clear and specific guidance about standards of disciplinary administration and man management.' Their instructions dealt with such routine matters as guards, inspections, parades, and fatigues

and emphasise the need to cut out unnecessary and time-consuming activities which make no real contribution to the efficiency and well-being of the unit and which discourage the keenness and interest of the soldier in the Army. The aim throughout the Army today is to promote mutual confidence between officers and men and to encourage in the soldier self-reliance and a sense of responsibility.[100]

The implication was that parades and inspections that had no other reason than to build a sense of corporate identity were now out of place.

The ways in which soldiers who fell foul of military rules and regulations were treated were also brought more into line with civilian practices after 1945. Soldiers accused of serious offences were still tried before a court martial composed of serving officers. However, after 1951 they had a right to appeal against a conviction to a superior civilian appeal tribunal.[101] By the mid-1950s courts martial were expected to vary sentences 'according to the requirements of discipline, but in ordinary circumstances, and for the first offence, a sentence should be light. Care must be taken to discriminate between offences due to youth, temper, sudden temptation or unaccustomed surroundings, and those

[97] PRO WO 32/16882. Memorandum, 18 Oct. 1956.
[98] IWMSA Accession No. 17679/2. P. J. Russell, reel 1.
[99] PP (1958–9), VIII. Cmnd. 545. *Report... of the Advisory Committee on Recruiting.*
[100] PP (1961–2), XXVI. Cmnd 1631. *Army Estimates 1962–63*, 12.
[101] Anon., *MML... 1956*, 587–92.

due to premeditated misconduct.'[102] COs who were reluctant to send a repeat offender before a court martial were likely to earn a reprimand on the grounds that their own summary punishments had obviously failed to reform the offender's behaviour.[103] But their powers of summary punishment underwent a significant diminution in 1962. Following hard on the abolition of National Service, they could no longer order that an offender be confined to barracks. In its place they could now impose fines as punishments.[104]

However, efforts to civilianize the daily life of the soldier only went so far. The perception remained that the army was a poor employer because its pay rates were too low. The army's need to recruit and retain skilled tradesmen in the inter-war period had caused anomalies in the pay code that became all too apparent during the Second World War.[105] Skilled tradesmen engaged in comparatively safe occupations at base depots were frequently paid considerably more than front-line soldiers who daily risked their lives.[106] In 1945 a new pay code was introduced for regular soldiers designed to rectify this anomaly and to ensure that a skilled fighting soldier could receive the same pay as a skilled tradesman. Even so, as the government White Paper introducing the new pay code candidly admitted, while a married private soldier in receipt of his pay and a marriage allowance would earn the equivalent weekly wage of a semi-skilled industrial worker, an unmarried private, even taking account of the free food and accommodation he received, would still be worse off than his civilian contemporaries.[107]

A soldier's earnings depended not only on wage rates, but also on his promotion prospects. Continued uncertainty about the size of the post-war army meant that the War Office did not reintroduce a peacetime promotion code for NCOs until 1952. The possibilities of promotion continued to be determined according to each unit's establishment.[108] But in other respects it was significantly different from the system that had operated since the Cardwell–Childers reforms, for the tight grip once exercised by the regimental system over the promotion of senior NCOs was relaxed. In the teeth arms up to the rank of sergeant, NCOs

[102] Anon., QR ... 1955, 200.

[103] PRO WO 32/14107. DPS to all GOCs-in-C, 6 Oct. 1950.

[104] War Office, KR ... 1955, 174–5; War Office, MML, 1972, 356–7; PRO WO 32/12177. Policy regarding the army system of summary punishment and reduction in rank, 1946; The Times, 13 Nov. 1959 and 3 Feb. 1961.

[105] PRO WO 163/47. Précis 21. H. J. Creedy, Army Tradesmen, 22 Mar. 1938.

[106] PRO WO 163/90/ECAC/P(43)55. Adj.-Gen., Formation of a standing committee on trade pay in the army, 10 May 1943.

[107] PP (1945–6), XVI. Cmd. 6715. Post-war pay code of pay, allowances, retired pay and service gratuities for members of the forces below officer rank, 7.

[108] PRO WO 32/13180. Minutes of a Director of Personnel Administration meeting held on 26 April 1948 to discuss the re-introduction of substantive promotion for regular other ranks.

continued to be chosen for promotion by selection, subject to their achieving the necessary qualifications and the recommendation of their CO. But following the introduction of the Brigade Group system in the infantry, senior NCOs above the rank of sergeant were selected from within the Brigade Group. Their chances of promotion were increased because they could now be cross-posted between units in the same Group.[109]

In the technical arms, where formal qualifications played a more important role, control of promotion was even more centralized, and all ranks were entered on a common roll.[110] But although the power of the regiment to pick and choose its own NCOs and WOs had been reduced, the military authorities were still a long way from having established a single standard system for the selection of senior NCOs that would ensure a uniform standard across the army. The influence of the regimental system persisted because as late as by 1958 there were still 194 separate promotion rolls for NCOs.[111]

National Service also had a significant impact on the career structure of the non-commissioned ranks. National Servicemen were eligible for promotion to NCO ranks but as they served for only two years, few of them rose above the rank of corporal.[112] In 1958 there were no National Service Warrant Officers, only ten National Service Staff Sergeants, and 1,101 sergeants, most of whom were filling tradesmen's jobs in the RAMC, REME, RAPC, and RAEC. There was also a rapid turnover at the level of corporal as National Servicemen completed their colour service and left the army. Ambitious and even moderately able regular soldiers were therefore likely to become corporals after only two years' service, and to become sergeants in their mid-20s.[113]

But if promotion prospects were good, pay, especially in the lower ranks, was not. The consequent turnover in regular personnel threatened the efficiency of the army by depriving it of the regular cadre that it needed to train and lead the National Servicemen. It also meant that National Servicemen had little financial incentive to convert to a regular engagement. With full employment and rising civilian wages, many National Servicemen found themselves worse off in the army than they had been before they were called up.[114] The military authorities

---

[109] PRO WO 32/13704. Col. C. H. Cree, for DPS, to all GOC-in-C, 5 Jan. 1949.

[110] PRO WO 32/16150. Vice Adj.-Gen., Introduction of a peace code of promotion for other ranks, 10 Mar. 1952.

[111] PRO WO 32/17657. AAG to DPA, The effect of the abolition of National Service and the reduction in the size of the army on promotion prospects of regular other ranks, 12 Jan. 1959.

[112] PRO WO 32/13180. Minute by DPA, 29 Apr. 1948.

[113] PRO WO 32/17657. AAG to DPA, The effect of the abolition of National Service and the reduction in the size of the army on promotion prospects of regular other ranks, 12 Jan. 1959.

[114] Barraclough, *National Service*, 15.

increased regular pay rates in 1950, 1954, 1956, and 1958 in an attempt to recruit and retain more regulars, but Treasury constraints meant that what they offered was usually too little and too late.[115] Finally, in 1960, with the end of National Service in sight, they made one more attempt. Henceforth a newly enlisted private soldier, if he was unmarried, earned £227 per annum, or £373 if he was in receipt of a marriage allowance. But this was still below the average annual wage of an agricultural labourer, which stood at £512 in 1960, and less than half that of a coalface worker.

It was only after a soldier had risen to become a senior NCO that his earnings became competitive with what he might earn in civilian life. A married infantry sergeant with between nine and fifteen years' service could earn up to £758.16 per annum, which put him ahead of all unskilled workers and many workers in skilled occupations such as bricklayers, carpenters, or bakers, although he would still earn less than an engine driver or engineering fitter.[116] However, the creation of an all-volunteer army was not an unalloyed gain for regular NCOs. The abolition of National Service and the concomitant reduction in the size of the Regular Army to only 165,000 men significantly reduced their promotion prospects. Competition amongst regulars to rise from corporal to sergeant became fiercer, and the time it took a private to become a corporal rose from about two years in the mid-1950s to about four years by the early 1960s. Units might have benefited by having more experienced NCOs, but the longer wait was hardly an incentive for men to remain in their regiment if they could earn better wages elsewhere.[117]

A second, equally intractable problem that confronted the military authorities as they struggled to make service in the army attractive after 1945 was housing. The Hore-Belisha programme to create modern barracks and married quarters had been cut short by the outbreak of war. The army entered the post-war world with little modern accommodation for either married or single soldiers, and instead a great many hutted camps that had been hastily constructed during the two world wars. In 1946 a War Office committee warned that in order to attract and retain volunteer recruits, army accommodation would have to match civilian standards.[118] But overcrowding was inevitable because, by 1949, the post-war army was some 50,000 men larger than in 1939 and shortages of capital meant that it was impossible to build the extra accommodation

[115] PP (1955–6), XXXII. Cmnd. 962. *Service Pay and Pensions*; *The Tank*, 40 (Mar. 1958), 1–3.

[116] Anon., *The King's Own Border Regiment* (Morecambe: The Morecambe Bay Printers, 1960), 51–61; Routh, *Occupation and Pay*, 101, 106–8.

[117] PRO WO 32/17657. AAG to DPA, The effect of the abolition of National Service and the reduction in the size of the army on promotion prospects of regular other ranks, 12 Jan. 1959.

[118] PRO WO 163/481. Committee on Army Life. Final Report, 25 July 1946.

it required.[119] By the late 1950s hutted camps, some of First World War vintage, were still being used despite the fact that they often lacked such basic amenities as effective heating systems, washing and sanitary facilities, proper mattresses, pillows, easy chairs, and writing tables.[120]

It was not until 1958 that the military authorities, driven by the need to attract and to retain men in an all-volunteer army, really began to improve the housing of the rank and file.[121] In 1958 a committee investigating how conditions of service would have to be modified following the end of National Service if the army was to recruit and retain enough volunteers to fill the ranks, emphasized the need to make barrack accommodation more comfortable.[122] Concerned at the reluctance of the Treasury to fund a large-scale building programme, the Army Board initially hesitated, but by the early 1960s improvements were slowly being introduced. In 1962, 2/Royal Green Jackets moved into the newly constructed Roman Barracks at Colchester, where they found that 'The barrack rooms with their coloured ceilings, bedside lights and Dunlopillo mattresses are a far cry from the barrack blocks of 15–20 years ago, and the cookhouse, central heating system and Junior Ranks' club look like exhibits from the Ideal Home Exhibition.'[123]

However, it was the incorporation of large numbers of long-service married men, both officers and other ranks, into the army in the 1950s that did more than anything to change the nature of regimental soldiering. By 1959 approximately 40 per cent of regular soldiers were married.[124] This had come about because, in order to train National Servicemen and place efficient units in the field, the army needed to recruit and retain a cadre of long-service NCOs. In 1952 the War Office therefore announced new terms of service for regular other ranks that were intended to offer prospective NCOs an attractive career until the age of 40, with senior Warrant Officers being allowed to continue serving until 55. Henceforth other ranks could enlist for a twenty-two-year engagement.[125] If this policy was to succeed, all restrictions on marriage had to be ended. All ranks serving on a regular engagement, regardless of

[119] PRO WO 32/13347/ECAC/P(49)84. QMG, Proposal to concentrate all isolated units and installations in the UK into garrison towns or areas, 3 Aug. 1949.
[120] PRO WO 32/13254. CIGS meetings with Home Army Commanders, 7 Jan. 1949; PP (1958–9), VIII. Cmnd. 545. *Report of the Advisory committee on Recruiting*; Poett, *Pure Poett*, 132–3; PRO WO 163/634/AC/P(57)1. QMG, Accommodation of the British army. Short term problem in the UK, 3 Jan. 1957.
[121] Baynes, *The Soldier in Modern Society*, 38.
[122] PRO WO 32/17698. Report of the Committee on the New All-Regular Army (Whistler Report), May 1958.
[123] *The King's Royal Rifle Corps Chronicle 1962*, 15–17.
[124] *The Times*, 5 Oct. 1959.
[125] *The Times*, 11 Mar. 1952.

their age, were eligible to receive a marriage allowance. Married officers over the age of 25 and other ranks over the age of 21 serving on a regular or short-service engagement were awarded local allowances for married couples and their families. They also received a family passage at public expense to and from overseas stations, a disturbance allowance paid when the family had to move home, the cost of educating their children in the UK when they were overseas, and the provision of married quarters.[126]

More generous allowances undoubtedly helped married families to withstand the rigours of army life, but by themselves they were not enough to stem the outflow of trained manpower. In 1954 a survey showed that 47 per cent of men who were refusing to extend their initial engagement did so because they were separated from their families, and 69 per cent of a group of 2,800 husbands questioned said their wives wanted them to leave the army as soon as possible. Many soldiers were also concerned that the life chances of their own children would be badly affected because their education was disrupted every time their father was posted to a new station.[127] One general concluded that family separation 'is knocking the bottom out of the regular content of the British Army'.[128]

Separation was caused by a chronic shortage of married quarters and frequent overseas postings. A report on the quality of married accommodation in 1958 highlighted how far it had again fallen behind civilian provisions and aspirations: they often 'lack privacy and are unattractive. They also lack refrigerators, garages for private cars and sufficient storage space for luggage.' The same committee recommended that complete villages of married quarters should be built around regimental depots so that when units were posted overseas on an unaccompanied posting, families would remain in place.[129] Shortage of funds made such a solution impractical and by 1965–6 the army in the UK needed 39,000 modern married quarters, but could only provide 24,000 such homes. Those families who did not live in official married quarters were accommodated in privately rented accommodation, much of which was substandard.[130]

[126] PRO WO 163/388. Committee on separated families, 2 Apr. 1954.
[127] PRO WO 32/17698. Report of the Committee on the New All-Regular Army (Whistler Report), May 1958.
[128] PRO WO 163/388/SFC/P(54)26. Report of the Committee on separated families, 2 Apr. 1954.
[129] PRO WO 32/17698. Report of the Committee on the New All-Regular Army (Whistler Report), May 1958.
[130] PP (1965–6), IX. Cmnd. 2902. *Defence Estimates 1966–67, for the year ending 31 March 1967*, 65.

The pre-1939 system, under which soldiers could expect to spend six or seven years abroad, was a thing of the past. By 1955 a normal overseas tour lasted for no more than three years, at the end of which officers and other ranks reverted to the home establishment, and every effort was made to give them a 'home posting' for at least eighteen months. But the only way to make this possible was to widen the definition of 'home' to include not just the UK but also Germany, Austria, Belgium, and Holland.[131] Even so, it was impossible to achieve these goals. Regiments did their utmost to sustain family morale when husbands were absent. Most units had their own 'Wives Club', usually presided over by the CO's wife. Its main function was to help wives and children cope with the inevitable periods of separation from their husbands and families in the UK that were common in army life.[132] But family separation was and remained a significant problem. By 1957 the incessant movement of units due to pressing operational commitments was encouraging so many soldiers to leave the army that the Army Council agreed that henceforth units would normally have an overseas tour of three years accompanied by their families, or a one-year overseas unaccompanied tour, followed by two years at a station where families could be united. Anything less would mean that the army would continue to haemorrhage married men at an unsustainable rate.[133]

The military authorities' efforts to attract recruits and to retain trained soldiers by civilizing daily life within the structures of the regimental system were at best only partially successful. For most of the period from 1945 to 1970 the Regular Army struggled to find sufficient volunteers to fill its ranks. A committee that investigated the treatment of National Servicemen in 1949 found: 'Suggestions that they might join the Regular Army are treated in most cases, with ridicule.'[134] By the middle of the 1950s, many National Servicemen regarded the experience as 'an infliction to be undergone rather than a duty to the nation'.[135] In 1965 the army was an all-regular force of volunteers. Its manpower ceiling for UK adult males was 20,360 officers and 160,770 other ranks. But it could muster only 19,210 officers and 156,781 other ranks, and almost half of the other ranks had signed on for an engagement of less than nine years. The re-engagement rate was worryingly low, a sign that soldiers were far

[131] War Office, QR ... 1955
[132] 'Families', The King's Royal Rifle Corps Chronicle 1965, 30.
[133] PRO WO 163/634/AC/M(57)2. Minutes of the 165th meeting of the Army Council, 4 Jan. 1957.
[134] PRO WO 163/497. First Report of the Army Working Day investigation team, 23 July 1949.
[135] PP (1956–7), XVII. Cmnd 35. Report of the Committee on the employment of National Servicemen in the UK.

from content with their lot. Only about 40 per cent of men at the end of a six-year engagement opted to re-engage, and only 35 per cent of those who had completed a nine-year engagement did so. They gave three reasons for being dissatisfied. One, low pay and allowances, would have been familiar to their grandfathers. But the other two reasons were revealing of how important family life and commitments had become, and how the greater freedom that soldiers now had to marry and establish a family had created divided loyalties in the minds of many of them. Their other two main reasons for leaving were the poor quality of so much army housing and 'the tempo at which our stretched forces are continually operating and the disturbance to family life, with long periods of separation, which this has entailed'.[136]

At the same time, the post-1945 reforms of barrack life had gone a long way to transform the ethos of the daily life of soldiers living inside the regimental system. By the early 1970s, once National Service had ended and the army had become an all-regular force, three out of five other ranks, and four out of five officers, were married, and most married soldiers also had children.[137] Changes in the disciplinary regime meant that their lives were no longer minutely regulated on a twenty-four-hour basis. Many married men were no longer willing to give twenty-four hours a day and seven days a week to the regiment. In the 1950s and 1960s army wives, following the example of their civilian counterparts, introduced a consumerist culture into the army. In a period of full employment having a job was increasingly taken for granted. What mattered now was being able to live comfortably as a family, to own a house, and to have sufficient time to enjoy family life, hobbies, and activities outside work. Consequently civilian notions that the working week should be restricted to five days a week, and the working day should run from 9 a.m. to 5 p.m., were increasingly prevalent. The army's insistence that officers and men be available for duty for the whole of every day of the year became increasingly untenable.[138] Soldiers assumed divided identities, as members of regiments or corps during the working parts of their lives, and as husbands and fathers when they were not on duty.

If the post-war period saw daily life in the regiment steadily approximate to the daily lives of civilians, it also saw an increasing professionalization of the regiment's officer corps. The very fact that the post-1945 army was more frequently engaged on active service than it had been before 1939

[136] PP (1965–6), IX. Cmnd. 2902. *Defence Estimates 1966–67*, 71–2.
[137] Baynes, *The Soldier in Modern Society*, 153.
[138] Dietz, *The Last of the Regiments*, 4–5.

was one reason why the regimental officer corps was more committed to soldiering as a profession than their predecessors before the Second World War. Units that regularly expected to see active service simply could not afford to carry 'passengers'.[139] But even had they wished to do so, changes in the ways in which regimental officers were trained and promoted would have minimized the possibility that they could do so.

During both world wars the military authorities were compelled to commission large numbers of men from outside the normal 'officer producing classes'.[140] This convinced some senior regular officers that leadership qualities were not synonymous with a public school education. In December 1943, the DMT, Major General J. A. C. Whitaker, decided: 'First rate leaders can come from any social class, provided they possess the right qualities, and are fully trained.'[141] However, other regular officers looked with disdain on the temporary wartime commissioned officers they had served alongside. In 1945 one wrote that

there is no blinking the fact that, as the War dragged on, apparently interminably, there was a marked deterioration in the standard of junior officers; this was of course inevitable with increased dilution and the supply of good officers consequently falling short of the demand. It is regrettable, however, that there was evolved a type of young officer not over careful in his turn-out and uncouth as to his manner, drawn from all walks of life and all types of schools. In many cases he had been neither bred nor educated to service and responsibility; his translation, via an O.C.T.U., from the ranks was too rapid to enable him to be trained other than technically as an officer, and the accompanying social and psychological training was irreducibly restricted.[142]

In his opinion such men were not acceptable as 'a potential representative of the officer corps of the Regular Army nor as a potential life-long comrade in an officers' mess'. The military authorities acted as if they agreed with him, for soon after 1945 officer recruiting reverted to the pre-war pattern. Between 1947 and 1958 two-thirds of the candidates for officer cadetships came from public schools, and a third of successful candidates came from just twenty-one schools.[143] A survey carried out in 1967 showed that the staff at Sandhurst remained committed to inculcating many of the same basic cultural values associated with the regimental system that had been common before 1939. The concept that officers had to be gentlemen, and leaders whom their followers trusted,

[139] Maj-Gen. D. Tyacke to the author, 18 Aug. 2002.
[140] Sheffield, *Leadership in the Trenches*, 30–1, 38–9; PRO WO 277/12. Maj.-Gen. A. J. K. Piggott, *Manpower Problems*, 81; PRO WO 277/16. Lt.-Col. J. Sparrow, *Morale*, 21.
[141] PRO WO 231/8. DMT, General Lessons from the Italian Campaign, 18 Dec. 1943.
[142] Corbally, 'The Officer-Producing Class', 205.
[143] PRO WO 163/531. Report of the Committee on the standard of officer cadets, Oct. 1951; PP (1958–9), VIII. Cmnd. 545. *Report of the Advisory committee on Recruiting*.

continued to be important.[144] Most cadets were strongly in favour of the system by which regiments and officers paired off according to their mutual likes and dislikes, rather than following the system employed by the French and US armies that allowed cadets to choose their regiments according to their place in the final order of merit. Most believed that leaders were born, not made, strongly supported the outward trappings of the regimental system such as regimental messes, and were opposed to the introduction of officers' clubs open to all officers in a district. They thought that 'Traditions should be respected' and placed leadership ability before technical competence as the main criteria for promotion.

So successful was Sandhurst at inculcating a new identity in cadets that the civilian teaching staff reported that even working-class cadets who arrived with strong regional accents left the college with upper-class ones. The one group of cadets who were in some respects an exception to this last generalization were those who had attended the army's own school, Welbeck College, which had been established in 1953 to give sixth-form boys sufficient grounding in scientific subjects so that they could, after Sandhurst and taking a degree, be commissioned into the RE, the RCS, or the REME. They were much more committed to the idea that the officer had to be technically competent before everything else.[145]

There was therefore no sudden or dramatic change in the social composition of the regular officer corps. However, once they had joined their regiment, their professional training and experience were very different from what they had been before 1939. From being a member of an occupation fit for a leisured gentleman before the Second World War, by the 1950s regular officers could quite reasonably see themselves as on a par with other white-collar professionals in terms of the commitment that their duties required of them. For one thing, those duties now occupied far more of their time than before 1939. This was partly because after 1945 the army faced long periods of operational overstretch as units were committed on active deployments across the globe. It was also because National Service meant that many officers were now occupied in training a constant stream of National Service recruits.[146] The long leave once granted to officers serving in India or the Far East, eight months every third year, was a thing of the past.[147] They also had less cash to indulge in the sometimes elaborate social life of

[144] M. Garnier, 'Changing Recruitment Patterns and Organizational Ideology: The Case of a British Military Academy', *Administrative Science Quarterly*, 17 (1972), 504–5.

[145] Garnier, 'Power and Ideological Conformity', 352–60; *The Times*, 7 June 1952.

[146] Brig. V. Boucher, 'Some Remarks on Opening a Battalion Officers' Study Period', *Army Quarterly*, LXV (1952), 123.

[147] Lt.-Col. B. S. Jerome, 'The Army as a Career', *Army Quarterly*, 60 (Apr. 1950), 74.

pre-war officers' messes or in expensive field sports.[148] Hunting had been becoming less popular since the end of the First World War and the gradual withdrawal from empire after 1945 virtually put an end to such sports as pig-sticking and polo.[149] By 1956, as one officer lamented, 'A couple of days hunting a week, even if one could afford to do so, is not quite the thing in these serious days.'[150]

But senior officers still expected their juniors to spend a part of their leisure time pursuing demanding and slightly dangerous physical activities.[151] Consequently, cheaper and more socially acceptable sports such as parachuting, skiing, and dinghy sailing, which were reckoned to develop in officers the same qualities of hardiness, quick decision, self-confidence, and courage that hunting and shooting had done, became increasingly popular.[152]

Before 1939 the officers' mess, with its often elaborate and expensive protocol, had been a powerful engine creating a sense of *esprit de corps* amongst the officers of every regiment. After 1945 the War Office sought to re-establish it as such, albeit on a less refined level. Their goal was to maintain the standards of comfort of 'the average pre-war mess of an inexpensive regiment'.[153] But there was a visible relaxation of pre-war rituals. Formal dinners were held no more than once a week, although all officers, married or single, were expected to attend. The evening meal, dinner for four nights and supper for the remainder, was no longer to be regarded as a parade.[154] Even so, junior officers still sometimes found the proceedings irksome. In 1963, an officer of 1/3 East Anglians forfeited half a guinea when he lost a bet with a fellow officer that 'he will not INTRODUCE "Desmond" [the donkey] to the public rooms of the officers' mess during the course of the evening after 7.30 o'clock on Wednesday 7th August 1963'.[155]

At the same time as the importance of the social and sporting trappings that surrounded the regimental officer corps were diminished, so other changes were fostering a greater professional commitment amongst regimental officers. The most important of these was the control that the

---

[148] Lt.-Col. L. H. Landon, 'The Financial Condition of the Army Officer', *Journal of the Royal United Services Institute*, 94 (1949), 417–19.

[149] MacKenzie, *Empire of Nature*, 195; Jerome, 'The Army as a Career', 74; C. MacKenzie, 'The Origins of the British Field Sports Society', *International Journal of the History of Sport*, 13 (1996), 177–91.

[150] Lt.-Col. J. A. H. Moore, ' "A Hunting We Won't Go" ', *Army Quarterly*, 66 (1956), 228.

[151] Kennard, *Loopy*, 92.

[152] ffrench Blake, *A History of the 17th/21st Lancers*, p. vi; Moore, ' "A Hunting We Won't Go" ', 228–9.

[153] PRO WO 32/12554. Committee on the future of officers' messes, 14 Aug. 1947.

[154] Ibid.; ERM. ERB 27. *Mess rules. The Depot, 3/East Anglian Regiment* (Depot Archive Copy, 1955), 2.

[155] ERM. ER 11268. Wager Book, 3/Royal Anglian Regiment, 8 July 1963.

regimental system had exerted over their promotion and training, which had begun to be relaxed even before 1939. Hore-Belisha introduced time promotion for all officers up to the rank of major, and in August 1938 nearly 2,000 regimental officers were promoted.[156] He also began to transform the training of officer cadets. In January 1938 he ordered the amalgamation of Sandhurst and Woolwich in the hope that if cadets were trained together they would be better able to work together on the battlefield. He also abandoned the attempt to operate the cadet colleges as universities and insisted that they revert to being military colleges where 'Cadets are to be taught to be soldiers'.[157] Finally, in March 1939, encouraged by the General Staff, he announced plans to establish a tactical school. All Captains who had not gone to the Staff College would be required to graduate from it before being promoted to Major. The school would disseminate a common tactical doctrine throughout all branches of the service, ensure that junior officers were prepared for the tactical tests in their promotion examinations, teach them how to teach, and encourage all-arms cooperation by giving officers the opportunity to mix with colleagues from other arms of the service.[158]

Coming as they did on the eve of the outbreak of the next war, many of Hore-Belisha's reforms were too late to have any real influence on the army's ability to conduct the battles they were shortly to confront. However, the principles that underpinned them were carried forward. In 1942, for example, the establishment of divisional battle schools represented a major step towards a common tactical training programme for junior officers, and this reform was institutionalized in the post-war era by the establishment of the School of Infantry.[159] By 1960 it was running regular courses for officers about to take command of companies and for recently commissioned platoon commanders, which placed great emphasis on all-arms cooperation. A squadron of tanks, a field battery, and a company of infantry were attached to the school, and much of the training took place in the field and was highly practical.[160]

---

[156] PRO WO 163/608. Committee on conditions of service of officers in RN, army and RAF, July 1938; Anon., 'Army Notes', *Journal of the Royal United Services Institute*, 83 (1938), 877–84.

[157] PRO WO 163/403. Report of the committee to consider the amalgamation of the RMA and the RMC, 31 Mar. 1939.

[158] LHCMA. Liddell Hart MSS 11/1937/79. Talk with Maj.-Gen. Sir R. Adam, 25 Oct. 1937; Anon., 'Army Notes', *Journal of the Royal United Services Institute*, 84 (1939), 205, 429–30.

[159] PRO WO 216/82. Report of a joint committee on instruction of officers and schools, 17 May 1942; T. Harrison-Place, *Military Training in the British Army, 1940–1944* (London: Frank Cass, 2000), 50–79.

[160] Maj.-Gen. D. Tyacke to the author, 7 Aug. 2002. Maj.-Gen. Tyacke became the Chief Instructor at the School in 1960.

Until the early 1960s the army retained the main features of the Hore-Belisha promotion system, although with some modifications. Time promotion became more rapid, officers being supposed to reach the rank of major after on average only thirteen years' service. This brought its own problems, for by the late 1950s some COs were complaining that junior officers spent so little time as subalterns and captains that they were unable to learn their jobs properly before becoming majors.[161] Promotion to lieutenant-colonel and above continued to be by selection.[162] But, in a departure from pre-war practice, the retirement age for officers passed over for promotion to lieutenant-colonel was to be cut from 47 to 45.[163] This was a compromise between two incompatible goals, the need to meet the expectation of regular officers that the army would offer them reasonable career prospects, and the lessons of both world wars, which indicated that the ideal unit commander was aged between 28 and 36.[164]

Commanding officers remained responsible for training their own subordinates when promotion examinations were reintroduced in 1950, although staffs at Command level were expected to provide more assistance than they had done before 1939, and the War Office provided a subsidy to enable officers to take correspondence courses.[165] Before 1959 officers who failed to qualify were given one more chance, and then faced premature retirement if they failed again. After 1959 their case was reviewed after their initial failure, and they could be prematurely retired even without being given a second chance.[166] However, in 1957 the Army Council had decided to abolish the qualifying examination for promotion from Lieutenant to Captain. They did so on the grounds that it was a sham. Officers who had a university degree found the written papers too easy, and too many of those who did not either paid a crammer to assist them or failed. Whereas before 1939 Lieutenants might have had as much as fifteen years' service before they took the examination, their post-war successors might have served for only four years. Henceforth Lieutenants were automatically promoted to Captain after six years' service and on the recommendation of their COs.[167] But the Captain to Major examination was retained and in 1959 it became even more important than it had been. For the first time it was assimilated

---

[161] PRO WO 32/17698. Report of the Committee on the New All-Regular Army (Whistler Report), May 1958.

[162] QR ... 1955 , 29, 43-4.

[163] PP (1945-6), XVI. Cmd. 6750. Post-war pay code of pay, allowances, retired pay and service gratuities for commissioned officers of the armed forces.

[164] Crang, The British Army and the People's War 1939-1945, 54.

[165] QR ... 1955, 23-4; PRO WO 32/17361. DGMT to all GOC-in-C 28 Mar. 1958.

[166] PRO WO 32/20174. War Office to all GOC-in-Cs 24 July 1958.

[167] PRO WO 32/14047. Promotion Examination (Lieutenant to Captain) Policy, 1957.

with the Staff College entrance examination, although the latter covered a wider field of knowledge and candidates had to attain higher scores to qualify for the College.[168] The syllabus continued to test each candidate's practical understanding of all-arms tactics at the unit level, his knowledge of the 'housekeeping' aspects of regimental service, and his ability to think beyond the confines of regimental soldiering to consider the role of the army in modern society.[169]

The abolition of National Service, the contraction of the army following the Sandys reforms, and the creation of an all-volunteer army required the wholesale reform of the officer promotion system. The army could no longer rely on conscripts to fill the ranks of the junior officer corps. It now required two types of officer. The first was the kind who wanted to make his whole career in the army and who, if he was sufficiently talented, could rise to the most senior ranks. In 1959, to attract and retain such men, the War Office abolished the separate retirement ages for different ranks of officers, and introduced the concept of full careers for officers to the age of 55. Suitably qualified Majors were to be selected for promotion to Lieutenant-Colonel after thirteen years' service, and Majors were to have a 60 per cent chance of being promoted to Lieutenant-Colonel by the age of 43.

Those officers who remained Majors and continued their careers were given jobs in static establishments rather than in mobile units. To ensure that elderly officers did not block the promotion of able younger men, pensions were granted to selected officers after they had completed as little as sixteen years' service. These proved so attractive that between 1960 and 1963 no fewer than 1,033 officers opted for early retirement.[170] But if too many officers were to opt for a full career commission, the middle ranks of the officer corps would become clogged with middle-aged men fit only for desk jobs. The second kind of officer that the army wanted was the type who wanted to serve for a comparatively short period before leaving to take up a civilian post. The military authorities, therefore, also instituted a system of short-service commissions so that at any one time 20 per cent of officers would expect to serve for between two to eight years before leaving the army for a civilian career.[171]

By the mid-1960s it was apparent that this system was not working. The army was losing too many able officers who had opted for a full

---

[168] PRO WO 32/16496/ECAC/P(57)23. DCIGS, Proposal to merge the promotion examination from Captain to Major with the Staff College entrance examination, 3 Apr. 1957.

[169] PRO WO 32/16496/ECAC/P(57)23. DMT to WO Directors, 16 Oct. 1957.

[170] PRO WO 32/20178. Assistant Military Secretary, MS2 to APA 6, 13 Aug. 1964.

[171] PRO WO 32/20995. Director of Manning (Army), Draft paper on officers for Committee on Future Structure of the Army, 15 Feb. 1967; War Office, *Notes on the British Army 1961* (London: War Office, 1961), 54–6.

career but who, after assessing their chances of promotion, their family responsibilities, and their qualifications, were deciding to seek a civilian job.[172] Consequently, in 1966 the Army Board lowered the average age of promotion to Lieutenant-Colonel from 43 to 40, and introduced wider age bands for promotion, thus enabling some officers to become Lieutenant-Colonels when they were only 37. It also improved the chances of promotion so that 70 per cent of Majors would become Lieutenant-Colonels. But even this had its shortcomings. Although it was comparatively easy to apply it to the main teeth arms, other arms of service, such as the Army Air Corps, Intelligence Corps, Army Catering Corps, and Royal Military Police, were so small that they did not have enough established posts to permit officers to advance as rapidly as their comrades in other arms.[173] Thus one facet of the Cardwell–Childers system did persist. The system of officer promotion still advanced some officers more rapidly than others according to their regimental affiliation.

But the post-1945 era did see a reduction in the influence of the regimental system on the post-commissioning training and education of regimental officers. There was more emphasis on school-centred training as compared to unit-centred training. By the 1960s, on leaving Sandhurst officers were divided into three categories. About half of all young officers, including those destined for the infantry or Royal Armoured Corps, divided their time for the next eighteen months between practical instruction with their unit and periods of instruction at their arm-of-service school. Officers destined for the technical arms were trained to degree standard at either the Royal Military College of Science at Shrivenham or at the University of Cambridge. They were also required to take long specialist courses applicable to their arm of the service. It might take them as long as five years after leaving Sandhurst before they became active practitioners, actually holding down jobs in real units. Finally, up to 10 per cent of officers spent three years reading for an arts degree at a civilian university.[174]

What did not change was that entry to the Staff College remained the goal of able and ambitious regimental officers trying to improve their promotion prospects, and competition to enter the College remained fierce.[175] Immediately after 1945, when the army had a plethora of Captains and Majors with experience of junior staff work, the Staff College course was reduced to six months. In 1950, when this supply

[172] Baynes, *The Soldier*, 133–5.

[173] PRO WO 32/20995. Director of Manning (Army), Draft paper on officers for Committee on Future Structure of the Army, 15 Feb. 1967; WO 163/691/AB/G(67)22. Adj.-Gen., Review of the officer career structure and promotion system—progress report, 12 April 1967.

[174] Baynes, *The Soldier*, 125–7.

[175] PRO WO 231/103. Defence Council Instructions (Army) 204–207/1964. 2 Oct. 1964.

was exhausted, the course was lengthened to a year, and the College was issued with a new directive. Its functions were now to train GSO2-grade staff officers and to fit them, after further experience, for command of their unit.[176] The course continued to provide mental stimulation and friendships that transcended narrow regimental loyalties.[177] By 1956 Camberley was producing 140 qualified British staff officers annually, more than twice the number it had produced before 1939, and in December 1962 the Army Council agreed to expand the number to 240.[178] This did help to narrow the gap between the regiments and the staff. It meant that after graduating, successful students, who continued to join the college in their late twenties or early thirties, were young enough to complete two tours of regimental soldiering before, in their early forties, they reached the rank of lieutenant-colonel and assumed command of their unit.[179]

The emphasis in the teaching was more heavily weighted than before 1939 to producing competent tactical and operational-level staff officers rather than higher strategists. Exercises at the College were normally at the level of the division or corps. In 1956, for example, students were set exercises concerned with operations in a limited-war scenario that involved allied forces composed of two corps, one British and one US, each consisting of no more than three divisions and supporting troops.[180] Battlefield tours, colloquially known as 'bottlefield tours', took them to Normandy, which

was designed to impart some real 'battle atmosphere' to the course. 'Guest Artists', from both sides, and at all levels of command, took us through a series of 'battle cameos' about Caen and leading up to the final breakout. It was fascinating stuff and brought to life the true realities of command.[181]

The syllabus also responded to changes in the army's commitments. In April 1956, for example, in reaction to a suggestion from the C-in-C East Africa, who was then engaged in suppressing the Mau Mau rebellion in Kenya, the college increased the amount of time it devoted to teaching imperial policing.[182]

---

[176] PRO WO 231/101. GSO2 Co-ordination, to Assistant Commandant, Staff College, 18 July 1957.

[177] Gen. Sir D. Fraser, *Wars and Shadows: Memoirs of General Sir David Fraser* (London: Allen Lane, 2002), 279–80.

[178] PRO WO 231/103. Rebuild—Staff College Camberley. Minutes of a meeting held at the WO at 1430 hrs on 13 Feb. 1963.

[179] PRO WO 32/19692. DGMT to British Military Attaché, Dublin, 17 Apr. 1963.

[180] PRO WO 231/101. Colonel GS 1 to all Directing Staff, Dec. 1955.

[181] Millman, *Stand Easy*, 65.

[182] PRO WO 231/101. Commandant Camberley to Under Secretary of State WO, 9 Apr. 1956.

The College also retained its pre-1939 commitment to encouraging students who had come from regimental soldiering to see their profession in a wider context and to acquire a broad grasp of the relationship between military force and the wider world. It did so by including what one commandant called 'Broadening subjects', taught 'with a view to stimulating students' interest and inducing them to further study in the library and to discussion'.[183]

However, by the late 1950s both the Directing Staff and some senior officers were unhappy about how the College had developed. The expansion of student numbers had only been made possible by reducing the length of the course from two years, which it had been before 1939, to one, with the result that the syllabus had become too crowded. Many students were reduced to learning by rote and were left with too little time to reflect on what they had been taught.[184] Secondly, the practice of taking students into the College in their early thirties and, *inter alia*, preparing them to take command of a unit, which they would not do for another decade, was wasteful. By the time they assumed command the doctrine they had learnt at the College might be out of date.[185] Finally, there was an increasing concern, perhaps fed by a pervasive belief in the rest of society that Britain was falling behind in science and engineering compared to other nations, that few senior officers had a real understanding of the probable impact that the latest scientific and engineering developments might have on the future conduct of war.[186]

The system of staff training, therefore, underwent two more major changes in the 1960s. First, the intellectual broadening of aspirant staff officers and commanders was taken a step further by requiring them to spend a period of between three to twelve months at the Royal Military College of Science at Shrivenham before going to Camberley. But from the point of view of the influence of the regimental system to determine how doctrine was interpreted, it was the second change that was of greater significance. Some of the crowding of the Staff College syllabus was relieved by dividing staff training into two parts. Suitably qualified officers in their early thirties who passed the competitive entrance examination were still selected to attend the full Camberley course. But from the late 1960s all officers between the ages of 26 to 29 were required to attend a Junior Command and Staff Course that was intended to fit them for

[183] PRO 231/102. Maj.-Gen. J. H. N. Poett to Under Secretary of State War Office, 1 Apr. 1958; GSO2 Co-ordination to Assistant Commandant Camberley, 18 July 1957.
[184] PRO WO 231/103. Minute, CIGS to Military Secretary, 21 Aug. 1957; PRO WO 231/101. A new order for Pinkland, n.d. but c. Mar. 1957.
[185] PRO WO 231/102. Assistant Commandant Camberley to all Directing Staff, 17 Apr. 1958; Review of the Staff College directive, 8 May 1958.
[186] PRO WO 32/17698. Report of the Committee on the New All-Regular Army (Whistler Report), May 1958; Marwick, *British Society Since 1945*, 69–70, 87.

senior captains' appointments at regimental duty, and Grade 3 staff posts, and to instruct them in the tactical employment of all arms up to a battalion/battle group level. By providing this element of centralized tactical training, the tactical parochialism engendered by the regimental system could be, to some extent, diminished.[187]

Even so the regiments had not lost all influence over training and doctrine. The General Staff still felt it was sometimes struggling to assert its hegemony. In 1969 the Commandant of the Staff College concluded: 'The formulation of all-arms tactical doctrine depends in the last resort on the ability to bang heads together, including the heads of the Arms Directors.' In his opinion, the best possible solution would be to create 'a proper Training Command for the Army. The GOC-in-C of the Command would be ideally placed to formulate tactical doctrine since Arms Directors and Schools would be under his command.'[188]

By 1970 a regimental system remained an integral and fundamental part of the British army and a superficial examination might suggest that many aspects of the system had continued largely unchanged. The amalgamations and disbandments of the post-1945 period did nothing to alter the importance, in the eyes of the military and regimental authorities, of the symbols of regimental distinctiveness. In 1936 the Army Council had agreed without demur that units that were exchanging horses for mechanized transport would retain their standards and guidons, and that on parade they would be carried by a tank.[189] Following the Sandys reforms in 1957 the Army Board agreed that 'in order to inculcate the pride of a Regiment in the new Amalgamated Regiments, new standards, guidons or Colours should be presented to amalgamated Regiments on a ceremonial parade as soon as possible after amalgamation'.[190] The new Brigades quickly produced their own short histories, designed to inculcate a brigade-wide *esprit de corps* into recruits. Thus soldiers who joined the Yorkshire Brigade were told that 'A soldier of the Yorkshire Brigade will feel, firstly a pride in the Regiment which he joins. At the same time, he will feel a pride in belonging to the Yorkshire Brigade, for the Brigade as a whole embodies all the fine traditions of the five old and famous Regiments which compose it.'[191]

---

[187] Baynes, *The Soldier*, 130; PRO WO 32/17362. Paper No. AB/P(68)12. Junior command and staff school, 10 Apr. 1968.

[188] PRO WO 231/102. Maj.-Gen. J. A. T. Sharp to Maj.-Gen. S. M. O. H Abrams, 5 Feb. 1969.

[189] PRO WO 32/4625. Mechanized cavalry regiments: standards and guidons for, 22 Apr. 1936.

[190] PRO WO 32/17324. Appendix A to AC/P(57)60, dated 19 Aug. 1957. Adjutant Gen., Standards, Guidons or Colours of amalgamated Regiments.

[191] Anon., *The Yorkshire Brigade* (Morecambe: Morecambe Bay Printers, n.d. but c.1959), 5.

Considerable effort was also devoted to amalgamating the customs and traditions of the new regiments. In 1958, following the amalgamation of 3rd and 7/Hussars to form the Queen's Own Hussars, the Officers Dress Committee agreed that officers who had served in 3/Hussars should be allowed to continue wearing a red side-hat, even though it might set them apart from their new comrades, but they could do so only when they were not on parade.[192] A year later, when the Highland Light Infantry and the Royal Scots Fusiliers were amalgamated to form the Royal Highland Fusiliers, the Colonel of the Regiment agreed that as officers in both regiments had habitually worn glengarries in the ante-room during the morning, they would continue to do so. The question of whether or not officers of the new regiment should or should not drink the loyal toast was more vexed. The Highland Light Infantry had been excused the obligation of doing so in the eighteenth century, but the Royal Scots Fusiliers had not. Eventually it was agreed that officers of the new regiment would drink the toast between October and April, but not between May and September.[193] Territorial units that were amalgamated in the reductions of the early 1960s followed suit by cementing their new identities with appropriate ceremonials.[194]

In another apparent throwback to the past that was more suggestive of continuity than change, the socially elite regiments of the army, the Brigade of Guards, the line cavalry, and the Rifle Regiments, had made a significant comeback since 1951. By 1970 officers from these regiments accounted for no less than a quarter of all general officers. Officers from the line infantry accounted for only a third. However, too much should not be made of this. First, the numerically dominant group in the senior ranks of the officer corps remained the generals from the 'teeth' corps regiments, although they now accounted for slightly less than 40 per cent of the senior officer corps. Secondly, the re-emergence of a larger cohort of officers from socially elite regiments at the top of the army did not mean that social prestige had taken the place of professional competence as the high road to command. Proven professional attainment was still crucial if an officer wanted to reach high rank. In 1970, 87.5 per cent of all general officers were Staff College graduates, and every one of the 'socially elite' generals had been to the Staff College.

[192] NAM 7708–20. Documents of 3rd Hussars. Minutes of the Queen's Own Hussars' Officers' Dress Committee, 4 Nov. 1958.

[193] Anon., *The Royal Highland Fusiliers*, 51–2.

[194] ERM. Brigadier C. M. Paton MSS 2. ER 8558. 4th/5th Battalion The Essex Regiment Territorial Army. Presentation of Colours by Her Majesty Queen Elizabeth the Queen Mother, Colonel-in-Chief, Warley, 25 July 1964.

Behind the outward show of customs and traditions, the regimental system as it existed in 1970 was very different from the one that Cardwell and Childers had established nearly a century earlier. The structure of the army was dominated by corps regiments, not by the line infantry or cavalry. Many of the restrictions that had once ensured that officers and other ranks could expect to spend their whole career within a single regiment had all but disappeared. Although the infantry did not constitute a single corps, the divisional system was but one step from it. The links between civilian life and army life were more tenuous than they had been for a century. Most recruits felt little attraction to their 'local' regiment, and localized, or even regionalized, recruiting was of less importance than it had ever been in the past. The merging of civilian communities and regimental communities that Cardwell and Childers had sought was fast receding. The army's footprint in civilian society was tiny compared to what it had been a hundred, or even fifty, years earlier.

Finally, the ethos of the regimental system had been transformed compared to what it had been before 1939. It no longer constituted a system of surveillance that oversaw every detail of the waking and sleeping lives of its members. Regimental officers had less time for leisure and devoted more time to their professional duties. Their careers were determined more than ever in the past by a promotion system designed to identify and reward merit. The army had not entirely become a nine-to-five job, but the presence of so many family men meant that the soldier's loyalty was now more clearly divided than it had ever been in the past between his military family and his real family. And the fact that so many soldiers, both officers and other ranks, did have family responsibilities also contributed to the fact that they increasingly saw the army as a career rather than a vocation.

In 1876 the Duke of Cambridge's insistence that 'in a volunteer Army the battalion is the family. The men wish to belong to a family; they have no home of their own, and their home is the battalion to which they belong, both as to officers and men' had a real and literal meaning.[195] But by the late twentieth century the meaning ascribed to the notion that the regiment *was* the soldier's family had changed. In the 1970s, as a result of the introduction of the 'military salary' and the greater provision of married quarters, increasing numbers of soldiers were marrying and they were doing so at a far younger age than in the past. This created a problem for the army, because the aspirations and attitudes of military families grew closer to those of their civilian counterparts. One result was that a growing number of servicemen left the army. Wives were more likely than in the past to have careers of their own which they were

---

[195] PP (1877), XVIII. C. 1654. *Report of the committee*, Q. 8810.

determined to pursue, and were much less willing than before 1945 to become absorbed into the corporate life of the regiment.[196]

Recruits were still issued with short pamphlets that outlined the history of their regiment. The pamphlets still held up past winners of the VC as exemplars. But they also usually contained far more material about the job opportunities, rates of pay and pensions, periods of paid leave, leisure activities, and comfortable barrack rooms awaiting them. 'Sunshine and golden sands near Tripoli' was the caption under one photograph printed in the handbook of the King's Own Border Regiment in 1960. It did not show, as might be expected, a platoon of infantrymen slogging across the North African desert in 1943. It showed a soldier and his family sunning themselves on a beach.[197]

[196] J. Scott-Clarke, 'The Military Wife', *Journal of the Royal United Services Institute*, 135 (1990), 69–74.
[197] Anon., *The King's Own Border Regiment*, 69.

Conclusion

The regimental system that existed in 1945 was still recognizably the same one that Cardwell and Childers had fashioned in the 1870s and early 1880s. Thirty years later, the British army was still organized on the principle of a regimental system, albeit one that was different in some significant respects from the organization that existed in 1945. This suggests that the regimental system had remarkable powers of survival. Anthropologists have argued that cultures, and by extension institutions, survive only if they overcome six basic challenges. They must be able to reproduce themselves. They must devise means to absorb and train newcomers so that they become functioning members of society. They must maintain order between their own members and between them and members of other societies and sub-cultures. They must motivate their members to engage in activities necessary for the survival of the institution. They must provide for the production and distribution of the goods and services deemed necessary to meet its basic needs. And finally, they must be able to adapt successfully to changes in the external environment.[1] The regimental system has persisted for so long because it successfully passed these tests.

Cardwell and Childers hoped that linking and territorialization would raise the status of service in the ranks, thus making it an attractive career for young men, and provide regiments with sufficient recruits from their own sub-districts. Their hopes were only partially fulfilled. The Regular Army limped along, finding just enough recruits to come close to filling its establishments, but rarely able to enjoy the luxury of turning away large numbers of otherwise unsuitable men except on medical grounds. The line infantry, the part of the army that had undergone the most thorough-going localization and territorialization, usually had the biggest shortages. For most of the line-infantry regiments, localized recruiting remained an aspiration rather than a reality. Even before the Boer War, most of them took their recruits on a regional rather than a local basis. Changes in the organization of recruiting after the Boer War, and again after the First World War, merely acknowledged that fact. The reality was that by the 1920s much recruiting, even for nominally localized regiments, was done on a national basis.

---

[1] Haviland, *Cultural Anthropology*, 47.

Cardwell and Childers were thus only partly successful in rooting the regiments firmly in the wider community, and thereby improving the status of the regular soldier and the esteem in which he was held by his civilian counterparts. After 1870 most civilians probably accepted that the army was a necessary institution, and that it was doing a worthwhile job. They were willing to cheer the soldier as he marched by, and to dip into their pockets to support his dependants when he was on active service. For the civilian public, regiments were sites of ceremonies, commemorations, and entertainments. They offered music and spectacle, and a vision of a reassuringly stable and hierarchical society for those who valued stability and hierarchy. But the presence of Regular Army depots and Volunteer and Territorial drill halls scattered across the country did not necessarily mean that civilians had much real knowledge of the everyday life of the soldier. What they did know they generally did not like. While some localities quickly took their local regiment to their communal heart, others did not. And even where communal identification with the local regiment was strong, it did little to raise a career in the ranks of the Regular Army in the esteem of the 'respectable' working classes. The soldier as an imperial icon may have been held in high public regard, but the army as an employer most certainly was not.

Cardwell and Childers had hoped that the auxiliaries would form a bridge between the civilian population and the regimental system. Young men who already had a home, a job, and a family, but still harboured martial ambitions, had ample opportunity to fulfil them in the Militia, the Volunteers, or the Territorials. But the linking of regular, Militia, and Volunteer units into territorial regiments in 1881 did not automatically create a common identity that united them. In some cases differences persisted even between regular battalions of the same regiments for many years after 1881. It was not really until the First World War brought about a massive expansion of the army, and accompanied it by blending together regular and auxiliary soldiers, that regiments really attained a common identity. In some cases that common identity persisted after 1918, while in others it faded quite quickly, to be replaced by a revival of the mutual suspicions that had characterized so much of the relations between regulars and auxiliaries before 1914.

But if regular units were not good at attracting more than the minimum manpower they needed to sustain themselves, they were extremely effective at transforming civilians into soldiers. The failure of most regiments to recruit more than a fraction of their men from their own sub-district meant that regiments were not primordial communities. Basic training for both officers and other ranks, therefore, had to perform two functions. It had to teach soldiers that as long as they were in the army they were men under discipline. It also began the process of instilling in them a notion of loyalty to a community larger and more permanent than the members of their barrack room, by inculcating in them a sense of regimental *esprit de corps*. The sense of 'specialness' that distinguished every regiment or corps did not emerge ready made from the county communities from which each regiment was supposedly drawn. It had to be deliberately manufactured by the leaders of each regiment or corps. Regimental 'traditions' were created and recreated with enormous gusto after the Cardwell–Childers reforms in an effort to provide regimental soldiers with a focus for their loyalties. The aim of their creators was to give officers and other ranks a cause with which they identified so closely that they would be willing to fight and die for it. Regimental loyalties also went some way towards ensuring the political apathy of the rank and file by providing a common interest that united officers, NCOs, and other ranks despite the obvious inequalities in access to power and privileges they enjoyed. But equally important in this respect was the fact that the Regular Army drew recruits for the ranks from those parts of the community that were unlikely to be politicized before they enlisted. Furthermore, when they were faced with concerted attempts to subvert the loyalties of their soldiers, the military authorities never relied upon the intangible attractions of the regiment alone. They also mobilized the weight of the law and the skills of the secret service. Regimental loyalties certainly did not depoliticize the officer corps. On the contrary, the defence of their regimental privileges was one thing that could sometimes cause them to behave in a highly political manner.

Regiments were equally successful at maintaining order between their own members and between them and members of other regiments. The Cardwell–Childers reforms were part of a Gladstonian programme to moralize the working classes. The reforms, as they effected recruiting, have often been accounted a failure. The Regular Army continued to have difficulties finding enough men to fill the ranks, and those it did attract tended to come from the bottom of the social pile. But such criticisms overlook the point that over time the reforms did change the behaviour of the rank and file for the better. Drunkenness, and the disorder which it had so often produced, were not eliminated, but by the Edwardian period their incidence was much reduced, and that decline became even more marked after 1919. The machinery of regimental soldiering operated to make the rank and file become 'respectable'. The possibility of conflicts arising between soldiers of the same regiment, or soldiers of different regiments, or between soldiers and civilians, was minimized by isolating each unit. Within the area marked out by the walls and fences that surrounded their barracks or cantonment, the regimental authorities maintained control over their subordinates, both officers and other ranks, by a combination of means. They appealed to their sense of reason, to their sense of tradition, and to their sense of loyalty to the regiment. They created a system of surveillance over almost every waking minute of their lives, a system that was only gradually relaxed from the late 1930s. They organized sports and better canteen facilities in a calculated effort to wean them away from harmful pursuits likely to lead to indiscipline. And when these means failed they resorted to formal disciplinary sanctions.

The authority of officers and NCOs was usually accepted without question by their subordinates. During basic training most soldiers came to learn that their superiors had a right to command them. This conferred a powerful degree of legitimacy on both officers and NCOs, and transformed the power that they could exercise into authority. Although some individuals did rebel against what they regarded as the intolerable constraints of regimental life, collective rebellions were rare. For most of the time, most soldiers were willing to find ways to accommodate themselves within the formal structures of their unit.

Regiments motivated their members in a variety of ways. They met the psychological needs of their members to feel that they belonged to a worthwhile community by developing elaborate and distinctive regimental identities. The deserving were rewarded with honours and promotions, and the undeserving were punished. Soldiers were not expected to die merely for tangible incentives. They were also offered symbolic rewards, medals for individuals, and battle honours for regiments.[2]

Even for regular soldiers, loyalty to, and identification with, 'the regiment' did not became all consuming. In 1879, just prior to their departure for the Zulu war, Maj.-Gen. Thomas Pakenham addressed the men of 94/Foot, telling them that

No doubt all of you are leaving relations and friends behind, Fathers, Mothers, Sisters, Brothers, perhaps sweethearts; when you arrive in Africa, you must for the time being forget all those, and think only of your duty to Queen and country, and, my advice is make your rifle your sweetheart, look well after it, in short take it to bed with you (a thing we did do for months) and when you go into action don't waste your ammunition, but let every bullet find its billet.[3]

His speech epitomized the military authority's conception of the role of the regiment in military life. For every soldier his regiment was to usurp the place of his biological family in his affections. The regiment was to be the conduit through which he gave his allegiance, and if necessary his life, to his Queen and Country. But the reaction of many of the men of the 94/Foot underlined the comparative failure of the military authorities'

---

[2] The best brief analysis of this process is K. Roy, 'Logistics and the Construction of Loyalty: The Welfare Mechanism in the Indian Army 1859–1913', in P. S. Gupta and A. Deshpande (eds.), *The British Raj and its Indian Armed Forces, 1857–1939* (Delhi: Oxford University Press, 2002), 98–124.

[3] NAM 7205-73. Papers of L/Cpl. H. James, n.d.

efforts to use loyalty to the regiment to impose a new identity on their men that would supersede their civilian personas. For no sooner had they fought their first action in South Africa than 'Many were the speculations about absent ones at Home, how long would this game last, and, would we be lucky enough to be sent to England at the termination of the campaign.'[4]

Despite the shared rigours of basic training, the construction of distinctive regimental cultures, and the constant surveillance to which officers and other ranks were subjected in barracks, loyalty to the regiment rarely entirely superseded a soldier's identification with other focuses of loyalty and identification. Few soldiers took their sense of identity—their understanding of who and what they were—simply and solely from the fact of their membership of a particular regiment. If they had done so they would have been unique. They would be the only people existing in a human society who had a single identity. Men did not immediately cease to be brothers or sons, Englishmen, Welshmen, Scots, or Irish, heterosexual or homosexual, the moment they donned a military uniform and wore the badges and buttons of a particular regiment or corps. The regimental system's claim to impose a single, overweening loyalty on each of its members was never entirely successful. Even regular soldiers before 1939, who were, for the most part, unmarried during their colour service, remained members of real families. They did not lose their identities as brothers, sons, or lovers when they put on a uniform. This was even more the case with the part-time soldiers of the auxiliary army, who expected to return home to their families at the end of their brief periods of training. After 1945, the ability of the regiment to call on the loyalty of its members crumbled still further, as the privilege of every soldier to marry on the strength was transformed into a right to do so.

When soldiers in action did give their loyalty to the 'regiment', it was very often not the metaphysical entity constructed by the regimental authorities. They identified with the human reality of a group of people sharing a common experience consisting at times of acute discomfort and physical and psychological terror. In 1999 a former soldier, who had served with the Fife & Forfar Yeomanry in North-West Europe in 1944–5, looked back on his experiences and concluded that

People probably never understand the link, or the bond that comes up that you generate in the service. It's always there. It's your family at the time. And I'm sure that most civilians could never understand it, but it's a link that's, that's seems to form and you're part of it, like it or not, you're part of it and eh now it's, it's very nice to pick up and look back. As I say even if it drives the wives barmy on the day.[5]

---

[4] NAM 7205-73. Papers of L/Cpl. H. James, n.d.
[5] IWMSA. Accession No. 18786/15. T. Boyne, reel 15.

On the battlefield regimental *esprit de corps*, albeit one construed in a rather different way from the ideal constructed by the military authorities, was, therefore, a powerful factor in persuading soldiers to fight. But of equal, if not more, importance in sustaining all types of soldiers when they faced real threats to their well-being on the battlefield was the quality of leadership offered to them by their immediate superiors, and the human relationships that they had struck up with the men next to them. This in turn points to an important proviso that must be noted in any consideration of the importance of the regimental system in sustaining morale in action. The ways in which soldiers conceived their regiment was not always consonant with the officially constructed notion of what constituted 'the regiment'.

Regular officers and long-service regular NCOs were more likely than other soldiers to subscribe to the official notion of the regiment as a metaphysical concept that would endure long after the individuals who composed it at any one moment had passed on. Wartime volunteers and conscripts often subscribed to a different notion. They identified less powerfully with the institution of the regiment and more powerfully with the people they had trained with, suffered with, and who may have died alongside them. Writing in 1981, Field Marshal Lord Carver, a former CGS and himself a regular soldier, but one who had commanded wartime conscripts and volunteers, asked

whether the emphasis, more intense in some parts of the army than others, on the maintenance of traditions and the *regimental* spirit is really necessary to good *unit* spirit. At the lowest level, it is being with his 'muckers', the comradeship of the small, closely-knit body of men at *company* level and below, that matters most to the soldier, and makes a man risk his life for the safety and esteem of that small group.[6]

An economist might not recognize a regiment as a unit of production, and so the immediate relevance of the test, a proven ability to produce and distribute the goods and services deemed necessary to meet its basic needs, might be difficult to apply. But regiments were required to produce a service, success on the battlefield. Few have questioned their ability to do this in the small colonial wars, and the even more common colonial policing commitments that confronted them during Britain's imperial heyday before 1939, or during the brushfire wars of the post-1945 period. But critics of its performance in big wars have abounded, and in their criticisms they have echoed many of the ideas of the nineteenth-century Radicals who focused their attention on the supposed shortcomings of the officer corps. Cardwell's supporters believed that the abolition

---

[6] M. Carver, 'All Muckers Together', *The Times*, 29 Oct. 1981.

of the purchase of commissions would open the way for officership to become a career open to talent.[7] It did, but only slowly. Promotion to the rank of Major by regimental seniority did not make the best possible use of the talent available in the officer corps as a whole. The fact that rates of promotion could vary widely between different regiments was a cause of much discontent. In 1936 the senior subaltern in some line-infantry regiments had served for only nine years, while in others he had served for as much as seventeen.[8] The differing private incomes required by regiments did not ensure that talent was evenly distributed throughout the regiments of the teeth arms.

But regimental officers were not, to a man, infused with an anti-modern and anti-professional spirit. Before 1914 they were expected to be gentlemen, but the military authorities increasingly also required them to have professional skills. Promotion examinations did establish a lowest common denominator of professional competence, although they gave little encouragement to the able to excel. Some officers resented the demands made on them, but the pressure on them to take their profession seriously increased and after 1918, to judge by the growing number of officers seeking entry to the Staff College, a substantial proportion of the officer corps responded positively to it. Regimental soldiering did obstruct the promotion of able officers, but for the ambitious and energetic there were ways around it. In the late nineteenth century there was a powerful correlation between membership of regiments that had a high social status and those officers who reached high rank in the army. By the Second World War that was no longer the case. In the seventy years after 1870 professional qualifications and attainments, as measured by an officer's ability to graduate from the Staff College, rather than membership of a fashionable regiment, increasingly became the passport for those officers who wanted to become generals.

One fact about the leadership cadre of the regimental system has too frequently been overlooked. That was that it produced a corps of qualified and professional NCOs able, in many cases, to perform functions that elsewhere were done by officers. Observers from the US army, for example, who visited British units training before D-Day in 1944 noted that much of the training was overseen by sergeants, rather than the commissioned officer, and that NCOs commanded the respect of their men, who were as orderly as if a commissioned officer had been present.[9]

---

[7] Capt. J. Spencer, 'Our Army Organisation of 1871: An Epitome of What It Is, and Results', *United Services Journal* (Dec. 1871), 560–3.

[8] PRO WO 32/3747. Minute by Military Secretary to Military Members of Army Council, 27 Jan. 1936.

[9] PRO WO 163/53/AC/G(44)19. Adj.-Gen., Inter-attachment of British and American Army Personnel in the United Kingdom, 1944.

It is also apparent that the extent to which different regimental cultures inhibited combined-arms cooperation on the battlefield has been exaggerated. Different regiments did often do things in different ways. But to ascribe the difficulties in cooperating on the battlefield that British troops sometimes experienced to these differences is to overlook the myriad of much more salient causes. British military doctrine was lacking in prescription because the multiplicity of different tasks facing the army was so great that too much prescription was as dangerous as too little. Combined-arms training was infrequent because of the peacetime pattern of deployment of the army. What is significant is that once units of different arms of the service did have an opportunity to train together and to work together in the field, regimental distinctions could easily be forgotten. Close cooperation was possible no matter what cap-badges they were wearing.

Finally, the regimental system was highly effective at adapting to changes in the external environment. While individual regiments might succumb one after another to government reform programmes, the system itself persisted. This quality of adaptability was built into the structures that Cardwell and Childers established, for they fashioned not one but four regimental systems. The first consisted of the line-infantry regiments. In 1881 they constituted the largest single component of the army, and were subjected to a thoroughgoing process of linking and territorialization. The second consisted of the two large corps regiments, the Royal Artillery and Royal Engineers, and the much smaller departmental corps. They had hardly been affected by localization or territorialization. The third consisted of the Horse Guards and line cavalry. They were not localized, and in 1881 were individual regiments. However, over the next fifty years they evolved into a close approximation to a corps of cavalry. The fourth regimental system consisted of the rifle regiments (the King's Royal Rifle Corps and the Rifle Brigade) and the regiments of Foot Guards. Parts of their organization were modelled on that of the line infantry, but other aspects were anomalous.

Cardwell and Childers had thus created a malleable structure that already contained so many contradictions that a few more were unlikely to undermine its foundations. This enabled it to endure even after the strategic circumstances that had shaped what Cardwell and Childers had fashioned were no longer relevant. In 1966, when an Army Board committee considered the future structure of the army, and examined the possibility of abandoning the existing structure of regiments and corps in favour of a series of functional corps, it decided that there was little need to do so. 'The Army List', it concluded,

is a memorial to the obsolete weapons and techniques of the 18th and 19th centuries—Fusiliers, Carabiniers, Lancers, Grenadiers—but there is little evidence that the abandonment of such weapons was in any way delayed by the fact that units were organised round them and even if it was it is hard to conceive of any organisation that would have made the adoption of new weapons any easier.[10]

Even in 1881 the regimental system was not very systematic. It was even less systematic ninety years later. By 1971, following the establishment of the divisional system, the Queen's Division had three large regiments, the Scottish Division consisted of six regiments and one regimental company, representing the Argyll and Sutherland Highlanders, the King's Division had six small regiments and one large one, the Light Division had two large regiments, and the Prince of Wales's Division had eight small ones and another regimental company. Such a hotchpotch, it was widely assumed in the press, could not last.[11] Surely the infantry would, in time, move towards a single corps of infantry? But in 1968 the CO of 3/Royal Anglian Regiment had wagered his most junior subaltern that in thirty-five years' time the regimental system would not have disappeared. At the time of writing his money still looks safe.[12]

The regimental system, or at least some aspects of it, remains the cynosure of many of the contemporary debates about the future of the British army. This is reflected in the army's own doctrine. According to *Soldiering: The Military Covenant*, published in 2000, 'Corps and Regimental Spirit' were still one of the major props of the army's morale.[13] Prominent politicians are still prepared to throw their support behind it. On 3 December 2003 Lord Howell of Guildford, a Conservative Party foreign policy spokesman in the House of Lords, told their Lordships that 'the regimental system is not yesterday's pattern, it is the framework on which the peculiar excellence of our Army and our frontline forces depends. In tomorrow's world, I believe that that will be even more the case.'[14] Nor is the notion that service in the army could be a school for the nation entirely dead. Contemporary British army doctrine suggests that the army, together with the other armed forces, has a particular place 'in the Fabric of the Nation'. They

promote the ideals of integrity, discipline, professionalism, service and excellence. This, together with their important role in providing training and experi-

[10] PRO WO 163/686/AB/M(66)5. Confidential Annex to minutes of 31st meeting of the Army Board, 9 June 1966.

[11] *The Times*, 27 May 1971.

[12] ERM. ER 11268. Wager Book, 3/Royal Anglian Regiment. 79th Wager; n.d. but *c*. Dec. 1968.

[13] MOD, *Army Doctrine Publications*, v: *Soldiering: The Military Covenant*. (London: MOD, 2000), 0315.

[14] *Hansard*, HL, col. 323 (3 Dec. 2003); accessed 15 Aug. 2004 at http://www.publications.parliament.uk/pa/ld200304/ldhansard/vo031203.

ence, contributes to national stability and cohesion. They also embody much tradition, which helps to promote a sense of regional and national identity.[15]

This was echoed in 1999 by the Director of Reserve Forces and Cadets, who opined that

Individually, Reserve service is a remarkable social and ethnic melting pot, a practical illustration that rights are matched by responsibilities and privileges by duties. Collectively, communities which support reserve units or subunits are involved with defence in a very real way. In my capacity as a Justice of the Peace I often encounter youngsters who have got into trouble because they like running in the wolf-pack of their mates. If only we could have given them a useful wheel to put their eager shoulders to![16]

In regiments themselves officers continued to cherish the small distinctions that made their regiments different from their neighbours, and to see a functional role for such differences. In 1994 the CO of 2/Royal Green Jackets insisted that the particular heritage of his regiment 'encourages constructive competition and, in a peacetime Army which is made up with volunteers, inter-Regimental rivalry is a key aspect of the maintenance of standards, high levels of self-respect and pride in our profession'.[17]

And regimental Old Comrade Associations continue to perform the function of allowing former members of regiments to celebrate their sense of belonging to a regimental community. Many old-soldiers regretted the amalgamations that saw the submergence of the regiment they had served with into some larger, more anonymous, entity.[18] Their service in the regiment was one of the emotional peaks of their lives. As one former member of the Royal Hampshire Regiment remembered:

You can go to Winchester on a Saturday in June—it's usually the second or third—when it's a get-together of the whole of the Comrades Association of the Royal Hampshire Regiment, when they have a service in the Memorial Gardens, a march through the city, a good dinner, the band playing, most of the officers and their guests there and the Mayor of Winchester. And it's one of those days when everything that was bad in the past is forgotten. And people only remember all the good things.[19]

---

[15] MOD, *Joint Warfare Publications (JWP) 0–01, British Defence Doctrine* (London: MOD, 1996), 5.10–5.11.

[16] Brig. R. Holmes, 'Volunteer Reserves: Usable and Relevant', *Journal of the Royal United Services Institute*, 143 (1998), 23.

[17] Lt.-Col. N. Parker, 'The Front Line: Operational Effectiveness and Resource Constraints—An Infantry Battalion Commander's Perspective', *Journal of the Royal United Services Institute*, 139 (1994), 12.

[18] IWMSA. Accession No. 17230. Maj. S. Horner, reel 18; IWMSA. Accession No. 004485/05. Lt.-Col. V. C. Magill-Cuerden, 40.

[19] IWMSA. Accession No. 004514/04. Major W. Parrott, 35.

But shortly after Lord Howell's speech the Labour government published a new defence White Paper. Its rationale marked the return to a strategic scenario that would not have been unfamiliar to Cardwell and Childers. The end of the Cold War, the threat of global terrorism, and the proliferation of weapons of mass destruction, created a security environment that was less, not more predictable. Consequently, like the Duke of Cambridge and Lord Wolseley, generals today have the utmost difficulty in determining exactly where and against whom the next war will be fought. The White Paper predicted that the possibility of a large-scale conventional attack on the UK has diminished almost to vanishing point.[20] The reorganization and re-equipment of the armed forces that the Defence Secretary, Geoffrey Hoon, announced was posited on the assumption that they were not likely to be involved in high-intensity operations in Central Europe or elsewhere against opponents equipped with the most up-to-date high technology weapons. Rather they would probably be engaged in a series of 'small wars' or expeditionary operations. Such undertakings would place a premium on the army's ability to deploy and sustain forces rapidly, and often concurrently, to a series of trouble spots outside the NATO area. Once they arrived in each new theatre of operations it was likely that they would find themselves engaged in a multiplicity of different kinds of operations, from peace support, peace-keeping, or peace-enforcing operations, to counter-terrorist activities, or high-intensity warfare, almost certainly in cooperation with allies. Future theatres of engagement, according to the Ministry of Defence, might be as diverse as the Near East, North Africa and the Persian Gulf, sub-Saharan Africa, or South Asia. They would call for armed forces that could 'engage proactively in conflict prevention and be ready to contribute to short notice peace support and counter-terrorist operations'.[21]

The emphasis the 2003 White Paper placed on the need to adjust organization, doctrine, and equipment to enable the armed forces to operate in conjunction with allies, particularly the USA and NATO, might have seemed strange in ministers and soldiers in the late nineteenth century. But the need to be able to project force far from the shores of Britain would have been entirely familiar, as would the notion that the most economical way of doing so was to rely on the most modern technology to act as a force-multiplier. And, confronted with the equally familiar problem of predicting who the next enemy might be and how to prepare against him, British army doctrine has continued to follow the

---

[20] Gen. Sir Michael Walker, 'RUSI Annual Chief of the Defence Staff Lecture', accessed 12 Dec. 2003 at http://www.rusi.org/cgi-bin/public/view.

[21] Cm 6041-I. *Delivering Security in a Changing World*, 7.

path of stating principles rather than defining a prescriptive dogma.[22] As in the past, this will not necessarily allow regimental idiosyncrasies to impede all-arms cooperation, provided there is time for units that will serve together to train together. The successful deployment of British forces in the Second Gulf War in 2003 was preceded in the autumn of 2001 by a large-scale exercise in Oman, Exercise Saif Sareea II, which taught valuable lessons that were later applied in combat. The 2003 Defence White Paper promised that the army, and the other armed forces, would continue to try to follow this path. There would not only be more emphasis on lower-level tactical training, and combined inter-service training, but there would also be larger-scale operational training exercises with allies.[23] This promise was welcomed by the National Audit Office when they examined the conduct of the forces deployed in Iraq. But, in a proviso that might have been worryingly familiar to many senior commanders in the past, they added that 'owing to their cost, such exercises will always be subject to affordability'.[24]

Thus the strategic scenario facing British soldiers at the start of the twenty-first century would not have been totally unfamiliar to their forefathers a century earlier. A second White Paper followed in July 2004 that spelled out in more detail what the MOD saw as the necessary changes in force structures. The aim of government policy, according to the Secretary of State for Defence, was to create 'flexible and adaptable armed forces properly supported to carry out the most likely expeditionary operations'.[25] The consequent restructuring of the army involved new roles being assigned to a number of artillery and armoured units and the reduction in the number of infantry battalions in the Regular Army's order of battle from forty to thirty-six by 2008. One battalion would be lost in Scotland and three in England. Consequently, the proportion of army manpower allotted to those standard bearers of the Cardwell–Childers regimental system, the infantry and cavalry, which had been 33 per cent in 1941 and had fallen to 31 per cent in 1996, would continue to shrink.[26]

A few days before the 2003 White Paper was published, the CDS had announced in a lecture that

---

[22] MOD, *Design for Military Operations—The British Military Doctrine* (London: MOD, 1996).

[23] Cm 6041-I. *Delivering Security in a Changing World*, 19.

[24] National Audit Office. HC 60 Session (2003–2004), MOD. *Operation TELIC—United Kingdom Military Operations in Iraq* (London: HMSO, 2003), 36.

[25] Cm. 6269. *Delivering Security in a Changing World. Future Capabilities*, July 2004.

[26] These statistics are derived from www.armedforces.co.uk/army/listings/10001.html, accessed on 15 Nov. 2003.

Our ability to develop an effective expeditionary capability will depend on our ability to sustain sufficient, trained and motivated Armed Forces Personnel. Developing and sustaining our 'personnel capability'—in parallel with our equipment and logistic capabilities—is essential and we are developing a new Service Personnel Plan to better manage delivery in this critical area.[27]

The possibility that for the army the quest to sustain sufficient trained and motivated personnel could take place through a strictly applied regimental structure seemed faint. 'The norm for Service Personnel', he added, 'will be individual mobility with frequent deployments and consequent separation from families.'[28] This was a far cry from the expectation of most soldiers who enlisted before 1939, and who expected to serve out their entire engagement in a single regiment. A statement by the CGS that accompanied the July 2004 White Paper made it clear that the infantry would continue to be organized on the divisional system established in 1960s. But, in a move that had more than a faint echo of the linking policies imposed on the army by Cardwell and Childers, the remaining single-battalion regiments were to be reorganized into large regiments of two, or preferably more, battalions. This would preserve some of the advantages of separate regimental identities by 'enhancing the advantages of geographical association'. But it would also ensure the most efficient use of exiguous manpower, for individual officers and other ranks would be able to move easily between units in their division, thus 'preserving the opportunity at an individual level to move between different roles'.[29] Each division was given until October 2004 to decide its own preferences, although the CGS message dropped a heavy hint that the Executive Committee of the Army Board favoured larger regiments of four or more battalions rather than small ones of only two. The Board also promised to issue 'final and definitive direction as to the future organisation of the infantry' by the end of the year. Finally, the Territorial Army was not to be left untouched, for whenever possible its infantry units would be integrated into the future large regiments, 'thereby restoring a true sense of identity at Territorial Army battalion level'.[30]

Despite the transformation that the regimental system had undergone since 1945 much of the rhetoric of the Cardwell–Childers system has survived. Some regiments still highlight their local and community ties in their recruiting literature. The Queen's Lancashire Regiment, whose recruiting area extends across the whole of Lancashire except for the

---

[27] Gen. Sir Michael Walker, 'RUSI Annual Chief of the Defence Staff Lecture', accessed 12 Dec. 2003 at http://www.rusi.org/cgi-bin/public/view.

[28] Ibid.

[29] Cm. 6269. *Delivering Security in a Changing World. Future Capabilities*, July 2004.

[30] Personal message from the CGS, General Sir Mike Jackson, to the Army, 21 July 2004, accessed at http://www.mod.uk/issues/security/cm6269/cgs.htm.

cities of Manchester and Liverpool, emphasizes that it represents 'a great Lancastrian team'.[31] The Devon and Dorset Regiment claim to be the 'county Regiment of both Devon and Dorset', and the Staffordshire Regiment emphasizes that they are 'the local Infantry Regiment for the County'.[32] Similarly, some regiments stress that they still constitute family communities. The Light Infantry insist that 'The Light Infantry prides itself as a family "from the Cradle to the Grave".'[33] Most regiments also tried to give some reality to the rhetoric. They worked actively, often using regimental funds to supplement MOD funding, to find recruits in their own recruiting areas. The Staffordshire Regiment maintained a Regimental Recruiting Team manned from personnel from within the regiment and equipped with vehicles 'which are imaged professionally on a corporate theme'.[34] The Royal Scots Dragoon Guards (Carabiniers and Greys) maintained a small team of recruiters at their Headquarters in Edinburgh and supplemented their efforts by allowing soldiers who were happy with their lot in the regiment to return home on leave to contact friends and relatives to persuade them to join the regiment.[35]

But, as in the past, demography and population density made this easier for some than for others, and those who had lost out had to look elsewhere. Some regiments maintained that the resulting diversity was a positive asset. The product of a series of amalgamations, the Queen's Royal Hussars, was recruited from three widely spaced parts of the British Isles, the West Midlands, Northern Ireland and the Republic of Ireland, and Surrey and West Sussex. The regiment claimed: 'The diversity of home areas gives a very cosmopolitan feel to the regiment, with a healthy intermingling of characteristics.'[36] Other regiments felt that they had no option but to proclaim that they were willing to throw their net very wide open indeed. The Duke of Wellington's Regiment, which has a recruiting area in South Yorkshire, actively encouraged recruits from the Commonwealth.[37] The Black Watch, with a recruiting area that stretched across Perthshire, Fife, Angus, and the City of Dundee, candidly admitted that it welcomed 'applicants from the UK and across the world. We currently have soldiers from Texas, Canada, New Zealand,

---

[31] http://www.army.mod.uk/qlr/recruitment_area.htm, accessed 8 Feb. 2004.

[32] http://www.army.mod.uk/devonanddorset/history.htm, accessed 8 Feb. 2004; http://www.army.mod.uk/staffords/index.html, accessed on 8 Feb. 2004.

[33] http://www.army.mod.uk/lightinfantry/today.htm, accessed 8 Feb. 2004.

[34] E-mail from the Regimental Recruiting Team of the Staffordshire Regiment to the author, rrt@1staffords.freeserve.co.uk, 9 Feb. 2004.

[35] Lt.-Col. R. J. Binks, Regimental Secretary, The Royal Scots Dragoon Guards (Carabiniers and Greys), to the author, 7 Apr. 2004.

[36] http://www.army.mod.uk/armcorps/qroyalhu/index.html, accessed 8 Feb. 2004.

[37] http://www.army.mod.uk/dukes/recruiting.htm, accessed 8 Feb. 2004.

Australia, England, Wales, Gibraltar and Fiji.'[38] In a period when the army was contracting, and when regiments that could not find enough recruits feared that they might be the target of the next series of amalgamations or disbandments, vulnerable regiments were willing to adopt a range of different strategies to find the men they needed. Emphasizing local connections, or the family atmosphere of the regiment, were only some of them.

The tension between regimental commitments and family obligations remained one of the army's major problems. By the late 1990s trained soldiers were leaving the army in worryingly high numbers as operational overstretch created unsustainable stresses between the demands of soldiering and the demands placed on the soldier by his family commitments. The rhetoric of the regimental community as a family could not in many cases overcome the pull of real family ties. In the 1970s, as a result of the introduction of the 'military salary' and the greater provision of married quarters, increasing numbers of soldiers were marrying, and they were doing so at much younger ages than in the past. This created problems for the army because military families shared many of the aspirations of their civilian counterparts. Wives were more likely than in the past to have careers of their own that they were determined to pursue, and they were much less willing than before 1945 to become absorbed into the corporate life of the regiment.[39] One result was that a growing number of servicemen left the army. The military authorities responded by insisting that real families could be incorporated into regimental families. The regiment, according to *Soldiering: The Military Covenant*, is 'regarded as a family—the military community in which most British soldiers do all their operational service and which embraces and cares for them and their families and dependants literally until death'.[40] But nonetheless the problem persists and in July 2004 the MOD at least seemed ready to make a serious effort to overcome it. It determined further to enhance 'the advantages of geographical association' by rooting regiments more firmly in a particular locality by ending 'The practice of arms plotting—moving infantry battalions and their families *en bloc* between roles and geographical locations every few years'. Henceforth, each unit could expect to be based within a particular geographical locality and families could expect 'to put down roots in the community within which they are based'.[41]

[38] http://www.theblackwatch.co.uk/recruitment/index.html, accessed 8 Feb. 2004.

[39] Scott-Clarke, 'The Military Wife'.

[40] MOD, *Soldiering: The Military Covenant*, 0316; A. Beevor, *Inside the British Army* (London: Corgi, 1991), 59–60; Cm. 5566, *The Strategic Defence Review: A New Chapter* (London: HMSO, 2002), i. 20.

[41] Cm. 6269. *Delivering Security in a Changing World. Future Capabilities*, July 2004.

It remains to be seen if these reforms will work. But in the meantime it is apparent that shortfalls in recruiting and the loss of trained manpower had led to a further erosion of regimental solidarities. By the late 1990s it was commonplace, according to the Army's Director of Personnel Services,

to top up units preparing for operational tours from those conducting routine training or recovering from earlier tours. This causes further gaps to appear elsewhere and serves to fragment the cohesion of our regiments and battalions, specially those not on operations who are training and conducting a host of other duties.[42]

During the Second Gulf War a number of units that deployed in the Gulf were so short of men that they had to be made up to strength by attaching to them whole companies from other regiments. Such a situation had clear echoes of what the army did in the late 1870s to prepare units for despatch to Zululand. The decision to link existing single battalion regiments has equally loud echoes of how Childers attempted to solve the same problem in 1881.

The CGS described the restructuring of the infantry as 'difficult and sensitive' and he was right.[43] Even before the publication of the 2004 White Paper, rumours abounded about the MOD's intentions. MPs of all parties and regimental associations, fearing that their 'local' regiments might be one of those to be cut, sought reassurances from Ministers.[44] Critics rose up in their wrath to defend the regimental system, or rather a vision of an idealized mythical version that was testimony to the success of those who had worked so assiduously in the past to construct the idea of 'the Regiment'. Before the July 2004 White Paper was published one Conservative front-bench spokesman insisted on the existence of 'often historic links deep inside the counties and cities from which they [the regiments] spring'.[45] And after its publication he reminded the Secretary of State 'that in these regiments are some of the qualities that set the British Army apart from all others, and that therefore the significance of the regimental system must be retained in any restructuring that takes

---

[42] Brig. A. S. Ritchie, 'Turning the Tide: Addressing Army Personnel Issues', *Journal of the Royal United Services Institute*, 144 (1999), 67.

[43] 'Personal message from the CGS, General Sir Mike Jackson, to the Army, 21 July 2004', accessed at http://www.mod.uk/issues/security/cm6269/cgs.htm.

[44] Hansard, col. 773 (Written answers) (6 Nov. 2003); col. 1267 (Written answers) (20 Nov. 2003), accessed 15 Aug. 2004 at http://www.parliament.the-stationery-office.co.uk/pa/cm200203/cmhansrd/vo031106; Hansard, cols. 3–5 (Oral questions) (19 July 2004), accessed 15 Aug. 2004 at http://www.parliament.the-stationery-office.co.uk/pa/cm200304/cmhansrd/cmo040719.

[45] Hansard, col. 4 (19 July 2004), accessed 15 Aug. 2004 at http://www.parliament.the-stationery-office.co.uk/pa/cm200304/cmhansrd/cmo040719.

place'.[46] Other MPs of all parties reiterated their belief that history and heritage were powerful forces impelling men to enlist.[47] But the fact that some MPs and regimental associations were sufficiently exercised by possible disbandments and amalgamations to ask questions in the Commons should not lead to the conclusion that regiments have retained the roots that Cardwell and Childers tried to plant for them in the wider community.[48] Although the regimental secretary of one English regiment was reported to have suggested that regiments threatened with amalgamation should organize a protest march on Parliament, protests against the White Paper were loudest in Scotland. This was an indication perhaps that public concern for the future of the regimental system only ran deep where it intersected with local nationalist sentiments.[49] By contrast, a petition organized in Huddersfield to protect the separate identity of the Duke of Wellington's Regiment collected only 300 signatures.[50]

By the end of the twentieth century the process of 'civilianizing' regimental soldiering that had begun in the very late 1930s was fast accelerating. One result was that many senior members of the army felt themselves increasingly beleaguered in a society that, whilst it was proud of their martial achievements, did not understand or necessarily share the army's culture. There were many reasons for this growing dissociation between army and community. Few civilians or politicians had any direct military experience. Societal values seemed to be changing in ways that were inimical to the culture of the armed forces. In 1999 the CGS complained that

In the past the conduct and values of society were perhaps more closely aligned with those required of a military force, but this is not necessarily the case today. The more libertarian values of modern Britain with their emphasis on the freedom of the individual rather than obligation to any collective identity are sometimes at odds with the values and behaviour needed to create the spirit and cohesiveness required in battle.[51]

[46] Hansard, col. 353 (21 July 2004), accessed 15 Aug. 2004 at http://www.parliament. the-stationery-office.co.uk/pa/cm200304/cmhansrd/cm040721.

[47] Hansard, cols. 363–4, 369–70 (21 July 2004), accessed 15 Aug. 2004 at http://www. parliament.the-stationery-office.co.uk/pa/cm200304; col. 543, 547 (22 July 2004), accessed 15 Aug. 2004 at http://www.parliament.the-stationery-office.co.uk/pa/cm200304/cmhansrd/ cm040722. G. Chamberlain and I. Johnston, 'Regiments Join Forces to Fight MOD Cuts', The Scotsman, 24 July 2004.

[48] Anon., 'Dukes Slam Plans to Merge Regiments', Huddersfield Daily Examiner, 20 July 2004; Anon., 'Duke's Battle Lines Drawn', Halifax Today, 6 Aug. 2004; P. Fleming, 'Save your Regiment', Westmoreland Gazette, 12 Aug. 2004.

[49] Chamberlain and Johnston, 'Regiments Join Forces'; 'Facing up to Defence Shake-up', BBC News, 21 July 2004, accessed at http://news.bbc.co.uk/1/hi/england/3912895.stm.

[50] Anon., 'You, the Readers, Rally to the Cause of Historic Regiment', Huddersfield Daily Examiner, 12 Aug. 2004.

[51] Gen. Sir R. Wheeler, 'Peacemakers Know that Britain Will Deliver', Journal of the Royal United Services Institute, 144 (1999), 7.

A year later the Chief of Defence Staff warned that legislation concerned with such issues as health and safety at work, working-time directives, and human rights 'might begin to erode the ethos of service and sacrifice. I do think the uniqueness of the Services is not always well understood and the modern concern for the rights of the individual sometimes have to be sacrificed in the military for the collective good of the team.'[52] His remedy, more frequent media briefings to communicate the armed forces' concerns, was a pale shadow of the Cardwell–Childers recipe of a military depot in every community. But the closure of army bases and the withering away of regiments meant that the army, like the other armed forces, had a much smaller footprint in society in 2000 than it had in 1881.[53] The bridge that the Militia, Volunteers, and Territorials had once formed between the Regular Army and civilian society had crumbled. In April 2001 the Territorial Army had been reduced to 40,300 men, organized into thirty-three teeth-arm units and forty-three logistics, medical, and communications units. Its main function was to reinforce regular units with individuals and specialist support units. Territorial Army centres were often the only military presence in a particular area, but in some areas there were hardly any of them: there were, for example, only two in mid-Wales, five north of the Highland line, and half a dozen west of Exeter.[54]

The CDS and his colleagues had some reason to be concerned at the growing divergence between their own interpretation of a desirable military ethos and wider societal values. A survey published in 1998 of the attitudes of regimental officers, NCOs, and rank-and-file soldiers showed that most were prepared to offer only qualified loyalty to the army or their regiment. Fifty-five per cent of respondents agreed that soldiers were different from other members society, but only 46 per cent thought that the interests of the army were more important than the interests of the individual. Sixty-two per cent thought that their willingness to serve their country led to them being exploited, and 77 per cent thought that they were in the same employment category as the police service, and so desired the same representation. But 62 per cent agreed that an organization akin to the Police Federation would have an adverse effect on the culture and ethos of the army, 60 per cent thought that it would have an adverse impact on discipline, and 55 per cent thought it might degrade the army's operational effectiveness.[55] It seemed that the

---

[52] Gen. Sir C. Gutherie, 'British Defence—The Chief of the Defence Staff's Lecture 2000', *Journal of the Royal United Services Institute*, 146 (2001), 7.

[53] C. Dandeker, 'On the Need to Be Different: Military Uniqueness and Civil–Military Relations in Modern Society', *Journal of the Royal United Services Institute*, 146 (2001), 4–9.

[54] Holmes, 'Volunteer Reserves', 23.

[55] R. Bartle, 'The Army in the 21st Century—Addressing the Final Taboo', *Journal of the Royal United Services Institute*, 143 (1998), 45–7.

army had moved a long way from the goal of Cardwell and Childers, that the regiment should be the focus of every soldier's loyalty, and that every officer and man should be willing to subordinate his own individual interests to those of his regiment.

In 1962 the novelist and former infantry officer Robert Graves wrote: 'It is the highly emotional regimental traditions, hoarded down the centuries, that alone account for smartness on parade, disciplined patience during civil disturbances, courage on the field.'[56] Graves was wrong. He was guilty of oversimplifying and overstating the case for the regimental system. It did play a part in sustaining morale and discipline, but it was never the only factor that did so, just as it was never the sole, or even the main, cause of the difficulty that the army sometimes experienced in both world wars in fighting in large combined-arms formations. The British army was, and is, a large and complex organization. It has routinely confronted large and complex problems. Reducing the reasons for its successes and failures to a single factor, and labelling that factor 'the regimental system', defies logic and belies reality.

[56] PRO WO 32/20366. Press cutting, undated, but c.10 Apr. 1962.

Bibliography

UNPUBLISHED PRIMARY SOURCES

National Archives, Public Record Office, Kew

Departmental Papers
Admiralty:
 ADM 1
Cabinet:
 CAB 1, 16, 23, 24, 27
Director of Public Prosecutions:
 DPP1, 2
Home Office:
 HO 45, 144
Ministry of Defence:
 DEFE 7
Ministry of Reconstruction:
 RECO 1
Security Service:
 KV2
War Office:
 WO 30, 32, 33, 38, 79, 93, 95, 106, 108, 123, 141, 147, 162, 163, 171, 190, 209, 217, 231, 260, 261, 277, 279, 293, 365

 Private Papers
 Edward Cardwell MSS
 Hugh Childers MSS
 Sir William John Codrington MSS

Bedfordshire Record Office

Bedfordshire and Hertfordshire Regiment Records

Private Papers
Lt.-Col. V. Russell MSS

Churchill College Cambridge
Field Marshal Lord Cavan MSS

Essex County Record Office

 Records compiled by J. W. Burrows for 'The War 1914–1919'
 Scrapbook of Brig.-Gen. Sir R. Colvin of Waltham Abbey

W. G. Green MSS
Maj.-Gen. Sir H. Ruggles-Brise MSS
H. Salmon MSS
J. T. de Horne Vaizey
Records of S. Watson of Shenfield

Essex Regiment Museum

Essex Regiment Records
Essex Yeomanry Records
C. D. Bacon MSS
A. E. Cooper MSS
Sgt. W. H. Green MSS
J. Howard MSS
Pte. R. A. Newbury MSS
Brig. C. M. Paton MSS
H. J. Staff MSS
Lt.-Col. H.C.N. Trollope MSS
2/Lt. H. R. Wardill MSS
Maj. C. A. Webb MSS
Cpl. E. J. Wymer MSS

Imperial War Museum, Department of Documents

Brig. E. E. F. Baker MSS
Maj. W. G. Blaxland MSS
Maj. J. H. Finch MSS
Pte. A. R. Gaskin MSS
Lt.-Col. G. E. A. Granet MSS
Capt. M. Hardie MSS
Col. F. W. S. Jourdain MSS
E. Lye MSS
Maj. D. A. Philips MSS
Jesse Short Collection
T. A. Silver MSS
J. C. Slater MSS
L. Waller MSS
Col. K. C. Weldon MSS
Maj.-Gen. D. N. Wimberley MSS

Imperial War Museum, Department of Sound Records

Maj. A. H. Austin
A. G. Avis
Col. A. R. Bain
A. R. Bale
Sir W. Barber
Brig. P. Barclay

A. C. Barr
D. F. Barrett
Maj.-Gen. H. L. Birks
K. W. Black
G. F. Blackmuir
Col. W. B. Blain
T. Boyne
A. H. Bradshaw
Maj.-Gen. H. E. N. Bredin
Lt.-Col. E. G. Brice
Brig. R. H. Bright
Col. U. B. Burke
H. W. Burnett
Capt. B. G. Buxton
R. J. Carriage
T. Chadwick
R. Clemens
Maj.-Gen. K. C. Cooper
W. Cousins
D. F. Cowie
Maj. F. Crocker
Reverend Maj. D. Davies
Brig. E. G. B. Davies-Scourfield
Brig. W. C. Deller
Maj. C. H. Ditcham
F. Dixon
Col. G. W. Draffen
Maj.-Gen. N. W. Duncan
Maj.-Gen. Sir C. Dunphie
R. F. Edwards
J. L. Fairhurst
Col. P. Featherby
Lt.-Col R. L. V. ffrench Blake
Sgt. M. Finlayson
Lt.-Col. R. C. Glanville
Maj.-Gen. F. W. Gordon-Hall
P. Gorman
J. Gray
Lt.-Col. M. R. L. Grove
Maj.-Gen. J. M. L. Grover
Col. J. Gunn
Gen. Sir J. Hackett
J. T. Hammond
Brig. R. N. Harding-Newman
Elizabeth Harrington
F. Hazell

J. E. Heyes
Brig. S. J. L. Hill
Maj.-Gen. P. R. C. Hobart
F. Hodges
D. J. Holdsworth
Lt.-Col. E. G. Hollist
Mrs. P. M. Hopkins
Maj. S. Hornor
Col. Sir A. Horsburgh-Porter
H. L. Horsfield
Maj. E. S. Humphries
F. H. Hunt
Maj.-Gen. H. P. W. Hutson
Lt.-Col. W. H. Hyde
Col. A. P. B. Irwin
Lt.-Col. A. C. Jackson
R. Jago
J. E. G. Jones
Col. G. J. Kidston-Montgomerie
Lt.-Col. R. King-Clark
Lt.-Col. M. E. S. Laws
Maj.-Gen. H. M. Liardet
T. W. McIndoe
Maj. D. C. McIver
Brig. J. F. McNab
Lt.-Col. V. C. Magill-Cuerden
Lt.-Col. A. M. Man
Col. F. O. Mason
F. Maurice
F. E. Mitchell
Maj.-Gen. J. Moulton
Col. P. R. M. Mundy
Lt.-Gen. Sir P. Neame
Lt.-Col. T. W. Nickalls
Col E. F. Offord
J. Packer
T. Pain
T. H. Painting
Maj. W. Parrott
G. Paterson
S. A. S. Phillips
N. Potter
Capt. F. J. Powell
Maj.-Gen. G. W. Richards
J. G. Rodger
P. J. Russell

L/Cpl. ? Rowden
P. B. Saunders
Col. K. E. Savill
Col. Sir D. Scott
Maj.-Gen. J. Scott Elliot
Brig. W. R. Smijth-Windham
H. Smith
Maj. H. J. Smith
Capt. P. Snelling
Brig. G. F. H. Stayner
F. T. Suter
Lt.-Col. J. R. V. Thompson
Lt.-Col. H. D. Thwaytes
F. M. V. Tregar
Maj.-Gen. G. F. Upjohn
R. Usher
Lt.-Col. W. O. Walton
E. G. White
E. O. L. Whitewick
A. S. Whitton
Lt.-Col. P. M. Wiggan

Liddell Hart Centre for Military Archives, King's College London

Lord Alanbrooke MSS
Lt.-Gen. Sir L. Kiggell MSS
Capt. L. C. King-Wilkinson MSS
Sir Basil Liddell Hart MSS
Field Marshal Sir A. Montgomery-Massingberd MSS

National Army Museum

Documents of 3rd Hussars
Formation of the Light Infantry
Historical Records 1/Royal West Kent 1849–1914
Historical Records 1/Royal West Kent 1882–1914
Historical Records, 50/Regiment of Foot, 1757–1882
Historical Records, 97/Regiment of Foot, 1808–1896
Records of the 88/Regiment (Connaught Rangers)
Record of Service of 94/Regiment and 2/Battalion Connaught Rangers
Royal Munster Fusiliers, Press cuttings
Scrapbook, Officer's Mess, 27/Foot, 2/Battalion Royal Inniskilling Fusiliers
Surrey Yeomanry, B Squadron, Woking Troop

Private Papers
Anon., *The Army and What it Offers*

Anon., Experiences of a soldier
Diary of Lt.-Col. Julius J. Backhouse
Maj.-Gen. W. O. Barnard MSS
Warrant Officer I. W. H. Davies MSS
Lt.-Gen. Sir Gerald F. Ellison MSS
Pte. J. A Facer MSS
Pte. P. Y. Grainger MSS
Diary of N. Hallam MSS
Sgt. H. Hopwood MSS
L/Cpl. H. James MSS
Lt.-Col. W. Lockhart MSS
A. Y. McPeake MSS
Col. A. M. Man MSS
Maj. St. J. W. T. Parker MSS
Pte. W. J. Putland MSS
Lt.-Col. A. J. Richardson MSS
Sir R. B. Stephens MSS
Col. G. C. Swiney MSS'
Field Marshal Sir G. Templer MSS
Captain Francis Warre-Cornish MSS
Lt. L. Wedd MSS
Sgt.-Major J. White MSS

National Library of Scotland

R. B. Haldane MSS

Royal Norfolk Regiment Museum

Norfolk Regiment Records
Anon., *Memorandum on the subject of social and official intercourse between British Officers and Indians* (Calcutta: Superintendent Government Printing, India, 1919). **Ch. 5**
F. W. Allen MSS
L/Cpl. C. Mates MSS
Cpl. P. C. Richards MSS
P. V. P. Stone MSS
Colour Sgt. John Wall MSS

Suffolk Record Office (Bury St Edmunds Branch)

Suffolk Regiment Records
Brig. I. L. Wight MSS

Websites

http://www.armedforces.co.uk/army/listings/10001.html. Accessed 15 Nov. 2003.

http://www.armedforces.co.uk/army/listings/10027.html. Accessed 8 Feb. 2004.
http://www.army.mod.uk/armcorps/qroyalhu/index.html. Accessed 8 Feb. 2004.
http://www.army.mod.uk/devonanddorset/history.htm. Accessed 8 Feb. 2004.
http://www.army.mod.uk/dukes/recruiting.htm. Accessed 8 Feb. 2004.
http://www.army.mod.uk/lightinfantry/today.htm. Accessed 8 Feb. 2004.
http://www.army.mod.uk/qlr/recruitment_area.htm. Accessed 8 Feb. 2004.
http://www.army.mod.uk/staffords/index.html. Accessed 8 Feb. 2004.
http://www.britains-smallwars.com/korea/Queens.htm. J. Copsey, 'Two Years for the Queen'. Accessed 28 Apr. 2002.
http://www.freespace.virgin.net/edward.nicholl/jacksonsdiary.htm. 'An Experience of Twelve Months Active Service on the Veldt, by 3213 Private John Jackson, 1st Battalion The Yorkshire Regiment (Green Howards)'. Accessed 18 Mar. 2000.
http://www.jwmilne.freeservers.com/speech.htm. No 8080 Private J. W. Milne, 1st Service Company Volunteers, Gordon Highlanders (1900), 'Looking back on the Boer War'. Accessed 8 July 2001.
http://www.mod.uk/issues/security/cm6269/cgs.htm. 'Personal message from the CGS, General Sir Mike Jackson, to the Army, 21 July 2004'. Accessed 30 July 2004.
http://www.rusi.org/cgi-bin/public/viewGen. Sir Michael Walker, 'RUSI Annual Chief of the Defence Staff Lecture'. Accessed 12 Dec. 2003.
http://www.theblackwatch.co.uk/recruitment/index.html. Accessed 8 Feb. 2004.

PUBLISHED PRIMARY SOURCES

Official Publications

ANON., *Appendix to the reports of the Select Committee of the House of Commons on public petitions. Session 1872* (London: House of Commons, 1872).
ANON., *Appendix to the reports of the Select Committee of the House of Commons on public petitions. Session 1874* (London: House of Commons, 1874).
Hansard's Parliamentary Debates.

Parliamentary Papers

PP (1861), XV. C. 2762. *Report of the Commissioners appointed to inquire into the present system of recruiting in the Army.*
PP (1862), XXVII. C. 5067. *Report of the Commissioners appointed to inquire into the condition of the Volunteer Force in Great Britain.*
PP (1867), XV. C. 3752. *Report of Commissioners appointed to inquire into the recruiting for the Army.*
PP (1875), XLIII. C. 1323. *General Annual Return for the British Army for the Year Ending 30 Sept. 1875.*
PP (1876), XV. C. 1569. *Report of the Royal Commission on Army promotion and retirement.*
PP (1877), XVIII. C. 1654. *Report of the Committee appointed to inquire into certain questions that have arisen with respect to the Militia and the present Brigade Depot system.*

PP (1878–9), XV. C. 2235. *Report of the Committee appointed by the Secretary of State for War to enquire into the Internal Organisation of the Volunteer Forces in Great Britain.*

PP (1881), XX. C. 2817. *Report of the Committee appointed to consider the conditions of a soldier's service as affected by the introduction of the short service system and other matters in connection therewith.*

PP (1881), XX. C. 2832. *Annual Report of the Inspector-General of Recruiting, 1 Feb. 1881.*

PP (1881), XXI. C. 2791. *Report of the Committee of General and other officers of the army on army reorganisation.*

PP (1881), XXI. C. 2792. *Memo by HRH the Field Marshal C-in-C on the proposal of the Secretary of State for War for the organization of the various military land forces of the country; and report of a committee on the details involved therein.*

PP (1881), XXI. C. 2792. *Supplementary report of Committee on the organisation of the various military land forces of the country.*

PP (1881), XXI. C. 2792. *Final report of committee on the organisation of the various military land forces of the country.*

PP (1881), XXI. C. 2792. *General Order 32 of 1873.*

PP (1881), LVIII. C. 2826. *Memorandum showing the principal changes in Army organisation intended to take effect from 1st July 1881.*

PP (1881), LVIII. C. 2922. *Revised Memorandum showing the principal changes in Army organisation intended to take effect from 1st July 1881.*

PP (1881), LVIII. C. 3083. *General Annual Return for the British Army for the Year 1880.*

PP (1882), XVI. C. 3167. *1882 Report of the Cavalry Organisation.*

PP (1882), XVI. C. 3168. *Report of Committee on Artillery Localisation.*

PP (1882), XXXVIII. C. 3405. *General Annual Return of the British Army for the Year Ending 30 Sept. 1881.*

PP (1883), XV. C. 3503. *Annual Report of the Inspector-General of Recruiting.*

PP (1888), XXV. C. 5302. *Annual Report of the Inspector General of Recruiting.*

PP (1890), XIX. C. 5922. *Report of the Committee appointed to enquire into certain questions that have arisen with respect to the Militia.*

PP (1890), XLIII. C. 6196. *General Annual Return for the British Army for the Year ending 30 Sept. 1889.*

PP (1892), XIX. C. 6582. *Report of the Committee on the terms and conditions of service in the army.*

PP (1892), XX. C. 6597. *Annual Report of the Inspector General of Recruiting for 1891.*

PP (1892), XX. C. 6675. *Report of the Committee appointed by the Secretary of State for War to consider the conditions of the Yeomanry.*

PP (1894), XV. *Report from the Select Committee on Volunteer Acts.*

PP (1894), LIII. C. 7483. *General Annual Return for the British army for the year 1893.*

PP (1897), LIV. C. 8558. *General Annual Return for the British Army for the Year ending 30 September 1896.*

PP (1899), LIII. C. 9426. *General Annual Return for the British Army for the year ending 30 Sept. 1898.*

PP (1900), XLII. Cd. 196. *Report of the Committee on War Relief Funds.*

PP (1902), X. Cd. 962. *Annual Report of the Inspector-General of Recruiting for the Year 1901.*

PP (1902), X. Cd. 982. *Report of the Committee appointed to consider the education and training of officers of the Army.*

PP (1902), X. Cd. 983. *Minutes of Evidence of the Committee appointed to consider the education and training of officers of the Army.*

PP (1903), X. Cd. 1421. *Report of the committee appointed by the Secretary of State for War to inquire into the nature of the expenses incurred by officers of the Army and to suggest measures for bringing commissions within reach of men of moderate means.*

PP (1903), X. Cd. 1494. *Minutes of Evidence of the committee appointed to consider the existing conditions under which canteens and regimental institutes are conducted.*

PP (1904), XXX. Cd. 2062. *Report of the Royal Commission on the Militia and Volunteers.*

PP (1904), XXXI. Cd. 2063. *Minutes of Evidence of the Royal Commission on the Militia and Volunteers.*

PP (1904), XL. Cd. 1790. *Minutes of evidence taken before the Royal Commission on the War in South Africa.*

PP (1904), XLI. Cd. 1791. *Minutes of evidence taken before the Royal Commission on the war in South Africa.*

PP (1906), XIV. Cd. 2693. *Annual Report of Recruiting for the year ended 30 September 1905.*

PP (1907), IX. Cd. 3365. *General Annual Report on the British Army for the Year ending 30 September 1906.*

PP (1907), XXXIX. Cd. 3515. *Principles to be kept in view in training the Territorial Force and the Special Contingent.*

PP (1907), XLIX. Cd. 3294. *Interim report of the War Office committee on the provision of officers (a) for service with the regular army in war, and (b) for the auxiliary forces.*

PP (1907), XLIX. *Army Commissions. Return as to the number of commissions granted during each of the years 1885 to 1906.*

PP (1911), XLVI. *General Annual Return for the British Army for the year ending 1910.*

PP (1914), XVI. *General Annual Return for the British Army for the year ending 30 Sept. 1913.*

PP (1914), LI. Cd. 7441. *Report of an inquiry by Mrs Tennant regarding the conditions of marriage off the strength.*

PP (1921), XX. *General Annual Reports on the British Army (including the Territorial Force from the date of embodiment) for the period from 1 October 1913 to 30 Sept. 1919.*

PP (1923), XIV. Cmd. 1941. *General Annual Report for the British Army for the Year Ending 30 September 1921.*

PP (1924–5), XVII. Cmd. 2342. *General Annual Report for the British Army for the Year Ending 30 September 1924.*

PP (1929–30), XIX. Cmd. 3498. *General Annual Report for the British Army for the year Ending 30 September 1929.*

PP (1930–1), XIX. Cmd. 3800. *General Annual Report for the British Army for the year ending 30 Sept. 1930.*

PP (1935–6), XVI. Cmd. 5104. *General Annual Report for the British Army for the year ending 30 Sept. 1935.*

PP (1937–8), XVII. Cmd. 5486. *General Annual Report for the British Army for the Year Ending 30 September 1937.*

PP (1937–8), XVII. Cmd. 5681. *Army Estimates, 1937–38.*

PP (1937–8), XVII. Cmd. 5696. *Statement relating to improvements in the pay and allowances etc of the regular army.*

PP (1945–6), XVI. Cmd. 6715. *Post-war pay code of pay, allowances, retired pay and service gratuities for members of the forces below officer rank.*

PP (1945–6), XVI. Cmd. 6750. *Post-war pay code of pay, allowances, retired pay and service gratuities for commissioned officers of the armed forces.*

PP (1952–3), III. *Reports of Committees. Army and Air Force Act. Report with Proceedings, Evidence and Appendices.*

PP (1955–6), XXXII. Cmd. 962. *Service Pay and Pensions.*

PP (1956–7), XII. Cmnd. 230. *The future organisation of the army.*

PP (1956–7), XVII. Cmnd. 35. *Report of the Committee on the Employment of National Servicemen in the UK.*

PP (1958–9), VIII. Cmnd. 545. *Report of the Advisory Committee on Recruiting.*

PP (1961–2), XXVI. Cmnd. 1631. *Army Estimates 1962–63.*

PP (1965–6), IX. Cmnd. 2902. *Defence Estimates 1966–67, for the year ending 31 March 1967.*

PP (1966–7), LIII. Cmnd. 3357. *Supplementary Statement on Defence Policy 1967.*

Cm. 5566. *The Strategic Defence Review: A New Chapter* (London: HMSO, 2002), i.

National Audit Office. HC 60 Session (2003–2004), MOD. *Operation TELIC—United Kingdom Military Operations in Iraq* (London: HMSO, 2003).

Cm. 6041-I. *Delivering Security in a Changing World* (London: HMSO, 2003).

Cm. 6269. *Delivering Security in a Changing World. Future Capabilities*, July 2004.

Manuals, Standing Orders, etc.

Adjutant-General, *Field Exercises and Evolutions of Infantry (1870)* (London: HMSO, 1870).

—— *Field Exercises and Evolutions of Infantry (1874)* (London: HMSO, 1874).

ANON., *Rules of the Royal Fusiliers Old Comrades Association and Royal Fusiliers Aid Society* (n.d. or publisher).

—— *Standing Orders of the 56th (West Essex) Regiment* (Bombay: Education Society Press, Byculla, 1874).

—— *The Standing Orders of the 47th (The Lancashire Regiment) of Foot* (Aldershot: William Clowes, 1876).

—— *The Standing Orders of the 1st Battalion, the Suffolk Regiment* (Chatham: Galen & Polden, 1888).

—— *Standing Orders of the First Essex Artillery Volunteers (EDRA)* (Stratford: Wilson & Whitworth, 1890).

—— *Standing Orders of the 1st Batt. 'The Queen's Own', late 50th Regiment* (Chatham: Gale & Polden, 1891).

—— *Standing Orders and rules of the 1st Volunteer Battalion Essex Regiment* (Brentwood: n.p., 1896).

—— *The Standing Orders of the 5th (Royal Irish) Lancers* (Aldershot: Gale & Polden, 1904).

—— *The Standing Orders of the 2nd Battalion 22nd (Cheshire) Regiment* (2nd edn., Madras, 1906).

—— *The Subaltern's Handbook of Useful Information* (London: Gale & Polden: first published Apr. 1916; 3rd edn., Jan. 1918).

—— *Rules of the Officers' Mess 1st Battalion South Staffordshire Regiment* (Aldershot: Gale & Polden, 1924).

—— *Standing Orders of the 1/Battalion The Norfolk Regiment* (Birmingham: The Birmingham Printers, 1925).

—— *Standing Orders of the Suffolk Regiment (The Twelfth Foot)* (n.p., 1925).

—— *1/Battalion Essex Regiment (44th Foot). Warrant Officer's and Sergeants Mess Rules* (Aldershot: Gale & Polden, 1926).

—— *The Standing Orders of the King's Royal Rifle Corps* (Aldershot: Gale & Polden, 1930).

—— *2/Battalion Essex Regiment (The Pompadours). Sergeants Mess Rules* (Aldershot: Gale & Polden, 1931).

—— *Standing Orders of the Durham Light Infantry* (Newcastle-upon-Tyne: J. & P. Beals Ltd, 1933).

—— *The Standing Orders of the 2nd Battalion The Royal Warwickshire Regiment* (Aldershot: Gale & Polden, 1934).

—— *Durham Light Infantry Standing Orders* (Newcastle-upon-Tyne: J. & P. Beals Ltd, 1941).

—— *Rules of the Royal Artillery Association, 1946* (n.d. or publisher).

—— *5th Royal Inniskilling Dragoon Guards. Officers Mess Rules* (Sennelager, Germany, no publisher, 1957).

—— *Handbook of the Cameronians (Scottish Rifles)* (Winston Barracks, Lanark, 1957).

—— *The Yorkshire Brigade* (Morecambe: Morecambe Bay Printers, n.d. but *c.*1959).

—— *The Royal Highland Fusiliers: Regimental Standing Orders* (Glasgow: Robert MacLehouse & Co. Ltd, *c.*1960).

—— *First Battalion of the York and Lancaster Regiment. Disbandment Ceremonies* (n.p., 1968).

Army Sports Control Board, *Games and Sports in the Army 1943–44* (London: War Office, 1944).

COLE, Maj. D. H., *Imperial Military Geography: General Characteristics of the Empire in Relation to Defence* (London: Sifton Praed, 1937).

General Staff, *Field Service Regulations. Part 1. Operations (1909)* (London: HMSO, 1909).

General Staff, *Training and Manoeuvre Regulations, 1909* (London: HMSO, 1909).
—— *Infantry Training 1911* (London: HMSO, 1911).
—— *Cavalry Training 1912* (London: HMSO, 1912).
—— *Infantry Training (4-Company Organisation) 1914* (London: HMSO, 1914).
—— *Infantry Training. Vol. I. Training, 1932* (London: HMSO, 1932).
—— *Training Regulations, 1934* (London: HMSO, 1934).
—— *Infantry Training (Training and War)* (London: HMSO, 1937).
—— *Training in Fieldcraft and Elementary Tactics. Military Training Pamphlet No. 33* (London: HMSO, 1940).
LEGGE, Maj. R. F., *Guide to Promotion for Officers in Subjects (a)(i) Regimental Duties* (London: Gale & Polden, 1915).
Ministry of Defence, *Manual of Military Law, Part 1, 1972* (London: HMSO, 1972).
Ministry of Defence, *Joint Warfare Publications (JWP) 0–01, British Defence Doctrine* (London: MOD, 1996).
—— *Design for Military Operations—The British Military Doctrine* (London: MOD, 1996).
—— *Army Doctrine Publications, v: Soldiering: The Military Covenant* (London: MOD, 2000).
MOORE, Maj. A. T., *Notes for Officers Proceeding to India. Revised and Corrected to March 1912* (Chatham: Royal Engineers Institute, 1912).
SPENCER, Lt.-Col. HON. A. A., *Standing Orders of the 44th or East Essex Regiment by Lt Col. Hon. A. A. Spencer* (Bombay: Education Society Press, Byculla, 1862).
War Office, *Regulations for the Volunteer Force. War Office 1881* (London: HMSO, 1881).
—— *The Queen's Regulations and Orders for the Army 1892* (London: HMSO, 1892).
—— *Manual of Military Law, 1899* (London: HMSO, 1899).
—— *Field Service Regulations. Part 1. Combined Training* (London: HMSO, 1905).
—— *Royal Warrant for the Pay, Appointment, Promotion, and Non-effective Pay of the Army, 1906* (London, 1906).
—— *Manual of Physical Training (1908)* (London: HMSO, 1908).
—— *Regulations for the Officers of the Special Reserve of Officers and the Special Reserve, 1911* (London: HMSO, 1911).
—— *King's Regulations and Orders for the Army, 1912* (London: HMSO, 1912).
—— *Manual of Elementary Military Hygiene 1912* (London: HMSO, 1912).
—— *Field Service Pocket Book, 1914* (London: HMSO, 1914).
—— *The King's Regulations and Orders for the Army and the Army Reserve, 1928* (London: HMSO, 1928).
—— *Royal Warrant for the Pay, Appointment, Promotion, and Non-effective Pay of the Army, 1931* (London: HMSO, 1931).
—— *The King's Regulations for the Army and the Royal Army Reserve, 1940* (London: HMSO, 1940).
—— *Royal Warrant for the Pay, Appointment, Promotion, and Non-effective Pay of the Army, 1940* (London: HMSO, 1940).
—— *Handbook of Military Hygiene 1943* (London: HMSO, 1943).
—— *Queen's Regulations for the Army 1955* (London: HMSO, 1955).

—— *Customs of the Army (1956)* (London: HMSO, 1956).
—— *Notes on the British Army 1961* (London: HMSO, 1961).
WOLSELEY, Sir G., *The Soldier's Pocket Book* (5th edn., London: Macmillan, 1886).

Regimental Journals

The Abbey Field Review. A Monthly Record of Garrison Life in Colchester.
The Black Horse Gazette. The Journal of the 7th Dragoon Guards.
The Eagle. The Journal of the Essex Regiment.
Eleventh Hussars Journal.
Essex Regiment Gazette.
'Faugh-a-Ballagh'. The Regimental Gazette of the 87th Royal Irish Fusiliers.
The Hampshire Regiment Journal.
Highland Light Infantry Chronicle.
Journal of the Honourable Artillery Company.
The Journal of the Household Brigade.
The Journal of the Queen's Royal Regiment.
The King's Royal Rifle Corps Chronicle.
The Lancashire Lad: The Journal of the Loyal Regiment (North Lancashire).
The Oxford and Buckinghamshire Light Infantry Chronicle 1910: An Annual Record of the First and Second Battalions. Formerly the 43rd and 52nd Light Infantry.
The Regimental Chronicle. The South Lancashire Regiment (Prince of Wales Volunteers).
St George's Gazette.
The 79th News.
The Sherwood Foresters Regimental Annual.
The Tank.
The Xth Royal Hussars Gazette.
The Wasp and the Eagle. Regimental Journal of the 3rd East Anglian Regiment (16th/ 44th Foot).

Newspapers

Halifax Today.
Huddersfield Daily Examiner.
The Scotsman.
The Times.
The Westmoreland Gazette.

CD-Roms

Soldiers Died in the Great War (Naval and Military Press, 1998).
Army Roll of Honour: World War Two (Naval and Military Press, 2000).

Contemporary Pamphlets and Memoirs, etc.

'A British Officer' [Capt. W. E. Cairnes], *Social Life in the British Army* (London and New York: Harper Brothers, 1899).

'A Field Officer', 'Modern Infantry Discipline', *Journal of the Royal United Services Institute*, 79 (1934), 464–74.

ADYE, Gen. Sir J., 'The Glut of Junior Officers in the Army', *Nineteenth Century*, 27 (1890), 258–69.

—— *Recollections of a Military Life* (London: Smith, Elder & Co., 1895).

ALEXANDER, Sir J. E., 'On Desertion in Canada', *United Services Journal*, pt. 2 (1842), 469–76.

ALTHAM, Lt.-Gen. Sir E. A., 'The Cardwell System', *Journal of the Royal United Services Institute*, 73 (1928), 108–14.

ANON., 'Army Notes', *Journal of the Royal United Services Institute*, 64 (1919), 757–8.

—— 'Army Notes', *Journal of the Royal United Services Institute*, 83 (1938), 877–84.

—— 'Army Notes', *Journal of the Royal United Services Institute*, 84 (1939), 205, 429–30.

—— 'Army Reform', *Edinburgh Review*, 153 (1881), 191–9.

—— [Douglas Galton], 'Article VIII. The Military Forces of the Crown', *Edinburgh Review*, 133 (1871), 207–42.

—— 'Desertion and Recruiting', *United Services Magazine* (July 1874), 296–307.

—— 'On Recruiting and Forming Reserves for the British Army', *United Services Magazine* (1875), 285–314.

—— 'Remarks on the Present Condition of the Army', *United Services Magazine* (1876), 209–13.

—— 'The Army, the Officer and the Horse', *Cavalry Journal*, 27 (1937), 244–5.

—— 'The Cost of the British Army and Recruiting', *United Services Magazine* (1875), 497–507.

ARNOLD, Sgt. CHARLES, *From Mons to Messines and Beyond: The Great War Experience of Sergeant Charles Arnold*, ed. S. Royle (Studley, Warwickshire: K..A. F. Brewin Books, 1985).

'Bantam', 'Reminiscences of Colchester Garrison', *The Abbey Field Review. A Monthly Record of Garrison Life in Colchester*, 1 (1926), 96–7.

BARCLAY, Brig. C. N., 'Editorial', *Army Quarterly*, 77 (1959), 131.

—— 'Editorial', *Army Quarterly*, 81 (1965), 1–2.

BARKER, Lt.-Col. A., 'The Recruiting Problem', *Army Quarterly*, 86 (1963), 192–7.

BARRACLOUGH, E. G., *National Service: An Insider's Story* (Durham: Pentland Books, 2001).

BARROW, Gen. Sir GEORGE DE S., *The Fire of Life* (London: Hutchinson, 1941).

BELCHEM, Maj-Gen. D., *All in the Day's March* (London: William Collins, 1978).

BELHAVEN, The Master of, *The War Diary of the Master of Belhaven 1914–18* (Barnsley: Wharncliffe Publishing Ltd, 1990).

BENSON, F. R., and CRAIG, A. T. (eds.), *The Book of the Army Pageant Held at Fulham Palace* (London: Sir J. Causton, 1910).

BIRDWOOD, Field Marshal Lord, *Khaki and Gown: An Autobiography* (London: Ward Lock, 1941).

BLACKER, Gen. Sir CECIL, *Monkey Business: The Memoirs of General Sir Cecil Blacker* (London: Quiller Press, 1993).

BOUCHER, Brig. V., 'Some Remarks on Opening a Battalion Officers' Study Period', *Army Quarterly*, 65 (1952), 123–6.

BOWMAN, J. E., *Three Stripes and a Gun* (Braunton, Devon: Merlin Books, 1987).

BRACKENBURY, Capt. C. B., 'The Military Systems of France and Prussia', *Journal of the Royal United Services Institute*, 15 (1871), 232–53.

CARRINGTON, P., *Reflect on Things Past: The Memoirs of Lord Carrington* (London: Fontana, 1989).

CARVER, Field Marshal Lord, *Out of Step: The Memoirs of Field Marshal Lord Carver* (London: Hutchinson, 1989).

CAVE THOMAS, Capt. W., 'The Establishment of County Military Training Schools; a Suggestion for Improving the Recruiting System', *Journal of the Royal United Services Institute*, 13 (1869), 143–50.

CHARRINGTON, Maj. H. V. S., 'Where Cavalry Stands Today', *Cavalry Journal*, 17 (1927), 419–30.

COLLINS, Maj.-Gen. R. J., 'Editorial', *Army Quarterly*, 61 (1949), 9.

COMPTON, Maj. Lord D., 'The Shortage of Officers in the Army', *Journal of the Royal United Services Institute*, 50 (1906), 785–97.

COOKE, Col. M., *Clouds that Flee* (London: Hutchinson, 1935).

COPPARD, G., *With a Machine Gun to Cambrai: The Tale of a Young Tommy in Kitchener's Army 1914–1918* (London: HMSO, 1969).

CORBALLY, Maj. M. J. P. M., 'The Officer-Producing Class', *Journal of the Royal United Services Institute*, 91 (1946), 204–8.

COWPER, Maj. L. I., 'Gold Medal (Military) Prize Essay', *Journal of the Royal United Services Institute*, 70 (1925), 202–21.

CRAIG, N., *The Broken Plume: A Platoon Commander's Story, 1940–45* (London: Imperial War Museum, 1982).

CRAWFORD, Capt. W. K. B., 'Future of Regimental Pride', *Army Quarterly*, 58 (1949), 240–6.

CUNNINGHAM ROBERTSON, Col. A., 'The Constitution of our Military Forces, and the Conditions of Military Service', *Journal of the Royal United Services Institute*, 13 (1870), 476–508.

DANIELL, Capt. J. F., 'Discipline: Its Importance to an Armed Force and the Best Means of Promoting and Maintaining It', *Journal of the Royal United Services Institute*, 33 (1889), 287–331.

DIXON, A., *Tinned Soldier: A Personal Record, 1919–26* (London: The Right Book Club, 1941).

DONNE, Col. BENJAMIN D. A., *The Life and Times of a Victorian Officer, being the Journals of Colonel Benjamin D. A. Donne*, ed. A. Harfield (Wincanton: The Wincanton Press, 1986).

DUNN, R., *Sword and Wig: Memoirs of a Lord Justice* (London: Quiller Press, 1993).

DYSON, S., *Tank Twins: East End Brothers in Arms* (London: Leo Cooper, 1994).

EDMONDSON, R., *John Bull's Army from Within: Facts, Figures, and a Human Document from One who Has Been 'Through the Mill'* (London: Francis Griffiths, 1907).

ERROLL, Col. the Earl of, 'The Defence of Empire. IV. The Dearth of Officers', *Nineteenth Century*, 339 (1905), 745–50.

ERSKINE, Maj.-Gen. G. W. E., 'The Territorial Army', *Journal of the Royal United Services Institute*, 93 (1948), 570–83.

FISHER, Brig. B. D., 'The Training of the Regimental Officer', *Journal of the Royal United Services Institute*, 74 (1929), 241–61.

FRANKLYN, Col. H. E., 'Training Troops on Foreign Service', *Journal of the Royal United Services Institute*, 79 (1934), 558–64.

FRASER, Gen. Sir D., *Wars and Shadows: Memoirs of Gen. Sir David Fraser* (London: Allen Lane, 2002).

FRASER, J., *Sixty Years in Uniform* (London: Stanley Paul, 1939).

FRASER, W., *In Good Company: The First World War Letters and Diaries of the Hon. William Fraser, Gordon Highlanders*, ed. D. Fraser (Salisbury, Wilts: Michael Joseph, 1990).

GIBBS, Capt. S., *From the Somme to the Armistice: The Memoirs of Captain Stormont Gibbs MC*, ed. R. Devonold-Lewis (Norwich: Gliddon Books, 1986–92).

GIBNEY, Capt. R. D., 'Recruiting', *United Services Magazine* (1874), 343–50.

GORE-BROWNE, W., 'Life in a Cavalry Regiment', *Nineteenth Century*, 28 (1890), 840–53.

GOSSETT, Col. M., 'Battalion Command', *Journal of the Royal United Services Institute*, 35 (1891), 469–86.

GOUGH, SIR H., *Soldiering On* (London: Arthur Baker, 1954).

GOW, Gen. Sir M., *General Reflections: A Military Man at Large* (London: Souvenir Press, 1991).

GRAVES, Col. F. J., 'Other Ranks Compared with Civilian Working Class Life—II. Recruiting Difficulties—III. The Condition of the Army Reserve', *Journal of the Royal United Services Institute*, 35 (1891), 573–601.

GREEN, L. J., *Gunner Green's War (1938–1946)* (Edinburgh: Pentland Press, 1999).

GUDGIN, P., *With Churchills to War: 48th Battalion Royal Tank Regiment at War 1939–45* (Stroud: Sutton Publishing, 1996).

GUINNESS, WALTER, *Staff Officer: The Diaries of Walter Guinness (First Lord Moyne) 1914–1918*, ed. B. Bond and S. Robbins (London: Leo Cooper, 1987).

GUTHERIE, Gen. Sir C., 'British Defence—The Chief of the Defence Staff's Lecture 2000', *Journal of the Royal United Services Institute*, 146 (2001), 1–8.

HAMILTON, Gen. Sir I., *Listening for the Drums* (London: Faber & Faber, 1944).

HARINGTON, Sir C., *Tim Harington Looks Back* (London: John Murray, 1940).

HARVEY, J. M. Lee, *D-Day Dodger* (London: William Kimber, 1979).

HAWKINS, FRANK, *Frank Hawkins: From Ypres to Cambrai. The Diary of an Infantryman 1914–1919*, ed. A. Taylor (Morley, Yorks: The Elmsfield Press, 1974).

HENNESSY, P., *Young Man in a Tank* (privately published, 1995).

HILLIER, J., *The Long Road to Victory: War Diary of an Infantry Despatch Rider 1940–46* (Trowbridge, Wilts.: privately published, 1995).

HITCHCOCK, Capt. F. C., *'Stand To': A Diary of the Trenches by Captain F. C. Hitchcock MC*, ed. A. Spagnoly (Norwich: Gliddon Books, 1937; repr. 1988).

HOGAN, G., *Oh, to be a Soldier: Recollections and Reflections of Seventy Years* (Braunton, Devon: Merlin Books, 1992).

HOLMES, Brig. R., 'Volunteer Reserves: Usable and Relevant', *Journal of the Royal United Services Institute*, 143 (1998), 21–3.

HORROCKS, Sir B., *A Full Life* (London: Collins, 1960).

HORTON, G., *A Brief Outline of My Travels and Doings whilst Serving in the Army from 1884 to 1918*, ed. A. E. Horton (Ts. memoirs. Produced by RHQ, Royal Irish Rangers, Belfast, 1982).

INNES, Col. T., 'Notes on Training the Militia', *Journal of the Royal United Services Institute*, 25 (1881), 123–56.

IRONSIDE, Maj.-Gen. Sir E., 'The Modern Staff Officer', *Journal of the Royal United Services Institute*, 73 (1928), 440–50.

JACK, Brigadier-General J. L., *General Jack's Diary 1914–1918: The Trench Diary of Brigadier-General J. L. Jack, DSO*, ed. J. Terraine (London: Eyre & Spottiswoode, 1964).

JARVIS, Maj. C. E., 'Regimental Tradition in the Infantry of the Line', *Journal of the Royal United Services Institute*, 96 (1951), 101–5.

JARY, S., *Eighteen Platoon* (Surrey: Sydney Jary, 1987).

JEROME, Lt.-Col. B. S., 'The Army as a Career', *Army Quarterly*, 60 (1950), 72–81.

KAULBECK, Lt.-Col. R. J. A., 'The Regiment', *Journal of the Royal United Services Institute*, 91 (1946), 257–65.

KENNARD, Lt.-Col. G., *Loopy: The Autobiography of George Kennard* (London: Leo Cooper, 1990).

KENNETT, A. C., *Life is What you Make it* (Edinburgh: The Pentland Press Ltd, 1992).

KINAHAN, Capt. C. E., 'The Need of Games in the Army: How they should be Organised', *'Faugh-a-Ballagh'. The Regimental Gazette of the 87th Royal Irish Fusiliers*, 6 (Jan. 1907).

KING-LEWIS, Brig. H., 'The Role of Territorial and Auxiliary Forces Associations in the Future', *Journal of the Royal United Services Institute*, 98 (1953), 585–93.

KITCHEN, Maj.-Gen. G., *Mud and Green Fields* (St. Catherines, Ontario: Vanwell Publishing Ltd., 1992).

KNOLLYS, Maj. W. W., 'The Army Promotion and Retirement Warrant', *United Services Magazine* (1877), 214–21.

—— 'Boy Soldiers', *Nineteenth Century*, 6 (1879), 1–9.

LAING MEASON, M., 'The Reorganization of our Army', *Dublin Review*, 6 (1881), 86–105.

LANDON, Lt.-Col. L. H., 'The Financial Condition of the Army Officer', *Journal of the Royal United Services Institute*, 94 (1949), 417–19.

LEAHY, Maj. A., 'Our Infantry Forces and Infantry Reserves', *Journal of the Royal United Services Institute*, 12 (1868), 310–58.

LIVERMORE, B., *Long 'Un: A Damn Bad Soldier* (Batley, West Yorks: Harry Haynes, 1974).

LOGAN, Capt. C. D. C., 'Problems of Infantry Re-organisation', *Journal of the Royal United Services Institute*, 114 (1969), 19–24.

LOYD-LINDSAY, Col. R., 'The Coming of Age of the Volunteers', *Nineteenth Century*, 10 (1881), 206–16.

LUCY, J. F., *There's a Devil in the Drum* (Sussex: Naval and Military Press, 1993).

LUNT, Maj. J. D., 'Post-war Conditions in the Army', *Army Quarterly*, 51 (1945), 89–98.

MACREADY, Gen. Sir N., *Annals of an Active Life* (London: Hutchinson, 1924).

MAITLAND, F. H., *Hussar of the Line* (London: Hurst & Blackett Ltd, 1951).

MARLING, Col. Sir P., *Rifleman and Hussar* (London: John Murray 1935).

MARSHALL-CORNWALL, Gen. Sir J., *Wars and Rumours of Wars* (London: Leo Cooper/Secker and Warburg, 1984).

MAYS, S., *Fall Out the Officers* (London: Eyre & Spottiswoode, 1969).

MEREDITH, J. (ed.), *Omdurman Diaries 1898: Eyewitness Accounts of the Legendary Campaign* (London: Leo Cooper, 1998).

MEREWOOD, J., *To War with the Bays: A Tank Gunner Remembers 1939–1945* (Cardiff: 1st Queen's Dragoon Guards, 1996).

MILEHAM, P. J. R., (ed.), *Yeoman Service by W. B and G. D. Giles: Contemporary Cartoons of the Suffolk Yeomanry Cavalry 1870 to 1910* (Tunbridge Wells, Kent: Spellmount, 1985).

MILLAR, W. M., 'Statistics of Deaths by Suicide among Her Majesty's British Troops Serving at Home and Abroad during the Ten Years 1862–1871', *Journal of the Statistical Society of London*, 37 (1874), 187–92.

MILLER, Capt. E. D., *Modern Polo* (London: Hurst and Blackett, 1911).

MILLMAN, C., *Stand Easy or the Rear Rank Remembers* (Edinburgh: The Pentland Press, 1993).

MILLS, B., *One For Grandad: The Really, Really, Real Dad's Army* (Salford, privately published, 1998).

MILLS, C. P., *A Strange War: Burma, India and Afghanistan 1914–1918* (Gloucester: Alan Sutton, 1988).

MONTGOMERY, Field Marshal Lord, *The Memoirs of Field Marshal Lord Montgomery* (London: Collins, 1958).

—— 'Morale in Battle', *British Medical Journal*, 2 (1946), 702–14.

MONTGOMERY-CUNINGHAME, SIR T., *Dusty Measure: A Record of Troubled Times* (London: John Murray, 1939).

MOORE, Lt.-Col. J. A. H., '"A Hunting We Won't Go"', *Army Quarterly*, 66 (1956), 228–33.

MORGAN, Gen. Sir F., *Peace and War: A Soldier's Life* (London: Hodder & Stoughton, 1961).

NEAME, Lt.-Gen. Sir P., *Playing with Strife: The Autobiography of a Sapper* (London: George Harrap, 1947).

NETTLETON, J., *The Anger of the Guns: An Infantry Officer on the Western Front* (London: William Kimber, 1979).

NICHOLSON, Col. W. N., *Behind the Lines: An Account of Administrative Staffwork in the British Army, 1914–1918* (London: The Strong Oak Press & Tom Donovan, 1939).

OGLE, W., 'Suicides in England and Wales in Relation to Age, Sex, Season and Occupation', *Journal of the Statistical Society of London*, 49 (1886), 101–35.

OUGHTRED, Capt. JACK, *Destiny: The War Letters of Captain Jack Oughtred M.C. 1915–1918*, ed. A. Wilkinson (Beverley: Peter & Christopher Oughtred, 1996).

PALMER, Sgt. A. V., 'What I Saw at Tel-el-Kebir: A Rejoinder', *Nineteenth Century*, 28 (1890), 148–56.

PARKER, Lt.-Col. N., 'The Front Line: Operational Effectiveness and Resource Constraints—An Infantry Battalion Commander's Perspective', *Journal of the Royal United Services Institute*, 139 (1994), 12–18.

POETT, Gen. Sir N., *Pure Poett: The Autobiography of General Sir Nigel Poett* (London: Leo Cooper, 1991).

PONSONBY, Sir F., *Recollections of Three Reigns* (London: Rye and Spottiswoode, 1951).

POULETT CAMERON, Col. G., 'The Royal Army Warrant and Explanatory Minute', *United Services Journal* (1871), 475–88.

PRYOR, A., and WOODS, J. K., (ed.), *Great Uncle Fred's War: An Illustrated Diary 1917–20* (Whitstable, Kent: Pryor Publications, 1985).

PYMAN, Gen. Sir H., *Call to Arms* (London: Leo Cooper, 1971).

RAVEN, Col.-Sgt. L., 'A Practical System of Ensuring Progressive Instruction throughout the Year's Training', *Essex Regiment Gazette*, 4 (1912), 48–51.

RAVEN-HILL, L., *Our Battalion: Being Some Slight Impressions of his Majesty's Auxiliary Forces in Camp and Elsewhere* (London: Punch Office, 1902).

REES, J. R., *The Shaping of Psychiatry by War* (New York, 1945).

RICHARDS, F., *Old Soldiers Never Die* (London: Faber & Faber, 1933).

—— *Old-Soldier Sahib* (London: Faber & Faber, 1936).

RITCHIE, Brig. A. S., 'Turning the Tide: Addressing Army Personnel Issues', *Journal of the Royal United Services Institute*, 144 (1999), 67–71.

ROBERTS, Field Marshal Lord, *Roberts in India: The Military Papers of Field Marshal Lord Roberts 1876–1893*, ed. B. Robson (London: Alan Sutton for the Army Records Society, 1993).

——, 'The Army—as It Was and as It Is', *Nineteenth Century*, 57 (1905), 1–26.

ROBERTSON, Field Marshal Sir W., *From Private to Field Marshal* (London: Constable, 1921).

ROBSON SCOTT, J., *My Life as Soldier and Sportsman* (London: Grant Richards, 1921).

ROUTLEDGE, Lt.-Col. R. W., 'A Volunteer Battalion', *Nineteenth Century*, 22 (1887), 742–7.

SAUNDERS, W., *Dunkirk Diary* (Birmingham: Birmingham City Council, Public Libraries Department, 1990).

SCOTT-CLARKE, J., 'The Military Wife', *Journal of the Royal United Services Institute*, 135 (1990), 69–74.

SECRETT, Sgt. T., *Twenty-Five Years with Earl Haig* (London: Jarrolds, 1929).

SEXTONE, D., *Reflections of an Idle Guardsman* (Sussex: The Book Guild, 1991).

SHEPPARD, Maj. E. W., 'Apprenticeship of Mechanised Cavalry', *Cavalry Journal*, 28 (1938), 165–70.

SHERIDAN, B., *'What Did You Do in the War, Dad?'* (Lewes, Sussex: The Book Guild, 1993).

SPENCER, Capt. J., 'Our Army Organisation of 1871: An Epitome of What It Is, and Results', *United Services Journal* (Dec. 1871), 560–3.

STEVENS, G., *With Kitchener to Khartoum* (London: William Blackwood & Sons, 1898).

TELFER, Capt. C. E. D., 'Discipline: Its Importance to an Armed Force and the Best Means of Promoting and Maintaining It', *Journal of the Royal United Services Institute*, 33 (1889), 333–73.

TILNEY, W. A., *Colonel Standfast: The Memoirs of W. A. Tilney 1868–1947. A Soldier's Life in England, India, the Boer War and Ireland*, ed. N. Murray-Philipson (Norwich: Michael Russell, 2001).

TREVELYAN, Sir C. E., *The British Army in 1868* (London: Longman, Green & Co., 1868).

TREVELYAN, R., *The Fortress: Anzio 1944* (London: Leo Cooper, 1956).

TUCKER, J. F., *Johnny Get your Gun: A Personal Narrative of the Somme, Ypres and Arras* (London: William Kimber, 1978).

TYACKE, Maj.-Gen. D., *A Cornish Hotchpotch* (King's Lynn: privately printed, 2002).

VAUGHAN, Maj.-Gen. J., *Cavalry and Sporting Memoirs* (London: The Bala Press, 1954).

WALKER, Col. W. W., 'Our Militia and How to Improve It', *Journal of the Royal United Services Institute*, 24 (1880), 445–78.

WARDLE, Maj. M. K., 'A Defence of Close Order Drill: A Reply to "Modern Infantry Discipline" ', *Journal of the Royal United Services Institute*, 79 (1934), 715–22.

—— 'The Development of Regimental Routine', *Journal of the Royal United Services Institute*, 81 (1936), 538–47.

WHEELER, Gen. Sir R., 'Peacemakers Know that Britain Will Deliver', *Journal of the Royal United Services Institute*, 144 (1999), 4–8.

WILKINSON, N. R., *To All and Singular* (London: Nisbet & Co., 1933).

WILSON, Sir H., *The Military Correspondence of Field Marshal Sir Henry Wilson 1918–1922*, ed. K. Jeffery (London: Bodley Head for the Army Record Society, 1985).

WINGFIELD, Col. M. A., 'The Supply and Training of Officers for the Army', *Journal of the Royal United Services Institute*, 69 (1924), 432–41.

WINGFIELD, R. J., *The Only Way Out: An Infantryman's Autobiography of the North-West Europe Campaign August 1944–February 1945* (London: Hutchinson, 1955).

WOLMER, LORD, 'A Militia Regiment', *Nineteenth Century*, 122 (1887), 566–75.

WOLSELEY, Sir G., 'England as a Military Power in 1854 and 1878', *Nineteenth Century*, 3 (1878), 433–56.

WYNDHAM, H., 'General's Inspection: Old Days and Old Ways', *Army Quarterly*, 74 (1957), 59–62.

—— *The Queen's Service: Being the Experiences of a Private Soldier in the British Infantry at Home and Abroad* (London: Heinemann, 1899).

SECONDARY SOURCES

ANDERSON, B., *Imagined Communities: Reflections on the Origins and Spread of Nationalism* (London: Verson, 1983; rev. edn. 1991).

ANDERSON, D., *Colonizing the Body. State Medicine and Epidemic Disease in Nineteenth-Century India* (Berkeley: University of California Press, 1993).

ANDREW, C., *Secret Service: The Making of the British Intelligence Community* (London: Heineman, 1985).

ANON., *The King's Own Border Regiment* (Morecambe: The Morecambe Bay Printers, 1960).

—— *The Royal Fusiliers in an Outline of Military History 1685–1926* (Aldershot: Gale & Polden, 1926).

—— *Royal Welch Fusiliers* (Aldershot: Gale and Polden, c.1919).

—— *A Short History of the Fifth Fusiliers from 1674 to 1911* (n.p.; c.1912).

—— *A Short History of the Royal Sussex Regiment (35th Foot–107th Foot), 1701–1926* (Aldershot: Gale & Polden, 1927).

—— *A Short History of the Somerset Light Infantry (Prince Albert's)* (Taunton: n.p., 1934).

—— *A Short History of 13th Hussars* (Aldershot: Gale & Polden, 1923).

ATKINSON, C. T., *The South Wales Borderers, 24th Foot* (Cambridge: University Press for the Regimental History Committee, 1937).

BABBINGTON, A., *The Devil to Pay: The Mutiny of the Connaught Rangers, India, July 1920* (London: Leo Cooper, 1991).

—— *For the Sake of Example: Capital Courts-Martial, 1914–1920* (London: Leo Cooper, 1983).

BADSEY, S., 'Cavalry and the Development of Breakthrough Doctrine', in P. Griffith (ed.), *British Fighting Methods*, 138–74.

BAILES, H., 'Military Aspects of the War', in P. Warwick and B. Spies (eds.), *The South African War* (London: Longman, 1980), 65–103.

—— 'Technology and Tactics in the British Army, 1866–1900', in R. Haycock and K. Neilson (eds.), *Men, Machines and War* (Waterloo, Ont.: Wilfried Laurier University Press, 1988), 21–48.

BAILEY, J., 'British Artillery in the Great War', in P. Griffith (ed.), *British Fighting Methods*, 23–49.

BAILEY, V., 'English Prisons, Penal Culture, and the Abatement of Imprisonment, 1895 to 1922', *Journal of British Studies*, 36 (1997), 285–324.

BALLHATCHET, K., *Race, Sex and Class Under the Raj: Imperial Attitudes and Policies and their Critics, 1793–1905* (London: Weidenfeld & Nicolson, 1980).

BARNES, Maj. R. M., *A History of the Regiments and Uniforms of the British Army* (London: Seeley Service, 1950; repr. 1962).

BARNETT, C., *The Desert Generals* (London: Allen & Unwin, 1983).

—— 'The Education of Military Elites', *Journal of Contemporary History*, 2 (1967), 15–35.

BARTLE, R., 'The Army in the 21st Century—Addressing the Final Taboo', *Journal of the Royal United Services Institute*, 143 (1998), 45–7.

BARTOV, O., *Hitler's Army: Soldiers, Nazis and War in the Third Reich* (Oxford: Oxford University Press, 1991).

BAYNES, Lt.-Col. J. C. M., *Morale: A Study of Men and Courage. The Second Scottish Rifles at the Battle of Neuve Chapelle 1915* (London: Leo Cooper, 1967).

—— *The Soldier in Modern Society* (London: Eyre Methuen, 1972).

BECKETT, I. F. W., *The Amateur Military Tradition 1558–1945* (Manchester: Manchester University Press, 1991).

BECKETT, I. F. W., 'Command in the Late Victorian Army', in G. D. Sheffield (ed.), *Leadership and Command: The Anglo-American Military Experience since 1861* (London: Brassey's, 1997), 37–56.

—— *Discovering British Regimental Traditions* (Buckinghamshire: Shire Publications, 1999).

—— 'The Territorial Army', in id. and Simpson (eds.), *A Nation in Arms*, 127–64.

—— 'Victorians at War—War, Technology and Change', *Journal of the Society for Army Historical Research*, 81 (2003), 330–8.

—— and SIMPSON, K. (eds.), *A Nation in Arms: A Social Study of the British Army in the First World War* (Manchester: Manchester University Press, 1985).

BEEVOR, A., *Inside the British Army* (London: Corgi, 1991).

BIDDULPH, Gen. Sir R., *Lord Cardwell at the War Office: A History of his Administration* (London: John Murray, 1904).

BIDWELL, S., and GRAHAM, D., *Fire-power: British Army Weapons and Theories of War 1904–1945* (London: Allen & Unwin, 1982).

BLACKER, Gen. Sir C., and WOODS, Maj.-Gen. H. G., *Change and Challenge: The Story of the 5th Royal Inniskilling Dragoon Guards* (London: privately printed, 1978).

BLAKE, Lt. Col. R. L. V. ff., *A History of the 17th/21st Lancers 1922–1959* (London: Longman, 1962).

BLANCH, M. D., 'British Society and the War', in P. Warwick and S. B. Spies (eds.), *The South African War: The Anglo-Boer War 1899–1902* (London: Longman, 1980), 210–38.

BLANCO, R. L., 'Army Recruiting Reforms, 1861–67', *Journal of the Society for Army Historical Research*, 46 (1968), 217–24.

BOND, B., *British Military Policy between the World Wars* (Oxford: Clarendon Press, 1980).

—— 'The Effect of the Cardwell Reforms in Army Organization, 1874–1904', *Journal of the Royal United Services Institute*, 105 (1960), 515–25.

—— 'Recruiting the Victorian Army, 1870–92', *Victorian Studies*, 5 (1962), 335–6.

—— *The Victorian Army and the Staff College* (London: Eyre Methuen, 1972).

BOURKE, J., *Dismembering the Male: Men's Bodies, Britain and the Great War* (London: Reaktion Books, 1996).

BOURNE, J., 'The British Working Man in Arms', in H. Cecil and P. H. Liddle (eds.), *Facing Armageddon: The First World War Experienced* (London: Leo Cooper, 1996), 336–52.

BOWMAN, T., *Irish Regiments in the Great War* (Manchester: Manchester University Press, 2003).

BRERETON, J. M., *The British Soldier: A Social History from 1661 to the Present Day* (London: Bodley Head, 1986).

—— 'Records of the Regiment: A Survey of Regimental Histories', *Journal of the Society for Army Historical Research*, 74 (1995), 107–20.

BROSE, E. D., *The Kaiser's Army: The Politics of Military Technology in Germany in the Machine Age, 1870–1918* (Oxford: Oxford University Press, 2001)

BRUCE, A., *The Purchase System in the British Army 1660–1871* (London: Royal Historical Society, 1980).

BUCHOLZ, A., *Moltke, Schlieffen and Prussian War Planning* (Oxford: Berg, 1993).

BURKE, P., *History and Social Theory* (Oxford: Polity Press, 1999).

BURNSIDE, Lt.-Col. F. R., *A Short History of the King's Own Hussars* (Aldershot: Gale and Polden, 1935).

BURROWS, P., 'Crime and Punishment in the British Army, 1815–1870', *English Historical Review*, 100 (1985), 545–71.

—— 'An Unreformed Army? 1815–1868', in D. Chandler and I. Beckett (eds.), *The Oxford Illustrated History of the British Army* (Oxford: Oxford University Press, 1994), 160–89.

CALABRIA, M. D., 'Florence Nightingale and the Libraries of the British Army', *Libraries and Culture*, 29 (1994), 367–88.

CAMPBELL, J. D., '"Training for sport is training for war": Sport and the Transformation of the British Army, 1860–1914', *International Journal of the History of Sport*, 17 (2000), 27–58.

CLAYTON, A., *The British Empire as Superpower, 1919–39* (London: Macmillan, 1986).

CLEMENTE, S. E., *For King and Kaiser! The Making of the Prussian Army Officer, 1860–1914* (New York: Greenwood Press, 1992).

CODRINGTON, Col. G. R., *The Territorial Army* (London: Sifton Praed, 1938).

COLLINS, M., 'The Fall of the English Gentleman: The National Character in Decline, c. 1918–1970', *Historical Research*, 75 (2002), 90–111.

COOK, Col. H. C. B., 'British Battle Honours', *Journal of the Society for Army Historical Research*, 59 (1979), 154–66.

CRANG, J., *The British Army and the People's War 1939–1945* (Manchester: Manchester University Press, 2000).

CUNNINGHAM, H., *The Volunteer Force* (London: Croom Helm, 1975).

CURTAIN, P. D., *Death by Migration: Europe's Encounter with the Tropical World in the Nineteenth Century* (Cambridge: Cambridge University Press, 1989).

DANDEKER, C., 'On the Need to Be Different: Military Uniqueness and Civil–Military Relations in Modern Society', *Journal of the Royal United Services Institute*, 146 (2001), 4–9.

DENMAN, T., '"Ethnic soldiers pure and simple"? The Irish in the Late Victorian British Army', *War in History*, 3 (1996), 253–73.

DENNIS, P., *The Territorial Army 1906–40* (Woodbridge: The Boydell Press and the Royal Historical Society, 1987).

DIETZ, P., *The Last of the Regiments: Their Rise and Fall* (London: Brassey's, 1990).

DIGBY, A., *The Evolution of British General Practice 1850–1948* (Oxford: Oxford University Press, 1999).

DINWIDDY, J. R., 'The Early Nineteenth-Century Campaign against Flogging in the Army', *English Historical Review*, 97 (1982), 308–31.

EDWARDS, Maj. T. J., *Military Customs* (Aldershot: Gale & Polden, 1950).

EVANS, N. R. H., 'Boer War Tactics Re-examined', *Journal of the Royal United Services Institute*, 145 (2000), 71–6.

EVANS, N. R. H., 'The Deaths of Qualified Staff Officers, 1914–1918', *Journal of the Society for Army Historical Research*, 78 (2000), 29–37.

FIELDING, S., 'What Did the People Want?: The Meaning of the 1945 General Election', *Historical Journal*, 35 (1992), 623–39.

FINLAY, R., 'National Identity in Crisis: Politicians, Intellectuals and the "End of Scotland", 1929–1939', *History*, 79 (1994), 242–62.

FOUCAULT, M., *Discipline and Punish: The Birth of the Prison* (London: Penguin, 1977).

FOWLER, S., 'Pass the hat for your credit's sake and pay-pay-pay': Philanthropy and Victorian Military Campaigns', *Soldiers of the Queen*, 105, (2001), 2–5.

FRASER, D., *And We Shall Shock Them: The British Army and the Second World War* (London: Hodder and Stoughton, 1983).

FREDERICK, J. B. M., *Lineage Book of the British Army: Mounted Corps and Infantry, 1660–1968* (New York: Hope Farm Press, 1969).

FREEDMAN, L., 'Defence Turning Point: The Sandys Defence White Paper', *Contemporary Record*, 2 (1988), 30–2.

FRENCH, D., 'Colonel Blimp and the British Army: British Army Divisional Commanders in the War against Germany, 1939–1945', *English Historical Review*, 111 (1996), 1182–1201.

—— 'Discipline and the Death Penalty in the War against Germany during the Second World War', *Journal of Contemporary History*, 33 (1998), 531–46.

—— '"An extensive use of weedkiller": Patterns of Promotion in the Senior Ranks of the British Army, 1919 to 1939', in French and Holden Reid (eds.), *The British General Staff*, 159–74.

—— 'The Mechanization of the British Cavalry between the Wars', *War in History*, 10 (2003), 296–320.

—— 'Officer Education and Training in the British Army, 1919–39', in Kennedy and Neilson (eds.), *Officer Education*, 105–28.

—— *Raising Churchill's Army: The British Army and the War Against Germany, 1919–1945* (Oxford: Oxford University Press, 2000).

—— 'Some Aspects of Social and Economic Planning for War in Great Britain, c. 1905–1915' (Ph.D. thesis, University of London, 1979).

—— and REID, B. HOLDEN (eds.), *The British General Staff: Reform and Innovation, c. 1890 to 1939* (London: Frank Cass, 2002).

FULLER, J. G., *Troop Morale and Popular Culture in the British and Dominion Armies 1914–1918* (Oxford: Oxford University Press, 1990).

GALLAGHER, T. F., 'British Military Thinking and the Coming of the Franco-Prussian War', *Military Affairs*, 39 (1975), 19–22.

—— '"Cardwellian mysteries": The Fate of the British Army Regulation Bill, 1871', *Historical Journal*, 18 (1975), 327–48.

GARNIER, M., 'Changing Recruitment Patterns and Organizational Ideology: The Case of a British Military Academy', *Administrative Science Quarterly*, 17 (1972), 499–507.

—— 'Power and Ideological Conformity: A Case Study', *American Journal of Sociology*, 79 (1973), 343–63.

GOOCH, J., '"A particularly Anglo-Saxon institution": The British General Staff in the Era of the Two World Wars', in French and Holden Reid (eds.), *The British General Staff*, 192–203.

GOODENOUGH, Lt.-Gen. W. H., and DALTON, Lt.-Col. J. C., *The Army Book of the British Empire: A Record of the Development and Present Composition of the Military Forces and their Duties in Peace and War* (London: HMSO, 1893).

GRAHAM, D., 'Sans Doctrine: British Army Tactics in the First World War', in T. Travers and C. Archon (eds.), *Men at War: Politics, Technology and Innovation in the Twentieth Century* (Chicago: Precedent Publishing, 1982), 69–92.

GRETTON, Lt.-Col. G. LE M., *The Campaigns and History of the Royal Irish Regiment from 1684 to 1902* (Edinburgh and London: William Blackwood, 1911).

GRIERSON, Lt.-Col. J. M., *Scarlet into Khaki: The British Army on the Eve of the Boer War* (London: Greenhill Books, 1899).

GRIFFITH, P., 'The Extent of Tactical Reform in the British Army', in id. (ed.), *British Fighting Methods*, 1–22.

—— (ed.), *British Fighting Methods in the Great War* (London: Frank Cass, 1996).

GROOT, G. DE, *Blighty: British Society in the Era of the Great War* (London: Longman, 1996).

GUHA, S., 'Nutrition, Sanitation, Hygiene, and the Likelihood of Death: The British Army in India, c. 1870–1920', *Population Studies*, 47 (1993), 385–401.

HACKETT, Gen. Sir J., *The Profession of Arms* (London: Sidgwick & Jackson, 1983).

HANHAM, H. J., 'Religion and Nationality in the Mid-Victorian Army', in M. R. D. Foot (ed.), *War and Society: Historical Essays in Honour and Memory of J. R. Western, 1928–1971* (London: Paul Elek, 1973), 159–82.

HARRIES-JENKINS, G., *The Army in Victorian Society* (London: Routledge & Kegan Paul, 1977).

HARRIS, J., *Private Lives, Public Spirit: Britain, 1870–1914* (London: Penguin, 1993).

—— 'Society and Civil Society in Britain, 1945–2001', in K. M. Burk (ed.), *The British Isles since 1945* (Oxford: Oxford University Press, 2003), 91–125.

HARRISON, M., 'Medicine and the Management of Modern Warfare', *History of Science*, 34 (1996), 379–409.

—— *Public Health in British India: Anglo-Indian Preventive Medicine 1859 to 1914* (Cambridge: Cambridge University Press, 1994).

HARRISON-PLACE, T., *Military Training in the British Army, 1940–1944* (London: Frank Cass, 2000).

HARVEY, A. D., 'Homosexuality and the British Army during the First World War', *Journal of the Society for Army Historical Research*, 79 (2001), 313–19.

HAVILAND, W., *Cultural Anthropology* (Fort Worth: Harcourt Brace College Publishers, 1996).

HENDRICKSON, K., 'A Kinder, Gentler British Army: Mid-Victorian Experiments in the Management of Vice at Gibraltar and Aldershot', *War and Society*, 14 (1996), 21–33.

—— *Making Saints: Religion and the Public Image of the British Army, 1809–1885* (London: Associated Universities Press, 1998).

HESS, R., '"A healing hegemony": Florence Nightingale, the British Army in India and a "Want of exercise"', *International Journal of the History of Sport*, 15 (1998), 1–17.

HICHBERGER, J. W. M., *Images of the Army: The Military in British Art, 1815–1914* (Manchester: Manchester University Press, 1988).

HOLMES, R., *Firing Line* (London: Penguin, 1987).

HOLT, R., *Sport and the British: A Modern History* (Oxford: Oxford University Press, 1989).

HOPE, J., 'Surveillance or Collusion? Maxwell Knight, MI5 and the British Fascisti', *Intelligence and National Security*, 9 (1994), 651–75.

HOPPEN, K., *The Mid-Victorian Generation 1846–1886* (Oxford: Clarendon Press, 1998).

HORN, P., *Pleasures and Pastimes in Victorian Britain* (Stroud, Glos.: Sutton, 1999).

HOULBROOK, M., 'Soldier Heroes and Rent Boys: Homosex, Masculinities, and Britishness in the Brigade of Guards, c. 1900–1960', *Journal of British Studies*, 42 (2003), 351–88.

HOWARD, M., 'Leadership in the British Army in the Second World War: Some Personal Observations', in G. Sheffield (ed.), *Leadership and Command: The Anglo-American Experience since 1861* (London: Brassey's, 1997), 117–28.

—— 'The Liddell Hart Memoirs', *Journal of the Royal United Services Institute*, 111 (1966), 58–61.

HUGHES, Maj.-Gen. B. P. (ed.), *History of the Royal Regiment of Artillery: Between the Wars, 1919–1939* (London: Brassey's, 1992).

HUGHES, D. J., *The King's Finest: A Social and Bureaucratic Profile of Prussia's General Officers, 1871–1914* (New York: Praeger, 1987).

HUSSEY, J., 'The Deaths of Qualified Staff Officers in the Great War', *Journal of the Society for Army Historical Research*, 75 (1997), 246–59.

JACKSON, L., 'Patriotism or Pleasure? The Nineteenth-Century Volunteer Force as a Vehicle for Rural Working-Class Male Sport', *Sports Historian*, 19 (1999), 125–9.

JACKSON HAY, Col. G., *An Epitomized History of the Militia (The 'Constitutional' Force)* (London: United Services Gazette, 1908).

JAMES, E. A., *British Regiments 1914–1918* (Heathfield, East Sussex: Naval and Military Press, 1998).

JEFFERY, K., 'The British Army and Internal Security 1919–1939', *Historical Journal*, 24 (1981), 377–97.

—— 'The Post-War Army', in Beckett and Simpson (eds.), *A Nation in Arms*, 211–34.

JOLLY, R., *Changing Step: From Military to Civilian Life. People in Transition* (London: Brassey's, 1996).

KEEGAN, J., 'Always a World Apart', *Times Literary Supplement*, 24 July 1998.

—— 'Regimental Ideology', in G. Best and A. Wheatcroft (eds.), *War, Economy and the Military Mind* (London: Croom Helm, 1976), 3–18.

KENNEDY, G. C., and NEILSON, K. (eds.), *Officer Education: Past, Present and Future* (Westport, Conn.: Praeger, 2002).

KENNEDY, Capt. J. R., *This, Our Army* (London: Hutchinson, 1935).

KENRICK, Col. N. C. E., *The Story of the Wiltshire Regiment (Duke of Edinburgh's) The 62nd and 99th Foot (1759–1959)* (Aldershot: Gale and Polden, 1963).

KERR, CAPT. W. J. W., *Records of the 1st Somerset Militia (3rd Battalion. Somerset Light Infantry)* (Aldershot: Gale & Polden, 1930).

KING, A., *Memorials of the Great War in Britain: The Symbolism and Politics of Remembrance* (London: Berg, 1998).

LARSON, R. H., *The British Army and the Theory of Armoured Warfare, 1918–40* (Newark, NJ: University of Delaware Press, 1984).

LEE, J., 'The British Divisions at Third Ypres', in P. Liddle (ed.), *Passchandaele in Perspective: The Third Battle of Ypres* (Barnsley: Leo Cooper, 1997), 215–26.

LEVINE, P., *The Amateur and the Professional: Antiquarians, Historians and Archaeologists in Victorian England, 1838–1886* (Cambridge: Cambridge University Press, 1986).

LIDDELL HART, B. H., *The Tanks: The History of the Royal Tank Regiment and its Predecessors. Heavy Branch MGC, Tank Corps and Royal Tank Corps*, i: *1914–1939* (London: Cassell, 1959).

LUMMIS, E., 'The English County Regiments', *Journal of the Society for Army Historical Research*, 74 (1995), 221–9.

MACDONALD, K. M., 'The Persistence of an Elite: The Case of British Army Officer Cadets', *Sociological Review*, 28 (1980), 635–40.

McGOWEN, R., 'Civilising Punishment: The End of Public Execution in England', *Journal of British Studies*, 33 (1994), 257–82.

McINNES, C., *Hot War, Cold War: The British Army's Way in Warfare 1945–1995* (London: Brassey's, 1996).

MACKENZIE, C., 'The Origins of the British Field Sports Society', *International Journal of the History of Sport*, 13 (1996), 177–91.

MACKENZIE, J. M., 'Empire and National Identity: The Case of Scotland', *Transactions of the Royal Historical Society*, 8, (1998), 215–31.

—— *The Empire of Nature: Hunting Conservation and British Imperialism* (Manchester: Manchester University Press, 1988).

MACLEOD, R., 'Sight and Sound on the Western Front: Surveyors, Scientists, and the "Battlefield Laboratory", 1915–1918', *War and Society*, 18 (2000), 23–46.

McPHERSON, J. M., *Battle Cry of Freedom: The Civil War Era* (Oxford: Oxford University Press, 1988).

MANGAN, J. A., 'Duty unto Death: English Masculinity and Militarism in the Age of the New Imperialism', *International Journal of the History of Sport*, 12 (1995), 10–28.

—— '"Muscular, militaristic and manly": The British Middle Class Hero as Moral Messenger', *International Journal of the History of Sport*, 13 (1996), 30–44.

MARWICK, A., *British Society since 1945* (London: Penguin, 2003).

MESSENGER, C., *For Love of Regiment: A History of the British Infantry*, 2 vols. (London: Leo Cooper, 1996).

MILEHAM, P., 'Moral Component—the "Regimental System"', in A. Alexandrou, R. Bartle, and R. Holmes (eds.), *New People Strategies for the British Armed Forces* (London: Frank Cass, 2002), 70–90.

MILLER, Maj.-Gen. C. H., *History of the 13th/18th Royal Hussars (Queen Mary's Own) 1922–1947* (London: Chisman, Bradshaw Ltd., 1949).

MILLER, S. M., *Lord Methuen and the British Army: Failure and Redemption* (London: Frank Cass, 1999).

MITCHELL, B. R., and DEANE, P., *An Abstract of British Historical Statistics* (Cambridge: Cambridge University Press, 1976).

MITCHINSON, K. W., 'Auxiliary Forces for the Land Defence of Great Britain, 1909–1919' (Ph.D. thesis, University of Luton, 2002).

MOREMAN, T., *The Army in India and the Development of Frontier Warfare 1849–1947* (London: Macmillan, 1998).

MURRAY, W., 'Armoured Warfare: The British, French and German Experiences', in id. and Millett, A. R., *Military Innovation in the Interwar Period* (Cambridge: Cambridge University Press, 1996), 6–49.

—— 'Does Military Culture Matter?' *Orbis*, 43 (1999), 27–42.

MYERLY, S. H., *British Military Spectacle from the Napoleonic Wars through the Crimea* (Cambridge, Mass.: Harvard University Press, 1996).

NASSON, W., *The South African War 1899–1902* (London: Edward Arnold, 1999).

NAVIS, M., '"Vested interests and vanished dreams": Duncan Sandys, the Chiefs of Staff and the 1957 Defence White Paper', in P. Smith (ed.), *Government and the Armed Forces in Britain 1856–1990* (London: Hambledon Press, 1996), 217–34.

OATTS, Lt.-Col. L. B., *Emperor's Chambermaids: The Story of the 14th/20th King's Hussars* (London: Lock, 1973).

O'CONNOR, M., 'The Vision of Soldiers: Britain, France, Germany and the United States Observe the Russo-Turkish War', *War in History*, 4 (1997), 264–95.

ODDY, D. J., 'Food, Drink and Nutrition' in F. M. L. Thompson (ed.), *The Cambridge Social History of Britain* (Cambridge: Cambridge University Press, 1990), ii. 251–78.

—— 'Gone for a Soldier: The Anatomy of a Nineteenth-Century Army Family', *Journal of Family History*, 25 (2000), 39–62.

—— 'Working Class Diets in Late Nineteenth Century Britain', *Economic History Review*, 23 (1970), 314–23.

OMISSI, D., *The Sepoys and the Raj: The Indian Army, 1860–1940* (London: Macmillan, 1994).

ORAM, G. C., *Military Executions during World War One* (Basingstoke: Palgrave, 2003).

OTTLEY, C. B., 'The Educational Background of British Army Officers', *Sociology*, 7 (1973), 191–209.

—— 'Militarism and Militarization in the Public Schools, 1900–1972', *British Journal of Sociology*, 29 (1978), 321–39.

—— 'The Social Origins of British Army Officers', *Sociological Review*, 18 (1970), 213–39.

PARIS, M., *Warrior Nation: Images of War in British Popular Culture 1850–2000* (London: Reaktion Books, 2000).

PERKINS, H., *The Rise of Professional Society: England since 1880* (London: Routledge, 1990).

POLLARD, S., 'Reflections on Entrepreneurship and Culture in European Societies', *Transactions of the Royal Historical Society*, 5th ser. 40 (1990), 153–75.

PORCH, D., *The March to the Marne: The French Army 1871–1914* (Cambridge: Cambridge University Press, 1981).

PUGH, M. D., 'The Rise of Labour and the Political Culture of Conservatism, 1890–1945', *History*, 87 (2002), 514–37.

PULSIFER, C., 'Beyond the Queen's Shilling: Reflections on the Pay of Other Ranks in the Victorian British Army', *Journal of the Society for Army Historical Research*, 80 (2002), 326–34.

RAMSAY, M., *Command and Cohesion: The Citizen Soldier and Minor Tactics in the British Army, 1870–1918* (Westport, Conn.: Praeger, 2002).

REES, W., 'The 1957 Defence White Paper: New Priorities in British Defence Policy', *Journal of Strategic Studies*, 12 (1989), 215–29.

ROBBINS, S., 'British Generalship on the Western Front in the First World War, 1914–1918' (Ph.D. thesis, University of London, 2001).

ROUTH, G., *Occupation and Pay in Great Britain 1906–79* (London: Macmillan, 1980).

ROY, K., 'Logistics and the Construction of Loyalty: The Welfare Mechanism in the Indian Army 1859–1913', in P. S. Gupta and A. Deshpande (eds.), *The British Raj and its Indian Armed Forces, 1857–1939* (Delhi: Oxford University Press, 2002), 98–124.

RUBIN, G., 'United Kingdom Military Law: Autonomy, Civilianisation and Juridification', *Modern Law Review*, 65 (2002), 36–57.

SAWCHUK, L. A., BURKE, S. D. A., and PADIAK, J., 'A Matter of Privilege: Infant Mortality in the Garrison Town of Gibraltar, 1870–1899', *Journal of Family History*, 27 (2002), 399–429.

SCOTT, L. V., *Conscription and the Attlee Governments: The Politics and Policy of National Service 1945–51* (Oxford: Oxford University Press, 1993).

SHEFFIELD, G. D., *Leadership in the Trenches: Officer-Man Relations, Morale and Discipline in the British Army in the Era of the First World War* (London: Macmillan, 2000).

SHOWALTER, D. E., '"No officer rather than a bad officer": Officer Selection and Education in the Prussian/German Army, 1715–1945', in Kennedy and Neilson (eds.), *Officer Education*, 35–62.

SIMKINS, P., 'Co-stars or Supporting Cast? British Divisions in the "Hundred Days", 1918', in P. Griffith (ed.), *British Fighting Methods*, 50–70.

—— *Kitchener's Army: The Raising of the New Armies, 1914–16* (Manchester: Manchester University Press, 1988).

SIMPSON, A., 'The Operational Role of British Corps Commanders on the Western Front' (Ph.D. thesis, University of London, 2001).

SIMPSON, K., 'The Officers', in Beckett and Simpson (eds.), *A Nation in Arms*, 63–98.

SKELLEY, A. R., *The Victorian Army at Home: The Recruitment and Terms and Conditions of the British Regular, 1859–1899* (London: Croom Helm, 1977).

SMURTHWAITE, D., 'A Recipe for Discontent: The Victorian Soldier's Cuisine', in M. Harding (ed.), *The Victorian Soldier: Studies in the History of the British Army 1816–1914* (London: National Army Museum, 1993), 74–85.

SMYTH, SIR J., *Bolo Whistler: The Life of General Sir Lashmer Whistler* (London: Frederick Muller, 1967).

SMYTH, SIR J., *Sandhurst: The History of the RMA, Woolwich, the RMC, Sandhurst, and the RMA, Sandhurst, 1741–1961* (London, 1961).

SPIERS, E. M., *The Army and Society 1815–1914* (London: Longman, 1980).

—— *The Late Victorian Army, 1866–1902* (Manchester: Manchester University Press, 1992).

—— 'Reforming the Infantry of the Line, 1900–14', *Journal of the Society for Army Historical Research*, 59 (1981), 82–94.

SPRINGHALL, J. O., 'The Boy Scouts, Class and Militarism in Relation to British Youth Movements 1908–1930', *International Review of Social History*, 16 (1971), 125–58.

STEINER, Z., and DOCKRILL, M. L., 'The Foreign Office Reforms, 1919–21', *Historical Journal*, 17 (1974), 131–56.

STERN, R., '"To rid the country of a scandal": The Uniforms Act of 1894', *Journal of the Society for Army Historical Research*, 71 (1993), 227–31.

STEWART, J., *A Brief History of the Royal Highland Regiment: The Black Watch* (Edinburgh: T. & A. Constable, 1912).

STRACHAN, H., 'The Battle of the Somme and British Strategy', *Journal of Strategic Studies*, 21 (1998), 79–95.

—— 'The British Army, its General Staff and the Continental Commitment', in French and Holden Reid (eds.), *The British General Staff*, 75–94.

—— *The Politics of the British Army* (Oxford: Oxford University Press, 1997).

—— *Wellington's Legacy: The Reform of the British Army 1830–54* (Manchester: Manchester University Press, 1984).

STRONG, K., *Intelligence at the Top* (London: Cassell, 1968).

TALBOT, P., 'The English Yeomanry in the Nineteenth Century and the Great Boer War', *Journal of the Society for Army Historical Research*, 79 (2001), 45–62.

THOMPSON, F. M. L., *Gentrification and the Enterprise Culture: Britain 1780–1908* (Oxford: Oxford University Press, 2001).

—— *The Rise of Respectable Society: A Social History of Victorian Britain, 1830–1900* (London: Fontana, 1988).

TOSH, J., *A Man's Place: Masculinity and the Middle-Class Home in Victorian England* (New Haven, Conn.: Yale University Press, 1999).

TRIMEN, Capt. R., *The Regiments of the British Army, Chronologically Arranged* (London: William Allen & Co., 1878).

TRUSTRAM, M., *Women of the Regiment: Marriage and the Victorian Army* (Cambridge: Cambridge University Press, 1984).

WALKOWITZ, J. R., *Prostitution and Victorian Society: Women, Class and the State* (Cambridge: Cambridge University Press, 1980).

WARD, S. R., 'Intelligence Surveillance of British Ex-servicemen, 1918–20', *Historical Journal*, 16 (1973), 179–88.

WEINER, M. J., *English Culture and the Decline of the Industrial Spirit, 1850–1980* (Cambridge: Cambridge University Press, 1981).

WESTON, D., 'The Army: Mother, Sister and Mistress: The British Regiment', in M. Edmonds (ed.), *The Defence Equation: British Military Systems—Policy, Planning and Performance since 1945* (London: Brassey's, 1986), 139–55.

WIENER, W. J., *Reconstructing the Criminal: Culture, Law and Policy in England, 1830–1914* (Cambridge: Cambridge University Press, 1990).

WINGEN, J. van, and TILLEMA, H. K., 'British Military Intervention after World War Two: Militance in a Second-Rank Power', *Journal of Peace Research*, 17 (1980), 291–303.

WINTER, J. M., *The Great War and the British People* (London: Macmillan, 1985).

WINTON, G. R., 'The British Army, Mechanisation and a New Transport System, 1900–1914', *Journal of the Society for Army Historical Research*, 78 (2000), 197–212.

WOOD, S., 'Temperance and its Rewards in the British Army', in M. Harding (ed.), *The Victorian Soldier: Studies in the History of the British Army 1816–1914* (London: National Army Museum, 1993), 86–96.

YARDLEY, M., and SEWELL, D., *A New Model Army* (London: W. H. Allen, 1989).

Index